Marvels of Charity

History of American Sisters and Nuns

George C. Stewart Jr.

Foreword by Dolores Liptak, RSM

Our Sunday Visitor Publishing Division
Our Sunday Visitor, Inc.
Huntington, Indiana 46750

ISBN: 0-87973-648-8
LCCCN: 94-66024

PRINTED IN THE UNITED STATES OF AMERICA

Cover design by Kathi Hilaski

648

With love and gratitude, this book is dedicated to
the women in my life:

Eugenia — my mother
Marie — my wife
Mary — my daughter
Louise — my daughter
Sisters — my teachers

and

Blessed Virgin Mary

Contents

Genesis
Benedictine Beginning
Monastic Life in the Middle Ages
Changes After Trent
The Franciscan Heritage
The Dominican Impact
The Ursuline Mission
The Carmelite Influence
The Visitandine Emphasis
Active Congregations
Proliferation in America
Summary
Endnotes

New Orleans
The Georgetown Poor Clares and the Pious Ladies
St. Elizabeth Ann Bayley Seton
Kentucky Foundations
Death of John Carroll
St. Rose Philippine Duchesne
First Order of Black Sisters
Barren Ground
Good Ground
Early Health Ministries
Port Tobacco Closed
Sisters of Charity Expand Ministries
Anti-Catholic Eruption
Endnotes

National Overview
Winds of Prejudice
Firestorm
Spreading Roots
Congregation of the Sisters of the Holy Family
Sisters, Servants of the Immaculate Heart of Mary

EDELWEISS

Begging for Alms
Heroic Service in Memphis
Occasional Conflicts Between Authority Figures
Unfinished Business
Endnotes

Rise of the APA and Related Groups
Immigration Patterns — The Ethnic Churches
Italian Immigrant Orders
Mother Frances Xavier Cabrini
Religious Sisters Filippini
Other Italian Orders
Polish Immigrant Orders
Felician Sisters
Sisters of the Holy Family of Nazareth
Bernardine Sisters of the Third Order of St. Francis
Sisters of St. Joseph of the Third Order of St. Francis
Franciscan Sisters of St. Joseph
Orders from Central and Eastern Europe
Other Immigrant Orders
American-Founded Orders
War-Nurses Again
End of an Era
Endnotes

Parochial Schools
High Schools and Academies
Colleges
Hospitals
Nursing Schools
Orphanages
Aged Poor
Ministry to the American Indian and Black Population
American Indian Sisters
Care of Poor Patients With Terminal Cancer
Foreign Missions
The Prayer Ministry
Other Ministries
Summary
Endnotes

National Events
Ku Klux Klan Attack
Growth of the Orders by 1945

Growth of Catholic Education
Support for High Schools
Growth of Colleges
Confraternity of Christian Doctrine
Health Care Growth
Service to the Aged Poor
New Ministries
Growth of Contemplative Orders
Sisters in Foreign Missions
The Rise of Maryknoll
China Missions
World War II
Summary
Endnotes

The American Catholic Scene
Women Religious
Franciscans
Sisters of St. Joseph
Dominicans
Sisters of Mercy
Mother Seton's Daughters
Benedictines
School Sisters of Notre Dame
Ursulines
Contemplatives
New Orders
Growth of Apostolates
Sister-Educators
Health Ministry
Foreign Missions
The Sisters Organize
Conference of Major Superiors of Congregations of Women Religious
The Sister Formation Movement
The Second Vatican Council
Endnotes

Impact of Vatican II
Impact of Secular Society
Drought
Final Words
Endnotes

Acknowledgments

✠ — ✠

NO AVERAGE CATHOLIC, the primary intended readership, could be less knowledgeable about the history of American sisters and nuns than I was at the outset of this book. However, abysmal ignorance was a distinct advantage in one respect — I unhesitatingly sought help from any and all sources throughout the research process. It is to the many kind, considerate, frequently inconvenienced, sometimes amused contributors that I owe more thanks than these few lines can convey. They are legion, making it impossible to list every name. But they know their input and will, I trust, realize and accept my gratitude.

Sheer luck attended the launching of what was only a concept toward reality in that each early contact with established authorities met with courtesy, sage advice, and, most importantly, encouragement. When I broached the subject to Robert P. Lockwood, President of Our Sunday Visitor Publishing Division, in 1988, he was positive and told me to proceed. That meeting was the critical moment of decision: I would do it.

Noted Catholic historians Fathers Harold A. Buetow and Wilfred P. Schoenberg, SJ, wrote encouraging words. Then, Father John Tracy Ellis, the premier American Catholic historian, and Sister Mary Ewens, OP, at the Cushwa Center at the University of Notre Dame, both suggested that I contact Dr. Margaret Susan Thompson of Syracuse University, a recognized expert, prolific writer, and sought-after speaker on the subject of women religious. Her advice, insights, and guidance on available resources have been invaluable. It might be said that Dr. Thompson was midwife at the birth of this book.

My luck held as I proceeded to contact hundreds of community archivists who filled out questionnaires, sent materials, answered queries, and reviewed extracts, correcting errors and skewed renditions, providing commentary. Some of the many helpful archivists were: Sister Constance Fitzgerald of the Baltimore Carmelites, Sister Aloysia Dugan of the Emmitsburg Daughters of Charity, Sister Henrietta Guyot of the St. Louis Daughters of Charity, Sister Margaret Warburton of the San Antonio Sisters of Divine Charity, Sister Barbara Misner of the School Sisters of St. Francis, Sister Mary Campion Kuhn of the Congregation of the Holy Cross, Sister Alice Lechnir of the School Sisters of Notre Dame, Sister Anna Margaret Gilbride of the Cleveland Ursulines, Sister Ann Courtney of the Sisters of Charity of New

York, Sister Rita Bergamini of the Sisters of Providence, Sister Ann Kathleen Brawley of the Sisters of Providence of Saint Mary-of-the-Woods, Sister Marie Laurence Kortendick of the Sinsinawa Dominicans, Sister Barbara Wills of the Mission Helpers of the Sacred Heart, Sister Elizabeth McLoughlin of the Sisters of Charity of Saint Elizabeth, Sister Joseph Marie Peplinski of the Sisters of St. Joseph of the Third Order of St. Francis, Sister Lillian Thomas Shank of the Dubuque Trappistines, Sister Mary Louise Sullivan of the Missionary Sisters of the Sacred Heart — and the list goes on. Sister Mary J. Oates of Regis College helped with Catholic women's colleges and Mr. Mark Unger of the Catholic Health Association helped with Catholic hospitals. Father Paul K. Thomas of the Baltimore archdiocese archives was most considerate and helpful in photocopying and forwarding requested materials.

Three authors whose manuscripts have since been published allowed me the use of their preliminary drafts. Sister Mary Denis Mayer lent her Civil War study of sister-nurses, *To Bind up the Wounds*; Sister Daniel Hannefin lent her history of the Daughters of Charity, *Daughters of the Church*; and Dr. Patricia Dunlavy Valenti lent her biography of Rose Hawthorne Lathrop, *To Myself a Stranger*. Such generosity is staggering.

As I came to realize how many different orders and congregations this history would entail, I retained assistant researchers who prepared background papers for my information. Natalie Beckert covered the Ursulines, Susan Casler the Benedictines, Marilyn Krug the Visitandines, Ruth Staben the Sisters of Charity, Xoan Nguyen the Poor Clares, Beverly McMahon the IHMs, and Mary Wilson the Franciscans. Sister Judith Wessels of the Cincinnati Sisters of Notre Dame de Namur researched a number of different congregations and performed various research assignments as well. Reverend Sheryl Jujawa of the New York Episcopal Church researched non-Catholic women religious and Sister Catherine Ann Curry of the San Francisco Sisters of the Presentation of the Blessed Virgin Mary researched and wrote the 19th-century sister-population report and provided counsel on all my drafts.

Still lucky, I met Dr. Christopher J. Kauffman, noted Catholic historian, Catholic History Professor at The Catholic University of America, and Editor of the *U.S. Catholic Historian*. He reviewed my early drafts, providing commentary, corrections, and most importantly, encouragement. He then did me the greatest favor I received throughout this entire project. He put me in touch with Sister Dolores Liptak, RSM. Sister Dolores is a highly regarded Catholic historian with numerous publications, an expert and professional consultant on archives science, and officer in numerous Catholic historical societies. To my delight, she agreed to act as mentor, becoming a taskmaster whose approval demanded constant checking, rechecking, and revisions. Without her input and oversight, this book would never have seen printer's ink. Her Foreword follows these acknowledgements.

Ann Marie Beal of Annapolis corrected technical errors and assisted in grammatical revisions. Susan Houston of Fayetteville also helped in this regard. Then, there is the "indispensable" one, Barbara Gonzalez, my secretary. She was a miracle locator, able to put her hands on any book, paper, article, correspondence, or other item needed on short notice. She compiled many of the statistics used throughout the book and is responsible for much of the data in the appendices. She prepared charts, spotted "glitches" in the drafts, and sought out detailed information by phone and correspondence. While most writers thank their secretaries as a matter of form, I can safely state that without Barbara this book would have been a year or longer in the making.

One acknowledgment rarely seen on pages such as this is for thanks for prayer support. In my case, many dozen individual women religious promised prayers. The entire community of Carmelite Nuns of Little Rock have consistently prayed for the success of this book as have the members of Madonna House in Canada where my son is a member. The Daughters of St. Paul in Charleston, South Carolina, and the Little Sisters of the Poor promised prayers as did Poor Clares in several monasteries. My hope is that they feel the final product justifies those prayers.

I want to thank each religious community who gave permission for photos from their archives to be reprinted here. They are the Maryknoll Archives, Maryknoll, New York; Missionary Sisters of St. Columban; Providence Archives, Seattle, Washington; Archives, Bertrand Hall-Saint Mary's, Notre Dame, Indiana; Daughters of St. Paul, Boston, Massachusetts; Missionary Catechists of Divine Providence, San Juan, Texas. A special note of thanks to Gonzaga University and the Milford Historical Society, Milford, Pennsylvania.

Then there is Marie, my wife and helpmate, whose patience, encouragement, and forbearance have been remarkable in view of my preoccupation and reduced participation in our mutual activities. She read the drafts, puncturing the inappropriate phrase, asking what this and that meant, pinpointed inept sentences and generally was a sounding board supreme; yet praising and supportive all the while. Although practically all writers credit their spouses (I suspect as much from wisdom as from conviction), I can truly affirm that Marie deserves all the credit that I can provide in limited space.

A final thought. The broad based support and assistance that so many gave to this undertaking was not because of me, but rather the subject itself; so dear to so many hearts. To each and every one, *Deo Gratias!*

Foreword

‡ — ‡

FOR OVER TWO hundred years, U.S. Catholic women have enthusiastically entered religious life. There is no movement in modern Church history, in fact, that can rival this vocational phenomenon in numbers, scope, variety of structures, or degree of accomplishment. At the beginning of the 20th century, so great was their example of selfless commitment that close to 50,000 young women had vowed to devote their lives in service to the church. By 1934, it was claimed that, in the United States, there was one sister for every one thousand Catholics; more than one half of these sisters taught in what had become the nation's most extensive private school system. Just thirty years later, religious life had reached its peak, with more than 200,000 sisters committed either to contemplative life or to ministries within educational, health, or social services.

Statistically significant, American sisters were also uniquely picturesque. Some, like the Carmelites, Dominicans, Benedictines, or Franciscans, were clothed in the soft garb of their ancient traditions. Others wore attire that suggested, by their distinctiveness, the degree to which adaptation to American circumstances had helped to create new styles of life and community. Regardless of colorful appearance or origin, it was what sisters were achieving on behalf of their fellow Catholics that really attracted attention. For, in the American setting, women religious found not only ministries that needed to be done but, more importantly, work that was worthy of their talents. It was here that countless bishops and clergy responded appreciatively not merely because of the labor they provided but because of the leadership that sisters commanded. Here, finally, their achievements received constant financial backing from admiring and enthusiastic laity.

A diverse force powerfully prompted by the Spirit, sisters today continue to comprise one of the most gifted corps ever to gather together on behalf of the Church's mission enterprise. More than simply contributing a work force, women religious have served as model teachers in many of the nation's most prestigious academies, directors of some of its most prominent hospitals, creators of many of its best social and health care facilities. Some 90,000 strong, and representing more than two hundred U.S. religious communities, they still bear witness to the transformative power of grace.

The abiding presence of women religious these two hundred years has been an overwhelming blessing to the American Catholic Church, to be sure. Yet the story of these women and their corporate mission has largely been left untold. To this day, too few American Catholics have had the opportunity, for example, to review the accomplishments of women religious, either individually or corporately, on behalf of the American Catholic Church. Few know any details of the sisters who established religious communities or of traditions initiated by these women that have inspired generations to follow. Few know of the ways in which women religious have been in the vanguard of evangelization. Few are aware of the leading role they have played in the establishment of diocesan schools, orphanages, homes for the aged or destitute, or hospitals. Still fewer Catholics have any idea of the degree to which women religious have been in the forefront of today's social justice movements.

Indeed, it is safe to say that the Catholic scholarly community has been very remiss in portraying the role of women religious and its significance in the creation of the U.S. Catholic Church. But why has a movement of such breadth and proportions not been carefully studied and evaluated? The reasons are varied. In the first place, sisters have not been, for the most part, the publicists of their own story. This was partly due to the lives of virtuous humility they chose to live. Victims of an exaggerated sense of modesty, all too many sisters chose to remain anonymous, giving credit for the schools, hospitals, or other apostolates which they established to the bishops or pastors who permitted their ministry. Besides, so great was the demand for sisters and so tremendous their challenge to educate or provide care that most sisters found little time even to keep records of what had been accomplished.

But there are other reasons for the scholarly lacuna. In a world where leadership in every field of secular or religious endeavor has been male, the story of what women accomplished in the Church has, quite frankly, been given little priority. Only since the mid-1970's have Catholic scholars seriously begun to study the role of lay or religious women within American Catholicism. This was first prompted by the fact that women had finally been permitted to enter the highest levels of education in both secular and Church-related universities. Armed with doctoral degrees in Church History, Historical Theology, American Studies, and Religious Studies, a number of these pioneer women scholars have been extremely active in providing new perspectives and in reinterpreting Church History, especially as it applies to the role of women.

Still, no Catholic university hosted a historical conference that emphasized the role of women in the U.S. Church until the 1980's. And it was not until 1989 that the first Catholic historical conference on the theme of religious women in the Church was ever held. Moreover, while more fine biographies and histories concerning women and women religious did begin to appear after the 1970's, few historians even considered writing one comprehensive history of American Catholic women religious. The sheer weight of data and the kaleidoscopic variety of congregations that need to be studied were reason enough to dissuade all but the bravest from taking on the project. Into the breach, the author of this monograph has entered, convinced that it is vital that the whole story be told.

For the past several years, George Stewart has committed himself to the Herculean task of rescuing from thousands of archival records and hundreds of biographies, histories, and chronicles, the collective story of women religious. These he has deftly blended into one narrative. His disarmingly simple approach combines complicated stories with biographical and statistical data that explain the numerical growth and geographical spread of religious communities throughout the United States.

This protean, panoramic view provides many details of the missing story. As told by Stewart, it is at once delicately beautiful, as a field of flowers, yet as tough as the solid institutional walls of brick and stone. It tells of the journeys and trials first embarked upon by such intrepid, saintly women as Elizabeth Seton, Elizabeth Lange, Rose Philippine Duchesne, Frances Cabrini, and Angela Truszkowska. It introduces us to heroic and often anonymous women who sometimes had to face up to church authorities; who were willing to place themselves at jeopardy in order to serve during times of war, pestilence, or civil need; who endured privation as well as prejudice for the sake of Catholic immigrant communities; who went on foreign missions; who took charge of hospitals, health care facilities, and colleges. This is a "story of stories" overwhelming in its depiction of what women religious, working side by side, have accomplished for the Catholic Church in the United States.

George Stewart realized that many would question why a layman should take up this kind of project. His answer, then and now, has been a simple disclaimer. His efforts were in tribute and acknowledgment. This book achieves this aim, and much more. Yet it is indeed a tribute — both to the sisters he has written about — and to himself. Because of his admiration for sisters, he has allowed us to see the hidden face of God in the countless women who have accomplished so much. Because of this text, we are challenged to remember and to marvel, as he has, at the extraordinary record of these several thousand women who have, since 1790, vowed service to the church in the United States. And he has reminded us of another phenomenon in the church — the unremitting generosity and devotion whereby the laity have enabled women religious to accomplish their remarkable goals.

Dolores Liptak, RSM
June 7, 1993

Preface

‡ — ‡

WELCOME TO A facet of American history of dynamic proportions and great vitality. For more than two centuries over a quarter of a million women, banded together in religious communities, have contributed enormously to the American commonwealth with their charitable, health, and educational ministries and institutions. Unfortunately, this history is unfamiliar to the general public, including the majority of Roman Catholics — today's 60 million would be far fewer had sisters and nuns not existed. This book is a modest effort to report that proud heritage and to increase awareness of their contributions to the Church and the United States.

Do not expect to encounter chapter after chapter of convent serenity, classroom vignettes, and sickroom sweetness. On the contrary, this history is rife with adventure, heroism, daring, dedication, struggles, perseverance, accomplishments, disappointments, victories, and defeats. Nor will the timid mice and tyrannical mothers-superior so dear to the hearts of Broadway and Hollywood scriptwriters be much in evidence. The role that sisters played in the Civil War, nursing both Union and Confederate sick and wounded, will be highlighted instead. Sisters died as a consequence of nursing the afflicted during the many epidemics of cholera, yellow fever, smallpox, and influenza of the 19th and early 20th centuries. They participated in the opening of the West, enduring hardships and dangers in remote outposts and on lonely Indian reservations. Their leaders were performing managerial and executive functions of major scope long before society opened these areas to secular women. Sisters founded and operated thousands of hospitals, schools, orphanages, colleges, and charitable institutions that have served untold millions of Americans. They acquired and managed extensive real estate holdings and ran the largest private school system ever known to the world. Missionary sisters have served in a multitude of foreign lands, enduring hardships and suffering, and facing violent deaths. In both the civic and religious arenas, sisters and nuns are an integral part of American history — their contributions and impact on national development too little known and appreciated.

We will see how sisters and nuns began their American existence and how with each passing decade they established an ever-increasing number of orders. Our story will parallel American history and illustrate the vital role sisters and nuns played in the growth of our country and its institutions. We will also look beneath the surface of what most see as a mysterious way of life to witness the dynamics of religious communal life, and how it influenced hundreds of thousands of women to dedicate their lives to the service of others. We will come to understand the tensions and problems they faced, their reaction to them and how they differ from most of the rest of us in perspective. Insights will emerge that partially explain why women adopt this counter-cultural way of life.

To date, only four United States citizens have been declared saints by the Roman Catholic Church. Three were women religious: Elizabeth Ann Seton, Rose Philippine Duchesne, and Frances Xavier Cabrini. Their lives and the orders they formed are detailed in the pages ahead. The works and sanctity of other sisters and nuns are under investigation to determine their qualification for this singular recognition. Outstanding women of talent and quite ordinary ones, motivated by deep religious convictions, have contributed more to society at large than any other clearly identified organized group of American women.

At the outset, it is important to clarify for whom this book is written. First, it is directed to Catholic laity in order to inform and enkindle a deeper appreciation for this marvelous and nearly forgotten heritage. Second, it is directed to those who treasure American history who will find herein an aspect of *Americana* not covered in overall fashion anywhere else. Third, it is addressed to those interested in Catholic history. Fourth, devotees of the new and expanding field of women's history who are not conversant with American Catholic history will find herein a gold mine of neglected information. Finally, this book will broaden the knowledge of the general non-Catholic public who have had little opportunity to learn about the role of American sisters and nuns in our country's development.

Conversely, it is not specifically written for sisters themselves, although their approval is desired and sought. Unfortunately, many will be sorely disappointed since it has been impossible to give fair and proper coverage to all the numerous religious orders, each of which cherishes its own particular traditions and history. Slight mentions and omissions will be sources of pain for many of today's sisters and nuns who naturally feel that their heroines merit prime coverage. There are simply too many orders and too many years. A legitimate assumption might be that large orders such as Benedictines, Franciscans, Dominicans, Sisters of St. Joseph, Sisters of Mercy, and others would receive coverage in proportion to their numbers and ministries. Giving them proper space would squeeze out too many smaller communities of sisters who have served without fanfare generation after generation; consequently, this reporter acknowledges the imbalance of coverage at the outset.

Those communities singled out for coverage in this 263-year journey must suffice to illustrate what was applicable to the many. Moreover, an apology is due archivists who gave or loaned me voluminous materials on the histories of their communities that are hardly mentioned in this book. Early drafts did use much of that information, but as the book progressed it became necessary to condense, even eliminate, a heart-breaking number of accounts.

Another unfortunate consequence of limited space is the inability to portray interesting experiences and the personalities of so many fascinating women. Some, about whom many biographies and accounts have been published, are only mentioned in passing. Imposed selectivity is an onerous burden, introducing the probability that the writer's personal attitudes and preconceived concepts will influence the numerous selection decisions, consciously or unconsciously. Unquestionably, many leaders, heroines, and holy women are missed along the way — I plead *nolo contendere* to charges brought on such grounds — and recognize that this undertaking is as risky as Hezekiah's inviting the Babylonians to inspect the temple (II *Kings* 20:13). It will require multivolume treatment by some future historian to present the full story in expanded detail.

Probably the most difficult aspect of this history has been reporting the foundations of the hundreds of orders, a critical part of sister-history, yet one that has a tendency to dull the subject after a few accounts. Again, I had to devise a method. I reported the foundings of all the antebellum orders and selected those established later that seemed exceptional or of particular interest. Although the sheer weight of detail may make those accounts seem encyclopedic, this is not the intent. Accounts and stories are meant to provide an overview of more than two centuries' experiences and convey adequate insights into religious life. Quite intentionally I gave space to and placed emphasis on "roots," American foundresses, ethnic sources, and early experiences since they set the patterns for successive generations to follow. As this history progresses, the reader will notice a gradual shift from specific accounts of communities to more general and inclusive coverage. In their totality, the accounts seek to convey the sweep of the history of American women religious so as to involve the reader.

Since this history covers over 200 years, I have attempted to assume the perspectives of each period being reported. It is important that the reader refrain from applying current attitudes and concepts to the events, customs, beliefs, self-images, and lifestyles of the past. The final chapters recount and attempt to explain the vast and fundamental changes that have absorbed the attentions of women religious this last half of the 20th century. I had to remind myself again and again that the sisters were women of their time and part of ongoing life wherever and whenever they existed. While their commitment to the religious life made them different in many ways, it did not alter their humanity.

On noting the absence of any overall history of American sisters and nuns, I first assumed that there was a dearth of source materials. What a blunder! The case is quite the opposite. I assure the reader that it would take many lifetimes to read all the available materials on this subject. Someone or some institution must take on the project of assembling some form of compendium listing all the known source materials. Sister Evangeline Thomas, CSJ, made a start on this in her *Women Religious History Sources: A Guide to Repositories in the United States,* a listing of the size and location of archival materials.

Most Catholics have little idea of how many different orders of sisters and nuns exist in the United States and are usually astonished to find out that they number in the hundreds. Anyone attempting to count orders encounters a problem because there are various methods of classification. Just when one has it tied down, one discovers that it does not apply to this or that group. Do not become discouraged; the accounts will clarify this multiplicity. Every religious order in the country, women and men, has a designated number in *The Official Catholic Directory* (OCD), published annually by P. J. Kenedy & Sons, Chicago, Illinois. Since the hundreds of orders have titles that tend to blur in the memory, they are identified in the text by the OCD number whenever there is a possibility of confusion, i.e., "Sisters of Mercy (2570)." At times the titles are shortened, such as "Franciscan Sisters (1450)," the OCD number properly identifying the specific Franciscan congregation, of which there are many. All orders use initials, such as "RSM" (Religious Sisters of Mercy) to identify themselves. Individual sisters use these initials following their title, i.e., "Sister Rose Marie, RSM." Appendix A lists the initials for every order in the United States. These technical details probably are of little interest to the general reader, but are necessary for historical accuracy and quite important to the sisters. The first time an order appears in the accounts, its full title, initials and OCD number are in bold print.

There are other textual guidelines peculiar to such a history. Many sisters assume a religious name when joining an order, such as "Sister Mary of the Incarnation," "Sister Joseph of the Holy Family," etc. With all due apologies to the sisters themselves, for the sake of simplicity and to avoid confusion, this history uses baptismal names with some frequency. Today, use of family and baptismal names is more common than in the past. Esoteric terminology applicable to sisters and nuns and their lifestyles is also necessary to some degree. The Glossary lists words, terms, and phrases that may be unfamiliar to the general reader. The first chapter, "Prologue," explains many of these terms, and their use throughout the text often clarifies the meaning.

No original research went into this book — no poring over old diaries, correspondence, and journals in community archives. Rather, it is the result of culling information from published works — a synthesis of the work of others, a *popular history*. During recent years, Catholic historians and scholars have performed a tremendous amount of serious research on the history of American sisters and nuns, which is ongoing. Books, dissertations, monographs, articles, and every manner of researched sister-history are pouring from Catholic and collegiate presses. The only important new information uncovered in my research is the total count of women religious in each era, statistics that have been generally under-reported in official Catholic publications. Almost all Catholic writers have used these sister-population figures without question. Appendix F provides the results of this investigation and will hopefully initiate a revision of official statistics for future use by Catholic historians.

Since most of the text was derived from published books, and most of the information is in the public domain, to identify all the sources for each fact such as appears in scholarly works would be impractical. Therefore, endnotes for each chapter are used to identify any single source of information for a lengthy account and to credit direct quotes. Endnotes also contain sidelights and items that do not fit neatly in the running text. Because of limited space, I have used statistics extensively to convey historical data more than I would have wished. While statistics do not directly address the human element of history, they do illuminate it to a remarkable degree.

The Selected Bibliography lists the works of the premier American Catholic historians. The first listing is an "entry" book into this subject, appropriately titled *An Invitation to American Catholic History*, by Professor Martin E. Marty (a Lutheran). Please note that all of those listed Catholic histories are deficient in coverage of women religious, something that skews vital Catholic history. Those omissions are a prime motivation for this book. The Selected Bibliography contains many of the sources consulted in my research. Also, in editing the drafts every effort was made to contact most of the archivists whose communities receive more than passing mention, and their correspondence was invaluable in the elimination of errors and revision of skewed renditions.

Since the Appendices contain considerable data of importance, many readers will want to refer to them for details. For example, Appendix B lists the founding dates for all original establishments in the United States in chronological order. This appendix is also a partial index. Appendix C lists sister-founded hospitals, Appendix D sister-founded colleges, etc.

To better appreciate the accounts, several prevailing winds in American history should be noted. Lest the reader forget, the United States has a long history of anti-Catholicism. Do not take umbrage at the rather frequent references to anti-Catholic prejudice; and do remember that it was prevalent for a long time. Sisters and nuns were often the objects of bias. In this ecumenical age, many would prefer to ignore the unpleasant events of the past.

A brief comment about the words "poor" and "poverty" is appropriate, since they appear so often. During much of American history, death from starvation, exposure to the elements, disease, malnutrition, accidents, violence, and plain neglect were common and stoically accepted as part of life. It was up to the local community, churches, charitable societies, religious men and women, good-hearted citizens, philanthropists, relatives, and other private persons and organizations to meet the needs of the desperate and poor. Thus the word "poor" had a stronger connotation than today's perceptions of poverty. This understanding is critical for appreciating the sisters' accomplishments.

The built-in authority structure of the Roman Catholic Church has sometimes pitted bishops against mothers-superiors of communities in decision-making and controlling destinies. Each had perceptions of his and her position, responsibility, and self-image, perceptions that were sometimes at odds. Since this is sister-history, events are described from their perspective. Although such conflicts were the exception and not the norm, exceptions seem to get attention.

Immigration and ethnic identity receive considerable attention. While the character of the Catholic Church in the United States was shaped in large measure by immigration, it had an even more noticeable effect on the sisterhood because so many communities began their American existence as immigrant groups. Ethnic characteristics in many of the communities were sharply defined during their early years, and the "Americanization" process they underwent provides an unusual insight into the sociological development of the United States.

While I have tried to produce an objective history, some readers may fault the editorial comments interjected here and there. Since it is almost impossible for a historian to avoid slants that reflect personal understandings, life experiences, and subconsciously fed attitudes, I have attempted to make my editorial comments patently obvious as such. These comments are intended to enhance the readership quotient of a popular history and to avoid a cold, dispassionate account without reference to the Divine or to the humanity of women religious.

Prior to plunging into the extensive research required to assemble the final contents of this book, I consulted several of the premier Catholic historians. Each advised something of a lesser scope. What I proposed was impossible — too many orders! If such were feasible, an established historian would already have done it. I now tend to agree with their assessments. No doubt, this work will elicit critical comments in some quarters. To this I only say, *"Mea culpa, mea culpa, mea maxima culpa!"*

I hope my effort will prod more skilled hands to produce superior versions of the "impossible" history.

With these caveats, the preliminaries done, enjoy an inspiring story still unfolding.

George Craig Stewart Jr.

CHAPTER 1

Prologue

‡ — ‡

NOWHERE HAVE women gained more importance in the Church than in the dedication of their lives as religious sisters and nuns. Before entering the fascinating realm that Catholic sisters and nuns have occupied in American history, we shall set the scene by briefly viewing the history of religious congregations from their origin in the Old World to the time when the idea was transported to the New where it flourished, extending an ancient legacy to our own day.

Genesis

Women have played a featured role in Christian history beginning with the Annunciation and the Nativity. New Testament accounts relate the devotion of women to the Savior, who favored them in many ways, involving them in a number of His miracles. Jesus paid the highest tribute to women in giving His mother Mary to humanity as He hung dying on the cross by His final instruction to John, "There is your mother!" It was women who discovered the tomb empty and heralded the Resurrection to the fearful disciples. Women were among those early Christians kneeling in the catacombs.

The first Christians recognized and accepted women's dignity and held holy widows and virgins in high esteem. Accounts of those days tell of women as benefactresses, catechists, deaconesses, and dispensers of community charities. Among the first recorded miracles performed by a disciple of Jesus occurred when St. Peter raised from the dead a woman, the young matron Tabitha. The roll call of dedicated women of the early Church echoes down the corridor of time: Thecla, Cecilia, Phoebe, Agnes, Perpetua, Anastasia, Paula, Lucy, Helena, Felicitas, Flavia, and Melania, just to mention a few. During the Roman persecutions some women refused to deny their faith and suffered horrible tortures and death. Piety and love for Jesus Christ have motivated and characterized numerous women during all of Christian history. In every age, men sneering at piety and religion have used the epithet "just a pastime for women!"

Gathering together to form communities for religious life was an evolutionary process. Withdrawing from the world to lead more spiritual lives began with men in the Egyptian desert. During the third and early fourth centuries hundreds of pious men became hermits in the desert seeking to deepen their spirituality, inspired by the teachings of Jesus Christ who often retreated to the desert for prayer and meditation. St. Anthony of Egypt (250-356), the prototype hermit, is often portrayed in Christian art. The early Church profited greatly from the example, theological speculations, and writings of these men. By the fourth century when the term "monk" (Greek *monachos*, "to live alone") came into wide usage, these hermits had begun to band together into communities for mutual support. Monks founded monasteries in Egypt, Palestine, Turkey, Syria, and Greece. From that time onward "monasticism" has been a great force in and a permanent feature of Christianity. St. Basil (329-379) is considered the father of Eastern monasticism since he formalized this institution with a "rule," a written statement of the spiritual purpose of the community and a prescription for its lifestyle and conduct.

Anchoresses, female hermits who did not necessarily live in the desert, appeared early in the third century, and monasteries for women arose in the fourth century. In 325, St. Pachomius (290-348) erected one for his sister and her companions in Egypt and later founded another monastery for a different group of women. St. Basil began a monastery for his sister Macrina and her companions. St. Augustine (354-430) established one in North Africa and composed a rule that is still widely used. Church records evidence the early existence of monastic communities of women; many of these attached to male monasteries for protection. The Fourth Ecumenical Council at Chalcedon (451), in addition to wrestling with various thorny issues such as the Nestorian heresy,[1] issued canons regulating the conduct of clerics and both male and female monastics. Thus we can say that the origins of women's monastic communities date back over 1600 years.

With this beginning, the evolution of women religious communities continued in Europe and eventually the United States. A brief summary of the European development, setting the stage for the American experience, follows.

Benedictine Beginning

In Europe, early records describe religious communities of women living together to pray and perform charitable works. Among them were those founded by St. Patrick in Ireland in 409, by Bishop Caesar in Arles, France in 525, and by St. Eanswythe, daughter of the King of Kent, in 630. Others appeared in Spain and Italy. Eventually, most of the surviving early female monasteries retained the Augustinian rule or adopted the Benedictine rule.

St. Benedict (480-546) founded the first permanent European monastery of monks at Monte Cassino, Italy.[2] His rule for the monastic life was so wise and flexible that it is still the primary rule of Western monasticism. He adapted his rule for women at the behest of his twin sister, St. Scholastica, who is credited with initiating the Second Order of St. Benedict, a term that denotes the female branch of a monastic order whose members are termed "nuns." St. Scholastica is often referred to as the "mother" of Western female monasticism. Hundreds of thousands of sisters and nuns have taken Scholastica as their religious name over the centuries. Numerous Catholic institutions bear her name.

Benedictine orders of men and women sprang up all over Europe, including Scandinavia, and spread as far as Iceland. They made tremendous contributions to the Church during the Middle Ages by civilizing the indigenous peoples, spreading Christianity, preserving records, restoring culture and learning, and producing beautiful manuscripts of scripture and the classics. Along with abbots, abbesses and prioresses enjoyed considerable status.[3] In England they were counselors to kings and bishops, exercising great sway. Their status deteriorated after William the Conqueror's victory at Hastings in 1066 because Normans held women in such low regard. However, in Germanic and Nordic lands, Benedictine abbesses continued to hold high status. Some of their monasteries even had subordinate components of monks under the control of abbesses. St. Walburga of Heidenheim (710-779), an English missionary to the Germans, is still venerated. Oil from a stone slab near her relics flows from October to February each year, is collected, and used for application to seriously ill patients during healing prayer services. St. Hildegarde of Bingen (1098-1179) was a mystic and prolific writer who exerted tremendous influence throughout Europe. She wrote morality plays, books on natural history and medicine, composed music, and corresponded with popes, kings, monks, nuns, and ordinary people of all social classes. Many of her works are preserved in the state library at Wiesbaden. The writings of St. Gertrude the Great (1256-1302), a Benedictine mystic in Saxony, have inspired seekers of a higher order of spirituality. While Benedictines have had a strong presence in France and Italy, Benedictine influence in the United States derives from its German and Swiss origins.

Monastic Life in the Middle Ages

All through the Middle Ages, the evolution of communities of women continued. Like their male counterparts, nuns began taking vows of poverty, chastity, and obedience, living by a prescribed rule in Church-approved monasteries. Some became members of groups that derived from the Benedictine order. Others joined new orders. For the most part, early monasteries were autonomous. Monks and nuns took a fourth vow of "stability" to specific monasteries, something the Church felt necessary to prevent dispersion of members when internal disputes arose. Because of a reversion to an earlier attitude of female inferiority, and to insure their protection, both state and Church laws began to impose "cloister" upon women, prohibiting the entry into a monastery by outsiders and restricting nuns' egress.

Within the wall of their monasteries, nuns occupied their time with prayer and contemplation, writing letters, gardening, manufacturing religious articles, and performing domestic duties. Cloister notwithstanding, some nuns were educators and performed numerous apostolic charities over the centuries. Local bishops often encouraged active ministries to meet critical needs. Nuns operated hospitals, orphanages, homes for the aged, hospices for pilgrims and the dying, as well as female academies within the confines of their convents. For example, in the 12th century the bishop of Paris established a hospital for the poor, the Hotel-Dieu, staffed by Augustinian nuns.

Communities usually required a dowry for admittance. Nuns sometimes became hardy farmers. Others manufactured artistic and religious products. However, it was dowries, tithes from land they owned, alms, gifts from benefactors, endowments, and inheritances that constituted the primary means of support for monasteries. Communities sometimes enjoyed the financial support of powerful patrons such as kings, queens, princes, aristocrats, professional men, guilds, and high Church officials. Sometimes, patrons endowed wealth in their wills. Over the centuries a number of monasteries accumulated large holdings of land. Throughout European history there are repeated instances of the suppression of religious orders and confiscation of their properties — a hazard of accumulation in times of social upheaval and political unrest.

During the Middle Ages it became the custom for ladies of rank or substance to bring a servant when joining an order; that servant normally became a community member. Since nuns had to read and understand Latin to pray the Holy Office, communities were divided into two groups. Those members who came as servants and illiterate members were categorized as "lay," doing most of the domestic work and acting as "externs" to perform tasks outside the monastery. Those who were literate, had paid the dowry, and could recite the Holy Office were classified as "choir," a term derived from the choir stalls where the nuns prayed aloud or chanted the Holy Office.[4] Often the habits were different to distinguish choir from lay. This ancient European caste system accompanied a few orders to America, where its elimination contributed to the "Americanization" process.

Scriptwriters, novelists, and even historians have often depicted women religious of the Middle Ages as entering religious life for less than noble reasons. Sometimes the age-old grasping for inheritance, particularly land, was a contributing factor for women being "put away" in convents lest the male heirs lose out. Since women could not engage in any honorable profession, being literate and educated could be a burden as well as a blessing in a society where less than five percent of the population could read or write, and a monastery was often the only satisfactory place for gifted women seeking an outlet for intellectual pursuits. At times, women of the nobility who posed a threat or inconvenience were "exiled" to convents or voluntarily retired there to extricate themselves from intolerable situations. Simple safety made these protected institutions desirable for widows and

Choir sister, Nuns of the Perpetual Adoration of the Blessed Sacrament (c. 1942).

Courtesy Gonzaga University

spinsters losing or lacking the security of a family. Such women often joined communities or rented rooms in the convent, thus providing needed income. Having boarders sometimes led to laxity of religious life and Church authorities totally eliminated the practice during various reforms. While the vast majority of the millions of nuns who lived during those centuries were pious and spiritually motivated, there were unquestionably some who did enter religious communities for mundane and practical reasons. Shakespeare's familiar quote from *Hamlet* "Get thee to a nunnery"[5] has some limited basis in historical fact.

The distinctive clothing worn by women religious, or "habit," dates back

Candidate for sisterhood. Daughters of Divine Charity (c. 1942).
Courtesy Gonzaga University

to the earliest days of monasticism. Founders and foundresses wanted the habit to distinguish their members from the laity and to give witness to their religious profession. They chose various colors and cuts — brown, white, brown with white cord about the waist, and differing headdress for the many black habits. Once a habit became standard within an order, tradition took over and community laws dictated continued use, some habits remaining unchanged for centuries. Most newly founded orders copied traditional garb.

Taking a religious name when making vows began as early as the sixth century, gradually taking hold during the Middle Ages. The idea springs from God's changing Abram's name to Abraham to signify the covenant between them (*Genesis* 17:3-9).[6] A religious name signifies the adoption of a new life; the replacement of family identity with a religious one. In time, the practice became so entrenched that, up until recent years, practically all sisters and nuns adopted religious names. Saints and biblical events have been popular name choices over the years, as the accounts ahead illustrate. The wearing of wedding bands, an ancient marriage custom dating back to Roman days, was the symbol of a nun's "marriage" to Christ.

The term "mother-superior," or simply "mother," indicates the elected or appointed superior of a group. In the larger communities with subordinate components, the overall superior was usually titled "mother-general," and the leaders of large subdivisions, normally called "provinces," used the title "provincial." There are variations on these titles but these were the most common ones.

A woman wishing to become a sister or nun entered into a formal process — formation. This was considered necessary in order to inculcate within her

Postulant. Daughters of Divine Charity (c. 1942).
Courtesy Gonzaga University

a higher level of spirituality, mold her attitudes, instill self-discipline, familiarize her with devotional and domestic routines, train her for the ministries performed by the community, teach her the history and charism of the community she joined and, most importantly, allow time for her to discern whether or not she had a true religious vocation.

Several terms were often used regarding formation. An "aspirant" was one who petitioned for admittance while a "postulant" was actually a candidate who physically moved into the convent; she typically retained this status for six months. A "novice" was an accepted postulant clothed with a "novice-habit" and preparing to take vows. The "novitiate" was the term used for the time period for formation, varying among the orders from six months to three years.[7] "Novitiate" could also indicate a convent or place where novices underwent formation. Normally a novice underwent her novitiate in the motherhouse of her community. The word "profession" referred to the actual taking of vows upon completion of the novitiate; with this step, the woman became a full-fledged member of the community. Profession was, in part, a religious ceremony marked by both joyful and solemn moments.

Since the vast majority of monasteries were autonomous, each required more than a rule for orderly life and smooth functioning. Something like a charter was needed to authorize its existence, approve its ministries, and define its relationship to Church authorities. No two autonomous communities were precisely alike; conditions varied from place to place and time to time. Hence, a detailed and precise official document was essential — a constitution. Items such as purpose for existence, method of electing officers, frequency of elections, duties of each officer, means of livelihood, community meetings (chapters), description of ministries, habits, specific types of devotions, relationships to higher authorities, and other matters were all

Professed. Daughters of Divine Charity (c. 1942).
Courtesy Gonzaga University

elements for a proper constitution. "Rule" and "constitution" are often used interchangeably. This history finds the word "rule" the most convenient in most instances.

Over time, another document came into common usage, the "custom book." This was an internal and informal document detailing "how we do things," covering a host of details concerning procedures and personal conduct in everyday life in the community. Custom books underwent frequent revisions because of their tendency to become overloaded with picayune prescriptions.

A question that has often piqued curiosity is how these women managed to live in the close physical contact of communal life and still maintain their serenity. The human dynamics at work would suggest that personality conflicts, irritating manners, power struggles, petty jealousies, and all the grist of human friction would make this impossible for any extended period of time. However, centuries of experience in communal living developed customs, rules, and practices that minimized the negative aspects and mitigated the tensions of group living. Mutual love, compassion, good humor, humility, gracious manners, trust, self-discipline, the vow of obedience, and the constraints imposed by deep spirituality governed their day-to-day living. While nuns at times had problems in maintaining harmony, they generally learned how to deal with tensions and resolve relationship problems. Because history has a way of highlighting disputes, struggles, contests, and personality clashes, the accounts ahead do report some of these exceptions to harmony.

Changes After Trent

The Protestant Reformation sent shock waves throughout the Catholic Church. Finally reacting in 1545, an ecumenical council convened in Trent, Italy. Because of internal disputes and wars, it took 19 years to complete its

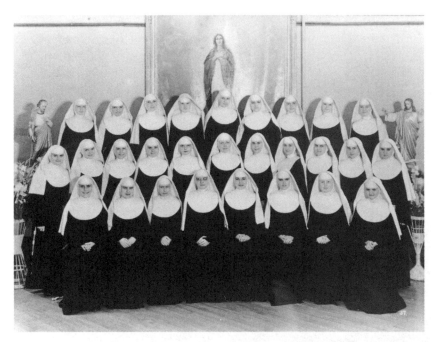

Group of novices. Sisters of Saint Francis of Mary (1940).
Courtesy Gonzaga University

25 sessions. The Council of Trent undertook to define Catholic doctrine more clearly, to eliminate clerical and episcopal abuses, and to reform the Church. Compliance and reform were not as rapid as the recent post-Vatican II experience, requiring many decades for full implementation. The council deepened the split between Catholics and Protestants although it was not a restoration of the Middle Ages Church and can be considered the beginning of a new Catholic era. The reformed Catholic Church crafted at Trent prevailed for the next 400 years.

In addition to other needed reforms, Church fathers determined to correct abuses that had crept into religious orders over the years. In this endeavor, the council legislated strict observance of enclosure for nuns in their monasteries and convents. Nuns practicing active ministries had to curtail or restrict them and Third Order sisters were required to live much as their Second Order contemporaries. However, this seemingly unfortunate circumstance of history had good results. Unpredictably and surprisingly, efforts accelerated to found new communities that would be free to practice active ministries and avoid cloister. Numerous communities appearing in the American saga sprang from these "new" congregations of sisters that arose as a result of reaction to the Council of Trent.

The United States became the rich inheritor of the variegated pattern of

Novice. St. Agnes Convent (c. 1942).
Courtesy Gonzaga University

communities of women religious that had developed in Catholic Europe since the fourth century. In the remainder of this chapter we will single out some of those founders and community members whose contributions had the greatest impact on the development of the Church in the United States.

The Franciscan Heritage

St. Francis of Assisi (1181-1226) is one of the saints and founders of religious communities most familiar to the American public. He was a deacon, never ordained a priest. As the world's first recorded great nature lover, he respected all of God's creation in a personal way. Even during his life he was considered a saint; popes and high Catholic officials gave him support. Today, his statues adorn flower gardens where he is often depicted talking to birds, and many Christians are familiar with his famous prayer for peace.[8] However, his impact on Christianity was much more profound. He made poverty and love the centerpieces of Christian living — demands that have challenged devout followers ever since. During his short life, he gathered thousands of followers and influenced the Church as few have ever since. By comparison, Mother Teresa of Calcutta has drawn around 3,000 members, half the number that Francis accrued, to her **Missionaries of Charity (MM-2710).**

Unlike the Benedictines, Francis' followers were not monastics. Rather they preached and mingled with the populace, depending on begging for sustenance. They initiated what came to be known as "mendicant" orders.[9]

Lesser known is Francis' female contemporary and friend, St. Clare (1194-1253), also a native of Assisi. Inspired by the Franciscan charism, this beautiful young woman defied her powerful family, withdrawing into a

Postulant. Home Mission Sisters of America, Glenmary Sisters.
Courtesy Gonzaga University

cloistered convent to lead a life of prayer. Other women soon followed her, resulting in the foundation of a community of Second Order Franciscans. St. Clare became the first woman to write a rule for women. Her spiritual descendants are orders of nuns called Poor Clares, most of whom live the contemplative life in monasteries. Eventually the Poor Clares split into two branches. We will encounter both in American history.

In addition to religious congregations, lay admirers organized into groups called "tertiaries" (Latin, "third") to apply Francis' spirituality to secular life. Some women who otherwise might have entered monastic life chose rather to become tertiaries and translate their spiritual impulses into active ministry while living "in the world." At first the tertiaries were simple associations for men or women or groups that combined both. Inspired by St. Francis' *Letter to All the Faithful*, tertiaries undertook to perform works of mercy and intensified their prayer life while maintaining loosely knit organizations.[10] St. Francis applied the term "Third Order" to these groups. Over time, some tertiaries gravitated to communal life that evolved into two categories: Third Orders Secular for laity, and Third Orders Regular for sisters, priests, and brothers.[11] Most Franciscan communities of women in the United States are Third Order Regular. Members of a Third Order are not technically nuns and are referred to as "sisters." In the American experience, Franciscan sisters ultimately became the most numerous group of women religious under one rule.

The Dominican Impact

The Order of Preachers, known as Dominicans and also a mendicant order, was founded by St. Dominic (1170-1221). Because the Fourth Ecumenical Lateran Council ordered that no more new rules be established, he adapted St. Augustine's for his new order.[12] A Spaniard by birth and an

Professed. Home Mission Sisters of America, Glenmary Sisters.
Courtesy Gonzaga University

ordained priest, Dominic became active in preaching in southern France where heresy was rampant. The Albigensian heresy had infected the clergy and populace.[13] Gathering some Cistercian[14] monks, he inaugurated a program of preaching; not just at Mass but in public places and in private homes. His concept for a new order solidified while he was visiting in Rome. Cardinal Ugulino (future Pope Gregory IX), who also supported St. Francis in establishing his order, was instrumental in securing papal approbation for St. Dominic's new order in 1216. St. Dominic dispersed his friars throughout Europe to gather followers and expand the ministry of vigorous preaching of the Gospel.[15] The Dominican order has a long proud history of vitality in the Church. Some traditions credit St. Dominic with originating the rosary at the instigation of the Blessed Virgin Mary. True or not, the Dominican order vigorously promoted its spread, making it the most popular and widely practiced of all Catholic devotions.[16] St. Thomas Aquinas (1225-1274), generally considered the Church's greatest theologian, was a Dominican.

While preaching in southern France in 1206, St. Dominic established a monastery of nuns whose mission was to support the preachers with prayer and to provide a haven for women converts from heresy. After founding the order, he established monasteries for nuns in Madrid and Rome and was in the process of forming another when he died. Thus began the Second Order of St. Dominic for nuns. The order expanded rapidly, establishing monasteries over most of Europe. Following the Franciscan example, Third Order Dominican sisters soon followed.

St. Catherine of Siena (1347-1380) was a Third Order Dominican famous in Catholic history.[17] One of 23 children, she displayed a vocation for religious life at an early age, joining the Dominicans at age 17. Her profound piety and active social work brought her followers called Caterinati that included priests, bishops, cardinals, aristocrats, and lay people. A miracle-worker, healer, converter, and a bearer of the stigmata,[18] she fostered many needed charities and instigated numerous conversions to Christian living with her compelling personality. Her letters, over 300 recorded and authenticated, attracted the attention of Church officials and the public.[19] She advised two popes and mediated disputes between warring states. Her letters and book, *Dialogue*, are her spiritual testaments to the world. Considered a saint during her short lifetime of only 33 years, she was canonized 81 years after her death. As we shall see, her Third Order spiritual descendants were prominent in American history since the early 19th century and the first Dominican community bears her name.

The Ursuline Mission

St. Angela Merici (1474-1540) founded the Order of St. Ursula in Brescia, Italy, in 1535, as a secular group of women dedicated to the education and Christian formation of future wives and mothers. In the beginning, her followers lived at home and wore no habits beyond "modest and maidenly" dress as they worked among their neighbors, quietly practicing their apostolate. Angela called them "Companions." They took no formal vows but adhered to the concepts of virginity, poverty, and obedience.[20] Too modest to allow her name to be attached to the group, Angela named her companions after a fourth-century virgin saint, the English princess Ursula, martyred at Cologne. Angela composed a primitive rule that among other things included this admonition for those to follow: "If, with change of time and circumstance, it becomes necessary to make fresh rules, or to alter anything, then do it with prudence, after taking good advice." After her death in 1544, the company became the first of its kind to receive Church approval.

Somewhat later, the bishop of Milan, St. Charles Borromeo (1538-1584), wrote a more formal rule for her followers. However, he did not enjoin cloister, gather them into groups, or in any way impose on them a form of communal life. While many of the consecrated virgins continued to live at home, gradually the necessity to care for homeless and aged members resulted in houses for community life. During the early 17th century, Ursulines were forced to choose between cloister or giving up the idea of profession as religious. Most Ursulines in Italy elected the latter. A group of French Ursulines formed the Congregation of Paris in 1612, after arriving at a compromise with Church authorities. They accepted cloister and solemn vows, but added a fourth one, "to employ themselves in the instruction of young girls." This made them an order of independent, not Second Order, nuns. The community grew in France, spread to other countries, and by the early 18th century numbered some 9,000 nuns.[21] Their establishment in continental United States occurred some fifty years before the Declaration of Independence.

The Carmelite Influence

Carmelite nuns came into being in 1452 when some existing nuns petitioned to join the Order of Carmelite friars as Second Order nuns. St. Albert of Jerusalem (1149-1214) had established the order on Mount Carmel in Palestine two centuries earlier. Some years after joining the Carmelite nuns in her native Spain, St. Teresa of Ávila (1515-1582) initiated a reform that led to the establishment of a more strictly enclosed monastery and a more intense spiritual life. Accepting the opposition and difficulties such a move presented, she broke away and founded 16 convents of nuns.[22] Termed Discalced, meaning "barefoot," her order symbolized the new more austere life, although in practice most wear sandals. She later founded a male branch of this order, making her the first foundress of a major men's order. The older order of Carmelites subsequently became known as Calced (shod) to distinguish between the two branches; their official title being Carmelite Nuns of the Ancient Observance. Both orders are present in the United States today.

St. Teresa is one of the most extraordinary women religious in history. During the 20th century, she and St. Catherine of Siena were declared Doctors of the Church, the only two women so honored. Requirements for this dignity are great sanctity, eminent learning, and proclamation by a pope or ecumenical council. This honor places St. Teresa and St. Catherine in the august company of only 30 others including St. Thomas Aquinas, St. Bonaventure, St. Augustine, St. Leo the Great, and St. Francis de Sales. St. Teresa's profound spiritual writings are studied worldwide in all branches of Christianity and remain popular devotional materials today. (Another Teresa, properly St. Thérèse of Lisieux, also a Carmelite nun and affectionately called "The Little Flower," is one of the most popular saints of the modern age among Roman Catholics.)

Following the death of St. Teresa, Discalced Carmelites quickly spread into other European countries. Catholic women who desired monastic religious life soon gravitated to this order. Spanish nuns established an English-speaking Carmelite monastery in Antwerp, Belgium. From Antwerp, English Carmelite nuns founded new convents in Hoogstraeten and Lierre.[23] Thus, Belgium became the center for English convents, monasteries, and seminaries during the 17th and 18th centuries as orders sought to accommodate English refugees from Protestant-dominated lands. During the colonial era, young American women seeking to enter such institutions traveled to Belgium to join English-speaking compatriots. Several of these women would return to the United States in 1790 to establish a Carmelite convent in Maryland.

The Visitandine Emphasis

In June 1610, St. Francis de Sales (1567-1622) and St. Jane Frances de Chantal (1572-1767) became founder and foundress of the Visitation Order in Annecy, France. At the outset, Francis de Sales intended that the nuns be contemplative but not cloistered, spending several hours a week visiting the sick and poor in their homes. He prescribed the admittance of any pious woman, young or old, virgin or widow, robust or in delicate health. However, the powerful Cardinal de Marquemont insisted that they become an order with solemn vows and papal enclosure, to which Francis de Sales reluctantly agreed. Consequently, they remained an enclosed order of nuns with primary emphasis on teaching girls within the confines of their convents. This was yet another order of independent nuns not associated with any male order. Co-foundress Jane de Chantal established over 60 Visitation convents in France. Margaret Mary Alacoque, a Visitation nun canonized in 1920, received visions of Jesus in 1763 and 1764 that popularized the ancient devotion to the Sacred Heart of Jesus which spread over the Catholic world and is a popular pious practice today. The order quickly spread to Italy, Switzerland, Poland, Belgium, and Germany. In the 18th century it established itself in Syria, England, Austria, Spain, and Portugal. In the 19th century it made foundations in South America and Czechoslovakia. In the United States, the Visitation rule was adopted by a group known as the "Pious Ladies" who then established the first Catholic academy for girls in this country.

Active Congregations

St. Vincent de Paul (1581-1660) was a French priest whose name will resound forever among Roman Catholic religious devoted to service to the sick, the poor, and the needy. The expression "Vincentian spirit" evokes his memory, as demonstrated by the thousands of hospitals worldwide named St. Vincent. He founded a congregation of priests and brothers called Vincentians, or Lazarists as they are known in Europe, to concentrate on preaching the Gospel to the poor and on performing basic charitable works. To ensure assistance to the poor in the rural parishes where he and his priests conducted missions, he organized confraternities of Christian charity for both men and women. He also started confraternities in Paris among women of wealth, but this initiative proved to be something of a failure since the ladies too often sent servants to perform the actual tasks.

St. Vincent was the first to devise an alternative to the type of convent life decreed by the Council of Trent. He became acquainted with a pious member of the aristocracy, St. Louise de Marillac (1591-1660), and over a period of years drew her into his charitable causes. After she became a widow in 1625, he sent her to visit the Confraternities of Charity in the country parishes to reanimate and guide them in their difficulties. When some of the pious country girls volunteered to serve in the confraternities in Paris, St. Vincent and St. Louise felt this was the solution for their problems in that city. The idea was to place them under the supervision of the ladies dedicated to the care of the poor. At first the girls lodged with the ladies or in convents. Later, St. Louise took three or four into her home where they lived under her direction, forming the nucleus of the Company of the Daughters of Charity whose founding date is November 29, 1633. These two saints, priest and widow, established the Daughters of Charity as a secular institution (confraternity) in order to avoid cloister and to practice their active ministries. Based on St. Francis de Sales' experience in founding the Visitation order and his advice, St. Vincent de Paul composed a rule that carefully defined their status as laywomen. Even today, the Daughters of Charity are technically a "society of apostolic life in community" and not an order or congregation in a strict canonical sense. In his words, the sisters would —

> *. . . have no monastery but the house of the sick, no cell but a hired room, no cloister but the streets of the city or the wards of hospitals, no enclosure but obedience, no grate but the fear of God, no veil but holy modesty. . . .*

St. Vincent de Paul cautioned his followers that the poor would only forgive the one who handed them bread in proportion to the love with which it was given. Animated by that spirit, the Daughters of Charity quickly became the largest social welfare organization of France, spreading into other European countries. Though outlawed during the French Revolution, they were among the last Catholic religious communities to be suppressed since their hospital work was so critical. During the Reign of Terror, 16 of them died on the guillotine for refusing to deny their faith. Both the spiritual and organizational descendants of St. Vincent de Paul and St. Louise de Marillac have flourished in America. They are prominent in the American experience.

In 1651 a French Jesuit priest, John-Pierre Medaille (1610-1669), formed a similar plan when he founded the Sisters of St. Joseph as a secular congregation. Father Medaille's memorable "Little Design" stated —

> *As our dear Savior in the Holy Eucharist appears to us as being nothing for self but all for God his Father and the souls redeemed by his Precious Blood, so, my dear daughter, our Little Design*

> *and the persons who compose it will be nothing for self, but whol-*
> *ly lost and emptied of self in God and for God; and furthermore,*
> *they will all for the dear neighbor and nothing for self.*[24]

Father Medaille composed a rule that remained essentially unchanged for 300 years. It approved ministries for any demonstrated need. The congregation expanded in France until almost destroyed by the Revolution, during which time most members waited for an end to persecution while they sought to live religious lives as private citizens. Jeanne Fontbonne (1759-1843) is known as the Second Foundress of the Sisters of St. Joseph. She and her sister Marie had joined the Sisters of St. Joseph at Bas-en-Basset in 1779, taking the religious names of Sister St. John and Sister St. Teresa. Sister St. John demonstrated leadership and became the mother-superior of the convent at Monistrol in 1785. Refusing to take the civil oath of the Revolution in 1791, she disbanded the convent and returned home. There the two sisters gave religious instruction to children until arrested in 1793. Condemned to death, the two awaited execution for 11 months. On the scheduled day of the guillotine they were suddenly released — Robespierre had been killed the previous day, ending the Reign of Terror. They returned home and waited for the rebirth of the community for 12 years. In 1807, Jeanne received an invitation from Cardinal Fesch of Lyons to restore the Sisters of St. Joseph as a diocesan congregation. Within nine years, there were 90 communities in various diocesan congregations operating schools, dispensaries, hospitals, homes for the aged and crippled children, and hospices for the insane. In a sermon, Abbé Piron, successor to Father Medaille, had predicted that the Sisters of St. Joseph would spread out everywhere and become as numerous as the stars. The Sisters of St. Joseph came early to the United States and although not as numerous as the stars, they did expand rapidly and spread out over the country.

Mary Ward (1586-1646), a notable pioneer of active and uncloistered women religious, organized a Jesuit-style community in England. Forced to flee Protestant persecution, the group moved to the continent. She and her followers wore no habits and lived without enclosure, a scandalous idea in those days. They focused primarily on teaching, establishing schools in Italy, Austria, Belgium, and Germany. Even today, members of her community, The Institute of Mary, are called *die Englisch Fraulein* in Germany. Unfortunately, her community was too closely identified with the Jesuits. Her sisters were even ridiculed with the nickname "galloping girls of the Jesuits" at a time when the Society of Jesus had accrued too many enemies. Losing favor with the pope, Mary Ward was forced to surrender authority over her community and was forgotten and almost lost in the footnotes of history until a recent Mary Ward "revival" among Catholic historians rescued her name.

The Daughters of Charity, the Sisters of St. Joseph, and the Institute of

Mary are just three examples of how the "new" congregations came to be. It was a continuing process that produced the Sisters of Mercy, the Sisters of Providence, the School Sisters of Notre Dame, and many, many more. We will witness the birth pangs of these and others in the chapters ahead.

Technically, the congregations founded after Trent were associations of laywomen without canonical status. Nonetheless, they wore habits, lived in convents, and received *de facto* recognition as women religious in the service of the Church. In 1745, almost 100 years after the Council of Trent, this proliferation of congregations prompted Pope Benedict XIV to issue a constitution (*Quamvis justo*) providing guides and norms for sisters in congregations with simple vows. The effect was to legitimize congregations without giving them full canonical status. He used the term "tolerate" in referring to them and made it clear that local bishops had full authority over congregations in their dioceses. This half-measure was the source of considerable confusion and consternation until the 20th century. In 1900, Pope Leo XIII issued his constitution *Conditae a Christo* giving full canonical status to congregations. He divided congregations with simple vows into two categories, those approved by the Holy See and those approved solely by bishops. This canonical charter gave specific regulations for each type, clearly defining the rights of bishops and those of congregations. As we shall see, during the American saga, the overriding power of bishops with regard to sisters in congregations sometimes created stress and problems.

As the curtain opened on the American drama, women religious fell into four broad categories: nuns of Second Orders, nuns of independent orders, sisters of Third Orders, and sisters of congregations. However, the distinctions were frequently blurred. Nuns often performed active apostolates, with cloister being more symbolic than actual. At different times and places, Third Order and congregational sisters lived more like nuns and practiced limited cloister.

Proliferation in America

How each of the hundreds of orders and congregations came to be is a special story, rooted mainly in autonomy and differing charisms. While many orders and congregations remain highly integrated organizations despite geographical dispersion and huge memberships, more commonly branch communities become autonomous once they are established and functioning. In their initial stages, these communities are referred to in this American history as "offshoots," since often they were still closely associated with their original motherhouses. With the passage of time and loss of close association because of distance and other factors, the tendency among some communities was to become not just autonomous but an entirely new order or congregation. The American experience clearly demonstrates this phenomenon.

Another explanation for proliferation lies in the collective personality or charism of orders, congregations, and even their subordinate communities. Charism, as now used, is considered a gift of the Holy Spirit, given to the community for the good of its members, for others and for the good of the Church. Charism is most clearly seen in the foundress or founder who exemplified that gift and reflected it by example, writings, leadership, inspiration to others, ministries practiced, devotional emphasis, teaching, and vision. Some examples of charisms are the peace and hospitality of St. Benedict, the love of poverty of St. Francis of Assisi, the preaching and study of sacred truth of St. Dominic, the intense prayer life and withdrawal from secular life of St. Clare and St. Teresa of Ávila, and the simplicity and love of the poor personified by St. Vincent de Paul and St. Louise de Marillac. Without such distinctions and differences, the orders and congregations would blend into sameness with little in the way of special character to appeal to differing inclinations and desires for personal commitment to religious life. These divinely inspired gifts demonstrate the many ways of pursuing the goal of holiness.

Summary

This brief historical overview from the Egyptian desert in the fourth century to the opening of the American experience in the 18th century only provides glimpses of the evolutionary development of women religious organizations of the Roman Catholic Church. Flashbacks in the accounts ahead will fill some of the voids of this abbreviated report and further clarify how the many institutions began, how they function, how they relate to the official Church, and why women join, devoting their lives to God and ministry to His people — across the United States.

Endnotes

1. The Nestorian heresy supported the doctrine that there were two separate Persons in the Incarnate Christ, the one Divine and the other Human, as opposed to the orthodox doctrine that Jesus Christ was a single Person, at once God and man.
2. The Benedictine monastery he founded at Monte Cassino became front page news during World War II when the Germans occupied it and used its dominating heights in resisting advancing American forces. Bombardment almost destroyed this ancient and active monastery. It has since been fully restored.
3. An abbess is the superior of an abbey, the highest ranking type of monastery. This title is peculiar to Benedictines and Poor Clares. In Benedictine tradition, a prioress is the superior of a lesser ranking monastery, a priory. Nuns in medieval

times were not as suppressed, as uneducated, and not as subject to male authority as is commonly believed. This is verified by research reported in many books, such as *Word and Spirit: A Monastic Review: Women in Monasticism* and *A New Song: Celibate Women in the First Three Centuries*, by Jo Ann McNamara.

4. The Holy Office, as it was formerly called, is the universal prayer of the Church, recited daily around the world. All priests and certain religious pray the Holy Office as do some pious members of the laity. It is now called the Liturgy of the Hours and is less demanding than the ancient monastic practice. The devotion probably derives from *Psalm* 118:164, "*Seven times a day I give praise to thee.*" The seven times of the day were termed Matins, Prime, Terce, Sext, None, Vespers, and Compline. The prayers themselves are mainly prescribed psalms that vary with the hours and seasons.

5. Act 3, Scene 1, ll. 131-138.

6. *New American Bible* (New York, NY: Catholic Publishing Company, 1970).

7. See Chapter 10 for a new category called "juniorate."

8. St. Francis' prayer:

> *Lord, make me an instrument of your peace.*
> *Where there is hatred, let me sow love;*
> *Where there is injury, pardon;*
> *Where there is doubt, faith;*
> *Where there is despair, hope;*
> *Where there is darkness, light;*
> *And where there is sadness, joy.*
> *O Divine Master, grant that I may not so much*
> *Seek to be consoled, as to console;*
> *To be understood, as to understand;*
> *To be loved, as to love;*
> *For it is in giving that we receive;*
> *It is in pardoning that we are pardoned;*
> *And it is in dying that we are born to eternal life.*

9. In theory, mendicant orders rely entirely on alms and benefactors for their support. The rejection of property and other forms of wealth was a revolutionary concept when introduced by St. Francis and St. Dominic. It appealed to thousands, drawing them to this higher level of Christian life. While the concept is retained in mendicant orders, over time it has been diluted by the practical demands of modern life. Some communities (e.g., Poor Clares and Carmelites) still strive for perfection in this regard.

10. In response to pleas from lay people for a rule, St. Francis wrote the letter about the year 1214. While he does not actually suggest the formation of a society, he lays down principles upon which religious life must be based. The letter ends with this exhortation:

> *I, Brother Francis, your little servant, beg and beseech you by*
> *the Love which is God, and desiring to kiss your feet, that you will*
> *humbly and lovingly receive these fragrant words of our Lord*

> *Jesus Christ and cheerfully put them into practice and observe them to perfection. Let those who cannot read have them read to them often, and let them keep them with them and carry them out unto the end, for they are spirit and they are life.* . . . See John A. Moorman, *A History of the Franciscan Order from its Origins to the Year 1517* (Chicago, IL: Franciscan Herald Press, 1968), p. 42.

11. Secular Franciscans, Dominicans, Carmelites, and other organizations of lay associates of religious orders are quite common today. The term "tertiary" is now used infrequently.

12. The stricture has remained in effect to this day. In a highly technical sense, there are only four Church-approved rules for religious orders: those of St. Basil, St. Augustine, St. Benedict, and St. Francis.

13. The existence of the Albigensian heresy seems unfathomable today because we do not realize how ignorant and superstitious a portion of the peasantry was in early medieval Europe. Traces of ancient paganism lingered for centuries after the Christian religion became paramount. Essentially, the Albigensian heresy held that there were two gods, one good but remote and the other evil but creative. The doctrine permitted ordinary people to live as they pleased while the prefects (leaders) lived ascetic lives of poverty. All that was required for salvation was to receive a special "sacrament" before death.

14. Cistercians were founded in 1098 under the rule of St. Benedict. Trappist monks and Trappistine nuns belong to this order, properly titled Cistercians of the Strict Observance.

15. There are four broad categories of Roman Catholic priests: (1) diocesan priests who serve under a diocesan bishop (called the "ordinary"), (2) friars, who may or may not live in a friary, give allegiance to a central director and can be sent anywhere, (3) clerics regular who live under community rule but engage primarily in the same activities as the diocesan clergy rather than the monastic life, and (4) monks who serve in or from a monastery, are attached to it, and obey the monastic superior (abbot).

16. The rosary is a guide for specified sets of prayers based on 15 "mysteries," honoring critical events in the lives of Jesus and His mother, the Blessed Virgin Mary. It has a crucifix and 5 beads on a single strand attached to a circular string of 53 beads by a small medal (substitute for 2 beads). The circular string has 5 sets of 10 beads, each set interspersed by a single bead. The prayers of the rosary consist of opening prayers (on the single strand) and 5 mysteries, each consisting of an Our Father, 10 Hail Marys, and a Glory Be. There are 3 sets of mysteries: Joyful, Sorrowful, and Glorious. Praying a set of 5 mysteries is considered a complete rosary.

17. The name Catherine seems popular among saints. The first St. Catherine (of Alexandria) was a martyr of the fourth century. In addition to St. Catherine of Siena, the 14th, 15th, and 16th centuries produced St. Catherine of Sweden (a Bridgettine nun), St. Catherine of Genoa (a laywoman), St. Catherine of Bologna (a Poor Clare nun), St. Catherine Thomas (an Augustinian nun) and St. Catherine De' Ricci (a Dominican nun). An American, Mother Katharine Drexel, founded

the Sisters of the Blessed Sacrament for Indians and Colored People. She has been beatified, a preliminary step for canonization.

18. A person with the stigmata bears the five wounds of Jesus Christ. They may be permanent or just appear on certain days. The wounds cause great suffering, but saintly persons with the stigmata consider it a special gift and an indication of Jesus' special love. The stigmata has been a recurring phenomenon throughout Christian history, even in our day.

19. An example of her writing is —

> *I long to see you, so engulfed and set on fire in Christ Jesus that you will be completely lost to yourself. But I don't see how you can unless your mind's eye rises above yourself in true desire to gaze into the eye of the divine charity with which God looked on His creatures before He created us. And so He still looks on us. For He looked at us within Himself and felt so boundlessly in love with us that for love He created us to share and enjoy the good He possessed in Himself.*
>
> *But because of Adam's sin His desire was not realized. So God, moved by the fire of divine charity, sent the gentle incarnate Word, His Son, to ransom us and rescue us from slavery. And His Son ran to surrender Himself to the shame of the cross. He eagerly associated with sinners, with publicans, with outcasts, with all sorts of people. For there is no putting laws or limits to charity: it is not self-centered or self-seeking. Since the first man had fallen from the height of grace through selfish love of himself, God had to act in the opposite way — so He sent this spotless Lamb with an indescribably greathearted charity, seeking not Himself, but only the Father's honor and our salvation* (Sr. Suzanne Noffke,OP, *The Letters of St. Catherine of Siena*, Binghampton, NY: Medieval & Renaissance Texts & Studies, 1988, vol. I, p. 47).

20. Today, such a group would be termed a "secular institute" (see the Glossary). There are 16 such groups for women in the United States at present and six more institutes for both sexes.

21. During the French Revolution, 35 Ursuline nuns suffered martyrdom.

22. Convent comes from the Latin word *conventus* (where people gather). A convent is simply a house where women religious live; it may or may not be a monastery. Some male religious also use the term "convent" for their house.

23. Carmelite nuns did not establish a monastery in Protestant England until the late 1700's when English law was ignored to accommodate nuns fleeing the French Revolution. Male Carmelites of the Ancient Observance made foundations in England in the 13th century. They were called "whitefriars" because of their white mantel and hood.

24. Patricia Byrne, CSJ. "French Roots of a Woman's Movement: The Sisters of St. Joseph, 1650-1836." Ph.D. Diss. Boston College, 1985, p. 53.

CHAPTER 2

Mustard Seeds
(1727-1833)

‡ — ‡

THIS AMERICAN HISTORY opens in 1790 in Belgium, then a possession of the Austrian Empire, which shortly bargained it away to revolutionary France. Four nuns of the Discalced Carmelite order — three Americans from Maryland and an Englishwoman — were about to leave Antwerp to establish the first Catholic convent in the original United States. The three Americans were members of the Matthews family, two blood sisters and their aunt, from Charles County in southern Maryland.[1] Little is known about the background of the Englishwoman, Frances Dickenson, except that she came from a Middlesex County family of substance and that she was well educated.

Why the Carmel would be established in Maryland is not surprising. Landed Catholic families of Maryland were among the wealthiest in colonial America despite intermittent religious suppressions and loss of their civil rights. Lord Baltimore founded this Catholic colony in 1634 and insisted that both Catholics and Protestants jointly settle it and live in harmony. The colonial legislature enacted the famous Act of Religious Toleration in 1639, but Catholics soon felt repercussions from religious and political persecutions in England. They fell under the thrall first of Puritan and then Anglican administrations in Maryland. Empowered by mandates from London, administrators enacted legal strictures removing Catholics' civil liberties and attacking the practice of their faith. However, like many of the Catholic rural gentry in England, Maryland Catholics stubbornly persevered in loyalty to their religion and in holding on to their lands. Denied chapels and public worship, ordinary Catholics on both sides of the Atlantic used Father Richard Challoner's *The Garden of the Soul*, a combination of devotional exercises and catechism, to instruct their children and preserve the faith.

Financially able Maryland families sent promising offspring to Europe for higher education, and Catholics evidencing religious vocations normally entered English-language convents and seminaries in Belgium. The expense of Atlantic passage and dowry made entry into convents impossible for ordinary women and restricted the numbers who could go regardless of any religious calling. Yet surprising numbers went to Belgium to become priests and nuns. Records from the 18th century before the American Revolution reveal that convents in Belgium and France admitted 36 women from Maryland, including the Matthews women who joined the Carmelite order in Belgium.[2]

In the years preceding the American Revolution, the Carrolls of Maryland were prominent Catholic leaders. In 1773, England granted religious freedom to Canadian Catholics in the Quebec Act, an action that aroused considerable resentment among the Protestant establishment in the American colonies. In 1776, the Continental Congress voiced its objections to free Catholicity in Canada in a resolution titled the Appeal to the English People and Appeal to the King — a strange stance from leaders who 15 years later would incorporate religious freedom in the Bill of Rights. This unfriendly and insulting action was not conducive to Canada's joining the rebellion. Even so, the Congress sent a delegation to Canada to seek its participation composed of Benjamin Franklin, Samuel Chase, and Charles Carroll, Maryland's signer of the Declaration of Independence. It also sent his cousin, Father John Carroll (1735-1815), a known patriot and prominent citizen, along as an advisor. The mission failed, but Benjamin Franklin and Father John Carroll became fast friends on the Canadian journey.

While Minister to France in 1784 and on hearing that the Roman Catholic Church was considering the appointment of a superior for the United States, Franklin was instrumental in having the Vatican name his friend John Carroll as Superior of the Mission (non-bishop superior of a territory). Four years later, the Vatican decided to create a diocese in the United States, and Carroll's fellow priests elected him as their candidate for the miter.[3] On August 15, 1790, Charles Walmesley, a Benedictine bishop, consecrated John Carroll a bishop at Lulworth Castle in Dorsetshire, England. His arrival home in 1790 marks the beginning of the official Catholic Church in the United States.

Catholics numbered around 30,000 out of 3,900,000 Americans in 1790 — less than one percent. There were only 33 priests, mostly aging ex-Jesuits, to serve them. Families often went months and even years without benefit of priest, Mass, the sacraments, or instruction for their children. Most Catholics lived in Maryland, with several thousand in Pennsylvania and lesser numbers in Delaware and New York. Small pockets of Catholics lived in the port cities of Boston, Norfolk, Charleston, and Savannah. Most were of English and Anglo-Irish extraction with a small admixture of Germans, French, and Irish. With the exception of the Maryland landed gentry and a few merchants, Catholics were concentrated in the lower working class. In light of these circumstances, it is remarkable that so many clung tenaciously to their faith.

Maryland was the first state to request a group of nuns. In 1788, Father Ignatius Matthews joined other Catholics of southern Maryland in petitioning the Bishop of Antwerp for a convent of Carmelites. As early as 1780, Mary Margaret Brent, prioress of the Carmelite convent in Antwerp and a Marylander, had been in contact with Ann Matthews, the prioress of the Hoogstraeten Carmel, planning for the Maryland establishment. However, Mother Mary Margaret Brent died in 1784. Her cousin, Father Charles Neale, chaplain of the Antwerp convent, was also deeply committed to the undertaking. Ann Matthews assumed the leadership mantle for the prospective mission. A native of Brussels, M. De Villegas D'Estainbourg, a great admirer of the Carmelites, helped raise funds for this venture and personally contributed a sizable amount. Father Neale added Frances Dickenson to the mission as he was quite impressed by her abilities and energy. When 1790 dawned, this small band of nuns was ready to take Carmel to America.

In Europe, the year 1790 was ominous. The Catholic Church was under attack in one form or another in practically every country of Europe. In France, the Bastille had fallen and radicals were seizing power. French revolutionaries would execute the king and queen, persecute and dismantle the Catholic Church, and unleash a series of wars that would ultimately consume all Europe. Emperor Joseph II of Austria considered monastic communities such as the Carmelites to be useless and suppressed those orders in his domain, confiscating their properties. His one concession to moderation was to exempt the "English" convents in Flanders because of their refugee status.[4] The Jesuits who had provided the church vitality and leadership for some 200 years had been suppressed in 1773. Malevolent winds of change emanating from the philosophies of Voltaire, Rousseau, and Diderot were blowing across Europe. Deism, the religion of "The Age of Reason" that elevated Man almost to parity with a vague and disinterested God, was in vogue in intellectual circles and threatened both religious and political structures. The year 1790 marked the opening of one of the darkest periods in European history for the Catholic Church.

But in the United States, colonial era anti-Catholicism had modified considerably as a consequence of Catholic participation in the Revolution and the assistance rendered by Catholic France and Spain. Marquis de LaFayette and Comte de Rochambeau were popular heroes throughout the country. While deep prejudice persisted, especially in New England, the rest of the country generally ignored or viewed Catholics benignly because their numbers were so insignificant. It should be remembered also that the majority of Americans at that time were unchurched. By some estimates, only around 17 percent belonged to any organized religion and Deism infected intellectual circles. It would remain for the early 19th century to witness a popular revival of religion. In this calmer atmosphere, Father Ignatius Matthews wrote his sister Ann: "Now is your time to found in this country, for peace is declared and religion is free."[5] One wonders if all this was confusing to the expatriates in Belgium, absent from home for so many years.

To leave a melancholy Europe and establish a convent of Teresians, as Carmelites are often called, in their hope-filled and beloved homeland must have been an intoxicating prospect for the three Maryland natives and intriguing for their English compatriot. It would be fascinating to know precisely how much Ann Matthews, her American nieces, and Frances Dickenson knew about contemporary history and current events on both sides of the Atlantic. Nonetheless, they must have been deeply moved as they prepared for their adventure; curiosity must have been keen for Frances Dickenson who was being uprooted for the second time.

The frigate *Brothers,* captained by a dour, crude, and stingy Scotsman, sailed from Texel, an offshore Dutch island, on May 1, 1790. The nuns and two priests — Father Charles Neale, their chaplain, and Father Robert Plunkett, an English ex-Jesuit who joined them for the crossing — were among the passengers. Had the mean Scottish skipper inspected the nuns' hold baggage he would have been surprised to find bolts of white linen and heavy dark brown cloth for future habits. Opening the book crates he would have been astonished by the hundreds of volumes of literature, classics, history, theology, devotional works, and the sciences.

For safety during the voyage the nuns wore fashionable silks and the two priests teased them for their supposed vanity. Two long months of bad food, rudeness from the captain, foul weather, and seasickness made the crossing a trial. When the ship anchored in the Canaries, the captain lost no time in spreading word that he had four escaped nuns running off with two priests aboard his ship. After Father Neale set matters straight with the authorities, some local Poor Clare nuns sent altar cruets and other gifts to cheer the Carmelites. Frances Dickenson maintained a diary of the voyage that is in the Baltimore Carmelite archives. The following typical entry is for June 8th:

> . . . *fair weather, fine brisk breezes went 6 miles an hour; in the 24 [hours] made 112 [miles]. mr. N & mr. P better. the rest pretty well. while we were conversing upon old monastical affairs & our [?] private concerns, down falls the hog into our room upon the table. the Dog had been worrying it. Miss Matthews fared the*

> *worst for the hog Scrambled till he rowl'd in her lap. She tossed him down & was not a little Startled to find Such an unwelcome guest so near her we were all more frightened than hurt. our Surprise being over we all laugh'd very heartily & the Scene Ended in merriment. . . .*[6]

Arriving in New York, they set foot on American soil July 2, 1790. Father Plunkett bid his farewells and the party continued on to Norfolk, then up the Potomac River by sloop, landing at Brentfield, home of Robert Brent, nephew of the deceased Mary Brent buried in Antwerp. Awaiting them was William Matthews, brother of Ann Teresa and Susanna, with news of the death of Father Ignatius Matthews who had ardently pursued the Carmelite establishment in America and was — sadly — unable to witness the actual event. In 1800, William Matthews became the first native-born American to be ordained a priest in the United States.

Back home at last! What joy the Matthews women must have experienced. After resting, the party moved on to the home of Father Charles Neale near Port Tobacco. He offered his ancestral home, Chandlers Hope, for a convent but it was deemed unsuitable. He then bargained for Durham, plantation and home of Mr. Baker Brooke, giving Chandlers Hope and 1,370 pounds for the trade. Despite the poor condition of the buildings, Durham was adequate for a convent and was the American Carmel for 41 years. In November, Elizabeth Carbery became their first postulant. She was 47 years old and had waited many years for an opportunity to join such a community. Her knowledge of farming proved invaluable in sustaining the nuns. Of the original four, all but Ann Teresa were buried in the Port Tobacco convent cemetery. She made the later move to Baltimore where she was buried.

Discalced Carmelite Nuns (OCD-0420) established at Port Tobacco the first Catholic women's religious institution in the original United States of America, a convent with pontifical rights and status. The minuscule Catholic population of this burgeoning pioneer land was in dire need of women religious to provide active ministries of charity and education. Instead, it got contemplative nuns who devote their lives to the prayer ministry.

Before leaving these nuns to their prayers, contemplation, farming, domestic duties, and copying and binding the prayer books composed by Frances Dickenson, we focus on several facts in their regard. First, just as tens of thousands came to these shores before them, and as millions more would come after them, they found a real and concrete "promised land" of religious freedom, not just a glamorized concept. Second, they were of English extraction and home-grown Americans, which somehow seems proper for the "first" American women religious in the former English colonies and new Republic. And last, they transported a mode of religious life from Europe that was alien to Protestant American perceptions and would arouse open hostility in the future.

New Orleans

Three French Ursulines and three sister-nurses of the Hospitalieres de Saint-Augustin went to Canada in 1639 to minister to the French settlers; the first women religious of North America. The Ursulines instructed Indians and wrote a catechism in the Huron language. Ursuline nuns were the first women religious both to the north and to the south of the 13 English colonies.

While Port Tobacco was the site of the first convent in the new country, it was not the first one in the present-day United States. Ursuline nuns founded one 63 years earlier in New Orleans. However, New Orleans did not become part of the United States until the Louisiana Purchase of 1803. This fact leaves two legitimate claims on "first." Although they were the first permanent communities, others came earlier for brief stays. In 1704, French Grey Nuns accompanied 23 girls from Paris to Mobile (Alabama) aboard the *Pelican.* The nuns remained until all but one girl married settlers. She returned to France with the nuns. A bit later, the 22 new brides became despondent over the crude food and stormed the governor's palace in the "petticoat rebellion." Whereupon, his housekeeper, Madam Langlois instructed the distraught brides on the proper preparation of native foods to please a French palate, ending the "rebellion." In 1721, three Daughters of Charity from Paris brought 81 potential brides for the settlers in Biloxi (Mississippi). All 81 quickly found husbands and the three sisters sailed back to France. There are no records indicating discontent among these brides.

In 1727, Mother Marie Tranchepain de St. Augustin led eight Ursuline nuns from France to recently founded New Orleans on a hazardous ocean voyage of five months. Perils faced on this crossing included running aground, pursuit by pirates, storms, and a brutal captain. On arrival, they almost drowned going ashore. In primitive and swampy New Orleans these refined French ladies experienced frontier culture shock. Broken promises by their sponsors and the crudest of accommodations constituted their welcome. Nevertheless, they persevered and remained to open an academy for girls, a free school for blacks and Indians, an orphanage, and later a hospital. The Ursulines began the adaptation of a restrictive rule and European modes of religious life to the harsh demands of frontier America — a tension between tradition and practical requirements that would involve numerous communities as American history unfolded.

The orphans and survivors of the Natchez Indian massacre of 1729 nearly overwhelmed the nuns, who later aided the Acadian refugees, cruelly driven from Canada by the British in 1755. Their travail was immortalized in 1854 by Longfellow with his famous poem "Evangeline." In the early years, authorities forbade the nuns from accepting postulants because of a shortage of brides for the settlers, an unwarranted imposition on the nuns and those desiring to join them. Only reinforcements from France kept them and their ministries active and vibrant. Mary Turpin was, however, an important exception to this rule. Born in present-day Illinois, she was the first native-born American to become a nun in the present-day United States on joining the New Orleans community in 1749. Earlier, a New England girl joined the Congregation de Notre Dame in Montreal. Indians raided Groton, Massachusetts, in 1694, kidnapping Lydia Longley who was subsequently ransomed by the French in Villa Marie and adopted by a local family. Later she converted to Catholicism and joined the nuns. These are the first known women born in the English colonies to join religious orders.

Louisiana became Spanish territory in 1769, which created some problems for the French nuns who came under the authority of the Bishop of Havana. The switch of Louisiana from Spanish back to French ownership in 1802 caused the 16 Spanish members of the Ursulines to quit New Orleans for Havana, leaving only eight French nuns to cover their boarding school, day school, and orphanage. With ownership transferred to the United States the next year, the nuns became deeply concerned about their future. They wrote President Thomas Jefferson expressing their apprehensions. He assured them that their rights could not be better protected than by the laws and Constitution of the United States. They probably did not realize that he had sent his own daughters to Catholic convent schools in Paris while Minister to France from 1785 to 1789. Their letter from Jefferson is a prized possession in the Ursuline archives today.

During the Battle of New Orleans in 1815, the nuns prayed fervently for an American victory. The Ursulines converted their academy into a temporary hospital — the first recorded American military hospital.[7] They cared for the sick and wounded of both armies, and General Andrew Jackson paid a personal visit to thank the nuns for their spiritual support and charity. Later, as President of the United States, he visited them again to renew his expressions of admiration and gratitude.

Today, the order is titled **Ursuline Nuns (OSU-4110)**.[8] Their convent on Chartres Street is the oldest surviving building in the Mississippi Valley, and Ursulines are an honored part of this city's heritage. Until 1987, when an American Civil Liberties Union (ACLU) lawsuit halted the practice, no nun or sister identified by habit paid fare on city buses and streetcars; a tradition going back to the heroic sacrifices of Ursulines, Sisters of Charity, and Sisters of Mercy during the vicious epidemics in which many sisters gave their lives nursing the stricken.

The Georgetown Poor Clares and the Pious Ladies

In 1794, three Poor Clare nuns appeared in New Orleans where the Ursulines graciously sheltered them for almost two years. How and why the Poor Clares got there is an intriguing story.

Because their convents had been seized, leaving them in acute physical danger from French revolutionaries, the nuns had fled to Havre-de-Grace and then sailed to Charleston, South Carolina. Their leader, Mother Maria de la Marche, former abbess of the convent in Tours, was accompanied by Mother Celeste le Blonde de la Rochefoucault and Mother Saint Hughes, former abbess in Amiens. From Charleston they went to Baltimore where Bishop Carroll received them kindly. After a brief stay with the Carmelites in Port Tobacco, the Poor Clares opened a school in Baltimore, but this venture quickly failed due to their poor command of English. Bishop Carroll recommended Louisiana as more suited for the foundation of a Poor Clare monastery among the French-speaking Catholic population. Agreeing, the nuns set out on October 10, 1793, on a journey fraught with danger and hardships.

Cloistered sister's habit. Poor Clare Colettines (c. 1942).

Courtesy Gonzaga University

While attempting to cross the Alleghenies by coach, the drunken driver deserted the nuns, who proceeded on foot in the cold rain until a kind Protestant minister lent them horses to get them to an inn. They reached Pittsburgh riding rented horses, but were stranded for two months awaiting a flatboat going south.[9] In December, they embarked and rode down the Ohio and Mississippi Rivers, spending almost two months experiencing accidents, encountering hostile Indians, and running aground in the icy river. On arrival at Sainte-Genevieve in northern Louisiana, they disembarked and remained until the end of summer. Local residents wanted them to establish a school but the Governor of Louisiana called them to New Orleans. Thus they arrived on the doorsteps of the Ursuline convent in the early fall. By any standards, then or today, this was a remarkable odyssey for three refined ladies wearing strange clothing and speaking little English. They had traveled 1,000 miles by coach, on foot, horseback, and flatboat.

During their stay with the Ursulines, the Poor Clares came to realize that their dream of establishing a monastery had little support from the local population. So they sailed to Cuba, where they received hospitality from local Poor Clares and funds from some wealthy men to further their plans for founding a monastery. When this project did not materialize, the French Poor Clares returned to Baltimore in the spring of 1797. Learning of the continuing poor conditions for religious in France, they temporarily gave up the idea of returning home. Once again they opened a school, this time in Georgetown (now part of Washington), where they purchased some land. Since the Poor Clares' command of English was still faulty, they relied on friends Maria Sharpe, Alice Lalor, and Frances McDermott, all of Philadelphia and known as the "Pious Ladies," to help with the teaching. However, this school also failed. The Poor Clares' crude sandals, coarse habits, and austere life frightened students away. Once again, the nuns failed to make a permanent establishment.

The Pious Ladies then determined to found a religious community themselves and made temporary vows in 1799. They began what would become an American community of **Visitation Nuns (VHM-4190).** They purchased the Poor Clare land and defunct school for a future convent and opened Visitation Academy, the first Catholic female academy in the original United States. Because of their association with the Pious Ladies and land sale, the Poor Clare nuns are often referred to by historians as the "Georgetown Poor Clares."

Ex-Jesuit Leonard Neale, who later succeeded Archbishop John Carroll, supervised Georgetown College and the community of the Pious Ladies. Ever since 1799 their objective had been to establish a proper Visitation community in full compliance with the spirit and rule of St. Francis de Sales and St. Jane Frances de Chantal. Napoleonic wars that interrupted communications with Rome, imprisonment of the pope, and the lack of prescribed Visitation documents and procedures for establishing a community combined to delay official recognition of the Pious Ladies and their companions. During the interim they taught young women, struggled to maintain their institution, and declined the offer to merge with Mother Seton's Sisters of Charity in Emmitsburg. In 1816, Archbishop Neale's urgent appeal to Rome for recognition resulted in special permission, an indult, allowing him to administer solemn vows. Mother Teresa Lalor and 32 women took solemn vows and officially became Visitation nuns.

In the meantime, Georgetown Poor Clare Mother de la Marche died in 1804. The other two nuns ultimately returned to Europe and apparently found a permanent home in a German convent.[10]

St. Elizabeth Ann Bayley Seton

It would almost seem that a novelist with an overly active imagination had conceived the wandering Poor Clares, whose adventures brought them into contact with all the first American nuns: Carmelites, Ursulines, and Visitandines. However, the Poor Clares failed to touch one base. Had they perchance gone to New York City around 1802, they might have encountered Elizabeth Ann Bayley Seton (1774-1821), daughter of a prominent physician, active Episcopal charity worker, mother of five children, and wife of merchant William Seton. This remarkable woman founded the first American congregation, the Sisters of Charity of St. Joseph, shortly changed to Sisters of Charity. It would remain another 50 years before the first American order of men was founded — the Paulist Fathers by Isaac Hecker in 1858. To date, Mother Seton is the only American-born person canonized a saint by the Roman Catholic Church.

It would be difficult to identify a more typical upper-class matron in the closing years of the 18th century than Elizabeth Ann Seton. Her father was the leading physician of New York, her grandfather had been a well-known Episcopal minister, and her husband was a member of a prominent merchant family. Elizabeth's mother died when she was three years old, and her father remarried a well-connected lady, Charlotte Barclay, daughter of Andrew and Helena Roosevelt Barclay.

Elizabeth grew up a somewhat lonely child, even in the midst of six half-brothers and half-sisters, and her sister, Mary. Her father was often in England studying medicine and was totally immersed in his practice when at home. Her stepmother generally ignored Elizabeth who devoted her growing years to learning music, French, social manners, the classics, and standard studies proper for a young lady of fine breeding. Somewhat introspective, she found delight in reading literature and the Bible and was attracted to religious subjects. When she was 19, she was courted by William Magee Seton, son of a successful New York merchant. William was well-educated, had studied in England and visited France, Spain, and Italy. He lived for a time in Livorno, Italy, with the Filicchi family, commercial contacts of the Seton firm. After a proper courtship, Elizabeth and William married on January 25, 1794. Bishop Samuel Provoost, one of the first three Episcopal bishops in the United States, conducted the nuptials. The newlywed's circle of friends consisted of bankers, lawyers, merchants, and ministers. During the next seven years, Elizabeth bore five children: Anna Maria, William Vincent, Richard, Catherine, and Rebecca. William was a good husband who loved his wife devotedly, writing her daily when away on business; theirs was a happy marriage in every respect. Elizabeth kept busy with the children, household duties, the servants, and attending the theater and social events. She was also active in a society caring for orphans and widows. Although close to her pastor, the Reverend John Henry Hobart, Elizabeth became enamored for a time with the writings of Rousseau and toyed with Deism.

Grave events soon closed in, beginning with the death in 1798 of William's father. He left seven children besides William, the oldest being only 18, and it fell to Elizabeth to help with a suddenly enlarged brood. Her own father, Dr. Bayley, died in the yellow fever epidemic of 1801. Next, William experienced a serious decline in both health and business. He had suffered for years with consumption (tuberculosis), which got progressively worse. Napoleonic wars, British mercantilism, loss of the experienced senior Seton to the business and a general economic depression combined to bring down the Seton firm.[11] Bankrupt and in desperate health, William accepted an invitation from the Filicchis to visit Italy where he hoped to improve his health in that milder climate. In October 1803, Elizabeth and Anna Maria sailed for Italy with William. Sea travel was particularly dangerous as Tripoli had declared war on the United States and had recently burned the *Philadelphia*. Barbary pirates attacked American shipping, causing Congress to authorize the arming of private commercial vessels for self-defense. Fortunately, this voyage was uneventful.

Elizabeth's half-brother Guy Carlton Bayley met them in Livorno where he was working in the Filicchi countinghouse. His greeting was the news that the ship and passengers were quarantined because of the yellow fever epidemic in New York, and the passengers were required to spend 30 days in the local lazaretto. The Seton's only visitor was Mrs. Philip Filicchi, the former Mary Cowper of Boston, who also sent an aged servant to stay and assist in those trying circumstances. Near death, William was released on the 30th day and taken to Pisa in a carriage where he died in Elizabeth's arms. At age 29, she found herself brokenhearted, in a foreign land, the mother of five fatherless children and in dire financial straits. In five short years, adversity had struck this genteel American lady with triple force.

The Filicchi family expressed solicitous interest in the forlorn widow and took her and Anna Marie into their home. Shipping delays caused the two to remain several months. During this sojourn, Elizabeth witnessed intense Catholic piety for the first time. This devout Christian family so impressed Elizabeth that she gradually became interested in Catholicism. She was drawn by the Eucharist that seemed so important to Catholics and found devotion to the Blessed Virgin Mary a source of great consolation. On a sightseeing trip to Florence with the Filicchi women, she was overwhelmed by the magnificent religious art and took to daily readings of Thomas à Kempis' *The Imitation of Christ*.[12] One day outside Livorno, they visited the hilltop chapel of Monte Nero for Mass, during which a boorish English tourist made loud derogatory remarks about the Eucharist and Catholics in general. Elizabeth was shocked to witness prejudice exhibited in such crass fashion and suddenly realized that she, most of her family, and practically all of her friends quietly nurtured the very same bias in a smug, sedate way. Although deeply drawn, Elizabeth did not embrace Catholicism in Italy.

Back in New York, she set out to secure a home for the children. The extended family rallied to her support and provided a small house for one year to allow time for adjustment to new circumstances. Her interest in the Catholic Church became known as she struggled for a decision. Both Antonio Filicchi, who accompanied her back from Italy, and her friend and pastor, John Henry Hobart, plied her with arguments and persuasions. Bishop John Carroll joined the fray with a letter of advice. Her friends and family were naturally opposed to such a step and made this clear. All during the travail she prayed incessantly, read scripture, sought advice and information, and experienced an internal tug-of-war. In the end she converted to Roman Catholicism and joined the Church on March 14, 1805, nine months after her return from Italy.

The following three years in New York were awkward for Elizabeth, being dependent on her sister and in-laws for support. She attempted both a school and boarding house for boys that for various reasons proved impractical. During this period, she became better acquainted with Bishop Carroll, who handled her confirmation and came to know her children. Antonio Filicchi approved her two sons' attending Georgetown College. Louis William Valentine DuBourg (1766-1833), a Sulpician priest who was then President of St. Mary's College invited her to move to thriving Baltimore and open a school.[13] With Bishop Carroll's approval, she accepted and moved in June 1808.

Her Paca Street school in Baltimore was mildly successful and supported Elizabeth and her three girls. During this time, Father DuBourg often spoke to Elizabeth about St. Louise de Marillac and the Daughters of Charity, whom he ardently desired to see established in the United States. Elizabeth expressed a fervent wish to have a part in this project and made private vows for one year before Bishop Carroll in March 1809. He gave her the title "Mother." By June, four women had joined her, referring to themselves as "Sisters of St. Joseph." Almost immediately other women were asking for admittance.

The Sulpicians wanted Mother Seton and her community to join the Daughters of Charity of St. Vincent de Paul, whose motherhouse was in Paris. However, since the Napoleonic wars had severed all communications with France, formal incorporation with that congregation was deferred. Meanwhile, all five women adopted a habit patterned after the widow's garb worn by Elizabeth.[14] This habit was their distinctive uniform until 1850 when they joined the Daughters of Charity and adopted the French habit.

Their most immediate need was for a motherhouse. Samuel Sutherland Cooper, former sea captain from a prominent Virginia family and a seminarian at St. Mary's, offered $7,000 to purchase land for the new sisterhood. The condition for this princely offer was the land's being in Emmitsburg, about 50 miles from Baltimore. Elizabeth considered this gift to be a manifestation of God's will and accepted. The small group moving to Emmitsburg consisted of Mother Seton, her seven followers, the three Seton girls, Elizabeth's two sisters-in-law who had followed her into the Catholic Church, and two boarders. They set up residence in the Stone House[15] on July 31, 1809 — the foundation date for the first recognized American-founded religious community, the Sisters of Charity of St. Joseph's, a short-lived title soon changed to Sisters of Charity.

This foundation raised the count to four communities of Catholic women religious in the United States with a combined membership of less than 100. The presence of these tiny cadres was hardly noticed in the land. Most Americans did not know they even existed.

Hardships filled the years in Emmitsburg for the early followers of Mother Seton. Death from consumption was common due to the cold dampness, harsh living conditions, and the destructive and contagious tuberculosis bacillus. Twelve sisters, all under 25 years of age, died from this disease before 1816.

The first order of business upon getting settled was to open a school, combination boarding and free. The free school is often called the first parochial school in the United States, although there were earlier false starts. In 1606, Spanish Franciscans opened a parochial school in St. Augustine, Florida, that lasted a few years. In 1800, parishioners operated a school at St. Peter's Church on Barclay Street in New York City. Still another parochial school operated in Philadelphia for a few years. None of these schools lasted and none involved sisters.

The boarding school quickly became a noted academy for girls, providing the main source of income for the free school. This combination arrangement, often including an orphanage, characterized numerous schools operated by sisters and nuns throughout the 19th century. Archbishop Carroll designated Father DuBourg superior for the new community but he soon resigned. Father John Baptist David, also a Sulpician, succeeded him. Mother Seton thought Father David cold and her relationship with him was difficult.

In 1808, the Vatican established four suffragan dioceses in the United States: Boston, Philadelphia, New York, and Bardstown (Kentucky). John Carroll became an archbishop. Sulpician Father Benedict Joseph Flaget, a friend of Mother Seton and her congregation, was designated Bishop of Bardstown. He strenuously resisted the appointment and went to France to seek relief from the miter by his Sulpician superiors. He failed in this effort but made contact with the Daughters of Charity in Paris. He obtained a copy of their rule and statutes plus a promise for French sisters to install those at Emmitsburg into the congregation properly. He sailed home in 1810, just before Napoleon suppressed both the Sulpician and Vincentian orders and took direct control of the Daughters of Charity, along with all religious orders that survived the Revolution. The outcome was that those promised sisters never sailed. Back at Emmitsburg, Father John Dubois had succeeded Father David as superior. He undertook to translate the rule and statutes, modifying them for American conditions, carefully specifying the difference between the French and American foundations. When Mother Seton adopted a constitution in 1812, she wisely made provisions for accepting tuition, prohibited by the French rule. Archbishop Carroll approved the amended constitution on January 17, 1812.

In 1814 the community established a mission away from Emmitsburg, the first of many hundreds for the Sisters of Charity; a title Mother Seton adopted around this time. Heeding the distressed call of Father Michael Hurley in Philadelphia for sisters to take over an orphanage in desperate need, Mother Seton designated Sister Rose White to take charge. Archbishop Carroll objected to her being sent away with the War of 1812 still raging, but Father Dubois reassured him. Sisters Susan Clossy and Theresa Conroy accompanied Sister Rose White to Philadelphia. They traveled so as to avoid British troops and arrived safely. They found the children in rags and running in the streets, the number of beds not half sufficient, and the orphanage $5,000 in debt. Boys and girls boarded together, a situation Sister Rose declared must be rectified by the establishment of separate houses. War conditions made their first year miserable — the sisters and orphans subsisted on a diet of potatoes and a drink made from corn. Gradually benefactors, mostly small shopkeepers and relatively poor people, came to the support of the orphanage. Sister Rose proved her mettle. Within three years the debt was paid, 25 orphans were decently housed, and the trustees promised a separate home for the boys.

Sister Rose White later took charge of another mission away from Emmitsburg when Bishop John Connelly of New York requested sisters to run an orphanage in New York City. Sisters Rose White, Cecilia O'Conway, and Felicita Brady took over a little house on Prince Street and the care of five orphans in 1817. Within a year they had 28 orphans. The promise of a separate house for the boys was not kept for 30 years, greatly disturbing the Sisters of Charity. An unusual source of support for the orphanage came from a black Haitian slave, Pierre Toussaint, the premier hairdresser of New York. He collected alms from his rich female clients and delivered them to Sister Cecilia on the first Tuesday of each month. Investigations into his life and sanctity are now in progress with a view to canonization.

Elizabeth Ann Seton suffered terribly during her final three years but remained composed, discharging leadership functions despite her pain. On September 24, 1820, she renewed her vows in the presence of her daughter Catherine, several of the sisters, and Father Simon Gabriel Bruté. Catherine was her only child present when she died on January 4, 1821, at age 46. Her life and the lives of the thousands of her subsequent "daughters" make the word Charity in the titles of their communities far more than symbolic. To those sisters gathered around her deathbed, she spoke these final words:

Be children of the Church; be children of the Church. Oh thankful . . . .[16]

The Vincentian spirit now planted in the United States is Mother Seton's memorial. All Americans can take considerable comfort that she lived when, where, and how she did. Pope Paul VI proclaimed Elizabeth Ann Seton a saint on September 14, 1975, not so much in recognition of what she did but in full realization of who she was: wife and mother, convert, educator, foundress, visionary, and pioneer of American-founded religious congregations. Spiritual writings contained in her journal and prolific correspondence provide profound expressions of her love of God and a depth of understanding of His love for her.

Kentucky Foundations

Mother Seton's friend and newly consecrated Bishop of Bardstown, Benedict Joseph Flaget, was so poor that he had to borrow money to make his way to Kentucky. He arrived in Louisville in 1811, ending the arduous trip riding a flatboat down the Ohio River from Pittsburgh. Making his way to Bardstown, situated in the north-central part of the state where Catholics were most concentrated, he found enough Catholics for him to see why the Vatican established the area as a diocese. As throughout the American westward movement, cheap land and fresh opportunity drew the settlers. While a trickle of pioneers started settling Kentucky earlier, a strong migration of Catholic Marylanders moved into the state in 1785, whole clans moving together. Most came through the Cumberland Gap, only discovered in 1750. This migration is sometimes termed the "Maryland Diaspora." Kentucky became the 15th state admitted to the Union in 1792 — first of the "Western" states.

Twenty years after the mass migration of Marylanders, Belgian priest Charles Nerinckx arrived in Kentucky. He was a large, powerful man whose untiring energies and prodigious work contributed enormously to the solid foundations of Kentucky Catholicism. For seven years he had hidden from French revolutionaries in an attic, much like Anne Frank in World War II. During those years he became intensely spiritual as well as rigid both religiously and politically — almost too much so for adaptation to the robust and independent pioneers in Kentucky. Despite these handicaps and the many disputes they occasioned, he was an effective priest with a burning concern about the lack of education and Catholic instruction for the children in his frontier parishes.

St. Elizabeth Ann Bayley Seton
Archives, Daughters of Charity, Emmitsburg, Maryland

Mary Rhodes arrived in Kentucky in 1811 to

visit relatives but remained to teach the local children. Tradition has it (fire destroyed the community records covering this period) that she was educated at Georgetown Visitation Academy. Her lessons in her brother's home included catechism, and so many children applied for the available space that a nearby log cabin was renovated for her school. Christina Stuart joined her. Quickly, the idea of establishing a religious community devoted to teaching took hold in their minds and they asked Father Nerinckx to write a rule for them. Joined by Ann Havern, the three formed a community on April 25, 1812, taking the title "Friends of Mary at the Foot of the Cross." Today, they are titled **Sisters of Loretto at the Foot of the Cross (SL-2360)**, commonly called Sisters of Loretto or Lorettines. Mary Rhodes' younger sister Ann, the youngest member of the new community, was elected first superior. However, she soon died of consumption and Mary Rhodes, considered the real foundress, was elected and held the post for the next 10 years.

Father Nerinckx' rule reflected his ascetic leanings, prescribing a severe regimen, to include going barefoot, sleeping in habits, and participating in lengthy devotions. In the group's first 11 years, 24 sisters under age 30 died. Bishop Flaget became seriously alarmed and wrote Rome when Father Nerinckx proved inflexible about making changes. The Vatican specified the adoption of the rule of St. Augustine, thereby alleviating Father Nerinckx's harsh prescriptions.

Father Nerinckx made the first Catholic effort towards racial integration when he brought several black girls into the community. Not totally transcending contemporary prejudice, these new sisters lived apart from the white sisters but joined in group devotions.[17] He left Kentucky in 1824, going to Missouri where he died the same year. After he left, the diocesan administrator sent the black women home, presumably feeling that the integration was an impractical innovation.

The Lorettines' academy became well-known throughout the territory and was visited by dignitaries such as Henry Clay who once gave an address to the students. While they did not include the care of orphans in their chosen ministry, they took many into their boarding school. A mother-superior of the time wrote that their school at Gethsemani "mothered so many orphans it was sometimes designated as an orphanage." They made their first foundation outside Kentucky, at Bethlehem in Perry County, Missouri in 1823, and three of those sisters made the second foundation in LaFourche, Louisiana, in 1825. Sisters of Loretto occupy a special niche in American Catholic history, as we shall see.

Kentucky was also the scene of the third American-founded congregation, established only six months after the Lorettines, in November 1812. On listening to Father John Baptist David preach about the need for Catholic

**Sisters of Loretto at the Foot of the Cross
(c. 1942).**

Courtesy Gonzaga University

education at St. Thomas parish, Teresa Carrico and Elizabeth Wells came forward, asking him for direction in establishing a teaching community. Catherine Spalding, a remarkable and highly talented woman, soon joined them. The young women elected her their first mother-superior. Today, Spalding University in Louisville bears her name. The women assumed the title **Sisters of Charity of Nazareth (SCN-0500)** and adopted the rule and statutes of the Sisters of Charity of Emmitsburg, although no affiliation existed and never has.

Father David was familiar with the Vincentian spirit, which he admired and desired for his charges. Unlike the Sisters of Loretto, these women were not adequately trained to undertake teaching immediately. Father David took their preparation under his personal direction and Ellen O'Connor, an accomplished teacher, joined the community. In 1814, the seven original members adopted a habit and opened a school. Because of an unclear title to the property in St. Thomas, the community moved in 1822. Their new home was in Nazareth near Bardstown, still the site of their motherhouse. From the beginning the sisters took orphans into their schools. When cholera struck Kentucky in 1833, leaving numerous parentless and one-parent children, Mother Spalding founded an orphanage in Louisville.[18] Despite pressures from Father David to join the Emmitsburg Sisters of Charity, the sisters were adamant on remaining autonomous. Mother Spalding prepared a petition that all the sisters signed, reading in part —

> *. . . it was much better for both our happiness and spiritual good
> that we should exist always as . . . a separate and distinct body. . . .*

> *Surely religion in Kentucky can be more extensively and effective-*
> *ly served by us as we now exist. . . .*[19]

Although the difference caused some ill feelings between them, this Kentucky pioneer priest and coadjutor bishop was buried among his beloved sisters at Nazareth when he died in 1841. In review, it seems that 1812 was a vintage year for American-founded congregations.

In 1822, Kentucky produced a third religious community, the **Sisters of the Third Order of St. Dominic (OP-1070-01)**, the first of many communities of Dominican sisters and nuns in the American experience.

Dominican priest Thomas Wilson promoted the foundation. On February 28 in the Church of St. Rose in Springfield he preached an impassioned sermon appealing to young women to consecrate their lives to the service of God and become Dominican sisters. He got a positive response, and on the morning of April 7 he clothed Maria Sansbury in the Dominican habit. That afternoon Judith McMan, Mary Carrico, and Severly Tarleton received the habit as they repeated the ancient formula of reception. Four months later he received six others into the community. Father Wilson adapted the constitution of the Second Order of St. Dominic to the circumstances and conditions of women living on the Kentucky frontier. The sisters were accorded permission to live in common with all the privileges and grants of nuns of the Second Order. The sisters elected Maria Sansbury, a native Marylander, their first superior and Father Wilson gave her the religious name "Angela." Their first convent was a crude log cabin near Springfield. Father Wilson and other Dominican priests undertook the sisters' religious training and instructions for teaching. When that log cabin proved totally inadequate for a convent, the sisters moved to a more spacious log cabin on Sansbury land near Cartwright Creek and renovated it for use as a convent, naming it St. Catherine in honor of their famous saint. A school was opened in an old still house — changed from distilling spirits to instilling knowledge. In July 1823, they opened St. Mary Magdalene Academy and enrolled 15 pupils. Over the next two years the community grew to 17 sisters, and once again the convent and school needed replacement.

To complete the building project the sisters borrowed $2,000, with Dominican Father Richard Miles, their chaplain and the future bishop of Nashville, signing the note. The debt created serious problems when Father Wilson died in 1824. Meanwhile, Bishop Fenwick of Cincinnati, who also filled a dual role as superior of American Dominicans, sought to have Kentucky Dominicans, male and female, transferred to his diocese. The sisters' new superior, Spanish-born Dominican priest Raphael Muños, was caught in the middle. Although he disapproved of the crude lives of the sisters who did their own farming and carpentry work and felt that the devotional life of the

Kentucky Dominicans needed improvement, he objected to their removal to the Cincinnati diocese. The sisters adamantly refused to sell their land, disband, or relocate to Ohio. They hung on. Father Stephen Montgomery, who replaced Father Muños in 1830, reassured the creditors and restored stability. The sisters paid the note in full in 1833 and received a state charter of incorporation in 1839, permitting them to enter into contracts without the signature of a priest. Thus began the first community of Dominican sisters in the United States, founded and populated by American-born women.

Their first daughter foundation away from the motherhouse was in Somerset, Ohio, in 1830, in response to a request from Bishop Edward D. Fenwick of Cincinnati. The sisters spent three weeks traveling by stagecoach, wearing secular clothing because of the prevailing anti-Catholic bigotry. Mother Angela joined this group in 1833. After fire destroyed the Somerset building in 1866, the community moved to Columbus, Ohio, and established themselves as an autonomous group, the Congregation of St. Mary of the Springs. Other Dominican communities would appear in the years ahead, both American-founded and immigrant.

Death of John Carroll

Archbishop John Carroll died in Baltimore on December 3, 1815, at age 80. He led the Catholic Church in the United States for over 30 years, bringing it from a tiny and despised minor religious group to a recognized denomination. His one diocese of 1790 grew to six during his episcopate. The 16,000 Catholics and 21 priests in 1784, when he became Superior of the Mission, grew to 120,000 Catholics and 60 priests by 1815. That year there were three Catholic colleges, two seminaries, three female academies, two orphanages, and six orders of women religious. Catholicism emerged during the Federalist period of American history to plant its feet firmly in the new Republic. Significant numbers of Catholics were no longer confined to Maryland and Louisiana, making their presence felt in New York, Pennsylvania, Massachusetts, Kentucky, Delaware, Virginia, and on the western frontier.

The first leader of the Catholic Church in the United States was a unique personality who lived at just the right moment of history, for no other man in America could have brought about this remarkable transformation. Only he had the prestige, character, stature, experience, and ability needed to shepherd his church safely into the 19th century. The title "Father" of the American Catholic Church belongs to John Carroll.

St. Rose Philippine Duchesne

France sent a saint to pioneer Missouri in 1818 in the person of Mother Rose Philippine Duchesne (1769-1852), who established the **Society of the Sacred Heart (RSCJ-4070)** in the United States. Born into an upper-class family in Grenoble, she attended the local Visitation academy and at age 17 joined the order. When revolutionaries suppressed the order, she returned home and devoted her life to visiting the sick, those in prison and to teaching religion to children. With religious freedom restored in 1802, she purchased the old Visitation convent with the idea of rebuilding the order in Grenoble. However, this proved impractical because the former nuns had dispersed, died, or joined other communities. She was inspired by St. Madeleine Sophie Barat (1779-1865), a remarkable woman who created an order that would eventually spread over the world. Now 33, Rose Philippine Duchesne and her few companions joined this order that used the Jesuit rule as a guide and dedicated itself to the spread of devotion to the Sacred Heart of Jesus. Members of this society take vows of stability and dedication to teaching young women in addition to vows of poverty, chastity, and obedience. Christian education was a desperate need following its near-destruction by the French Revolution and Reign of Terror.

In 1812, a visiting Trappist who had been in Kentucky in 1805 spoke to the nuns about his frontier experiences and the Indians who were without missionaries.[20] At that moment, Rose Philippine Duchesne determined that she would become such a missionary. A close kinship existed between Mother Duchesne and Mother Sophie Barat, who agreed to her desired ministry — some day. Twelve years later, Mother Seton's old friend and the bishop of the vast diocese of New Orleans, Bishop Louis W. DuBourg, visited Mother Barat in Paris begging missionary sisters.[21] While sympathetic she felt she could not spare nuns at that time. Disappointed, Bishop DuBourg was about to depart when Mother Duchesne appeared and falling to her knees pleaded, "Your consent, Reverend Mother, give your consent."[22] Mother Barat sensed that God was sending her a message and reversed her decision.

On May 29, 1818, Feast of the Sacred Heart of Jesus, five nuns[23] with Mother Duchesne designated the superior landed in New Orleans after a miserable 11-week voyage. Welcomed and sheltered by the Ursulines on Chartres Street, Mother Duchesne waited patiently for word from Bishop DuBourg, now residing in St. Louis. After five weeks without hearing from him, she decided to go to St. Louis anyway. The small band embarked on the crude *Franklin*, only the eleventh steamboat to ply the dangerous Mississippi River route, unmarked by buoys or other navigational aids and filled with shifting shoals and floating trees. It took 42 days to reach St. Louis. Had she received a letter the bishop sent, she might not have been so bold. In it he commented:

> *You say you have come to seek the cross. You are so well placed*
> *to find it that you will not have far to seek. If I were not assured of*
> *finding in you these blessed dispositions, I would tremble and not*
> *rejoice at your arrival. . . .*[24]

At age 49 it seemed that converting the Indians was not to be for Mother Duchesne. Rather, it was the education of young women and meeting the challenges of poverty on the frontier that demanded all her abilities, energies, and perseverance. These she had in abundance.

At that time St. Louis was a small town with a population of 5,000 — a mixture of French-speaking and English-speaking settlers and merchants catering to the needs of passing pioneers as they prepared to move further into the West. Because of land costs in St. Louis, Bishop DuBourg sent the nuns some 15 miles away to St. Charles, close to where the Mississippi and Missouri Rivers join. The small crude cabin that the bishop rented became their first convent and school, a site cherished by the Society to this day. These refined French ladies performed farm chores, gathered firewood, repaired the cabin, and met the daily demands of life on the frontier. Prices for basic needs were exorbitant; even drinking water cost pennies. Here, the nuns established the first free school west of the Mississippi, teaching Creole, French, and American children of the rugged but poor inhabitants.

The following year, 1819, the bishop moved the small colony to Florissant, a few miles distant from St. Charles,

St. Rose Philippine Duchesne.

despite objections from Mother Barat in France who wanted a foundation in St. Louis. The first American postulant, Mary Layton, joined the community in Florissant in 1820, and soon others applied for admittance.[25] Thus began an educational ministry in the Sacred Heart tradition that would eventually influence and help mold thousands of American young women.

Despite the poverty, Mother Duchesne never ceased planning for future convents, academies, orphanages, free schools, and a novitiate. Over the next 22 years, local vocations and reinforcements from France enabled her to establish six convent schools stretching from New Orleans to St. Louis.[26] John Mullanphy, their benefactor, leased a house and 24 acres of land (for 999 years!) to Mother Duchesne in St. Louis, where she established an orphanage, academy, convent, and parish school — much to Mother Barat's delight.[27] Each of these foundations was a struggle with poverty, overcome by the dedicated nuns under Mother Duchesne's leadership and wise guidance.

In 1840, the 71-year-old Mother Duchesne finally relinquished her position as superior and fulfilled her dream by securing permission to minister to Indians. Father Pierre J. De Smet (1801-1873), the most famous of the Jesuit "blackrobe" missionaries to the Indians, invited her to present-day Kansas to found a school and live with the Potawatomis. Taking two sisters with her to Sugar Creek, this elderly nun ministered to the children of a tribe cruelly forced by the government to move from their lands in Indiana. On arrival, protocol demanded the sisters shake hands with every member of the tribe — all 700 of them. Sadly, Mother Duchesne was too old to learn the language. However, she was able to teach domestic skills to the women and nurse the sick. Because of her intensive prayer life, the Indians called her Quah-kah-ka-num-ad, "the woman who prays always." The tale is told of how an Indian boy could not believe that she prayed without moving from her knees for hours at a time. One day he slipped up behind her and placed corn kernels on the back edge of her habit, draped on the floor as she knelt. Returning four hours later, he discovered that not a single kernel had moved. Perhaps Bishop Charles Joseph Chaput, a Potawatomi who is now the Bishop of Rapid City, South Dakota, is a descendant of that awestruck boy.[28]

When Mother Duchesne's health deteriorated, the new mother-superior in St. Louis ordered her back to St. Charles, where happily she recovered. Despite her pleas, she was not permitted to return to her beloved Potawatomis, spending her final prayer-filled years in the convent she had founded.

Rose Philippine Duchesne died in 1852 at age 83, leaving the Society of the Sacred Heart firmly established in the United States. The mission at Sugar Creek moved to St. Mary's, Kansas, in 1847 where the Society ministered until 1876. Its cemetery is the final resting place for seven missionary nuns; the site and identity of these early Kansas pioneers almost forgotten.

Mother Duchesne's achievements, devotion to education and Indians, the testimony of contemporaries, and her voluminous correspondence attest to her holiness, confirmed by miracles that led to her beatification in 1940 and to her canonization in 1988. America was blessed by the life of Mother Rose Philippine Duchesne, leader, educator, and "woman who prays always."

First Order of Black Sisters

Revolution and anarchy in the French colony of Haiti erupted in 1791, resulting in the final withdrawal of French forces in 1804. Severe violence and killing marked the upheavals. Because of the turmoil, considerable numbers of educated blacks and mulattos emigrated to the United States. Most were Roman Catholic. Baltimore became the center of a sizable colony of these free blacks, many of whom brought skills and some wealth from Haiti. Others lived at a bare subsistence level. Regardless of their financial status, free blacks could not attend public schools in Maryland as it was against the law to teach blacks to read and write. Sometime prior to 1828 — the date is uncertain because of secrecy — Miss Elizabeth Lange, who had immigrated from Cuba, and several black women from Haiti began teaching black children in a private school. This effort attracted the attention of Father James H. Joubert, a Sulpician, who encouraged Elizabeth Lange, Maria Magdaleine Balas, and Rosine Boegue to form a religious community of black sisters with education and religious instruction for young black girls as its primary ministry. On July 2, 1829, four sisters made their first profession of vows and founded the **Oblate Sisters of Providence (OSP-3040)**. The fourth foundress was Marie Therese Duchemin, a remarkable lady who reappears later in this history. Thus began the first congregation of black sisters and the ninth order established in the United States.

Their early years were remarkably calm considering the times and public attitudes towards blacks, slave and free. Their combination day and boarding school prospered, taking in orphans and poor as well as the black elite of Baltimore. It kept alive the tradition of educated free blacks and produced many future teachers. It is difficult today for people to appreciate how courageous and tenacious Mother Elizabeth Lange and her companions had to be to found a community of black sisters in the milieu of 1829 in a slaveholding state. Although her community was and remains small, she is assuredly one of the great American foundresses.

Barren Ground

During 1812, the year the United States went to war with England, several groups of women religious attempted to make foundations and each failed. While some Trappist monks who left Kentucky in 1809 were in New York City, a second contingent of Trappists from Europe arrived in Boston bringing a Trappistine nun with them. The monks left her in Boston and joined the other Trappists in New York. The leader of these wandering Trappists, Dom Augustine, established a convent in New York City for Trappistines and sent for the nun in Boston. Several more Trappistines arrived from Europe at about this time. Soon a Trappistine convent, "productive of much good," was founded in New York City and received American postulants. However, with the fall of Napoleon, Dom Augustine decided to return to France with his entire company.[29] The American-born nuns were given the option of remaining or going to Europe. The convent closed and four of the nuns joined the Sisters of Charity at Emmitsburg. Trappistine nuns are properly titled **Cistercian Nuns of the Strict Observance (OSCO-0670)**. They did not reestablish their order in the United States until 1949.

The second failed attempt also occurred in New York City. Father Anthony Kohlmann, a Jesuit who had been appointed administrator of the New York diocese in 1812, had ambitious plans for his Catholic flock, including the establishment of a college for young men, an academy for girls, a free elementary school for the poor, and a home for orphans. For the academy, he secured three Ursuline nuns from Blackrock Convent, Ireland: Christina Fagan, Sarah Walsh, and Mary Baldwin. His intent was to secure Presentation sisters in Ireland for the poor school and orphanage, but before he could carry out his plans he was reassigned to Georgetown College.

Oblate Sisters of Providence (c. 1942).
Courtesy Gonzaga University

The Ursuline academy, situated near what is now Third Avenue and 15th Street, was a popular asset for New York. However, the house that the nuns thought was a gift turned out to have a lien of $2,000. Since young women desiring admittance into the Ursuline order could not afford a dowry and tuition was barely enough to support the nuns, the Ursulines could not pay for the house. Moreover, a chronic shortage of priests at that time did not permit daily Mass, a standard devotion the nuns had expected when leaving their convent in Ireland. In 1814, Father Kohlmann moved to Georgetown College and the Trappists left for France.[30] These departures created a vacuum for the nuns and, combined with the original condition imposed by Ursuline superiors in Ireland that they secure postulants, resulted in their recall and return to Ireland in the spring of 1815.

Later, yet another failure involved Poor Clares. Bishop Edward Fenwick of Cincinnati, while on a begging trip in Europe in 1825, secured two Colettine Poor Clares in Bruges, Belgium: Sisters Marie Francoise Vindevoghel and Marie Victoire de Seilles. They arrived in Cincinnati in August 1826 and opened a school with 70 pupils. Their abbess back in Belgium became distressed because this active ministry violated their rule and was contrary to her expectations that her nuns were to found a cloistered monastery. It seems that the bishop became disappointed with the nuns, feeling that they were incapable of conducting a school, so the Poor Clares departed Cincinnati and went to Pittsburgh. Joined by two other religious from Belgium, they opened the first Catholic female academy in Pennsylvania.[31] By 1830, the community had grown to 14 members. They opened a branch in Detroit in 1833 where their academy was highly successful for the next six years. They opened a free school as well and several nuns went to Green Bay, Wisconsin, to found a school.

Disputes over spheres of influence surfaced. Bishop Résé of Detroit and Sister Marie Francoise clashed in 1835. The details are somewhat murky but revolved around her refusal to accept an aspirant he sent from Detroit. She maintained that his authority covered the Detroit convent but not Pittsburgh, while he maintained he had powers over the Pittsburgh convent as well. Before the dispute could be settled by Rome, the bishop put the convent under interdict, thereby denying the nuns sacraments and Mass. They supported themselves with needlework while the case brewed and anti-Catholics seized on the trouble to create scandal. Eventually the Vatican ordered Bishop Francis P. Kenrick of Philadelphia to restore the sacraments to the nuns and canceled Bishop Résé's authority over the Poor Clares in Pittsburgh. By the time Sister Marie Francoise returned from Rome, where she had gone to further the appeal, Bishop Résé had resigned. However, friction arose between Bishop Kenrick and the superior.

In the end, Sister Marie Victorie de Seilles and eight professed American Poor Clares disbanded the American community and went to Belgium to enter a convent. Sister Marie Francoise Vindevoghel remained in the United

States and is lost to history. This failure highlighted the tension between monastic life and active ministry and the inherent conflict between the powers of a community superior and those of the local bishop. The day in the American sun for Poor Clares was still 36 years away.

These false starts, sad but nonetheless interesting, illustrate the difficulties faced by women religious in the earliest days of the Republic and make the successes all the more admirable.[32]

Good Ground

John England (1786-1842), Bishop of Charleston, South Carolina, was possibly one of the most competent and talented bishops ever to wear the miter in the United States. Rome handpicked this dynamic Irish priest to go to America in 1820 and become bishop of one of the smallest dioceses in the world, as measured by Catholic population. It was also one of the most troubled. In 1816, lay trustees of St. Mary's, Charleston's only Catholic church, refused to accept the French priest lawfully appointed by Archbishop Neale, who then placed the church under interdict. His appointee, Father de Cloriviere, opened another church for the loyal Catholics. The schismatics then attempted to form an independent church in 1819 with a rogue priest from Holland.[33] Archbishop Ambrose Marechal, Neale's successor, dispatched Father Benedict Fenwick to Charleston to sort out matters.[34] Mildly successful, he returned to Baltimore and later became Bishop of Boston. The Vatican then detached North Carolina, South Carolina, and Georgia from the Baltimore diocese to create the new Charleston Diocese and sent John England to make something of it.

Upon arrival in his newly established see in December 1820, Bishop John England began to demonstrate his competency. Initially, he issued the first pastoral letter by an American bishop and immediately set about visiting his scattered flock in all three states, reportedly numbering 5,000 — fewer Catholics than in his old parish back in Ireland. He had only four priests to support him. He quickly grasped the spirit of America and its concept of separation of church and state. His many sermons over the years, from Protestant as well as Catholic pulpits, hammered on the theme that Catholics were loyal Americans and should not be deemed by their neighbors, or consider themselves, second-class citizens. He addressed the legislatures of both North and South Carolina and later became the first Catholic clergyman to address the U.S. Congress.

One of his first acts was to compose a catechism and an English-language missal, distributed to all known Catholics. Aided by his blood sister, he founded *The United States Catholic Miscellany* in 1822, the first Catholic newspaper in the United States. It enjoyed national circulation and an international reputation. That same year he founded a seminary to train priests, handling most of the instruction himself. With few native vocations, he recruited priests in Ireland. This seminary existed until 1851. He devised a constitution for his diocese in 1823 that effectively defused the trustee problem, setting the pattern for other bishops facing similar problems. Almost from the day of his arrival in America, he urged a convocation of all the bishops to establish policy and coordinate activities. Archbishop Ambrose Marechal and the other French-born bishops ignored this advice, and it was not until 1829 that the First Provincial Council was convened under Archbishop James Whitfield, fourth Archbishop of Baltimore.

Bishop England planned to visit Ireland to recruit Ursuline nuns for his diocese but problems prevented the journey. He met the lack of sisters in another way. While in Baltimore for the council, he came into contact with four women who wanted to become religious. They agreed to form a community under his direction and moved to Charleston. These were Mary O'-Gorman, age 34; Honora O'Gorman, age 29; Mary E. Burke, age 23; and Mary Teresa Barry, age 14. While it was quite common for girls in their teens to join religious communities, the Barry girl is the youngest one recorded in this era. Mary Burke was a native-born American from Maryland and the other three were born in Ireland. In December 1829, Bishop England moved the sisters into a small house on Legare Street and designated them Sisters of Our Lady of Mercy; now known as the **Sisters of Charity of Our Lady of Mercy (OLM-0510).** Mary O'Gorman became first mother-superior. Their habit was the widow's dress and cap worn by Mother Seton's Sisters of Charity in Emmitsburg. Bishop England officially notified the Vatican of this new institute, writing —

> *In Charleston four nuns are living a religious life under a rule which I drew up for them. They were established towards the end of last year under the title of Our Lady of Mercy, and they desire to take simple vows each year and to dedicate themselves to teaching young girls, in instructing the negro slaves in faith and morals, and for caring for the sick and infirm. . . .*[35]

Five more women entered the community during 1830: Ellen Rugan, Rose Hughes, Catherine McKenna, Ellen Clarke, and Marie Kennedy. Although American in foundation, this congregation was remarkably Irish in membership. Their first ministry was a school that opened with six pupils. Honora O'Gorman's assignment was to care for the domestic concerns of St. John the Baptist Seminary.

The early years were difficult as with almost all newly founded communities. Their problem was not so much the cruel demands of the frontier as simple lack of money. Poverty inhibited their ability to take in orphans or even maintain the new house that the bishop rented for them. Since tuition was inadequate for their expenses, they suffered considerable privation. In 1831, they received a godsend in the person of a 66-year-old postulant, Julia Datty. This remarkable woman, a native of Haiti and educated in Paris, brought a sizeable dowry, teaching experience, and a citywide reputation with her. For many years, Sister Datty had operated a school in Charleston that was fashionable as well as academically excellent. During those years she practiced ministries of kindness, visiting the sick and assisting the needy and was, in essence, a secular Catholic religious. Her membership brought a whole new dimension to the community. Both day and boarding pupils increased and the sisters were able to take in a few orphans. Bishop England appointed Julia Datty mother-superior in 1833 despite her advanced age. The community moved into a larger house on Beaufain Street the next year, where they enjoyed a private chapel for the first time with the Blessed Sacrament available for adoration. By 1834, the community had 14 members.

One of Bishop England's few failures was not writing a constitution for his young diocesan community. He had promised to do so as his letter to Rome indicated, but his many commitments and long absences from the diocese caused him to procrastinate and he never did effect this vital function. No religious community can operate smoothly for long without either close supervision by the foundress or a constitution to regulate internal functioning. Such governance is essential. Bishop England's appointment as Apostolic Delegate to Haiti in 1833 by Pope Gregory XVI initiated a series of long absences from his diocese, during which internal frictions evolved among the sisters for lack of supervision or a constitution to guide them. Happily, the sisters did resolve the problems among themselves. Bishop Ignatius Reynolds, successor to Bishop England, wrote a constitution for this congregation in 1844. This relatively small diocesan community[36] has engaged in the care of orphans, care of the sick, and Catholic education in South Carolina ever since. However, as we shall see, they became involved in nursing during the Civil War, experiencing perils and high adventure.

Back in Ireland, Mary Francis Clarke and four companions wanted to serve God in some teaching capacity. The needs of Catholics in the United States were widely recognized in Ireland and the women decided to go there. They sailed in 1833 from Liverpool, the port of departure for millions of Irish immigrants during the 19th century. All their money was entrusted to one companion who got so excited on approaching New York that she dropped her handbag overboard — something of a harbinger of the vow of poverty. After arriving in Philadelphia, they met an Irish priest, Father Terence J. Donaghoe, the pastor of St. Michael's church. Anxious to establish a parochial school, he considered their arrival a godsend. The women submitted to his spiritual guidance and he secured permission from Bishop Henry Conwell to form a religious community. They chose **Sisters of Charity of the Blessed Virgin Mary (BVM-0430)** as their title. Father Donaghoe drew up a rule and arranged for a convent in the parish. He appointed Mary Francis Clarke the superior. The sisters opened a school, and with numerous aspirants wishing to join, they established a novitiate. As we shall see, this community later moved to Iowa where this important teaching congregation prospered and expanded.

Pauline Marie Therese Bazire and Athanais Haincque, with the guidance and encouragement of Father Charles Boutelou, founded the **Congregation of Our Lady of Mount Carmel (O.Carm-0400)** in France in 1824 as an offshoot of a Third Order group affiliated with the Avranches Carmelites. Because of his known monarchist sympathies, Father Boutelou was forced to flee France during the short revolution of 1830 that deposed King Charles X. Father Boutelou went to Louisiana and became pastor in Plattenville. In 1832, Bishop Leo de Neckere of New Orleans invited two members of the Sisters of Mount Carmel to make a foundation in his diocese. In response to his appeal, Mothers Therese Chevrel and St. Augustin Clerc crossed the Atlantic to establish the 12th foundation of women religious in the United States. On arriving and learning that Bishop de Neckere had died in a yellow fever epidemic, they went to join Father Boutelou in Plattenville. There they operated a girls' school and taught for five years before the new bishop, Anthony Blanc, called them to New Orleans because he needed the school property for a seminary. He assigned the sisters to a school for free black girls that remained in operation until 1897 when it was transferred to the Sisters of the Holy Family.[37] The Carmelites also initiated an academy for white girls in 1840. By 1885, the sisters had 13 schools in operation.

The congregation of Our Lady of Mount Carmel was not formally affiliated with either branch of Carmelites until 1930, when it was accepted as a Third Order Regular congregation of the Calced Carmelites. Active-contemplatives, the sisters engage in a variety of ministries, including education and health care, mainly in southern Louisiana and the Philippine Islands.

Early Health Ministries

The Daughters of Charity in Europe had a long tradition of medical care, and the American Sisters of Charity readily adopted this ministry in the Vincentian spirit, having gained considerable medical experience by caring for orphans and treating their own members. Sisters of Charity from Emmitsburg began their first work in medical institutions at the Baltimore Infirmary in 1823. Father Dubois, their superior, always the careful contractor for the sisters' services, insured proper conditions before allowing them to work in the infirmary where Dr. Robert Patterson needed them. The infirmary had three physicians and four surgeons, a special ward for diseases of the eye and one for sailors which later expanded into a separate Marine hospital.[38] The doctors were affiliated with the medical faculty at the University of Maryland. Working under their supervision, the sisters learned about medicines and treating illnesses and wounds — medical skills they later put to use in their own hospitals.

Bishop Joseph Rosati of St. Louis requested sisters from Emmitsburg to staff a hospital in 1828, and Catholic benefactor John Mullanphy offered land, $150 for transportation, $350 to furnish the hospital, and two houses for rental income. With this request and assurances, four sisters departed on what turned out to be an adventurous and difficult journey, traveling by carriage, farm cart, steamboat, and on foot after their horses ran away leaving them deserted in the wilderness. On arrival in St. Louis, they found the bishop away and no one expecting them. Mother Duchesne provided hospitality pending his return. That year, the sisters opened the first permanent Catholic hospital in the United States.

Then the dreaded epidemics began.[39] A cholera epidemic struck the United States in 1832 with devastating force, killing thousands as it spread to various sections of the country. While cholera had erupted in different localities previously, this was the first nationwide epidemic. Practically all communities of sisters and nuns became involved in caring for victims. Three Sisters of Charity of Nazareth died in this service: Joanna Lewis, Patricia Bamber, and Generose Buckman. The Sisters of Charity suffered 13 deaths in nursing service: Emeliana Pigot (a native of Scotland) in St. Louis,[40] Mary Frances Boarman and Mary George Smith in Baltimore, Sister Gabrielle in Philadelphia, and nine unnamed sisters in New Orleans. The epidemic came late to Charleston, in 1836, and Julia Datty of the Sisters of Charity of Our Lady of Mercy died serving the citizens of that city. All the above, and perhaps others, died as a direct result of tending to the stricken. The motherhouse in Emmitsburg received the following unsolicited letter:

> *Boston, November 7, 1832*
>
> *Madam Superior:*
>
> *Although a stranger to you permit me to make a most respectful inquiry. A short time ago, I saw in the public papers of the day, a notice that while the awful pestilence was raging in Philadelphia, several of the ladies of your institution, volunteered their kind personal assistance to the sick and dying strangers in that city, while*

the stricken were deserted by their friends and neighbors. This, in my opinion is the greatest marvel of charity ever manifested in America!

Many of my friends, as well as myself, are desirous to know more about these interesting individuals; the name of each, her native place, by whom the plan was suggested, etc.; and we should be exceedingly gratified to have their several signatures inclosed to us. We feel that the influence of such examples of charity should extend to the end of time.[41]

It took almost four years for this first of the nationwide epidemics to run its course. American women religious nursed hundreds of victims, many got sick themselves, and a number died. They inherited numerous orphans that the epidemic spawned. The opening of the St. Louis hospital and emergency nursing during the epidemic initiated a health care ministry that would entail the devotion and labors of thousands of the successors to these early American sister-nurses.

Port Tobacco Closed

Economic necessity forced the Carmelite nuns at Port Tobacco to move to Baltimore in 1831. Mr. Baker Brooke had traded Durham plantation to Father Neale in 1790, and years of litigation with Mr. Brooke's heirs over title to their land drained the nuns' resources. Roger Brooke Taney, future Chief Justice of the Supreme Court and a Catholic, successfully defended the nuns' claim.[42] However, the plantation was so run down by 1831 that Archbishop James Whitfield, successor to Archbishop Neale, insisted they move to Baltimore where he provided a brick house with a lovely garden. The Sisters of Charity welcomed them with a fine meal and prepared their new home for occupancy. The last of the Port Tobacco land was sold in 1836, excepting one acre of cemetery. In 1976, Carmelite nuns made a new foundation at Port Tobacco. With the help of benefactors and supporters, the nuns resettled the site, 186 years after the original foundation.

Bishop John Carroll had obtained a rescript from Rome in 1790 to allow the Carmelite nuns to teach, hoping they would accept this active ministry, but respected their wishes to continue their vowed monastic life of contemplation and prayer. By 1832, however, economic pressures in Baltimore caused Archbishop Whitfield to seek a renewal of the rescript and, with reluctance, the nuns opened an academy. The following extract from the prospectus is indicative of the educational level provided by the Carmelite nuns in the academy:

The Sisters having charge of this institution propose a course of

> *instruction which comprises Orthography, Reading, Writing, Arithmetic, Book-Keeping, Grammar, English Composition, the use of maps and globes, Sacred History, Ancient and Modern History, Chronology, Mythology, Botany, Rhetoric, Natural Philosophy, Astronomy, French, Vocal and Instrumental Music, Drawing and Painting in Water Colors, Painting on Velvet in Oil Colors, Plain and Ornamental Needle Work, Embroidery in Gold and Silver, Tapestry, Lace Work, Bead Work, etc.*[43]

They successfully operated this academy until 1851 when Archbishop Francis Patrick Kenrick insisted that an active apostolate was not consonant with their charism and the nuns were able to resume the enclosed monastic life prescribed by their rule.

Sisters of Charity Expand Ministries

In the years after Sister Rose White went to establish the orphanage in New York in 1817, the Sisters of Charity grew both in membership and missions away from the motherhouse. By 1834, they numbered 135 sisters. During the 17 years between 1817 and 1834, they opened free schools in Frederick, Baltimore (two), New York, Albany, Washington, Harrisburg, Cincinnati, New Orleans, Alexandria, Boston, Brooklyn, and St. Louis. They opened orphanages in Baltimore, Frederick, Boston, Washington, Cincinnati, and St. Louis. When the school in New Orleans for black girls failed, the sisters opened an orphanage. They also established a second orphanage in Philadelphia and one in Wilmington, Delaware, to care for orphans whose parents were killed in explosions at the DuPont gunpowder mills. When reading historical accounts of how this or that order spread rapidly, one tends to be a bit skeptical. Yet here is an example of dynamic expansion and spread of apostolic activities.

Anti-Catholic Eruption

As is so often the case, events in Europe had repercussions in the United States. Parliament passed the Catholic Emancipation Act in 1829 restoring full civil liberties to English Catholics, including the right to hold public office. American newspapers reported on the debates preceding final passage, marked by high emotions and much bitterness. The debates, published tracts, news accounts, and final passage aroused resentment against Catholics in the United States by the Anglo-Protestant establishment, still feeling a strong kinship with the English Protestant establishment. This coincided with the "Second Great Awakening" of Protestantism (the First Great Awakening occurred in the 1730's). Church attendance soared and preaching reached new heights of oratory. Crowds of 20,000 to 30,000 were not unknown at revivals where renowned preachers delivered spellbinding sermons. A favorite subject was "popery" and its evils. These factors focused attention on American Catholics and resurrected anti-Catholicism, an intrinsic element of colonial culture.

A steady flow of Irish immigrants also aroused resentment. Their unwashed presence and competition for jobs created antagonism among the laboring classes and overt discrimination in all areas of social life. Irish Catholicity sparked dislike and even hatred, especially in the large cities of the East. Anti-Irish riots rocked Boston in the 1830's.

Another factor that contributed somewhat to anti-Catholic attitudes was the creation in Europe of Catholic charitable organizations raising money for foreign missions. Pauline Jaricot, a devout Frenchwoman, founded the Society for the Propagation of the Faith in 1822. Triggered by an effort to raise money to support Bishop DuBourg of Louisiana, the concept was expanded to cover worldwide missions. By 1836 the society existed all over Catholic Europe and raised considerable annual contributions. The United States was the principal beneficiary of this fund for the next 50 years. In 1829, the Emperor of Austria created the Leopoldine Society in memory of his daughter. Funds raised by this society were earmarked for missionary endeavors in the United States among German-speaking immigrants. These organizations intensified Protestant belief that European Catholics and monarchs were attempting to undermine the republican principles of the country. These events and conditions combined to load the anti-Catholic tinderbox.

Ursuline nuns in Boston who had only wished to establish an academy for young ladies became early victims of Protestant prejudice. The story begins with Reverend John Thayer, a Presbyterian minister of Boston, who visited Rome around 1803, converted to Catholicism, and became an ordained priest. He strongly desired to found an Ursuline convent in Boston to teach young women and sought nuns in Ireland for this project. Because of the 1812 failure in New York, the Ursulines in Cork declined another attempt. While in Ireland, Father Thayer interested two blood sisters, Mary and Catherine Ryan, in the project and planned for them to make their novitiate at the Three Rivers Ursuline convent in Canada. He died in 1815, but in 1817 the Ryan sisters went to Three Rivers anyway, completed their novitiate, and opened a convent in Boston. Another blood sister and a cousin joined them. By 1822 the new Ursuline community numbered nine members and their academy enjoyed a fine reputation, drawing students from as far away as the West Indies and deep South.

Since the convent and school were situated in an unhealthy section of town, Bishop Fenwick purchased land across the Charles River in Charlestown for a new convent and expanded academy. Mount Benedict, their new home, was located in a staunchly Protestant area. The nuns moved at four o'clock in the morning in order to avoid notice because they had heard that some neighbors planned to tear down their house before they moved in. Once settled, the Ursulines resumed teaching. The majority of their students were young ladies from upper-class Protestant families. The academy's good reputation for educational excellence spread until August of 1834.

Revivalist preacher Lyman Beecher, a dynamic orator, delivered three impassioned anti-Catholic sermons in Boston on Sunday, August 10. Just 12 days before Beecher's sermons, Sister Elizabeth Harrison, in one of her occasionally recurring fits of mental derangement, slipped out of the convent and ran across the street to the home of Edward Cutter. At first, she refused to see the bishop who was called but finally returned to the convent. The Cutters visited the convent to check on her but were refused entry due to the nun's breakdown. They suspected that her reputed mental condition was an excuse for restraining her against her will. Bishop Fenwick promised an investigation and the Cutters were permitted to inspect the convent and interview Sister Elizabeth. Afterward Mr. Cutter drafted a statement expressing his satisfaction.

On Monday, August 11, selectmen of Boston inspected the convent for three hours, including the cellar where infants were reputed to be buried. They interviewed Sister Elizabeth and verified that she was not being kept a prisoner. They checked the garden where the nun escorting them was reportedly buried, much to her amusement. Fully satisfied, they drafted a public statement for Tuesday's newspaper. Mr. Cutter's statement, the bishop's statement, and the public report of the selectmen all came too late. That night, a mob violently attacked and burned the Ursuline convent school. The rioters even desecrated the graves in the small cemetery. Terrified, the nuns shepherded their 60 wards through the garden and over the wall, finding temporary refuge in the home of the nearby Adams family.[44] Mr. Cutter assisted in their flight. No firemen, policemen, or citizens came to their aid. The next day the nuns and students took shelter in the convent of the Sisters of Charity. Fortunately, only one Ursuline nun, 20-year-old Sister St. Henry, died later as a result of that night of terror.

Official investigations of the vicious attack clearly demonstrated that the authorities ignored the potential for riot and purposely failed to lift a hand to perform their obvious duty. City officials and the local press piously deplored the disgrace, especially after it received national and international press coverage. Yet the Concord, New Hampshire, *Freeman* printed: ". . . old Massachusetts is no longer disgraced by a nunnery and its accomplishments. . . ."

A farce trial ensued. No rioter was punished and Bishop Fenwick was insulted in court. Restitution for damages was never made despite Bishop Fenwick's efforts with support from some fair-minded citizens. Back home in Cincinnati, Lyman Beecher did his best to make the Mississippi valley the scene of religious war.[45] The Ursuline nuns shook the dust of Charlestown from their sandals and withdrew, some to Three Rivers in Canada and others to the New Orleans community.

This example of anti-Catholic prejudice introduced an era of violence that would sorely test the courage and stamina of the mustard seeds that were the early American sisters and nuns.

The tinderbox was lit!

Endnotes

1. Ann Matthews, the aunt and prioress of the Antwerp Carmel, was known in religion as Mother Bernardina Teresa of St. Joseph. Her niece Susanna Matthews was known as Sister Mary Eleanora of St. Francis Xavier. Ann Teresa Matthews, the other niece, was known as Sister Mary Aloysia of the Blessed Trinity. Frances Dickenson, the Englishwoman, was known as Mother Clare Joseph of the Sacred Heart.

2. Most men, some 43, joined the Jesuits, including John Carroll, Leonard and Charles Neale, and Ignatius Matthews. Edward Fenwick entered the Dominican seminary in Brussels, another became a Benedictine, one a Franciscan, and three were ordained as secular priests. Nine of the 33 American women joined the Carmelites, including the Matthews. Seven entered the Benedictine monasteries, five entered Poor Clare monasteries, four became Dominicans, and eight became Canonesses of the Holy Sepulcher. Two of the Benedictines, Mary Anne and Henriette Hagan, were imprisoned during the Reign of Terror in Compiègne. Reflecting their English heritage, Anglo-Saxon and Anglo-Irish surnames predominated, including: Brent, Neale, Matthews, Hill, Parnham, Wharton, Digges, Brooke, Pye, Boone, Rozer, Semmes, Spalding, Edelen, Dougherty, and Hagan. See Chapter I, contributed by James Hennesey, SJ, in N. Minnick et. al., *Studies in Catholic History in Honor of John Tracy Ellis* (Wilmington, DE: Michael Glazier, 1985), pp. 1-26.

3. Authority for designating bishops was a problem throughout the Middle Ages, referred to by historians as the "Investiture Conflict." Popes contested with emperors and kings over this right, most often settled by the monarch naming the candidate and the pope retaining veto power. A bishop was often elected by fellow priests who submitted his name to Rome for confirmation. This was the case with John Carroll. Since the late 19th century, the Vatican has had the exclusive right to name bishops worldwide.

4. French revolutionaries did not honor the refugee status of the Carmelites. In fear for their lives, the Antwerp community fled to England in 1794 and settled in Lanhern, Cornwall, in a house donated by Lord and Lady Arundell where the

community is still located. The Hoogstraeten community also fled in 1794 and spent some years in Poole, Dorsetshire. Due to poverty and loss of their house, the Carmelites moved to Normandy in 1825, but returned to England in 1870 and built a permanent convent near Chichester, Sussex.

5. Rev. Charles Warren Currier, *Carmel in America: A Centennial History of the Discalced Carmelites in the United States* (Darien IL: Carmelite Press, 1989), p. 56.

6. Sr. Constance FitzGerald, OCD, ed., *The Carmelite Adventure: Clare Joseph Dickenson's Journal of a Trip to America and Other Documents, Carmelite Sources, Volume II* (Baltimore, MD: Carmelite Sisters, 1990), p. 69. The original journal, which this author was privileged to examine, is in the archives of the Carmelite Monastery, Baltimore, MD.

7. The Ursulines' contract with the Company of the Indies in 1727 called for them to staff the military hospital in New Orleans.

8. Today, most Ursuline communities belong to either the Roman Union (4410) or the Congregation of Paris (4120).

9. River pirates posed a constant danger to flatboats well into the 1820's. Those vicious criminals would await the flatboats hanging up on a shoal, or lure them near shore, then attack and kill the crew and passengers and steal the cargo. Flatboats were large rafts with a shack for shelter. They rode the currents while the crew used long poles for steering and for pushing when needed. The logs making up the flatboat were normally sold on arrival at a southern destination.

10. Abbe Jean Desobry, *Memoires de la Societe des Antiquaires de Picardie* (Amiens, France: Au Siege de la Societe, 1986), p. 132.

11. Between 1775 and 1790 the American economy fell by 40-50 percent, an amount comparable to that experienced during the Great Depression of 1931-1937. See Thomas K. McCraw, "The Strategic Vision of Alexander Hamilton," *The American Scholar* (Washington, DC, Winter 1994), p. 43.

12. Written in the 16th century, the *Imitation of Christ* is the most widely published religious book in the world outside the Bible itself and is still a popular devotional manual throughout the Christian community. John Wesley, founder of the Methodist Church, deemed it the best summary of the Christian life. Ignatius Loyola, founder of the Jesuit order, read a chapter each day. Thomas Merton acknowledged that it initiated his conversion. Pope John Paul I died with the book in his hand.

13. Archbishop John Carroll invited French Sulpician priests fleeing the Revolution to establish a seminary in the United States, a desperate need. They founded St. Mary's Seminary in Baltimore in 1791. This first American seminary is still in operation. Archbishop Carroll had ordained 30 priests by 1815. The Society of St. Sulpice was founded in 1642 by French priests to carry out the mandate of the Council of Trent for better education of priests. The society has always been small but has exerted a major influence on the training of seminarians throughout the Catholic world.

14. Several communities later adopted the habit worn by Mother Seton and her sisters.

15. The Stone House is now a museum on the grounds of the motherhouse in Emmitsburg.
16. Sr. Daniel Hannefin, DC, *Daughters of the Church: A Popular History of the Daughters of Charity in the United States 1809-1987* (Brooklyn, NY: New York City Press, 1989), p. 14.
17. James K. Kennelly, *The History of American Catholic Women* (New York, NY: Crossroad, 1990), p. 55.
18. These sisters were familiar with epidemics. Sister Harriet Gerdner, SCN, died in Vincennes, Indiana, in 1826 as a result of nursing victims during a Yellow Fever epidemic.
19. This petition is in the Nazareth Archives. Dr. Margaret Susan Thompson, Syracuse University, has reported on it in her writings.
20. A band of Trappist monks fleeing the French Revolution arrived in Kentucky in 1805 after years of wandering over Europe, including Russia. They remained in Kentucky for four years, moved to Illinois and then to New York. Kentucky got a permanent Trappist monastery in 1848 at Gethsemani, made famous by the writings of Thomas Merton.
21. Louis William Valentine DuBourg (1766-1833), Mother Seton's friend and mentor, is prominent in early American Catholic history. He was the third president of Georgetown College, founder of St. Mary's College, and Bishop of New Orleans. In 1826, he returned to France and became Archbishop of Besançon.
22. Sr. Louise Callan, RSCJ, *The Society of the Sacred Heart in North America* (New York, NY: Longmans, Green and Co., 1937), p. 32.
23. The four nuns accompanying Mother Duchesne to the United States were Octavie Berthold, Eugénie Audé, Catharine Lamarre, and Margaret Monteau. Sister Octavie's father had been Voltaire's personal secretary. As a young woman, Sister Eugénie enjoyed life in high society. One evening on returning home after attending a ball she stood admiring herself in the mirror when she received a vision of Christ's tormented face. This caused her to seriously examine her life. Afterwards she joined the Society of the Sacred Heart.
24. Marjory Erskine, *Mother Philippine Duchesne* (New York, NY: Longmans, Green and Co., 1926), p. 149.
25. One of the early novices was Mary Aloysia Hardey (1809-1886) who had attended the Sacred Heart Academy in Grand Coteau, Louisiana, opened in 1821. Mary Hardey became one of the great leaders of the Society of the Sacred Heart, founding convents and academies in numerous locations in the United States, Canada, and Cuba. She rose to become assistant mother-general of the order. Buried in France where she died, her body was quietly removed to the United States in 1905 when the order was suppressed by the French government.
26. During the Civil War the Sacred Heart Academy in Grand Coteau, Louisiana, founded by Mother Duchesne, was spared destruction from a raging nearby battle. Union General Nathaniel P. Banks ordered his troops to protect the academy. His daughter had attended the Sacred Heart Academy in New York and he held the sisters in high esteem.
27. John Mullanphy (1758-1833), a fascinating character, was born in Ireland,

served in the Irish Brigade of the French Army but left France when the Revolution broke out. He and his wife emigrated to the United States in 1792. After living in Baltimore, Philadelphia, and Kentucky, they went to New Orleans. He fought in the War of 1812 and was with Andrew Jackson at the Battle of New Orleans. He then made a fortune in real estate and cotton in St. Louis, becoming Missouri's first millionaire. A devout Catholic, he contributed a large portion of his fortune to religious orders, orphanages, convents, churches, and a hospital.

28. When I wrote Bishop Chaput about this comment, he denied any knowledge of the connection but expressed amusement in granting permission to include it.

29. The ship bearing the Trappists back to Europe anchored in Halifax, Canada, and a monk, Father Vincent de Paul Merle, went ashore to purchase provisions. The ship sailed before he returned. After eight years of struggles, he founded a Trappist monastery in Antigonish, Canada. It moved to Rhode Island in 1900.

30. While still in New York in 1813, Father Kohlmann returned some stolen goods taken by a penitent. The owner petitioned the court to require Father Kohlmann to reveal the name of the thief which he refused to do, citing the seal of the confessional. Father Kohlmann lost the case but appealed the decision to a higher court which upheld him. The case attracted national attention, resulting in numerous states enacting statutes protecting the secrecy of the confessional. This case set precedents for protection of privileged information that are still operative in our legal system.

31. These were probably Beguine sisters, as the Poor Clare archives in Belgium contain no record of other Poor Clares joining the group in Cincinnati or Pittsburgh. Beguines arose in the Low Countries during the 13th century and were quite numerous and active for 200 years. They were an anomaly, living the common life but without vows and dedicating themselves to good works and prayer, although without affiliation with any established order and without a rule. Lacking canonical status, some bishops encouraged them because of their openness to destitute widows and their ministries. In time many drifted into heresy, resulting in suppression and persecution. Those that submitted to episcopal authority survived as lay religious, but greatly diminished in numbers. A dozen or so groups existed in the early 19th century and today there are only a handful in Belgium.

32. Sr. Mary Christiana Sullivan, MA, "Some Non-Permanent Foundations of Religious Orders and Congregations of Women in the United States (1793-1850)," *Historical Records and Studies, United States Historical Society, Vol. XXXI* (New York, NY: 1941), pp. 12-53. Most of the information about "failed orders" is derived from her accounts.

33. Because of the dislocations and breakdown of Church administrative systems caused by the French Revolution and its aftermath in Europe, bad priests often evaded Church supervision and discipline, sometimes going to the United States where their backgrounds were unknown. While some reformed and ministered effectively with this second chance, others created problems when they secured positions in American churches. The term "rogue priests" applies to those miscreants.

34. Father Benedict Fenwick was a cousin of Bishop Edward Fenwick, future Bishop of Cincinnati.
35. Sr. Anne Francis Campbell, OLM "Bishop England's Sisterhood, 1829-1929" (Ph.D. Diss., St. Louis University, 1968), p. 15. Indiscriminate use of "sister" and "nun" is not so new after all. Much of the information in this account is derived from that dissertation.
36. Two offshoots from this community later became Sisters of Mercy. The group in Savannah, Georgia (2580), adopted the Mercy rule in 1892 and the Belmont, North Carolina (2570) group did so in 1913.
37. New Orleans had a sizable colony of free blacks of both pure and mixed blood. They could own property, make legal agreements, own slaves, and become educated. However, their semi-citizenship status barred them from voting, holding office, or marrying whites. While the marriage law was observed in a legal sense, it was openly violated by "arrangements" with all the essential elements of marriage. White fathers acknowledged and supported their children from these common law marriages.
38. In 1804, Congress passed a law requiring every merchant seaman to pay 20 cents per month, deducted from his wages, to underwrite the care of sick and disabled seamen. Marine hospitals sprang up in the major ports, and over the years Catholic sisters served in some of these institutions.
39. City officials in New York became so concerned about cholera that they declared July 4, 1832, a day of fasting and prayer instead of a celebration of Independence Day. The following list of dates for major epidemics of the 19th century conveys some idea of how often they occurred and involved Catholic sisters in nursing:
    Cholera: 1829, 1832-35, 1849-50, 1854, 1871, 1879, 1897.
    Yellow Fever: 1816, 1843, 1849, 1855, 1867.
    Small Pox: 1865, 1878, 1880-81, 1886.
    Typhus: 1847, 1890.
40. Louis, one of three Nez Percé Indians from the Northwest, was another victim of the epidemic. The three came down the Missouri and Mississippi Rivers by canoe to St. Louis seeking "blackrobes" to instruct the tribe. Later, in 1877, under Chief Joseph, the Nez Percé fought several engagements with the U.S. Army while attempting to flee to Canada. General Howard cut them off just short of the border and forced the tribe onto a reservation.
41. Barbara Misner, "A Comparative Social Study of the Members and Apostolates of the First Eight Permanent Communities of Women Religious Within the Original Boundaries of the United States, 1790-1850" (The Catholic University of America, Ph.D. Diss., 1980), p. 232. There is no record of the reply to the writer of this letter, a Mr. Levi Barlett of Boston.
42. In 1857, Judge Taney wrote the Supreme Court decision in *Scott v. Sanford*, the so-called Dred-Scott Decision. This held that slaves were not citizens and that a free state could not refuse to return a runaway to its owner in a slave state. This decision helped precipitate the Civil War.
43. Misner, p. 272.
44. One of the nuns was Mary Barber (Sister Mary Benedicta), the oldest daughter

of Virgil Horace Barber (1782-1847), a Jesuit priest. Father Barber, a former Episcopalian minister and president of a seminary, converted to Catholicism after his only son, Samuel, joined the Jesuits. The entire family converted and became religious. Mrs. Barber joined the Visitandines in Georgetown, daughter Abigail joined the Ursulines in Quebec, daughter Susan joined the Ursulines in Three Rivers, and youngest daughter, Jane, joined the Visitandines.

45. One of the Beecher daughters, Harriet Beecher Stowe, wrote the famous *Uncle Tom's Cabin.*

CHAPTER 3

Spreading Roots (1834-1861): American Initiatives

✠ — ✠

TORCHING OF THE Ursuline convent ignited a firestorm, signaling the worst outbreak of overt anti-Catholicism in United States history. It manifested itself in various forms: riots, harassment, and threatened violence against women religious and priests, and economic and social discrimination against Catholics and immigrants. It spawned a social movement termed "nativism" and a political party popularly called the Know-Nothings. The firestorm raged for two decades, only dissipated by the passions leading to the Civil War. Because of their little understood role in American society, sisters and nuns often found themselves the main focus of anti-Catholic hatred and rage. They nonetheless continued performing their ministries and were not intimidated. Existing communities expanded and dozens of foundresses established new ones.

In some respects the era from 1835 to 1861 was the most memorable and remarkable in sister-history. While facing a constant threat of violence, sisters and nuns increased from fewer than 1,000 to almost 5,000, added 44 new orders and congregations to the 12 already existing in 1834, began to take their ministries to the Far West, and opened schools, academies, hospitals, orphanages, and charitable houses wherever they served. Concurrently, the Catholic Church, fed by large numbers of Irish and German immigrants, grew to 43 dioceses. By 1850, Catholics had become the largest denomination in the country, claiming 10 percent of the population. Sister-history of this era is better understood when considered in four categories: (1) the assaults of anti-Catholicism, (2) the domestic establishment of nine new congregations, (3) the performance of ministries, and (4) the arrival of 35 immigrant communities from Europe and Canada. In this chapter we examine the first three categories. The fourth category, immigrant orders and congregations, requires extended coverage and is reported in the next chapter. While this approach examines the same 27-year span from two different perspectives, domestic- and immigrant-founded religious orders, the reader will find it provides for greater clarity in understanding a tumultuous and rather complex part of American history.

National Overview

A brief overview of the national experience — scene by scene — sets the stage for sister-history 1835 to 1861. President Andrew Jackson (1767-1845) reshaped the political landscape by exploiting the populist tendencies of the voters in the new western states, displacing the oligarchy of the Federalist period. He devised a "removal policy" whereby the government cruelly forced Indian tribes east of the Mississippi River onto reservations in the Oklahoma Territory and to other places in the West while settlers eagerly seized their lands. Disputes with England over the Canadian border brought the nation to the brink of war and popularized the slogan "54-40 or Fight." Another slogan, "Remember the Alamo," stirred Texans in their fight for independence while the Mexican War (1846-1848) added vast territories to the nation.

Mines were dug and forests cleared. Vigorous construction of roads, railroads, and canals linked the nation's cities while the infrastructure of growing metropolises expanded at a feverish pace. The Industrial Revolution took hold in the United States, intensifying the demand for cheap skilled labor. Steam power came into wide usage. Agriculture and ranching expanded. Discovery of gold at Sutter's Mill sent 80,000 Forty-Niners to California in one year alone. Abolition and states' rights stirred political passions. King Cotton enriched Southern planters and prolonged the institutional hold on slavery. Abraham Lincoln rose from obscurity to become president at the most critical moment in American history. Wagon trains trekked the Oregon Trail as settlers moved into the opening West. Ten new states joined the Union as the burgeoning population, swollen by immigration, moved ever westward.[1]

Immigration was not a major factor in national development before 1835, averaging less than 25,000 arrivals per year, mostly from Ireland, England, Scotland, Germany, and Canada. Napoleonic wars, economic depression, and the War of 1812 restricted immigration to a mere trickle. After 1815, however, immigration gradually increased each year, reaching 65,365 newcomers in 1834 and 114,371 in 1845. Thereafter and until the Civil War brought a sudden halt, the annual count of immigrants ran in the hundreds of thousands, hitting an antebellum peak of 427,833 in 1854. During the 1845-1861 period, the Irish constituted 39.5 percent of immigrants and Germans

32 percent. English immigrants dropped to a mere 15.7 percent. The other 12.8 percent was a mixture of Canadians, French, and assorted other nationalities.[2]

A small but steady stream of Irish came to America during the 18th century, mainly as indentured servants and laborers. Most were either Protestants from Ulster or became Protestant for lack of priests and religious instruction, especially in the South. When the Great Potato Famine devastated Ireland in 1845, followed by more crop failures in succeeding years, thousands of Irish starved to death. The English government and people provided only token aid. The population of Ireland decreased by 2.5 million in just 10 years. *It was emigrate or die!* Hundreds of thousands fled to England, Australia, Canada, New Zealand, and South America, but the majority went to the United States. An anomaly of Irish immigration, unmatched by any other ethnic group then or since, was the large number of unmarried women — 54 percent of the total — something that may have influenced vocations.

Irish immigrants were severely handicapped in several ways. English social and economic repression and religious persecution, dating back to Queen Elizabeth I and Cromwell, had reduced most Irish to near serfdom. Savage enforcement of the infamous Penal Laws kept the population in thrall until late in the 18th and early 19th centuries when a series of Relief Acts gradually eased the yoke. Upper-class Anglo-Irish and a small middle class managed decent living standards, but most of the lower classes were illiterate tenant farmers. In 1841, less than half the Irish population could read or write. Many of those who could learned in the illegal "hedge" schools — secret sessions for children in some hidden place taught by an educated adult.

Despite these handicaps, Irish immigrants had assets that eventually salvaged their situation in the United States. First, they spoke English, easing their integration into the work force and assimilation into the general population. Some spoke Gaelic but understood English and adapted easily to its everyday use. Second, they accepted the challenges facing them, fully aware of far worse conditions in Ireland. Third, they were willing hard workers ambitious to improve their status. Fourth, they had an instinct for politics and quickly grasped the power of the ballot and block voting. Finally, they were sustained by deep religious conviction ingrained by generations of resistance to English religious and ethnic persecution.

Labor contractors, professional politicians, and Catholic priests, most of Irish extraction, were among the few who sought to assist the needy and often wretched arrivals. They met the boats, directed to relatives, located housing, found jobs, provided food and fuel, registered the voters, and arranged bail when needed. Priests ministered spiritually, read and wrote letters for the illiterate, arbitrated disputes, gave advice, and by default became authoritative father figures. This paternalistic role was accepted as normal among the Irish for most of the 19th century.

Germans immigrated in a small but steady stream beginning in the early 18th century. Pennsylvania and North Carolina enjoyed the early concentrations of these hardy farmers, skilled artisans, and thrifty tradesmen. Near-famine conditions in Europe in 1817 triggered a wave of emigration which, starting in the 1840's, increased substantially, further stimulated by revolutions in 1848, wars, fear of conscription, and economic hardships in Europe. All told, around 1.5 million German immigrants landed between 1790 and 1860. Catholics from the Rhineland and Bavaria and Protestants from other sections of Germany came in near equal numbers, although a sizeable number of Protestants were Free Thinkers without formal affiliation with any established church. This denominational ratio pertained until the flood of German Catholics fleeing *Kulturkampf* arrived in the 1870's and 1880's (see Chapter 6).

German immigrants differed from the Irish in several respects. First, they generally came as family and clan groups. Second, they tended to come from the lower-middle and middle classes, were literate, and often well-educated. Third, they normally arrived with funds and skills. Fourth, they tended to remain only briefly along the Atlantic seaboard before settling in the Midwest where land was cheaper and farming a surer venture although numbers settled in cities of the East. Finally, they clung tenaciously to their German language and cultural traditions. Lutherans and Catholics alike avidly sought German-speaking pastors and teachers for their children.

While Irish and Germans constituted the majority of immigrants, a mixture of other nationalities was drawn to the expanding and developing United States by the Industrial Revolution, the discovery of gold in California, and vast stretches of available farmland. People came from Canada, Poland, Belgium, France, Switzerland, the Scandinavian countries, and even far-off Australia. During these years, the United States was in the early stages of forming a pluralistic society, a not altogether popular development among the Anglo-American Protestant majority.

Winds of Prejudice

Anti-Catholic prejudice, deeply rooted in the Anglo-American Protestant psyche and intensified by the upsurge of Catholics and non-Anglo immigrants found an outlet for its resentments, expressing itself in the "nativist" movement. This in turn took political form in the American Party. The settled majority deplored the immigrant tendency to cling to ethnic culture and language which further fueled the growing resentment against immigrants and Catholics.

Anti-Catholic literature became popular fare in England during the 1820's and 1830's, an outgrowth of the public debates over Catholic civil emancipation that Parliament enacted in 1829. Those debates triggered a glut of English literature that played heavily on Gothic tales of nuns as captives in convents. These books found a ready readership in the United States, fanning the flames of smoldering anti-Catholic sentiments.

On this side of the Atlantic, counterparts to these vicious books took the form of bizarre fictions of convent life. In 1829, the Boston Ursulines received a young postulant, Rebecca Reed, who was unsuited for religious life and released after six months. This woman spread rumors of weird goings-on and mistreatment of nuns within the convent. Publicity surrounding the convent burning made her 1835 book, *Six Months in a Convent*, a minor sensation, intensifying the existing hostility against the Catholic women religious. However, it was another American book of that genre that became the most scandalous and notorious literary hoax in modern history.

It appeared in 1836 under the title *Awful Disclosures of Maria Monk, as Exhibited in a Narrative of Her Suffering During a Residence of Five Years as a Novice and Two Years as a Black Nun in the Hotel Dieu Nunnery at Montreal.*[3] In later editions it appeared simply as *Awful Disclosures of Maria Monk*. Its ghastly lies made *Six Months* seem trivial by comparison. Ghostwritten by Reverends J. J. Slocum, George Bourne, and Theodore Dwight, it portrayed secret tunnels, dungeons, infanticide, nuns as the sexual slaves of priests (with uncooperative ones subject to torture or death) and various other macabre scenes. A smashing success, it sold over 300,000 copies in just 15 years, a huge circulation for that time. It was also printed and circulated in England, attracting a wide readership. This vicious book focused public attention on nuns who were increasingly misunderstood.

The ghostwriting ministers took Maria Monk on tour of the lecture circuit where she drew immense crowds. The three preachers garnered large sums of money and gave little to Maria. As a counter measure, Bishop John Hughes of New York instigated an official investigation, as did Canadian authorities. Both investigations established that Maria Monk had never been a nun, had been under treatment for mental disorders, was a prostitute, and had not even been in Canada during portions of her tale. Despite the official reports and the fact Maria became pregnant while on tour, her drawing power remained undiminished. Years later her daughter wrote a book disclosing the full truth which received scant circulation.[4] Meanwhile, Lyman Beecher, the instigator of the convent burning in Charlestown, published an anti-Catholic diatribe titled *Plea for the West* from his Midwest stronghold.

Unscrupulous fundamentalist preachers noting how Maria Monk filled lecture halls and collection baskets initiated a genre of anti-Catholic preaching that remained a pulpit crutch well into the 20th century. Fulminations against the pope, Jesuits, and nuns were always dependable topics for rousing a congregation. Another ploy was the "ex-nun" and "ex-priest" as speakers on the lecture tour. A few were actually apostates, but most were simply impostors.

Adding to the ferment, another anti-Catholic stimulus emanated from England. The Oxford Movement (1833-1845), brilliantly advocated by John Henry Newman, called for restoration of sacramental and other "Catholic" practices to the Church of England.[5] The anti-Oxford movement was a strong reaction by those wanting the Anglican Church to be even more "Protestant" in form and practice. Supporters of the anti-Oxford movement stirred strong sympathies in the United States and contributed to the rekindling of indigenous anti-Catholic prejudices.

During most of the 19th century, Protestant churches promoted a theme of domesticity as proper for women, resulting in an unconscious aversion to the role of unmarried women. This translated into prejudice against Catholic sisters and nuns who were considered to be leading unnatural lives. Although women were highly influential in most Protestant denominations, they were discouraged from the Catholic tradition of forming female religious societies, especially those including single women (see Appendix G, Non-Catholic Women Religious).

One of the most bizarre incidents in the history of the United States Army intensified anti-Irish and anti-Catholic sentiments during the Mexican War. As war loomed, the Army posted a battalion, partially composed of newly arrived Irish immigrants, to Texas near the Mexican border. Incompetent, politically appointed officers encamped the battalion in a miserable location and were quick to use the lash for minor offenses. They openly insulted Sergeant Major John Riley, an experienced soldier who attempted to advise them. He had taught at West Point and knew his business.

Drawn by promises of land and money and led by Riley, several hundred members of the battalion deserted and joined the Mexican Army. Some of the deserters were Irish immigrant Catholics, although the press and later some historians exaggerated their numbers. Using the deserters, Mexican military authorities created the St. Patrick Battalion, better known as the San Patricios. Sergeant Major Riley was the acknowledged leader and their unit colors featured a harp and shamrock. The San Patricios fought valiantly in several battles; American troops bitterly resented their inflicting casualties on ex-comrades. Many San Patricios died in battle and eventually the U.S. Army captured most of those still alive and tried them. Fifty were hanged.

Riley was flogged and branded. Because of the Irish names among the San Patricios, nativists seized on this unfortunate bit of military history to claim that Irish-Catholics were not patriotic Americans.[6]

Firestorm

As a result of these anti-Catholic factors, Catholic sisters found themselves the objects of public antipathy and even violence. Movement outside their convents, orphanages, schools, academies, and other institutions could be dangerous. They were frequently insulted, spat upon, pelted with mud or rocks, and vocally threatened. In one illuminating minor incident when two sisters went walking one day, a Yale college student boldly picked up one of the sisters and carried her a full city block. Setting her rudely down and grinning from ear to ear, he rejoined his companions to collect his wager winnings. Other incidents were far more serious.

Sisters and nuns routinely wore secular clothing for extended travel. Those forced to walk daily from convent to school or hospital sometimes wore secular garb in public, changing on arrival and again before returning. Sisters who were too poor to purchase decent secular clothing used flour sacks to make dresses, some so ludicrous they drew more attention than the habit. Any unusual noise at night outside the convent or a strange knock on the door was cause for alarm. Living a peaceful, routine life during these years was sometimes difficult.

One may wonder at so few reports of abuse of priests. They felt the same pressures and did receive bad treatment at times. However, in those days priests wore secular clothing, similar to the dark conservative garb of the Protestant clergy, and they were not easily identifiable in public as Catholic priests.[7] Because mature, self-confident men are a far less attractive target for a cowardly mob than pious women, there were fewer assaults against priests. One memorable exception was the experience of Jesuit priest John Bapst, whom nativists tarred and feathered in Ellsworth, Maine, in 1854. While priests did not avoid their responsibilities, they were simply not that visible, and nativists focused their hatred on the sisters.

Catholic laity felt pressures as well. Deemed second-class citizens, they daily contended with the dislike and suspicion of their neighbors, discrimination in employment, and the possibility of violence. Signs in storefronts and on factory gates reading "No Irish Need Apply" were everyday reminders.

The grass-roots nativist movement gradually assumed formal status. The Order of the Star Spangled Banner organized in New York in 1849 as a secret elitist society and actively anti-Catholic, evolved into the American Party, organized in 1854 as a political party. The title "Know-Nothings" was applied to this political party because of the secret oaths and members' habit of saying "I know nothing" when queried about their party. Secret societies were deemed "un-American," and such groups as Masons, Mormons, and the Cincinnati were severely criticized.[8] Nonetheless, for a few years in the 1850's the American Party became powerful, winning numerous elections in New England and other localities. Its support was derived primarily from working-class Protestants holding strong anti-Catholic views. The party platform called for barring Catholics and immigrants from public office and for extending the period for naturalization from five to 25 years. In a letter to Joshua Speed in 1855, Abraham Lincoln wrote:

> *As a nation we began by declaring "all men are equal." We now practically read it "All men are created equal, except negroes." When the Know-Nothings get control it will read, "All men are created equal except negroes, foreigners, and Catholics." When it comes to this, I shall prefer emigrating to some country where they make no pretense at liberty. . . .*[9]

Neither major political party endorsed the Know-Nothings in 1856 and their power faded quickly when passions leading up to the Civil War riveted the public's attention and overshadowed Know-Nothing influence. Yet during its heyday, it posed a serious threat to Catholics in general and women religious in particular.

The firestorm even approached one Catholic city stronghold. In 1839 an unbalanced Carmelite nun, Isabella Neale, ran away from her convent in Baltimore. Word quickly spread that a nun had "escaped" and a mob formed. The mayor and some prominent citizens kept matters calm until troops could be summoned. After three days of high tension, troops dispersed the mob and calm returned to Baltimore, the most "Catholic" city in the United States. At her brother's request, Protestant doctors examined Sister Neale and found her "not sound of mind." Sisters of Charity cared for Sister Neale in their hospital for the rest of her life.

Anti-Catholic riots threatened Cincinnati, Louisville, Albany, and other cities; the worst outbreak occurred in Philadelphia. After some disputes between the bishop and public education authorities, the first of a series of riots erupted in 1844. Before peace returned at least 15 people had been killed and over 50 injured. The mob burned to the ground two Catholic churches and a seminary and used 5,000 books from the Augustinian library as fuel for a bonfire. Thirty houses went up in flames. A letter from Sister Gonzaga Grace to Mother Xavier Clark in Emmitsburg during the height of the riots grimly illustrates the terror:

> *We are in the midst of frightful dangers; a great portion of our peaceful city is the scene of riot and bloodshed; two of our churches*

> *burned to the ground. St. Michael's up in Kensington this after-*
> *noon, and St. Augustine's about half-past nine tonight. St. John's*
> *has been guarded since Monday night, and St. Mary's is now sur-*
> *rounded by a strong detachment of the military, besides a patrol. . . .*
> *Three police officers now guard our Asylum, and we know not at*
> *what moment our dear little ones must be roused from their peace-*
> *ful slumbers to fly for their lives. Threats have been made positive-*
> *ly to destroy St. John's tonight; and in consequence the sisters and*
> *Orphans have been obliged to retire to some good families for a*
> *shelter, because if the church were burned the Asylum would cer-*
> *tainly catch . . . I am fearful it will be worse tomorrow night. The*
> *military are out on duty, but it seems no use. They have burned*
> *whole rows of houses, and shot many as they passed along. Do*
> *pray very hard, Mother; for what would become of us if the*
> *Asylum were attacked? How could we escape with ninety nine*
> *children, seventy of whom would not be able to assist themselves*
> *even out of the mob?*[10]

Alarmed by the Philadelphia riots and fearful they would spread to his city, Bishop John Hughes of New York secured an interview with the mayor and mayor-elect. Demanding troops to protect Catholic property, he bluntly warned them if any Catholic churches or institutions were damaged the Irish would burn the entire city to the ground. He did not come by the nickname "Dagger John" without reason.[11] The mayor promptly dispatched troops and peace prevailed in New York.

Sensationalism fanned the firestorm. In the mid-1850's, the Emmitsburg Daughters of Charity received a postulant named Josephine Bunkley. She ran away one night and asked strangers for help in returning to her father in Virginia. The *Frederick Examiner* printed stories of her "captivity" and "escape." Explanations by the mother-superior that anyone could leave at any time had no effect. Mr. Charles Beale wrote an anti-Catholic book about Josephine's experience and published it without consulting her and she later sued him. Josephine never returned to religious life, but regretted her actions and remained a Catholic. Upstaged by the vehemence of the slavery debates, this book was soon forgotten.

In 1853, Archbishop Gaetano Bedini, representing the Vatican, visited the United States with a view to investigating the "trustee" problem and the establishment of diplomatic relations. His presence and false accusations by an Italian ex-priest were enough to create havoc. Mobs formed wherever he went. In the end he had to be smuggled out of the country aboard the *Atlantic* in New York harbor. In 1855, Louisville experienced a riot. Instigated by Know-Nothings just before an election, it resulted in 20 deaths and hundreds wounded.

Thus, well into the 1850's, a number of factors coincided to stimulate latent anti-Catholicism, making the late antebellum years the most difficult ones for Catholics in American history. As the Civil War neared, abolitionist and pro-slavery political passions diverted public attention and the nativist movement faded.

Spreading Roots

Yet all the negative factors did not deter women religious from founding new orders and congregations or from practicing their ministries. Eight communities with American founders and foundresses arose between 1835 and 1861 as Catholic women continued to spread the roots of religious life. Each foundation was a different story.

Congregation of the Sisters of the Holy Family (SSF-1950)

The second order of black sisters arose in New Orleans. While still a teenager, Henriette Delille (1812-1862), a free black woman (whose father was white), began ministering to the city's poor and teaching religion to black children in St. Mary's parish. She often mentioned to her pastor, Father Etienne Russelon, her desire to found a community of black sisters. During the antebellum years, New Orleans had developed a reputation as a debauched seaport. Although it had a large population of free blacks, including some who were quite wealthy, it was teeming with black slaves. Although she was a stunning beauty, Henriette refused to attend the annual Quadroon Ball where wealthy white men surveyed girls of mixed blood with common law marriage in mind. Instead, she drew Juliette Gaudin and Josephine Charles into her plans for a religious community and secured the financial backing of a wealthy Frenchwoman, Marie-Jeanne Aliquot, who spent her American years serving the poor blacks of New Orleans. When Bishop Anthony Blanc finally granted permission, Henriette founded the Congregation of the Sisters of the Holy Family, based on the Rule of St. Augustine. It was a moving moment when Henriette stood before the congregation of St. Augustine's parish church to make her proclamation that day in 1842 after ten years awaiting permission from Bishop Anthony Blanc: "I, Henriette Delille, in the name of Our Lord Jesus Christ . . . consecrate myself to God and I vow poverty, chastity, and obedience. . . ." The sisters had moved into their convent and begun communal life in 1832, ten years earlier.

From the first day they cared for aged homeless women. In 1847, a Louisiana law decreed that organizations with a minimum of six would be incorporated or disbanded. The small band of three brave women were saved

Holy Family Sisters (c. 1942).

Courtesy Gonzaga University

by free people of color who formed the Association of the Holy Family with Mother Henriette as president, included other members for financing and work assistance, secured a constitution, and erected a new building. The home is listed as the first incorporated Catholic home for the aged in Louisiana — and in the United States. It continues today, still enjoying the distinction of top quality service. With increased membership, the Holy Family sisters opened orphanages and schools in other cities and towns in Louisiana, Texas, Florida, Oklahoma, Arkansas, California, Belize, and Nigeria. Today the congregation has pontifical status.

In 1988, the process of study for Mother Henriette Delille's beatification began. It would be difficult to imagine a greater source of pride for black Catholics of the United States than for the country's fifth canonized saint to be Mother Henriette Delille, servant of the poor of New Orleans.

Sisters, Servants of the Immaculate Heart of Mary (IHM-2150)

Another black woman, Teresa Maxis Duchemin, helped found the Sisters, Servants of the Immaculate Heart of Mary. Only recently has her distinction as "foundress" been seriously considered. Her story follows a tortuous path.

Teresa's Haitian mother, Marie Ann "Betsy" Maxis Duchemin, was orphaned at age 10 during the 1793 slave uprising and taken in by the Duchemins, a French Catholic family who treated her as a daughter. The family left Haiti that year and settled in Baltimore where Betsy was educated and trained to be a nurse. In 1810, Betsy bore a daughter, Teresa. The father was Arthur Howard, an English Army officer whom Teresa later glimpsed once at a distance when she was eight or nine years old. While only one-eighth black, Teresa was raised as a "person of color." The Duchemins provided a first-class education at Miss Lange's school, and Teresa became fluent in French. Being religious by nature, she decided to join Mary Elizabeth Lange as one of the founding sisters of the Oblate Sisters of Providence. Betsy followed her daughter into the order in 1831, only to die while nursing during the cholera epidemic the next year.

While Teresa was serving as superior in 1843, she met Father Louis Florent Gillet, a French-speaking Redemptorist who celebrated Mass for the Oblate sisters at various times. Around this time he accepted an invitation from Bishop Peter P. Lefevere of Detroit to work in that diocese. While preaching a mission in Grosse Pointe, he met Theresa Renauld, who would become one of the first three members of a new congregation.

Assigned as pastor of St. Anthony parish (he changed the name to St. Mary in honor of the Immaculate Conception), Father Gillet became concerned about the lack of Catholic education for the children of his parish and those in the nine mission stations the Redemptorists served in southern Michigan. While on a visit to Toledo, Ohio, he learned that Father Rappe (later a bishop) had secured teaching sisters. This inspired him to remark that if he could not secure sisters he would make some. In the summer of 1844, while on a visit to Baltimore he shared his vision with Sister Teresa Duchemin. Since the Oblate sisters had not been able to renew their vows during these "sad years" when they felt abandoned by church authorities and threatened by nativists, she readily agreed to go to Michigan and help found a new congregation.

The following year Sister Teresa and another Oblate, Charlotte Schaaf (Sister Ann Constance), joined Theresa Renauld of Grosse Pointe to form a new Sisters of Providence community in Monroe, Michigan. At this time, Sister Teresa determined never again to consider herself black. She kept the religious name Sister Teresa, Charlotte Schaaf assumed the name Sister Ann and Theresa Renauld became Sister Celestine. A fourth member, a widow named Josette Godfroy-Smyth, joined them five months later and became Sister Alphonsine. November 10, 1845, is the recognized founding date for this congregation.

Father Gillet wrote a constitution based on the Redemptorist rule, adapted to the apostolic mission of teaching. Bishop Lefevere approved it and appointed Sister Teresa the superior. In 1847, a woman accused Father Gillet of solicitation following her confession. She was convicted of perjury in court, but broken-hearted, Father Gillet felt his reputation was soiled and he left Monroe, secured dispensation from his Redemptorist vows, and spent the next 10 years performing priestly duties in various dioceses. He returned to France in 1858 and joined the Cistercian order, taking the religious name Father Celestin. Because the congregation changed its title in 1847 to Sisters, Servants of the Immaculate Heart of Mary, it was not until two years before his death in 1891 that he learned that the congregation he helped found still existed. Working together, Cistercians and Sisters, Servants of the Immaculate Heart of Mary, transferred Father Gillet's remains to Monroe in 1929 where he now rests among "his" sisters.

After providing a series of directors for the sisters, Redemptorists withdrew from Monroe in 1855. At that point, Bishop Lefevere reappointed Sister Teresa mother-superior and named Father Edward Joos, a diocesan priest, the director of the congregation. Both Mother Teresa and Father Joos rejoiced when four sisters went to Susquehanna County, Pennsylvania, in 1858, to serve in a boys' school in Father John O'Reilly's parish. This mission was their first outside Michigan.

Mother Teresa made further contacts with Bishop John N. Neumann of Philadelphia, aware that he was a Redemptorist for whom the sisters felt a strong kinship. He sent a letter asking for sisters to serve in Reading. Mother Teresa was enthusiastic but Father Joos was indifferent, so she went to visit Bishop Lefevere. During the interview he learned that she had made the investigations without his knowledge and was thinking of establishing a novitiate in Pennsylvania. He decided that the sisters could not accept any further invitations from Philadelphia.

When a letter arrived informing Mother Teresa that her presence was needed in Susquehanna, Bishop Lefevere refused permission for her to go. When she complained to Father Joos, he characterized her appeal a "revolt" and informed the bishop. On April 1, 1859, the bishop arrived at the convent, discharged Mother Teresa from office, appointed Sister Mary Joseph Walker her successor and directed Mother Teresa to leave for Susquehanna the following Monday. He permitted her to take two sisters with her and wrote demanding the return of three of the sisters sent earlier.

When Sister Teresa arrived in Susquehanna, she learned that Father O'Reilly had refused to return the three sisters to Monroe, relying on the original written agreement. While both bishops wanted a peaceful solution, Father O'Reilly was adamant. Bishop Neumann died shortly thereafter and

Bishop Lefevere issued a letter declaring a canonical separation of the two groups, forbidding all correspondence and association between them.

While Mother Teresa was attempting to establish a school in Reading, Pennsylvania, Bishop Wood, successor to Bishop Neumann, suddenly recalled her to be superior in Susquehanna. Since she ardently desired to return to Monroe, she secured his permission for Sister Celestine and herself to leave the congregation. Whereupon they went to Canada and stayed with the Grey Nuns of Ottawa, awaiting an opportunity to visit Monroe. Bishop Lefevere accepted Sister Celestine's return to the community but refused readmission for Mother Teresa. She returned to Canada where the compassionate Grey Nuns provided extended hospitality.

The balance of her story revolves around years of attempting to mend relations with her old community, seeking readmission. In 1886, at age 70, she was permitted to rejoin, spending her final seven years as a happy member of the congregation that she had helped found. Few foundresses have traveled such a twisted road.

Today, there are three distinct branches of the "IHM's," as they are popularly called: the Monroe congregation (2150), the Immaculata branch, formerly West Chester (2170), Pennsylvania, and the Scranton, Pennsylvania, branch (2160), which was formed from the Philadelphia diocese shortly after the establishment of the Scranton diocese. All three congregations have played a prominent role in Catholic education.

Dominican Sisters of Sinsinawa (OP-1070-03)

In 1847 a remarkable Dominican priest, Samuel Mazzuchelli, scion of a banking family of Milan, founded the Dominican Sisters of Sinsinawa, a large and important congregation.[12] While a seminary student at Santa Sabina in Rome, he developed an ardent zeal to become an American missionary upon hearing the appeal and invitation of Dominican Bishop Edward Fenwick of Ohio who was recruiting missionaries. Without waiting to be ordained, Mazzuchelli sailed for the United States in 1828. Bishop Fenwick welcomed him to Cincinnati where he continued his studies at Somerset. The bishop ordained him in 1830, then sent him 600 miles north to his first mission, Mackinac Island, where he labored among the French-Canadian traders, Indians, and settlers. Father Mazzuchelli covered a huge territory, larger than several of today's states, founding as many as 20 churches. In 1831, he established the first Catholic church in Wisconsin at Green Bay. Later, he converted numerous Indians of the Winnebago and Menominee tribes and published a Winnebago prayer book and a Chippewa Almanac in 1832. The first book published in Wisconsin, it is now preserved in the Library of Congress.

Fatigued from his labors of 13 years and in frail health, Father Mazzuchelli returned to Italy. While there, his Dominican superiors empowered him to establish a new province of the Dominican order in Wisconsin. With financial support from the Society of the Propagation of the Faith in France and donations from his family and friends in Italy, he traveled back to the United States and took the first step at Sinsinawa. In 1846, he built St. Dominic Church and founded Sinsinawa Mound College for men. Keenly conscious of the ever-pressing need for sisters to educate young women, in 1847 he clothed four local women in the Dominican habit: Mary Fitzpatrick, Margaret Conway, Judith Cahill, and Ellen Conway. He personally undertook their training and preparations for teaching. The four novices professed their vows two years later and several more women joined them.

That auspicious beginning almost ended in disaster. One of the sisters lost heart, recommended that the group disband, and departed to join the Ursulines. Two other novices also withdrew. The four remaining prayed ardently for a full day and then allowed their youngest member, Sister Rachel (Ellen Conway), to decide for them. She expressed love for and confidence in their community and preserved it for posterity, declaring, "In the name of God let us remain together in our present community."[13]

Another setback for the infant community occurred in 1849 when Father Mazzuchelli resigned as President of Sinsinawa Mound College and transferred all his responsibilities to the Kentucky Dominicans. Various problems with the clergy at the college brought Father Mazzuchelli to the realization that he could not continue in the roles of both missionary and provincial. Convinced of his own incompetence in governance, he surrendered jurisdiction over the sisters. To their dismay, he moved to Benton, 14 miles from Sinsinawa, and took over as pastor of the local church. Two years later the new Dominican superior asked Father Mazzuchelli to bring the sisters to Benton and resume responsibility for their welfare. The community reunited with their beloved founder, teacher, and friend.

In 1854 Father Mazzuchelli sought sisters from the Somerset Dominican community to assist in the religious formation of this young congregation. He had trained the novices earlier but wanted sisters from an existing community to assure complete formation while he composed a constitution. He moved the motherhouse to Benton where it remained until 1867. One of their students, Ellen Power (Sister Mary Emily) later joined the community and became the superior at age 23. She borrowed $20,000 to purchase land when the college closed in 1866 and led the sisters back to Sinsinawa and opened St. Clara Academy for girls. The motherhouse has remained in Sinsinawa ever since. This foundation demonstrated the power of dedicated youth guided by a holy priest. The Dominican Sisters of Sinsinawa prospered and by the early 20th century had become the second largest women's Dominican group in the United States. Their ministries have included teaching in parochial schools, operating academies, and a host of charitable endeavors.

Sisters of St. Francis of Philadelphia (OSF-1650)

John Nepomucene Neumann, a native of Bohemia later canonized a saint, became Bishop of Philadelphia in 1852. While visiting Rome for the declaration of the dogma of the Immaculate Conception of the Blessed Virgin Mary he received word that three Philadelphia women had offered themselves as religious to perform works of mercy. Pope Pius IX advised him to establish them as Third Order Franciscans.

One of the women was Marie Anna Boll Bachmann. Born in Bavaria in 1824, she received a sound basic education and as a teenager helped her father operate his small village store. At age 20 she married Antony Bachmann, who had been a coachman for King Ludwig. In 1847, the couple and their first-born child emigrated to the United States where Anna bore two more children. While she was pregnant again in 1851, Antony was mortally wounded in a quarry blast triggered by nativists.

In 1855, young Widow Bachmann (Sister Francis), her blood sister Barbara Boll (Sister Margaret), friend Anna Dorn (Sister Bernardine), and Bishop Neumann co-founded the Sisters of St. Francis of Philadelphia. The sisters' appearance in the Franciscan habit on the streets of Philadelphia in 1855 during the height of the Know-Nothing rage created hostility, so Father Hespelein, their parish priest, ordered them to wear secular clothing in public.

Their ministry was to serve wherever a need existed. In 1858 they nursed smallpox patients in the convent and people's homes because hospitals refused patients with communicable diseases. This experience led to their opening a 20-bed hospital, St. Mary's, in 1860, something that paid dividends when the sisters answered the call for nurses during the Civil War. In 1858, they accepted their first school, St. Alphonsus in Philadelphia, and a little later established a home for working girls. On Bishop Neumann's advice, Mother Francis Bachmann placed her two boys with relatives to rear, while her two daughters continued living in the convent under the care of Sister Margaret. Relinquishing the immediate care and direction of her children was for Mother Francis the supreme sacrifice. When the sisters opened missions in New York in 1861, Sister Margaret was one of the pioneers and took the young Bachmann girls with her. Both girls became Franciscan sisters in the Buffalo foundation (1180). Mother Francis' youngest son was ordained a priest in the Buffalo diocese and the oldest one died of typhus in 1864 contracted while serving in the Union Army.

Bishop Neumann died in January 1860 and two months later, Mother Francis Bachmann sent six sisters to Syracuse to minister to Germans. That community grew and became autonomous in 1861. She also sent founding sisters to New York in 1861. Mother Francis died in 1863. Her foundations expanded and sent out three offshoots. These six congregations are often called the "Neumann Franciscans" and live on as a memorial-in-service to a holy widow and sainted bishop.

Congregation of the Sisters of St. Agnes (CSA-3710)

Father Caspar Rehrl, an Austrian, came to Wisconsin in 1845 and was successful in founding parishes throughout the state. Because he was absent so much from his home parish in Barton, he determined to organize a society of women to handle the religious education of parish youth. He founded the Congregation of the Sisters of St. Agnes in 1858 with a nucleus of three women. They initiated a long tradition of teaching and transferred their motherhouse to Fond Du Lac in 1870. Their first mother-superior, Mary Agnes Hazotte, elected at age 17, was such a remarkable leader that she headed the order for the next 40 years, until her death in 1905.

Franciscan Sisters of Allegany, New York (OSF-1180) and Congregation of the Third Order of St. Francis of Mary Immaculate, Joliet, Illinois (OSF-1710)

The Franciscan Sisters of Allegany trace their beginnings to April 25, 1859, when Father Pamfilo da Magliano gave the Franciscan habit and religious name, Sister Mary Joseph, to Mary Jane Todd. Italian Franciscan, Father Pamfilo, had joined Bishop John Timon to aid in the development of that new diocese.[14] The bishop asked this Franciscan friar to "seek for sisters of the Third Order" to provide education for young women of the area. His search led him to form a new congregation in Allegany, New York.

Three months after the induction of Sister Mary Joseph, Ellen Fallon joined, taking the religious name Sister Mary Brigdet. Several months later,

15-year-old Mary Anne O'Neil joined. Father Pamfilo had encountered her in the Fort Lee, New Jersey, parish and had challenged her to seek a vocation — a challenge she accepted, taking the religious name Sister Mary Teresa.

The three sisters formed the nucleus of the new community which soon attracted others. In 1865, the community held its first chapter (meeting), electing Sister Mary Teresa the General Superior, a post she held for the next 55 years (two by appointment and 53 by election). She is often referred to as the "co-foundress." In 1860, the sisters began branching out, opening schools in Connecticut, New York, and other states in the East.

In 1879, three sisters went to Jamaica as missionaries, making this community the first to send sisters to foreign missions. They later sent missionaries to Brazil and Bolivia. Beginning in 1880, the sisters expanded their apostolates to include operating hospitals, homes for young and elderly, pastoral and social work of various descriptions. Once again we witness how a holy priest, dedicated women, and a dynamic teenager combined to form a religious community to serve God's people.

Father Pamfilo also instigated the foundation of the Congregation of the Third Order of St. Francis of Mary Immaculate, Joliet, Illinois. That foundation is covered in the account of Mother Alfred Moes, Chapter 6.

Sisters of Charity of Leavenworth, Kansas (SCL-0480)

In the 1840's Bishop Richard P. Miles of Tennessee was pressuring the Sisters of Charity of Nazareth for more jurisdiction over the group serving in his diocese. His aim, not unlike that of many bishops of the period, was to have a diocesan community under his direction. In 1851 five sisters agreed to leave Nazareth and form a small community in Nashville. To this Mother Catherine Spalding reluctantly agreed.

Father Ivo Schacht, appointed spiritual director for the group, had housing for them, but their rapid growth demanded more space. To provide this he bought land and built a motherhouse, orphanage, and an academy, using monies deposited by the parishioners. The sisters occupied these in 1856 unaware of the deep trouble between Bishop Miles and Father Schacht. To their consternation, this resulted in Father Schacht's leaving the diocese.

The parishioners, learning of his departure, began demanding their money, but there was none to give them. This problem should not have affected the sisters, but it did since the now ailing bishop refused to honor the debt. So it was in 1857 when the sisters in Nashville found themselves burdened with a debt not of their making. They then weighed the problem, considered the alternatives, and decided to pay off the debt. To meet it they sold almost everything they had: buildings, land, furniture, and some supplies.

Although they were almost penniless and certainly homeless, their resolve to be of service to people was strengthened, not dampened by this ordeal. To ensure their resolve, Mother Xavier Ross journeyed to St. Louis where Father de Smet, the Jesuit missionary to the Indians, arranged a meeting with Bishop John B. Miege of Kansas Indian Territory.

When Bishop Miege asked Mother Xavier what requirements the community had, she asked that they be allowed to live by and carry out the rule of St. Vincent de Paul and their constitution, and that the ordinary of the diocese always be their ecclesiastical superior. He was well satisfied by their answer. It was a successful meeting for the two found mutual satisfaction in their desire to be of service as well as a genuine promise of support. "Come north as soon as possible," the bishop urged. It would be Kansas for these sisters and new congregation — the Sisters of Charity of Leavenworth.

In 1858, Leavenworth, "where the West begins," was filled with a conglomeration of trappers, hunters, Indians, half-breeds, settlers heading West, frontier merchants, scouts, gamblers, and soldiers stationed at nearby Fort Leavenworth. These were years of terror and violence in the Kansas Territory as pro-slavery and anti-slavery factions contended for supremacy. Such a milieu seemed out of place for religious women to begin a new congregation, but the stark contrast fertilized new growth. Mother Xavier and a friend of the community, Mrs. Farrell, went to Leavenworth to ascertain if it would be a suitable place for the sisters. Satisfied, Mother Xavier returned to Nashville to complete their business affairs and close out the debt.

On November 11, 1858 the first contingent of nine sisters and an orphan girl arrived at the wharf in Leavenworth having traveled by train and riverboat from Louisville. The other sisters soon followed: a total of 16 sisters constituting the founding group. Within the first week the sisters began teaching in the boys' school, arranging to open an academy for girls and caring for the sick in their homes and in the wagon trains. They taught the black children whose families had fled to the free state of Kansas and they took orphans into their already crowded quarters.

In 1864 the sisters opened the first private hospital in Kansas with Sister Joanna Bruner at its head, the first trained nurse in the territory. She was the first woman in Kansas to run a hospital. She trained other sisters in nursing skills.

In 1869 five sisters and a music teacher, Rosa Kelly, traveled to Montana territory to open a hospital in Helena, the first of their many missions in the West, and simultaneously an orphanage as well as a school. Though they had no living quarters provided them on their arrival, they made do as they had before and would many times again. Hardship was never so much a calamity as a challenge to be faced.

In 1873, Mother Xavier Ross and Sister Joanna visited Denver in response to an invitation from Bishop Joseph Machebeuf to found a hospital. Although confronted with severe poverty, Sister Joanna was able to open and operate St. Joseph Hospital, Denver's first, three years before Colorado was a state. The hospital continues to this day to provide its best care to the sick, the poor, and the needy. St. Joseph is a far cry architecturally from that first small structure, but exemplifies the same spirit of its founders. Sister Joanna later opened another hospital in Laramie, Wyoming, and still later a school for the Arapahoe children at the St. Steven's Mission at Wind River, Wyoming.

In 1963 the sisters went to northern Peru where today young Peruvian women have joined them to serve their own people as Sisters of Charity of Leavenworth. In the United States, community members serve in Arizona, California, Georgia, Kentucky, Maryland, Missouri, New Mexico, Nebraska, Oklahoma, Oregon, South Dakota, Texas, and Washington.[15]

Mother Seton's Daughters

In 1834, Simon Gabriel Bruté became bishop of the new diocese of Vincennes, Indiana.[16] He had been Mother Seton's spiritual director from 1812 until her death in 1821 and was residing in Emmitsburg when named bishop. Much like Kentucky's Bishop Flaget before him in 1811, Bishop Bruté was penniless and needed help from friends to get to Indiana. The Sisters of Charity presented him with Mother Seton's personal Bible and a local doctor gave him a watch. When the Sisters of Charity of Nazareth recalled their sisters from Vincennes in 1837, Bishop Bruté turned to his old friends in Emmitsburg for help. Sisters Benedicta Parsons and Mary Margaret Cully volunteered. Within a year they had a 40-student school and 10 orphans, all that the two sisters could manage. A student, Ann Brown, joined them later to become the first Indiana native Catholic sister.

In 1835, Emmitsburg sent sisters to establish missions in Utica and Pittsburgh while adding a second mission to Philadelphia. Because Samuel Cooper, their early benefactor, had specified that the order must never refuse sisters to his home state of Virginia, sisters made foundations in Norfolk, Richmond, Alexandria, and Martinsburg (now West Virginia) in 1834. They withdrew from Norfolk in 1840, returning in 1848. Their stay in Martinsburg was for a longer period. The Richmond foundation prospered with an orphanage and free school.

When Sister Rose White moved from Philadelphia to New York in 1817 to care for orphans, she assumed that other provisions would be made for boys since the Vincentian practice was limited to girls. In this and other orphanages it was by exception not rule that the sisters cared for boys of school age. The anticipated separate facilities did not materialize for 29 years, becoming a source of friction with the leadership in Emmitsburg, acerbated by Bishop John Hughes' repeated requests for more sisters and even greater control over their activities. In 1846, the leaders at Emmitsburg made a decision to withdraw their sisters from New York because of his uncooperative attitude.

At the same time, arrangements for affiliation with the Daughters of Charity in Paris were in progress. This union had been quietly fostered by Sulpician priests whose apostolate was training priests, not sisters, and they sought to transfer oversight to Vincentian priests who also favored the union. Most sisters had been unaware of the proposed merger.

The Sisters of Charity was the largest congregation in the United States at this time with almost 300 members. Their independence, so carefully

Sisters of Charity, Greensburg, Pennsylvania (c. 1942).
Courtesy Gonzaga University

provided for by Father Dubois and approved by Archbishop Carroll, irritated some bishops who desired more direct control over the sisters functioning in their dioceses. It may have seemed to many of the upcoming Irish clergy and hierarchy that the Sisters of Charity were unduly influenced by French-born Sulpician and Vincentian priests and bishops.[17] The sisters were often caught in the middle of these debates. Many wanted their congregation to remain distinctly American, as it had been founded, feeling that substituting a French Vincentian rule for the one composed for Mother Seton was a denial of their American heritage and an affront to her memory. Such factors came into play in the contest between Bishop Hughes and the motherhouse of the Sisters of Charity in Emmitsburg, brought to a head by the "boy problem."

In submitting suggestions for the upcoming Third Provincial Council in 1846, Bishop Hughes wrote to Archbishop Samuel Eccleston on November 24, 1845 —

> *Again, altho' it is a matter perhaps foreign to the deliberations of the Council as such, still, I think the numbers of the Sisters of Charity who are far removed from their centre, the Mother House, would seem to call for a modification of their system.*[18]

Bishop Hughes wrote Father Louis Regis Deluol, the Sulpician superior of the Sisters of Charity, that he desired to erect a separate diocesan community with the sisters then serving in the New York diocese. Other bishops had founded communities with four or five sisters, but Bishop Hughes was ambitious for his diocese. He wanted 52 — a sixth of the entire congregation. On June 17, 1846, Father Deluol, speaking for the Council of the community and for himself, wrote Bishop Hughes —

> *We may be mistaken, but we consider this step of yours as calculated to inflict a deep and dangerous wound on the community, and if the example be imitated, and every bishop in the Union had the same right, we would consider it mortal. Appointed as we are to watch over the conservation and to promote the welfare of the community, we can neither approve of nor even connive at the measure.*
>
> *Therefore, we consider it our bounden duty to recall to the Mother House all the Sisters of Charity who are actually in your diocese. . . .*[19]

He also wrote to all the sisters to explain why the Council took the action, saying —

> *It would not be for Its [The Community's] good to parcel it out. This has never been allowed in France, where the Sisters of Charity have existed for upwards of two hundred years. This was refused thirty years ago to the Venerable Bishop Flaget of Kentucky, by Bishop Dubois and Mother Seton. This we cannot ourselves allow. . . .*[20]

Father Deluol gave the sisters in New York the choice of remaining a part of their community or joining the new diocesan congregation to be formed by Bishop Hughes. The bishop used every means at his disposal to influence the decisions. This tug-of-war placed the sisters in New York in an intolerable situation. They had either to abandon their orphans and ministries on which they had expended a generation of love and grueling work and return to Emmitsburg, or separate themselves from the beloved community they had joined. Tension built. When the election slips were tallied, 29 had chosen to remain and the rest had elected to return to Emmitsburg.[21]

The new diocesan congregation assumed the title of the **Sisters of Charity of St. Vincent de Paul, of New York (SC-0650)**. Mother Elizabeth Boyle became first superior of the new congregation, which went on to become large and prominent in its own right. The first motherhouse was at 109th Street and 5th Avenue, land now part of Central Park. In 1849, the sisters established New York's third hospital, St. Vincent's. When the city's plans for Central Park became known, Mother Angela Hughes, Bishop Hughes' sister and successor to Mother Elizabeth Boyle, purchased a 55-acre estate overlooking the Hudson River, named it Mount Saint Vincent-on-Hudson, becoming the motherhouse of this community.

Devastated by the blow that divided the community over which he had charge, Father Deluol aggressively pursued affiliation with the Daughters of Charity. On July 18, 1849, the Council of the Daughters of Charity in Paris voted to admit the American community. They were no doubt influenced by a vision of the Blessed Virgin Mary to one of their sisters (St. Catherine Labouré[22]) in 1830, in which Our Lady said:

> *When the Rule shall be in vigor, another community will come to be joined to your own. This is not customary, but I also very much love this community, and you are to say they are to be received. God will bless them and they will enjoy great peace. And thus your community will become very large.*[23]

After the vote of acceptance, Superior-General Etienne, the head of the entire Vincentian family that included the Daughters of Charity, wrote to the sisters in Emmitsburg —

> *. . . a nominal union and one of friendship does not suffice. You yourselves have already understood that life should come from the source. . . . You are grafted on the tree planted by the Holy Founder. In order to receive sap from it, that you may bear fruit. . . . Your union with the Mother House, my very dear Sisters, requires that you become Daughters of Charity absolutely like those of Paris, Madrid, Turin, Rome, Warsaw, Leopoldstade, Mexico, Syria, Algiers, Egypt, Brazil, China. . . .*[24]

Four sisters went to Paris to become imbued with the spirit and practices

**Sisters of Charity of St. Elizabeth,
Convent Station, New Jersey (c. 1942).**
Courtesy Gonzaga University

of the congregation. Upon their return to Emmitsburg in 1858, the formal incorporation was consummated. Mother Seton's foundation now became the **Daughters of Charity of St. Vincent de Paul (DC-0760)**, the American province of this international congregation. Donning the new habit with its distinctive white headdress and removing the widow's "weeds" passed down from Mother Seton was an emotional experience.

Meanwhile in Cincinnati, another drama took place. Six sisters did not agree to the union, maintaining that Mother Seton had founded an American order and it should remain so. With nativism rampant, criticism of being un-American was a sore subject with all Catholics, but sisters received the brunt of nativist hostility. In 1852, Bishop John Purcell accepted them as **Sisters of Charity of Cincinnati, Ohio (SC-0440)**. In 1870, that community sent founding sisters to Pennsylvania who became **Sisters of Charity of Seton Hill, Greensburg, Pennsylvania (SC-0570)**.

The New York community sent sisters to Halifax in 1849, which in turn became an independent congregation in 1855, titled **Sisters of St. Vincent de Paul, Halifax (SC-0640)**.[25] In 1858, Bishop James Roosevelt Bayley, Mother Seton's nephew, asked the New York community to send sisters to train novices for a new community he was founding. Because the New York community had none to spare at the time, the novices went to the Cincinnati Sisters of Charity for novitiate. Upon their return, the New York community sent two sisters to act as superiors and guides. Thus the **Sisters of Charity of Saint Elizabeth, Convent Station (SC-0590)** formed from two groups cooperating with Bishop Bayley. This community also grew into a large and prominent congregation, performing numerous ministries.

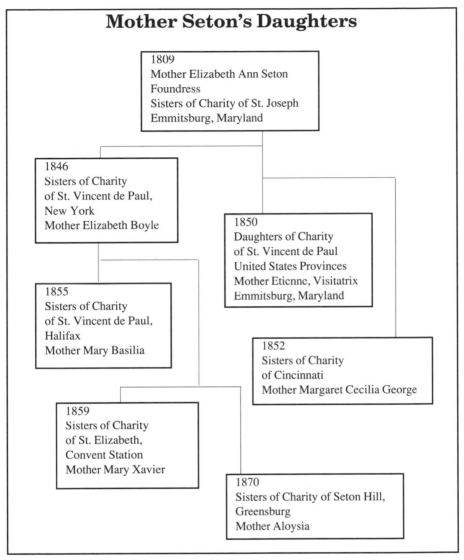

Mother Seton's Daughters

1809
Mother Elizabeth Ann Seton
Foundress
Sisters of Charity of St. Joseph
Emmitsburg, Maryland

1846
Sisters of Charity
of St. Vincent de Paul,
New York
Mother Elizabeth Boyle

1850
Daughters of Charity
of St. Vincent de Paul
United States Provinces
Mother Etienne, Visitatrix
Emmitsburg, Maryland

1855
Sisters of Charity
of St. Vincent de Paul,
Halifax
Mother Mary Basilia

1852
Sisters of Charity
of Cincinnati
Mother Margaret Cecilia George

1859
Sisters of Charity
of St. Elizabeth,
Convent Station
Mother Mary Xavier

1870
Sisters of Charity of Seton Hill,
Greensburg
Mother Aloysia

Table I

These six independent communities are followers of St. Vincent de Paul and are St. Elizabeth Ann Seton's "daughters." Table I illustrates the various foundations.

Thus, in addition to the eight new domestically founded communities, four new congregations emerged from Mother Seton's original foundation during this era. Meanwhile, other communities were arriving from Europe and Canada, as we shall see in the next chapter. All communities, both domestically founded and immigrant, found the need overwhelming for their ministries and devoted their talents, energies, and religious lives to meeting those demands.

Catholic Schools and Academies

"School" and "academy," words appearing repeatedly in recounting the sisters' story, are not synonymous. They indicate two distinct types of education. While either institution might be a day school, boarding school, or combination, they differed in the level and quality of instruction and sex of the students. Schools were normally open to both boys and girls although initial efforts were made to keep the sexes separate. Sisters taught the basic subjects of reading, writing, arithmetic, history, and geography plus the fundamental devotional practices and tenets of Catholicism. Prior to the Civil War a curriculum equivalent to today's sixth or seventh grade constituted the highest level of basic education sisters provided in their schools.

Between 1727 and 1852, women religious also founded 133 schools for girls.[26] Most of them qualified as academies. These institutions were similar to today's high school but taught a broader range of subjects suitable for young women, including domestic arts. Orders of priests and brothers conducted equivalent institutions for boys.[27] The prospectus issued by the Carmelites for their academy is an example of the curriculum offered in girls' academies. French and music were popular and considered desirable cultural subjects for young ladies from good families. Throughout the 18th and 19th centuries French was the language of culture and diplomacy; working knowledge of French was considered *de rigueur* for educated people. Protestant laywomen also operated academies in the larger cities. However, the upper classes accepted the fact that the best education for girls was to be had from the nuns, especially French-speaking ones. Proof of this reputation was that they sent daughters to attend these academies. At times, Protestants outnumbered the Catholic girls, as was the case at the Ursuline academy in Charlestown in 1834. An Englishman writing of his observations of the United States in 1852 stated —

> *In this country, the education of all the first classes of Protestants seems to be entrusted to the Catholic priests and nuns. . . . The parents say that their children are better taught and looked after than they would be in any other schools; the teachers say that they do not interfere with the religious opinions of the non-Catholic pupils; and that without such indiscriminate admission of all, they would not be able to support their establishments. Three-fourths of the boarders in many convents are Protestants.*[28]

Income from Protestant students was critical because it underwrote costs for poor Catholic girls and subsidized the free school and/or orphanage, often operated in conjunction with the academy. While they feared that their daughters might convert to Catholicism, which did occur at times, Protestant parents still enrolled daughters in large numbers. This phenomenon had an impact on the fortunes of the Catholic Church little recognized by Catholic historians. After being educated by the nuns, young Protestant women returned home with an understanding of Catholicism and lifelong affection for their teachers. They transmitted these attitudes within their families and later mellowed the anti-Catholic outlooks of their husbands. Sons entered the world of business, the professions, the military, and politics with a more benign attitude towards Catholics; daughters did the same within their new families. With the exception of the most bigoted anti-Catholics, respect and admiration for nuns were widespread in upper-class circles and had a positive effect in ameliorating anti-Catholicism in the 19th century. Some credit for weak support for nativism and the American political party (Know-Nothings) by the social and economic establishment of the day can be attributed to the influence exerted by Protestant products of Catholic female academies.

A parochial school *system* as understood today did not exist in this era. The growth of antebellum parochial schools resulted from the uncoordinated efforts of individual foundresses, mothers-superior, priests, bishops, and lay people. Despite Catholic poverty and a shortage of teaching sisters the count of parochial schools in 1861 was surprisingly large, approaching 1,500. Wherever sisters operated, they emulated Mother Seton's first parochial school in Emmitsburg. However, the vast expansion of these schools did not begin until after the Civil War.

Religious communities established a significant number of "free" schools that the academies subsidized, many of which later converted to parochial status. Since many constitutions brought from Europe specified teaching of girls, this restriction limited the number of boys admitted into the sisters' schools. American-founded congregations were far freer to provide for boys, but the majority of teaching women religious concentrated on female students.

Orphanages

Since antebellum national and state governments deemed orphans the responsibility of relatives, churches, benevolent societies, and local communities, there were only eight recorded orphanages in the United States before 1800. This attitude continued well into the 19th century even though orphans became an ever mounting social problem because of epidemics and immigration. Protestant and civic agencies who contended with the problem deserve credit. With an increasing Catholic population especially vulnerable to early adult deaths, thus creating large numbers of orphans, the sisters faced an urgent need demanding Christian charity in action. They responded by opening orphanages.

Before the cholera epidemic of 1832, the United States had never experienced a nationwide killing epidemic, although devastating local ones broke out from time to time. In 1832, the country was totally impotent to control or contain the epidemic. Victims overran limited health facilities. Treatment consisted of little more than bed rest — the strong survived and the weak perished. Cholera destroyed whole families and neighborhoods while fear gripped the healthy, who sometimes fled and abandoned the sick. Dead sometimes lay unburied for days. Following this first national health catastrophe, epidemics recurred periodically, some widespread and others restricted to cities or sections of the country. Yellow fever, small pox, typhus, influenza, and cholera were the killers of the 19th century. Consumption (tuberculosis) never reached epidemic proportions but was a steady killer. Each epidemic left thousands of orphans in its wake.

Shipboard conditions for poor immigrants of the 1840's and 1850's were horrible. Bad food, filth, and vermin were constant companions of the poor, who had saved just enough for passage. Packed in steerage they contracted whatever disease any one passenger brought on board. Mini-epidemics occurred at sea and survivors often carried the sicknesses ashore. Children leaving Liverpool with parents would arrive in New York, Philadelphia, or Boston as orphans.

Grinding poverty and early deaths dashed the dreams of many immigrants. Depression and hunger drove some women to prostitution and desertion of their families. It was routine for priests at the end of Sunday Mass to ask if anyone in the congregation would adopt an orphan. Abandoned babies of unwed mothers were often taken to the sisters regardless of their willingness or ability to receive them. At times, civil authorities placed orphans with families who wanted them for work on the farm or in the shop. In some localities they lodged young orphans in the county poorhouse among the mentally retarded, the aged, and alcoholics. Abuse of child labor was common. Young homeless girls were particularly in danger of sexual abuse. Orphans were a social problem unimaginable today. Most communities of sisters became deeply committed to the care of these unfortunate children. Some religious communities accepted this ministry on a temporary basis but found it impossible to relinquish later when faced with pitiful children. Others found it fitted their rule perfectly and embraced it joyfully as a permanent ministry. From the middle decades of the 19th century, Catholic sisters were the largest single agency in the United States caring for orphans.

Epidemics and the consequences of immigration left many children orphaned.
Missionary Sisters of the Sacred Heart, Center for Migration Studies, Staten Island

But even the sisters could not accommodate them all. A big percentage were identified as Catholic, while many were "religion unknowns."

An innovation of the Sisters of Charity was to open technical and industrial schools for teenage orphan girls. The first was St. Philomena's opened in St. Louis in 1846. Here they learned sewing, laundry work, cooking, housekeeping, dressmaking, and fancy needlework. A unique feature was that it was self-supporting from the income the girls earned catering and making shirts and uniforms. Seeing this success, the Sisters of Charity opened similar schools in Utica in 1848 and New Orleans in 1855. Most convents housing teenage orphan girls went to some pains to teach employable skills, even qualifying some to become teachers. These ministries saved literally thousands of young women from commercial exploitation, or worse.

Nursing

Increasing numbers of sisters engaged in nursing and operating hospitals. The first were Sisters of Charity from Emmitsburg. Several other orders also founded hospitals. While most orders continued to concentrate on education and the care of orphans, nursing became an important ministry because of the many epidemics. When they struck, sisters would normally close their schools to visit and care for the sick. When people abandoned the sick, afraid to enter their houses, sisters went inside and nursed. The cholera epidemic of 1850 so depleted the Dominican sisters in Memphis that they had to forfeit their autonomy and reaffiliate with the motherhouse at St. Catherine's in Kentucky, once again becoming a dependent mission house.

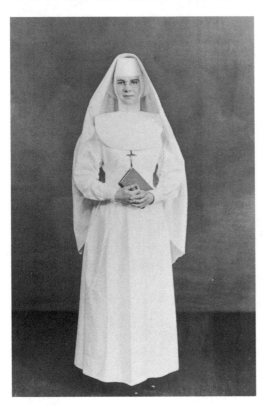

Nursing habit. Sisters of St. Joseph of Newark (c. 1942).

Courtesy Gonzaga University

Almost every order engaged in temporary nursing during various epidemics. Each has its accounts and heroines; many dying in the line of duty while nursing. Following the cholera epidemic of 1832, the Trustees of the Poor in Baltimore publicly commended the Sisters of Charity for their heroic nursing services. However, the Trustees commended the black Oblate Sisters of Providence privately, even though Sister Betsy Duchemin died as a result of her nursing.

Because of the historical, social, and religious circumstances just outlined, caring for orphans, teaching and, to a lesser extent, nursing constituted the primary ministries of Catholic women religious during the antebellum years.

Early Ministry in the West

Most of the activities reported so far have been confined to the eastern half of the United States. The 1840's and 1850's also witnessed sisters beginning to establish themselves in the West, where Canadian sisters were first on the scene. The Daughters of Charity were first of the American-founded orders to send sisters to the Far West. Others quickly followed.

At the time of the First Plenary Council of Baltimore in 1852, San Francisco was promoted to the rank of archdiocese and Bishop Joseph Alemany was elevated to the pallium.[29] While in Baltimore for the council, he visited

Emmitsburg to plead for sisters. Sister Francis McEnnis and six Daughters of Charity sailed to San Francisco by way of Panama on the Ohio. Crossing the isthmus required a three-week trek on muleback through the jungles. When Sister Corsina's balky mule ran off into the dense foliage, the only way the mule skinners could track her was the sound of her loudly singing a psalm. Dysentery, yellow fever, and malaria decimated overland travelers going from the Atlantic to the Pacific side. Sisters Mary Ignatia Greene and Honorine Goodman both perished. Captain Ulysses S. Grant, crossing the isthmus at the same time with a party of soldiers and their families bound for Oregon, lost 100 of his charges to those deadly diseases.

After embarking on the Pacific side, the sisters sailed to San Francisco where Father John McGinnis met them, presenting 15 orphans for their care. He then led the group to a shanty, their first convent/orphanage/school. Within a year, the sisters had 90 girls in their school.

A second contingent of Daughters of Charity arrived in San Francisco in 1855, crossing the Isthmus of Panama on the newly constructed railroad. No one contracted a disease. In order to accept boys into the school, they built a new structure on the site of the present-day Palace Hotel. It accommodated 75 orphans and 300 day students. A third group of sisters arrived in 1856 and established an orphanage and day school in Los Angeles. In order to raise funds they sponsored an annual Orphans Fair on Steamer Day, when the monthly steamship arrived bearing ice. This gala event featuring fresh-made ice cream developed into one of the big social events of Los Angeles. Steamer Day was made especially exciting in 1858 by the arrival of the first overland stage, making a 21-day run from St. Louis.

The sisters' small hospital begun in a tool shed became the official county hospital — the only one in southern California. Teresa Fox, California's first postulant for the Daughters of Charity, made the difficult trip to Emmitsburg for her novitiate in 1859. This long journey prompted the Council in Paris to approve a novitiate for California that opened in Los Angeles in 1861 with six postulants.

Mother Matilda Mills led a group of six Loretto sisters westward to Santa Fe in 1852. En route, Mother Mills and Sister Monica Bailey contracted cholera. Mother Mills died and was buried in Independence, Missouri. Sister Monica, too weak to continue, remained behind and eventually recovered, joining her companions in Santa Fe three years later, where she served until her death in 1865. The Sisters of Loretto established Our Lady of Light Academy, which became a permanent feature of Santa Fe.[30] In 1855, the Loretto motherhouse sent reinforcements who experienced a harrowing 10-week trip. One day a war party of 200 Indians accosted the wagon train, threatening attack. The wagon-master ordered the sisters into their wagon with all the canvas pulled down. There they sweltered for hours when the hot sun turned their wagon into a veritable broiler. The Indians finally departed after receiving gifts of blankets, calico, cotton, sugar, tobacco, and molasses. The party proceeded without further threats.

These and similar incidents signified the beginning of sister-ministry in the West. Immigrant orders also sent missionary sisters; their Western adventures are covered in the Chapter 4.

Progress of the 12 Orders Founded Before 1834

First-founded, the Ursulines confined their ministries to New Orleans for 117 years until Mother-Superior Seraphine agreed to send nuns to Galveston, Texas, in 1844 at the request of Bishop John Odin. The two nuns selected for the mission died before they could leave New Orleans, and Mother Seraphine notified Bishop Odin that the Ursulines would donate the property they had purchased in Galveston to any other order he might secure. Not to be denied, he replied, "I will have no other order. I desire educators." Mother Seraphine relented and sent eight nuns. Because German, Spanish, French, and English were all widely spoken in Texas at that time, good instruction in English was critical. On hearing the reports of difficult conditions in Galveston, Mother Seraphine dispatched two more nuns, both excellent English teachers. That academy became a permanent feature of Galveston. In 1855, rumors of a secret passage in the convent aroused the suspicions of local Know-Nothings who harassed the nuns. The mother-superior announced an open house and invited the malingerers to inspect every nook and cranny, pleasantly answering all their questions. Her openness laid to rest the rumors and permitted a peaceful life for the nuns and growth of the academy.[31]

The New Orleans Ursulines apparently favored Bishop Odin because they also sent a founding group to San Antonio in 1851 at his request. The four nuns' arrival was unexpected, and consequently they lodged in a crude shack crawling with scorpions and filled with mosquitos and ants. The nuns placed the legs of chairs, tables, and beds in pans of water to keep from being devoured. The first day of school was bedlam as the children were undisciplined and not very respectful. Sounds of several languages spiced with Indian words and local slang echoed in the classrooms. However, those Ursulines knew their business and quickly brought order out of chaos, going on to establish a quality educational program famed throughout Texas and down into Mexico.

America's only order of contemplatives in this era, the Discalced Carmelites of Baltimore (originally Port Tobacco), operated an academy from

1832 to 1851, as noted, and then returned to their monastic life. It would remain for the Baltimore Carmelites to send foundresses to St. Louis in 1863, at the height of the Civil War, to make the first new foundation.

In 1861, Mother Seton's "daughters" constituted the largest groups of women religious in the United States. The Daughters of Charity and the Sisters of Charity were teaching in parochial schools, operating academies and orphanages, nursing, managing hospitals, and performing a host of charitable works.

The Georgetown Visitation order secured pontifical status when recognized by Rome in 1816. Pope Gregory XVI extended that privilege to all Visitation institutions in the United States in 1840. Georgetown Academy had a rocky beginning and almost failed before achieving its "flagship" status. Sister Ignatia (Maria Sharpe), one of the founding Pious Ladies, was the only qualified teacher at the start but she died in 1802, still a young woman. Mary McDermott, another Pious Lady, died in 1820. During a bleak period for the academy as it struggled to survive, Father Joseph P. Cloriviere became superior in 1819. He immediately set about upgrading and ensuring quality education. Visitandines consider this priest their Second Father-Founder. He spent his personal fortune in this endeavor, building a beautiful chapel (now a National Historical Building), auditorium, and monastery. Working with Sister Mary Austin, a professionally trained teacher, he instituted a program of teacher training. They issued the first prospectus in 1822. After Father Cloriviere died in 1822, Sulpician Father Michael Wheeler succeeded him and continued the upgrading, personally spending $2,000 for science lab equipment, unheard of for a female academy at that time. President Andrew Jackson visited the academy in 1829 and issued an invitation to the students to visit him in the White House that the girls gleefully accepted.

By 1832 the Visitandines numbered 60 nuns, and Mother-Superior Madaline Augustine accepted the invitation of Bishop Michael Portier of Mobile to found an academy. She personally led the founding group and established the Academy of the Visitation, a combination day/boarding school. That community was autonomous as are all new Visitation convents once established. Mother Agnes Brent led a founding group to Kaskaskia in southern Illinois in 1833 and founded Menard Academy, named after their principal benefactor. Even so, it was a struggle in this isolated area. The St. Louis diocese split in 1843, placing Kaskaskia in the new Chicago diocese. Bishop Peter R. Kenrick of St. Louis wanted Visitandines for his diocese, and in a compromise solution Mother Brent moved to St. Louis, taking two nuns along to make a foundation. Two weeks after their departure, a major flood destroyed the Kaskaskia convent and most of the town. Boats evacuated the nuns from the second story of the convent. They moved to St. Louis and made a second foundation in that city. The two merged in 1846 and operated one academy.

The Georgetown Visitation community also sent founding nuns to Baltimore in 1837, to Frederick in 1846, to Philadelphia in 1848, to Washington, D.C., in 1850, and to Catonsville, Maryland, in 1852. The Baltimore convent in turn sent foundresses to Wheeling in 1848 and Brooklyn in 1855. Frederick sent a founding group to Parkersburg in 1864. All established and operated female academies of outstanding excellence and wide reputation. Alice Lalor, foundress and Pious Lady, served as mother-superior at Georgetown until 1819 when she stepped down. She lived as an obedient and humble nun until her death in 1846 — last of the Pious Ladies.

Sisters of Charity of Nazareth from Kentucky went to Nashville in 1842 to open a school for young girls and orphans. They established a hospital in 1848, just in time to help during an outbreak of cholera. As we have already seen, Bishop Miles initiated actions to break these sisters away from their motherhouse and form a diocesan community. In 1851 an alarmed Mother Spalding recalled her sisters. However, six of them chose to remain and became the nucleus of a short-lived diocesan community that broke up in 1858. Three sisters joined the group going to Kansas to form the eminently successful Sisters of Charity of Leavenworth.[32] Catherine Spalding, foundress and magnificent Kentucky pioneer, left a congregation of 300 sisters when she died in 1858.

Sisters of Loretto at the Foot of the Cross continued their ministries of teaching and caring for orphans in Kentucky. They operated four institutions in addition to the motherhouse at Loretto and ran a school for the hearing and speech impaired from 1840 to 1843. Why it was discontinued is unknown (fire destroyed the motherhouse and records in 1858). Mother Bridgit Hayden led a mission to the Osage Indians in 1847. These sisters are reputed to be the first white women to settle permanently in the Kansas Territory. The school they established and operated remained open until 1895. Trappist monks purchased the Loretto property at Gethsemani in 1848 and erected their famous monastery. Co-foundress Mary Rhodes died in 1853; Mother Ann Havern, co-foundress, died in 1862.

From the start, Mother Duchesne's Society of the Sacred Heart was pontifical. Thus she operated with considerable independence, even pulling out of locations. Normally she transferred facilities and ministries to other orders when leaving. One suspects that she kept a wary eye on any acquisitive bishops. This order increased from fewer than 100 nuns in 1834, mostly Frenchwomen, to 464 members in 1860, growth fueled by American vocations. Their foundations grew at an amazing rate: Sugar Creek, Kansas ('41 —

Mother Duchesne finally going to her beloved Indians), New York City ('41), McSherrystown, Pennsylvania ('42 — transferred to Sisters of St. Joseph in '52), Montreal ('42 — transferred to Sisters of St. Ann in '52), Philadelphia ('47), Natchitoches, Louisiana ('47), Detroit ('51), Albany ('52), St. Joseph, Missouri ('53), and Chicago ('58).

An interesting tale concerns their efforts to purchase the Lorillard estate in New York for a convent and academy in 1847. The heirs wanted $70,000 but the nuns only dared commit to $50,000. Students, parents, friends, supporters, and the nuns barraged heaven with 20,000 Memorares.[33] In the end, the heirs took the $50,000, throwing in an extra 20 acres of choice land. Rose Philippine Duchesne died in 1852 in St. Charles, Missouri, in the land of her girlhood dreams, joining Elizabeth Ann Seton as an American saint.

Kentucky's third group, the Dominican Sisters, also continued the work of teaching and caring for orphans. Their mission in Somerset, Ohio, became autonomous but cooperated in sending sisters to join in the new Memphis foundation. That community suffered severe losses in the cholera epidemic of 1850, as noted earlier. Somerset sent founding sisters to Zanesville, Ohio, and lent sisters to assist with the religious formation of the Dominican Sisters of Sinsinawa, Wisconsin. Kentucky sisters also made a foundation in Nashville in 1860. The motherhouses at St. Catherine's (Kentucky) and Somerset sent petitions to Rome in 1848 requesting adaptation of their constitutions to include elements of both Second and Third Orders. There is no record of the response, but they remained Third Order Dominican sisters. Mother Angela Sansbury, one of the founding group and the first mother-superior, moved to Somerset in 1833, and after 1836 acted as mother-superior until she died in 1839. She was buried at Somerset but was exhumed and moved along with the rest of the sisters buried there when the motherhouse moved to Columbus, Ohio.

The story of the Oblate Sisters of Providence during these years was the saddest of any order. From their founding in 1829 to the mid-1840's, this quiet community of black sisters practiced their ministry of educating free black children, both poor and well-off, even though teaching blacks to read and write was illegal in Maryland. After Father Joubert's death in 1843 left them without a protector, Archbishop Eccleston indicated he desired them to disband. However, Sulpician priest Father Deluol encouraged them to persevere. Their continued existence was in doubt during the six years between 1843 and 1849. Their historian described this period as follows:

> *We pass over these sad years. To many it seemed as if the good*
> *work was to be abandoned. The good Father Deluol did all in his*
> *power but no one dared come forward to take up the work. . . . Of*

> *the sorrow and deep distress of the Sisters in the years following*
> *[Father Joubert's death] we draw a veil. . . .*[34]

Since Sulpician superiors in France were withdrawing their American priests from directing communities of sisters, a Redemptorist priest, Father Thaddeus Andwader, with the backing of his superior, Father John N. Neumann (later bishop and now a canonized saint), took charge in 1849. Father Anwander effected a complete turnaround. By 1857 students increased, additions were made to school and convent, and a new school for boys opened; quality education for black youth survived the trials. That quality was attested to by the Commissioner of Education in his 1871 annual report to the Congress where he praised the pre-Civil War teachers in the District of Columbia who were graduates of the Oblate Academy in Baltimore.

Bishop John England founded the Sisters of Charity of Our Lady of Mercy in Charleston, South Carolina, but gave them little authority and failed to provide a constitution. Between his many visits to Haiti, he imported a group of Ursuline nuns from Ireland in 1835. They established an academy, and the Sisters of Charity of Our Lady of Mercy were relegated to the teaching of poor Irish and free blacks. When that school for blacks opened, the citizens of Charleston demanded it be closed. Bishop England said he would if all other such schools operated by Protestant denominations did likewise. Unfortunately, they called his bluff and all schools for free blacks ceased operation. The sisters operated a small hospital between 1838 and 1841 and a contingent went to Augusta, Georgia, in 1839 to nurse cholera victims. Bishop John England died in 1842 at age 56. His successor, Ignatius Reynolds, wrote a constitution for the Sisters of Charity of Our Lady of Mercy. They convened their first official council meeting in 1844, 15 years after being founded. They sent sisters to Savannah in 1845 and that community became autonomous in 1847. It joined the Sisters of Mercy of Savannah in the 1890's.

All during these years the sisters of the Congregation of Our Lady of Mount Carmel founded in New Orleans in 1833 continued their quiet teaching ministry. During the yellow fever epidemic of 1853, they nursed the stricken and solaced the dying; their spiritual director, Father Megret, was a victim. They established new convents in Thibodaux and Algiers, Louisiana.

Mary Francis Clarke, that indomitable Irishwoman, led four companions in 1843 to Philadelphia, where they became Sisters of Charity of the Blessed Virgin Mary. In 1836, Mathias Loras became bishop of the new diocese of Dubuque, Iowa. He and Father Donaghoe, sponsor of the order's founding, became friends over the years. When nativist activities in Philadelphia created so much hostility, Father Donaghoe considered moving the sisters away from the city. Bishop Loras was a classmate of the famed Curé of Ars in France, a miracle-worker and today the patron saint of parish priests. Perhaps emboldened by that association, he asked Father Donaghoe to provide sisters for his new western diocese. Father Donaghoe agreed and designated five sisters for that mission territory. In 1843, together with the bishop who came to Baltimore to attend the Fifth Provincial Council, the sisters journeyed to Iowa by carriage, rail, canal, and steamboat. No unpleasant incidents are reported for the trip. Before departing, Bishop Loras purchased a large bell for his future cathedral and on nearing Dubuque had it mounted on the riverboat deck. As they approached the landing the pealing of the bell heralded their arrival, much to the delight of the citizenry, doubly thrilled at the sight of sisters.[35]

They immediately opened an academy for boarders and day students, serving a wide area of the still primitive territory. Meanwhile back in Philadelphia the riots and Know-Nothing hostility prompted Father Donaghoe to consider moving all the sisters, a course Bishop Loras urged him to follow.[36] The Philadelphia sisters joined the group in Dubuque and made that city their permanent home. Shortly afterwards Father Donaghoe also answered the call of the West and transferred to Dubuque as vicar-general, once again becoming their spiritual director. For complex reasons it took an inordinate amount of time for this new congregation to receive canonical recognition.[37] The Vatican finally approved their constitution in 1877.

Although the next order to be discussed was established in the United States during the Civil War, the story of its unusual American foundress centers on the antebellum years and is included here.

Cornelia Connelly (1809-1879)

A small group of English sisters arrived in Towanda, Pennsylvania, in 1862, to establish the **Sisters of the Holy Child Jesus (SHCJ-4060)** — the first founding group to come from England. A dishonest agent had sold the order's English benefactor badly rundown property, making the sister's first two years in Towanda miserable. Snow drifted through the cracks of the deteriorated house, covering the sleeping sisters. In 1864 they left Towanda, moving to Sharon Hill outside Philadelphia where they founded an academy and operated successfully thereafter. The story of their foundress, Cornelia Connelly, is highly unusual.

Born into a well-to-do Philadelphia family, Cornelia Peacock at age 23 fell madly in love with a brilliant young Episcopal minister, Pierce Connelly, and married him against her family's wishes. As her portrait and statements of contemporaries testify, Cornelia was a beautiful young woman. The array of tutors provided by her parents gave her a superior education. Cornelia spoke several languages and was an artist and musician. Once married, she set her mind on pleasing Pierce as an ideal wife. In Natchez, Mississippi, where Pierce was stationed as rector, she bore three children while Pierce became a local celebrity with his wit, preaching, and charm.

Pierce got caught up in the religious debates of the day instigated by the Oxford Movement in England and undertook a study of Catholicism to bolster his arguments. To the astonishment of his family, friends, and congregation, he announced that he had become a convinced Roman Catholic. Resigning from his church, he moved the family to Louisiana where he secured a teaching post. Cornelia also took up the study of Catholicism, converted, and was received into the Church. However, Pierce's sense of self-importance demanded that he go to Rome and be inducted by the highest dignitaries. Taking the entire family, the Connellys successfully stormed high society and were interviewed by the pope. Pierce finally joined the Church with much fanfare and publicity.

Back in Louisiana, after his triumphant Roman sojourn, Pierce became withdrawn, moody, and restless. One afternoon he suddenly announced to Cornelia his desire to become a Catholic priest. The obvious sacrifice he was asking was that she become a nun, the only possible way he could be ordained. He plied her with arguments, applying all his considerable persuasive skills, catering to her devotion to him and her love of Jesus. Sad and frightened, Cornelia spent weeks in prayer and agonizing self-examination. She finally agreed, provided she could remain a novice and keep the children with her until they became of age. The family packed up and returned to Rome.

Months of examinations and legal procedures ensued. Pope Gregory XVI liked and supported the Connellys, which helped shorten the formalities. After both parties signed the required documents with all their promises and commitments, Cornelia entered the convent of the Society of the Sacred Heart in Rome, taking the children with her. Pierce was ordained with extensive publicity in England and the United States. He then went to England to join the household of Lord Shrewberry, one of England's richest and highest ranking Catholic peers, as tutor to the Shrewberry son and family chaplain.

Two year's residence in the Sacred Heart convent convinced Cornelia that her vocation was not with this order. When Pope Gregory XVI asked her to go to England and found a teaching order, she accepted without hesitation. There, Cornelia founded the Society of the Holy Child Jesus in Derby in 1846. Meanwhile Pierce was promoting himself to be appointed England's first cardinal since the Reformation. However, his overweening ambition soon became apparent to Vatican officials who ignored him.

During the next year Pierce sorely missed Cornelia, and contrary to all agreements, he attempted to visit her, supposedly to assist in the composition of the constitution for her new order. When she refused to receive him, he departed the convent in a rage. Having temporary custody of the children, he removed them from England in an attempt to blackmail Cornelia into meeting with him. When this ploy failed, he filed for restoration of conjugal rights in the Anglican Court of Arches. To Pierce's astonishment, the devoted and pliable young wife had become a woman of iron will.

The case caught the attention of the press, which made it into a sensational *cause célèbre* widely reported in England and the United States. It pilloried Cornelia and made her seem to be an unnatural mother and faithless wife. Mortified and hurt, she maintained her silence. Pierce won the case. Cornelia then appealed to the Privy Council, a higher and non-ecclesiastical court. After two years the Privy Council handed down a verdict favoring her position. During these trials she suffered excruciating spiritual pain, humiliation, and sadness. English Catholics found her an embarrassment and expressed wishes that both she and Pierce would return to the United States. Despite her hurts, she paid Pierce's legal expenses to keep him from debtors' prison.

Pierce formalized his break with the Catholic Church and secured the post of rector of the American Episcopal church in Florence, Italy, where he ministered to rich American and English tourists. He was successful in turning the children against their mother and spent his remaining years writing anti-Catholic tracts and false reports about Cornelia.[38] She, on the other hand, continued building her order, overcoming a variety of difficulties concerning money, disputes with Cardinal Nicholas P. Wiseman, and problem sisters. In 1868, Cornelia visited the American sisters at Sharon Hill, her first return to Philadelphia since becoming a religious. During all the years of her trials and suffering,

Society of the Holy Child Jesus (c. 1942).

Courtesy Gonzaga University

Cornelia protected the privacy of her spiritual and devotional life. Many of her contemporaries considered her a living saint. Sufficient evidence has recently been uncovered attesting to her deep holiness and supporting her cause for sainthood.[39] Her order is represented in many countries. It helped establish an autonomous community in Nigeria in 1930, the Handmaids of the Holy Child Jesus, and later another in Ghana named the Sisters of the Infant Jesus. The American branch of the Society of the Holy Child Jesus grew, spreading out to teach in numerous states. Few orders have come into existence under such unusual circumstances.[40]

Summary

Having seen the firestorm of anti-Catholicism, how American women religious coped under those trying conditions, the domestic foundation of new orders, the expansion of existing ones and the opening of ministry in the West, we leave the American founders and foundresses of this era for accounts of the 29 immigrant orders from Canada and Europe that arrived and established themselves during the same 1835-1861 years, providing a different perspective on this fascinating early period of American history.

Endnotes

1. The 10 new states were Arkansas ('37), Michigan ('37), Florida ('45), Texas ('45), Iowa ('46), Wisconsin ('48), California ('58), Minnesota ('58), Oregon ('59), and Kansas ('61).

2. Civil War in Quebec in 1837 sent the first of many waves of French-Canadians south, mainly into New England. This was a reversal of the American Revolutionary experience when American Tories loyal to the Crown moved to Canada in considerable numbers.

3. One of the two copies in this writer's possession does not provide the name of the author or sponsors. It simply states "Toronto, Published for the Trade." The other was published by the Menace Publishing Company Inc., Aurora, Missouri. That publisher specialized in anti-Catholic materials during the first two decades of the 20th century, including reprints of *Maria Monk*. Reprints appeared in London as recently as 1969. Even today, crude extracts sometimes appear on post office counters and in other public places.

4. Bernard J. Delaney, *The True History of Maria Monk* (London, England: Catholic Truth Society, nd [mid 1940's]), p. 27.

5. John Henry Newman (1801-1890) was elected a fellow of Oxford University in 1822 and was ordained an Anglican priest in 1825. His studies led him to Catholicism after his efforts failed to reform the Church of England. He was ordained a Catholic priest in 1847 and named a cardinal in 1879. His writings and sermons mark him as one of the intellectual giants of the 19th century. The impact of the Oxford Movement in the United States was rather brief although for a

few years it aroused considerable interest among intellectuals and the educated Protestant clergy. As a result, many of them engaged in historical research, theological investigations, debates, and serious reflections on Protestant dogmas. A surprising number of this group converted to Catholicism (see "Cornelia Connelly," p. 124).

6. Robert Ryal Miller, *Shamrock and Sword: The Saint Patrick's Battalion in the U.S.-Mexican War* (Norman, OK: University of Oklahoma Press, 1989), p. 174.

7. Catholics are sometimes surprised to learn that priests were normally addressed as "Mister" rather than "Father" in antebellum America. Bishops were often addressed as "Doctor," reflecting their academic degrees. Archbishop Nicholas Patrick Wiseman (1802-1865), later the first English cardinal since the Reformation, directed the English clergy to wear Roman collars and he directed the laity to address them as "Father." American Catholics quickly adopted these innovations following the Civil War.

8. Although not specifically anti-Catholic, the Society of the Cincinnati was very elitist. It was formed by officers of the American Revolutionary Army (not militia) at the end of the war. Because of its provision for hereditary membership, the society was severely criticized as elitist. The city of Cincinnati was named in its honor and George Washington served as president until his death. The society still exists, with one male descendent per original officer eligible for membership.

9. James Hennesey, SJ, *American Catholics: A History of the Roman Catholic Community in the United States* (New York, NY: Oxford University Press, 1981), p. 126.

10. Sr. Daniel Hannefin, DC, *Daughters of the Church: A Popular History of the Daughters of Charity in the United States, 1809-1987* (Brooklyn, NY: New York City Press, 1989), p. 67.

11. A journalist coined "Dagger John" as a derisive nickname and anti-Irish slur. Traditionally, bishops pen a cross before their signatures and Bishop Hughes' cross looked more like a dagger than a cross. These facts and his fiery temper perpetuated the nickname.

12. Today there are 30 congregations of Dominican sisters listed in the OCD under number 1070. The appended "-03" to the number for the Dominican Sisters of Sinsinawa indicates that this was the third Dominican foundation. The original Kentucky group has "-01," the Somerset, Ohio, group "-02," the California group "-04" etc.; all are in chronological order of foundation.

13. Sr. Mary Nona McGreal, OP, *Samuel Mazzuchelli, OP: A Kaleidoscope of Scenes from His Life* (privately printed by the Sinsinawa Dominicans), p. 51. Most of this account is derived from this book.

14. Father Pamfilo da Magliano is also remembered for founding what later became St. Bonaventure University. An Irish-American, Nicholas Devereux, was a great benefactor to Catholic ventures and was behind the invitation to Father Pamfilo to come to America. A Devereux daughter joined the Sisters of Mercy and was an outstanding leader.

15. Sr. Julia Gilmore, SCL, *We Came North, Centennial Story of the Sisters of*

Charity of Leavenworth (Meinrad, IN: Abbey Press, 1961). Also, see Sr. Mary Buckner, SCL, *History of the Sisters of Charity of Leavenworth* (Kansas City, MO: Hudson-Kimberly Publishing Co., 1898; printed in paperback in 1985).

16. Now an archdiocese, the original diocese transferred from Vincennes to Indianapolis in 1898.

17. There was considerable tension between the Irish and French clergy throughout the antebellum years when French-born bishops predominated in the hierarchy. One small example concerns the admission policy at St. Mary's Seminary in Baltimore, one of the nation's few seminaries. The rector, French-born Sulpician priest Louis Deluol, wrote his superiors in France:

> *"The Gentleman answered that the number of seminarians would be as large as one could wish, if they accepted all those who applied; formerly, there was a large number of seminarians because a large number of Irishmen were admitted; experience proved that those subjects, in general, proved unsatisfactory, that many thought of the Seminary only as a stopping off place, and they left us soon as they found something to do in town; others misbehaved; so it was decided that they would admit subjects of that nation only with discretion and with fitting precaution. . . ."*
>
> (James M. White, *The Diocesan Seminary in the United States: A History from the 1780's to the Present*, Notre Dame, IN: University of Notre Dame Press, 1989, p. 37).

An example of the opposite view was expressed by Bishop John England of Charleston, South Carolina, who stated —

> *"The French can never become American. Their language, manners, love of la belle France, their dress, air, carriage, notions, and mode of speaking of their religion, all, all are foreign. . ."*
>
> (Ibid., p. 53).

18. Hannefin, p. 88.

19. Ibid., p. 88.

20. Ibid., p. 89.

21. Some records indicate that 26 sisters remained in New York and that 26 returned to Emmitsburg. Another indicates that 31 remained and 28 returned. See Sr. John Mary Crumlish, DC, *The Union of the American Sisters of Charity with the Daughters of Charity, Paris* (Emmitsburg, MD: St. Joseph's Provincial House, 1950), p. 46.

22. The Blessed Virgin Mary instructed St. Catherine Labouré to promote the wearing of a new medal which she described in detail. That medal, popularly called the "Miraculous Medal," has hung from the necks of literally hundreds of millions of Catholics since the apparition in 1830.

23. Ibid., p. 91.

24. Ibid., p. 92.

25. This Canadian foundation later established three provinces in the United States. Two are located in Massachusetts and one in California.

26. The Catholic University of America, *New Catholic Encyclopedia* (Washington, DC: 1967), Vol. 5, p. 138.
27. These accounts give little notice to the educational efforts of Catholic brothers. Christian Brothers (Institute of the Brothers of the Christian Schools) came to the United States as early as 1819. Franciscan Brothers and Xaverian Brothers were also active in teaching boys. By 1873, approximately 900 brothers were teaching in more than 100 schools (mostly boys' academies).
28. Mary Ewens, *The Role of the Nun in Nineteenth Century America* (Salem, NH: Ayer Company, Publishers, Inc. 1971), p. 141.
29. The pallium is a narrow circular band made of pure white wool and worn around the neck. The symbol of metropolitan authority, its use dates back to the 8th century.
30. In 1873, the Sisters of Loretto at the Foot of the Cross constructed a beautiful chapel in Santa Fe costing $30,000, a huge sum in those days. When the work was well advanced, it became apparent that the architect had erred badly in not allowing space for a staircase to the choir loft. Workmen tried to fit one in, but abandoned the effort as hopeless. About this time a bearded carpenter appeared leading a donkey carrying his tools. He offered to help. Working quietly for six months, he constructed a spiral staircase, without nails, and architecturally perfect. It is without support except from the floor and attachment to the choir loft. When finished, he disappeared without payment. No one knew who he was or where he came from. All that the sisters would allow was that they had been praying a novena to St. Joseph. The staircase is a design marvel, impossible to duplicate; theoretically, it should collapse. X-ray analysis proves the absence of nails, and the shaping of each individual piece of wood would require computer calculations. The wood itself is not native to North America and its species remains unknown. This staircase is a major tourist attraction today.
31. Modern archaeological excavations have been made in an attempt to explain an ancient large drain beneath the old Ursuline convent. It seems the Know-Nothings of 1856 were on to something after all.
32. One of the original Sisters of Charity of Nazareth changed her mind and returned to Nazareth in 1853. Two others died in 1854 and were buried in Nashville.
33. This is a short intercessory prayer to the Blessed Virgin Mary. It begins, "Remember O most gracious Virgin Mary. . . ." Hence, the title "Memorare."
34. Barbara Misner, "A Comparative Social Study of the Members and Apostolates of the First Eight Permanent Communities of Women Religious Within the Original Boundaries of the United States, 1790-1850" (The Catholic University of America, Ph.D. Diss. 1980), p. 48.
35. Mother Clarke and her sisters did not wear habits at this time, adopting them in 1858.
36. These years were a particularly difficult period for the Philadelphia diocese. The "trustee" problem was severe and poorly handled by Bishop Henry Conwell (1745-1842). The Vatican permitted him to remain in office but gave full administrative authority to Coadjutor Bishop Francis P. Kenrick (1796-1863).

Bishop Conwell constantly attempted to undermine Bishop Kenrick's administration. Bishop Kenrick became Archbishop of Baltimore in 1851.

37. The Sisters of Charity of the Blessed Virgin Mary had recognition problems in Philadelphia where Bishop Henry Conwell did not extend public approbation and his powerful coadjutor Bishop Francis Kenrick referred to the sisters as "Donaghoe's pious ladies." After they moved to Iowa, Bishop Mathias Loras only extended "quasi-diocesan" status. Suggestions that they join an established congregation came from all quarters. Bishop Loras wanted them to amalgamate with the Daughters of Charity in Emmitsburg, Father Samuel Mazzuchelli wanted them for his new Dominican foundation in Sinsinawa, and Bishop John Hughes wanted them for his newly formed Sisters of Charity in New York. However, Father Donaghoe and Mother Clarke successfully defended the sisters' independence (Sr. Mary DeCock, BVM, "Turning Points in the Spirituality of an American Congregation," *U.S. Catholic Historian, vol. 10*, Baltimore, MD, pp. 62-63).

38. The Connellys had five children. One died very young in a tragic accident. Their older son, Mercer, died in New Orleans of yellow fever at age 20. Their daughter, Adeline, visited Cornelia several times but remained with Pierce until he died. She then returned to the Catholic faith. Their other son, Frank, became a noted artist and sculptor. He maintained sporadic contact with Cornelia but blamed the Catholic Church for spoiling his childhood and ruining his parents' lives. Their daughter, Marina, married into the Borghese family in Rome and became a princess.

39. Even after 100 years, some of the English hierarchy and clergy are not in favor of Mother Connelly's canonization. They feel that her case caused scandal that still rankles their English sense of propriety. Her pain lives on, even in death. Nonetheless, she was declared Venerable in 1992.

40. Juliana Wadham, *The Case of Cornelia Connelly*, (New York, NY: Pantheon Books, Inc., 1957). Most of this account is derived from this book.

CHAPTER 4

Spreading Roots (1834-1861): European and Canadian Initiatives

‡ — ‡

ON JULY 17, 1794 — at the height of the Reign of Terror — the dreaded death carts approached the Place de la Revolution in Paris, still lighted by the midsummer's fading sun although it was near eight in the evening. For almost 100 days the vile prosecutor Antoine Quentin Fouquier-Tinville had been condemning victims with little more than brief mock trials. He treated nuns no differently. The day's victims were 16 Carmelite nuns from Compiègne, condemned to death that morning simply for being Catholic religious. En route, they sang the *Miserere, Salve Regina, Te Deum*, and *Veni Creator*.[1]

The singing grew louder as the tumbrels neared the square. Hardened by months of bloody executions, the huge crowd thirsted for the day's spectacle. They gradually ceased jesting as the singing became perceptible. Slowly at first, then rapidly, the clear notes took hold and soared over the assembled onlookers, finally assuming complete dominance. Not even the king's execution had produced such quiet by the mob. Before mounting the horrible killing machine, the Carmelites renewed their vows and forgave their executioners, to the fascination of the morbid audience. This done, they resumed singing. Sister Constance, the youngest, went first. She held her head high and approached the guillotine like a queen passing before the court. No hand touched her as she knelt down to place her head on the block. Quickly the knife fell and her head toppled into the basket. One by one at about two-minute intervals the other Carmelite nuns followed, all with total dignity. Each fall of the blade reduced the singing's volume and the spectators strained to hear. Finally Mother Teresa, who had asked to go last, took her turn and the crash of the blade ended the singing. Complete silence hung over the square. Abruptly, the stillness was pierced by a small, clear female voice in the crowd. A young woman picked up where Mother Teresa had ceased. All alone she sang the final words of the *Veni Creator*:

> *Deo patri sit gloria*
> *Et filio, qui a mortuis*
> *Surrexit ac Paraclito*
> *In saecularum saecula.*[2]

She had not yet finished the last note when the mob, now awakened and maddened, fell on the unidentified girl and furiously tore her to pieces.[3] This scene so full of pathos was just one of many that witnessed the deaths of some 40,000 French Catholics, condemned for refusing to deny their religion during the Revolution.

In Paris alone 23 ex-Jesuits and hundreds of secular priests died in prison in the so-called "September Massacres" of 1792 when they were stabbed, shot, and clubbed to death by blood-frenzied revolutionaries. The Daughters of Charity lost 16 members to the guillotine. Similar scenes were repeated in various sections of France. The execution of women religious was only one facet of a revolution that changed the world forever. Its underlying philosophy spawned the evil concept that destruction of existing society is justified by the need to make way for the new, regardless of the violence and killing required — a total liberation from ethics. In 1917, Lenin asked: "Where shall we find our Fouquier-Tinville?" Joseph Stalin fit the bill. Today in America, we tend to misunderstand or forget the profound and worldwide effects of the French Revolution.

Out of turmoil in Europe came aid for America. Their experiences of persecution made French Catholics highly sensitive to the troubles of their counterparts in the United States. Before 1835, only three American orders had French origins: the Ursulines of New Orleans, Mother Duchesne's Society of the Sacred Heart, and the Calced Carmelites in Louisiana. During the next 26 years, however, 18 orders and congregations arrived from French-speaking Canada and France. The guillotine had spewed blood that seeded a new land.

The burning in 1834 of the Ursuline convent in Charlestown, Massachusetts, received broad press coverage that created shock waves throughout Catholic Europe, especially in France, where it sounded all too familiar. Napoleon had re-legalized the Catholic sisterhood in France but barely tolerated it. Following his downfall in 1815, a tremendous religious revival swept the country. Old religious orders revived and new ones sprang up.[4] The calamity at Charlestown rasped on the nerves of French women religious, triggering positive responses to calls for help from across the Atlantic.

Earlier, Bishop John Carroll had taken advantage of the availability of exiled French priests and imported French Sulpicians to found a seminary and train American priests. Other French priests fleeing the Revolution also came to America. As late as 1850 nine out of the 30 American bishops were French-born. While the French-speaking population of the United States was relatively small, the Louisiana Purchase of 1803 brought the French-speaking Catholics of New Orleans into the population, and the greater Mississippi Valley and Great Lakes regions contained thousands of scattered and unnoticed French-speaking settlers, traders, and descendants of earlier trappers. They were Catholic, but most had been without priests and religious help for generations. Even thousands of Indians whose ancestors had been converted by the Jesuits considered themselves Catholic. Scattered, poor, and untutored, these nominal Catholics lived outside the mainstream of American life well into the 19th century. Only inherited fidelity qualified most as Catholic before the arrival of priests and women religious.

French immigration never approached that of the Irish or Germans, although French-Canadians migrated during the first half of the 19th century, drawn by employment opportunities in New England where higher paying jobs were a magnet for the poor rural workers of Quebec.[5] Political and ethnic tensions and civil unrest were also factors sending settlers south of the border. Most settlers had sound basic education, were religious, and tended to be clannish, learning just enough English to get by. Bigoted New Englanders applied the derogatory nickname "Canucks" to these quiet, pious Catholics who needed spiritual nourishment.

Post-Napoleonic era French Catholic religious orders, keenly aware of the horrors of persecution, were receptive to appeals for support for American Catholics. French-born clergy and bishops in the United States, their numbers far out of proportion to French-speaking Americans, knew how to exploit sympathies and gain assistance from sisters and nuns back in France. These situations explain in some measure why so many French-speaking women religious came to the United States between 1835 and 1861.

Because of centuries of persecution, Ireland did not have many long-established congregations of women religious engaged in active ministry able to support the hordes of their countrymen emigrating to the United States. Only two relatively new congregations sent foundresses. Yet so many Irish immigrants and Irish-American women joined other communities that they assumed an Irish complexion.

The motivational pull that brought German-speaking women religious during these years was somewhat different. It was based on response to appeals for educational services for German-American Catholics and their children, something that German-Americans considered critical for preservation of their culture. Having covered the foundations of domestic orders in the previous chapter, we now focus on immigrant orders arriving during the same 27-year span. The new French-language foundations are reported first, then the Irish, and finally the German orders and congregations.

FLEUR DE LIS

Sisters of St. Joseph of Carondelet (CSJ-3840)

On March 5, 1836, six members of the Sisters of St. Joseph arrived in St. Louis from France. The arrival of what would ultimately become the second largest congregation in the United States was the result of a combination of factors. Mother St. John Fontbonne, who barely escaped the guillotine in 1794 and became the "second foundress" of the congregation, wanted to send missionaries to the United States. The motherhouse was in Lyons, also the headquarters of the Society of the Propagation of the Faith whose publication, *Annales*, often featured reports from the American frontier submitted by Bishop Joseph Rosati of St. Louis pleading for missionaries and funds. His European agent was Father Charles Cholleton who also happened to be the spiritual director for the Sisters of St. Joseph in Lyons. The wealthy Countess de la Rochejacquelin who took an interest in the Society for the Propagation of the Faith and the needs of America was a friend of the Sisters of St. Joseph. Thus, when Bishop Rosati wrote Father Cholleton seeking sisters, these factors came into play. The countess offered to underwrite such a mission and in fact provided financial support to the mission for many years. Mother St. John accepted eight of the many volunteers for the mission and designated her niece, Sister Febronie Fontbonne, the superior. Sisters Celestine Pommerel and St. John Fournier remained in France to study sign language before going to the United States.

The six sisters landed in New Orleans where they rested with the ever hospitable Ursulines who persuaded them to wear secular clothing for the trip up the Mississippi for fear of nativists. Arriving in St. Louis, they remained with the Sisters of Charity until three of the sisters were dispatched to Cahokia, Illinois, to open a school. A bit later the other three sisters were posted to the village of Carondelet,[6] a few miles south of the city. This site became their motherhouse.

Anne Eliza Dillon, the first American-born postulant, joined the order in

1837 and the two sisters who had remained behind arrived the same year. They made the first Catholic effort in the United States to minister to the hearing and speech impaired. Four deaf girls arrived at the Carondelet convent in 1838, the first beneficiaries of a ministry that continues to this day. The sisters opened St. Joseph's Academy in St. Louis in 1840 and assumed management of St. Joseph's Orphanage and St. Vincent's parochial school in 1845. When they purchased property for a school for black girls, this action created such a commotion in St. Louis that the project had to be abandoned. Nonetheless, the sisters provided Sunday school instructions for these victims of prejudice.

Because of the difficulty of communications between the two distant motherhouses, the American community separated from Lyons in 1847, becoming autonomous. Around 1860, during negotiations with the Vatican for papal status, the congregation adopted the title of Sisters of St. Joseph of Carondelet.

As the community expanded it established its first mission away from the motherhouse in Philadelphia in 1847. They established a hospital in Wheeling in 1853 and one in St. Paul in 1854. After disastrous floods ruined Cahokia in 1856, they abandoned that location. When cholera struck St. Louis in 1849 and again in 1851, the sisters nursed the sick and dying, losing several of their own to this plague. Because of the losses in membership due to the cholera epidemics and increased numbers of orphans, pleas went out to Lyons for reinforcements. That mother community could not spare sisters at this time and contacted the St. Joseph community at Moutiers, which sent a band of volunteers to supplement the growing numbers of American-born postulants. French sisters continued arriving into the 1880's. Foundations were made in Buffalo in 1854, in Brooklyn in 1856, and in Erie in 1860.

Mother Celestine, superior for many years, encouraged the establishment of other foundations for the Sisters of St. Joseph which grew into separate congregations. She died in 1857 at Carondelet. With the passage of years, the Sisters of St. Joseph of Carondelet founded hospitals, academies, schools, and orphanages and practiced multiple other charitable ministries. A heroic "second foundress" and a wealthy countess sent more than just eight missionaries to the United States.

Sisters of Notre Dame de Namur (SNDdeN-3000)

Two very unlikely women co-founded this congregation in Amiens in 1804 — one a cripple and the other a viscountess. St. Julie Billiart, devout even as a child, suffered a crippling nerve disorder as a teenager and for many years was confined to bed where she taught religion to neighborhood children. When her teaching attracted the attention of authorities during the Revolution, her family hid her and then spirited her away to Compiègne for safety. While in hiding, Julie received a vision of the crucified Christ surrounded at the foot of the Cross by nuns wearing unfamiliar looking habits. Later, she said that she often recognized faces from the vision when interviewing candidates for her order, and the vision also inspired the habit she adopted.

As soon as it was safe, Julie, now miraculously cured, began the foundation of a new congregation. It was at this time Viscountess Francoise Blin de Bourbon rejected a promised life of luxury, prestige, and pleasure to join Julie. Like Jeanne Fontbonne, foundress of the Sisters of St. Joseph, she had been saved from the guillotine by the death of Robespierre. The two women adopted a rule that was unusual for that day in several respects. It eliminated the distinction between lay and choir sisters and centralized governance under a superior-general. As their primary ministry, they assumed education of poor adolescent girls. Because the Bishop of Amiens found fault with this rule and would not approve it, they moved the congregation to Namur, Belgium, in 1808 where they have maintained their motherhouse ever since.

When Bishop John B. Purcell of Cincinnati visited Namur in 1839 seeking sisters for his diocese, he was able to secure eight volunteers there, shepherded by Mother Louise de Gonzague, the appointed superior. Arriving in Cincinnati in 1840, they rested with the Sisters of Charity and purchased a house for a convent, free school, and academy. Reinforcements arrived from Namur in 1843, enabling them to open a mission in Toledo and another in Boston in 1848.

During the same period Father Pierre De Smet, the Belgian Jesuit missionary to the Indians, visited the motherhouse in Namur and asked for sisters to serve in far-off Oregon. Six sisters volunteered and accompanied him on a seven-month sea voyage that included a perilous rounding of Cape Horn amid violent storms, icebergs, and fog. After arriving in 1844 they founded a girls' school at St. Paul, Oregon. No mail arrived for two full years, and their feelings of isolation were intense. Finally a packet of letters forwarded by Namur sisters in Cincinnati arrived to gladden their hearts in remote Oregon. Archbishop Francis N. Blanchet returned from a begging trip to Europe in 1848 with seven more sisters from Namur, enabling the opening of schools in Oregon City and Willamette.

Then came the discovery of gold at Sutter's Mill and the gold rush of '49 that practically depopulated the Oregon territory. Catching the fever, people deserted entire districts and villages. In 1853 the sisters decided that their services were more important elsewhere, and the entire community moved to

San Jose, California, joining four Namur sisters who came from Cincinnati in 1851. This enlarged group opened a novitiate for postulants and initiated the establishment of several schools and academies. Being so far from Namur, they became an independent province under the leadership of Mother Mary Cornelia, who acted as superior for 40 years. Today, she is considered the California foundress. The Sisters of Notre Dame de Namur ultimately became a large teaching order, famous throughout of the United States.

Sisters of Providence of Saint Mary-of-the-Woods, Indiana (SP-3360)

This American congregation was a branch of the French congregation founded at the beginning of the 19th century at Ruille-sur-Loir in the diocese of Le Mans by Abbe Jacques-Francois Dujarié as part of his contribution towards overcoming the spiritual and material effects of the French Revolution. Father Celestine de la Hailandière visited Ruille-sur-Loir in 1839 seeking Sisters of Providence for the Vincennes Diocese (now Indianapolis). Later that year he became the bishop upon the death of Bishop Simon Bruté. Mother Mary Lecor agreed to the request, provided that her choice, Sister Theodore Guérin (1798-1856), baptized Anne Thérèse, would be the superior of this group and any foundations made from it. She further stipulated that the Bishop of Le Mans and the Bishop of Vincennes would both have to agree to any changes to these arrangements.

Arriving in Indiana in 1840, the six sisters found the intended convent still under construction. Together with four local postulants who had awaited their ar-

Novice. Sisters of Providence of St. Mary-of-the-Woods, Indiana (c. 1942).
Courtesy Gonzaga University

rival they moved into a small room in the farmhouse of a Catholic family. That farm was deeply forested and Bishop Bruté had named the local parish Saint Mary-of-the-Woods after the town of that name in France — for this reason, "of-the-Woods" is individualized in the title of the congregation.

The postulants who had awaited the coming of the sisters taught English to the French sisters while they themselves experienced formation. In due time the community acquired the farm property, which became motherhouse, novitiate, and academy. The academy opened in 1841 with 12 girls. It grew and flourished, eventually leading to the establishment of the well-known Saint Mary-of-the-Woods College. While the sisters considered higher education of women an important ministry, they opened and staffed elementary and secondary schools, orphanages, and other charitable institutions from coast to coast over the years.

In 1843, Mother Theodore returned to France seeking funds and more sisters. While there, she received letters indicating that Bishop de la Hailandière was not keeping to the original agreements and was interfering in internal affairs of the community. Returning to the United States, she learned that he had called for an election in her absence. Still the sisters reelected her unanimously. That was not the end of the discord. Bishop de la Hailandière deposed Mother Theodore in 1847 while she was away tending to community affairs in Vincennes, ordering her to leave Indiana and not return. Meanwhile the motherhouse in France determined on a separation because of the distance and difficulties in communications, effectively eliminating the Bishop of Le Mans from a position of authority. This severe blow struck Mother Theodore as she sought the continuance of the congregation and to preserve its rule. She endured trials of the most painful and unexpected nature during the

Professed. Sisters of Providence of St. Mary-of-the-Woods, Indiana (c. 1942).
Courtesy Gonzaga University

seven years she contended with the bishop who opposed, reprimanded, and falsely accused her.

Dispirited, the sisters considered residence elsewhere. Fortunately for them, Bishop de la Hailandière suddenly resigned. His successors, John Bazin and then Maurice de Saint-Palais, respected the sisters' constitution in every regard. The congregation then enjoyed tranquility and progressed rapidly with Mother Theodore restored to her lawful office. During her 16 years as superior, she erected 18 establishments in Indiana, including two orphanages. The motherhouse and academy were permanently established at Saint Mary-of-the-Woods. Suffering frequently from poor health, she died in great pain in 1856. Because of her dedication, personal sanctity, and extensive sufferings, her cause for beatification has been introduced and is in progress.[7]

On the white cross over Mother Theodore's grave an inscription reads: "I sleep, but my heart watches over this house which I have founded." Today her "house" has over 800 sisters serving Catholic education and a vast array of charitable ministries. In 1920 they were the first community to send American missionary sisters to the interior of China. Mother Theodore's heart still beats among her spiritual descendants.

Congregation of the
Sisters of the Holy Cross (CSC-1920)

This congregation is descended from one of the many founded in France during the dynamic revival following the Revolution. Father Basil Anthony Moreau founded the Congregation of Holy Cross for priests and brothers, but the need for sisters soon became apparent and he organized the Marianites of Holy Cross in 1841.

Father Edward Sorin, a Holy Cross priest, and six brothers of the order came to the United States in 1841 in response to the pleas of Bishop de la Hailandière. Father Sorin founded the University of Notre Dame in South Bend. When he sent word to France that sisters were needed, four came to Indiana in 1843. Initially the sisters performed domestic chores for the Holy Cross fathers and the college, but the need for a novitiate soon became apparent when aspirants requested admission into the community. Father Sorin moved those sisters involved in formation of postulants to a house in Bertrand, Michigan, seven miles distant and just over the state line, but they returned to South Bend in 1855. Their first ministries included operating a "select school," instructing the hearing impaired, caring for orphans, and briefly teaching Potawatomi children.

Eliza Maria Gillespie (1824-87) joined the community in Bertrand in

Congregation of the Sisters of the Holy Cross (c. 1942).

Courtesy Gonzaga University

1853. She was educated by the Dominican Sisters in Somerset, Ohio, and at the Visitation convent in Georgetown. She was a cousin of Senator Thomas Ewing of Ohio, a cousin of James Gillespie Blaine,[8] and a distant relative of the wife of General William T. Sherman. Noted for her beauty and intelligence, Eliza was a Washington socialite. At age 29, she determined to join the Sisters of Mercy, but while visiting her brother at Notre Dame, Father Sorin persuaded her to join the Sisters of the Holy Cross. She was given the religious name of Sister Mary of St. Angela and is normally referred to as Mother Angela.

After returning from France in 1854, where she had gone to learn sign language in order to teach the deaf, she became directress of St. Mary's Academy and moved it to property across the road from the University of Notre Dame, where it still functions on the banks of the St. Joseph River as Saint Mary's College, a highly regarded institution. During the Civil War, she organized sister-teachers to work as nurses. Under her leadership, they operated eight military hospitals and served on the hospital ship *Red Rover*. In 1869, the Vatican recognized the community as an independent congregation. Mother Angela became the first mother-superior and is considered the foundress of the American branch. A famed educator, she compiled two sets of readers for Catholic schools. During her tenure as mother-superior, the congregation founded 35 schools and other institutions. In 1865, she helped found and edit the widely read Catholic journal, *The Ave Maria*, the first periodical in the

United States devoted to the Blessed Virgin Mary. Saint Mary's College and Mother Angela are both renowned in American Catholic history.

Congregation of Marianites of Holy Cross (MSC-2410)

This congregation is the only branch of Holy Cross sisters still affiliated with the motherhouse in Le Mans, France. In 1848, sisters and brothers from the motherhouse in South Bend went to Bardstown, Kentucky, to help at St. Mary's College. When the college suffered financial difficulties, the priests withdrew but the sisters remained, their difficulties mounting because of lack of contact with France and Notre Dame. About this time Holy Cross Father Drouelle arrived from France and observed their unhappy condition. He also visited New Orleans where Archbishop Anthony Blanc asked him for Marianite sisters to operate an orphanage. In April 1848 three sisters left Bardstown with six Holy Cross brothers for New Orleans. The orphanage was in deplorable condition and the sisters suffered great privation. Ursulines provided them food the first six months and benefactors eventually stepped forward, led by Mrs. Jourdan. Several other sisters from the Indiana community joined in the New Orleans foundation.

While these sisters had no involvement in military nursing during the Civil War, they felt the cruel impact of the conflagration. Union troops quartered in their convent in Plaquemine, Louisiana, practically destroyed the building, even stabling horses on the ground floor.[9] Sister Mary of the Five Wounds harried General "Beast" Butler, commander of the Union Army occupying New Orleans, successfully begging him to provide food for their orphan girls. Following the war, the sisters resumed their primary ministry of teaching. At the present time these Marianites serve in numerous dioceses and have missionaries in Chile and India.

The community of Marianites of Holy Cross in Canada separated from France in 1883 and assumed the title of Sisters of Holy Cross and Seven Dolors. They sent sisters to New Hampshire in 1881 and to Connecticut in the 1890's. This third descendant of Father Moreau's foundation is now titled the **Sisters of Holy Cross (CSC-1930).** Both the New Orleans and Indiana communities aided in this foundation, which is still active in New England and has missions in Bangladesh, Haiti, Peru, Mali, and Cameroon. Thus the United States enjoys three separate groups of sisters from Father Moreau's original founding of the Congregation of Holy Cross in France.

Sisters of the Good Shepherd (RGS-1830) and Contemplatives of the Good Shepherd (CGS-1830)

Five Good Shepherd sisters left France for Louisville, Kentucky, in 1842. Reflecting the international character of their order, each sister was of a different nationality: French, German, Belgian, Spanish, and Italian. The order of Sisters of the Good Shepherd is most unusual. St. John Eudes (1601-1680) founded it to care for and work for the salvation of the souls of girls and women endangered by immoral circumstances. In addition to the three regular vows, the sisters and nuns take a fourth one stating their primary apostolate. French revolutionaries believed they had permanently destroyed the order, but the remarkable Sister Mary Euphrasia Pelletier (Rose Virginie) refounded it in Angers in 1835. Since then it has spread over the world, has 145 provinces with 6,788 members (752 in the United States) and operates hundreds of institutions. In their 148 years of ministry in this country, they have lovingly tended the lives and salvaged the souls of thousands of women.

The order of Contemplatives of the Good Shepherd, initially called Magdalenes, then Sisters of the Cross, is their complementary group of nuns who provide prayer support for the active ministry. They led a strictly cloistered life in the Carmelite tradition.

From Louisville, the order spread rapidly, and within 25 years there were convents in New York, Cincinnati, St. Louis, Philadelphia, Columbus, Brooklyn, New Orleans, Chicago, St. Paul, Boston, and Baltimore. Such rapid expansion indicates the desperate needs of girls and women and illustrates how meeting obvious charitable demands generates vocations.

In many ways, the Sisters of the Good Shepherd anticipated modern professional counseling and psychological therapy. Their organization was structured for this ministry. Orphans and destitute young girls were kept separate in the Preservation Class while the Penitent Class was for wayward girls and prostitutes. Some came voluntarily, while parents, guardians, law officers, and social workers brought others. The sisters educated girls in the Preservation Class and taught them employable skills. Penitent Class women lived separately and did laundry work and other income-producing chores. If they requested it, Penitents were allowed to wear a simple black habit but did not take vows. Some eventually joined the contemplative branch. The nature of their work with troubled women sometimes subjected the sisters to malicious charges. Such misunderstanding has plagued the endeavors of these dedicated women religious over the years.

Today both branches maintain institutions in the United States, although their ministries have evolved considerably. Some newer ministries are care of battered women with children, family counseling and services, care of women newly released from prison, service to migrants, refugees, and troubled teenagers. The international motherhouse of this order is now located in Rome. The five American provinces are headquartered in Cincinnati, Ohio; Jamaica, New York; Washington, D.C.; St. Louis, Missouri; and St. Paul, Minnesota.

Ursuline Nuns of the Congregation of Paris (OSU-4120)

In 1845, Ursuline convents in Boulogne-sur-Mer and Beaulieu sent founding nuns to the United States, the first group going to St. Martin's in Ohio. Three were English-speaking nuns from Boulogne-sur-Mer and eight were French-speaking nuns from Beaulieu. In 1850, another group from Beaulieu went to Cleveland. Both were ultimately successful, establishing academies and expanding to other locations from their American motherhouses. Each group was led by an Englishwoman, and each had unusually difficult early years in the United States.

Ursuline Nuns, St. Martin, Ohio (c. 1942).
Courtesy Gonzaga University

Father Amadeus Rappe, an American-based priest who had been the Ursulines' chaplain at Boulogne-sur-Mer, was responsible for bringing them to the United States. Bishop John Baptist Purcell (1800-1883) had assigned him to Toledo and at Father Rappe's urging Bishop Purcell requested Ursuline nuns from the Boulogne-sur-Mer convent. When the mother-superior agreed, she named Julia Chatfield (1809-1878) the superior of the group because of her leadership qualities and command of English. Julia's father, an English Army officer, had sent her to France to study with the Ursulines. At age 19, when she converted to Catholicism, he withdrew her from the academy, hoping the social life in London would make her change her mind. At age 21, Julia defied her father and returned to Boulogne, joined the Ursulines and took the religious name of Sister Julia of the Assumption. Her father disowned her.

In 1845, when the nuns first arrived in Cincinnati, Archbishop Purcell (now elevated) offered Mother Julia her choice of sites in Ohio in Dayton, Chillicothe, St. Martin's in Brown County near Fayetteville, or Louisville, Kentucky. Monsignor Machebeuf (later bishop) showed her Chillicothe and St. Martin's and was prepared to show her the other locations when Mother Julia asked the archbishop to decide.[10] He designated St. Martin's in Brown County, although it was in the countryside far from any urban center and most potential students. That disappointment was the first of many.

Archbishop Purcell was indecisive about the Ursulines. Were they to go to Father Rappe in Toledo as originally anticipated or to remain in Brown County? He would not say. He refused Mother Chatfield's requests to relocate in spite of the sufferings caused by the local poverty or to clarify the Ursulines' canonical status. When a nun went on mission to Louisiana and later left the order, he refused to allow her to rejoin St. Martin's, despite Mother Chatfield's pleading.[11] When Bishop Reynolds of Charleston, South Carolina, set the Ursuline nuns there adrift, Archbishop Purcell asked Mother Chatfield to take them in, which she graciously did. Gradually the academy's reputation spread, and by the time of the Civil War, had students from both the North and South. In 1863, Morgan's Raiders invaded this section of Ohio. Riding past the Ursuline convent at night and seeing no lights they rode on. The nuns and pupils were inside praying for their lives.

Archbishop Purcell is famous in Ohio Catholic history as a leader and builder of churches and Catholic institutions. He imported numerous orders of priests and sisters, expanded a small Catholic newspaper to national prominence, contested with the Know-Nothings, and founded a German-language newspaper. The archbishop's debates with Reverend Alexander Campbell, leader of an anti-Catholic movement termed "Campbellism," were classic victories that won many converts to Catholicism, including a surprising number among the Protestant clergy.[12] During the Civil War, he flew the Union flag from his cathedral, a not altogether popular action, while just 100 miles to the south in Louisville, Bishop Martin John Spalding flew the Confederate flag. Archbishop Purcell's main fault, especially as he aged, was indecisiveness. In the face of his constant indecision, Mother Julia of the

Assumption maintained her composure, lived up to her vows, and was obedient and patient. However, the many pressures finally broke her health and she died in 1878. Not long afterwards the archbishop resigned.[13] He lived out his few remaining years at the Ursuline convent at St. Martin's and is buried there.

Boulogne-sur-Mer sent its second contingent to America in 1850, with the other Englishwoman, 32-year old Mary Beaumont (Sister Mary of the Annunciation), as superior. Like Julia Chatfield, she left England for her education with the Ursulines and then joined the order. These two English nuns were friends in France and even closer ones in Ohio. Mother Beaumont's group of four nuns went to the Cleveland diocese of Bishop Rappe (now elevated), their former chaplain in France. Arabella Seymour accompanied the nuns and on arrival joined the community, becoming the fifth co-foundress.

Poverty made the early years extremely difficult for the new Ursuline group; they were only able to continue functioning because of a monetary gift from the Brown County Ursulines. They opened an academy and taught in numerous parochial schools in the Cleveland district after being excused from cloister. They also sent nuns to make foundations in Toledo, Tiffin, and Youngstown. Mother Beaumont led the community for over 30 years and in 1871 founded Ursuline College, Ohio's first chartered college for women. She died in Cleveland in 1881, three years after her devoted English Ursuline friend. Both established communities that have made enormous contributions to education, missionary work, and charity.

Charleston's Bishop Patrick Lynch asked the Irish Ursulines who were now living with Mother Chatfield's French nuns to return to South Carolina. In 1858 they resettled in Columbia together with the Irish nuns at the Ursuline convent in Covington, Kentucky. Having their own convent did not end their trials, however. The violence of war would strike the Ursulines several years later.

Dominican Sisters (OP-1070-04)

Spanish-born Dominican priest Joseph Sadoc Alemany (1814-1888) served in Dominican missions in Ohio, Kentucky, and Tennessee before going to Rome on Dominican business in 1849. While there, the pope designated him Bishop of Monterey, California. Before leaving Europe to assume his new post, he sought sisters in Ireland and France for far-off California. He enlisted Belgian-born Sister Mary Goemaere and two Dominican novices in Paris.

The new bishop and the sisters visited the Dominicans in Somerset, Ohio, before leaving for California. The two French postulants remained in Ohio while English-born Sister Francis Stafford and Virginia-born Sister Aloysa O'Neil joined the western trip.[14] Their trek across Panama by muleback and canoe was difficult and dangerous, but none of them contracted a disease. They sailed for California after reaching the Pacific side.

Arriving in San Francisco on December 6, 1850, the sisters went to Monterey to open the first convent school in California in March 1851. They moved north to Benicia in 1854 and later to San Rafael. Their early years were marked by poverty but steady growth. Maria Concepcion Arguello, the first California postulant at age 60, was the daughter of a former Mexican governor of California. Another Dominican congregation, from Brooklyn, was established in San Jose in 1876.

Sisters of Charity of St. Augustine (CSA-0580)

In 1850, Bishop Amadeus Rappe of Cleveland was once again searching for sisters, especially some nuns to operate a hospital. Friends directed him to Mother Bernardine Cabaret, the superior of St. Louis Hospital in Boulogne-sur-Mer. She was enthusiastic and volunteered to go herself, securing remittance of the remaining part of her term as superior. Taking Sister Francoise Guillement and two postulants, she sailed for the United States on September 24, 1851. The Ursulines in Cleveland received them as guests and provided religious training for the postulants. Within two weeks, the Augustinian sisters began visiting the sick and poor in their homes, unofficially becoming Cleveland's first public health nurses. Having learned basic English from this experience, they moved into their new convent in the spring of 1852 and opened St. Joseph's, the city's first hospital. In the fall of 1852, Sisters Bernardine and Francoise returned to France, leaving the novices without a superior. Ursuline Mother des Seraphines took over as temporary superior.

Bishop Rappe, desperate for sisters to operate a hospital, remembered an Ursuline novice that he had witnessed nursing during a cholera epidemic some eight years earlier. Although about to become a professed Ursuline, Elizabeth Bissionette (Sister Ursula) agreed to assume charge of the tiny community and accept the rule of the Sisters of Charity of St. Augustine. Under her direction, the sisters opened an orphanage.

In 1865, they reentered the hospital field and opened St. Vincent Charity Hospital. After such a tenuous beginning, these sisters went on to open additional hospitals, nursing schools, and charitable homes in Ohio.[15]

Daughters of the Heart of Mary (DHM-0810)

Marie Adelaide de Cice and Jesuit priest Pierre Joseph de Cloriviere founded this society in 1790 during the French Revolution.[16] Because of the circumstances of their foundation and the fact that they did not wear habits, they were known only to a few church officials. Their primary objective was to preserve religious life during the persecution; their secondary goal was to offer the consecrated life to women of any age or profession. Members ministered alone or in groups as a corporate body, as the situation dictated.

Bishop Amadeus Rappe, the quintessential recruiter, requested this unique congregation to minister in Cleveland. Three members arrived in 1851 under the leadership of Anna Romaine Pance and founded St. Joseph's Orphanage in Cleveland to meet a desperate need resulting from epidemics. It was their first corporate work in the United States.

Daughters Ernestine Nardin and Victoria Boucher came from France in 1857. Ernestine established free schools and an academy in the Buffalo area. Those unfamiliar with their status called them "the ladies" or a similar appellation. They were known as the "Nardines" in Buffalo.

As their numbers increased — some from France and others from American vocations — their congregation established 17 Indian missions around the perimeter of Lake Huron. These foundations included schools, social centers, catechetical centers, and a hospital. With increased numbers, they were able to establish themselves in the East by the 1860's. Archbishop Michael Corrigan of New York accepted them in 1887, and they were permitted to live according to their chosen lifestyle, similar to other provinces in different parts of the world.

This international order is unique in several ways. Its members are often unknown as religious to all but the hierarchy and selected members of the clergy. They do not use the title "sister," rather whatever is acceptable for laywomen in any milieu. They may live alone, with family or in a group, and have always worn contemporary dress. They attempt to meet the needs of the Church and the world in whatever capacity they can. However, today those members serving in corporate ministry in the United States are usually known as religious.[17]

Today, 2,400 Daughters of the Heart of Mary serve in 30 countries and the 175 American members serve in 16 states. They minister in teaching, retreat work, catechetical instruction, social service, health care, spiritual direction, and technological pursuits in both foreign and domestic service. While today it might seem that other communities have adopted the lifestyle of the Daughters of the Heart of Mary, this society's particular charism is unique and historic.

Sisters of Providence (SP-3350)

Two Canadian-born brothers who became bishops are famous in the early history of the Pacific Northwest. Francis Norbert Blanchet became vicar-apostolic of the Oregon Territory in 1843; in 1846 he was elevated to archbishop of the newly designated archdiocese of Oregon City. The same year, his brother Augustin Magloire Alexander Blanchet (normally identified by the initials A. M. A.) became Bishop of Walla Walla, Washington Territory.

At this time the Northwest was thinly settled with French-Canadians, retired employees of the Hudson Bay Company, trappers, and a sprinkling of American settlers. Jesuit priests traveling over the vast territory worked among the Indians. Both bishops, poor themselves and presiding over equally poor and scattered Catholic communities, set records for begging trips. This was remarkable considering the numerous European-born American bishops and priests who constantly besieged Europe with pleas for money and personnel. During their many years as archbishop and bishop in the Northwest, the Blanchets traveled to Europe, South America, Mexico, and Canada many times pleading for help.

The year 1852 found Bishop A. M. A. Blanchet in Montreal appealing to the Sisters of Providence. Trans-Canadian travel through the Rockies was not then possible, making it necessary to sail to Panama, cross the isthmus and then sail north in order to get from Montreal to Oregon. Five sisters volunteered and, accompanied by a chaplain, made the long, tiring trip. On arrival they found the archbishop absent in Mexico on a begging trip and the territory practically deserted because of the earlier gold rush to California. This emigration had caused the Sisters of Notre Dame de Namur to depart. In a state of panic, the sisters sailed to San Francisco. A priest told them of a man in Chile with a boat going around the Horn. Intending to return later to Oregon, they sailed to Chile. There, both the local archbishop and the government entreated them to remain and minister. They stayed, founded a convent, and became a permanent Chilean institution. Although long separated from its wellsprings in Canada, that community faithfully followed the Providence rule, handwritten from memory and passed down from generation to generation. Over a 100 years later, in 1970, the Chilean sisters reunited with the Montreal community.

While stopping over in Montreal en route to Baltimore for a bishops' meeting in 1856, Bishop Blanchet again approached the Sisters of Providence, gingerly in view of the previous misadventure, although aware that a promise had been made to replace the lost sisters. Once again, Mother

Caron most generously permitted five volunteers to accompany the bishop back to Oregon. She appointed Canadian-born Esther Pariseau the superior.

Esther Pariseau (1823-1902), professed as Sister Joseph of the Sacred Heart, had learned carpentry, metalworking, and other shop skills working in her father's carriage shop. At age 20, she prevailed on her devoted father to take her to Montreal to be presented to Mother Emilie Gamelin, foundress of the Sisters of Providence in Canada.[18] When Mother Gamelin asked Monsieur Pariseau if he was willing to give up his daughter, she was startled and pleased by his answer: "Certainly, Madame. She is our Christmas gift to the Divine Child." Sister Joseph and the other four sisters made the trip to Oregon without serious hazard on the new railroad across the Isthmus of Panama. They rested in San Francisco where the Sisters of Mercy there gave them the treasured gift of an accordion.

On arrival in Vancouver, Washington Territory, the sisters slogged from the wharf up the hill in mud, knee-deep in places. When they asked why they had stopped before such an unimposing structure, they were told it was the bishop's "palace." No place had been arranged for them. Their first night was spent in a musty attic that they merrily cleaned of many months' accum-

Bronze statue of Mother Joseph placed in Statuary Hall — Washington, D.C., May 1, 1980.
Courtesy of Sisters of Providence Archives, Seattle, Washington

Spreading Roots (1834-1861): European and Canadian Initiatives

ulation of odds and ends. They long remembered and often laughed about their first night "in the attic."

Not long after, a 16- by 24-foot crude wooden building was erected for their convent. Sister Joseph, now commonly referred to as Mother, immediately put her carpentry talents to work building an altar and making a tabernacle from a candle box. Three weeks later, an infant appeared on their doorstep whom they named Emily Lake. This orphan child later became the first pupil in the first permanent school in the Northwest. Unlike the earlier sisters who departed soon after arrival, these sisters remained to teach, provide for orphans, and minister to the sick and poor.

That humble convent became the provincial house from which the Sisters of Providence made foundations over the Washington Territory. During the next 46 years, Mother Joseph erected 11 hospitals, seven academies, five Indian schools, and two orphanages.[19] She is acclaimed as the first architect of the Pacific Northwest, for she designed and supervised the construction of numerous structures. We will hear more of Mother Joseph in Chapter 6.

Each state of the Union is entitled to two statues of its heroes in the National Statuary Hall in the Capitol in Washington, D.C. Mother Joseph, representing Washington State, is one of the six women and the only Catholic woman so honored. Monsieur Pariseau not only gave a precious Christmas gift to the Divine Child, he honored the United States, and its Northwest.[20]

Sisters of Charity of Montreal, "Grey Nuns" (SGM-0490)

In 1737, Madame Marguerite d'Youville, a widow, and three companions began the Sisters of Charity of Montreal in her home, where they cared for the sick poor. Because of quarrels stemming from the time she was still married, some neighbors now opposed Madame d'Youville and her sisters, dubbing them "*les soeurs grises*" or the "drunken nuns." Nonetheless, they persevered and became a respected congregation. In 1775 the nuns chose to wear grey habits and have been called Grey Nuns ever since. This was something of a play on words as *gris* means both "drunk" and "grey" in French.

Father Augustine Campion, then vicar-general of the Cleveland diocese, prodded Bishop Rappe into requesting Grey Nuns to take over the orphanage in Toledo. His timing was excellent as the community was experiencing an abundance of recruits and was receptive to new missions. Sister Blondin and three Grey Nuns came to Toledo in 1855, assumed charge of the orphanage, opened a hospital, and took care of the elderly. The headquarters of the American province of this Canadian order is located in Lexington, Massachusetts. Today, some of the American sisters work in Bogota and La Parada, Colombia.

Mother d'Youville was declared "Blessed" by Pope John XXIII in 1959. He referred to her as the "Mother of Universal Charity." She is the first Canadian to be beatified, and on December 9, 1990, Pope John Paul II canonized her. Canada, the United States, and her congregation are all delighted to have a *"gris"* saint in heaven praying for them.

North American Union of the Sisters of Our Lady of Charity (NAU-OLC-3070)

On June 1, 1855, Sister Mary Jerome Tourneux and three sisters went to Buffalo, New York, at the invitation of Bishop Timon. These sisters were a different branch of St. John Eudes' Sisters of the Good Shepherd. In keeping with their primary mission of meeting the needs of troubled young women, they established homes for girls in need of a temporary new environment. This critical ministry of the 19th century attracted vocations. The congregation spread into Canada and Mexico as well as numerous states, forming autonomous communities. Fourteen groups federated in 1944 and secured approval from Rome to form the Union in 1978. Three communities remain independent: Dallas-Fort Worth, Little Rock, and Steubenville.

With the passage of time, these sisters expanded their ministries to include day care centers, nursing homes, pastoral work, schools, religious education programs, and the care of orphans, neglected children, migrants, and minority groups.

Sisters of St. Joseph of Medaille (CSJ-3880)

While visiting in Paris, Father Buteux, a parish priest in Bay St. Louis, Mississippi, met Father Chaldon, the vicar-general of the diocese of Metz. Recounting his adventures as a missionary priest in Indiana, Father Buteux mentioned that he always carried the Blessed Sacrament with him on his travels over the countryside. Father Chaldon asked how he carried the hosts. On hearing that they were simply wrapped in paper and tucked into a saddle bag, Father Chaldon was shocked. He promptly handed Father Buteux some gold coins and told him to purchase a proper receptacle for the Blessed Sacrament. Returning to France years later, Father Buteux looked up his old benefactor, now Bishop of Belley. He asked for assistance for his poor parish in Bay St. Louis. That kindly bishop prevailed on the Sisters of St. Joseph in Bourg to send three sisters.

The Sisters of St. Joseph of Bourg came from that French city to the United States in 1855. The Bishop of Natchez met Mother Eulalie Thamet and her two companions in New Orleans and conducted them to Bay St. Louis, where they joined Father Buteux and opened a school. Reinforcements from France arrived later to bolster their ministry.

Rome officially declared the three American provinces of the Sisters of St. Joseph of Bourg a separate congregation in 1977 with the title of the Sisters of St. Joseph of Medaille, honoring the original founder. A close relationship still exists between the American and French branches, both of which trace their origins back to LePuy, France, and the year 1650, when this institute first received canonical recognition.

Sisters of the Holy Names of Jesus and Mary (SNJM-1990)

The year 1859 found Archbishop Francis Norbert Blanchet, the quintessential beggar, once again appealing for help in Montreal. This time he approached a newly formed congregation, the Sisters of the Holy Names of Jesus and Mary which had grown to 72 sisters in just 15 years. Showing great generosity, Mother Theresa Martin designated 12 sisters for the mission.

By the time they sailed from New York the party had grown to 16. The archbishop and Holy Names sisters were joined by two Sisters of Providence to reinforce the convent in Vancouver, British Columbia, and two St. Ann sisters headed there also. "Enough sisters to make believers of all the heretics in Oregon!" exclaimed the happy archbishop as they sailed out of New York harbor.

General Winfield Scott (1786-1866) of Mexican War fame was also on board the *Star of the West*. His solicitous attentions puzzled the sisters until they learned his poignant story. Years earlier his only daughter, who had converted to Catholicism, revealed her desire to become a nun. The general objected strenuously and sent her abroad in an effort to thwart her intentions. Realizing at last that he was destroying her happiness, he relented and she joined the Visitandines. However, she died shortly afterwards and was buried in the cemetery of Visitation Convent in Georgetown.[21] Afterwards he was never quite the same. The sight of any sister or nun reminded him of his lost daughter, and he constantly sought to make amends. In addition to the many courtesies they received aboard ship, all the sisters crossed the Isthmus of Panama in the general's private railroad car, something those earlier sisters crossing the isthmus on muleback could only envy.

Sisters of St. Ann (c. 1942).
Courtesy Gonzaga University

When *The Northern* docked at Vancouver, Washington, the passengers were thrilled by the cannon salute and a large crowd gathered to greet the general. Mother Joseph of the Sisters of Providence was on hand to embrace her two new sisters. After the passengers disembarked, the archbishop celebrated Mass. The two Sisters of St. Ann then sailed for Canada and the 12 Holy Names sisters re-embarked for Portland.

Portland, Oregon's largest town, had a population of only 2,874 souls in 1859. Archbishop Blanchet purchased the badly run-down Lownsdale House for the sisters' convent. The seller felt he had made a coup, but the farsighted archbishop bought the property for its location. On the night of arrival, the sisters went immediately to work restoring the house. Named St. Mary's, that convent and school became famous in 1925 when the U. S. Supreme Court found in their favor in *Pierce v. Society of Sisters*, the landmark decision reversing Oregon's compulsory public school attendance law. The order grew, and although they concentrated their ministries in the Pacific Northwest over the years, they also made foundations in Albany, New York, Key West and Tampa, Florida, Oakland, California and other sites.[22]

Congregation of the Incarnate Word and Blessed Sacrament (IWBS-2200)

Bishop Odin of Galveston who had been so successful in securing nuns from the New Orleans Ursulines applied his persuasive powers in Lyons, where he prevailed on the Incarnate Word Sisters to give four of their number to teach in Brownsville, Texas. This congregation, under the Rule of St.

Augustine, became a permanent Texan community. They specialize in teaching and hospital work and have a mission in Kenya.

Daughters of the Cross (DC-0770)

When the Vatican erected the Natchitoches Diocese in northern Louisiana in 1853, Auguste Martin was named bishop. He immediately set out for France to beg for money, priests, and sisters. Daughters of the Cross responded with 10 sisters. Mother Mary Hyacinth led them to Cocoville in 1855 and then moved the community to Shreveport. This teaching order is still active in Louisiana.

Sisters of the Congregation de Notre Dame (CND-2980)

Founded in Montreal in 1653 by Marguerite Bourgeoys, now a canonized saint, this congregation sent sisters to Bourbonnais, Illinois, in 1860 to teach

and minister to the local French-speaking population. This order, under the Rule of St. Augustine, founded an academy there and, later the same decade, one in Waterbury, Connecticut, and in other locations. The provincial headquarters of this Canadian congregation is in Ridgefield, Connecticut.

The French Connection

These orders from France and Canada, the offshoot in Louisiana and the three already established in the United States, brought the total of French-speaking sisters and nuns to 21 separate communities. Taken together, they constitute a remarkable set of foundations in a country with such a small French-speaking population. While some German,

Daughters of the Cross (c. 1942).
Courtesy Gonzaga University

Irish, and Anglo-American elements in the Church may have resented the dominance of French-born prelates during the antebellum years, they had to admire and give thanks for their skills and persistence as beggars. Without their European and Canadian forays, the nation and Church would have been the poorer. Of all the evil consequences emanating from the French Revolution, the United States would seem to be one of the few beneficiaries of that conflagration. As unfortunate as the convent burning in Charlestown seemed at the time, it motivated French sisters to send help to the United States.

Judge Fouquier-Tinville would be astounded to know how his persecution of nuns had pollinated a rebirth of French orders that transplanted Catholic women religious shoots to the United States.

SHAMROCKS

Ireland was emerging from centuries of English oppression during this era. While the various Relief Acts lifted the yoke somewhat, Ireland still had to struggle to catch up with European educational and economic standards.

Daughters of the Cross (c. 1942).
Courtesy Gonzaga University

After centuries of suppression, the few existing orders of sisters and nuns expanded and others appeared, but in limited numbers since poverty retarded the growth of new foundations. Because of the potato famines that prompted hundreds of thousands to emigrate, by the late 1850's few families in Ireland were without a relative in the United States, and all Ireland was keenly conscious of what was transpiring in that promised land. The need for religious assistance for their displaced countrymen was pressing and obvious. While Ireland had little money for assistance, it did have holy women in abundance.

Two great Irishwomen born in the 18th century managed to establish religious communities despite the hostile environment of their time and place. Each of their congregations grew to spread over the world. Both made significant contributions to the United States as they attracted hundreds of Irish-American women to their ranks during the antebellum years. Honora Nagle and Catherine McAuley are high on the roster of memorable foundresses.

Sisters of the Presentation of the Blessed Virgin Mary (PVM-3320)

Honora "Nano" Nagle (1718-1784) grew up during the era of English domination described earlier. Her family, members of the landowning class, sent her to France to be educated because the Penal Laws forbade Catholics to teach Catholics in Ireland. Following her father's death in 1746, Nano returned after having lived an active social life in Paris. Conditions in Ireland and the example of her sister Ann's charitable works for the poor of Dublin caused Nano to examine her own life and her attachment to luxury and the social scene. Her initial reaction was to enter a convent in France, but she soon realized that her true vocation was helping the poor children of her native land where the only schools available were the Charter Schools of the Church of Ireland (Anglican). The government subsidized these schools and was using them to proselytize Catholic children. On returning to Ireland, she used her inheritance to found schools in Cork for both girls and boys. This was around 1755, the precise dates being unknown because of the secrecy surrounding the illegal nature of her activities. In addition to reading, writing, and religion, her schools sought to provide salable skills such as arithmetic, fine sewing, and glove-making. After a few years, Nano sought a religious order to take over her schools so as to guarantee continuity. She financed and supported the founding of Irish Ursulines for this purpose, using girls she had sent to France for novitiate with the Ursulines. However, Nano was not overly pleased with the school operated by her Ursulines in 1772, so in 1776 she founded her own congregation, naming it the Sisters of Charitable Instruction of the Sacred Heart of Jesus.

Sisters of the Presentation of the Blessed Virgin Mary (c. 1942).
Courtesy Gonzaga University

Nano assumed the religious name of Sister Mary of St. John of God but could not decide among several rules before her death in 1784. Rome approved this institute in 1805 under the title of Sisters of the Presentation of the Blessed Virgin Mary. They adopted the rule of St. Augustine. This young order, inspired by its foundress, grew rapidly and spread over Ireland and into England. Their first foreign mission was in Newfoundland in 1833. They also spread to Australia and India. During the 20th century, they expanded to New Zealand, Africa, New Guinea, the Philippines, Central America, and South America. Their first United States foundation was on the Pacific coast.

Representing Archbishop Alemany, Father Hugh Gallagher went to Ireland in 1854 to recruit priests and sisters for the Far West and appealed to the Presentation sisters at their Midleton convent. He explained that since the gold rush had attracted people from many countries, California was now home to children who spoke a variety of languages and needed education and religious instruction. Four sisters from the Midleton convent and one from the Kilkenny convent responded to his call.

Mother Mary Joseph Cronin led the party of five sisters to San Francisco, arriving on November 13, 1854. They opened a free school for several hundred children in San Francisco. When Mother Mary Joseph returned to Ireland, Sisters Mary Teresa Comerford and Xavier Daly carried on, opening schools in Berkeley and Sonoma. Other groups of Presentation sisters came directly from Ireland, establishing themselves in New York City and in Dubuque in 1874. In 1880, another group came directly from Ireland to the Dakotas, finally settling in Fargo, where they opened an academy and school, marking the beginning of systematic teaching in the Dakotas. The earthquake of 1906 destroyed the Presentation facilities in San Francisco and they rebuilt. Today over 1,000 Presentation sisters serve in more than 20 states, with centers in the dioceses of San Francisco, Dubuque, New York, Albany, Fargo, Savannah, Sioux Falls, Phoenix, and Worcester.

Sisters of Mercy (RSM-2580)

Catherine McAuley's (1778-1841)[23] Catholic father died when she was only seven years old. Her mother, nominally Catholic, only returned to the faith on her deathbed; Catherine was 11 years old. After living with several families, she made a permanent home with Quakers Dr. and Mrs. William Callahan, distant relatives by marriage on her mother's side. They treated Catherine as a family member. All the while Catherine maintained her father's Catholic faith which made a deep impression on the Callahans. Upon their deaths, Catherine inherited a fortune valued in today's currency at nearly one million dollars.

Now 44 years old, she was free to pursue her charitable instincts. Her plans were to find ways of caring for servants seeking employment, mothering orphan girls, and educating the poor and neglected. She went to France to investigate such institutions. On returning, she constructed a large house on Baggot Street in Dublin to shelter poor young working women of good character. Catherine taught them skills such as sewing and glove-making. That house later became the motherhouse of the Sisters of Mercy. Some cultured women in Dublin joined Catherine and helped at the house.

By 1830, clerical criticism made clear to Catherine that if her work was to continue it required canonical status. After making arrangements with the Bishop of Dublin, Catherine and two companions received novitiate training with Mother Honora Nagle's Presentation Sisters. Now a vowed religious at age 50, Catherine returned to Baggot Street. On December 12, 1831, together with the two sisters who had shared novitiate with her, Catherine founded the Sisters of Mercy. This congregation would ultimately become the largest English-speaking women's religious congregation in the world and one of the largest congregations in the United States.[24]

Michael O'Connor, a parish priest in County Cork, witnessed the foundation and work of the Sisters of Mercy before leaving Ireland to work in the Pittsburgh area. When Pittsburgh became a diocese, he became its first bishop and went to Rome for consecration. On the way back, he visited Ireland and appealed to the Sisters of Mercy in Carlow for help. Mother McAuley had died in 1841 and one of her close companions, Mother Francis Xavier Warde (1810-1884), was superior of the convent. She agreed to help and led seven sisters to the United States, accompanying Bishop O'Connor to Pittsburgh, where in 1843 they instituted their first foundation in the United States.

Initially they worked among the poor Irish of the city, visiting in the homes and providing spiritual counseling to Catholic women. The next year they opened a school. Bishop O'Connor and the city fathers were concerned about the lack of a hospital. In an unusual joint effort, the Church and city raised the needed funds for the first hospital in western Pennsylvania. Constructed in 1846, the hospital was turned over to the Sisters of Mercy for operation.

Mother Seton's Sisters of Charity left Pittsburgh at the end of the school year in 1845. This abrupt departure created a vacuum and the need for more sisters. In 1846, Mother Warde went to Ireland for reinforcements and returned with new recruits. Later that year she went to Chicago with six sisters where she opened a convent.

Ever alert for sisters, Bishop John Hughes of New York hoped to secure some from the Mercy convent in Dublin, but Mother Cecilia informed him she had none to spare. She suggested he try their convent in London. The Bishop of Westminster was not disposed to lose any sisters, but "Dagger John" was persistent and persuasive.[25] He left London with Mother Agnes O'Connor and seven sisters in tow.

These sisters took up their normal ministries in New York of visiting the sick, teaching, and visiting prisons. Their first postulant was Catherine Seton, youngest daughter of Mother Elizabeth Ann Seton. Catherine had determined to enter an order other than the one founded by her mother. For 25 years, as Sister Josephine, she prepared Catholic condemned criminals in New York for death and eternity, earning the nickname of "the prison sister." This New York community sent founding sisters to Brooklyn in 1855 and to St. Louis in 1856.[26]

Meanwhile Mother Warde's community in Chicago expanded rapidly and she again agreed to lead a founding group. In 1851, Bishop Bernard O'Reilly of Hartford asked Mother Warde to make a foundation in Providence, Rhode Island. She felt this mission was critical due to the virulent anti-Catholicism in New England and agreed to his request. The sisters entered the city quietly wearing secular clothing and began their ministries despite open public hostility.[27] The community grew rapidly in membership and sent sisters to Little Rock, Arkansas, to supplement foundresses from the Mercy convent in County Naas. Francis Warde founded communities in Hartford and New Haven, Connecticut in 1852; in Rochester, New York, in 1857; in Manchester, New Hampshire; and in St. Augustine, Florida, in 1859. The New England establishments thrived despite the unfriendly environment. The Little Rock community struggled but managed to survive. Blind during the last months of her life, Mother Warde died in 1884 at the Manchester, New Hampshire, convent that she had founded.

The final antebellum establishments by the Sisters of Mercy were made in Cincinnati and San Francisco. A laywoman, Mrs. Sarah Peter, with the approval of Archbishop Purcell, visited the Mercy convent in Kinsdale in 1856 seeking sisters to minister in her city. These were promised but there would be a delay. The resourceful Mrs. Peter used the time to visit Germany, where she secured Franciscan Sisters of the Poor (1440). Thus the triumphant dowager returned to multi-ethnic Cincinnati in 1858 with two orders of sisters, one Irish and one German. Mrs. Peter was a generous benefactor to both groups. She gave her home to the Franciscans, retaining lifetime use of several rooms.

When Father Gallagher secured Presentation sisters for California, he also recruited Mercy sisters from Kinsdale and brought both groups to San Francisco. Sister Mary Baptist Russell, the Mercy leader and member of a prominent Irish family, provided dynamic leadership for her group. Despite bigotry forcing the closing of one school and difficulties in establishing a hospital, the Sisters of Mercy persevered. When cholera struck in 1854, being the only people with experience in treating the stricken, the sisters nursed during the raging epidemic, saving hundreds of lives. This ministry is still remembered as an important milestone in California Catholic history. Once the epidemic subsided, they adopted ministries of visiting the sick in their homes and the prisoners at San Quentin. In 1857, they opened St. Mary's Hospital in San Francisco and a convent in Sacramento. Despite suggestions from the archbishop, Mother Russell adamantly refused to allow her sisters to take teacher certification examinations from public school authorities or to permit sisters to wear secular clothing in order to secure public funds. As a result of these experiences, the California Sisters of Mercy never became as deeply involved in education as those in the East and Midwest; in the West they concentrated more on health services and aid to the poor.

"Daughters" of both Nano Nagle and Catherine McAuley came to the United States, bringing their Irish charm, deep devotion to religious life, and their ministries. These two particularly remarkable religious foundresses showered America with shamrocks that still sprout.

Dominican Sisters (OP-1070-08)

American-born women established Dominican communities in Kentucky and Wisconsin, as we have seen. A French foundress established the California Dominicans and Bavarian Dominicans settled in New York. In 1860, Irish Dominican sisters arrived from Dublin, under the direction of Mother M. John Flanagan. They came to New Orleans, adding yet another ethnic source of this ancient order.This community has concentrated on education at all levels and social services ever since.

The Irish Connection

Catholic France and Canada would seem to be the fountainheads of women's religious communities in antebellum America; indeed the majority of orders and congregations had such French origins. The Irish congregations just described formed a distinct minority of communities. Yet, Irishwomen were pivotal in a number of domestically founded communities such as the Sisters of Charity of Our Lady of Mercy in Charleston, South Carolina, and the Sisters of Charity of the Blessed Virgin Mary in Philadelphia. During this period, Irish-American women predominated in practically all the other domestically founded communities, such as Mother Seton's "daughters." Even with reinforcements from France and French-speaking Canada, a number of the French-origin orders and congregations quickly took on something of an Irish flavor since the majority of American vocations came from Irish-American families.

EDELWEISS

In the 1840's, German-Americans constituted the second largest ethnic element of the American Catholic population. Since no German-founded orders or congregations had been established in the United States prior to 1844, German-American women experiencing vocational impulses joined existing domestically-founded and French orders. German surnames appeared with regularity on the rolls of most of them. However, beginning in 1844, German foundresses and groups came in rapid succession, adding yet another ethnic source of American religious communities.

Sisters of the Precious Blood (C.PP.S-3260)

Italian priest Gaspar del Bufalo (1786-1837) founded the Society of the Precious Blood in 1815 to promulgate and spread this ancient Christian devotion. Anna Maria Brunner (1764-1836), a devout Swiss widow and mother of six, two of whom were priests, visited Rome in 1832. While there she met Father Bufalo and decided that she had a calling to spread this devotion. That same year one of her priest sons, Francis de Sales Brunner (1795-1859), purchased Castle Loewenberg in Canton Graubunden. Father Brunner had been a Benedictine priest for 17 years, but left that order to become a Trappist. When French revolutionaries suppressed his Trappist monastery in 1830, he returned to Switzerland, purchased the castle, and opened a boys' school. He was a powerful preacher with a magnetic personality, famed throughout the Catholic cantons of Switzerland and nearby sections of France for his retreats and parish missions. Mother Brunner, as she is affectionately remembered, left Italy and moved into the castle with her son. She invited two of the maids working in the castle to join her in practicing spiritual exercises. The maids in turn invited friends in Baden to participate. By simple example, this devout elderly widow initiated a religious community with its principal spiritual exercise being devotion to the Precious Blood of Jesus Christ. The year 1834 is considered the founding date for this congregation, and Anna Maria Brunner its foundress.

When his mother died in 1836, Father Brunner took Anna Maria's community under his personal supervision. Elizabeth Meisen, now called Sister Clara, took over as superior of this infant religious community and the local bishop recognized the simple rule which Mother Brunner had composed.

Still technically a Trappist, Father Brunner visited Rome in 1838. While there he secured dispensation from his vows as a Trappist and joined the Missionary Institute of the Precious Blood. Returning to Castle Loewenberg, he established a foundation of the Precious Blood in Switzerland for men, the first non-Italian branch of that order. He was successful in recruiting a group of priests, postulants, and men wishing to become brothers in the new order. He now had two communities under his supervision, one of men and the other of women.

China attracted his attention for future missionary endeavors, but he experienced delays in securing permission to venture there. Instead, Father John M. Henni, representing Bishop John Baptist Purcell of Cincinnati, visited Father Brunner in 1843 and convinced him of the need for German-speaking missionaries in Ohio where cheap and fertile farmland was a magnet for German immigrants. The sisters at Castle Loewenberg slaved to help raise funds to send Father Brunner and his band of eight priests and seminarians to Ohio. These devoted women sewed and begged, selling their chapel vestments and sacred vessels. The men arrived in Cincinnati on December 31, 1843. Bishop Purcell posted them to the north-central part of the state where German settlers were without priests.

In the meantime, Frances Bauer, a former member of the Sisters of Divine Providence who had fled the French Revolution, was living the life of a hermit in rural north-central Ohio, near New Riegel, the new home of the Fathers of the Precious Blood. For years she had championed the building of a log church in the wilderness and arranged for priests to visit several times a year to confer sacraments and offer Mass. She was ecstatic over the newly arrived priests and provided them special treats from her garden and kitchen. On learning that they had a community of sisters back in Switzerland, she harried Father Brunner unmercifully, agitating to have them brought over. One can scarcely blame her since she was the only woman religious in a territory as large as Ireland.

Finally acquiescing, Father Brunner sent summons to Castle Loewenberg. Three sisters arrived on July 22, 1844: Mother Mary Ann Albrecht, her teenage daughter, Sister Rosalie (see Chapter 6 for more about the Albrechts), and Sister Martina Disch. The men constructed a convent in Peru near New Riegel. After Father Brunner sold Castle Loewenberg in 1850, the rest of the community moved to Ohio.

His Trappist instincts led him to impose a severe regimen on the sisters. They lived a semimonastic life with perpetual adoration of the Blessed Sacrament coupled with harsh living and working conditions. Their food was plain — cornmeal every day. When corn and potatoes remained the only fare, Father Brunner's only solution was to find different ways to prepare them. Nonetheless the community expanded. In addition to spending long hours in daily devotions, the sisters taught, cared for orphans, and provided domestic services for priests and seminarians. They ultimately spread to 14 states and Canada (no longer there) and sent missionaries overseas. In retrospect, it is somewhat awesome to consider the power of pious example, as exemplified by Mother Brunner.

School Sisters of Notre Dame (SSND-2970)

Karoline Gerhardinger (1787-1879), known in religion as Mother Mary Teresa of Jesus, was one of the great foundresses of 19th-century Germany. Educated by the Canonesses de Notre Dame who were suppressed in 1809

School Sisters of Notre Dame (c. 1942).
Courtesy Gonzaga University

by the Bavarian government when secularization inspired by the French Revolution swept over Europe, Karoline became a teacher in a village school. This was sponsored by Bishop George Michael of Ratisbon and Father Francis Sebastion Job[28] whose ultimate aim was to establish a congregation modeled on the suppressed Canonesses de Notre Dame, with certain modifications to the old rule. When conditions improved sufficiently, they established the School Sisters of Notre Dame in 1833 and designated Karoline the first superior. For the next 44 years she led the congregation which spread over Germany, Austria, and into the United States. Today the congregation has 21 provinces located in 31 countries on five continents, and their general motherhouse is in Rome.

Mary Josephine Friess (1824-1892), known in religion as Mother Caroline Friess, was one of the most dynamic foundresses and leaders of 19th-century America. Educated by tutors and Benedictine nuns, she determined to become a religious at an early age. Based on the advice of a bishop and clerical friends, she elected to join the newly founded School Sisters of Notre Dame.

All during the 1830's and 1840's Bavarian, Austrian, and German religious communities were besieged with requests for money, priests, and sisters to support the large and growing German-speaking settlements in the United States. Mother Teresa, keenly aware of the needs, was receptive to a request from Redemptorist fathers for teachers in Pennsylvania. Deceptive accounts of conditions in St. Mary's made by Count von Schroeder to King Louis of Bavaria, the Archbishop of Munich, and Mother Teresa herself finally persuaded her to send sister missionaries. Mother Teresa led the founding group in order to inspect conditions and decide on the location of the American motherhouse. From the many volunteers she chose three professed sisters and a novice to accompany her. Her first choice was Sister Mary Caroline Friess, one of her former pupils in whom she detected the promise of future greatness.

On arrival in New York on July 31, 1847, Mother Teresa made immediate contact with local Redemptorist priests. They were appalled by their sisters' intended destination, St. Mary's, in sparsely settled northwestern Pennsylvania. Thereupon, Mother Teresa went to Baltimore to consult with the Redemptorist provincial, Father John N. Neumann (future bishop and canonized saint). Suspicions mounted concerning Count von Schroeder, his growing descriptions of St. Mary's, and his handling of the sisters' money. However, since a commitment had been made, Mother Teresa determined to go to St. Mary's and see for herself.

Tragedy struck early. The novice, Sister Emmanuel, became ill on the trip and died in Harrisburg. Following the funeral, they proceeded to St. Mary's. Meanwhile Count von Schroeder disappeared with all their funds. On arrival, Mother Teresa's worst fears were confirmed by the isolation and primitive conditions; she determined that this was no place for the motherhouse although she agreed to operate a school. During her *pro forma* visit to the local ordinary, Bishop Michael O'Connor of Pittsburgh, she learned that he had no prior knowledge of their coming, another von Schroeder falsehood.

Leaving Sisters Seraphine and Barbara to manage the school, Mother Teresa, Sister Caroline, and Sister Magdalene went to Baltimore in October to assume management of a school in the Redemptorist parish of St. James.

Thus Baltimore became the site of their first American motherhouse. After receiving several American postulants, the arrival of eleven more missionaries from Bavaria, and opening another school, Mother Teresa and Sister Caroline, accompanied by Father Neumann, visited Redemptorist parishes in Pittsburgh, Detroit, Milwaukee, Rochester, Buffalo, New York City, and Philadelphia. Priests and Catholics in all locations pled for German-speaking teaching sisters, something Mother Teresa determined to provide as quickly as resources allowed.

Mother Teresa returned to Bavaria in July 1848 after naming Sister Seraphine the American superior, passing over Sister Caroline because she was the youngest of all the sisters. However, Mother Teresa put Sister Caroline in charge of schools and made her responsible for opening new ones. Ten more sisters arrived in January 1849. They were the last Bavarian sister-missionaries. Growing numbers of American applicants and postulants facilitated growth thereafter.

By 1850, it was obvious that restrictive congregation rules concerning enclosure had to be modified to meet conditions in America, a common problem with many communities. Mother Seraphine directed Sister Caroline to return to Bavaria in order to secure the needed modifications. Since Mother Seraphine neglected to send a traveling companion, write Mother Teresa notifying her of the impending visit, or provide Sister Caroline proper documents, her Bavarian reception was less than cordial. However, she gradually convinced the Archbishop of Munich who in turn persuaded Mother Teresa of the necessity of the change. This accomplished, Mother Teresa appointed Sister Caroline the Vicar to the Superior General and placed her in charge of the American branch of the congregation. Now titled Mother Caroline, she returned to the United States and launched one of the greatest foundation careers in American Catholic history.

Bishop John Martin Henni of Milwaukee had visited Bavaria several times seeking support for his diocese bursting with German Catholics. This paid off when Mother Teresa directed her newly appointed vicar to relocate the motherhouse in Milwaukee. With funds supplied by the King of Bavaria,[29] Mother Caroline purchased the "house with four chimneys," as it became known. Today Milwaukee is headquarters for one of six American provinces of the School Sisters of Notre Dame.

Under Mother Caroline Friess' leadership, the community expanded and became a prime contributor to the emerging parochial school system in the United States. In addition to the numerous German-American women who joined the community, many non-German aspirants applied for admission. Rather than operating academies like so many other orders, they concentrated on parochial schools. From the outset they accepted Jewish and

Protestant children. The sisters taught in Polish, Czech, Italian, and other ethnic parish schools in addition to serving the German-American communities. Their College of Notre Dame of Maryland, established in 1896, was one of the earliest Catholic women's colleges in the United States (see Chapter 8).

At Mother Caroline's death in 1892, the American branch numbered over 2,000 sisters who were operating 200 schools in 30 dioceses while caring for some 2,000 orphans. By 1965, they numbered 7,057 members and were operating 665 schools. In some ways it is remarkable that a German order only 14 years old would send founding sisters to the United States and that both communities would grow at such phenomenal rates. Explanations point to Mothers Teresa and Caroline Friess, two remarkable women.[30]

Ursuline Nuns of the Congregation of Paris (OSU-4120)

To this point, Ursulines from France and Ireland had made American establishments. Now German Ursulines entered the picture. When Archbishop Kenrick of St. Louis found his German Catholic population growing by leaps and bounds, he dispatched Father Joseph Melcher to Europe in 1846 to locate teachers. Father Melcher approached the Ursuline convent at Odenburg. Mother-Superior Magdalene Stehlin agreed to accompany Father Melcher and personally led three nuns in 1848 to St. Louis, where they stayed temporarily with the Visitation nuns. They opened an academy when the convent was completed. More sisters came in 1849 from the Ursuline convent in Landshut, Austria.

Still another Ursuline foundation originated from Germany. Bishop Martin J. Spalding sent a priest, Father Leander Streber, to recruit German-speaking women religious to teach the children of the growing German population in Kentucky. He met success at the Ursuline convent in Straubling, Bavaria. Mother Mary Salesia Reitmeier and two nuns arrived in Kentucky in 1858. Three more came in 1859 and the nuns opened a novitiate in 1860 to accommodate American postulants. Two foundations emanated from Louisville: Paola, Kansas, in 1895 and Maple Mount, Kentucky, in 1912. Two communities affiliated with the Louisville foundation — Columbia, South Carolina, in 1938 and Pittsburgh in 1958. Although the nuns remained semicloistered for many years, they began missions in a number of states and later sent missionaries to Peru.

Sisters of the Third Order of St. Francis of Assisi (OSF-1705) and The Congregation of the Sisters of the Third Order of St. Francis of Perpetual Adoration (FSPA-1780)

Father Francis Anthony Keppeler, a local pastor in Ettenbeuren, Bavaria, and his assistant, Father Mathias Steiger, emigrated to Milwaukee in 1849 with 14 of their parishioners, eight laywomen and six laymen, all Franciscan tertiaries. It was the priests' intention to found a religious congregation of sisters as well as one of brothers when they arrived in America. The brothers' foundation eventually failed as original members dropped out and vocations failed to materialize. But the women's congregation, which they established in 1849 shortly after their arrival in America, survived. This was the first of many communities of Franciscan Sisters founded in the United States, bringing St. Francis of Assisi's charism to these shores.

Ottilie Duerr (Mother Aemiliana) was chosen first superior when the sisters established themselves near Lake Michigan and pronounced vows in 1853. Their early ministries consisted of educating German immigrant children, domestic duties at St. Francis de Sales Seminary, and the care of orphans.

Led by Mother Antonia Herb, they moved the motherhouse to Jefferson, Wisconsin, in 1864 and then to La Crosse in 1871 at the invitation of Bishop Michael Heiss. In 1873, because of friction with seminary officials and the sisters working there, Mother Antonia proposed that the Milwaukee sisters form a province. Instead, they chose to be independent of La Crosse, becoming the Sisters of the Third Order of St. Francis of Assisi. The bishop of Milwaukee approved the transfer to La Crosse and the keeping of their vows. The sisters elected Sister Crescentia Nondorf their mother-general. Thus, one foundation split into two congregations. With the passage of the years, the Sisters of St. Francis of Assisi, besides their domestic duties at the seminary, performed like services for the hierarchy, staffed numerous parochial schools, cared for orphans, conducted a school for the deaf, began a ministry for the mentally handicapped, and established a mission in China. In 1946, they instituted perpetual adoration of the Blessed Sacrament at their motherhouse and continue it today. These sisters presently serve in many different social and parish ministries in the United States, Taiwan, and Japan. They sponsor a secondary school for girls and the Cardinal Stritch College in Milwaukee, and operate institutions for the care and education of developmentally disabled.

The Franciscan Sisters of Perpetual Adoration established the practice at the motherhouse in 1878 and to this day they maintain that devotion. Their ministries have included staffing parochial schools and diocesan secondary schools, the care of orphans, and missionary work in China, Guam, and El Salvador. Today they serve in parish ministry and sponsor hospitals and facilities for the aged, for unwed mothers, for the addicted, and for the emotionally and mentally disturbed. They are also involved in higher education in Zimbabwe and the Marshall Islands. They sponsor Viterbo College in La Crosse, the Franciscan Spirituality Center, and the Center for Holistic Living. In 1989, the two communities jointly celebrated the 140th anniversary of their common founding.

Congregation of the Sisters of the Third Order of St. Francis, Oldenburg, Indiana (OSF-1730)

This preeminent teaching congregation resulted from the efforts of a pioneering priest and the acceptance of challenge by an Austrian Franciscan sister. A native of Alsace, Francis Joseph Rudolph, was ordained in 1839 and answered the mission call to the United States in 1842. After two years as pastor in Fort Wayne, Indiana, he was posted to Oldenburg, the center of a German settlement, where he served until his death in 1866. Concerned for the Catholic education of the parish children, he established a school but desperately needed teaching sisters. Unable to secure any, he wrote Rome in 1849 asking permission to found a community of the Third Order of St. Francis, a request readily granted. Thereupon, Father Rudolph wrote a German Franciscan missionary in New York for help. Visiting Europe, the Franciscan, Father Ambrose Buchmaier, contacted a community of Third Order Franciscans in Vienna, Austria.

Two sisters volunteered, Theresa Hackelmeier and another sister who later changed her mind. Known in religion as Mother Theresa, this intrepid Franciscan crossed the Atlantic alone, traveled to Indiana and presented herself to a delighted Father Rudolph on January 6, 1851. Thus began the third establishment of Franciscan sisters in the United States, all three German founded.

Awaiting Mother Theresa was a crude log cabin and three aspirants. The heavy concentration of German settlers in this section of Indiana is indicated by the names of the aspirants: Elizabeth Lindemann (Sister Michaela), Louise Ehret (Sister Gabriela), and Walburga Speir (Sister Josepha). In June, a highly educated young Swiss lady arrived to join the infant community. A friend of Father Rudolph happened to know Theresa Dreer and that she was considering a religious vocation. He wrote her in Switzerland describing the needs in Oldenburg and the new community. Theresa Dreer, known in religion as Mother Antonia, accepted the invitation, adding a whole new dimension to the community. She became Mother Theresa's successor when the latter died in 1860.

As the community grew, membership remained predominantly German-American throughout the 19th and into the 20th century. For many years they taught in both German and English. By 1900, the community numbered 500 members and were operating 76 parochial schools and 10 academies. While originally concentrating on education at all levels, this community was open to outreach. Sisters were provided to minister to the Crow and Cheyenne Indian tribes. Later the congregation sent sisters to the foreign missions in China, Papua (New Guinea), Mexico, and Africa.

In retrospect, it seems highly unlikely that a pioneer priest and an Austrian Franciscan sister, thousands of miles apart, could join forces to establish a thriving congregation in a rural setting. Yet, improbable accomplishments characterized St. Francis, as they have his spiritual descendants to our own time.

Benedictine Sisters of Pontifical Jurisdiction (OSB-0230)

The American beginning for Benedictine women religious was quite shaky and involved clashes between two strong-willed people, Abbot Boniface Wimmer (1809-1887) and Mother Benedicta Riepp (1825-1862).[31]

Two lay benefactors of Baltimore purchased a large tract of land in Elk County in western Pennsylvania in 1844 with the idea of establishing a Catholic "colony." In 1846 Boniface Wimmer, a Benedictine monk from the monastery in Metten, led a group of monks to Pennsylvania to minister to German-speaking immigrants. They settled on the purchased land in Latrobe near Pittsburgh and established St. Vincent's monastery which was promoted to a priory in 1852, to an abbey in 1855, and archabbey in 1892. Benedictine monks also set up two independent priories — one in Collegeville, Minnesota, and the other in Atchison, Kansas. The monks elected Wimmer president of the Latrobe abbey in 1855 and Rome appointed him abbot for life in 1858.

Mother Benedicta was born in Waal, Bavaria, daughter of the town glassblower. Educated by Benedictine nuns at St. Walburga's in Eichstatt, she entered that monastery at age 19 and pronounced final vows in 1849, taking the religious name Benedicta. The School Sisters of Notre Dame who rested at St. Walburga's while on their way to the United States in 1847 in-

Benedictine Sisters of Pontifical Jurisdiction (c. 1942).

Courtesy Gonzaga University

spired in Sister Benedicta a desire for the missions. When Boniface Wimmer appealed for sisters for western Pennsylvania, she was first to volunteer. Designated superior, she sailed with two other sisters, arriving in St. Mary's in 1852.

Conditions in this "colony" did not match the descriptions Abbot Wimmer had given the nuns at St. Walburga's, and the reasons for the precipitous departure of the School Sisters of Notre Dame in 1849 quickly became apparent. St. Mary's was isolated and sparsely settled, the inhabitants poor, and accommodations for the sisters crude. Nonetheless, Mother Benedicta determined to fulfill her mission and bargained with the local school board for a salary of $25 per month for her sisters. They taught 60 pupils in German half a day with a lay teacher instructing in English the other half. The sisters suffered from lack of decent food during the first years. Bread, potatoes, buckwheat cakes, and on rare occasions a piece of fruit made up their meals. For Christmas Mother Benedicta cooked a large kettle of mush, allowing the sisters to eat all they wanted. Conditions of their charges were not much better as Mother Benedicta wrote King Ludwig in appealing for funds. The pupils, she wrote —

> *. . . came to school half clothed and stiff from the cold, forced to sit all day with nothing to eat but a piece of black bread. . . .*[32]

When Abbot Wimmer ordered Mother Benedicta to open a novitiate to receive 12 girls he had recruited, Mother Benedicta objected because St. Mary's was a dependency of St. Walburga's and lacked proper authorization to accept postulants. But Wimmer insisted and the novitiate opened. He brought one or two recruits each time he visited despite the overworked and overcrowded sisters. Mother Edwarda at St. Walburga's also objected. What was worse, the abbot took control of funds[33] intended for the nuns and applied them to the men's priory. These events set the scene for conflict.

Much distressed and without permission from Abbot Wimmer who considered himself to be her lawful superior, Mother Benedicta accepted an invitation to move to Minnesota in 1856 and took five sisters with her. They were delayed in Erie, Pennsylvania, where Bishop Josue M. Young invited them to make a foundation in his diocese. After he made arrangements for them to stay, the Erie community became the first Benedictine women's religious foundation outside St. Mary's. Sister Scholastica Burkhardt became superior. Mother Benedicta returned from Erie to St. Mary's and a furious Abbot Wimmer. Their disagreements about controlling funds and other matters escalated. Mother Benedicta and six sisters departed immediately upon receipt of the annual payment from Bavaria before Abbot Wimmer could seize it. Arriving in Erie in 1857, she sent seven sisters to Minnesota to make a foundation while she departed for Europe with Sister Augustine Short in hopes of resolving the problems with Abbot Wimmer.

She got a cool reception at St. Walburga's and was practically ostracized for returning without proper permission from Church authorities. She was severely criticized for accepting novices against all the rules. Finally she secured an interview with the Archbishop of Munich to whom she presented five questions for decision. These were: (1) Who would decide on candidates and novices? (2) Who would decide on the fitness of those desiring final profession of vows? (3) Would solemn vows be permitted without enclosure? (4) Would Abbot Wimmer appoint superiors or would the sisters elect them? (5) Who would control the finances of the sisters' houses? She then sailed for the United States and the archbishop referred the propositions to Rome for decision. Arriving back at St. Mary's, she found Abbot Wimmer had replaced her as superior and denounced her to the other priories. She transferred to Minnesota with his permission.

Vatican authorities resolved the questions posed by the Archbishop of Munich in 1859. They relieved Abbot Wimmer of jurisdiction over the Benedictine sisters and transferred authority to the local bishop where each priory was located. Inasmuch as cloister was near impossible and active ministry was being performed, they prohibited solemn vows. This resolution of the disputes between Mother Benedicta and Abbot Wimmer applied to all Benedictine communities in the United States.[34] It was a mixed blessing. In the years ahead various bishops at various times interfered in the internal affairs of Benedictine communities and imposed unwanted decisions.

Mother Benedicta was relieved of all authority and ordered back to Eichstatt, but was too ill to travel. Bishop Young, ever considerate of Mother Benedicta, petitioned to allow her to stay in St. Cloud where she remained until dying of consumption in 1862. Shortly before her death she wrote a priest friend:

> *I have one great favor to ask you, namely, that you be so kind and in my stead beg the right Reverend Lord Abbot (Wimmer) to forgive me for the displeasures I have caused him. . . .*[35]

By the time of Mother Benedicta's death, seven communities of Benedictine sisters had been established and were engaged in teaching, primarily to German-speaking children.[36] Switzerland and Bavaria provided most of the early Benedictines in the United States, both men and women religious. For example, Maria Rickenbach monastery in Switzerland sent foundresses to Clyde, Missouri in 1874 and numerous monasteries have emanated from that foundation. For the women, the move to America resulted in a change of status from nun to sister, something that troubled Benedictine women for decades. Although Benedictine sisters would have become important in any event, Mother Benedicta's stubborn persistence laid the groundwork for the vast expansion of Benedictine convents and apostolates over the United States. The majority belong to the Benedictine Sisters of Pontifical Jurisdiction (0230) with 45 autonomous monasteries while a smaller group of contemplatives belong to the **Congregation of the Benedictine Sisters of Perpetual Adoration of Pontifical Jurisdiction (OSB-0220)** with five monasteries. There are also seven independent small Benedictine groups with various origins (see Appendix B).

Mother Benedicta was the bearer of Western Christianity's most ancient order of women religious to the United States, where it produced a bountiful harvest.

Dominican Sisters (OP-1070-05)

The first German Dominican sisters in the United States came from the Holy Cross Monastery[37] in Ratisbon in 1853. They were Second Order nuns, although their spiritual descendants in the United States are Third Order sisters. While Abbot Boniface Wimmer was visiting his cousin in Ratisbon in 1851, he appealed to the prioress for sisters to minister to the German-speaking Catholics in his area. Two choir nuns and two lay nuns responded and the four, with Mother Josepha Witzlhofer as superior, set out for the mission aboard the *Germania*. A Bavarian mission society paid their expenses, with the understanding that they might return to the cloister in Ratisbon if the American venture did not work out. Wearing secular clothing for fear of

Nativists, about whom they had heard terrifying reports, they arrived in New York on August 28, 1853.

They disembarked along with other passengers and waited patiently on the dock for Abbot Wimmer or his representative, who was to meet and escort them to St. Mary's, Pennsylvania. Finally, the last of the passengers departed with friends, leaving the four nuns standing forlorn on the dock. They spoke not a word of English and knew nothing of how to handle themselves in this strange country. However, they did have a letter identifying a Redemptorist priest in New York. It was most probably a ship's officer who finally secured a carriage and dispatched them to the Redemptorist priest's address.

The astonished priest had no accommodations for sisters and made arrangements for their temporary shelter with German Catholic families. A parish priest from the Williamsburg district of Brooklyn came to the Redemptorist rectory. Like most pastors, he had been looking for teaching sisters and took advantage of Abbot Wimmer's blunder. Within three weeks the nuns were teaching girls in the Most Holy Trinity parish school. By 1859, the number of Dominicans had increased sufficiently for them to send sisters to St. Nicholas parish school on Second Street in New York City, with Mother Augustine, one of the four foundresses, as superior. Still considering themselves cloistered nuns, they built a monastery in the open fields near St. Nicholas Church — land that is today covered with skyscrapers.

From this Dominican foundation, located in Williamsburg, New York, instead of St. Mary's, Pennsylvania, came ten other American congregations of Dominican sisters who eventually numbered in the thousands.[38]

Franciscan Sisters of the Poor (SFP-1440)

As reported earlier in this chapter, when Mrs. Peter of Cincinnati went to Ireland in 1856, the mother-superior informed her it would be two years before any Sisters of Mercy were available. Mrs. Peter used that time to visit Germany and work on securing German-speaking sisters for her bishop. This small congregation of Franciscan sisters had only been formally organized a short time before being approached by Mrs. Peter. Nonetheless, they sent six sisters to America in 1858. Three more followed in 1859. The Franciscans had nursing experience and soon opened a hospital in Cincinnati and another one in Covington, Kentucky, in 1861. Their congregation in Germany included a branch of contemplatives, three of whom arrived in Cincinnati in 1860, where a chapel was reserved for their Perpetual Adoration devotions. Not long after their arrival in Cincinnati, the doughty Mrs. Peter personally led "her" Franciscan Sisters of the Poor on the military transport boat *Superior* to pick up wounded from the Battle of Shiloh.

Sisters went to Brazil in 1960 in response to the pope's appeal to provide ministries, and in 1978 they answered the appeal of the Bishop of Kaolack, Senegal, for help. Ever attuned to the needs of the poor, these Franciscans serve where most needed. After several moves their generalate is now located in Brooklyn, New York.

The German Connection

Ministry to their German brethren was the clear motivation for the eight foundations just described. They were not fleeing persecution or famine nor did they have strong missionary impulses. In practically every instance their foundations were expressions of apostolic mission in response to pleas for German-speaking women religious to teach German-American children and otherwise serve that ethnic group. These German foundresses were also the first to plant the seeds of St. Francis of Assisi on these shores. With the exception of the Dominicans in New York, all settled in the Midwest, mirroring the German immigrant tendency. Irish and Irish-American women did not join these orders to the degree that they did the French and domestic communities. These immigrant communities retained their distinct German flavor far longer than most other ethnic immigrant orders.

Summary

The 28 immigrant orders introduced here consist of French and Canadian lilies, Irish shamrocks, and German edelweiss. Such an analogy, beautiful flowers to heroic women, is appropriate for pioneers planting Catholic roots in fertile land and cultivating them with courage, blood, sweat, and love. Domestically founded communities, one might call them American Beauty roses, complete the antebellum panoply of women religious foundations.

Antebellum Reflections

Shells cannonading Fort Sumter in Charleston harbor on April 12, 1861, abruptly ended the antebellum period of American history. Along with the rest of American society, sisters were caught up in the violence of regional warfare. Before following the sisters into that cauldron of blood, pain, and death, some reflections on their antebellum history are in order.

This infant nation, the infant Roman Catholic Church and the infant institution of women religious each groped for direction, permanency, and self-identification during the antebellum years. Thoroughly intertwined, they reacted to one another in striving for existence and vitality. The antebellum period is important, interesting, and critical in sister-history.

Ursuline nuns wading ashore in French New Orleans in 1727 and the Carmelites landing at Port Tobacco in 1790 are both firsts; the one in the present-day United States and the other in the original 13 states. Both orders transported across the Atlantic ancient and honorable heritages that traced back to saints — St. Angela Merici of Brescia in Italy and St. Teresa of Ávila in Spain. Each of these American beginnings became a fountainhead for new foundations across the land that have perpetuated the charisms of their foundresses.

Who in 1790 could have envisioned such women as Elizabeth Ann Seton, the Pious Ladies, the Kentucky foundresses, or Elizabeth Lange? Most European, and for that matter most American, observers would probably have considered it preposterous to think that American women could found orders and congregations without foundresses and aid from established European orders. Yet that is what happened. Eight of the first 12 foundations were distinctly American in origin with American foundresses. This is indeed memorable, and the remarkable women who did it were even more memorable.

The age-spread is something of a surprise. While foundresses such as Mother Seton, the Pious Ladies, Mother Duchesne, Mother Theodore Guérin, Mother Angela Gillespie, and other foundresses were mature women, the many teenage leaders are unusual. Mother Henriette Delille, Sister Teresa Duchemin, Dominican Sister Rachel, Mother Agnes Hazotte, and Mother Mary Anne O'Neil are some of the teenagers who demonstrated the kind of leadership that captivates the imagination.

Each of the first 10 motherhouses was located where slavery was legal — some sisters came from slave-holding families and brought slaves when joining communities. Is the Southern complexion a historical accident? Not exactly. Maryland, the fountainhead of American Catholicity, was a natural setting for the early foundations as was adjacent Georgetown. The Maryland diaspora with its large Catholic element spilled over the mountains into Kentucky, a slave-holding state. New Orleans and Charleston were Deep South and the entire Mississippi River valley contained Catholics, descendants of the French trappers and settlers. St. Louis had a large Catholic population from the earliest days. These conditions combined to lend a Southern flavor to the early foundations. However, starting in the 1820's, Irish and Irish-American women joined these societies in increasing numbers, rapidly becoming predominant. Yet, the Southern complexion of most of the first 10 communities, while distinct, was relatively short-lived.

Black Catholic women founded the ninth American congregation. Considering the effects of slavery, restrictive laws for free blacks, disinterest of Church authorities, and lack of public support, black foundresses had to be remarkable women. Both Mother Lange's Oblate Sisters of Providence and Mother Delille's Congregation of the Sisters of the Holy Family have long and honorable American histories.

Accounts often describe three or four sisters, never more than a dozen, establishing communities. Just as frequently, they disclose how these foundations sent out missions and sprouted offshoots, seemingly overnight. Vocations fueled expansion. While reinforcements from Europe were often critical for survival in the early stages of a community's life, their impact on the overall expansion was marginal. On arrival at a new location, founding sisters characteristically discovered both teenage and mature women awaiting their arrival to join them. Latent vocations abounded. Frequently the local priest or bishop had already recruited aspirants. Impassioned sermons primed pious women to consider seriously a vocation in the anticipated community or in an existing one.

Sisters and nuns concentrated their ministries on the education of girls. Sisters' examples as holy, independent, caring women exerted a profound influence on their charges and resulted in many vocations, these in turn becoming multipliers. Catholic immigrants finding sisters already in America was a pleasant surprise; joining a community was not something to be dreaded or discouraged with daughters. Observing the horrendous needs of the poor also stimulated vocations. Good-hearted young women found that postulancy answered their inner urgings to "do something" for fellow humans and God.

Some modern writers examining the vocation phenomenon of the 19th century have put forward a variety of sociological factors to explain it, among them: escape from poverty or brutality, distaste for marriage and childbearing, dread of spinsterhood, an unhappy home situation, rootless widowhood, desire for respect and status, opportunity for education and professional training, an outlet for talents, sheer loneliness or boredom, sense of adventure, need for security, and other nonreligious motivations. All these very human factors doubtlessly played some part in individual decisions. But such sociological answers ignore or gloss over the primary factor, the "call from God," without which vocations could hardly stand the test of time. Correspondence, diaries, journals, and eyewitness accounts all bespeak of piety and deep spirituality as a common denominator. Departures from religious life did occur with about 23 percent of those joining religious communities.[39] Yet, fidelity and perseverance were the rule, not the exception.

It is difficult today to grasp the passion and intensity of anti-Catholicism in the antebellum period. Threats, overt violence, riots, and convent-burning are all matters of record. Dislike by neighbors and antipathy from all quarters simply for being Catholic had a depressing and smothering effect. Nativism was not built on any well thought-out principles but rather on visceral, grassroots, deep-seated hatred of Catholicism, antipathy towards its adherents and resentment and dislike of immigrants. Books such as *Awful Disclosures of Maria Monk* and macabre tales by English authors, the Act of Emancipation of 1829, and the Oxford Movement in England, and impassioned diatribes against "popery" by fire-breathing preachers inflamed nativists, who resorted to violence and focused their attentions on the most visible target — the sisters. Day-to-day life in such a milieu is hard to imagine. Yet the sisters lived through more than three decades of this hostile environment.

Like many negative forces, this one had some positive effects. For one, the nativist movement acted as a purgative for pent-up inherited prejudice, allowing it to reach a climactic stage and then partially burn itself out. For another, it shamed decent Americans of all religious persuasions, who gradually diluted their anti-Catholic antipathy. The Anglo-American

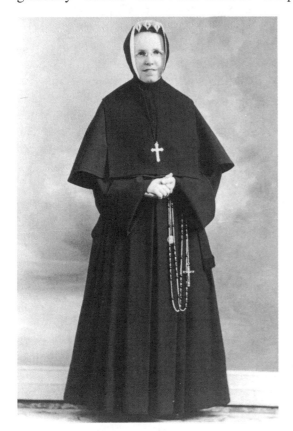

Deaf-Mute Sisters (c. 1942).
Courtesy Gonzaga University

Catholics of Maryland had emulated Catholics in England who commonly sought anonymity and avoided public notice insofar as possible. But French and especially Irish Catholics of the new Republic faced anti-Catholicism openly, refusing to retreat into second-class status. The challenges posed by nativism evoked positive responses. Targeted sisters displayed courage, dignity, and determination, thereby accruing respect, admiration, self-confidence — and vocations.

The sight of nuns in habits — target identification — only seemed to increase vocations. While Church authorities sometimes discouraged the wearing of the habit in public, sisters were reluctant to surrender the "holy habit" and did so only under strong pressure. This witness bolstered Catholic morale and made a deep impression on girls, affecting their consideration of religious life. Reports circulated widely during epidemics about sisters in habits nursing and entering infected homes when no one else would. Even lukewarm Catholics swelled with pride on seeing sisters going about their business. The "witness of the habit" had a profound impact.

With few exceptions, founding sisters faced extreme poverty. For immigrant religious the hardship began aboard small sailing vessels that took many weeks, even months, to cross the stormy Atlantic. Several accounts mention pirates and running aground. Seasickness, terrible food, and cruel captains compounded the stresses. Various terms describing poverty and hardships become redundant as they appear in the accounts: "shack," "snow through the cracks," "bad food," "consumption," "early deaths," "lost in the wilderness," "no money," and other descriptive words and phrases. Repetition should not dull the senses — the sisters experienced true poverty and real hardships. Other pioneer women of the 19th century often endured the same, but they had parents, husbands, and offspring to share the burdens.

Great distance from home, family, friends, and even motherhouses was more the rule than the exception. Only companionship within the community, deep faith, and conviction that their lives counted for something important in God's eyes offset the debilitating effects of loneliness and depression. Their sacrificial lives, simple yet profound, stir feelings of the deepest admiration.

Sisters and nuns sometimes labored under self-imposed burdens when they attempted to conform to the rules and constitutions of the settled convents of Europe. Bishops and priests frequently mandated modifications as a matter of common sense and compassion. Superiors sometimes felt compelled to seek modification from motherhouses in Europe or Rome. The ancient tension between the monastic life and active ministry continued in the new Republic. Adaptation to American conditions was often much too slow.

During the antebellum years (and ever since), women religious have supported themselves financially in various ways. Dowries, tuition, music lessons, tutoring fees, gifts from families and benefactors, aid from European missionary societies, and the manufacture of religious articles and supplies constituted sources of income. They earned whatever wages they received from parishes and institutions, pitifully small in most instances. It is a little recognized fact that women religious have never enjoyed substantial financial support from the official Church. While bishops and priests have often given monies to women religious communities over the years, no central financial support programs existed.

The sisters were first and foremost educators. If the Catholic population was to retain its faith and rise from the lowest economic and social classes, Catholic education was mandatory. The Catholic establishment recognized this and strained every resource to address the need. Most of the burden fell on the shoulders of the sisters and nuns. They carried it as best they could, which was astonishingly well.

Orphans demanded special attention, and this ministry, second only to education, involved proportionally more sisters in the antebellum era than in later years. Immigrant deaths at sea, epidemics, early deaths among the impoverished and the shortage of public facilities all combined to create orphans in inordinately large numbers, relatively more than in any other period of American history. Catholic sisters constituted the primary agency addressing this problem. Girls received special attention from the sisters who salvaged thousands for productive lives.

Health care was next in importance. Congregations such as the Daughters of Charity, Sisters of Mercy, and Franciscan Sisters of the Poor entered hospital work early. They were operating 28 hospitals by 1861 (see Appendix C). They nursed the stricken during the vicious epidemics; they were the only organized groups of female nurses in antebellum America. This ministry would pay huge dividends in the years immediately ahead.

Miscellaneous ministries also received attention from women religious. These included instructing the deaf and mute, visiting poor homes and prisoners, caring for wayward girls, counseling those with spiritual needs, operating homes for the aged, supporting seminaries with domestic services, and providing religious instruction and music in parishes. Their agenda was open to all needs.

American women religious came to the West late in the antebellum period; the Daughters of Charity from Emmitsburg were first on the scene. Canada sent Mother Joseph and her Sisters of Providence and the Sisters of the Holy Names of Jesus and Mary. Dominicans, Sisters of Mercy, and Sisters of the Presentation of the Blessed Virgin Mary from Ireland also made Far West foundations. Sisters of Charity of Cincinnati and Sisters of Loretto came to Santa Fe. These tiny cadres broke ground, but it remained for the post-Civil War years to see significant results.

When 60 orders and congregations are mentioned as the total in 1861, this figure does not include the numerous autonomous communities that emanated from the original foundations. For example, the Georgetown Visitation convent sent founding nuns to Mobile and Kaskaskia in 1833, to Baltimore in 1837, to Frederick in 1846, and to other cities during the 1850's. The Baltimore convent sent founding nuns to Wheeling in 1848 and to Brooklyn in 1855. Frederick in turn sent foundresses to Parkersburg in 1864. All are "offshoots": some "daughters" and others "granddaughters."

While each is an independent community, all are listed under one classification. The same applies to other orders that practice autonomy for mission communities when they become self-sustaining. This classification distinction and the word "offshoot" is used throughout this entire sister-history. While total foundations for 1861 is listed as 60, the number of independent communities was actually greater.

American bishops went begging for sisters. Hat-in-hand they approached mothers-superior in Europe and Canada — with considerable success. Bishops played on sympathies, aroused missionary fervor, contacted old friends, described the plight of ethnic parishes, challenged, and otherwise begged for their poor American dioceses. French-born and German-born bishops and priests were especially active and successful in this regard. Irish bishops and priest were also increasingly active in recruiting in the homeland. Some bishops made numerous forays; practically all of them used their *ad limina* visits to prowl Europe seeking help. They also sent priests and even laypersons such as the resourceful Mrs. Peter of Cincinnati to recruit sisters. Numerous American orders and congregations are a direct result of those begging trips.

Each reader will retain a different set of images from the brief coverage of the many personalities and events in antebellum sister-history. Will it be singing Carmelites going to the guillotine, the English Carmelite Frances Dickenson, Mary Turpin the first native American nun, the Georgetown Poor Clares, the Pious Ladies, St. Elizabeth Ann Seton, Rose White, Mary Rhodes, Maria Sansbury, Catherine Spalding, Elizabeth Lange, Betsy and Teresa Maxis, Julia Datty, St. Rose Philippine Duchesne, her awestruck Potawatomi friend, 15-year-old Mary Anne O'Neil, Henriette Delille pronouncing vows, or perhaps the youngest Dominican saving her community? The personalities and events of antebellum American sister-history are fascinating.

With these ruminations, the antebellum period closes and sister-history enters the traumatic Civil War years.

Endnotes

1. *Miserere*, "Have Mercy. . ."; *Salve Regina*, "Hail, Holy Queen. . ."; *Te Deum*, "To You O God We Give Praise. . ."; *Veni Creator*, "Come Holy Spirit. . . ."
2. In English the final verse of the Veni Creator translates:
   > *To God the Father be glory*
   > *And to the Son, who from death*
   > *Has risen, and to the Paraclete*
   > *Unto the age of ages.*
3. Gertrude Von Le Fort, *The Song of the Scaffold*, translated by Olga Marx,

(Kirkwood, MO: Catholic Authors Press, 1933). The account is taken from this novel based on the historical facts of the execution. The singing girl may be fictional. An opera, *Dialogues Des Carmelites*, by Francois Paulence is also based on this event.

4. Between 1815 and 1900, some 400 women religious orders and congregations were founded or restored in France, with a peak membership of about 400,000 women.

5. Today, some 15 million Americans trace their ancestry back to Quebec. One-third of the inhabitants of Vermont are descendants.

6. Carondelet is named for the first Spanish governor of Louisiana. Unlike French pronunciation with the final consonant dropped, the "let" is sounded.

7. On July 11, 1992, Pope John Paul II accorded her the title of "Venerable," the first step in the canonization process.

8. As the Republican candidate in 1884, James Blaine was victimized by the slogan "Rum, Romanism, and Rebellion." It alluded to Irish drunkenness, Catholicity, and the Confederacy.

9. This incident mirrors the near destruction of Leonardo da Vinci's (1452-1519) painting, *The Last Supper*, by French troops in Milan in 1499 who stabled their horses in the refectory of Santa Maria delle Grazia.

10. French-born Joseph P. Machebeuf (1812-1889), the first bishop of Denver, was one of the great pioneer priests of the West. He joined Bishop Lamy at Santa Fe in 1851 and traveled extensively over New Mexico, Arizona, and into Mexico. Later, he was sent to Denver as bishop where he established numerous Catholic institutions and vitalized the diocese.

11. This nun returned to Boulogne, which she had left in 1845. She later went on mission to England where she died.

12. Alexander Campbell (1788-1866), like his father before him, was an active religious leader and founder of the Disciples of Christ. He wrote extensively on religious subjects and was the founder of Bethany College.

13. Unfortunately, toward the end of Archbishop Purcell's life, the private diocesan bank operated by his brother (a priest) failed, causing a major scandal. The archbishop resigned although he was not personally involved with the bank.

14. Sister O'Neil was the adopted sister of General William T. Sherman's wife.

15. Sr. M. Michael Francis, OSU, *The Broad Highway: A History of the Ursuline Nuns in the Diocese of Cleveland, 1850-1950* (Cleveland, OH: The Ursuline Nuns, Cleveland, Ohio, 1951), pp. 114-115.

16. Father Pierre J. Cloriviere associated himself with the Russian branch of the Jesuits that escaped suppression when Empress Catherine II refused to allow the edict to be promulgated in Russia and ordered the Jesuits to continue teaching in their schools. He restored the order in France after the papal restoration of the Society of Jesus in 1814. His nephew, Joseph P. de Cloriviere, emigrated to the United States and was the so-called "Second Father-Founder" of the visitation convent in Georgetown. Two other Jesuits associated with the Russian group, William Strictland and Marmaduke Stone, reestablished the order in England in 1804.

17. Today, the Daughters of the Heart of Mary have three spiritual centers: Marian Center, Holyoke, MA; Regina Maria Retreat House, Plattsburgh, NY; and Maryhill Renewal Center, St. Paul, MN.

18. Marie Emilie Gamelin (1800-1851) endured numerous personal tragedies and sufferings before founding her order in 1843. She was inspired by the spirit of St. Vincent de Paul and had a special devotion to Our Mother of Sorrows. When Mother Gamelin died, the community numbered 46 sisters. It totals over 1,700 worldwide today with nearly 400 in the United States.

19. St. Joseph's Hospital was started in 1858 in a small 20- by 16-foot building by the Sisters of Providence with the help of an association of laywomen, the Ladies of Charity. It is one of the oldest hospitals in the Northwest and the first permanent one in the Washington Territory.

20. Sr. Mary of the Blessed Sacrament McCrosson, SP, in collaboration with Sr. Mary Leopoldine, SP, and Sr. Maria Theresa, SP, *The Bell and the River* (New York, NY: Pacific Books, Inc., 1957). Most of this account is derived from this book.

21. During the Civil War, General Scott refused to allow the quartering of troops at Visitation Academy despite the nuns' willingness. He felt that would be disrespectful to his daughter's grave.

22. Sisters of the Holy Names of Jesus and Mary, *Gleanings of Fifty Years* (Portland, OR: Press of Glass & Prudhomme Co., 1909). Sr. Mary Flavia, SNJM (1856-1945), was the actual author. Humility prevented her from affixing her name to the work. Most of the account is derived from this book.

23. No birth certificate or baptismal certificate has ever been located. However, the date of birth of 1778 is generally accepted by historians.

24. Before she died in 1841 at age 63, Catherine McAuley had been involved in the foundation of 12 convents in Ireland and two in England. During the 25 years following her death, the Sisters of Mercy opened over 200 convents in Ireland, England, Newfoundland, Scotland, the United States, Australia, New Zealand, and Argentina.

25. The title Bishop of London belongs to the Anglican bishop. While the Catholic bishop's see is also London, he uses the title Bishop of Westminster.

26. Both the New York and Pittsburgh communities became fountainheads for the tremendous growth and expansion of the Sisters of Mercy during the 19th century. Each sent out offshoots that in turn produced daughters, granddaughters, and great-granddaughters. In addition, Irish convents in Naas, Kinsale, Ennis, and Moate sent sisters to the United States to make small foundations. The family trees of these foundations are too complex for display in this volume, but nonetheless intriguing. Further compounding simple explanations, some motherhouses moved to other locations while some foundations did not last. In short, the history of the growth and expansion of the Sisters of Mercy in the United States is a story in itself, requiring book-length coverage.

27. Mr. Knowles, the mayor of Providence, informed Mother Warde that he would be powerless to prevent the Know-Nothings from violence against her community. She calmly informed him that if she were the chief of municipal affairs

she would know how to control the populace. Then she organized the local Irish, who armed themselves and intimidated the mob that formed outside the convent. After this, the sisters were no longer molested. Account taken from Edward A. Ryan, S.J., "The Sisters of Mercy: An Important Chapter in Church History" (Woodstock, MD: *Theological Studies*, Vol. 18, June 1957), p. 267.

28. His *The Spirit of The Constitutions of the Poor School Sisters of Notre Dame* became the foundation for this congregation's rule of life. The word "poor" in the title was soon discarded.

29. He established the *Ludwig Missionsverein* as a fund-raising society for missionaries. He financed the School Sisters of Notre Dame's initial entry into the United States and the fund provided an annual stipend of $1,800 beginning in 1855, later increased to $1,840. Their last grant was in 1866. See Sr. Florence Deacon, OSF, *More than Just a Shoe String and a Prayer: How Women Religious Helped Finance the Nineteenth Century Social Fabric*, privately printed, Cardinal Stritch College, Milwaukee, WI, 1992.

30. A School Sister of Notre Dame, Mother Caroline and the School Sisters of Notre Dame in North America (St. Louis, MO: Woodward & Tiernan Co., 1928). Most of the account is based on that book.

31. Abbot Wimmer witnessed nine Benedictine women professing solemn vows in 1855, the first and last to do so until 1922 when the Vatican recognized the title of "Benedictine Sisters of Pontifical Jurisdiction." Charter communities of the Congregation of St. Scholastica included: Atchison, Kansas; Erie and St. Mary's, Pennsylvania; Chicago and Lisle, Illinois; Elizabeth, New Jersey; Ridgely, Maryland; Cullman, Alabama; and Guthrie (later Tulsa), Oklahoma.

32. Sr. M. Grace McDonald, OSB, *With Lamps Burning* (St. Joseph, MN: St. Benedict's Priory Press, 1957), p. 11.

33. The *Ludwig Missionsverein* made two grants intended for the nuns, one for 8,000 florins and another for 3,000 florins. Mother Benedicta never saw any of this money. See Margaret Susan Thompson, Chapter Seven, *Women, Feminism and New Religious History: Catholic Sisters as a Case Study*, Philip VanderMeer and Robert Swierenga, eds. (New Brundswick, NJ: Rutgers University Press, 1991), p. 147.

34. Although Abbot Wimmer fares poorly in this account, he was a dynamic leader, even if autocratic and stubborn. During his abbacy he provided priests for churches throughout the country. Monks from St. Vincent's Abbey in Latrobe established 10 other monasteries. Archabbot Wimmer is honored and regarded as the abbot-founder of Benedictines in the United States.

35. Sr. M. Louise George, OSB, *Mother Paula O'Reilly* (Pamphlet, 1985), p. 116.

36. The seven monasteries were St. Joseph's in St. Mary's, PA (1852), Mount St. Benedict's in Erie, PA (1856), St. Benedict in St. Cloud, MN (1857), St. Scholastica in Newark, NJ (1857), St. Walburga in Covington, KY (1859), St. Scholastica in Chicago, IL (1861), and St. Gertrude in Shakopee, MN (1862).

37. Holy Cross Monastery was founded in 1233 and continues as a Second Order cloistered community to this day. It is the oldest monastery in Germany with an unbroken existence in Ratisbon. Basically contemplatives, the nuns were forced

by the local ruler to open a school in their monastery after the French Revolution.

38. Sr. Lois Curry, OP, *Women After His Own Heart: The Sisters of St. Dominic of the American Congregation of the Sacred Heart of Jesus, Caldwell New Jersey, 1881-1891* (New York, NY: New City Press, 1981), pp. 24-28.

39. Most departures occurred in the first several years of membership. See Barbara Misner, "A Comparative Social Study of the Members and Apostolates of the First Eight Permanent Communities of Women Religious Within the Original Boundaries of the United States, 1790-1850" (Ph.D. Diss., The Catholic University of America, 1980), p. 92.

CHAPTER 5

Sister War-Nurses

AT 6 A.M. ON October 15, 1874, the six Dominican sisters teaching at St. Patrick's parochial school in Jacksonville, Illinois, were in their chapel for morning devotions. Father M. P. Burke suddenly burst in, highly excited and clutching two telegrams: one from President Ulysses S. Grant and the other from Bishop Peter J. Baltes, ordinary of the diocese of Alton. President Grant's was an invitation to Mother Mary Josephine Meagher and another Dominican sister of her choosing to unveil the new Lincoln Monument in the state capitol of Springfield at 10 a.m. that same morning. National attention was focused on this ceremony honoring the country's "savior" with its new imposing monument, the most expensive ever erected in the United States up to that time. Springfield was 40 miles away and the ceremony was scheduled in just four hours.

Unbeknownst to the sisters, President Grant had expressed a wish at the previous day's planning session for Catholic sisters to do the unveiling. He felt that their Civil War nursing services had never been properly recognized and that this was a perfect opportunity for the nation to express its gratitude. On hearing that an invitation to local Ursuline nuns had been politely declined for reasons of humility, General William Tecumseh Sherman stated his personal preference for Dominican sisters. Father P. J. Macken, pastor of St. Patrick's in Jacksonville, overheard the remark and stated that he had Dominican sisters (1070-10) teaching in his parish. President Grant immediately wired Bishop Peter J. Baltes for the proper episcopal approval and ordered his personal train to bring the sisters from Jacksonville.

Mother Josephine was specifically named because Father Macken was aware of her nursing at the Battle of Perryville in Kentucky. Mother Josephine chose Sister Mary Rachel Conway, another war-nurse, as her companion. The two sisters raced to the station in Father Burke's carriage and sped to Springfield on the president's train. They were then hustled into an imposing carriage and joined the entourage en route to the ceremony. Their carriage was second in line behind the president's as they passed the tens of thousands of spectators gathering for the event. Their white Dominican habits contrasted sharply with the morning coats and top hats worn by the civil dignitaries and with the colorful uniforms worn by the generals. These contrasts served to rivet attention on the two sisters.

After Governor Richard J. Oglesby of Illinois delivered a lengthy oration, he motioned the sisters forward for the unveiling. At the agreed signal, Mother Josephine pulled on the cord and the silken covering of the 100-foot tall monument fell in folds into the sisters' arms. The throng of witnesses sent up a deafening roar of approval.

Millions of Americans read the details in their newspapers the following morning. The general reaction was positive. That same morning also found Mother Josephine back in Jacksonville teaching the older boys in class and Sister Rachel teaching harmony in the music room.

That ceremony in Springfield in 1874, nine years after the end of the Civil War, is long forgotten. Yet it represented a profound and permanently changed perception of Catholic sisters and nuns by the American public and a noticeable reduction of Protestant hostility towards them. These feats were brought about by a mere handful of Catholic sisters, affectionately remembered as the "Nuns of the Battlefield."[1] Thousands of men and around 3,200 women acted as nurses during the war. The approximately 640 Catholic sister nurses is a relatively small proportion of that number. This fact raises questions of why they were so important and their service so significant, warranting President Grant's invitation to unveil the Lincoln Monument and to merit a statue in their honor in the nation's capitol. Before recounting the episodes that answer these questions, a look into the background of nursing in the United States during the antebellum period and its status in 1861 is helpful.

Pre-Civil War Nursing

Since the idea of decent women attending to the intimate personal needs of strange men was not acceptable in antebellum America, nursing was not considered a respectable profession for women. Consequently, except for Catholic sisters who had a centuries-old tradition of nursing, there were only a limited number of qualified and experienced female nurses in the country. Rudimentary nursing in hospitals was handled by men and low-class women, including prostitutes and alcoholics. This state of affairs reflected English practices. During and following the Reformation, the English government suppressed Catholic orders, destroying quality nursing in the process. Despite quantum leaps in medical knowledge in the late 18th century and first half of the 19th century, the quality of nursing only improved marginally in England and the United States.

During the Crimean War (1854-1856), Florence Nightingale and Sisters of Mercy from convents in England and Ireland became world famous for their roles in military nursing for the British Army. International newspaper coverage made these women familiar household names and helped change attitudes toward female nurses in England. Although the Civil War came too soon for Miss Nightingale's example and concepts to be implemented in the United States, both the public and medical establishment were in the process of revising their negative attitudes. Nursing by women gained acceptance more quickly and widely in the North than in the South, where tradition and resistance to change were stronger.

Catholic sisters were operating 28 hospitals when the war erupted and constituted the only clearly identifiable groups of nurses in the country. A few private and public hospitals had made tentative efforts to train female nurses. Lutheran and Episcopal church groups had initiated small programs. However, there were probably fewer than 100 of these non-Catholic nurses, and they were not organized in groups as were Catholic sisters. Only a small proportion of sick people were treated or nursed in hospitals in those days. Most received treatment in the home with mothers, wives, sisters, daughters, and female servants doing the nursing, usually quite satisfactorily. While no pool of experienced nurses existed in 1861 other than Catholic sisters, many women had home experience and could make the transition to hospital nursing with limited training, adequate supervision, and on-the-job experience.

Catholic sisters made ideal nurses for reasons other than training and experience. They viewed nursing as a religious ministry rather than a profession and felt deeply that their *raison d'être* was to motivate repentance for sin, to convert, to baptize, and prepare the dying for eternity. The nursing ministry was seen as a Christian duty to humanity and a God-given means to an end. This self-image manifested itself in compassion, devotion to duty, patience, tenderness, and extra physical exertions — all qualities of the ideal nurse. The sisters' religious vows of poverty, chastity, and obedience further enhanced their suitability for war service. They cheerfully accepted harsh living conditions, asking for no remuneration beyond subsistence, having been inadvertently prepared for such a rough life by years of physical hardship and poverty. Doctors and medical officials had no fears about romantic involvements with patients or staff and were delighted to have holy women setting the tone in the wards, often filled with rough soldiers accustomed to vulgar language and bawdy conduct. Even sisters' habits, startlingly unfamiliar to most non-Catholic patients, were an asset in asserting discipline and controlling unruly patients. Sisters' respect for the office and authority of doctors came naturally to women living the vow of obedience and made them highly popular with medical personnel. The virtue of humility, prized and generally practiced by the sisters, pleased and won the admiration of doctors and patients alike. The practice of always appointing or electing a superior for any group activity or endeavor enabled the sisters to make timely decisions and act cohesively and efficiently, abilities that were essential under the chaotic conditions of war. The outbreak of the Civil War in 1861 found Catholic sisters the only source of organized, experienced, available, and dedicated female nurses in the United States.

Medical Facilities During the Civil War

The Civil War was the most traumatic event in American history. The opposing forces fought over 2,000 battles, ranging from small unit skirmishes to major engagements between large armies. Soldiers' deaths exceeded the *combined total* of other American wars from the Revolution through World War II. Within a four-year span, 620,000 men died. The Union lost 360,000 of its 2,100,000 soldiers and the Confederacy lost 260,000 of its 850,000 fighting men. Since the census of 1860 listed 5,919,380 males between the ages of 20 to 49, the country lost 10.47 percent of its vital manhood — a terrible price to pay for unbridled political passions.

On April 6 and 7, 1862, a total of 25,000 men on both sides fell at Shiloh, the greatest loss in battle in American history up to that time. The 26,000 casualties at Antietam on September 17, 1862, marked the bloodiest single day in American history. The 51,000 casualties in three days of combat at Gettysburg on July 1, 2, and 3, 1863, surpassed the carnage of any other battle in American history. Some 8,000 Union soldiers fell at Cold Harbor, Virginia, on June 3, 1864, *in just eight minutes* in the bloodiest charge of the war.

Most fighting was at close range and ferocious. While shrapnel and grapeshot fired from cannons were murderous, it was mainly the minnie ball from accurate rifle fire that killed and maimed. The soft-lead minnie ball was fired at low muzzle velocity, causing it to flatten and spread on entering flesh, inflicting horrible wounds. Pistol, saber, and bayonet killed and wounded relatively few combatants, contrary to battle scenes depicted in motion pictures. Bombardment from heavy cannons mounted on warships and in permanent forts did tremendous property damage and created numerous casualties.

Fighting took place in many parts of the country, including the frontier areas of the Southwest. The heaviest and most decisive battles were fought in what Civil War historians call the East and West theaters of the war. The East theater encompassed Virginia, West Virginia, Maryland, Pennsylvania and the Carolinas. The West theater included Kentucky, Tennessee, Missouri, Mississippi, Arkansas, Texas, Alabama, Georgia, and Louisiana. The heaviest battles were fought in the East between the Confederate Army of Northern Virginia commanded by General Robert E. Lee and the Union Army of the Potomac under a series of generals culminating with Ulysses S. Grant. These large armies, often close to 100,000 men on each side, clashed in Virginia, Maryland, and Pennsylvania. Heavy battles in the West were fought for control of the Mississippi River in pursuit of the Union strategy of splitting the Confederacy. Although not on the scale of the battles fought in the East, more battles and naval engagements occurred in the West. Centralized command and control structures including medical support evolved more quickly and effectively in the North than in the South.

This war was exceptionally brutal for many reasons, not the least of which was archaic medical care. Wounded men who might have lived with better medical planning, facilities, and attention died by the tens of thousands. It was common for the wounded to lie unattended on the battlefield for many hours, even days. Retreating armies often left casualties lying where they fell for the victors to treat. While both sides honored this responsibility, these unfortunates were usually the last to receive help. Chloroform and ether were often in short supply, especially in Confederate units. Out of ignorance, doctors failed to sterilize sponges, bandages, and surgical instruments, causing infections that resulted in deadly gangrene and tetanus. It was not until 1876 that American medical establishment fully comprehend that germs caused infection and began routine sterilization of surgical instruments and hands.

Casualties were taken to regimental field hospitals set up in primitive surroundings close to the fighting. Due to the prevalence of gangrene, surgeons routinely amputated wounded arms and legs as a precaution. Hasty surgical procedures performed in tents, temporary sheds, and barns compounded the suffering and resulted in numerous agonizing deaths. Thousands died from bleeding or exposure to intense heat or cold before being removed from the battlefields in crude ambulance wagons that jolted over rutted roads and cross-country. Others expired in evacuation rail cars and ships removing them to rear area hospitals. It is a commentary on the times that military and civilian authorities considered such primitive medical treatment quite normal. Common soldiers accepted these conditions, considering it their lot.

Despite the large numbers of battlefield casualties, disease was the greatest killer. A total of 414,000 men died from typhus, smallpox, dysentery, measles, chicken pox, malaria, pneumonia, and camp fevers — *five times* the civilian rate. Hasty induction into the armies with little or no medical screening threw thousands of men into close quarters where even one infected recruit could cause an epidemic. Because germs were not yet understood as carriers of disease and infection, soldiers often failed to maintain proper hygiene and sanitation standards despite the accumulated knowledge from previous wars. During the first two years of the war, regiments were commonly unable to muster half their numbers for march or battle because of sickness. Dietary deficiencies and near-malnutrition often weakened soldiers, rendering them susceptible to whatever disease was rampant.

On April 12, 1861, the only Federal military hospital was a 41-bed unit at Fort Leavenworth, Kansas. The Army Medical Corps consisted of 98 personnel, some of whom soon left to join their Southern brothers. The Confederacy had only 24 medical officers. Neither side had ambulances.

During the first year of war, both sides operated on the premise that it would be short. As a result, provisions for medical support were limited to immediate needs. By the spring of 1862, one year into the war, the heavy fighting in Virginia and the bloody engagement at Shiloh caused civilian and military leaders on both sides to conclude that the war would be long and bloody. Thereafter the buildup of medical support was tremendous. By 1865 the Union was operating 204 military hospitals and the Confederacy 150. Satterlee Hospital in Philadelphia, designed to accommodate 3,500 patients, was the largest and best planned Union facility. When it opened on May 1862, it had 25 Daughters of Charity as nurses; by the end of the war the number had increased to 90. Chimborazo Hospital in Richmond ultimately expanded to handle 8,000 patients, making this Confederate facility the largest hospital in world history. Ambulance units were organized and railroad cars were refitted with litters for evacuation. First conceived by the U.S. Sanitary Commission, waterborne hospitals came into wide use in both the East and West.

Tens of thousands participated in providing medical support: doctors, surgical and medical assistants, litter bearers, grave diggers, ambulance drivers and assistants, animal handlers, cooks, bakers, food service personnel, supply and storage personnel, laundry workers, pharmacists, housekeepers, clerks, orderlies, ward masters, matrons, and nurses. In the North and the South, hundreds of thousands of women worked in patriotic aid societies that raised money and gathered, prepared, and delivered bandages, clothing, books, food, and other necessities and comforts to the soldiers. Broad-based civilian support filled a critical need for both sides despite the occasional friction with doctors generated by well-intentioned women.

Buglers, regimental musicians, drummer boys, the lightly wounded or mildly sick and convalescent patients were pressed into temporary service as litter bearers in the heat of battle. They received no training and simply learned by experience. During the last two years of war, the Union Army organized an ambulance corps to pick up wounded, provide first aid, and remove them to field hospitals. Confederates operated far more informally with each unit resolving its own problems.

Male nurses, who were alternately called orderlies or attendants, performed basic nursing in the field units and predominated in the general hospitals, outnumbering females by a large margin. They normally worked under the supervision of ward masters, matrons, and female nursing superintendents such as Catholic sisters. With a few notable exceptions that we shall see, female nurses did not accompany troops in the field or tend wounded on the battlefields.

In addition to the 3,200 female nurses, some 6,000 to 7,000 women assisted in hospitals, acting as nurses' assistants, cooks, laundresses, and housekeepers. This figure does not include wives who appeared occasionally to succor their husbands nor does it include camp followers and casual day laborers.[2] The 3,200 true nurses, as the term is understood today, cleaned wounds, stemmed bleeding, applied and changed bandages, assisted doctors in examinations and surgery, administered medicines, fed and bathed incapacitated patients, assisted the feverish, and monitored serious cases. They also managed kitchens, supervised orderlies, and generally controlled supplies and the wards. Turnover of female nurses was high. Consequently, not all of the 3,200 women were on duty at any given time during the war.

Some women who gave heroic and dedicated service are famous. Mary Livermore and Mary Ann Hoge did remarkable work with the U.S. Sanitary Commission. Cordelia Perrine Harvey, widow of a Wisconsin governor, also worked for the Sanitary Commission. She persuaded President Lincoln to authorize military hospitals in Wisconsin for that state's patients. Mary Ann Bickerdyke, with full backing from General Grant, aggressively attacked filth and poor nutrition in the Union armies fighting in the West. The troops called this unusual and controversial woman "General Bickerdyke." Clara Barton, later foundress of the American Red Cross, was renowned for going onto battlefields to help the wounded. Louisa May Alcott, author of *Little Women*, achieved fame from writing about her war experiences, although she spent less than six months in actual nursing. Mary Walker is remembered as the only female doctor to serve with a military unit, as surgeon for the 52nd Ohio Regiment. On the Confederate side, President Jefferson Davis commissioned Sally Louisa Tompkins a captain so her infirmary could qualify as an Army hospital, making her the only female officer in the Confederate Army. Kate Cummings and Ella King Newsome were Southern nursing heroines. Hundreds of other women on both sides nursed with devotion.

Sources of Female War-Nurses

The South never formally established an Army nurse corps as did the North, although the Confederate Congress enacted a law in September 1862 authorizing the employment of female civilian nurses and matrons for military hospitals. The approximately 1,000 female nurses in Southern hospitals were a combination of hired women, volunteers, and Catholic sisters; male orderlies, including some slaves, performed most of the nursing in the field. One factor that somewhat relieved pressure on facilities and resources was the proclivity of Confederate sick and wounded to return home for care and convalescence within the bosom of the family. Conversely, the Union appointed official female Army nurses from the start. Aside from Catholic sisters who were a special category, the Union Army used these sources for nurses: Superintendent of U.S. Army Nurses (Dorothea Dix), the Surgeon-General of the Army, the U.S. Sanitary Commission, and local military and civilian authorities. Their intertwined roles require some explanation.

On April 15, 1861, when President Lincoln issued a call for 75,000 volunteers to put down the "insurrection," an unusual woman left home for Washington to offer her services. Miss Dorothea Lynde Dix (1802-1887) grew up in Boston, taught school, wrote children's books, and tutored the children of noted Unitarian minister and writer, William Ellery Channing. She became interested in the care of the mentally ill and visited every institution in Massachusetts where these unfortunates were confined in 1841. Her report horrified the state legislature, which promptly enacted laws to improve conditions. She expanded her activities to neighboring states and eventually the nation. Within a dozen years, 15 special institutions for the care of the insane sprang up in the United States and Canada. She was already renowned for this work when she visited Europe inspecting insane asylums. There, Pope Pius IX called her "another Saint Teresa."

Upon her arrival in Washington, she was designated Superintendent of U.S. Army Nurses by President Lincoln, an appointment many came to regret bitterly as the war progressed. Miss Dix had always operated as a lone investigator and activist promoter of her cause. She was a poor executive who caused considerable confusion, even chaos, in her area of responsibility. Swamped with patriotic volunteers, she dispatched hundreds of unqualified women to nurse in military units and hospitals. Within weeks of her appointment, the Surgeon-General issued an order forbidding these women to march with the regiments or live in camp. The "Dix Ladies," as they were called, were prone to criticize doctors and conditions in the confusion of mobilization, so doctors generally resented them. Turnover was high. Eighteen months into the war, the Secretary of War issued General Order # 351 giving the Surgeon-General as well as Miss Dix the right to appoint Army nurses.

This order, effectively undermining her authority, corrected some of the administrative problems she was causing. Contemporaries saw Dorothea Dix as arbitrary, stubborn, prudish, and deeply anti-Catholic. She refused to appoint Catholic women as nurses and resented the fame the sisters achieved. In later years she asked to be remembered for her work for the insane and not her Civil War activities.

The U.S. Sanitary Commission was a quasi-official organization composed of doctors, church organizations, volunteers, and prominent citizens. Congress approved and endorsed it on June 13, 1861, although President Lincoln dubbed it a "fifth wheel." Empowered to investigate and advise, it grew rapidly under outstanding leadership. Because of the confusion and disruption of war, it soon expanded its activities beyond merely investigating and advising. It became the Union's main civilian umbrella organization, coordinating the efforts of thousands of local benevolent aid societies. It raised huge sums of money and furnished medical and other supplies in large quantities. This group was the first to use waterborne hospitals in the evacuation of wounded and helped improve sanitation and hygiene in the camps. Additionally, it procured and trained nurses. The exact number they provided is difficult to determine because many women were actually appointed by Miss Dix and the Surgeon-General. Probably, more than half of the 3,200 nurses originated with the Sanitary Commission and in the main most of those nurses performed well.

Local authorities such as state governors, city mayors, and military officers often assumed the initiative in establishing medical facilities for their military constituents, especially during the first two years of war. States furnishing volunteer units felt responsible for their citizens, and city mayors near the fighting often faced up to the need to care for casualties pouring into their communities. Military commanders acted to provide medical facilities where necessary, including nurses. Each case was different. As the war progressed into the second year and beyond, the Federal Government in Washington assumed most of these responsibilities as did Confederate authorities in Richmond.

Nursing Sisters

In 1861, there were almost 5,000 Catholic sisters and nuns in the United States. The majority were situated in the East and Midwest, but orders were also situated in the Southwest, California, and the Pacific Northwest.[3]

The smallest numbers were in the Deep South. While most sisters teaching and caring for orphans continued these ministries uninterrupted throughout the war, some communities supplying war-nurses closed or restricted their schools, left their orphans with reduced staffs, or transferred them to other institutions. In each of those cases, the sisters either responded to the "greater need" for skilled nurses or reacted to uncontrollable events. Communities in physical proximity to hostilities suffered serious disruption, especially in the South.

Most communities assumed nursing duty during the first year of war and constituted the most effective nursing force on the scene. As the war progressed, sisters' visibility, experience, organization, and effectiveness contrasted sharply with the multitude of well-meaning but untrained, disorganized, and untried volunteers. By the end of 1862, some 18 months into the war, female nurses originating with the U.S. Sanitary Commission, Miss Dix, and the Surgeon-General became the majority and their numbers increased for the balance of the war. Catholic sisters never furnished significant additional numbers beyond those early commitments either because they were not asked, or because of their inability or unwillingness to abandon pupils and orphans, or because of their remoteness from the war scene. Also, many bishops were opposed to sisters' leaving their convents and ministries for the uncertain and possibly dangerous arenas of warfare.

Well aware of the reputation of Catholic sisters as competent nurses, doctors frequently expressed a preference for them and sought to secure their services. This image was so strong in knowledgeable circles that even non-nursing sisters were asked to assume that role since it was common knowledge that sisters from many teaching communities served as nurses during epidemics. It is not surprising, therefore, that 10 of the 20 communities furnishing war-nurses were teaching orders.

Scholars estimate that around 640 sisters engaged in military nursing at one time or another during the Civil War, although only 584 names are definitely established. Unfortunately, records in the archives of the communities involved are not always complete for this period. Additionally, the sisters themselves felt no compulsion to record the details of names, places, events, movements, assignments, and critical historical data. Their correspondence, memoirs, and diaries most often detail religious ministry rather than the chronicles of war.

The "nuns of the battlefield" came from 20 different communities representing 12 religious orders:

> 1 - Daughters of Charity of St. Vincent de Paul (0670) —
>   Emmitsburg, Maryland.
> 2 - Sisters of Mercy (2570) — Pittsburgh, Pennsylvania.
> 3 - Sisters of Mercy (2580) — Cincinnati, Ohio.
> 4 - Sisters of Mercy (2580) — Vicksburg, Mississippi.
> 5 - Sisters of Mercy (2580) — Chicago, Illinois.
> 6 - Sisters of Mercy (2580) — Baltimore, Maryland.

7 - Sisters of Mercy (2580) — New York, New York.

8 - Sisters of Mercy (2580) — Little Rock, Arkansas.

9 - Congregation of the Sisters of the Holy Cross (1920) — Notre Dame, Indiana.

10 - Sisters of Charity of Cincinnati (0440) — Cincinnati, Ohio.

11 - Sisters of Charity of St. Vincent de Paul of New York (0650) — New York, New York.

12 - Sisters of Charity of Nazareth (0500) — Nazareth, Kentucky.

13 - Franciscan Sisters of the Poor (1440) — Cincinnati, Ohio.

14 - Dominican Sisters (1070-01) — Springfield, Kentucky.

15 - Dominican Sisters (1070-07) — Memphis, Tennessee.

16 - Sisters of St. Joseph (3830) — Wheeling, West Virginia.

17 - Sisters of Charity of Our Lady of Mercy (0510) — Charleston, South Carolina.

18 - Sisters of Providence (3360) — St. Mary-of-the-Woods, Indiana.

19 - Sisters of Our Lady of Mount Carmel (0400) — New Orleans, Louisiana.

20 - Ursuline Nuns (4110) — Galveston, Texas.

These sisters participated in a veritable kaleidoscope of action. Some communities served throughout the war, others lesser times, and several groups had only brief involvement. For those interested in fuller detail, a highly recommended book is Sister Mary Denis Maher's *To Bind up the Wounds: Catholic Sister Nurses in the U.S Civil War*. Other books devoted to this topic are identified in the bibliography. This chapter only touches on the highlights of Catholic sister-war-nurses.

In 1861, the 800 members of the Daughters of Charity of St. Vincent de Paul — commonly referred to as "Sisters of Charity" — comprised the largest religious community in the country. They were also the most active order in medical work, operating 19 hospitals — 12 of their own and seven public hospitals. They furnished close to 300 nurses, who served almost continually for four years. Since the services of many of the other sisters were shorter, even temporary, the Daughters of Charity effectively furnished well over half the war-nursing services provided by Catholic sisters. They operated in numerous locations and served both the Union and Confederacy.

The second largest number, approximately 100, came from seven communities of the Sisters of Mercy, also active in hospital work. A teaching order, the Sisters of the Congregation of the Holy Cross from Notre Dame, Indiana, were third in number, supplying 80 sister-nurses. The smallest group were the 12 Ursuline nuns in Galveston, Texas, whose small convent/academy was twice converted into a temporary hospital. The other 10 communities furnished nurses in varying numbers and for different periods and under a variety of circumstances. Each contributed in full measure, according to the circumstances of their involvement. Places and types of service rendered by the sisters to military patients included general hospitals, hospital ships, temporary and field hospitals — and on battlefields.

Service in Military Hospitals

Washington was in close proximity to many of the major battles fought in the East. Manassas, just 25 miles away, was the scene of the First and Second Battles of Bull Run. At the time of the First Battle of Bull Run (July 1861) few beds were available in the 16 hospitals in the Washington area. By 1865 there were 85 federal hospitals using converted churches, homes, public buildings, hotels, schools, and tent complexes. The city became one tremendous hospital, processing and treating tens of thousands of wounded and sick. Numerous battles occurred within just a day or two's ride from Washington.[4]

The Sisters of Mercy from Baltimore were operating an infirmary in Washington when hostilities began. They offered this institution for military use on April 19, 1861, giving them the distinction of being the first of the "nuns of the battlefield." Mother Colette O'Connor remained in charge throughout the war. When this facility burned to the ground in September 1861, the sisters and patients barely escaped with their lives. Officials moved them first into an armory and shortly afterwards into the old Stephen Douglas mansion, renamed Douglas Hospital, where they nursed during the rest of the war. On one occasion when food provisions ran low and an official in the War Department refused to supply them, two Sisters of Mercy went directly to the White House and reported the news to President Lincoln, who responded as follows:

> *To Whom It May concern:*
>
> *On application of the Sisters of Mercy in charge of the Military Hospital in Washington furnish such provisions as they desire to purchase, and charge same to the War Department.*
>
> *(Signed) ABRAHAM LINCOLN*[5]

On June 10, 1861, the Daughters of Charity opened Providence Hospital as a civilian facility. It remained the only hospital in Washington for civilians throughout the war but accepted and treated military patients as well. Its first military patient was Leopold Charrier, 25th New York Volunteers, shot in the arm on the drill field, and the first Union soldier to receive a pension. The sisters received their first prisoner-of-war patient, one J. A. Wingfield, suffering from "general debility" in August. During 1862, a year of many heavy battles in Virginia, casualties filled the hospital proper and tents in the courtyard. The Daughters of Charity also furnished the nurses for the large Eckington, Cliffburn, and Lincoln Hospitals in Washington.

The Sisters of the Congregation of the Holy Cross from Notre Dame, Indiana, nursed in Washington at St. Aloysius Hospital for a year. Sisters of Mercy from Pittsburgh nursed at Stanton Hospital. A poignant tale from Stanton Hospital concerns a dying soldier from Pittsburgh who pleaded with a Sister of Mercy to get a message to his wife, Mary. He objected to doctors operating on the newborn son he had never seen who had two little fingers on one hand. Sadly, the soldier died before his identity could be established, making it impossible to deliver the message. Twelve years later in Pittsburgh, the sister came across an orphaned street urchin with two little fingers on one hand. The orphan remembered that his mother's name was Mary and he had hidden his only possession, a family Bible. With these clues, the sister established his identity, cared for him, and saw to his education.

During the early hectic days of the war, the Sisters of Charity of Nazareth, Kentucky, answered the call for hospital nursing service. General Robert Anderson,[6] commander of the Department of Kentucky, was overrun with sick and casualties from the skirmishes at Bardstown and Louisville. Bishop Martin Spalding of Louisville made an offer for the sisters' services that the general immediately accepted. The sisters went to Louisville and nursed in three converted factory-warehouse hospitals. Conditions were deplorable with filth everywhere; wounded men lying untreated and in agony. These teaching sisters took charge and brought physical relief, order, and cleanliness out of chaos. General Anderson was totally supportive and issued this order:

> *The Sisters of Charity will nurse the wounded under the direction of the Army surgeons without any intermediate authority or interference whatever. Everything necessary for the lodging and nursing of the wounded and the sick will be supplied to them without putting them to expense; they giving their services gratuitously. So far as the circumstances will allow, they shall receive every facility for attending to religious and devotional exercises.*[7]

The Sisters of Charity of Nazareth staffed a hospital for Confederate prisoners at Baptist College in Bardstown. More sisters nursed at Paducah. Here Sister Lucy Dosh, still a young woman of 22, contracted cholera from a patient she volunteered to tend. She died the third day after Christmas 1862. A truce was declared and an honor guard composed of an equal number of Union and Confederate soldiers accompanied her casket to a riverboat flying a white flag. It bore her young body up the Ohio River for burial at St. Vincent's in Union County, Kentucky. On another occasion, 12 weary Confederate soldiers came to the convent at Nazareth to secure sisters to nurse the sick and wounded in Lexington, Kentucky. The sisters answered the appeal that same night. The band of soldiers and sisters walked for two days under a flag of truce to Lexington.

The Sisters of Charity of Cincinnati nursed in Cumberland, Maryland, and in Calhoun, Kentucky. An extract from a letter written from Cumberland in February 1862 is typical of the reaction to Catholic war-nurses wherever they served:

> *Already, I have been informed, the good fruits of the Sisters' labors are manifest with regard to the patients confined in the two hospitals under their charge. The sick men seem astonished and cannot comprehend the devotedness, the zeal and unwearying patience of the Sisters. Some declared that had the Sisters been here from the beginning, not a man would have died. The cleanliness of these two hospitals, the improvement in the patients, the great change for the better in the cooking and preparation of food suitable for the delicate constitution of the sick, are subjects of grateful remarks by the patients, and all combine to sound the praises of their inestimable nurses. No doubt the citizens of Cumberland of all denominations, will, ere long, be convinced of the justness of the praise accorded to the Sisters of Charity.* . . . *Would that the wishes that I myself have heard expressed by brigade and hospital surgeons, could soon be gratified, by the arrival of more Sisters to take charge of two or three more hospitals.*[8]

The Sisters of St. Joseph in Philadelphia had operated a hospital from 1849 to 1859 before turning it over to the Daughters of Charity. Dr. Henry Smith, Surgeon-General of Pennsylvania, was aware of their past medical experience and asked for sisters to nurse at Camp Curtin near Harrisburg where an epidemic had erupted among the recruits. Mother Monica Pue led a group of sisters who immediately set about the usual tasks of organizing wards, cleaning up filth, and establishing order. The sisters received fine treatment and their only complaint was that everyone called them "sisters of charity" regardless of explanations that they were Sisters of St. Joseph, not Charity. The camp closed in 1862 and the sisters transferred to the general military hospital at Fortress Monroe, Virginia. Some of the same sisters served on the hospital ships *Whilden* and *Commodore* that retrieved wounded from the Battle of Yorktown, taking them to Philadelphia. When Confederates threatened the *Commodore* during a trip up the James River to retrieve wounded from the fighting near Richmond, the ship's captain paraded the sisters on deck to demonstrate that this was indeed a hospital ship, normally considered a "truce

Providence Hospital, Washington, D.C.

Daughters of Charity, Emmitsburg, Maryland

ship." The Confederates held their fire. Camp Curtin reopened briefly later in 1862 and the sisters nursed there once again.

On June 1, 1861, another of Mother Seton's "daughters," the Sisters of Charity of Cincinnati, responded to a request from Governor Dennison of Ohio for nurses at Camp Dennison, where newly mobilized volunteers were sick with various diseases. Sister Anthony O'Connell led a group to the camp of 12,000 soldiers in training. Sister Magdalene Cooper went along as German interpreter, an indication of how heavily this ethnic group had settled in Ohio. All went well with the sisters except for the mud that often came over the tops of their boots. For the first time in the war a newspaper, *The Cincinnati Commercial*, referred to Catholic sisters as the "Florence Nightingales of America."

In contrast to these early outpourings of patriotic fervor, the Mayor of New York refused the offer of a vacant academy building from the Sisters of Charity of St. Vincent de Paul of New York for use as a hospital. He was fearful the city would have to bear the expense instead of the Federal Government. Nevertheless, that building became a military hospital, and Secretary of War Stanton appointed the Sisters of Charity official Army nurses. Mother Seton's grandson, Captain William Seton, was seriously wounded and became a patient of his grandmother's "daughters." Here the sisters set up a special ward for sick and wounded buglers and drummer boys. One sister called the "Irish Nightingale" took sweets to the boys each evening and sang for them in her beautiful voice.[9] Memoirs concerning these youngsters are heart-rending.

Bishop Hughes opposed sending any sisters to act as war-nurses outside his diocese. Regardless, the Sisters of Mercy from St. Catherine's Convent in New York City sent a contingent to Beaufort, North Carolina, in May, 1862, to operate a hospital after Union forces seized that small port. The steamer ran aground in the shallow Pamlico Sound and the sisters transferred to a tug during a torrential storm that soaked their woolen habits. When they alighted in Beaufort, the locals took them to be widows seeking the bodies of their dead husbands. Mother Augustine McKinna and Dr. John Upham were aghast at the conditions they found in the Atlantic Hotel housing 200 sick and wounded Union soldiers.[10] Dried blood and filth covered the inside of the former resort hotel. As in so many other instances, the sisters went to work cleaning and restoring decent conditions for the patients. Gradually the suspicious town residents came to admire and support the sisters in their nursing ministry.

In the fall of 1862 after Union forces captured New Bern, the sisters departed Hammond Hospital (Atlantic Hotel) although it continued to function under military control. Convalescent patients operated the hospital under the supervision of military doctors. Moving inland to New Bern, the sisters converted the John Wright Stanly House into the new hospital. The house had been a former governor's mansion when New Bern was the colonial capital of North Carolina. During this North Carolina sojourn, Sister Catherine Seton, Mother Seton's daughter and the "prison sister" of New York, kept the sisters informed with frequent chatty letters about conditions on the "home front."[11] When the need for their services declined in 1863, the sisters returned to New York with the satisfaction of having both extended the hand of mercy and done their duty.

Sisters of Charity of Our Lady of Mercy from Charleston, South Carolina, answered a call from Bishop Lynch of Charleston and Bishop McGill of Richmond in December 1861 to nurse in a Confederate hospital at Greenbrier White Sulphur Springs, Virginia (now West Virginia). The day before their scheduled departure Charleston experienced the worst fire in its history. Only the combined efforts of Protestant and Catholic friends saved the convent and orphanage. A week later Mother Teresa Barry (one of the original foundresses at age 14) led five sisters and their chaplain, Father Lawrence O'Connell, to Richmond where they stayed with the Daughters of Charity, observing their hospital operations. The hospital in Greenbrier was a converted hotel under the management of Miss Emily Mason, who soon moved to Charlottesville, Virginia, to manage another hospital. Six months after their arrival Union forces threatened Greenbrier, and the hospital and sisters moved to Montgomery White Sulphur Springs, Virginia, where they remained to nurse the rest of the war. Patient loads varied widely, at times only 200 to 300 and at others nearly 1,000 sick and wounded.

Unhappily, several anti-Catholic doctors attempted to have the sisters removed. Confederate authorities investigated and questioned allegations against the other doctors who supported the sisters and found the charges to be unfounded and false. When the war ended, these sisters were too poor to purchase passage back to Charleston, but managed to secure a ride to Washington where a priest helped them get to New York. There, the local Catholics took up collections to enable them to sail home. The sisters who remained in Charleston during the war later received recognition from the U.S. Congress for ministering to Union prisoners confined under deplorable conditions in and around the city. Congress awarded them $2,000 in compensation for the destruction of their convent during the siege, but the Ursulines of Columbia, South Carolina, received no compensation for their convent, destroyed by fire when Union troops set the city ablaze in 1865

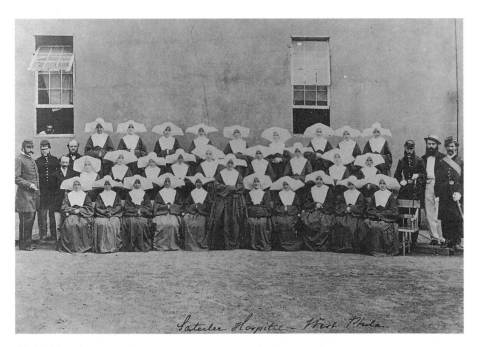

Civil War, Saterlee Hospital, West Philadelphia.
Daughters of Charity, Emmitsburg, Maryland

During the siege of Charleston in 1863, the bombardment was so heavy that the sisters took their orphans and students to Sumter, South Carolina, for safety. This small congregation gave outstanding war service. In 1856, the Sisters of St. Joseph of Wheeling, (West) Virginia, opened a 100-bed hospital.[12] They also operated an orphanage and school and taught Sunday school in the two local parishes. This section of Virginia was pro-Union and took initial steps to secede from Virginia in 1861. The U.S. Congress accepted the new state of West Virginia in June, 1863. Tensions between partisans of the North and South in Wheeling during those eventful days gave the sisters pause when they remembered the French Revolution and how cruel anarchy could be to innocent bystanders. They treated military and civilian patients alike in their hospital and visited the city jail to minister to Confederate prisoners. The Federal Government assumed control of their hospital in 1864 converting it into a general military hospital — something of a blessing for the sisters who were now privy to government rations and supplies. Casualties poured into Wheeling and almost overwhelmed the sisters, who gave up their beds and slept on the floor. Mother Mary de Chantal (Jane Keating) became superior in 1864 and managed the hospital, orphanage, school, and other activities during these pressure-packed days.

A teaching order, the Sisters of Providence of Saint Mary-of-the-Woods, Indiana, was asked to take over the city hospital in Indianapolis. In May 1861, just weeks after the outbreak of hostilities, Mother Cecilia led a band of sisters to that city and took charge. The Indianapolis hospital functioned under their care throughout the war. They also sent several sisters to Vincennes, Indiana, to care for recruits at the camp infirmary. For several months during 1862 they operated a hospital in a converted seminary. When cholera broke out and the hired help deserted in terror, the half-dozen sisters chopped wood, washed linens, cooked, cleaned the wards, hauled water, washed pots and bedpans, and performed all the other housekeeping chores without help — in addition to nursing the 100 delirious patients. None of the sisters contracted cholera although they were in physical contact with the carriers. Eventually the patients recovered and the hospital closed.

Confederate authorities asked the Dominican Sisters in Memphis, Tennessee, to assume nursing control of City Hospital in the summer of 1861. Here they found deplorable conditions and not enough food for the patients. An appeal to the citizens of Memphis corrected this. Shortly after the Battle of Shiloh, Sister Mary Alberta Rumph was nursing in a ward when she heard the familiar call "more wounded." Her young Confederate brother was among the stricken. Quickly noting his condition, she passed him by to tend a far more seriously wounded Union soldier. She returned to his cot only after attending to those with greater needs. The hospital became a Union installation after Memphis surrendered.

The Sisters of the Congregation of the Holy Cross nursed for a time at St. Aloysius Hospital in Washington.[13] Mother Angela Gillespie also led sisters to Mound City, Illinois, to nurse.[14] Sisters from this congregation nursed in general hospitals in Memphis, Tennessee, St. Louis, Missouri, and Cairo, Illinois, throughout the war. On arrival in Cairo in December, 1861, the sisters found:

> . . . *every room on the first floor was strewn with human legs and arms. As the wounded were brought in from the battlefield, they were laid anywhere and amputations took place. Some of the wards resembled a slaughter house, the walls were so splattered with blood. . . .*[15]

The sisters went to work washing the floors and walls while soldiers carried away the amputated limbs. Later, Mary Livermore of the U.S. Sanitary Commission deemed the Mound City hospital to be outstanding. When the Mississippi River flooded their hospital in the spring of 1862, the sisters moved all patients to upper floors. Sister M. Elise O'Brien, still a novice, died from natural causes during the flood, and her companions watched sadly as an honor guard took her body away in a boat to the train station for transport to Notre Dame for burial.

Before the war, the Franciscan Sisters of the Poor, who had previous medical experience in Germany, established hospitals in Cincinnati, Ohio, and Covington, Kentucky. During the war, they managed and nursed in four military hospitals in Cincinnati and one in Columbus. They opened an orphanage in Covington for children of fallen soldiers of both sides. The Franciscan Sisters of the Poor in Cincinnati, personally led by the same Mrs. Peter who had secured them in Germany, worked on the hospital ship *Superior* that went to Shiloh. Mother Schervier, foundress of the order in Germany, visited her daughters in Cincinnati in late June 1863, shortly before Gettysburg and the fall of Vicksburg.

Father Charles Menard, the pastor in Thibodaux, Louisiana, established a 40-bed hospital in June 1862 to minister to Confederates. Sisters of the Congregation of Our Lady of Mount Carmel from Thibodaux supplied a dozen sisters who nursed throughout the war treating Confederate and Union patients alike. As happened to so many Southerners in the final years of the war, poverty haunted these sisters, and only the generosity of the equally poor local population kept them functioning. In October 1862 shortly after the battle of Labadieville, a nearby unit of Union soldiers heard the ringing of the convent bell and assumed it was an alarm of some kind. The commanding officer sent a squad in haste to ascertain the danger. Sister St. Hyacinth, her hand on the rope, calmly said: "Do you not know the sound of the Angelus? This is the call to prayer." The soldiers sheepishly made their report back to headquarters.

Crossing Enemy Lines

Just weeks after hostilities began, Mother Ann Simeon Norris of the Daughters of Charity in Emmitsburg received a telegram from Confederate authorities in Richmond. It was a request for the sisters who had recently opened St. Francis de Sales Infirmary to receive Confederate sick and wounded. Mother Simeon and the council agreed. Daughters of Charity in Norfolk, Virginia, who were also operating a hospital opened its doors to Southern military patients. Confederates abandoned Norfolk in May 1862, destroying naval stores as they left, including the ironclad *Virginia* that had fought the Union ironclad *Monitor*, revolutionizing naval warfare. The sisters then began to accept Union patients and staffed a marine hospital in nearby Portsmouth. Both facilities functioned for the balance of the war.

Another telegram from Richmond in 1861 asked for nurses to assist General J. E. Johnson's Confederate forces located at Harper's Ferry. A small group from Emmitsburg set out to join this Army and accompanied it to Winchester, Virginia, operating in temporary hospitals as they went. From Winchester, the sisters left the field and joined the Daughters of Charity operating in Richmond. Casualties from the First Battle of Bull Run filled the city. Confederate authorities asked the Daughters of Charity to staff a newly opened general hospital. Despite some hesitation on the part of Bishop John McGill of Richmond, they accepted the invitation and nursed there the balance of the war.

Since replacement and rotation of sisters between the Southern stations and Emmitsburg were necessary, the Daughters of Charity found themselves forced to cross both Union and Confederate lines. In late 1861, a spy scare in Baltimore created something of a crisis. Responding to a letter of accusation by Major General John A. Dix (Dorothea's brother), Mother Simeon and the council penned a reply on December 20, 1861, stating that —

> *... at no time under no circumstances, directly or indirectly, have any Sisters belonging to said community gone to Virginia or any other state for political purposes, or carried documents or messages having political tendencies. The only object for which the Sisters were sent to Virginia was to nurse the sick and wounded soldiers. The Sisters now in Richmond passed lines at various times via Harper's Ferry or by Bay to Norfolk, but furnished with passports by General Banks, Major General Scott, or*

the Secretary of State. The first two bands that crossed at Harper's Ferry had no pass, none then being required. . . .

The fact that the Sisters went to nurse soldiers in the South could not be interpreted as dissatisfaction for the Government, since the Sisters from the same society were, at the request of General Rathbone, sent to Albany where they took charge of the sick soldiers and remained at the hospital until their services were no longer required. At the request of General Fremont, the Sisters went to attend and are still attending the sick soldiers at the Military Hospital in St. Louis. They also gave their attendance to the sick and wounded soldiers at the infirmary in Baltimore until they were removed to some other locality; also at the Troy Hospital, Milwaukee, and other places. In a word: the sisters have responded to every call without distinction of creed or politics, and are ready at the moment to give their services if asked by the proper authority; nay, they are willing to suspend their schools and diminish their number in hospitals and orphan asylums for the purpose of nursing the sick and wounded. Of about eight hundred Sisters of Charity, there is not one but would readily obey the first summons for the same work of charity. . . .

We take the liberty to remark that the duty of the Sisters of Charity is to strive to save their souls by the exercise of charity towards their fellow-creatures, the poor and suffering of every nation, independent of creed or politics. . . .[16]

This letter apparently resolved the problem, but spy scares involving Catholic sisters occurred from time to time. There is strong evidence to suggest that Confederate spies wore habits and posed as sisters in order to cross lines and infiltrate enemy centers. Accusations of aiding the enemy were leveled against the sisters a number of times because of their insistence on treating Union and Confederate patients equally and because of their persistent practice of visiting prisoner-of-war camps to minister. Nonetheless, Catholic sisters moved about quite freely in all war zones. The military on both sides treated Catholic sisters with respect and courtesy. There are no recorded instances of their being refused permission to cross from one side to the other.

Sisters were not able to answer all calls for nurses. For example, Dr. E. Burke Haywood, in charge of the military hospital located on the state fairgrounds in Raleigh, North Carolina, asked for Sisters of Charity of Our Lady of Mercy of Charleston, South Carolina. He promised a large room in a house where the sisters would be free from intrusion or insult and under military guard, with the services of a Catholic priest. The request was denied because no sisters were available.

Service on Floating Hospitals

Some of the most demanding and grueling nursing duty of the war took place on water-borne hospitals. These converted ships, boats, and barges evacuated casualties from much of the fighting in Virginia, especially in 1862. In the West, starting with Shiloh and continuing with the fighting for control of the Mississippi River, hospital boats plied the Ohio, Tennessee, and Mississippi Rivers bearing wounded to the medical centers in St. Louis and Mound City, Missouri; Cincinnati, Ohio; Louisville, Kentucky; and other Midwestern locations. Employment of these floating hospitals normally followed heavy fighting when casualties piled up in large numbers with little advance notice. In order to save lives, doctors performed immediate surgery aboard ship despite highly unsatisfactory conditions. Crowding of wounded and dying men in limited deck space magnified the screams and horror. Several accounts of these scenes serve to illustrate these experiences. A Daughter of Charity wrote —

> ...when men, sisters, provisions, horses, etc. were all on board, we were more like sinking than sailing. . . . Here misery was in her fullness and her victims testified to her power by the thousand-toned moans of bitter waves. . . . Here our Sisters shared with their poor patients every horror except that of feeling their bodily pains. They were in the lower cabins; the ceiling low, and lighted all day by hanging lamps or candles; the men dying on the floor with only space to stand or kneel between them. . . . [17]

And a Sister of Charity of Cincinnati wrote —

> At one time our boat deck looked like a slaughter-house, wounded everywhere. I have seen Dr. Blackman cut off arms and limbs by the dozens and consign them to a watery grave. Accompanied by Miss Hatch or a Sister I would pick my steps among the wounded bodies to follow the doctor, dressing the wounds of those brave boys. . . .The groans of those poor boys as they lay on the deck in that pool of blood would rend the stoutest heart. . . . [18]

Another Sister of Charity of Cincinnati recorded —

> At Shiloh we ministered to the men on board what were popularly known as floating hospitals. We were often obliged to move farther up the river, being unable to bear the stench of the dead bodies on the battlefield. This was bad enough, what we endured on the field of battle while gathering up the wounded is beyond description.The soldiers were remarkably kind to one another. They went around the battlefield giving what assistance they

could, placing the wounded in comfortable places, administering cordials, etc., until such time as the nurses could attend to the wounded and sick. I remember one poor soldier whose nose had been shot off, who had almost bled to death and would have been missed had we not discovered him in a pen, where some kind comrade had placed him before he left the field, every other place of refuge being occupied. . . .[19]

Major General Jacob D. Cox of the U.S. Volunteers, an ex-governor of Ohio and ex-secretary of the Interior, wrote this description of that scene:

The Sisters of Charity, under the lead of Sister Anthony, a noble woman, came out in force, and their black and white robes harmonized picturesquely with the military surroundings as they flitted about under the rough timbered framing of the old barn, carrying comfort and hope from one crude couch to another.[20]

In addition to these harsh demands, sisters serving on floating hospitals in the East frequently had no access to Mass and the sacraments for weeks at a time. Eventually Father Francis Burlando, Superior of the Daughters of Charity, felt compelled to withdraw them from that duty. He left those working on the riverboats in the West at their posts inasmuch as they were in and out of major cities where they had access to Mass and the sacraments. He wrote this letter to the motherhouse in Paris on September 1, 1862:

Those floating hospitals were, however, very frightful; more than four or five hundred sick and wounded lay heaped on one another; the bottom, middle and hold of the ships were filled with the sufferers. Willingly would we have continued our service, but our sisters were deprived of all spiritual assistance; no mass or communion; even when they entered the port, it was hard for them to go to church, either because they did not know where there was one, or because the distance would not allow them. We were therefore obliged to remove and place them in the organized hospitals on land, where they can at least rely on the assistance of a priest. . . .

The spectacle presented by our Sisters on these floating hospitals was an object of surprise and admiration amid so much wretchedness and suffering. Everyone is struck likewise by the good order which reigns in the hospitals and ambulances which they attend. If we had a thousand Sisters at our disposal, we should have more than sufficient work for them, merely in attending to the poor wounded. The Sisters of Charity are now known everywhere, they can go to any place without a passport, and are everywhere respected. I think that amid all these disturbances I

> *foresee a brilliant future for our province; but we must learn to*
> *suffer in the transition. We will let God do His own work, while we*
> *pray and fix our eyes on the divine will, holding ourselves ready to*
> *follow it in all.*[21]

U.S. Navy records credit four Holy Cross Sisters and five black nurses with being the forerunners of the U.S. Navy Nurse Corps, not formally established until 1909. These women nursed on the *Red Rover*, a captured Confederate ship converted for evacuation on the Mississippi and fitted out to carry 200 patients. Sisters of Mercy from Chicago worked on the *Empress*.

Confederate evacuation by water was on a much smaller scale because of the geography of war. Boats went from Memphis in November 1861 to retrieve wounded from the Battle of Belmont, Missouri, and were used in a few other instances. No sisters nursed on any of these rare Confederate hospital boats.

Service in Temporary Hospitals

Sisters frequently moved from one location to another. For example, in 1864 the Daughters of Charity left Richmond to nurse Confederates in Marietta, Georgia, moved on to Atlanta and then back to Richmond. Each place where sister war-nurses operated, well over 100, is a story in itself. Most temporary hospitals were little more than converted facilities of some type such as homes, churches, and public buildings. Common themes running through the annals indicate that on arrival at a new location the sisters invariably encountered filthy conditions, poorly tended patients, and welcoming doctors. They often encountered initial hostility from patients and local citizens based on ignorance or bigotry; as time passed those individuals normally reversed their opinions once they came to know the sisters and saw them in action.

In early 1862, the mayor of Cumberland, Maryland, called on the Sisters of Charity of Cincinnati to help in some of the 12 hospitals in his city. Another group went to Nashville in March 1863 and took over a hospital in an old cotton mill. They also nursed in New Creek, Kentucky, for three months before moving with Union forces to Culpeper, Virginia. Following in ambulances, they set up makeshift field hospitals in tents. Confederates drove this Army back to Washington and the sisters returned to Cincinnati. Later, the sisters from Cumberland went to Richmond, Kentucky, to care for wounded Indiana casualties at the request of that state's governor.

The Sisters of Mercy, established in Vicksburg, Mississippi in 1859, transformed their new school into a hospital in December 1862 when the siege of this key Mississippi River city produced numerous Confederate wounded. The 48-day siege ended July 4, 1863, the same day Lee retreated from Gettysburg. The siege was a horror story for civilian inhabitants as well as military defenders. Shelling sent the populace fleeing into caves for safety and hunger neared famine proportions. Given an offer to leave under a flag of truce, the sisters refused to abandon their patients. However, they did obey an injunction from the bishop: "Sisters, do not go out all together, for I do not want you all to be killed. Decide and work in different directions so that some of you may escape." Following General Grant's victory, the arrival of a fleet of hospital and supply ships blessed the city. The ships also brought nurses from the U.S. Sanitary Commission and Catholic sisters from several communities.

The Sisters of Mercy departed Vicksburg, moving with the Confederate Army as it retreated. First they set up in Mississippi Springs, then in Jackson. When that city came under attack, they moved into Alabama and took over a hospital in Shelby, where they nursed for the balance of the war. Enduring incredible poverty, their annals note that Mother de Sales Browne had to gather wood at night to keep the hospital stoves burning because the day's nursing left no time for such chores.

In addition to work in general hospitals in Washington, Mound City, Memphis, and Cairo, Holy Cross sisters from Notre Dame, Indiana, nursed in Paducah and Louisville, Kentucky and Franklin, Missouri. When Vicksburg fell, sisters working on the *Red Rover* bringing relief heard the sounds of the final battle as they approached the city.

The Daughters of Charity, in addition to working in military general hospitals and on hospital ships and taking military patients into their own institutions, nursed in a number of temporary hospitals: Frederick, Maryland; Lynchburg, Virginia; Monroe, Louisiana; White House, Virginia; Marietta and Atlanta, Georgia; St. Louis, Missouri; Sharpsburg, Maryland; Alton, Illinois; and numerous temporary stations in the field. One account concerns the sisters who were operating an orphan asylum in Natchez, Mississippi. While that city was under bombardment from Union gunboats on the river, Confederate General Albert Blanchard asked for sisters to take over a hospital in Monroe, Louisiana. To get there, the sisters had to cross the river in the dead of night for fear of the Union gunboat *Essex*. They crowded into a small skiff, and two Confederate soldiers paddling as quietly as possible got them across the river. The sisters alighted in deep mud and proceeded in the dark.

The Sisters of Mercy from Chicago attempted to go to Lexington City, Missouri, in 1861 to care for patients from the Illinois Irish Brigade. Their ship, the *Sioux City*, came under Confederate fire that prevented them from reaching their destination. So they went to Jefferson City, Missouri, where Mother Monholland accepted an invitation from the U.S. Sanitary Commission to take charge of a hospital. They nursed there until that hospital closed in April 1862.

Service on Battlefields

When the Sisters of Charity of Cincinnati and the Franciscan Sisters of the Poor went on hospital ships to Pittsburgh Landing following the bloody Battle of Shiloh, they prowled the battlefield locating and tending to wounded and ensured their transportation to the hospital boats. One sister recorded that the unseasonable cold reduced bleeding and saved many lives. With 25,000 dead and wounded from both sides, the sisters performed critically needed field nursing.

The Dominican Sisters who represented all Catholic sister war-nurses at the monument unveiling in Springfield in 1874 sent their students home from the academy at St. Catherine's after some Texan Confederate raiders were about to steal the sisters' horses. But the teenage academy girls shamed the raiders into returning them. The sisters fed the Texans the first hot meal they had eaten in many weeks. The Dominican Sisters were also close to the enemy armies clashing at Perryville, Kentucky, on October 8, 1862. In this inconclusive battle the Union Army suffered 4,200 casualties and the Confederates 3,400. Sisters went to the battlefield while fighting was still in progress to minister to fallen Union troops since their convent was under General Buell's control. They worked the battlefield all during the night using lanterns and pine knot torches. The following day, Confederate General Bragg left his wounded behind when he retreated, and the sisters included them in their endeavors during daylight. They converted their convent and academy dormitory into a hospital and continued searching the battlefield without rest until all the wounded had been located and removed. As each wagon carrying one sister and the wounded arrived at the temporary hospital, other sisters unloaded the pitiful cargo, taking charge of their care. Dominican priests and brothers from nearby St. Rose Monastery served beside the sisters, taking wounded to the monastery which they converted into a temporary hospital.

Sharpsburg, Maryland, site of the bloodiest day in American history — the Battle of Antietam on September 17, 1862 — is only 30 miles from Emmitsburg. When word of the battle reached the Daughters of Charity, a small group set out immediately with a wagon of medical supplies. They set up in a local home and searched for men still alive. Like Shiloh, the area was littered with dead, dying, and wounded awaiting help. The sisters gave first aid to the wounded and comforted others until litter bearers arrived.

The greatest number of Daughters of Charity who served on a battlefield was at Gettysburg, where 51,000 men fell during the three-day battle. First alert of impending battle came on June 27 when a large force of Union troops marched into Emmitsburg and camped around the motherhouse. General George Gordon Meade, Commanding General of the Army of the Potomac, set up headquarters there for two days. He posted guards to protect the sisters and their female pupils and every courtesy was observed. A minor crisis arose when Southern girls in the academy leaned out their dormitory windows to taunt Union troops by singing patriotic Confederate songs. The sisters hastily suppressed this exuberant outburst. Union troops moved north on June 29. Southern girls could not be prevented from expressing their joy when Confederate patrols arrived the following day.

Confederate forces left on June 30. The next day the sounds of battle were clearly audible. Emmitsburg is only nine miles from Gettysburg, just over the Pennsylvania line. The thunder of cannon and rattle of musketry reverberated for two more days — then silence. On Sunday morning, July 4, the first group of sisters under the care of Father Burlando ventured towards Gettysburg in a wagon filled with supplies. There an incredible scene unfolded. No American battle has ever resulted in so many dead and dying men in so small an area. In addition to human carnage, dead horses, wrecked cannons, wagons, and implements of war littered the landscape. *It was a vista from hell.*

Citizens of Gettysburg ventured from their basements and places of safety and responded to the obvious needs. Military medical personnel worked feverishly. Help arrived hourly from as far away as Washington and Baltimore. Special trains brought help and evacuated casualties. Before it all ended, over 72 crude temporary hospitals functioned in houses, barns, churches, a seminary, and under whatever shelter could be found.

Additional Daughters of Charity from Emmitsburg and Baltimore joined those already on the scene. Saving the lives of the wounded was the overriding requirement and every hour counted. Local citizens and Union medical personnel passed over Confederate casualties until Union wounded could be treated. The sisters found themselves practically the only ones ministering to the Southerners. When they depleted the supply of bandages, the sisters ripped their undergarments into strips to bind wounds. They jumped ditches to reach the fallen. They pulled boards from broken fences to erect makeshift lean-to shelters. They loaded wounded in their wagon and took them to the local Methodist church for surgery. Pews were used as litters and planks across pews served as an operating table. Orderlies shoved the dead under pews until the bodies could be removed. Severed arms and legs and blood covered the floor. Orderlies supported the surgeons when they became too exhausted to stand. This grisly scene of agony and death finally faded as the flow of casualties diminished and then ceased. Sisters offered baptism to the dying and administered this sacrament to those wounded who desired it.

Daughters of Charity remained to nurse in Gettysburg a number of weeks. Thousands of military personnel and volunteers aided in saving lives, burying the dead in mass graves, and tending and evacuating the survivors to hospitals all over the East. The distinctive habits of these few dozen Daughters of Charity, clearly distinguishable among the masses of military and civilian laborers amid the holocaust, magnified the appearance of their contributions and attracted press attention. Dual victories at Gettysburg and Vicksburg on almost the same day ensured eventual Union victory and totally eliminated chances for diplomatic recognition by the great European powers for the Confederate States of America.[22]

Mother St. Pierre Harrington was superior in Galveston, Texas, when the city came under Union blockade in 1861. She offered the small Ursuline convent/academy for hospital use to Confederate General Magruder. This port city came under bombardment twice during the war, in 1861 and again in 1864. Both times that Ursuline convent/academy became a hospital. Because of Galveston's exposure to naval shelling, all the other local hospitals moved inland to Houston. The Ursuline nuns alone refused to leave. A quote from a Confederate soldier who was present during the first battle reads:

> *The first fight I was in was one at Galveston, and a pretty stiff little fight it was. Both sides kept up a hot fire and the air above our heads seemed thick with bullets. I had been shot in the face and was pretty badly hurt myself. It was gathering light now and one could see fairly well. I raised my head and looked down the line, and I saw to my bewilderment some women moving down there. I said to my companion lying beside me. "My God! Look at those women. What are they doing down there? They'll get killed." He raised his head a little and said, "Oh, those are the Sisters. They are looking for the wounded. They are not afraid of anything. . . ."[23]*

Physical Danger

While several Catholic priests acting as chaplains in Confederate units were killed in action, no Catholic sister or any other female nurse was killed or wounded by gunfire at any time in the war. This fact is remarkable in view of the many perils these women faced. In several instances, sisters were aboard ships that came under fire but luckily came to no harm. Sisters of Mercy nursing Confederates near Pensacola Bay, Florida, in 1861 had their hospital shelled by Union forces at Fort Pickens, nearly killing one sister. Sisters nursed patients with highly contagious diseases when others were unwilling, even moving into isolation wards for extended periods.[24] Lucy Dosh of the Sisters of Charity of Cincinnati died as a direct result of nursing a diseased soldier, as did Sister Mary Consolata Conlon of the Daughters of Charity who contracted typhoid aboard a hospital ship in 1862. Sister Appolonia McGill of the Sisters of Charity of Nazareth also died of typhoid at the 8th Street Federal Hospital in Louisville, Kentucky. Sisters Angela Brooks, Philippa Pollock, and Catherine Malone of the Sisters of Charity of Nazareth all died while serving in military hospitals. Other sisters died after field service; the reasons are unknown today, but exhaustion and run-down constitutions probably contributed.

A distinct danger lurked on battlefields where hundreds of unexploded shells lay scattered, some ready to explode with the slightest disturbance. Even so, sisters did not shirk moving about among the wounded on battlefields, joining military medical personnel and even local civilians in responding to the desperate needs of the fallen.

During the times that Galveston, Charleston, Mobile, Memphis, and Vicksburg came under siege and bombardment, sisters serving in these cities were in constant danger. To their credit, they continued to minister when offered safe conduct out of those cities. In sum, Catholic sisters conducted themselves with honor in the face of danger.

Prejudice Endures

Not only did the sisters face the dangers of the battlefield, but also the unfriendliness of some of the citizenry, especially in the South. While the Know-Nothing political movement faded in the 1850's, its underlying anti-Catholic and anti-immigrant attitudes remained deeply rooted in the American consciousness. When Catholic sisters left the relative safety of their convents to venture into the highly public arena of war, they fully realized that they would most likely encounter hostility but refused to be intimidated. They traveled widely, often in small groups of only three or four, wearing habits. A number of accounts describe reactions to sisters in small Southern towns.[25] For example, in 1863 Mother Euphemia Blenkinsop, Assistant to Mother Simeon at Emmitsburg, went to check on the sisters stationed in the South. At one train stop she attracted a large crowd that wondered aloud if she was a new kind of soldier and cheered when she spoke. A crowd of the curious gathered outside the hotel dining room to peer through the window as she ate. Movement with armies in the field exposed sisters to strangers in areas where no sister had ever been seen. However, there are no recorded instances of their ever being molested, which speaks well for the basic decency of all Americans and the respect that women, not just Catholic sisters, enjoyed in that era. Military and civilian leaders were concerned for the safety of the sisters and often took personal interest in seeing to their protection, as this note sent by the president to Mother Columba in 1861 attests:

> *Let no depredation be committed upon the property or posses-sions of the Sisters of Charity of Nazareth, near Bardstown, Ky.*

> *(signed) A. LINCOLN*[26]

Most accounts dealing with anti-Catholicism concern the initial reactions of patients, the vast majority of whom were unchurched or Protestant. Sisters recorded over and over that newly arrived patients were either fearful of them or hostile. Ignorant soldiers covered their heads and were afraid of what they had heard were diabolical demonesses with horns. Some patients spat on the sisters and others refused treatment or medication from them. The sight of women in strange "costumes" with beads hanging from their waist and obviously in full control often made ignorant rural boys nervous or fearful. The sisters practiced patience and compassion, explaining why they were not married and worked without pay. Typically, hostility melted and changed to respect, even affection. Some soldiers assumed the role of "protector" and informed newly arriving patients about the sisters. This self-appointed role helped shorten and modify hostility. The unwavering insistence by the sisters that Union and Confederate patients receive equal treatment mitigated hostility and had a profound effect on fighting men who respected each other. Eventually, word-of-mouth passed among the troops that one would be lucky to be nursed by a "sister of charity" when sick or wounded. By the third year of the conflict, the hostility of arriving patients had decreased significantly.

Antipathy extended to some doctors and other nurses. A few doctors were openly hostile towards Catholic sisters, like the Confederate doctors working in West Virginia with the Sisters of Charity of Our Lady of Mercy from Charleston. In another case, the doctor in charge of the military hospital in Cairo, Illinois, refused to accept sisters. He reversed his decision later when he was in desperate straits and short-handed. Mother Angela Gillespie of the Congregation of the Sisters of the Holy Cross let him cool his heels for a week before sending sisters. Their performance then changed his mind and healed the former breach. Doctors, including those who had been unfriendly at first, were generally the strongest boosters of Catholic sisters as nurses. Some female nurses, especially the "Dix Ladies," resented and opposed them. A few nurses from the U.S. Sanitary Commission refused to work under the supervision of Catholic sisters.

Probably the greatest "carriers" of anti-Catholicism were women in local aid societies. Groups of these women visited hospitals regularly in both the North and South. Many were Protestant church-connected and often felt a responsibility to ensure that sister-nurses did not influence good, Protestant boys with diabolical Catholic doctrines. Religious tracts that depicted the evils of convent life, such as *Maria Monk*, appeared regularly at bedsides. At times these women were overbearing and officious. Once a visiting lady in Memphis seized and shook a sister she thought was not properly caring for a patient because he was a Protestant. In another case, a group of "Dix Ladies" arriving at Point Lookout, Maryland, were surprised to find Daughters of Charity already nursing there and a sister wrote —

> ... *the women have greatly annoyed us, but their duties were sufficiently apart from ours. They were as hostile to Catholicity as was the North and South to each other....* [27]

Care of enemy patients sometimes aroused the ire of female visitors. For example, Daughters of Charity nursing in Lynchburg, Virginia, encountered fierce hostility from Southern women because of the care given to Union patients. Sister-nurses received equally antagonistic reactions in Frederick, Maryland, from Northern ladies resenting the treatment of Confederate patients. All in all, both doctors and sisters would have been happier to receive the supplies and gifts from these organizations without the bearers. One such hostile visitor, Mrs. Pomeroy, wrote of the Holy Cross sisters nursing at St. Aloysius Hospital in Washington —

> *This order wear black woolen dresses and capes, white muslin caps or bonnets, with black woolen veils hanging negligently graceful over the back; thick boots and checked aprons. A heavy leaden cross, and quite a large leaden heart, are suspended from the neck. What looking objects to wait upon our sick and dying boys!* [28]

Opposition and resistance from military authorities were infrequent and mostly concerned the sisters' insistence on visiting and ministering to prisoners-of-war. Several unpleasant episodes resulted from such opposite outlooks on charity. When Union forces occupied Little Rock, Arkansas, they treated the Sisters of Mercy shamefully because they had nursed Confederate sick and wounded. They quickly reversed this attitude when the sisters tended Union patients. Again, the commanding officer at Camp Chase near Cincinnati would not allow a Catholic priest to enter the camp out of prejudice. Archbishop John Purcell called on the Franciscan Sisters of the Poor, who were able to get into the camp and to minister to Catholic sick and dying. In another case, a Union squad led by Lieutenant James invaded the convent of Dominican Sisters in Memphis, Tennessee, on Christmas Eve 1862. He was insulting and demanded entrance to search for Confederates. Considering the vastness of this war, such incidents were remarkably few.

Generals on both sides were solicitous for the welfare of their men and coveted the benefits provided by Catholic sister-nurses. Among generals who wrote letters praising Catholic chaplains and nursing sisters after the war were Robert E. Lee, George B. McClellan, George P. Meade, P. G. Beauregard, Joseph E. Hooker, Ambrose E. Burnside, William S. Rosecrans, Philip H. Sheridan, Irwin W. McDowell, George M. Schofield, and the Surgeon-General of the Union Army, William Hammond.[29]

After the war, President Jefferson Davis of the Confederate States of America went out of his way to personally thank Catholic sisters for the ministrations to Confederate sick and wounded. While there is no record of President Lincoln having written a letter of appreciation, he and Mrs. Lincoln personally thanked the Daughters of Charity during his many visits to Lincoln Hospital in Washington. He also visited and thanked the Sisters of Mercy at Stanton Hospital. Had he lived, there is every reason to believe that he would have given public recognition to Catholic sister-nurses.[30]

Press reports familiarized the entire nation with Catholic war-nurses, using such titles as "Florence Nightingales," "sisters of mercy," "sisters of charity," "angels of mercy," "angels of the battlefield," and "nuns of the battlefield" to portray them.

Religious Ministry

Dix Ladies and others sometimes accused the sisters of proselytizing patients to Catholicism. To some degree the sisters were guilty. Existing records left by the war-nurses concentrate on accounts of baptizing the dying while ignoring critical historical data such as dates, places, etc. Letters, journal entries, and memoirs repeatedly mention instances of how this or that patient was moved to repent, accept divine forgiveness, become Catholic, and be baptized before dying. Redeeming fallen-away Catholics gave the sisters special satisfaction. Sisters also provided the unchurched fragmentary religious instructions and baptized them quickly on their deathbeds. It should be remembered that many sisters of this era firmly believed that only Catholics could go to heaven. It was always the dying who received the sisters' religious attentions, whether on a battlefield or in a ward. They took pride and solace in counting how many baptisms they administered. One sister recounts, "400 in just three months," another, "dozens on the ground" and still another, "at least 20 that night on the ship." Sisters did not vigorously proselytize patients not in danger of death.[31] They left it up to their example to trigger questions asking for information and explanations of the Catholic faith.

Sister-nurses maintained cordial relations with Protestant ministers and hospital chaplains and did not hesitate to send for them to minister to dying

Protestant patients. Accusations against the sisters originated with zealous lady visitors, not the Protestant clergy working side by side with them. There are no known records of complaints from those ministers. Typically, they reported their admiration and respect, at times expressing a desire to see similar Protestant female religious organizations. Methodist minister Reverend George W. Pepper from Ohio who served as an Army chaplain throughout the war included this observation in a speech:

> *The War has brought one fine result, it has shown that numbers of the weaker sex, though born to wealth and luxury, are ready to renounce every comfort and brave every hardship, that they may minister to the suffering, tend the wounded in their agony, and soothe the last struggles of the dying. Scores of these devoted ladies — Sisters of Charity — are consecrating themselves, heart and soul, spending and being spent in the services of God and humanity. If we look at the Army of the Potomac, at the Army of Tennessee, we find these angels of piety diffusing gladness and joy in every hospital. . . .*[32]

Hidden Lamps

Nursing became a respectable profession for women in the United States as a result of the war experience in which Catholic war-nurses led the way. This new status would have been achieved eventually, but the services and example of the sisters hastened the process. The war highlighted the need for formal nursing training. In the 1870's and 1880's, nursing educational institutions sprang up rapidly under Protestant, Catholic, and governmental auspices.

This brief coverage of an involved and complex story addresses the question of why the President of the United States would insist on Catholic sisters being honored at the 1874 unveiling of the monument in Springfield, Illinois, dedicated to martyred Abraham Lincoln. Ulysses S. Grant, along with hundreds of thousands of veterans, was aware of the services rendered by the sister war-nurses. Florence Nightingale, still active in England, must surely have been pleased with further vindication of the suitability of female nurses for both civilian and military nursing.

After the Civil War, Catholic sisters wearing habits could go out in public without fear of insult or assault and received respect and courtesy everywhere. Along with the work of the sisters, the participation of Catholic chaplains and hordes of Irish-Catholic and German-Catholic soldiers raised the prestige of the Catholic Church to a degree that it would have taken decades to achieve in peacetime. Anti-Catholicism would revive in various forms in the latter part of the 19th century and during the 20th century, but sisters would never again be the primary target of violence.

As a result of nursing experiences, several teaching orders branched out into hospital work. This was a distinct advantage when the orders sent sisters to the opening West where medical services were almost nonexistent. The 28 sister-operated pre-war hospitals multiplied into hundreds in the decades following the war. Exposure to American life in the raw and close contacts with a cross section of the population benefited the sisters considerably. They gained confidence and became more adept at dealing with non-Catholic officials and in putting non-Catholics at ease. These qualities were invaluable as the sisters moved into the primitive communities of the West.

One bothersome question lingers. Why is this magnificent story so little known, especially among Catholics? Answers are elusive and complex, but the following facts offer a partial explanation:

> *The sisters hid their lamps under bushel baskets.* Following the war, they quietly resumed their basic ministries of teaching, caring for orphans, hospital work, and dispensing charities. They felt no compulsion to write about their experiences in detail. Archbishop Martin J. Spalding said of them: "They did much and wrote little."
>
> *Their reaction to praise was that God's pleasure was ample reward.* Whereas the three million veterans formed national associations with local chapters, gloried in reunions, parades, and conventions, and lobbied for pension benefits, the sisters had no such desires.
>
> *New challenges appeared quickly and pressures mounted.* Massive immigration, heavily Catholic, strained resources and personnel. Ministering in the opening West was a new drain. Increased demand for teachers was overwhelming. These and other factors combined to dim the memory and bury the story of the "nuns of the battlefield" until it was almost totally forgotten.

We now enter the so-called Age of Immigration, the opening of the West and a new facet of American Catholicism engendered by yet another European convulsion.

Endnotes

1. Ellen Ryan Jolly, LLD, *Nuns of the Battlefield* (Providence, RI: The Providence Visitor Press, 1927). The account of the unveiling of the Lincoln statue in Jacksonville and various other details were taken from this book. Dr. Jolly worked on it for ten years and is primarily responsible for the "Nuns of the Battlefield" statue in Washington, D.C., located at the intersection of Rhode Island and Connecticut Avenues.

2. The word "hooker" (prostitute) derives from the camp followers of Union General Joseph E. Hooker's Army.
3. Three immigrant orders arrived during the Civil War, two settling in Pennsylvania and one in New York. In addition to Mother Cornelia's Pennsylvania establishment of the Society of the Holy Child Jesus (4060), the entire community of the **Sisters of the Humility of Mary (HM-2110)** left France in 1864 and resettled in Lawrence County, Pennsylvania. The Belgian **Sisters of St. Mary of Namur (SSMN-3950)** made a foundation in Lockport, New York in 1863. An offshoot of the Humility sisters, the **Congregation of the Humility of Mary (CHM-2100)**, later settled in Iowa. In December, 1865, shortly after the war ended, three Italian Franciscans, led by Mother Gertrude, arrived in New York City to make a foundation. They were the **Franciscan Missionary Sisters of the Sacred Heart (FMSC-1400)**.
4. The battles close to Washington included First Bull Run (July '61), Yorktown (May '62), Seven Pines (May '62), Mechanicsville (June '62), Gaines' Mill (June '62), Malvern Hill (July '62), Second Bull Run (August '62), Antietam (September '62), Fredericksburg (December '62), Chancellorsville (May '63), Gettysburg (July '63), Spotsylvania (May '64), Cold Harbor (June '64), and the fighting around Richmond and Petersburg in 1865.
5. Jolly, p. 245.
6. General Robert Anderson commanded Fort Sumter in Charleston harbor when Confederates bombarded it to open the Civil War.
7. Jolly, p. 4.
8. Jolly, p. 44.
9. Sr. Marie De Lourdes Walsh, SC, *The Sisters of Charity of New York, 1809-1959,* Vol. III (New York, NY: Fordham University Press, 1960), p. 173.
10. Constructed in 1859, the Atlantic Hotel quickly became a noted resort for North Carolina society. The three-story structure with triple porches was built on pilings out over the water. After the war, the owners renovated the hotel and once again it became a socially popular resort. The railroad to Morehead City, just across the Newport River from Beaufort, brought guests from as far away as New England and the hotel prospered. In August 1879, a vicious hurricane destroyed the building and two men died attempting to save guests. Governor and Mrs. Jarvis as well as many other guests lost all their personal belongings. The Gatling jewels were washed out to sea and one local found a silver service that washed ashore. See Virginia Doughton Pou, *The Atlantic Hotel* (Raleigh, NC: privately printed, 1991).
11. After her mother's death in 1821, Catherine Seton spent the next 25 years as a socialite and world traveler, mingling with prominent friends and relatives. She was a beautiful woman reputed to be exceedingly charming. She toured Europe several times and lived in Florence for a time. She never married. Not wishing to join her mother's order, she joined the Sisters of Mercy in New York in 1846, the first American postulant choir sister to join the Irish group that Bishop John Hughes brought to New York. She was extremely active in charitable works the rest of her life, gaining the title "prison sister" for her work with condemned

criminals and others in New York's jails. Upon her death, *The New York Catholic News* in its April 5, 1891, issue printed —

> *No one probably ever acquired such influence and control over the thieves and robber class of New York. Though complete information was seldom the reward for her zeal and prayerful labors, she was able to prevent much evil and inspire much good in the minds and hearts of this dangerous and apparently irreclaimable class. They came to her for years to seek advice and guidance, they endeavored to make her the trustee for their wives and children, so implicit was their confidence in her. She would be called to the (convent) parlor to meet at the same time some relative moving in the best circles, and perhaps some unfortunate whose steps to the convent door had been followed by a detective.*
>
> Sr. Ann Miriam Gallagher, RSM, "Catherine Seton (1800-1891): Mercy Prison Sister," Paper delivered at History of Women Religious Conference, Marymount College, Tarrytown, NY, June 29, 1992, pp. 12-13.

12. A group of Sisters of St. Joseph of Carondelet went to Wheeling in 1853. They became autonomous in 1860 as the Sisters of St. Joseph (CSJ-3830-17).

13. In the early days of the war, the government confiscated churches in Washington for conversion into hospitals. The pastor of St. Aloysius Church, Jesuit priest Bernadine Wiget, offered to build a hospital on church grounds to avoid the loss of the church. Parishioners and other volunteers constructed a 250-bed hospital in just eight days in conformity with government building plans. The Sisters of the Congregation of the Holy Cross nursed in this hospital.

14. Their first chaplain, Father Julian Bourget, recently arrived from France, died of malaria his first year at the hospital.

15. Rev. James T. Connelly, CSC, "Holy Cross Communities in the Civil War." Paper delivered to the 1993 Conference on the History of Holy Cross, Austin, TX, 1993, p. 6.

16. Sr. Daniel Hannefin, DC, *Daughters of the Church: A Popular History of the Daughters of Charity in the United States, 1809-1987* (New York, NY: New City Press, 1989), p. 112.

17. Sr. Mary Denis Maher, CSA, *To Bind up the Wounds: Catholic Sister Nurses in the U.S. Civil War, Women's Studies #107* (Westport, CT: Greenwood Press, 1989), p. 102. Sister Denis kindly provided me the preliminary drafts of this book that contained much material not in the published version. Much of this chapter is derived from her book and manuscript.

18. Archives, Sisters of Charity of Cincinnati, "Memoirs of Sr. Theodosia."

19. Maher, preliminary draft.

20. Jolly, p. 47.

21. Hannefin, p. 116.

22. Confederate President Jefferson Davis appointed Bishop Patrick N. Lynch of Charleston, South Carolina, the Confederate Emissary to the Papal States and the pope received him in this role. This reception was not the diplomatic recognition

that many considered it to be, a common misconception even today, although the Vatican was the friendliest of any European state to the Confederacy. Resentment of this in the North affected United States relations with the Vatican for years afterwards. President Davis also sent Father John Bannon of St. Louis to Ireland to explain the Confederate cause. He was so successful that he was not permitted to return to his parish after the war.

23. Maher, preliminary draft.
24. Losses suffered by the Sisters of Charity of Nazareth were probably representative of the other nursing communities. They record that:
    Sister Appolonia McGill died of typhoid fever at the 8th Street
        Federal Hospital in Louisville in 1862.
    Sister Catherine Malone died of broken health after nursing in #1
        Federal Hospital in Louisville in 1862.
    Sister Angela Brooks died of unknown causes while nursing in
        Confederate Hospital in Lexington in 1863.
    Sister Philippa Pollock died of broken health after nursing at #4
        Federal Hospital, Louisville in 1864.
25. The Confederate government registered 59,000 churches. Only 2,200 were Catholic (3.7 percent).
26. Maher, preliminary draft.
27. Maher, preliminary draft.
28. Anna L. Boyden, *Echoes from the Hospital and White House* (Boston MA: Lathrop, 1869), pp. 140-141. Mrs. Pomeroy's description of the habit is distorted. The Sisters of the Congregation of the Holy Cross did not wear a "heavy" cross, but rather a silver heart that was only two and a half inches long. Their woolen capes were only waist length.
29. Many of these letters are preserved in the library at Notre Dame University.
30. Abraham Lincoln's first cousin, Mordecai Lincoln, married Mary Mudd, a Catholic, and joined the Church. Their children, Abraham's second cousins, were all Catholic. While never close to this branch of his family, Abraham knew them and appreciated their support in his political campaigns. It is reasonable to presume, based on this relationship and other incidents, that President Abraham Lincoln respected the Catholic Church and its adherents.
31. Father Edward Sorin, superior of the Holy Cross communities in the United States, recorded that the Holy Cross sisters had administered the sacrament of baptism to 1,800 soldiers by the end of 1863. See Edward Sorin, CSC, *The Chronicles of Notre Dame du Lac* (Notre Dame, IN: University of Notre Dame Press, 1992), pp. 255-274.
32. Maher, preliminary draft.

CHAPTER 6

The Garden Expands (1866-1889)

‡ — ‡

After placing our journey under the protection of Saint Joseph, we left Walla Walla for Idaho City. . . . In Idaho City, and in the mines of that locality we collected the amazing sum of $3,000. . . . The miners came to meet us and, in order to make our passage through the mines easier, went with us by easy stages from one mine to another. . . . Spent with fatigue we arrived in Missoula in September. We then resumed the work of collecting funds in the mines to the south. We met with considerable coolness here, yet succeeded in obtaining $2,000.

This time we were to travel neither by boat nor by stagecoach; only on horseback could we get through the dark forests that lay between us and our own lower Columbia country. To spare us further expense, the sisters at St. Ignatius loaned us their saddles and riding habits. The Jesuit fathers furnished us with horses. . . . After a cheerful supper and a short, fervent evening prayer, each one would wrap up in a blanket, taking saddle or pack for a pillow. The tent was assigned as shelter for Sister Catherine and me. . . . After this fashion we spent eighteen long days and nights out of doors. . . . We had a good supper on venison which Father Saint-Onge had killed during the day. We then said an earnest evening prayer and had just wrapped ourselves in our blankets when a terrifying howl frightened us almost out of our wits. Hurriedly Father Saint-Onge took his revolver and Sapiel seized his knife. The Indian quickly cut firewood to start a blaze around the camp. They knew that wolves do not ordinarily pass the line of fire, and that generally they do not attack singly but call out to each other as a signal for attack. The first terrifying call was answered in the distance by another and then another . . . and then on every side. A half-hour after that first howl, we were surrounded by half a hundred of these furious beasts. Our horses were tethered inside the line of fire. I cannot describe the fright of those poor animals . . . some of the provisions burned, our tent caught fire several times and our saddles were damaged. But finally the night of horror passed and with daylight the wolves left.[1]

THE YEARS 1866-1889 were some of the most exciting in American history, as illustrated by this account from a journal kept by Mother Joseph Pariseau of the Sisters of Providence on her begging trip to the mining camps. After that terrifying incident, an Indian war party accosted the group. Fortunately the painted warriors spared the party because of the presence of the "blackrobe" priests whom the Indians seldom if ever harmed. Not long after, a rampaging grizzly bear, the most dangerous animal in North America, came close to charging into their camp. On another occasion, Mother Joseph was traveling to Denver by stagecoach with Sister Mary Augustine when bandits robbed the passengers at pistol point. Mother Joseph survived all these trials and adventures and enlightened many an evening back at the Sisters of Providence convent in Vancouver.

These years begot some of our most unforgettable sisters. In the pages ahead we will meet the controversial Mother St. Andrew Feltin of Texas, the freewheeling Mother Alexia Hoell of Wisconsin, the long-suffering Sisters of the Most Precious Blood, countesses who permanently established the Poor Clares, and Mother Moes, who was a member of four congregations, foundress of two of them. These years saw Sister Blandina Segale befriending Billy the Kid and taming her corner of the Wild West; Mother Amadeus forging her way on the lonely Western frontier and in Alaska. We will witness the incredible distances and dangerous circumstances coloring the treks of sisters going to assigned missions in the West. Yellow fever epidemics in Memphis during the 1870's once again demonstrated the heroism of sister-nurses, around 30 of whom died striving to care for the stricken. On the other side of the ledger, we will also meet the infamous Bishop William G. Mc-Closkey of Louisville, who lashed out with the worst treatment women religious ever received from a bishop in this country.

Overall, during the quarter-century following the Civil War, the climate for sisters and nuns was much improved over the antebellum years. Sisters no longer traveled in secular clothing or felt fearful about their convents being violated and were generally respected by the public. In large measure, it was sister-nurses and Catholic soldiers of the Union and Confederacy who effected the change. While still embedded in the American psyche, anti-Catholicism took on more muted forms. These welcome developments coincided with momentous events in sister-history.

Catholic Growth and National Overview

Membership in religious communities exploded. The 6,000 sisters and nuns of 1866 grew to 32,000 by 1890 — a *five-fold* increase in just 25 years. Each new convent became a magnet for aspirants to religious life, attracting thousands of second- and third-generation ethnic Irish and German girls and mature women. Large Catholic families and the flood of Catholic immigrants broadened the base of potential vocations. Fifty-four new immigrant orders appeared and reinforcements from Canada and Europe for existing orders fueled the expansion. In 1890, the end of this era, Carmelites celebrated their centennial — 100 years in the United States. Despite the sometimes hostile soil, the mustard seeds represented by the four Carmelites of Port Tobacco and the eight Ursulines of New Orleans had sprouted into sturdy plants.

Academies and parochial schools constituted the primary sources of vocations. As these institutions increased they generated even more vocations as the cycle repeated itself. In 1884, the Third Plenary Council of Baltimore mandated a parochial school in every parish, instigating an unparalleled expansion of Catholic education. By 1890, sisters were teaching 800,000 pupils. An increasing number of orders entered the health care field as well; sister-operated hospitals sprouted over the country.

The Church grew apace. By 1890 Bishop John Carroll's lone diocese of 1790 had expanded to 72 dioceses in nine archdioceses. Over 9,000 priests ministered to more than 8 million Catholics, their numbers swollen by massive immigration from Europe. From less than 1 percent of the population in 1790, Catholics had grown to 14 percent by 1990. Thousands of churches, some quite imposing and beautiful, convents, hospitals, orphanages, academies, schools, colleges, and charitable institutions attested to the Catholic presence in the land.

Logically, the wrenching experience of the Civil War should have left the nation exhausted, drained, spent, and in need of a generation or two to recover its former vitality. Such was the case for the defeated South, punished by the severity of Reconstruction and prolonged economic depression extending well into the 20th century. However, the rest of the nation vibrated with economic energy, experiencing fantastic population growth, territorial expansion, and progress in every field of endeavor.

Railroads snaked across the plains, linking the nation from Atlantic to Pacific, sending out spurs to every region, joining cities and towns, creating new trade centers in the process. The shift from rural and agrarian to urban and industrial continued. Manufacturing doubled and doubled again. Exports boomed. Financial panics caused depressions, but trade and commerce grew nonetheless. The Atlantic cable to England was completed in 1865; the United States purchased Alaska from Russia in 1867 for $7.2 million. The introduction of barbed wire, the "sod-buster" plow, and new agricultural machinery enabled a vast expansion of farming west of the Mississippi, extending to the Rockies. Gustavos F. Swift put the newly invented refrigerator rail car to work and transformed the meat packing industry. The first mail-order house, Montgomery Ward, began retailing to a huge and widely scattered clientele. Inventors such as Thomas Alva Edison and Alexander Graham Bell led the parade into a new mechanical age.[2] Newspapers proliferated using advanced printing presses; entrepreneurs controlled newspapers in multiple cities with syndicates linked by wire services. Robber barons broke new ground in capital accumulation, manipulated the stock market, and bilked investors. They created huge corporations in railroads, steel, oil, mining, utilities, coal, and other industries. Some of the new rich made disgusting displays of their wealth with lavish entertainment and pretentious mansions. Labor unions organized, despite strong opposition. Strikes against railroads and mine owners cost lives and lost wages, but business usually won with the backing of police, hired detectives, and strike breakers.

It fell to the lot of the United States Army to "win the West" from the Indians for land-hungry settlers, avid miners, ranchers, and expanding railroads. Broken treaties, invasion of their hunting grounds, and slaughter of the buffalo provoked nomadic Plains Indians into warfare. When the Sioux and Cheyenne made the mistake of fighting too well, defeating General Custer and the Seventh Cavalry, the federal government had the needed excuse to justify all-out war against the Indians. The Army defeated the tribes, driving them onto miserable reservations and into the hands of corrupt Indian agents who mistreated and cheated them. The federal government did not respect the treaties or reservations, carving away choice portions for settlers, miners, and ranchers. By 1890, the tribes were thoroughly subdued and living in abject poverty, generally ignored by most Americans. The last holdout, Apache chief Geronimo, based his surrender on the solemn pledge of an Army lieutenant. When the lieutenant's word was not honored by the government, he refused the Medal of Honor from Congress in protest, resigning his commission. Fortunately, Geronimo was not murdered as was Crazy Horse after Custer's defeat. The slaughter of defenseless Indian women and children at Wounded Knee was the epitome of terrorism. Even the Oklahoma Territory that was set aside for displaced tribes proved too enticing and was opened up for settlers in 1889; "Sooners" sneaked in early to stake out claims to the best land.

Hordes of settlers including immigrants rapidly filled the West. Nebraska, Colorado, North Dakota, South Dakota, Wyoming, and Idaho gained statehood. It was the age of wagon trains heading West over the Oregon trail,

Indian raids, and stout pioneers, the gunfighter (OK Corral) and outlaw (Jesse James), cowboys driving longhorn cattle over the Chisolm Trail from the plains of Texas to the railhead at Abilene, Kansas, the prospector seeking the "glory hole," — raw material for today's romanticized fiction, movies, and television.

American literary lights shone with the likes of Mark Twain, Oliver Wendell Holmes, Bret Harte, Robert Louis Stevenson, Louisa May Alcott, Ralph Waldo Emerson, and Lew Wallace. International writers such as Henrik Ibsen, Jules Verne, Karl Marx, Feodor Dostoevski, Thomas Hardy, Leo Tolstoy, Charles Darwin, and Friedrich Nietzsche added to the intellectual ferment.

Education expanded rapidly with the firm establishment of the public school system. Illiteracy decreased rapidly except among Indians, freed slaves, and some newly arrived immigrants. The number of private colleges and universities continued to expand. States vied with one another in establishing their own institutions.[3] Clearer distinctions among primary, secondary, and collegiate levels replaced the old overlapping grade system. State-supported education became something of a civic religion deemed central to democracy and true Americanism. However, many school systems were infused with Protestant and anti-Catholic overtones. Catholic bishops fought a losing battle for state support of parochial schools.

The Ku Klux Klan, born in 1865 in Pulaski, Tennessee, spread rapidly throughout the South. It terrorized blacks and kept them from the polls and under the economic and social control of Southern "Bourbons." With the end of Reconstruction in the 1880's, the Klan faded and did not seriously revive until the 1920's, when it added Jews, labor unions, and Catholics to its target list.

Immigration Patterns

Immigration drove the American engine of growth and expansion, fueling a huge increase in population, engendering tremendous industrial growth. Immigration, which slowed momentarily during the Civil War, resumed with a vengeance once it ended, with 10 million immigrants landing during the era. During the 25 years from 1866 to 1890, America's population *more than doubled,* increasing from 31 million to 63 million. Whereas Irish, English, Scotch-Irish, and Scots immigrants had predominated in the antebellum years, Germans became the largest ethnic group in the 1870's and 1880's. Poles and Italians also began to appear in significant numbers in the 1880's. Table II illustrates this changing pattern.[4]

As the statistics make clear, the immigration pattern took on a distinct German shape. Although the Irish continued immigrating in large numbers,

Immigration Statistics — 1860-1889

	1860-69	1870-79	1880-89	Totals
Britain	532,956	578,447	810,900	1,922,303
Ireland	427,419	422,264	674,061	1,523,744
Germany	723,734	751,769	1,445,181	2,920,684
Canada	117,978	324,310	492,865	935,153
Italy	9,853	46,296	267,660	323,809
Poland*	1,886	11,016	42,910	55,812
Central Europe	3,375	60,127	314,787	378,289
Eastern Europe	127	319	7,222	7,668
Russia**	1,670	35,177	182,698	219,545
Others***	262,263	512,412	1,010,284	1,784,959
Totals	2,081,261	2,742,137	5,248,568	10,071,966

* Poland was not an independent country. It was divided among Prussia, Austria, and Russia. The Immigration Service misclassified tens of thousand of Poles as Germans and other nationalities. In 1900, the Census Bureau listed 383,388 Poles under the category of "foreign-born."

** Includes Latvians, Lithuanians, Estonians, Finns, Poles, Ruthenians, Armenians, and both Polish and Russian Jews.

*** Scandinavians, French, Belgians, Dutch, Hispanics, Greeks, Lebanese, Orientals, and others.

Table II

the Germans became the largest immigrant group — the majority of whom were Catholics. Thus sister-history in this 25-year era features new German foundresses and their communities.

Kulturkampf — German Immigration

The consolidation of the German Empire and other European developments caused the Teutonic influx. Prince Otto von Bismarck, the Iron Chancellor, led Prussia in its drive to unify the German states and create a cohesive country. He crowned his success in 1870 when Prussia defeated France, drawing the last of the holdout German states into the Prussian-led German Empire. He then turned his attention to humbling the Roman Catholic Church that had resisted him in Prussia and in occupied Poland. Germany would be Prussian and Protestant. With this in mind, he initiated *Kulturkampf,* literally translated as "struggle for civilization" and more commonly recognized as the state versus the Catholic Church.

Bismarck opened his attack in 1871 with the Pulpit Law penalizing any criticism of the state from the pulpit. His offensive reached full force with the passage of the infamous May Laws, legalized suppressive acts against the Church that he rammed through the *Bundestag* in May 1873 and in May 1874. Armed with these statutes, he exiled and imprisoned bishops, closed seminaries, emptied thousands of parishes of priests, suppressed religious orders, and broke diplomatic relations with the Vatican. Only those women religious engaged in nursing escaped suppression; the German Army insisted that they be exempted in order to ensure adequate medical care for its soldiers.

Isaac Hecker, the leading American Catholic intellectual of this era, foresaw the ultimate outcome when he wrote the following observation in the *Catholic World* in July 1873:

> *There is the law, and it is sure to be carried out. Well, the bishops will go to jail, will pay the fines, or become exiles. They will continue to ordain priests and educate them, irrespective of that power called the state. And the real difficulty begins now. The Catholics cannot yield; sooner or later the state must. . . .*

While persecution motivated Catholic emigration, other Germans also had reasons to emigrate. Accelerated industrialization pushed workers from farms and villages into crowded factory towns with their slums and poverty, as had happened earlier in England. Strong population growth, periodic economic depressions and fear of conscription into the Army all contributed. Almost three million Germans emigrated to the United States, a majority of them Roman Catholic. *Kulturkampf* also triggered emigration fever in occupied Poland, producing a small stream of immigrants that would expand into a flood a few years later.

Women religious joined the exodus and 16 German-origin orders appeared in the United States during this era.[5] Each foundation is a story in itself. All these orders were vibrant and later several had substantial memberships. Numerous individual refugee sisters joined existing ethnic German religious communities such as the School Sisters of Notre Dame and Benedictines.

Earlier, some of the first German *émigrés* found their way to Texas, an independent republic from 1835 to 1845. President Sam Houston was anxious for dependable people to settle the land and strengthen the new republic against Indian raids and Mexican incursions. He made provisions for land grants to groups that met rigid requirements of stability and financial sufficiency. An unusual entrepreneur, Henry Castro, contracted for a land grant in 1842. He agreed to provide 600 families or men over 17, all to be situated within three years. He turned to the Rhineland and the French province of Alsace to find willing pioneers. All were ethnic Germans. He settled them in several increments 25 miles from San Antonio and named the new town Castroville. Thus, Texas joined Pennsylvania as hospitable locales for German immigrants.

Ursulines were the first women religious in Texas, brought there by Bishop Odin of Galveston in 1847. When he visited France in 1853, he secured the Sisters of the Incarnate Word and Blessed Sacrament. There were around 60 sisters and nuns in Texas in 1866 when Bishop C. M. Dubuis of Galveston made one of those typical begging trips to Europe. He secured the help of two Polish priests,[6] several seminarians, and reinforcements in Lyons for the Sisters of the Incarnate Word and Blessed Sacrament. While in Lyons, he persuaded Mother Angelique to train three women for hospital and orphanage work in Texas. They became the nucleus of the **Congregation of the Sisters of Charity of the Incarnate Word (CCVI-0470)** and have the distinction of being the only European order founded specifically for service in the United States. Bishop Dubuis also visited the motherhouse of another order, seeking German-speaking recruits for Texas.

Mother St. Andrew Feltin (1830-1905)

Before Bishop Dubuis left France, he visited the Sisters of Divine Providence in St. Jean-de-Bassel. The French Revolution had almost destroyed the community, but it survived due to the dogged loyalty of the sisters who went home or into exile to await better days. When the Church was formally reestablished by treaty, the Concordat of 1801, the sisters returned to religious life. Complex French law and ethnic histories caused the congregation to develop into two branches, one French-speaking and the other German-speaking. The motherhouse of the German-speaking Sisters of Divine Providence was in St. Jean-de-Bassel. The congregation was disposed to send sisters to the United States, fearing hostilities between Prussia and France and wanting to make a foundation in a safe location. Louise Feltin joined the Sisters of Divine Providence in 1849, assuming the religious name of Sister St. Andrew. Her two priest brothers, Nicholas and Celestine, went to Texas in 1852, but Father Celestine died the next year. Father Nicholas served as a pastor for many years. Their brother Lewis came later and settled in Castroville. Because of her brothers, Sister St. Andrew was predisposed for ministry in Texas when Bishop Dubuis asked for teaching sisters. Sister St. Andrew volunteered as did Sister Alphonse Boegler. Mother Constantine designated Sister St. Andrew the superior and gave her a departing charge "to found everywhere rural schools for girls."

Bishop Dubuis returned to the United States with 28 missionaries. He remained in Baltimore while the two Sisters of Divine Providence, four Ursulines, three Sisters of the Incarnate Word (just founded), and 19 priests and seminarians went on to Texas. The bishop had returned from quite a successful begging trip.

On their arrival in Galveston on October 25, 1866, recruit Caroline Spann Rice greeted the two Sisters of Divine Providence and welcomed them to the United States. The three went to Austin, where Father Nicholas Feltin was preparing a convent. Two years later, nine sisters were operating schools in Austin, Corpus Christi, and Castroville. When Holy Cross sisters (1920) came to Austin in 1874, the two remaining Divine Providence sisters in Austin left, joining other orders. One was Sister Caroline Spann Rice, the first American-born member of the Sisters of Divine Providence.

Membership grew under the leadership of Mother St. Andrew. During the 20 years following her arrival, the congregation increased to 195 sisters, who staffed 22 schools. Much of the increase resulted from her three recruiting trips to Europe where she secured reinforcements from the motherhouse in St. Jean-de-Bassel and candidates in Alsace, the Rhineland, and Ireland. Some of the increase came from Texas girls who were sometimes hastily inducted and not properly formed for religious life due to the intense pressure for sister-teachers. This fact later became a factor in Mother St. Andrew's "troubles."[7]

Bishop Dubuis died in 1881. The Vatican split Texas into two dioceses and designated French-born Jean Claude Neraz the Bishop of San Antonio. The Sisters of Divine Providence were now part of his diocese. His desire to reclassify the Divine Providence community from a branch of the motherhouse in France to a diocesan community did not become apparent until 1883.

While on a visit to France, Bishop Neraz called on the motherhouse and spoke with Mother Constantine, the superior-general. She commented on the difficulty of communication with the community in far off Texas. Bishop Neraz used this remark as justification for separating the group from the motherhouse of St. Jean-de-Bassel. When he returned to Texas, he announced that the community was no longer a branch of the European house but a diocesan congregation. This decision violated the sense of the agreement made between Mother St. Andrew and Bishop Dubuis. It was entirely contrary to the constitution she brought from St. Jean-de-Bassel in 1866 that had governed the conduct of the congregation ever since. Meanwhile the motherhouse in Europe had no inkling that such a move was underway and continued furnishing reinforcements to its Texan "branch."[8]

The scene was set for a contest between a bishop and a mother-superior-foundress. Situations, mishaps, and misunderstandings put Mother St. Andrew at a disadvantage in this unequal struggle. There was an intense demand for more schools and the Sisters of Divine Providence strained to supply teachers. Mother St. Andrew as superior of the congregation had full authority over teacher assignments, curriculum, and school administration. On the other hand, pastors felt they had full authority over what transpired in schools in their parishes. Mother St. Andrew's control over teacher assignments sometimes created friction between her and priests — frictions that escalated over the years.

A minor spat between two blood sisters, both Sisters of Divine Providence stationed at St. Joseph's in San Antonio, got out of hand and created considerable embarrassment for Father Feltin and Mother St. Andrew. While home for a visit, the Koehler sisters got into a heated dispute. Returning to the convent, Sister Angela persuaded Mother St. Andrew to transfer Sister Virginia away from Father Feltin's parish where she was also choir director. Father Feltin objected to the transfer. Mr. Koehler, the sisters' father, got involved and sided with Sister Angela. He accused Father Feltin of attempting to poison him and filed charges. Newspapers in San Antonio printed the story and accused Mother St. Andrew of having caused her brother Nicholas' arrest. Although the court dismissed the charges for lack of evidence and the newspapers retracted their accusations against Mother St. Andrew, the harm to her reputation had already been done.

In another incident, a priest named Father Gapes started a controversy because of his visits to the sisters stationed in New Braunfels, supposedly because of a certain Sister Christine. Mother St. Andrew discussed the matter with several sisters and wrote a letter to the New Braunfels superior, who disclosed its contents, stoking the fires of gossip. Local priests became incensed when they heard the story. The upshot was a letter to Bishop Neraz from a Father Pefferkorn, demanding the deposition of Mother St. Andrew. He claimed the priests' honor had been challenged by her. It listed Father Feltin's arrest and stated that Father Gapes had taken the "shortest way out" — he had abandoned the priesthood. The letter also accused Mother St. Andrew of warning her sisters "to beware of all priests" in her instructions.

The bishop called for a trial. Two of the four priests sitting in judgment were among those she had supposedly harmed — a stacked deck. Mother St. Andrew denied all the charges except her comments about the frequent visits of Father Gapes to the convent and an offhand remark she had made to the effect that she was not afraid of any trial, even by the pope. Their report to the bishop was lengthy but clearly demanded her removal. It also included a threat by the priests to leave the diocese if this was not done.

Bishop Neraz deposed Mother St. Andrew and called for the election of a new superior. Nevertheless, the sisters voted for her. When Bishop Neraz threatened to appoint the new superior, Mother St. Andrew withdrew and urged them to vote for Sister Florence Walter, elected on the next ballot.

Sister Florence was in France at the time recruiting 20 candidates. When she arrived back in San Antonio, Bishop Neraz and Father Pefferkorn greeted her with the news of her new position. Since Bishop Neraz had imposed the stricture that Mother St. Andrew could not be superior of a school or mission convent, she went to Galveston. Another sister, Sister Arsene, left Castroville without permission and joined her.

Mother St. Andrew contacted Bishop Nicholas A. Gallagher of the Galveston diocese, offering to establish a new congregation of the Sisters of Divine Providence. He agreed and stipulated the new motherhouse be located in Galveston. Mother St. Andrew wrote Bishop Neraz seeking the approval that was necessary under canon law. Instead of answering her, he wrote to his fellow bishop. Bishop Gallagher then sent for Mother St. Andrew, revoked his earlier approval, and counseled her to submit to Bishop Neraz.

At this point, Mother St. Andrew and Sister Arsene left for California with the objective of establishing a branch of the congregation in the Los Angeles diocese. She remained a few days and returned to Texas to seek Bishop Neraz's approval. He refused once again, directed her to remain in the Castroville convent, and ordered her to await the decisions of Mother Florence and her council. He even denied Holy Communion to Mother St. Andrew until such time as she agreed in writing to submit to her superiors and return money and articles she had taken to California.[9] She met all the conditions and was posted to Clarksville as a classroom teacher.

In March 1887, Mother St. Andrew once again departed for California without permission. The pastor in Anaheim was delighted and looked forward to the establishment of a parochial school with sister-teachers. Mother Florence, ever solicitous for Mother St. Andrew, gave Sister Arsene permission to join her. When Bishop Neraz learned her whereabouts, he wrote the vicar-general of Los Angeles and informed him of Mother St. Andrew's status. Bishop Gallagher also condemned her. These letters killed any prospect of her founding a community and she was forced to leave. Before returning to Texas, she pleaded for an interview in a long letter to Bishop Neraz. He refused and directed Mother Florence to send her away from the convent.

She moved in with her brother, Lewis, and his family in Castroville. His wife died the next year, leaving seven motherless children. Mother St. Andrew moved the family to San Jose, California, and opened a grocery store to support them since Lewis had an alcohol problem and did not seem able to hold a job. She operated the store for 10 years and ensured that the children were educated and learned a trade. When the oldest, Mary, became a schoolteacher and could support the younger children, Mother St. Andrew

Sisters of Divine Providence, Our Lady of the Lake Convent, San Antonio, Texas (c. 1942).
Courtesy Gonzaga University

took steps to return to Texas since Bishop Neraz had died in 1894 and Father Pefferkorn had returned to Europe.

Mother St. Andrew wrote a letter to Mother Florence in 1900 asking permission to rejoin her order. Mother Florence read it to the entire congregation gathered at the motherhouse for summer retreat. With tears all around, the sisters unanimously voted for her return. The diocesan administrator approved and word was sent to Mother St. Andrew to "come home."

On October 27, 1900, Mother St. Andrew Feltin pulled her old habit from her trunk and put it on before pronouncing vows for the second time. She was 70 years old. She lived five more happy years, holding a venerated place in the Castroville convent. On hearing that she had returned, many of her old friends came to visit. Mother Florence took her to see the new motherhouse at Our Lady of the Lake in San Antonio.

When she died in 1905, the **Sisters of Divine Providence of San Antonio, Texas (CDP-1010)** numbered 250 members and were operating 52 schools. The congregation continued to grow and expanded its ministries to numerous dioceses in the United States, Brazil, and Mexico. Our Lady of the Lake University was a testimonial to the community that owes its existence to Mother St. Andrew. Sister Joseph Neeb, a close friend of Mother St. Andrew, wrote the following description about her:

> *If a life could voice the blessedness of sacrifice, it would be that of Mother St. Andrew. Through what trials, hardships, persecutions, sorrows and sufferings had she not passed, from the first days of the foundation of the Congregation in Texas until the hour in which she was to be most sorely tried. But in a moment of weak-*

> *ness she determined to cast aside the crosses that seemed too heavy for her to bear; and in that hour of temptation she left the Congregation that for so many years had been so dear to her heart, a step for which, as she often said in her later years, each night of her long exile from her own she wet her pillow with bitter tears of regret.*[10]

Very few congregations have had such a difficult beginning, and seldom have such tragic struggles produced such beneficial results. Sister/bishop, sister/priest, and sister/sister conflicts might well have destroyed a lesser group of women in their efforts to persevere in their vocations and ministry. The Sisters of Divine Providence of Texas and their German-American foundress, Mother St. Andrew, deserve special recognition for victory over adversity.

Mothers Alexia and Alfons

Presently, the largest of the German-founded orders from this era, the **School Sisters of St. Francis (OSF-1680)** was founded in New Cassel (now Campbellsport), Wisconsin, by three adventurous women. They were Francesca Hoell (Mother Alexia), Paulina Schmid (Mother Alfons), and Helena Seiter (Sister Clara). Their story opens as the *Koeln* sailed from Bremen in August 1873. In fear of the authorities and the May Laws, the Franciscans' bishop had instructed the sisters in Schwarzach to disband and return home, join another order, remain as laywomen to care for their orphans, or seek a new life elsewhere. Three Franciscans elected to try America. Their shipboard companions included 40 **Sisters of the Most Precious Blood (CCPS-3270)** who were also emigrating to the United States. This group of Precious Blood sisters was the last of their community to leave Gurtweil, Germany. They earlier sent Mother Albertine Bogg to Belle Prairie, Illinois in 1870 to establish an American foundation, and now left Germany to join her. The three Franciscans spoke not a word of English, had no recommendations and possessed only $70. The Immigration Service counted them among the 460,000 arrivals of 1873 — an average of 8,846 per week. Sister Alfons had a brother in Philadelphia, so the three spent the last of their $70 for train tickets. Fortunately the brother could provide shelter and food. The three sisters quickly put their sewing skills to work making vestments that quickly sold. Receiving no encouragement for a community in Philadelphia or Baltimore, they determined to try Chicago, a German center like Milwaukee, St. Louis, and Cincinnati.[11]

Sister Alexia had an uncle and aunt in Chicago, so once again they prevailed on relatives for food and shelter. They immediately began to sew vestments and to teach lace work to local girls. Meanwhile, they sought an opening for their vocations. After several disappointments they received two invitations the same day, one from Bishop Louis M. Fink in Leavenworth, Kansas, and the other from Bishop Michael Heiss in La Crosse, Wisconsin. They were inclined to go to Leavenworth, but a priest who was befriending them had a dream the night before the two invitations arrived. In it, St. Joseph appeared and said: "Tell the Sisters that I want them to be in Wisconsin. I have already made preparations for them and everything will be well." That settled the issue.

Before going to La Crosse, they stayed with the School Sisters of Notre Dame in Milwaukee. Established in 1847, this German-founded order now numbered 600 sisters and was operating 126 schools. There Mother Caroline Friess was kind and supportive. In La Crosse, however, the three Franciscan sisters found conditions unsatisfactory. Since there were already German Franciscan sisters there, they concluded that St. Joseph had another location in mind. Without enough money for fare back to Milwaukee but trusting in God, they bought tickets for as far as it would go. A kind conductor covered the balance and paid their carriage fare to the School Sisters' convent. For the next three months, the sisters studied English and awaited another call. It came from Father Anton Michels, a 32-year-old German priest from Treves, Germany, now the pastor of St. Matthew in New Cassel, a flourishing parish which was without a parochial school because Mother Caroline had no sisters to spare.

Awaiting the three Franciscans was a convent in an unfurnished building containing exactly one chair. The first night, they ate while kneeling, using a board found in the yard for a table. They slept on the floor. After Father Michels informed parishioners the next day, a stove, furniture, food, and kitchen utensils arrived. On their first Sunday in New Cassel, the three sisters renewed their vows after Mass before Father Michels. Once again they were proper religious although without a rule or recognized order.

Trusting in God and St. Joseph, Mother Alexia did not concentrate on preparing the schoolroom connected to the convent for fall classes; instead she contracted with John Fellenz for the erection of a new school for $10,950 despite the fact that she had no money. After recovering from shock, Father Michels purchased 10 acres on a lovely hill at the edge of town for $500. Help came from many sources. Parishioners pitched in, hauling bricks and lumber in wagons while others helped dig foundations and unloaded the wagons. The sisters sewed furiously at night and begged during the day. The school opened that fall with 80 students in the first building. The sisters taught alternately in German and English and two lay teachers taught some classes. Construction continued into the winter. The sisters moved into the still unfinished school/convent after Christmas. At this point Mother Alexia unveiled her next objective. With future vocations in mind, she would conduct a boarding school in addition to the parish school. Wisely, she dedicated the new building to St. Joseph. She needed all the help she could get.

The boarding school opened in January 1875 with 30 students. Many came from Chicago, the result of a recruiting trip by Sister Alfons. The curriculum was solid but not sophisticated. The academy's reputation spread and students came from Milwaukee, Chicago, and small towns in Wisconsin. A young teacher, Susanna Loewel became the first American postulant. When Mother Alexia needed help in supplying sisters for two schools, it came from the original source — Germany. A priest friend wrote from Buehl that he knew of several young women anxious to join a community such as theirs in New Cassel. Thereupon Mother Alfons went to Germany and returned with five postulants. This brought the infant community up to 11 members: three professed sisters, three novices, and five postulants. Four more postulants joined almost immediately, raising the total to 15.

School Sisters of St. Francis, Bellevue, Pennsylvania (c. 1942).

Courtesy Gonzaga University

Mother Alexia was a superb teacher and a sensitive novice-mistress who placed great stress on formation for religious life. While insisting on obedience and humility, she explained the meaning and sublimity of religious life, encouraging by word and example the open expression of joy and cheerfulness. Franciscan poverty dominated their lives and she taught its meaning and how to treasure it. Mother Alexia's formation of these first sisters in the new order was copied and repeated over the years by novice-mistresses, explaining in large measure the fantastic growth and stability of this congregation.

Mother Alexia made her second recruiting trip to Germany in 1879. She left New Cassel by train, without Atlantic passage money. In New York, she stayed at St. Mary's Hospital in Hoboken, operated by the Franciscan Sisters of the Poor. When a sister asked how she would secure a ticket to Europe, Mother Alexia answered that St. Jude would take care of it. The Poor Franciscan who had to haul supplies daily to the hospital with a hand cart replied, "If you can get a pass, maybe St. Jude can get me a horse."

The story goes that after Mother Alexia visited the manager of the North-German Lloyd Steamship Company the next day and returned with a round-trip pass, the Poor Franciscan decided to put St. Jude to the test and also visited the manager. When she asked for a horse, he demanded, "And I suppose you want a cart too?"

"Oh, yes, if you have one to give."

It so happened that the company was phasing out horse-drawn carts at this time and the Poor Franciscan sister returned gleefully with both a horse and a cart. St. Jude had passed the tests with flying colors.

Mother Alexia returned from Germany with 23 postulants. Six more came in 1880 and Sister Alfons went on a successful hunt in 1881. Sadly, that year was also marked by the death of the humble self-effacing Sister Clara. Sister Theresa made recruiting journeys in 1882, 1884, and 1889. Ten years after the first postulant was received in 1875, the order numbered 114 professed sisters, 18 novices, and 10 postulants. However, 13 sisters had died, including Sister Clara. Polish surnames now mingled with German names.

As the numbers of schools and sisters grew, Mother Alexia determined that a new larger motherhouse was needed and in a larger city. After looking over Milwaukee and Kenosha, she decided on a third city, Winona, because of its beauty and similarity to a Rhine River town. She had no inkling that the taste of honey would turn to gall.

Based on the invitation of Bishop Thomas Grace of St. Paul, Mother Alexia made a bold decision to build. She bought an 11-acre tract of land for $5,850 and contracted for a large two-story convent with a chapel and basement. The dedication ceremony on March 15, 1885, was long remembered. Bishop John Ireland, the new Bishop of St. Paul, replacing Bishop Grace, attended. After the dedication the party went to the dining room for a banquet. Mother Alexia's dinner partner, the "consecrated blizzard of the Northwest," startled her.

Bishop Ireland, the famed Americanist, was highly intelligent, an accomplished orator and expert financier, who would later become an archbishop.[12] He was also blunt, tactless, and thought nothing of riding roughshod over those who opposed his positions. German-American Catholics of this era considered him their archenemy. Polish, Ukrainian, and other ethnic Catholic groups reached the same conclusions in the 1890's. At the banquet, Bishop Ireland plied Mother Alexia with searching questions. Were the postulants from Minnesota? From Germany? What training did the sisters receive? Where were the sisters teaching? Were these predominantly German-speaking parishes? Did Mother Alexia realize how important it was for the Church in America to be American, not foreign? Were the sisters certified teachers? As Mother Alexia answered each question she became increasingly disturbed by their trend. Even so, she was not prepared for the shock of the bishop's final statements. His ultimatum was that the motherhouse could only be established in his diocese provided no further postulants be accepted from Europe, no sister be sent to teach until certified, and that the community would be "diocesan." At that moment the brand new Winona building became an academy, not a motherhouse.

Mother Alexia found these stipulations intolerable and directly opposed to her view of a community unlimited by geography. She sold the boarding school in Winona to the Sisters of St. Joseph (3840) for a hospital, which was not a success. The postulants in Winona returned to New Cassel riding in a freight car for lack of fare money. As most spirited young girls would, they considered this ride a lark and sang, joked, and smiled at the passing countryside. Meanwhile, Mother Alexia looked for a new location for the motherhouse. Milwaukee, passed over earlier, now became the best choice.

Tragedy struck the Milwaukee motherhouse shortly after it opened in 1890 when a fire destroyed the entire structure. Sister Blanka, trapped on the fourth floor, jumped and died from her injuries. After the tears and funeral, Mother Alexia began anew. Some sisters moved back to the extremely crowded conditions in New Cassel, while sisters in Milwaukee took up full-time serious begging. This assignment was particularly hard on the younger sisters who felt humiliated when people slammed doors and insulted them. This disappointment was offset by the extreme generosity of working people and help from the business community. Frugal living went so far that novices whitewashed their black shoes for the vow-taking ceremony rather than buy white ones to match their bridal dresses. These efforts and the insurance money enabled Mother Alexia to pay for a new motherhouse, opened in 1891.

The congregation continued to grow. In 1895 it numbered 429 members with 300 sisters teaching in 65 schools. By 1905 it had grown to 540 sisters staffing 98 parochial schools in a number of states. Mother Alexia resigned as superior-general in 1907 and returned to Germany to found a province, a reversal of the usual procedure. Mother Alfons became the new superior and held the post until her death. After encountering difficulties in Germany, Mother Alexia established the European province in Luxembourg. To earn money, the community got into the sanitarium business in the United States and Europe, with mixed results.

Sisters from the German province sent missionaries to the Caroline Islands in 1906 where they ministered until 1918. The Japanese military seized the islands from Germany during World War I, treated the sisters brutally, and drove them out.

Before Mother Alexia died in 1918, she attempted to make a foundation in Romania that fortunately was canceled at the last moment. She established convent/sanitariums in Erlenbad, Strasbourg, and San Remo (Italy). Mother Alfons died in 1929. Foundresses of a great Franciscan order, these two women were truly remarkable. America can be grateful for an unexpected bonus from *Kulturkampf.*[13]

Valiant Women — From Switzerland to Oregon

In March 1887, in the small rural community of Sublimity, Oregon, Archbishop William Gross received the vows of five young German-speaking women and accepted five others as novices, recognizing them as Sisters of the Most Precious Blood. The story of how these young women came to this moment is one of the most bizarre and heroic accounts in the annals of American sisters.

The Sisters of the Precious Blood arrived in Ohio from Switzerland in 1844. Father Francis de Sales Brunner, founder of a branch of the Precious Blood order, brought his entire community, male and female. The sisters of this order consider his mother to be their foundress. The section of Ohio assigned to them for ministry had been settled by German-speaking farmers. The German-speaking Swiss sisters were basically rural and not highly educated.

Joseph Albrecht, a strange, driven man and well-to-do farmer was an admirer and benefactor of Father Brunner back in Switzerland, and Joseph's family determined to join Father Brunner in religious life. Joseph's wife and daughter joined the female order and came to Ohio with Father Brunner. However, Joseph dallied about fulfilling his promise to become a priest, finally joining the group in Ohio in 1848 where he was ordained the next year with practically no training.[14] Bishop Rappe of Cleveland failed to verify proper preparation, but quickly recognized this folly and revised the regulations and qualifications for ordination. For the next 16 years, Joseph Albrecht filled his role as priest with mixed results.

Albrecht was a powerful preacher, had a magnetic personality, was generous with his money, and developed a strong following among the local

German families. He was, however, contentious and difficult with his superiors and fellow priests. Because of some bad experiences in Switzerland, he held all bishops in disdain. His antagonism resulted in numerous disputes and his demotion to a small parish after he had built and managed a large monastery. As the years went by, he became progressively more ill-tempered and rebellious.

Father Albrecht heard about a successful colony in Wisconsin much like a modern-day "commune" that a Father Ochwald established for Catholic families. Father Brunner was dead (1859), and Joseph's daughter had died shortly after arriving in Ohio. When his wife, Mother Mary Ann, died in 1864, he lost his last emotional tie to the Precious Blood Society. He decided that with his money and following he could found a colony like Father Ochwald's.

An incident in 1866 triggered the final break. One Sunday he became infuriated when some young girls appeared at Mass wearing the latest fad — hoop skirts and ribbons in their hair. He ordered them out. When they reappeared in church for evening services still wearing the "immodest" attire, he drove them out with a switch. This action split the parish and caused the archbishop to order an apology — a directive Albrecht ignored.

In October 1866, Albrecht left Ohio with 14 sisters, six brothers (one defected in Chicago), and five large families. Six of the sisters had taken vows and considered Father Joseph to be their lawful superior. The other eight were postulants, members of the families who left. Another girl, eight-year-old Emma Bleily, left her family and joined the group at the moment of departure because she could not bear to be separated from her closest friend, Julia Boedigheimer. The entire community — priest, brothers, sisters, and families — settled in the backwoods of Minnesota at Rush Lake near Otter Trail. The archbishop in Ohio revoked Albrecht's priestly authority and the bishop in Minnesota excommunicated Albrecht when he rebuffed overtures for restoration of his good offices and regularization of his community.

During the 20 Minnesota years, the sisters lived in a log cabin convent. Albrecht forbade contact outside their community. Under the guidance of the six vowed sisters the small community led what they considered a proper religious life.

Joseph Albrecht died in 1884 still at odds with ecclesiastical authorities. His will gave all his property and complete authority to three "trustees," the heads of the families. The trustees decided to leave Minnesota, escape "persecution" and go to Oregon where good land was cheap. When the time came to leave, the trustees removed Albrecht's coffin from its crypt, placing it in a packing crate. Loading all their possessions in three boxcars, the community left for Oregon, Albrecht's coffin concealed in its crate in one of the boxcars. The party consisted of 79 people, two of the original Ohio vowed sisters (four had died), 14 teenage aspirants, four brothers, and the families. The trustees exercised dictatorial control.

Bishop Martin Marty, the famed Benedictine missionary bishop, boarded the train in Montana. Hearing there were sisters aboard, he approached them asking for help for his pioneer vicariate. However, the trustees prevented further contact. In Montana, the summer heat alerted railroad workers to Albrecht's odor. It cost the trustees $2,000 in bribes to continue with the coffin aboard. In Portland, Oregon, the trustees prevented the sisters from visiting a nearby Catholic church. However, Father Dominic Faber spotted the sisters in the train station, spoke to them, and promised a later visit. The party moved on to Jordan in Lynn County.

A crude structure became the sisters' convent and practically their prison. Albrecht's coffin, placed across the rafters, provided overhead decoration. No contact with outsiders was permitted. As promised, Father Faber appeared one day and was shocked — no Mass, no sacraments, and no priest to minister to the sisters. The trustees forcibly took him to the train station and threatened dire harm if he should ever return. Emma Bleily (the eight-year-old runaway) protested and later wrote the following description of the sisters' lives:

> *The trustees, each of whom had one or more daughters among the girls, now came to regard themselves as their superiors. When the girls insisted on receiving the sacraments, telling the men that the catechism stated that they must make their Easter duty, one of the trustees gave them a lecture. He said that St. Paul stated that they must be governed by the spirit as the letter killeth; that if they loved God and obeyed them, they would be alright. They obeyed but sent many prayers to heaven for the consolation of religion, Mass, Holy Communion and the Blessed Sacrament. The girls knew little about religious life. None of them had ever been confirmed, but they did desire with their whole souls to serve and to love God alone. To appreciate the attitude of the girls towards the trustees it must be remembered that the trustees, besides being the fathers of a greater number of the girls, had been appointed by Father Joseph as their guardians. Also, the girls had to look to the trustees for their support since they had the control and management of their property.*[15]

When yet another priest visited and said Mass, the infuriated trustees increased the sisters' labors on the farm, working them like slaves. About this time another of the vowed Ohio sisters died without benefit of the last sacraments. The trustees ignored her pitiful pleas for a priest.

Matters came to a head when Prior Adelhelm Odermatt, superior of the local Benedictine monastery, and Father Werner Ruttiman, a Benedictine priest, appeared at Jordan with fire in their eyes. They even intimidated the trustees. The priests interviewed the girls one at a time and found all in good faith and wishing to serve God as religious. Thereupon they allowed each one to sign the following statement:

> *We the undersigned do solemnly swear to uphold our allegiance to the Roman Catholic Church, and to its representatives on earth. We also promise to become members of a new religious congregation, subject to the Metropolitan of Oregon City, His Excellency Archbishop Gross. No one has forced this statement on us. With our own free will, we have signed it and have severed all connections with the trustees of Jordan. Signed. . . .*[16]

When Emma Bleily signed, Prior Adelhelm recognized her name and asked if she were related to the Bleily family in Missouri. She stated her uncle had built a Benedictine monastery in Clyde. This clue put her in touch with the mother she had not seen or heard from since running away in Ohio.

The scene following this interview was dramatic and somewhat poignant. The priests summoned the trustees who came smiling, sure of their authority. Prior Adelhelm read the signed statement and then called upon those sisters who wished to do the archbishop's work to stand. All rose. Then each trustee in turn demanded that his daughter come with him. When Anton Bender's daughter refused, Prior Adelhelm said she was of age and could not be forced. Christof Sibernagel's daughters also refused. However, his youngest daughter, Matilda, was not of age and was afraid of her father. Prior Adelhelm arranged for her to hide with a Catholic family and sent for her later. The third trustee, Victor Eifert, had three daughters in the group and only the underage Elizabeth obeyed her father. At the last moment, five of the girls lost their nerve and changed their minds. Immediately afterwards, eight sisters climbed into wagons and went to the Benedictine monastery, where they were kindly received and placed under the supervision and care of two Benedictine nuns.

In preparation for becoming proper Catholic religious, the girls engaged in the ancient tradition of choosing new names. Emma Bleily, soon to be designated superior, became Sister Mary Wilhelmina. Some priests in the diocese opposed these girls' becoming a new order and insisted that they join established communities. Joseph Albrecht's odor had filtered into the Oregon clergy, but the archbishop kept his promise contained in the oath the girls had taken at Jordan.

After a period of orientation and training for proper religious life, 10 sisters (Matilda Sibernagel rejoined the group and a postulant from Sublimity joined) were formally inducted by Archbishop Gross, who received their vows as Sisters of the Most Precious Blood. They set up in Sublimity and opened a bilingual school, teaching in German and English. Sister Clara was the only remaining member of the Precious Blood sisters in Ohio, although they all considered themselves members of that society. In 1905, for complex reasons including a lack of formal affiliation with the Precious Blood Society, Archbishop Christie (Gross had died) redesignated them **Sisters of St. Mary of Oregon (SSMO-3960)** and gave them a new rule. The order grew, opened an orphanage in Beaverton, sent missionaries to Peru, and taught in rural schools among the German-speaking farm families. Sisters of St. Mary of Oregon trace their lineage back to "Mudder" Brunner in Switzerland, to Ohio, to Minnesota, and finally to Oregon.

In view of their lives of isolation under Joseph Albrecht and then near-slavery under the trustees, it is remarkable that they persevered in vocations to religious life. These seemingly simple girls, only mildly educated and deprived of church ministrations, were indeed valiant women.

Mother Alfred Moes (1828-1899)

When a devastating tornado struck Rochester, Minnesota, in 1883 killing 31 people, injuring hundreds, and destroying much of the town, Franciscan sisters aided the injured and homeless. Mother Alfred Moes, foundress and mother-superior of the **Sisters of the Third Order Regular of St. Francis of the Congregation of Our Lady of Lourdes (OSF-1720)**, was concerned that Rochester had no hospital. She convinced Dr. William W. Mayo (1819-1911) of the need and he agreed to serve as house physician if she built the hospital. With great effort and sacrifice by her community, Mother Alfred raised $20,000 and opened St. Mary's Hospital in 1889. Dr. Mayo and his two physician sons treated the patients. Mother Alfred added two wings to the hospital during the next 10 years as the fame of the Mayo brothers and their clinic spread across Minnesota and beyond. Since then, St. Mary's Hospital and the Mayo Clinic have grown together, and today Rochester is one of the best known medical centers in the world.

Marie Catherine Moes was born in Remich, Luxembourg, one of 10 children. She and her sister Catherine[17] emigrated to the United States in 1851 with the intention of joining a religious community. They spoke both German and French and joined the German-oriented School Sisters of Notre Dame in Milwaukee and quickly learned English. Records are unclear as to their intention to remain permanently in this community as neither pronounced vows. They left and almost immediately joined the Congregation of the Sisters of the Holy Cross in Notre Dame, Indiana. Here they became permanent members, pronounced vows, and took the religious names of Mary Alfred and Mary Barbara.

During the next eight years, the Moes sisters taught in parochial schools. While she was the school principal in LaPorte, Indiana, Sister Alfred got involved in local ethnic tensions and a priest wrote Bishop John Henry Luers complaining about her. Sister Alfred in turn wrote the bishop a furious letter defending her conduct and honor. The upshot was her transfer to another school as punishment for "disobedience." In 1863, she wrote Father Pamfilo da Magliano, founder of the Franciscan Sisters of Allegany, New York, indicating that she, her sister, and two other Holy Cross sisters wished to join the Franciscans. He authorized their initiating a new Franciscan community in Illinois. Again, the records are unclear as to exactly why and how the Moes sisters severed relations with the Holy Cross community.[18] In any event, they went to Joliet in 1865 and founded the **Congregation of the Third Order of St. Francis of Mary Immaculate, Joliet, Illinois (OSF-1710)**, the first Franciscan community in Illinois. Mother Alfred was now a foundress. The community prospered and within 11 years had 116 members who taught in schools in Illinois, Ohio, Missouri, Wisconsin, and Tennessee.[19] Mother Alfred was a good businesswoman unafraid to invest in property and take risks in building.

At the time of the foundation, Bishop James Duggan was ordinary of the Chicago diocese and was disposed to leave oversight of the Franciscan sisters to Franciscan friars. In 1870, he was succeeded by Bishop Thomas Foley, a prelate highly jealous of his prerogatives and authority, with strong ideas about oversight. Mother Alfred and the new bishop crossed swords almost immediately over trivial matters. Bishop Foley ordered the election of a new superior in 1876 and prohibited Mother Alfred's reelection, although she had founded the community and had supervised it for 11 years. The shocked sisters elected Mother Alberta, a sister unaccustomed to administration and financial management. She leaned heavily on Mother Alfred, who continued to administer the congregation from her position as assistant to the superior while Mother Alberta left the motherhouse and returned to her convent in Chicago. When Bishop Foley heard of this arrangement, he was furious and ordered Mother Alberta to stay in Joliet and personally manage the community. Tensions ran high throughout the congregation as a result of these unhappy events.

Mother Alfred led a group of sisters to Minnesota about this time in response to an appeal for sisters to found a girls' academy and parochial schools. This move extricated her from the uncomfortable situation in Joliet where the sisters had split loyalties. She founded schools in Owatonna and Rochester. Meanwhile, after Mother Alberta's one-year tenure as superior ended, the sisters elected Mother Alfred to her old position. This election was conducted secretly for fear of Bishop Foley's ire. When he learned of it, he arbitrarily appointed Sister Francis Shanahan superior and ordered that no more sisters be sent to Minnesota and that no financial assistance be given those missions despite earlier commitments. When a dispute arose over title to the property purchased in Minnesota, Bishop Foley forbade Mother Alfred and the sisters in Minnesota to return to Joliet and ordered a break in contact between the two groups. Mother Alfred then organized a new Franciscan congregation with 24 sisters from the Joliet community. Sister Barbara also left the Joliet community that she loved dearly to join Mother Alfred. This new community grew rapidly and by 1889 had 112 members. Mother Alfred sent sisters to open schools in Ohio and Kentucky as well as in Minnesota.

The sisters lived frugally to help finance Mother Alfred's projects, including St. Mary's Hospital. When some discontented sisters complained to Archbishop Ireland of St. Paul, he ordered a new election for superior, declaring Mother Alfred ineligible. When all the sisters voted for her anyway, he appointed Sister Matilda Wagner. In later years, Archbishop Ireland admitted that he had done an injustice to Mother Alfred Moes.

Mother Alfred retired in 1890 and lived with Sister Barbara in Ironton, Ohio. When Sister Barbara died in 1895, Mother Alfred moved into the convent of the sisters teaching in St. Paul. Here she led a quiet, prayerful, and contemplative life in the order she founded. She visited the Joliet community and had a joyful reunion with the charter members who had always retained their love for her. That community is proud to claim Mother Alfred Moes as foundress. Although twice victimized by high-handed bishops, she never complained and constantly offered prayers for anyone she might have offended. Builder and foundress of two congregations and a member of two others, Mother Alfred Moes led an unusual life. When she died in 1899 at the age of 71, she left two Franciscan congregations and a world-renowned medical center as her memorials — a remarkable woman religious in an age of remarkable women religious.[20]

Sisters of Notre Dame (SND-2990)

In 1850 an order was founded in Germany beginning with the friendship of two young women, Aldegonda Wolbring and Lisette Kühling. Trained by the renowned educator Bernard Overberg, Aldegonda and Lisette began teaching in Coesfeld, Germany. Taking in a small group of orphans, the two women resolved to devote their lives to God in teaching and caring for children. Thus began the Sisters of Notre Dame. From 1850 to 1855 three sisters from Amersfoort, Holland introduced the steadily growing community in Coesfeld into the spirit and rule of the Amersfoort congregation as they had received it from the Sisters of Notre Dame de Namur, founded by St. Julie Billiart.

The pressures of *Kulturkampf* in 19th-century Germany forced the sisters to expand to other continents. In 1847, Mother-Superior Mary Chrysostom Heck and Sister Mary Aloysia (Aldegonda Wolbring) led founding sisters to the United States. Though they were invited by Covington's Bishop Augustus Toebbe, brother to one of the order's members, the sisters first settled in Cleveland, Ohio. There, as well as in Covington, Kentucky, Toledo, Ohio, and California, they labored in schools, orphanages, and hospitals, though their primary apostolate is in education. Over the next 10 years some 200 members came from Germany. Mother Chrysostom later reestablished the generalate in Mülhausen, Germany; in 1946, it was transferred to Rome. The Sisters of Notre Dame are now serving in 12 countries.

In 1883, the German government admitted the failure of *Kulturkampf*, restored diplomatic relations with the Vatican, began the process of rescinding the May Laws, and in 1886 permitted exiled women religious to return if they wished. German Catholicity enjoyed a fresh burst of vitality.

These selected accounts of immigrant German foundations indicate the profound effects of *Kulturkampf* on American women religious orders. The number of German-American communities and their overall memberships surged. Like most orders in their American beginnings, they experienced adversities but persevered. Thus Prince Otto von Bismarck unintentionally strengthened the Catholic Church in both Germany and the United States — often the proverbial result of persecution and suffering.

Other Foundations

During this quarter-century, American, Canadian and non-German European foundresses were also active. The sources of these foundations include: the United States with 17, France and Canada each with 11, Italy with seven, Ireland, England, and Switzerland each with two, Spain, Poland, and Holland each with one (see Appendix B for the listings).

As *Kulturkampf* phased out in Germany during the 1880's, France took a decidedly anticlerical turn. Freemasons and agnostic forces assumed control of the Third Republic following France's defeat in the Franco-Prussian War of 1870. The new government expelled the Jesuits — always the first to go — and initiated suppressive steps against the Church, including seizure of sisters' properties. The government revoked documents in 1880 that had been recognized as certificates of teachers' competence and ruled that all teachers had to be French citizens. It opened normal schools and banned the establishment of new religious orders. The final blow fell in 1904 when religious were banned from teaching altogether. These factors account for the

11 immigrant orders at a time when French immigration was a mere trickle. Once again, America profited from persecution and tragedies in Europe.

Permanent Poor Clares

Twice we have seen Poor Clares from Europe come and go. This time they came from Italy and Germany, this time they were led by countesses, and this time they put down permanent roots. Today 24 Poor Clare monasteries are located in 18 different states.

In 1873, Pope Pius IX directed two Poor Clare nuns, blood sisters from a noble family, to go to the United States and establish the Poor Clare order. The nuns were Mothers Maria Maddalena (Countess Annetta Bentivoglio) and Maria Constance (Constanza Bentivoglio). After landing in New York in 1875, they spent almost a year in a frustrating effort to secure approbation for a foundation. Archbishop Corrigan treated them coldly. Mother Maddalena recorded his reception:[21]

> *He would not receive us because our form of life was against the spirit of the country....*[22]

The Drexel family, however, (see Chapter 8) and Archbishop James F. Wood in Philadelphia were kind and supportive. The latter even provided a house, but then abruptly changed his mind and withdrew permission for a Poor Clare foundation. His reasons are obscure, but it seems that the antipathy towards contemplatives by his clergy and previous misconduct by some Italian Franciscan friars swayed him. Then came an invitation from New Orleans from Archbishop Napoleon J. Perche who had wanted a convent of Poor Clares for some years. The nuns' Franciscan superior, German priest Father Gregory Janknecht, was not favorably disposed because of a lack of Franciscan friars in New Orleans, but finally agreed. Conditions in New Orleans proved highly unsatisfactory. After several visits, Father Gregory ordered them to leave and go to Cleveland where the bishop would welcome them. The nuns (now four with two postulants) were saddened at this apparent failure, whereupon Mother Maddalena promised that one day Poor Clares would return to New Orleans. The Poor Clares found the Cleveland house well suited for use as a convent and the local Franciscan community made them feel welcome.

Meanwhile in Germany, *Kulturkampf* was priming another community of Poor Clares to send nuns to the United States. The May Laws made continued functioning of the Dusseldorf community impossible and it moved to Holland. Father Gregory was familiar with this community and invited them to Cleveland. Delighted, Mother-Superior Marie of the Immaculate Conception sent five nuns in 1877. She designated Mother Veronika von Elmendorff (a countess) the superior of the group.

On the night before the arrival of the German nuns, Father Gregory informed the Italian nuns and their American novices that the Colettine Poor Clares from Holland would arrive the next day. They were aware that he had invited them to make a foundation in the United States, but this sudden arrival came as a surprise. Father Gregory indicated that Mother Maddalena would remain as abbess and Mother Constance her first assistant, but he informed the nuns that they would have to conform to the customs and religious devotions of the Colettines, pray together in German, and wear Colettine habits.[23] During the ensuing two months the Italian nuns and their novices attempted to adjust to the German language and different devotional practices. Although the two groups lived in harmony with mutual respect and affection, the strains of differing cultures, languages, and religious customs made continuing life together too difficult. Mother Maddalena determined to make yet another attempt at a permanent foundation, and the Bentivoglio group departed Cleveland.

As always, money was a major obstacle in making a permanent foundation, so Mother Maddalena put her nuns to work begging alms. Mother Constance visited Omaha in this endeavor while the others worked in New York. While still a priest, Bishop James O'Connor of Omaha had encountered the nuns in Philadelphia in that unsuccessful attempt and agreed they could come to Omaha.

John Creighton provided their first home and was their constant benefactor.[24] A strong friendship developed between Mother Maddalena and Mr. Creighton. One day a business friend visiting from Chicago complained that both he and his wife were sad because they had no children. Mr. Creighton told him not to worry further because he would have the Poor Clares pray for them. Several months later, a telegram arrived from Chicago: "Twins! Call off the Poor Clares!"

In 1885, Mother Maddalena sent founding nuns to New Orleans, fulfilling the vow she made in 1875. Today there are nine Poor Clare convents in the United States that grew out of the original Colettine foundation in Cleveland, plus two in Brazil and a community of Byzantine Poor Clare nuns. Fourteen communities arose from Mother Maddalena's Omaha convent. Her cause for beatification is underway.

Opposition to the contemplative way by American clergy and bishops, *Kulturkampf*, Colettines fleeing Germany, sheer persistence by countesses, stark poverty, a devout burly businessman benefactor, American novices, alms-begging, and halting English — a strange blend of factors that colored the Poor Clares' permanent foundation in the United States. The Georgetown Poor Clares would understand and applaud.

In 1990, six Colettine Poor Clares from the Monastery of Our Lady of Guadalupe in Roswell, New Mexico, established a new monastery in El-shout, Holland. The citizens welcomed the nuns with a band, parade, festivities, smiles, tears, and love. American nuns were repaying that land of refuge from *Kulturkampf* for sheltering their spiritual ancestors. Surely St. Clare herself would approve such gracious remuneration.

The West — Treks to Santa Fe and Tucson

Chronicles such as contained in Mother Joseph Pariseau's journal covering the missions and establishments made by sisters in the West during this period are fascinating. Adventure, danger, hardship, and devotion characterize so many episodes that it raises the question of why many intriguing stories have not been dramatized. Few epochs and few groups of women offer such a rich lode of factual raw material for dramatic exploitation.

The list of orders sending sisters into the opening West is long and their ministries wide and varied. They established hospitals where there were none, succored Indians on lonely outposts, opened schools in shacks, lived on the edge of starvation, suffered loneliness and frustration, mothered orphans, begged in the mining camps, stood up to outlaws, and dealt with gamblers and rough cowboys. Catholic sisters made a difference in this raw, untamed part of the country. A few examples must suffice to illustrate this little-known phase of the history of American sisters and nuns.

In 1867, Bishop John Baptist Lamy of Santa Fe secured two Sisters of Charity of Cincinnati and three Sisters of Loretto as reinforcements for their sisters already at the mission.[25] They joined a party leaving Leavenworth, Kansas, by wagon train that had to cross 600 miles of territory inhabited by Comanches, Apaches, and Kiowas. They almost made it without incident, but on July 30 their luck ran out and Kiowas attacked. To compound difficulties, even though within sight of a river, the wagon party could not secure water for themselves or their animals. In the midst of the attack, 18-year-old Loretto Sister Alphonsa Thompson and a young man suffered the final climax of cholera. She died almost immediately. Charity Sister Augustine, braving a hail of arrows, crawled under one wagon to the next in order to reach the sick man and minister to him in his dying moments. That night the wagon-master called for volunteers to sneak a barrel of whiskey across the small river, which they did. As intended, the Kiowas found the trove and quickly got drunk. The wagon train then slipped away and arrived in Santa

Fe safely. Sister Alphonsa and the young man lie buried in unmarked graves that have never been located.

In another exciting saga, seven members of the Sisters of St. Joseph of Carondelet traveled from St. Louis to San Francisco by rail, to San Diego by ship and to Arizona by wagon, arriving in Tucson on May 26, 1870. All 4,000 citizens turned out to welcome them with fireworks, torches, cheers, pealing of church bells, joyous shouts, and the firing of guns into the air. Few if any sister-teachers ever covered such a long distance in the United States to report for a school assignment.

Sister Monica Corrigan led her group from the motherhouse at Carondelet, Missouri, on April 20, 1870, to St. Louis, where they boarded the train that would take them over 2,000 miles to San Francisco. The Central Pacific Railroad working eastward and the Union Pacific Railroad working westward had just linked at Promontory Point, Utah, creating the first transcontinental railroad.[26] After resting with the Sisters of Mercy in San Francisco for a week, the band sailed to San Diego aboard the *Arizona*. On May 7th the party departed San Diego with a Mexican wagon driver who did not speak English. Their 600-mile journey took them through some of the most desolate terrain in the Southwest. These uninformed sisters left civilization little prepared for what lay ahead.

Some nights they spent in the open. Howling wolves terrified the sisters who prayed for deliverance. One night a horse licked Sister Euphrasia's face and she woke up screaming. Another night, a cold Sister Martha went prowling around the edge of the camp looking for firewood. Spotting a likely looking log in the dim light, she pulled it vigorously towards the fire. The driver woke up screaming as she tugged on his leg. Other nights they spent at remote ranches. At one such stopover, the ranchers were exceedingly sociable and ended up proposing marriage. They were sincere, there being no white women in the region. At another ranch, they had to sleep in the stable with 40 men, many of them drunk and obnoxious. The Mexican driver acted as guardian in this situation.

Their passage through the desert was an eye-opener. A vicious sand storm had killed thousands of cattle and sheep, and a stagecoach with seven passengers had been buried by the storm. The 125-degree heat bore down mercilessly. They stayed in the wagon when it crossed the Colorado River on a toll ferry. The wagon almost upended in the deep running water and only the counter-weight of a falling horse prevented the crude raft from spilling the sisters into the river. It seemed that death lurked everywhere.

After reaching Yuma, Arizona, the sisters rested. A priest joined the party for the final and most dangerous leg of the journey — through Apache territory. Providentially, as they approached Picacho Pass, a notorious haunt of hostile Apaches, a troop of 16 soldiers joined them to accompany the sisters the final 65 miles. As they entered Picacho Pass everyone prepared their firearms. Noting signs of Indians nearby, the party sped up and the soldiers began shouting to warn the Indians. The caravan passed through the pass safely; the sisters arrived in Tucson the following evening, almost six weeks after leaving Carondelet.

Bishop John Baptist Salpointe welcomed them to their new home. If the bishop, priests, and the people of Tucson were happy with the safe arrival of the party, the sisters were ecstatic. This trek opened a long relationship between the Sisters of St. Joseph of Carondelet and the people of Arizona.[27]

Virginia City

In 1859, the discovery of silver deposits in Nevada resulted in a boom town named Virginia City that expanded rapidly, reaching a population of 15,000 by 1864.[28] A local priest, Father Patrick Manogue, asked the Daughters of Charity for sisters to operate a school and orphanage, since there was no school and mine accidents were creating orphans. Despite the community's deep involvement in war nursing, they dispatched three sisters to Virginia City. In short order they had 90 pupils, but fierce winter blizzards forced the closing of the school for most of the first winter. By July of 1865, they had 112 pupils and 25 orphans under their care. The entire operation (orphanage, school, convent) was conducted in a one-room structure. Nevada paid a small sum per pupil, but it was tuition, an annual orphans' fair, and donations from local Catholics that enabled continued operations. One of their orphans, Katie Malone, later joined the Daughters of Charity and as Sister Stanislaus became a famous sister-nurse in New Orleans (see Chapter 8).

By the time the Comstock lode played out in 1872, that one-room school and orphanage had grown two large and two small brick buildings. As miners departed and the town shrank, the sisters closed their school and returned to the motherhouse for other assignments.

Sister Blandina

Italian-born Sister Blandina (Rosa Maria Segale, 1850-1941) left Cincinnati for the remote hamlet of Trinidad, Colorado, in December 1872. This member of the Sisters of Charity of Cincinnati — only 21 years old — was directed by her superior to travel alone and join other sisters from their community ministering to the Mexicans, Indians, and settlers in this isolated area just north of the New Mexico state line. Her 21-year sojourn in Trinidad, Santa Fe, and Albuquerque was a mixture of adventure and dedicated ministry.

Traveling by train and stagecoach, Sister Blandina arrived safely in Trinidad on the banks of the Purgatoire River, then a small rough town of several hundred inhabitants. Billy the Kid and his gang kept the citizens of Trinidad in a constant state of fright intensified by occasional Indian raid scares. There Sister Blandina remained for the next four years helping to build a schoolhouse, learning Spanish, teaching, and applying her considerable charm and courage to saving lives.

Sister Blandina received a rude introduction to frontier justice. She was shocked when the local sheriff allowed a lynch mob to murder a drunken get-rich-quick land grabber who had shot and killed an innocent passerby. The next time this situation arose, she took control. The father of one of her pupils shot a man and the sheriff arrested him. The usual mob formed, awaiting the victim's death so they could act. Sister Blandina visited the dying man and asked if he would forgive his assailant if he came to beg pardon. The mortally wounded man agreed. Sister Blandina then visited the jail, where with considerable difficulty she persuaded the terrified assailant to walk down the street with her and the sheriff to the dying man's room. The glowering mob parted to allow the threesome to pass only because of Sister Blandina. Forgiveness was asked and granted. The sheriff then returned the culprit to jail to await trial and the mob dispersed.

On another occasion one of Billy the Kid's outlaw gang was wounded and came to town seeking help. Sister Blandina was the only person who would help. As he approached death, she gently and cleverly turned his thinking toward eternity and Divine forgiveness. It was a tense moment when Billy and his gang showed up as she was nursing. Because of her kindness, Billy asked if he could do her any favor. Aware of his intent to kill the town's four doctors for refusing to treat his companion, she asked for the doctors' lives. Billy felt tricked by this tiny woman who was only five feet three inches tall, but abided by his promise. These two, sister and outlaw, formed something of a friendship. Her presence saved lives when she was with a group riding across the plains. The gang, intent on robbing and killing them, rode off when they saw Sister Blandina. Later in Santa Fe she visited Billy in jail, although she was never able to convert one of the most violent murderers in the West.

While stationed in Albuquerque, Sister Blandina and a companion attempted to visit a distraught woman whose husband had deserted her and their children. The pair got lost in a snowstorm and only the mule's instincts got them to a railroad construction camp. Here they encountered stark fear: some 22 terrified men huddled in a tent awaiting an Apache attack. Because a drunken worker had shot and killed an Apache, the tribe was sending out scouts in preparation for attack. When two scouts in full war regalia appeared at the edge of camp, it was Sister Blandina who went to parlay with them. Holding aloft the crucifix on her rosary, she boldly walked up to the warriors and asked what the problem was. After broken conversation in Spanish, English, and sign language, she convinced the Apaches that the murderer was not in this camp. The scouts believed her and asked where the murderer was. She told the truth. He was in the next camp down the line. The Apaches departed and the grateful railroad workers immediately took up a collection for the sisters. Sister Blandina said afterwards that she never wanted to know what happened to the drunken killer at the other construction camp.

While in New Mexico, Sister Blandina arranged the building of a three-story hospital, an industrial school, and several primary schools. Her activities took her into the homes of poor Mexicans as well as the mansions of rich landowners. She maintained close contacts with Archbishop Lamy, Governor Lew Wallace, General Carleton and the various Indian tribes. Not only was she a good organizer but her knack for converting dying men salvaged many souls in their final moments.

When recalled to Cincinnati in 1894, Sister Blandina and her blood sister, Sister Justina, assumed responsibility for ministering to local Italian-Americans, mostly immigrants. She spent the next 35 years operating a social center, distributing clothes and food, opening schools, handling juvenile court cases, finding employment, reclaiming homeless women and girls, and initiating scout troops and various civic and social organizations. She became famous for her social apostolate to Cincinnati's Italian-Americans.

At her death, all Cincinnati mourned the loss of this amazing sister with her two-part career, frontier missionary and big-city social worker. Her final words were: "My Jesus, Mercy . . . Gesu . . . Madre."[29]

Mother Amadeus Dunne

When the Cheyenne refused to move to the Indian Territory in Oklahoma in 1879, General Nelson A. Miles forced them to settle on reservations in Montana. Bishop John Baptist Brondel, Vicar-Apostolic of Montana, wrote the bishops back East asking for sisters to work on the reservations. Bishop Richard Gilmour of Cleveland published the request, and 36 Ursulines from the Toledo convent volunteered. He wrote Bishop Brondel: "I am sending you six Ursulines for a Christmas present and Mother Amadeus, the flower of my flock, is at their head." Sarah Theresa Dunne (1846-1920) joined the Ursulines in Toledo in 1864 after attending Ursuline Academy in Cleveland and took the religious name Sister Mary Amadeus of the Heart of Jesus. She is remembered today as Mother Amadeus.

When the six nuns arrived at Miles City, Montana, on January 17, 1884, the temperature was minus 40 degrees. Bishop Brondell had ridden 500 miles from Helena on horseback to be on hand to greet them along with Indians, border ruffians, cowboys, gamblers, and the other inhabitants of Miles City — the "wicked little city of Montana" as the Eastern press termed it. Three of the nuns remained in Miles City to open a school. They were so poor that help from the motherhouse in Cleveland was all that kept them functioning. One day someone asked a small boy with 10 cents why he was buying scraps of liver. He replied that they were for the nuns who were on the edge of starvation. Word spread and the local populace contributed what they could.

Mother Amadeus and the other two Ursulines rode in a mule-drawn Army ambulance for four days to reach the Jesuit mission outpost at the confluence of Otter Creek and Tongue River. Their convent/chapel was the small 16-by-22 foot end room of a 3-room log cabin. The middle room was to be a school, and the far end room a rectory for the priest. Pages from the *Police Gazette* served for wallpaper. Mice found the paste delightful and became a plague, forcing the nuns to switch rooms with the "rectory." Because of its utter poverty, the nuns dedicated the mission to St. Joseph Labre (1748-1783), the "beggar of Rome" who initiated the Forty Hours devotion that spread over the Catholic world.

The Cheyenne remained an untamed tribe, prone to leaving the reservation for raids on settlers. Poor health and the pressures of dealing with the Indians caused the priests to depart, leaving the nuns alone in the wilderness without Mass and sacraments. The howling of wolves and an occasional whoop from a carousing Indian were the only carols for the nun's first Christmas Eve at the mission.

With patience and compassion, Mother Amadeus won admiration and respect from the chiefs who permitted her to remain in peace and minister to the tribe. Bishop Brondell secured funds to build a decent school, named the White House. It became a haven for refugees during several uprisings by the Cheyenne. In a few short years Mother Amadeus learned the language and gained the confidence of the entire tribe. She extended her influence to other tribes and opened several schools, including one for the Crow in 1887 near the old Custer battlefield. During her 23 years in Montana, she founded 12 flourishing missions.[30]

Mother Amadeus attended the first general chapter of the Ursulines in Rome in 1900 and was elected provincial-superior of the Ursuline Nuns of the Roman Union for the northern sections of the United States. Popes Leo XIII, Pius X, and Benedict XV held her in high esteem. In 1905, she sent nuns to open a mission in the Yukon delta of Alaska to minister to the Innuits and joined them in 1907. Facing incredible hardships, she founded a mission at St. Michael's and later one at Valdez. In 1918, while she was recovering from an injury at St. Michael's, the building caught fire and she and the other nuns barely escaped with their lives. Never fully recovering from these shocks, she died in Seattle two years later.

With the title "Teresa of the Arctic," Mother Amadeus is considered one of the great women religious of this era. Indians and Eskimos sent delegations to her funeral in Seattle, joining hundreds of bishops, priests, sisters, and admirers in mourning the passing of a beloved mistress and benefactor. For the Indian and Eskimo mourners, Mother Amadeus was much more than the flower of Bishop Brondell's flock.[31]

Begging for Alms

Moving into the sparsely populated areas of the West compounded the normal problem of obtaining money for sisters. Because of poor bishops, meager help from some of the motherhouses and the lack of established Catholic businessmen, sisters often had to beg. Communities sent sisters "back East" to plead for funds. For the most part, priests allowed them to solicit in their parishes and furnished leads to potential benefactors. The sisters sometimes met refusal or a demand from a pastor or bishop for a percentage of the proceeds, a stipulation the sisters often ignored. While direct one-on-one begging can be degrading, the sisters perceived it as a spiritual exercise and offered their humiliations as a sacrifice to God.

Sisters riding on mules and horses or in wagons became a common sight in and around the mines and railroad construction and lumbering camps, where their alms-seeking usually got a generous response. We have seen how Mother Joseph fared. Practically all women religious who operated in the West during these years had similar experiences, if not quite so dramatic.

Sisters opened and staffed hundreds of schools, hospitals, and mission stations on Indian reservations during this era. A more detailed listing of those foundations is provided in Appendix C. Meanwhile, "back East," sisters and nuns were contending with a very different challenge.

Heroic Service in Memphis

In 1900 Major Walter Reed discovered that the dreaded yellow fever was transmitted by the female *aedes aegypti* mosquito. Prior to that time, most people attributed the disease to swamp water and "vapors." Once contracted, victims suffered horribly and usually half of them died within five days. Although Memphis was built on a bluff overlooking the Mississippi River, the city was surrounded by swamps and frequently flooded low lying areas —

prime breeding grounds for the deadly carriers. Memphis experienced three yellow fever epidemics during the 1870's.

When the first outbreak occurred in 1873, 25,000 of Memphis' 40,000 citizens fled to safer locations, leaving the poor, mostly Irish and blacks, to fend as best they could. While many Protestant ministers left, along with their congregations, Catholic priests, brothers, and sisters remained in the city to minister. The pattern repeated in the 1879 epidemic when 5,150 victims died and the final outbreak in 1879 with 600 deaths.

Two orders had sisters in Memphis in 1873: the Dominican Sisters (1070) and the Congregation of the Third Order of St. Francis of Mary Immaculate, Joliet, Illinois (1710). A number of other communities sent sisters to help, especially during the vicious 1878 epidemic, including the Franciscan Sisters of Mary (1415), the Franciscan Sisters, Daughters of the Sacred Hearts of Jesus and Mary (1240), the Daughters of Charity (0760), and the Sisters of Good Shepherd (1830). The deaths of 21 priests and around 30 sisters attests to the price paid for dedication to ministry. Four Episcopalian sisters also died in service, giving witness to Christian charity in action.

The figure, around 30, for sister deaths is probably close to the truth. Writers at the time placed those deaths at 50, but only 27 names are established, including 14 Dominicans and four Joliet Franciscans. Quite possibly, some infected sisters returned to their permanent convents only to die there. Most of these sisters and the priests who died were volunteers, offering their lives to save others.[32]

Occasional Conflicts
Between Authority Figures

Previous accounts have illustrated the tension between the demands of active ministry and the restrictions of Old World constitutions and customs. We have observed the Americanization process gradually resolving much of this tension. While many of the European orders brought the custom of two classes of sisters, choir and lay, with them to America, this system died out gradually in most communities. For example, 14 of the 16 Benedictine convents still maintained the two classes as late as 1879, but 24 years later only four of the 22 Benedictine communities continued to observe the distinction. A few Carmelite convents maintain the classes to this day. As Abbot Innocent Wolf of Atchison said: "The institution of lay sisters dies out in America when they cannot get foreign girls any more."[33] Whatever the internal tensions resulting from the class system, they were relatively minor and destined to fade in the American milieu.

However, other tensions increased with the passage of the years. An ongoing cause of stress was the demand of a number of bishops that sisters perform domestic work in seminaries, willing or not. The foregoing accounts indicated some tensions between various mothers-superior and bishops. For example, the accounts have highlighted Bishop John Hughes of New York versus the Sisters of Charity in Emmitsburg, Bishop Richard Miles of Nashville versus the Sisters of Charity of Nazareth, Bishop de la Hailandière versus Mother Guérin, Bishop Jean Neraz versus Mother St. Andrew, Abbot Boniface Wimmer versus Mother Benedicta,[34] Archbishop John Ireland versus Mothers Alexia and Alfred Moes.[35] Each of these incidents is a complex story involving special circumstances. While the individual conflicts are of historical interest, struggles between these two authority figures arose for several reasons.

The basic cause for ongoing tension is rooted in the nature of religious community and clerical status. The great majority of bishops had been secular priests with little or no personal experience in the dynamics of religious life; some bishops were insensitive to the deep rooted self-images and attitudes of women religious.[36] They wanted full control over all religious matters and activities within their dioceses, which is their responsibility. However, some of them carried this desire to extremes and created unnecessary confrontations with mothers-superior. Some bishops demanded complete control over communities located within their dioceses, including personnel assignments, designation of superiors, specifying ministries, oversight of community life, financial management, and even the acceptance or rejection of candidates. Those episcopal ambitions sometimes translated into determination to change a local community's status to diocesan — not subject to a motherhouse outside the diocese. Conversely, mothers-superior in both American and European motherhouses were determined to maintain the integrity of their orders and not surrender affiliation to bishops to whom they had graciously furnished sisters.[37] These clashing concepts set the stage for a number of struggles, ranging from mild arguments to outright disputes. For example, Bishop Peter Baltes of Alton, Illinois, sought to separate a community of the Sisters of Notre Dame de Namur from their motherhouse in 1874 and later expelled a community of the Adorers of the Blood of Christ for refusing to break ties with their motherhouse. During the 1870's, Bishop Vincent V. Ryan of Buffalo meddled outrageously in the affairs of the Sisters of Mercy in his diocese. The continuing breakups of dioceses into more and smaller ones as the Church grew further compounded the problem of jurisdiction and community status, especially among diocesan communities.

Lest all the blame for the tension be placed on bishops, it should be noted that sisters in local communities with a stronger attachment to their local bishop and churches than to far off motherhouses sometimes agitated for autonomy and for diocesan status. It bears repeating that most bishops were highly supportive, cooperative, respectful, kind, and solicitous for the welfare of women religious in their dioceses.

Yet no account of American sister-history would be complete without a description of how one particular bishop carried his episcopal authority over sisters and nuns in his diocese to extremes. This notorious bishop single-handedly did more to harm sister-bishop relations than anyone in the American experience. He was William George McCloskey (no relation to John McCloskey, the first American cardinal).

William George McCloskey was the first rector of the North American College in Rome, but was eased out because of his autocratic methods. He became Bishop of Louisville, Kentucky, in 1868 through one of the worst blunders by the Church in selection of bishops in the 19th century. Disputes with priests, other bishops, laity, and sisters marked his 41-year tenure. The growth of the diocese is more a testament to the vigor of Kentucky Catholicism than to his leadership.

Women religious abandoned the diocese whenever possible. For example, the Little Sisters of the Poor founded a home for the elderly poor in 1869 but left in 1875; the Sisters of the Third Order Regular of St. Francis left in 1890; in 1897 all the School Sisters of Notre Dame withdrew from the diocese. He deposed Mother Innocence Schlangen at the motherhouse in Louisville and forbade her and some other Ursulines to vote for her successor. Her offense was crossing the Ohio River into Indiana to inspect some property. He had directed that no sister might leave the diocese without his personal permission. Following some minor infraction of his orders, he addressed a council meeting of the Sisters of Loretto. One wrote of this lecture —

> *The 18th of July — Day never to be forgotten Oh! Oh! The reproachful lecture the Council got at St. Benedict's. Traduced, Abused, I cannot write more. Oh! Cruel man! May the Lord give us grace to forgive. Treated with utmost contumely. And not permitted to a word of explanation. . . .*[38]

In 1904, Bishop McCloskey committed the most famous of his outrages. He objected to the caretaker living in the same house as the chaplain of the Sisters of Loretto and ordered the caretaker to move out. During the summer while the chaplain was on vacation and Mother Praxedes[39] was in Rome pursuing Vatican approval of the revised rule, Mother Francisca directed the caretaker to move back in so as not to void the insurance on the building because of non-occupancy. When he learned of this, Bishop McCloskey sent a priest to remove the Blessed Sacrament from the chapel and declared the convent under interdict. On returning from Rome, Mother Praxedes wrote asking for an explanation. The bishop wrote her stating —

> *You have disobeyed our decree regarding the removal of Mr. John Elder from the priest's house by reinstating him. . . . We have withdrawn the Reverend Father Riley and we hereby forbid any ecclesiastic whatsoever to offer up the Holy Sacrifice at Loretto without our permission in writing.*[40]

Now under interdict, Mother Praxedes wrote back to the bishop:

> *The sister who died here yesterday barely escaped not receiving the last sacraments. . . . Even if the Council were guilty, the penalty seems to be quite disproportionate to the offense and includes the innocent as well as the guilty. . . . We protest against this injustice and therefore hold you responsible for all the lost graces, holy Mass and the sacraments.*[41]

Mother Praxedes agreed to remove the caretaker, but refused to accept the return of the chaplain who had attempted to sow discord among the sisters. She appealed to Archbishop Sebastiano Martinelli, the apostolic-delegate in Washington. Abbot Edmond Obrecht of the Trappist monastery at Gethsemani sped to Washington to plead her case. Two weeks later, Archbishop Martinelli ordered Bishop McCloskey to lift the interdict. Over Bishop McCloskey's protest, the Vatican later approved the revised rule of the Sisters of Loretto and they became a pontifical order with a cardinal-protector.[42]

Although tensions and disagreements between bishops and mothers-superior sometimes created disputes, no known confrontations involved abuses that match those of the infamous McCloskey. To the dismay of his fellow bishops he activated aggressive action for pontifical status by numerous orders. The McCloskey legacy is well known and remembered by women religious to this day.

Unfinished Business

What we have witnessed in this chapter is only part of the story. *Kulturkampf* and German immigration opened the Age of Immigration, 1870-1917, during which time many millions came to the United States. We will examine that phenomenon and its impact on women religious in more detail in Chapter 8. Again we reserve the consequences of The Third Plenary Council of Baltimore of 1884 for the chapters ahead.

Recounting the lives, struggles, and achievements of just a few sisters and nuns of this era must suffice to illustrate a dynamic period of outstanding service and growth. In 1890, the 126 orders and congregations[43] with 32,000 members made the American sisterhood the largest component of the Catholic Church, a force of influence on the lives of millions. Having observed how first the French, then the Irish, and then the Germans helped shape the Catholic Church in the United States, we now turn our attention to the next sizable influx of Catholics — Italian and Polish immigrants.

Endnotes

1. Sr. Mary of the Blessed Sacrament McCrosson, SP, in collaboration with Sr. Mary Leopoldine, SP, and Sr. Maria Theresa, SP, *The Bell and the River* (New York, NY: Pacific Books, Inc., 1957), pp. 190-193.
2. Alexander Graham Bell invented the telephone in 1876. The first exchange was located in New Haven, Connecticut, in 1878. The Sisters of Providence of Saint Mary-of-the-Woods in Indiana were among the first Catholic sisters to install a telephone, which cost them $120 per year.
3. In 1865 alone, Maine and Kentucky founded state universities, and private groups established Cornell, Purdue, and the Massachusetts Institute of Technology. Land-grant provisions by the federal government stimulated a veritable explosion of new colleges starting in the 1870's. Protestant groups joined the college-foundation urge with dozens of small institutions, some of which later expanded into major universities. Jesuits continued setting the pace for Catholic colleges.
4. Historical Statistics of the United States, Colonial Times to 1970, *Part 1* (Washington, D.C: U.S. Department of Commerce, Bureau of the Census, GPO, 1975), pp. 105-109.
5. They were —
   > Sisters of Divine Providence of San Antonio, Texas (CDP-1010).*
   > The Sisters of Divine Providence of Kentucky (CDP-1000).**
   > Sisters of Divine Providence (CDP-0990).***
   > Poor Handmaids of Jesus Christ (PHJC-3230).****
   > Adorers of the Blood of Christ (ASC-0100).
   > Franciscan Sisters of Mary (OSF-1415).
   > Sisters of Christian Charity (SCC-0660).
   > School Sisters of St. Francis (OSF-1680).
   > Sisters of St. Francis of Penance and Christian Charity (OSF-1630).
   > Sisters of St. Francis of Perpetual Adoration (OSF-1640).
   > Sisters of the Third Order of St. Francis of the Holy Family
   >   (OSF-1570).
   > Hospital Sisters of St. Francis ((OSF-1820).
   > Franciscan Sisters of the Sacred Heart (OSF-1450).

Franciscan Sisters, Daughters of the Sacred Hearts of Jesus and
  Mary (OSF-1240).
Sisters of Notre Dame (SND-2990).
Ursuline Nuns (OSU-4110).

* Since the provinces of Alsace and Lorraine were German from 1870 to 1918, and were again incorporated briefly into Germany by Hitler, most of the sisters coming to Texas considered themselves German.

** They came from the same motherhouse as San Antonio group.

*** The entire community fled from Mayence, Germany, in 1876 and settled in Pittsburgh. They had no connection to the Alsatian sisters.

**** Like so many others, these sisters endured extreme poverty in the early years. One day Mother Rose, the American foundress, went into Fort Wayne, Indiana, to secure some food. Back at the convent in Hessen Cassel, a sister decided to cheer her dejected companions. She climbed atop an upturned flour barrel and launched into a mock oration complete with flamboyant gestures. Loudly she intoned, "O Mother Rose, we have no flour! O Mother Rose, we have no potatoes! O Mother Rose, we have no. . .!" With splintering and loud cracking of wood, the orator disappeared into the barrel. The paeans of hilarious laughter replaced the pangs of hunger.

6. One was Father Barzynski, who later became famous in Chicago (see Chapter 8).
7. A "failed order" was one of the problems she faced. In 1872, three German-speaking sisters went to Panna Maria and St. Hedwig where Father Felix Zwiardowski was pastor. Around eight young Polish girls joined the Sisters of Divine Providence as a result. When Mother St. Andrew sent two Polish-speaking sisters to replace the German-speaking ones, Father Felix refused the exchange. Since a new bishop had not jet arrived, she had to await his arrival to appeal. Being unfamiliar with conditions, Bishop Anthony D. Pellicer favored Father Felix, granting him permission to establish a new order. In 1875, Father Felix formed a branch of the Sisters of the Immaculate Conception, despite objections by Mother-General Marcellena in Poland. By 1879, the community had grown to 30 members, 11 from Mother Andrews's community. The end came when Father Felix's arbitrary governance and neglect of the sisters resulted in angry and threatening Polish parents. The bishop lost confidence and the clergy turned against Father Felix. The community disbanded with some joining the Sisters of Divine Providence and the rest returning home.
8. When the Sisters of Divine Providence at St. Jean-de-Bassel made a foundation in Kentucky in 1889, they took great care to clarify the community's status before sending sisters. Sister Arsene, Mother St. Andrew's friend and companion, served in Kentucky after returning from Texas.
9. The community provided this money for the establishment of a convent in the Galveston diocese. It also represented the amount of Mother St. Andrew's dowry, spent for the construction of the Castroville convent.
10. Sr. Mary Generosa Callahan, CDP, *The History of the Sisters of Divine*

Providence, San Antonio, Texas (Milwaukee, WI: Catholic Life Publications, Bruce Press, 1954), p. 156. The entire account is based on this book.

11. The three cities of Cincinnati, St. Louis, and Milwaukee delineated the so-called "German Triangle." It encompasses some of the richest farmland in the United States and was a magnet for Germans immigrants.

12. Archbishop John Ireland (1838-1918) was and remains a controversial figure. Doubtlessly one of the most capable and intelligent prelates in American Catholic history, his accomplishments are legion. He organized and effected a plan to resettle poor Irish families from Eastern cities on farmland in Minnesota. Between 1876 and 1881 he settled 4,000 families. He became the main spokesman for the Catholic Total Abstinence Society and was nationally recognized as a brilliant speaker. He was the leading spokesman for Catholic accommodation with American democracy, and for "shared time" for Catholic schools. Popes and presidents considered him, along with Cardinal James Gibbons, to be the leading Catholic in the United States. Leader of the liberal wing of the American hierarchy, he exerted considerable influence in Rome. He was, however, intolerant of those who did not agree with his positions, ruthless with those who opposed him directly, disdainful of European ethnic cultures being perpetuated in the United States, an enemy of "national churches," and the bane of German, Polish, and Ukrainian Catholics.

13. Sr. Francis M. Borgia, OSF, *He Sent Two: The Story of the Beginning of the School Sisters of St. Francis* (Milwaukee, WI: The Bruce Publishing Co. 1965). Most of the account is derived from this book.

14. Prior to the Third Plenary Council of Baltimore in 1884, training of priests in the United States was sometimes haphazard, ranging from excellent preparation at such outstanding seminaries as St. Mary's in Baltimore to informal studies under the supervision of a bishop. The need for priests was so great that many received just the bare minimum of philosophical and theological training. Fortunately, most of these priests were devout and performed their basic functions satisfactorily. Many of the foreign-born priests had excellent educations and were effective priests, although a handful of "rouge" priests left Europe in disgrace and created problems in the United States.

15. Rev. Wilfred P. Schoenberg, SJ, *These Valiant Women: History of the Sisters of St. Mary of Oregon, 1886-1986* (Beaverton, OR: Sisters of St. Mary of Oregon, 1986), p. 92. This entire account is based on that book. Father Schoenberg was kind in making suggestions and encouraging my work.

16. Ibid., p. 101.

17. The similarity of names (Catherine) sometimes caused confusion for the two sisters as well as future historians. Mother Alfred often used the name Josephine in legal documents to avoid mixups.

18. The Congregation of the Sisters of the Holy Cross (1920) suffered considerable stress during this era because of jurisdictional disputes between Father Sorin at Notre Dame and Father Basil Moreau in France, the founder of the congregation. Bishop Luers became involved and sided with Father Sorin. Another factor not mentioned in the records is that most of the Holy Cross sisters at this time were

French and the Moes sisters were German-speaking Luxembourgers, raising the possibility of ethnic tensions. Sisters were certainly not immune to these ethnic prejudices, which followed them across the Atlantic during the Age of Immigration.

19. See Chapter 6 and Appendix G for accounts of the yellow fever epidemics in Memphis. Two of the six sisters from Joliet died giving heroic service there in 1873.

20. Sr. Carlan Kraman, OSF, *Odyssey in Faith: The Story of Mother Alfred Moes, Sisters of St. Francis* (Rochester, MN: Sisters of St. Francis, 1990). Most of the information about Mother Moes is taken from this book.

21. Archbishop Corrigan's opposition to contemplatives is questionable. He became acquainted with Mother Mary of Jesus (Julia Crooks) in France while still a young priest. His brother married one of her nieces. While Bishop of Newark, he arranged for four Dominican nuns to come to Newark in 1880 where they established a cloistered monastery.

22. Rev. Albert Kleber, OSB, STD, *A Bentivoglio of the Bentivoglio: Servant of God, Mary Maddalena of the Sacred Heart of Jesus, Countess Annetta Bentivoglio, 1834-1905* (Evansville, IN: Monastery of St. Clare, 1984), p. 96.

23. Both branches of Poor Clares followed the Primitive Rule of St. Clare, but had different constitutions. While essentially alike, they have different devotional practices and wear different habits.

24. John Creighton was a great benefactor of Catholic institutions. Creighton University in Omaha is named for him, and Pope Leo XIII made him a papal knight.

25. Willa Cather wrote a fictionalized account of Bishop Lamy, *Death Comes for the Archbishop*.

26. Engines and supplies for the Union Pacific Railroad came from the East by clipper ship around Cape Horn to San Francisco. Thousands of Chinese laborers built the line.

27. Sr. Aloysia Ames, CSJ, *The St. Mary's I Knew* (Tucson, AZ: St. Mary's Hospital of Tucson, Inc., 1970), pp. 132-150.

28. Virginia City was the site of the first Catholic Church in Nevada, established in 1860.

29. Sr. Blandina Segale, SC, *At the End of the Santa Fe Trail* (Milwaukee, WI: The Bruce Publishing Co., 1948). The entire account is based on this book.

30. When Mother Amadeus became ill one year, Mother-Superior Stanislaus left Toledo to care for her, bringing Mary Fields with her to help. Mary was quite tall and ample (over 200 pounds) and totally uninhibited. When Mother-Superior Stanislaus returned to Toledo, Mary remained in Montana and became a legend in her own lifetime. She was one of the first female postal drivers in the United States and performed admirably. On her rounds she carried a shotgun and pistol, fought off wolves, and intimidated hostile outlaws and Indians. Modern Western films often feature caricatures of the gruff but lovable Mary Fields.

31. This account was based on a variety of sources. See Convent Annals, *Life of the*

Rev. Mother Amadeus of the Heart of Jesus (New York, NY: The Paulist Press, 1923) and Sr. M. Michael Francis, OSU, *The Broad Highway: A History of the Ursuline Nuns in the Diocese of Cleveland, 1850-1950* (Cleveland, OH: The Ursuline Nuns, 1951).

32. See Thomas Stritch, *The Catholic Church in Tennessee: The Sesquicentennial Story* (Nashville, TN: The Catholic Center, 1987), pp. 193-202.

33. Joel Rippinger, OSB, *The Benedictine Order in the United States: An Interpretive History* (Collegeville, MN: The Liturgical Press, 1990), p. 154.

34. As noted in the foundation account in Chapter 3, the Vatican gave full authority over Benedictine women religious in the United States to the local bishop where the convents were located. This decision had some very unhappy results. For example, in 1881 and again in 1883 Bishop Tobias Mullen of Erie, Pennsylvania, overturned the election of the superior and appointed his choice.

35. Archbishop John Ireland's blood sister, Mother Seraphine of the Sisters of St. Joseph in St. Paul, Minnesota, could do no wrong in his eyes. Priests in trouble with the archbishop often sought her intervention.

36. Margaret Susan Thompson, Chapter Seven, *Women, Feminism, and New Religious History: Catholic Sisters as a Case Study,* Philip VandeMeer and Robert Swierenga, eds. (New Brunswick, NJ: Rutgers University Press, 1991), p. 145.

37. Clyde F. Crews, *An American Holy Land: A History of the Archdiocese of Louisville* (Wilmington, DE: Michael Glazier, Inc., 1987), p. 222.

38. Clyde F. Crews, *An American Holy Land: A History of the Archdiocese of Louisville* (Wilmington, DE: Michael Glazier, Inc., 1987), p. 222.

39. Mother Praxedes Carty is famous in Loretto history. While still a novice she was sent to New Mexico where she established a reputation for competence and loving compassion. After several assignments in New Mexico, she was posted to Denver to save a floundering academy. Meanwhile, back in Kentucky, Bishop McCloskey was interfering with the internal affairs of the congregation. The apostolic delegate appointed Bishop Thomas S. Byrne of Nashville to investigate the situation. In the end, he called Mother Praxedes from Denver and appointed her mother-general. After the difficult battles with Bishop McCloskey and approval of the new rule, the sisters elected her mother-general, reelected her; she served for 22 years in that post. During her tenure, the Sisters of Loretto established 51 schools, two colleges, and sent sister-missionaries to China.

40. Crews, p. 224.

41. Ibid., p. 224.

42. The designation of a cardinal as "protector" of a religious order is an ancient custom initiated by St. Francis of Assisi in the 13th century. Upon achieving pontifical status and making the request, an order is granted a cardinal as protector by the Vatican. Thus the order has a high-level advocate to whom it can turn for assistance when it feels the necessity.

43. Here, as elsewhere throughout this book, the total count of orders and congregations is based on the "original foundations" as listed in Appendix B. Offshoots

became autonomous and the numbers rose. Communities became independent, split, re-affiliated, sent out more offshoots, and formed associations. Changes were in constant flux, making coordinated dates and totals of independent communities too involved a subject for detailed treatment in a book such as this.

CHAPTER 7

New and Different Flora (1890-1917)

‡ — ‡

DRAMATIC AS WAS the expansion of the sisterhood from 1866 to 1890, the growth during the next quarter century was truly fantastic. When the United States declared war on Germany in 1917, sister-population stood at 84,000, an increase of 52,000. Some 98 new orders raised the total of original foundations to 224, plus their many offshoots. Italian, Polish, and Slavic foundresses made fresh foundations as floral additions to American beauty roses, French fleur de lis, Irish shamrocks, and German edelweiss. The number of sister-founded hospitals, nursing schools, colleges, and charitable institutions increased in like proportion.

Contemplatives found congenial space in the American sun. Sisters continued operating the expanding network of parochial schools. During these years lifestyles, operating practices, and patterns settled into the forms that would govern the sisterhood for the next half century. By 1917, most ministries were firmly established excepting foreign missions, and these would soon involve increasing numbers of sisters.

By 1917, Catholics had increased to 16 percent of the American population. Even 19,000 priests were hardly sufficient for a denomination swollen by millions of new members, many of whom did not speak English. "Brick and mortar" bishops and priests erected cathedrals, churches, schools, rectories, social centers, and convents by the thousands. Irish working girls reputedly financed from their wages the construction of cathedrals such as St. Patrick's in New York and St. Joseph's in Hartford. This oversimplification indicates how generally poor lower- and middle-class working Catholics strained to support "their" church. Catholic presence was pervasive in many towns and cities. Ten of the 14 new dioceses were in the West, illustrating the development of that section as it joined the mainstream, bringing the total number to 100. John Carroll would have been astounded.

These were not peaceful years among the hierarchy. Disputes among bishops broke into the open before the puzzled and sometimes bemused gaze of the general public. Archbishop John Ireland disputed openly with Archbishop Michael Corrigan of New York and Bishop Bernard McQuaid of Rochester. Factions contended over public funding of parochial schools, the German and Polish demands for better representation in the hierarchy, and the status of secret societies that imitated the American practice of taking oaths. One, the Knights of Labor, was not condemned by the Vatican as a result of the intervention of American and Canadian prelates. The Catholic University of America was another bone of contention between conservative and liberal elements. Cardinal James Gibbons of Baltimore, the most universally respected and accepted Catholic leader in the United States, moderated and controlled these opposing factions and prevented their disputes from getting out of hand. Only occasionally did the controversies interrupt the activity and interests of women religious or the overwhelming mass of ordinary Catholics who went about their business, exercising their religious impulses in devotional ways. Novenas, Forty Hours devotion, stations of the cross, benediction of the Blessed Sacrament, group rosary recitation, adoration before the exposed Blessed Sacrament, daily Mass, Feast Day processions, missions, retreats, and other devotions completed the panoply of Catholic religious life. Some Catholic historians refer to the Church of these years as the "devotional Church."

On the international stage, the era opened with Emperor William II's dismissal of Chancellor Otto von Bismarck, much to the delight of German-American Catholics[1], and closed with America's entry into World War I. In between, the pace of events quickened. Catholic German emigration decreased. Anti-Semitic persecution triggered emigration by hundreds of thousands of Jews who joined other minority groups leaving Imperial Russia for the United States and Canada. France continued repressive measures against the Church and religious orders, occasioning new immigration to the United States. Italy experienced population explosion and economic depressions. Poland writhed under the iron heels of Germany, Russia, and Austria. Labor versus industry struggles characterized England, still enjoying the international power it achieved during the Victorian Age. European powers divided Africa among themselves and by 1912 had control of the entire continent excepting Ethiopia and Liberia. They continued staking out economic and colonial spheres in the Far East.

The United States asserted its power with victory in the Spanish-American War, military incursions into Mexico in 1914 and 1916, and the occupation of Haiti by U.S. Marines. Despite strong opposition from Irish-Americans, German-Americans, and other elements favoring neutrality, the

United States joined the Allies in declaring war on Germany in 1917. The executions and deportations following the abortive Easter Rebellion in Ireland in 1916 had aroused bitter resentment among Irish-Americans, while German-Americans opposed entry into the war for ethnic reasons. In the end, Anglophiles in the State Department and President Woodrow Wilson had their way.

Trade expanded, cities sprang up, and new states joined the Union. One of the greatest engineering feats of all time, the Panama Canal, was completed in 1914 and cut thousands of miles off shipping transit between the Pacific and Atlantic Oceans. Oklahoma, Utah, New Mexico, and Arizona achieved statehood. Cleveland, Los Angeles, Denver, Salt Lake City, Kansas City, Seattle, and Minneapolis joined the ranks of major metropolitan centers. New York vied with London and Paris for prestige with its high-rise buildings, elegant shops, opera, symphony orchestras, museums, zoos, parks, theater, literature, publishing houses, art galleries, libraries, and cultural and sports activities. New York's financial institutions assumed power and influence second only to those in London. Washington's international political importance was on a par with Berlin, Paris, Moscow, and London.

The census of 1890 reported 9,249,547 "foreign-born" who constituted 15 percent of the 62,622,250 Americans. It also uncovered one startling fact: it was now impossible to locate a continuous Western frontier line beyond which population thinned out to less than two people per square mile. This inspired historian Frederick Jackson Turner to remark —

> *. . . four centuries from the discovery of America, at the end of a hundred years under the Constitution, the frontier has gone and with its going has closed the first period of American history. . . .*[2]

The shift from agrarian and rural to industrial and urban continued uninterrupted. Social unrest grew as labor unions developed strength and called for strikes against railroads, mines, and industrial exploiters. Optimism, rugged individualism, entrepreneurship, and the cult of success became major forces in shaping American attitudes. Colleges proliferated. Anthropology and the writings of Darwin brought Biblical accounts into question, promoting agnostic beliefs. Although the stable middle class continued to expand, working lower classes still constituted the great majority of the population and grew even faster with ever fresh contingents of immigrants. Recovery from devastation of the Civil War and punitive Reconstruction was slow in the South which slumbered in economic depression.

In the North, Midwest, and Far West, immigrant waves swamped labor markets and school systems, overwhelmed charitable institutions and re-aroused nativism. Anti-Semitism became rampant. Between 1880 and 1924, some 2.3 million Jews arrived from Europe, mainly from Russia and Poland. They differed from the earlier Jews from Western Europe and the Iberian peninsula. Clad in long black coats, sporting unruly looking beards, and speaking Yiddish, these new Jews seemed strange even to the older American Jewish stock. Assimilation of all these new and "different" immigrants was far more difficult than in earlier decades. Roughly half of the newcomers were Catholic, sealing yet another title, "the Immigrant Church." Because of sheer numbers and their being "different," immigrants of this era aroused tremendous resentment, and the fact that so many were Catholic stimulated latent anti-Catholic sentiments.

Rise of the APA and Related Groups

The Protestant majority viewed this influx with mixed emotions ranging from admiration and respect to dislike, mistrust, scorn, fear, and hatred. In 1891, Pope Leo XIII dismayed a thoroughly Protestant financial and industrial leadership with his historic encyclical, *Rerum Novarum*, which enunciated the Catholic position on the dignity of work and the rights of labor. It gave solace and formal backing to the millions of workers, many of them Catholic, in their struggles to unionize and secure fair treatment from industry and business.

Know-Nothings and the post-Civil War Ku Klux Klan with their anti-Catholic and anti-immigrant activities had come and gone. But their mean spirit gradually revived as the 19th century coursed to an end and the early decades of the 20th century unfolded. While women religious were not terrorized by riots or violence, they became, once again, the centerpiece of anti-Catholic legal efforts. A new anti-Catholic organization arose in 1887, the American Protective Association (APA), founded in Clinton, Iowa, by Henry F. Bowers. It was never powerful on the national level but did considerable mischief, especially in the South and in many rural communities over the country. Economic depressions, the unprecedented waves of immigrants, and plain ignorance enhanced the association's appeal.

The APA used the time-proven exploitation of the ex-priest and ex-nun on the lecture circuit. For example, it brought Margaret Shepherd to Omaha in 1897 to speak.[3] The fact that Margaret had been committed to a Good Shepherd home in Bristol, England, for prostitutes and alcoholics did not deter them. The APA predicted an uprising of Catholics led by the Knights of Columbus and Jesuits to slaughter heretics on September 5, 1893, mistakenly thought to be the feast day of the Jesuit founder, Ignatius Loyola.[4] In the face of such blatant and outrageous prejudice, the Democratic Party included a condemnation of the APA in its 1894 platform. Thereafter, the APA gradually faded from the scene, but its emotional appeal and spread of misinformation had residual effects well into the next century.

In 1911, a new anti-Catholic association, the Guardians of Liberty, arose in upstate New York, adding its voice to another small anti-Catholic group named the Patriotic Sons of America. A national magazine, *The Menace*, with a monthly circulation of 1.5 million in 1915, devoted its issues to anti-Catholic propaganda. These groups and their paper concentrated on furthering legislative restrictions on Catholic schools and sisters, reviving objectives that the APA had so ardently pursued. Alabama and Georgia passed "convent inspection" laws in 1915 and Florida followed in 1917. Never seriously enforced, those statutes were efforts to threaten Catholics and mollify fundamentalist constituents. Anti-Catholic legislators introduced convent inspection and religious garb bills in a number of other states, including Michigan, Minnesota, Iowa, and Pennsylvania. Again there was more sound than fury.

The Sisters of the Good Shepherd were sometimes a target for slander because of their ministry to delinquent young women. The courts often sent them to the sisters instead of prison. This apostolate exposed the sisters to false testimony from some of their charges, making them vulnerable to vicious rumors. Some bishops even found their ministry an embarrassment. Sisters sometimes found it necessary to invite civic authorities to inspect the convents in order to allay their suspicions and disprove false charges.

While anti-Catholicism made frequent appearances during the 1890-1917 years, it never grew into a serious menace. Prejudice took on non-violent forms, including denial or loss of employment, exclusion from prestigious law firms, bank boards, brokerage houses, and top management positions in business and industry, and social rejection. Conditions varied from social class to social class, from city to city, and from state to state. The primary institutions where anti-Catholic prejudice was nearly nonexistent were the armed forces — the Army, Navy, and Marine Corps.

Immigration Patterns — The Ethnic Churches

Almost 16 million immigrants arrived at the reception center on Ellis Island during the 1891-1917 era. Interpreters of the Immigration Service questioned newcomers in dozens of languages, making the center sound like the Tower of Babel. Most of the arrivals were poor and ill-clad. A fortunate minority arrived with funds and friends or relatives to greet them. Medical inspectors processing the arrivals sent diseased immigrants back to Europe, ignoring their pitiful pleas. Officials often misspelled the strange sounding names, entering them incorrectly on the entry forms. Immigrants usually adopted the new spelling with resignation. While relatives were sometimes on hand to greet new arrivals, most often benevolent ethnic societies, church-related groups, or prospective employers were the ones to assist the new-comers in getting settled or directed to intended locations. Table III indicates the diversity and newness of origins for the millions of immigrants as outlined in Table III:

Immigration Statistics
(1890-1917)

Central Europe*	3,730,569
Eastern Europe**	275,264
Italy	3,705,015
Russia***	3,017,157
Great Britain	1,091,112
Germany****	989,095
Ireland	863,266
Canada	744,463
All Others	1,353,632
TOTAL	15,769,573

*Includes present day Czech Republic, Slovak Republic, Hungary, and Austria.
**Includes Romania, Bulgaria, former Yugoslav states, and European Turkey.
***Also includes Estonia, Lithuania, Latvia, Ukraine, Ruthenia, Armenia, and Poland. Russia occupied a large section of Poland. Numerous Jews are included.
****Germany and Austria occupied the balance of Poland. These numbers include Poles, Jews, and some Slavs.

Table III

Irish-Americans remained the largest Catholic ethnic group with German-Americans the second largest. By 1890, many second- and third-generation ethnic Irish were well assimilated, many having joined the middle class and even the upper classes. Although newly arriving and first-generation Irish still had to work up from the lower middle class, they now received support from established ethnic brethren and relatives. Young Irish-American men entered West Point and Annapolis, attended Catholic, state, and private colleges and entered the professions in ever increasing numbers. Although signs reading "No Irish Need Apply" could still occasionally be seen in New England, it could be said in 1917 that, to a certain extent, the Irish had "arrived."

Most Irish-Americans were fiercely loyal to the Roman Catholic Church.

With generous contributions from savings and wages, they helped finance cathedrals, churches, schools, and charitable institutions and supported the clergy and women religious. Irish children routinely attended parochial schools. Sons and daughters became the mainstay of the clergy and sisterhood. By 1890, Irish bishops constituted the majority of the American hierarchy. Consciously or subconsciously, most Irish assumed a proprietary attitude towards the Catholic Church — it was "their" church. John Lancaster Spalding (1840-1916), the famous Bishop of Peoria, best expressed the Irish self-image:

> *The general truth is that the Irish Catholics are the most important element in the Church in this country. . . . Were it not for Ireland Catholicism would today be feeble and non-productive in England, America and Australia. . . . No other people . . . could have done for the Catholic faith in the United States what the Irish people have done. . . . No other people had received the same providential training for this work; of no other people had God required such proofs of love. . . .*[5]

While overblown, there was a strong element of truth in this statement.[6] On the other hand, the less numerous German-American Catholics had been in America as long as the Irish and were equally supportive of the Church. Some deeply resented Irish domination of the hierarchy and its efforts to "Americanize" them by suppressing the use of the German language in parochial schools and religious rites. Liturgy, singing, music, and preaching in German parishes followed Old World forms, traditions, and customs, quite different from Irish churches that the Germans saw as cold and flat. In short, there was considerable antipathy between these two major ethnic elements of the Church, and the arrival of Polish, Italian, and Ukrainian Catholics only magnified the resentment of Irish domination.

Germans concentrated in the Midwest where they formed closely knit communities and established "national" churches. They went to great lengths to secure German-speaking priests for pastors and German-speaking sisters to teach their children. In 1915 for example, 95 percent of their parishes had German-language parochial schools. With considerable justification, Germans resented Irish opposition to their national churches. The German clergy formed associations in a losing battle to lodge complaints and make appeals for relief at the Vatican. Irish political skills outmaneuvered them and ready Irish wit soothed Roman fears. The Irish position for "Americanization" dominated, with final victory sealed by the United States declaration of war with Germany in 1917.

At the height of the German-Irish controversy came millions of Catholic Italians, Poles, Ukrainians, Lithuanians, Hungarians, Slovenes, Czechs,

Slovaks, and other Catholic immigrants. As best it could, each group sought to follow the German example and form its own national church. Because new immigrants usually clustered in ghettos, such churches were a natural outgrowth just as they were for Germans. Although the Irish were the best assimilated and most scattered over the country of all Catholic ethnic groups, in most large cities they still lived in clearly Irish neighborhoods. While some Irish-American bishops expressed concern that the influx of new and different immigrant Catholics represented a giant step backwards in terms of Americanization, many Irish bishops supported the ethnic newcomers in a transition phase, aiding their national churches. As a result, the response of the Irish hierarchy was to expedite the Americanization process — gently if possible, but forcibly if necessary.[7]

While Germany, France, and Canada continued to represent major sources of immigrant women religious orders, the new Polish, Italian, and Slavic orders broadened the ethnic base of the sisterhood and provided stimulating diversity. The story of the foundresses and some details of the communities that originated as a result of their pioneering seems the best way to recount how the sisters and nuns came to the United States from 1891 to 1917. This is offered with reference to the specific immigrant experiences of these newer groups.

Italian Immigrant Orders

During the antebellum period and immediately after the Civil War, a trickle of Italian immigrants came to the United States, usually as artists, merchants, architects, vineyard growers, wine makers, artisans, musicians, and craftsmen of fine musical instruments. Italian Jesuit priests were active in the Pacific Northwest and Italian Dominican priests helped establish Catholic parishes in the Midwest. A small number of Italian Franciscan friars and Vincentian priests also came. Prior to the 1890's, the scattered Italian priests were in general proportion to the small Italian population, but there were no Italian women religious orders during those years, although individual Italian-American women joined various orders. Some Italian and Italian-American sisters were noted academy educators, particularly in schools operated by Mother Duchesne's Society of the Sacred Heart.[8] However, the flood of Irish and Germans during the 1840-1890 years overwhelmed any presence made by Italian immigrants and their priests.

As the foregoing immigration statistics reveal, Italians became the largest ethnic group arriving between 1890 and 1917 — 3.7 million in just 27 years. For various reasons, these immigrants had an extremely difficult time adjusting to life in the United States. Unlike earlier Italian arrivals, this wave comprised few intellectuals, professionals, artisans, craftsmen, or accomplished farmers. The great majority came from Sicily and the impoverished provinces of southern Italy with expectations of achieving quick prosperity in the United States. However, 54.2 percent of Italian immigrants arriving between 1899 and 1909 could not read or write and most lacked salable job skills. Actual conditions dashed the unrealistic hopes of the poor and uneducated immigrants who found access only to the lowest paying jobs, usually as common laborers for the railroads and construction companies building canals, dams, and roads. Italian-American labor contractors (*padrones* and *bordanti*) shamefully exploited their fellow countrymen.[9]

Males predominated, comprising about 65 percent of Italian immigrants. Their intent was to accumulate enough money to send for families and relatives or to return to their native villages and be "somebody." More Italians returned to the homeland than any other ethnic group, often crossing the Atlantic several times before settling down in the United States. They spoke dialects and sometimes had difficulty communicating with Italians from other districts. Clustered in "Little Italys" in large cities, many immigrants and especially women confined in the home were slow to learn English. A tiny criminal strain joining such societies as the Black Hand and Mafia tarnished the Italian image for generations. Authorities in Italy routinely falsified records in order to rid the country of these undesirables by sending them across the ocean as immigrants.

In those parts of Italy whence so many came, religion was at a low ebb. Many of the local clergy were indolent and ignorant. Rural village Catholicism was devotional and emotional, bordering on superstition and vastly different from the Catholicism practiced in the United States by the Irish and Germans. Since the Italian government paid clerical salaries and maintained the churches, Italian immigrants found church support an alien concept. Their failure to provide even minimal financial support infuriated American Catholics ministering to their needs. Recent political events in Italy fostered an anticlericalism that infected many immigrants. Difficulties in preserving the faith among these immigrants and their children were commonly referred to among the hierarchy and clergy as the "Italian problem."

Further compounding the difficulties, there was a severe shortage of Italian-speaking priests, essential for the formation of national churches that were so instrumental in easing the transition into the American culture for other ethnic groups. The limited number of Italian and Italian-American priests were swallowed up by the immigrant hordes, so national churches never blossomed to the extent of the Irish, German, Polish, and some Slavic churches. Existing parishes normally absorbed Italians. Another symptom of the strains between the Church and Italians was the frequent refusal by Italian parents to send their children to parochial schools. Even when free tuition was offered, many still chose public schools because they resented the discrimination directed towards their children by other Catholics. At times prejudice was noxious. All too often Irish pastors relegated Italians to church basements for services. Middle-class Catholics, especially the Irish, looked with scorn on Italian devotionalism and their colorful celebrations of feast days of favorite saints.

As city neighborhoods gradually became Italian, local parishes took on an Italian complexion, with or without an Italian pastor. Protestant societies targeted Italian immigrants for a major proselytizing effort — the most serious effort ever made against an immigrant Catholic group — without significant lasting results.[10] Italians slowly made the difficult transition to Americanization as education and economic advancement lifted them from the lowest economic and social levels. Anticlericalism gradually faded. Inherent decency and a deeply ingrained Catholic heritage reasserted themselves, and the great majority of second- and third-generation Italians remained loyal Catholics.

Italy at this time had more women religious than any country in the world. Yet they did not come to minister to their countrymen in the United States in significant numbers. The reasons are complex. Educational and other ministries in Italy consumed most of their resources. Those already committed to missionary endeavors felt that support for existing missions in South America, Africa, and Asia had priority over the United States. Cloistered and semicloistered lifestyles, typical among most Italian communities, also inhibited missionary efforts. Yet 13 orders did come to the United States during this era. The most famous was led by a tiny north Italian sister.

Mother Frances Xavier Cabrini (1850-1917)

On July 7, 1946, a throng of dignitaries, friends, relatives, and members of the **Missionaries of the Sacred Heart of Jesus (MSC-2860)** gathered in Rome for a banquet. They came to celebrate the canonization of Mother Frances Xavier Cabrini. During the speeches extolling this new saint of the Roman Catholic Church, the master of ceremonies introduced a young man named Peter Smith who made this short statement: "I for one know for certain that the age of miracles has not passed." This brought the audience to its feet with a resounding roar of applause. Peter Smith was the beneficiary of the crucial miracle needed for canonization.

Peter was born in 1921 in New York's Columbus Hospital, established by Mother Cabrini's Missionary Sisters of the Sacred Heart. Following normal post-delivery procedure, the nurse on duty swabbed the baby's eyes with what she thought was a solution of one percent nitrate. Two hours later she noticed that his eyes were inflamed and that his face was covered with blisters. She immediately had the solution analyzed. To her horror, it was *50 percent* nitrate. Drs. John Grimley and Paul Casson examined the baby and both declared unequivocally that he was permanently blinded. Nonetheless, the sister-superior in the hospital placed a relic of Mother Cabrini over the baby's eyes, and all the Missionary Sisters of the Sacred Heart of Jesus spent the entire night in prayer.[11] They prayed to Mother Cabrini to procure a miracle from God and petitioned the Sacred Heart of Jesus. The following morning, an examination by the doctors disclosed no damage to the eyes and that the blisters were rapidly receding. An eye specialist confirmed these findings. The doctors certified that a miracle had occurred.

Peter, however, developed pneumonia and ran a temperature of 109 degrees, as high as the thermometers would register. The doctors announced that death was imminent and that severe brain damage had occurred. Once again, the sisters spent the night in prayer. They could not believe Mother Cabrini had obtained such a marvelous miracle only to then have the baby die of pneumonia. In the morning Peter was well, and with the fever gone; he returned to normal. Not all miracles are as dramatic as these, but few other saintly people led such a spectacular life.

Francesca, as she is affectionately called, was born on July 15, 1850, in the Lombard district of Italy in a suburb of Lodi. The area was under Austrian occupation at this time and had an excellent school system. One of 11 children of pious middle-class parents, Francesca was first tutored by her older sister Rosa, then excelled at the local school. Francesca was blond and blue-eyed with a fair complexion, but frail and small, reaching only five feet in height. Very early she set her mind on the religious life and missionary work, dreaming of converting the Chinese. At age 19, she applied to the Daughters of the Sacred Heart, but they rejected her because of her delicate health. The Canossian Sisters likewise refused her application for health reasons.

Francesca secured her teaching certificate and taught in the village school for two years. Knowing her religious desires and impressed by her teaching abilities, a priest recommended her to the Bishop of Codogno, who had a problem and needed someone like Francesca. A local laywoman, Antonia Tondini, was operating an orphanage at her own expense. The problem was that she wore a habit, called herself a nun, was ill-tempered, and not receptive to supervision. Unwisely, the bishop had allowed this situation to continue in consideration of the orphans. His solution was to inject a teacher who had his backing and unofficially represented him. Francesca seemed the answer.

Although the prospect did not appeal to Francesca, she agreed to give it a two-week trial. Those two weeks stretched into six years during which time she endured bullying and scandalmongering by the hateful and jealous Antonia Tondini. Treasuring the religious virtue of obedience, she complied with all Antonia Tondini's commands. In later years she wrote to her sisters —

> *Obedience! Oh, precious word!... Word of revelation, ray of clarifying light that diffuses upon us from the Father the manifestation of the Divine Will through His representative in the world! Whoever does the will of God feels great peace, presages heaven in his own soul! ... Before the precept of obedience all fear ceases, for confidence enters the soul and reassures it. ...*[12]

One speculation about the six years under the harsh control of Antonia Tondini is that Francesca considered this her novitiate and time of religious formation. She learned to give complete obedience before she ever demanded it of others. In the years to come, Mother Frances Xavier Cabrini would walk with the famous, make a companion of any social status feel comfortable, charm the great and powerful, captivate those she met, and convert opponents into supporters.

When the bishop finally had enough of Antonia Tondini, he closed the orphanage but permitted Francesca to take seven of the sisters who had gathered about her. With this core group, Francesca began her religious community. She combined her missionary ambitions with her special devotion to the Sacred Heart of Jesus in the title of the new order, the Missionaries of the Sacred Heart of Jesus. Although finally approved, the word "missionary" created problems, inasmuch as no order for women religious had ever had that word included in its title. She bought a rundown warehouse in Codogno and turned it into their first convent. Although the start of the order was poor and inauspicious — food, fuel, and the other basic needs of life were often scarce — this little band of eight women would grow to thousands and minister to millions all over the world.

Word of Francesca's order spread. She enthralled the country Lombard girls who investigated this new order and joined in ever increasing numbers. Francesca asked the Daughters of the Sacred Heart to refer rejected applicants to her; some she found quite suitable. Early ministries included teaching and caring for orphans. During the first eight years, Francesca built her new order to 145 members and established seven convents.

Most important to Francesca's missionary plans was to begin a foundation in Rome. Because Rome was overrun with convents, it took special permission to establish a new one, a procedure normally taking two to three years. With only a sister-companion and without contacts, Francesca went to Rome in 1887. Within a matter of months, she gained support from powerful cardinals and the required permission for a convent. In January 1889, she had an interview with Pope Leo XIII. Francesca left it with a pope as supporter and friend, a relationship that endured and intensified over the years.

Because Francesca envisioned an international missionary order, she felt it important to establish a foundation in Rome. That city was overrun with convents and it took special permission to establish a new one, a procedure normally taking two to three years. While in Rome, Francesca met a remarkable bishop, Giovanni Battista Scalabrini (1839-1905), the strongest voice in Italy agitating for assistance to Italian immigrants overseas. His personal contributions to this cause were the foundations of the priestly order of Scalabrinians, the **Missionary Sisters of St. Charles Borromeo (MSSCB-2900),** and the lay Society of St. Raphael. He also co-founded the **Apostles of the Sacred Heart of Jesus (ASCJ-0130)** that sent sisters to Boston in 1902. He traveled to North and South America investigating conditions and choosing assignments for his priests and sisters. Since Archbishop Michael Corrigan of New York had asked him for sisters to help Italians in that city, he put the archbishop in contact with Francesca. She wanted to go to China, but her new friend Pope Leo XIII insisted that she to go to the United States and minister to Italian immigrants. She wrote Archbishop Corrigan that she would arrive no later than May 1889.

Eager to begin, Francesca and seven sisters sailed on the *Bourgogne* in March. When no one met them at the dock in New York, they jammed into a taxi and rode to a Scalabrinian parish rectory. The Italian priests greeted them but had no bedrooms to spare, so they sent the sisters to an unfamiliar neighborhood boardinghouse. Mother Cabrini and her companions spent their first night in the United States trying to sleep while sitting up because of the vermin and filth.

In the morning, they were off to see the archbishop. Francesca was astounded when he coldly told her that he had written her not to come and that they were to return to Italy. The letter missed her because of the early start in March instead of May. Looking straight into his eyes, Francesca responded, "No, Your Grace, that is impossible. I have come here with permission of the Holy See and here I will remain." Unaccustomed to such forthright talk, especially from a sister, Archbishop Corrigan reassessed this tiny Italian lady and compromised. They could remain but could not operate the orphanage planned for them. He escorted them to the convent of the Sisters of Charity, whose hospitality they enjoyed for several weeks.

The archbishop's problem stemmed from the location of the house that

Mother Frances Cabrini, foundress of the Missionaries of the Sacred Heart of Jesus.

Missionaries of the Sacred Heart

the Countess di Cesnola, wife of the Director of the Metropolitan Museum of Art, had bought for an orphanage for Italian children. Its location was in one of New York's most fashionable neighborhoods, and the thought of bothersome Italian orphans' offending his benefactors horrified Archbishop Corrigan. He only relented after the countess pled with him on her knees. Francesca made a dress out of a habit for the first little Italian orphan girl to arrive. As it turned out, the house was too small and unsuitable for use as an orphanage, so as soon as she could, Francesca moved the orphans to an Italian neighborhood. Archbishop Corrigan came to call and celebrate Mass, displaying his growing fascination with Francesca.

Over the years, Francesca opened hospitals in New York, Chicago, and Seattle and charitable homes, orphanages, and schools in such places as Denver, Los Angeles, and New Orleans. She was constantly on the move — to new cities, across the Atlantic, to Central America, to South America, and to different European countries. Her first concern was ministry to Italian immigrants, but her foundations were open to all. Her practice was to send for Italian sisters to start a mission and then build with local vocations. In a matter of just five or six years, the majority of sisters in American convents were native-born Americans.

Francesca was a shrewd businesswoman. Desperate for money when founding her first hospital in New York, she hit on the idea of naming it Columbus in honor of America's discoverer instead of giving it the name of a saint or a clearly Catholic title. This ploy secured the backing of the Italian government and aid from anticlerical elements of the Italian-American community. She did the same in Seattle and Chicago, although today the hospitals in New York and Seattle have been renamed "Cabrini." On another occasion, an Italian businessman in New Orleans boastfully promised a large sum of money for her charitable works in that city. Quickly Francesca had a lawyer draw up legal papers that the startled businessman signed. As she had anticipated, his anticlerical friends later persuaded him to withdraw the offer, but Mother Cabrini enforced the legal agreement.

Early one morning in Chicago, a bemused police officer on his beat observed two sisters measuring distances along the sidewalk with a school ruler, chalk, and string. Francesca was in the process of purchasing property for her next Columbus Hospital and she examined the title papers minutely at the sale closing, comparing the measurements her sisters had made with those in the documents. Looking at the agents, she declared that the title papers were inaccurate. They first assured her they were correct, but when she produced the measurements that her sisters had made, they shamefacedly admitted the attempted fraud and corrected the documents to include all the land she was purchasing.

Now an ardent supporter, Archbishop Corrigan informed Francesca of some beautiful property up the Hudson River from New York City that was for sale and perfect for a motherhouse, orphanage, and school. It belonged to Jesuits who wanted to sell because of a water problem. The well gave only enough water for drinking; the rest had to be hauled up a long hill. The price was right and Francesca purchased without hesitation, renaming it West Park. She walked over the property and examined the ground inch by inch. She then directed the drilling of a new well on the spot she indicated. It produced copious amounts of pure water. Francesca loved West Park and said she wished to be buried there.

Francesca later wanted the orphanage moved from West Park closer to the city. One day while touring, she spotted a boys' school in Dobbs Ferry that looked perfect. She asked for the owner, but he was absent. Instead, his son received her. When she announced her desire to purchase, he informed her it was not for sale. Finally, to be rid of this persistent Catholic sister, he said his father might consider $100,000. She said that this was too much, but secured his promise to give her card to his father. On the way out, Francesca secreted a St. Joseph medal in a flower bed and remarked to her companion: "You will see. St. Joseph will drive those boys away." Eventually, she bought the school at an attractive figure.

Money was often short and the till empty when Francesca initiated some new foundation, but a benefactor always appeared at the last moment to bail her out. Only her implicit faith in God justified such audacity, but faith she had in huge quantities. One example of a poverty-stricken beginning concerns the New Orleans foundation. In the spring of 1891, someone murdered the chief of police. The local press blamed Italians. After being acquitted at their trial, a mob formed and dragged 11 Italians out of the jail and hanged them. The authorities were brought in after President Harrison rejected a protest from the Italian government, saying it was a local affair, at which point Italy broke diplomatic relations with the United States. When Francesca investigated the situation she found local Italians in pitiful circumstances, even worse off than the poor blacks. She promised Archbishop Francis Janssens and Father Gambera of the Scalabrinians that she would send help.

Returning to New York, she selected three sisters to establish the mission. After sitting up the entire 52-hour trip, they arrived in New Orleans in the dead of night with no idea of where to go. One sister jestingly suggested they do what St. Francis of Assisi had instructed Brother Leo to do in similar circumstances centuries ago. In imitation of that legend, she spun around until dizzy and pointed in the direction she faced. Off they went up the dark street. A carriage passed, stopped, and turned around. The driver asked if they were the sisters coming to help the Italians. When they answered yes, he loaded them in the carriage and delivered them to Father Gambera's house farther up the very same street. That night the sisters refused to use mosquito nets, saying it violated their vow of poverty. When they awoke the next morning covered with bites, they reassessed the application of the vow to mosquitoes. As usual, the beginning was difficult. Francesca returned to New Orleans to help and joined the sisters in begging for alms to finance the mission. She later said that begging was humiliating and the hardest penance she ever had.

Some Italians emigrated to South America where they became the second largest ethnic group in Argentina and had strong representation in Brazil, Chile, and several other countries. For this reason, Francesca always had South America in her plans. She headed for Argentina in 1895 with a traveling companion, Sister Chiara, an older and rather retiring sister. (Francesca required her sisters to travel in pairs or more.) They sailed down the Pacific coast of South America and disembarked in Chile where both religious and civil authorities cordially welcomed her. She was disappointed to learn that the passes over the Andes to Argentina were closed until the annual thaw and disturbed by the news of the death of the Archbishop of Buenos Aires, who had invited her to Argentina.

The trip over the Andes was an unforgettable adventure. She and Sister Chiara rode the train up the mountains and then joined the first mule caravan of the season for the crossing. The dizzy heights terrified poor Sister Chiara, who lay limp on her mule with her eyes closed so as not to look at the chasms thousands of feet deep and just inches off the narrow trail. A muleskinner with a strong resemblance to depictions of St. Joseph made sure the sisters did not fall into the ice crevasses when they had to dismount and continue by foot. He saw to their comfort and acted as their protector in the rustic inn filled with drunken mountaineers and travelers.

Mother Cabrini took Argentina by storm. The new archbishop and local priests were charmed; she soon sent to New York for sisters to establish an academy. She was filled with joy by a reunion with her brother, Giovanni Batista, a resident of Rosario. Years later, her sister Rosa retired from teaching and sailed to Argentina but died shortly after arrival. As was Mother Cabrini's custom, she walked every street in Buenos Aires in search of a house appropriate for her needs. Having spotted the right one, she purchased it despite warnings that the neighborhood was not safe. It turned out to be perfect for an academy. Seven years later, Mother Cabrini sent founding sisters to Brazil, a fortuitous decision on her part since today Brazil is the greatest source of vocations for the congregation.

Mother Cabrini's other foundation trips read like a travel itinerary: Paris in 1898, Madrid in 1899, four places in Italy in 1900, Spain in 1900, Argentina again in 1901, England in 1902, the United States 1902-1906, Italy and Spain in 1906, Brazil in 1908, England in 1910, Italy in 1911, France in 1914, and England in 1915. She was constantly on the move.

While information on Mother Cabrini's foundations and travels is well-documented, information about her private spiritual life is based on her retreat notes and letters. She guarded her personal sanctity carefully. Her writings concentrated on correspondence to individual sisters and to the 67 convents she founded. These letters of instruction and admonition provide the major sources for insights into her spirituality.

Her governance of the order was a combination of tender solicitude and stern demands for obedience to the rules, spiritual exercises, and the customs of the order. Somehow she kept informed about the spiritual condition of each sister and of any problems. When Francesca visited a convent, she would spend hours with any troubled sister, helping to resolve the problem. However, she did not countenance slackness and could be quite firm. On one occasion, a sister about to sail from Italy to a mission complained aloud to her parents in Francesca's hearing about the hardships ahead. Francesca immediately sent her back to Codogno to review her vocation and commitment.

Francesca had a special devotion to the pope, writing about him in an instructional letter to the convents:

> *He is the visible head of the Church of Jesus Christ on earth, the representative of God, the oracle of the Most Holy Trinity, the embodiment of the Holy Spirit, the audible trumpet of the Holy Redeemer, the mouthpiece of God, the Work of God. The pope is the beacon of Divine Wisdom; and, thus his word and blessing are like a straight column of fire to me, a flame which guides me through every danger and beyond every difficulty. Speak! Oh, daughters, speak to everyone about the pope, so that all who have erroneously left him may come back to him; for it matters not how far one has fallen away from the right path, one may rise and walk again on the road to God. Remind everyone that the pope is a fruitful vine and those who remain faithful to him will produce copious fruits in the mystical vineyard....*[13]

Mother Cabrini devoted most of her time and energies to her order and making new foundations, but she always made time for sisters from other orders seeking her help and advice. Several orders secured pontifical status as a result of her contacts in Rome and knowledge of the ways of the Vatican. She provided invaluable help for Mother Katharine Drexel and was a close friend of Helene de Chappotin, Mother Mary of the Passion, who founded the **Franciscan Missionaries of Mary (FMM-1370)**. That order made a foundation in the United States in 1903 from its convent in India. Her relationship with Pope Leo XIII was close; cardinals and archbishops claimed her friendship as well. The press reported on her regularly. Francesca understood English very well, but spoke with a heavy accent and generally had her speeches read for her. Even so, it was not until Mother Teresa of Calcutta gained fame that a living Catholic sister has been as widely known and admired as was Mother Cabrini.

Francesca's love affair with the United States was lasting. It was her first mission. She sought citizenship and was naturalized in 1909. At its zenith, her order had close to 1,400 members working in a number of countries. In 1926, a wealthy Chinese merchant offered to finance a mission in China, and Mother Cabrini's sisters brought her girlhood dream to pass. Unhappily, the Communists expelled the sisters in 1949 and only two of the eight native Chinese sisters remained behind while the others made their way to safety.

During her last visit to Italy, Francesca sought out Antonia Tondini, the woman who had first tested her vocation to religious life. Going to her and falling to her knees, Francesca asked forgiveness for any unhappiness she had caused. Now 80 years old, poor old Antonia pulled Francesca to her feet and the pair embraced. During this tearful reunion, Francesca told Antonia that she had prayed for her every day since their separation over 30 years earlier. Antonia said that if she had been a better "nun," Francesca might still be tending orphans in Codogno instead of ministering to the world. Antonia knew that Francesca was a saint.

Frail and frequently ill, Mother Cabrini spent her final months in Chicago. Her always concerned sisters noted an unusual tenderness and kindness — omens of her impending death. Even so, Francesca explored the countryside outside Chicago looking for a suitable farm to supply produce to Columbus Hospital and the convent. In fact she closed a deal after personally inspecting the property and cows, as a good Italian country girl should do.

On December 22, 1917, at the age of 67, Mother Cabrini received Extreme Unction and died. Chicago mourned; as did the world. Outpourings of sorrow and love arrived from the pope, cardinals, archbishops, mothers-general of other orders, chiefs of state, senators, congressmen, societies, medical associations, Italian-American organizations, and thousands of individuals. Mother Cabrini lay in state in Chicago as thousands passed her coffin in grief. Her sisters accompanied her body to New York for the requiem Mass and burial. The turnout there was even greater. Mother Cabrini's sisters interred Francesca at West Park as she had requested. Dressed in pure white and each carrying a white lily, 100 orphan girls accompanied the coffin to the grave.

Investigations into Mother Cabrini's cause for sainthood uncovered a whole series of minor "miracles." On more than one occasion a distraught sister came to her because she lacked money to buy bread or pay a pressing bill. Francesca would instruct her to look in her pocket or in a certain drawer. Exasperated because she had already looked several times, the sister would nevertheless obey and look once more only to find the money in the exact amount needed. While strolling down a street or across a city square, Francesca would occasionally remark to her companion that a girl they noticed would one day join their order. Invariably that person applied. On one of her many Atlantic crossings, the ship's engines broke down in the evening and the crew worked all night to repair them. Dawn revealed a veritable forest of icebergs surrounding the ship, much farther south than normal. Had the ship continued plowing ahead in the dark, it could well have crashed into one. Interesting though these "miracles" may be, none was of the caliber needed to certify sainthood. Peter Smith's cure would do that.

Canonized by Pope Pius XII in 1946, Frances Xavier Cabrini became the first American citizen to be canonized. Her memory lives on in the United States in the many parish churches and charitable institutions named for her.

In 1950, the Vatican designated Mother Cabrini the Patroness of Emigrants. All Americans, as well as those of Italian ancestry, have a saint to inspire them and to bolster pride.[14]

Religious Sisters Filippini (MPF-3430)

In the late 17th century, St. Lucy Filippini (1672-1732) founded this order in Italy to teach girls from poor families.[15] Over the years, the order grew into one of the great teaching communities of Italy. Monsignor Luigi Pozzi, the pastor of St. Joachim Church in Trenton, New Jersey, visited Rome in 1910 and with persistent efforts finally secured five Filippini sisters to teach in his parochial school. They departed Rome in 1910 after an audience with Pope Pius X and sailed to the United States.

One thousand jubilant Italians welcomed the sisters with a marching band. As with so many newly arrived immigrant groups, the early years of the Filippini sisters in Trenton were marked by severe poverty. Their paltry pay forced them to exercise extreme frugality. Nonetheless, they were at first successful in their purpose.[16] A parochial school was started. But two years after the sisters arrived, Father Pozzi became ill and Father Edward C. Griffin took over as the new pastor. The climate of the school suddenly changed. He wanted American sisters to operate the school and the Italian sisters to restrict their activities to teaching catechism and Italian. When this plan faltered, he threatened to rent the school building to the city and use the income to pay on the parish debt. At this point, the parishioners rebelled. A large group of women, with sticks hidden under their aprons, taunted him with these words: "Why did you come here? You get out of this parish. Woe to you if you dare send our sisters away!"[17] The men of the parish who were members of the Holy Name Society waited outside as reinforcements. Intimidated, the pastor agreed to keep the sisters. But he soon returned to his old ways, again attempting to send the sisters away, and publicly insulting them by citing their lack of diplomas and declaring that they were not fit to wear the habit. A parish committee submitted an article published by *Italo-Americano* recounting the biased conduct of Father Griffin. A group of parishioners approached Bishop James McFaul. He also was not supportive, telling them, "You have a debt of $50,000 on your church. When you bring the money, you can have an Italian pastor." In the end however, Father Griffin was transferred and the parish got its Italian pastor.

Youngest of the five sisters who sailed from Italy in 1910, Sister Ninetta Ionata became superior in 1916. In this period, the sisters were seriously considering abandoning the mission when, in 1918, Bishop Thomas Joseph Walsh (1873-1952) became the new ordinary.[18] Bishop Walsh took a solicitous interest in these Italian sisters and their parish school; it was the dawning of a new day. On hearing that the superior-general in Rome was recalling the sisters, he sent her this wire: "The government forbids departure." Not knowing which government the wire meant, she withdrew the recall order.

With Bishop Walsh's backing and encouragement, the community expanded with reinforcements from Italy and local vocations. Under Mother Ninetta's dynamic leadership, the school expanded to include 1,000 students. Sisters were sent into Italian neighborhoods without parochial schools to teach catechism and minister to the poor. During the influenza epidemic of 1918, Mother Ninetta sent sisters to nurse the stricken in their homes. Bishop Walsh was highly supportive and arranged for a motherhouse and novitiate on the banks of the Delaware River at the old Fiske estate, purchased with a gift of $50,000 from financier James Cox Brady. Mother Ninetta became the American provincial in 1938 and superior-general of the international congregation in 1954.

By 1960, the community numbered over 500 sisters teaching 50,000 first- and second-generation Italian-American children. Perseverance and the support of a great archbishop combined to overcome prejudice and poverty. Today, the community operates 40 schools in four states and has missionaries in Brazil, India, and Ethiopia. If Mother Cabrini earned the title of "the Patron Saint of Immigrants," others suggested that Mother Ninetta had earned the title of "the Angel of Immigrants."

Other Italian Orders

An order of contemplatives, the **Religious of the Passion of Jesus Christ (CP-3170)**, arrived from Italy in 1910. Commonly called Passionist Nuns, this order is not directly related to the male Congregation of the Passion or to the **Sisters of the Cross and Passion (CP-3180)**, although all three trace their origins back to St. Paul of the Cross, an Italian saint-founder of the 18th century. Mother Mary Louise Campanari and four companions came from Italy and established the first monastery in Pittsburgh. Five additional monasteries have flowered from that original foundation: Scranton, Pennsylvania; Owensboro, Kentucky; Erlander, Kentucky; Ellisville, Missouri; and Hyogo-Ken, Japan. These nuns lead secluded lives in cloister and support themselves by baking altar breads, sewing, printing holy cards, and providing facilities for retreats. They take five simple vows: poverty, chastity, obedience, enclosure, and grateful remembrance of the Passion and Death of Jesus Christ.

Other Italian communities arriving in this era were quite small and grew slowly. Not all assumed the teaching ministry. The **Daughters of Mary Help of Christians (FMA-0850)**, commonly called Salesian Sisters, specialized in youth work. This group came to New Jersey in 1908. The **Daughters of St. Mary of Providence (DSMP-0940)** arrived in Chicago in 1913 to minister to retarded girls. Italian remained the "in-house" language for many years, and this resulted in delightful confusion when non-Italian postulants and novices misunderstood instructions. All these orders function today with the same spirit of cheerful devotion.[19] Over the years, Italian-American young women also joined many of the non-Italian orders. Language barriers and prejudice, even from fellow Catholics, did not deter Italian-American women with a religious vocation.

The **Servants of Mary (Servite Sisters) (OSM-3590)** of Ladysmith, Wisconsin, is an American-founded order with an interesting Italian connection. An Austrian-born Servite priest, Boniface Efferen, conducted a retreat for the Sisters of St. Joseph (3830-02) of La Grange, Illinois in the spring of 1912. He discovered that this community had more sisters than its academy required, and that some were anxious for more active ministry. He described the needs of the parish in Ladysmith for a parochial school. Five sisters under the leadership of Sister Mary Alphonse Bradley expressed a desire to accept the challenge and become Servite sisters. With the permission of the Archbishop of Chicago and after being dispensed from their vows, the five went to Ladysmith and began teaching in the new school. It opened with 95 pupils. The demands in Ladysmith made it impossible to send sisters to Pistoia, Italy, for formation as Servites, so the Italian motherhouse sent Sisters Mary Louise and Benjamin to Ladysmith to inculcate the American sisters with the Servite charism.[20] Two years later the Italian sisters went to Chicago to open a school for Italian children. Two Italian sisters from Pistoia replaced them and remained until 1919. That same year, the local bishop in Wisconsin formally recognized the sisters at Ladysmith as a diocesan Servite community independent of Pistoia. The Servite Order in Rome did the same two years later. In addition to teaching in parochial schools, the community built a hospital and nursing home and is active in operating a convalescent home. They established Mount Senario College in 1962, named after the mountain in Italy where Servites built their original monastery. Today, the sisters are active in education, social work, parish ministry, caring for the sick and elderly, and working for the poor and disadvantaged.

Another Servite community, based in England, came to Indiana in 1893 and established their motherhouse in Omaha, Nebraska. The **Servants of Mary (OSM-3580)** are often called the "Omaha Servites." They remain affiliated with the Servite generalate in Rome.

The third Servite community, the **Mantellate Sisters, Servants of Mary of Blue Island (OSM-3570)**, was established by the two Italian Servite sisters who left Ladysmith in 1916 and went to Chicago to teach. This community is an American province of the Italian Servite order.

The Servite order is ancient. It was founded in 1233 by seven Florentine businessmen at the bidding of the Blessed Virgin Mary to serve the ill and needy. Beginning as a confraternity, it evolved into an order with both male and female branches. The United States continues to draw dividends from those Florentine businessmen of the 13th century.

Although disproportionate in size to the huge numbers of Italian immigrants arriving during this era, Italian sisters and nuns made solid foundations under the leadership of such dynamic women as Mothers Cabrini and Ninetta. These grew as first- and second-generation American-Italian women joined those communities.

Polish Immigrant Orders

Polish fidelity to the Church has been remarkable since Poles believe that their Catholicity is a basic element of their ethnic identity. In some ways, Polish-Americans can easily claim to be even more Catholic than the Irish. The United States has profited by the industry and civic contributions of the Polish immigrant and descendants, not the least of which has been stout performance in the armed forces during wartime.

In pre-Revolutionary days, there were already a small number of Polish immigrants in Pennsylvania as parish records containing Polish surnames document. Generals Thaddeus Kosciuszko and Casimir Pulaski assisted George Washington during the Revolution. General Pulaski was killed in the fighting at Savannah; Robert E. Lee constructed a fort there named for him. Felix Millaszewicz commanded privateers raiding British shipping. During the Civil War, rosters of both Union and Confederate regiments contained a scattering of Polish surnames.

As noted in the account of Mother St. Andrew Feltin and the Sisters of Divine Providence, the first Polish group to make a permanent American settlement was in Texas in 1854.[21] However, significant Polish immigration did not begin until after the Civil War, when Prussian oppression and abortive uprisings against the Russians sent thousands of Poles seeking refuge elsewhere. As happens in most unsuccessful revolts, numerous intellectuals had to leave precipitously and many of them came to the United States. What began as a stream in the 1870's and 1880's became a torrent from 1890 to 1914. It is impossible to pin down specific immigrant numbers since the Immigration Service of that time classified most Poles as Austrian, Russian, or German. Interpolation of Immigration Service figures and Census Bureau reports of foreign-born indicate that around one million Poles had arrived by 1900 and two million by 1910. Some support for these estimates comes from recorded establishments of Polish national churches: 16 during the 1860's, 74 in the 1870's, 170 in the 1880's, 330 in the 1890's and a total of 700 by 1914.

Much like the Germans, Poles had a strong tendency to migrate to the Midwest. Available jobs also drew them to the coal fields of Pennsylvania and the industrial cities in the East. Detroit, Milwaukee, Pittsburgh, Cleveland, and Chicago, quickly became Polish centers. For example, the 1900 census shows Chicago with a population of 1,698,575 of whom 587,112 (34.5 percent) were foreign-born. Sizable numbers of Poles also settled in New York, New Jersey, and Connecticut.[22] Poles were reliable, hard workers whom industrial managers favored. They found employment in meat packing houses, foundries, coal mines, smelteries, furniture fabrication plants, textile mills, slaughterhouses, and heavy industry. As mass production assembly plants developed in Detroit and other industrial centers, Polish workers moved onto the assembly lines. Since many Poles in this era came from rural backgrounds, some naturally sought farming opportunities. Wisconsin was especially popular for land-seeking farmers, as were Michigan, Iowa, Minnesota, and Illinois. Like the Italians, some Polish immigrants originally intended to return to the homeland once they achieved financial security, but few actually did because of unsettled conditions in Poland, failure to realize financial success, and World War I.

Poles cherished traditions, loved their native language, and wanted no part of the Irish-inspired drive for Americanization. Once settled in a rural community or city ghetto, the first thing they sought was a Catholic environment, especially one that included a Polish pastor and sisters to teach their children. A study of this period by Rudolph Vecoli[23] discloses that the Poles gave the most per capita to church support of any ethnic group. Polish laity usually initiated the move for new parishes. They purchased land, built church and school, and then sought a Polish pastor. This procedure caused not a few disputes with bishops and priests since the laity were often reluctant to surrender control of the church they had financed and built. This "trustee" problem — a throwback to the 1830's — contributed to defections to the Old Catholic Church and the Polish National Church, a breakaway splinter denomination, although these desertions were not numerically significant.[24] Polish parishes were highly cohesive and pulsated with religious and social activities; more than any immigrant group, Poles had a sense of parish and community identity. They gave their pastors, but not necessarily other priests, tremendous support and obedience and looked upon them as father-figures. These tendencies only gradually faded.

Chicago was a magnet for Poles and St. Stanislaus Kostka parish is famous. Father Vincent Barzynski left Panna Maria, Texas, in 1874 and took over the parish, presiding there until his death in 1902. As a result of the massive influx of Poles into Chicago, the parish grew to be the largest one in the entire United States. In 1898 for example, it contained 40,000 members with 3,000 children in its parochial school. When fire destroyed the school in 1906, parishioners built a new one with 54 classrooms for its 3,819 pupils — the largest primary school in the United States. Parishes in other Polish communities, if not so large, enjoyed equally strong support.

Women religious orders of Polish origin became prominent in the Midwest and Northeast from the 1890's onward. Beginnings were often difficult due to poverty and language. Yet in putting down roots, each foundress and group hit fertile soil, rich with devout Polish Catholics and potential Polish female vocations. The vibrant Catholicity of Polish women enabled unparalleled growth of their congregations. The first Polish order came to Wisconsin in 1874, and, although the account of their foundation requires a flashback to the 1865-1890 era, it best fits into this overview of the Polish experience.

Felician Sisters

The first order of Polish sisters to establish themselves in the United States was the **Congregation of the Sisters of St. Felix of Cantalice, Third Order of St. Francis (CSSF-1170)**, commonly referred to as the "Felicians."[25] Mother Mary Angela Truszkowska (1825-1899) founded this Franciscan congregation in Warsaw in 1855. During an uprising against the Russians in 1863, the sisters cared for some wounded rebels and the czar ordered the community disbanded. They fled to their center in Crakow, in the Austrian sector. Mother Angela governed her order until stricken by poor health in 1869 and spent her final 30 years in retirement, devoting her hours to prayer and letters. After two wars and many upheavals, the Felician motherhouse removed to Rome where it presently functions. Cardinal Archbishop of Crakow, Karol Wojtyla (Pope John Paul II), opened the apostolic process for beatification of Mother Angela in 1967 and beatified her when he became pope.

Father Joseph Dabrowski is inexorably linked to the early history of the Felicians in the United States. A hunted revolutionary, he fled Warsaw and entered a seminary in Rome. Following ordination, he accepted the invitation of Bishop Melcher of Green Bay, Wisconsin, to minister to the many Poles settling there. Before going to the United States, he went to Crakow to visit his mother and became acquainted with the Felicians. He promised to send for teaching sisters once he got settled. Mother Angela was happy knowing that the Felicians were expanding and rejoiced to know that the sisters would be ministering Poles in the United States.

Father Dabrowski's first assignment was a Wisconsin country parish in

Poland's Corner. Several months after his arrival in 1874, he wrote Mother-Superior Magdalene as follows:

> *The sisters are to be charged with responsibility for schools and orphanages, else all is lost for God and for the Polish people. By the help of God, the sisters may organize a novitiate here from which all Polish parishes could receive ministries. . . . We must conform to standards set for public schools; it would be a misfortune if we ranked lower than the Protestants. . . . [In America] the church is completely free; the government does not assist religion, but, thanks to God, does not interfere either. The school is independent; one teaches what one likes in whatever language. One is free to build churches and convents; the government expresses no concern. In America the sisters will find a wide field of work; teaching religion to growing children so that they may live the faith in everyday life and helping abandoned orphans by taking their religious direction in the school and day nursery. Without a Catholic school here for the Polish child of immigrants, all will be lost for God and country. A day nursery for the Polish children will provide care for many orphans, wresting them from Protestant influence and saving their souls for Christ.*[26]

Mother Magdalene and the council approved the mission and designated five sisters. Sister Mary Monica Sybilska was chosen superior. Their trip through Germany was uneventful despite *Kulturkampf*; they even received free train tickets to Hamburg. But Father Dabrowski was not prepared for their arrival in Poland's Corner. An upper room of the small rectory had to serve as their first convent. School opened downstairs with 30 pupils. A week later, Antonina Zaracz became their first postulant.

Fires destroyed the church in 1875 and again in 1876. The sisters had to beg alms to supplement the insurance. The presence of taverns open on Sundays motivated Father Dabrowski to relocate the parish church to Polonia, two miles from Poland's Corner. He set up a printing press since no Polish-language textbooks were available. He and the sisters composed and printed 45 different books between 1877 and 1904. A highly educated, talented teacher, Father Dabrowski taught the postulants religion, Catholic Church history, world history, Polish history, geography, arithmetic, Latin, physics, chemistry, and drawing.[27] Mother Monica took care of spiritual formation. She wisely refused calls for Polish language teachers from other parishes until the sisters had completed a full novitiate.

The order moved its American motherhouse to Detroit in 1880. There they opened an academy, orphanage, home for the aged, and later established the first Polish-operated hospital in the United States in Manitowac, Wiscon-

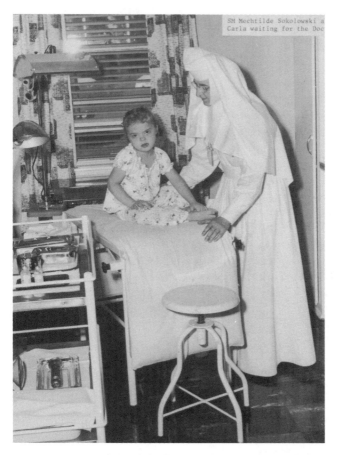

Sister Mary Mechtilde Sokolowski and Carla waiting for the doctor, Felician Sisters, Buffalo, New York.

Courtesy Felician Sisters

sin. By 1881, they had sisters teaching in six locations outside Wisconsin; by 1900, they were operating 40 schools in 11 states. Such growth is unusual. Starting with five sisters in 1874 in a small rural community, the order grew to 400 members by 1900. Factors that promote vocations were strong in the Polish immigrant community: family piety, deep respect for priests and religious, strong ethnic identity, example, and traditional love of the Church. The Felician congregation became multicultural beginning in the late 1940's but cherishes its Polish heritage and culture.

Felicians did not limit their ministries to teaching, health services, and orphanages. They helped staff St. Joseph's Home of Immigrants on Ellis Island until 1913. They established St. Joseph Patronage for Working Girls in New York City which remained in operation until the 1970's. Felicians spread over the country and today have provinces in Buffalo, New York; Chicago, Illinois; Lodi, New Jersey; Coraopolis, Pennsylvania; Enfield, Connecticut; and Rio Rancho, New Mexico. Vice-provinces developed by American Felicians were located in Canada and Brazil; both autonomous provinces since 1988. American Felicians are the largest of all the many Franciscan congregations in the United States and at their zenith numbered around 4,500 members.

Sisters of the Holy Family of Nazareth (CSFN-1970)

The second order of women religious of Polish origin to arrive in the United States landed in New York on July 4, 1885. The order's foundress, Frances Siedliska (Franciszka Anna Jozefa, 1842-1902), led the group of 11 sisters to Chicago in response to an invitation from Father Vincent Barzynski, who had asked for sisters to teach Polish children and care for orphans. St. Josaphat's parish welcomed them with 10 orphans and a delightful Polish feast prepared by the ladies of the parish. Mother Mary Frances (Mother Mary of Jesus the Good Shepherd) remained in the United States three months, during which she called on the archbishop, appointed Mother Raphael Lubowidzka the American superior, and settled the sisters in three Polish parishes: St. Josaphat, St. Adalbert, and St. Stanislaus Kostka. Three months later, the sisters opened a novitiate to accommodate novices who came from the motherhouse in Rome and the anticipated American vocations.

Few immigrant orders have had a more successful start and enjoyed greater growth during their early years in this country than the Holy Family of Nazareth sisters. Soon after arrival in Chicago, their knowledgeable,

sophisticated, capable leader, Mother Frances, called on Archbishop Patrick Feehan. She was accustomed to dealing with high church dignitaries in Rome, and even had an audience with the pope. She impressed the archbishop. They worked out a written agreement stating that the sisters would not be asked to do anything contrary to their rule and that the internal workings of the com-

Polish Cultural Center, Polish Saturday class with Sister Mary Amalia, Felician Sisters, Buffalo, New York.

Courtesy Felician Sisters

munity would be handled by the mother-superior without clerical interference. It also stipulated appropriate recompense and means of support. Father Barzynski and the other two pastors signed the document. Her wise precautions enabled the Sisters of the Holy Family of Nazareth to avoid many pitfalls.

Born into a wealthy family in Poland, Mother Frances had grown up with servants, tutors, and governesses amid a life of social activities befitting her family position. She vacationed in Switzerland, Germany, and France. Her parents were not overly religious and were dismayed when she evidenced deep spirituality at a young age. Her mother gradually became devout and sympathetic, but her father fought against her religious tendencies almost to the end — converting just before his death.

Capuchin priest Lendzian Leander was her spiritual advisor during her teenage and early adult years. Father Leander was skeptical when a Capuchin brother reported receiving a vision in which Frances was to found a religious order and base it in Rome. However the priest gradually became convinced of the validity of the vision and guided Frances in becoming a religious. She opened a convent in Rome and one in Crakow and gradually built up the congregation. She chose the simple ordinary life of the Holy Family in Nazareth as the source of inspiration for the new order. Mother Frances returned to the United States twice during the following 11 years to support and inspire her sisters. She became an American citizen in 1897 in order to be more effective in the United States. Before her death in 1902, she opened a convent in Paris, one in London, and three more in Poland in addition to the American foundations.[28] Mother Frances was declared venerable 1935 and beatified in 1989.

As the American congregation expanded with local vocations and reinforcements from Poland and Rome, it made a fourth foundation in Chicago in 1889, one in Scranton in 1890, one in Brooklyn in 1891, and one in Philadelphia in 1892. By 1902, the congregation was operating 20 establishments, including a hospital in Chicago. The motherhouse and novitiate moved to Des Plaines, Illinois, in 1908. Eventually, the American congregation grew to almost 1,800 members with four provinces and a vice-province. Over the years, the congregation founded and operated hospitals, a nursing school, two colleges, homes for the aging, and a number of academies. They also taught in primary and secondary schools and performed numerous charitable works.

While the original American settlement was made to serve Poles in Chicago, the congregation readily served other ethnic groups. In fact, Mother Frances disliked her daughters being referred to as "the Polish Sisters" since hers was an international order with English, French, German, Italian, and other nationalities. Today Australia, Asia, Latin America, Europe, and the United States are all beneficiaries of the charity of Mother Frances' spiritual daughters. On her deathbed, she called out "charity" in five languages: Polish, Italian, German, French, and English.[29]

Bernardine Sisters of the Third Order of St. Francis (OSF-1810)

The Bernardines were the third Polish order in the United States to gain many recruits and expand extensively. The community derived from an old order in Poland, founded in 1453 by St. John Capistran. Then, the Bernardines were cloistered sisters with one active ministry — teaching girls in their boarding school. In the early 1890's, the order sent several extern sisters to the United States to seek help for their economically strapped community. American Poles, no matter how recently arrived, were better off than most of their countrymen in Poland and responded to such appeals from their meager earnings. Father Thaddeus Jachimowicz, pastor in Mt. Carmel, Pennsylvania, became acquainted with the begging sisters and asked that the order send teaching sisters. In response to this request, Mother Veronica Grzedowska (1843-1916) and four sisters came in 1894 to teach 300 children at Mt. Carmel. That year was a busy one as the sisters taught school while they themselves learned English. Unhappily, their relations with Father Jachimowicz deteriorated rapidly when he demanded they perform duties outside their rule. They were essentially contemplatives and required time for devotions, precluded by full-time teaching and domestic tasks that he required. Mother Veronica wrote Mother Jadwiga, her Franciscan superior in Poland, about the difficulties. Mother Jadwiga wrote back directing them to find another situation or return to Poland. Her instructions were clear and allowed for no other options.

Two sisters who spoke good English went to inform Bishop Thomas McGovern of Harrisburg of the unhappy situation and to seek permission to look for another position. When informed of Mother Jadwiga's instructions, he agreed and the two sisters left for Mt. Carmel. They missed connections in Reading and were forced to take shelter in a nearby church where the pastor, Father Malusecki, listened to their story and invited them to bring the group to his parish. Mother Veronica joyfully accepted.

Life in Reading was an improvement, although the convent was small and some distance from church and school. Father Malusecki was kind and supportive. Shortly after their arrival, a parishioner deposited a small girl for their care. More orphans soon appeared and Mother Veronica secured a state charter allowing for their care. She accepted postulants, although she had no authority to admit them into the order. She longed for a proper convent and orphanage and set about securing one. The sisters went from town to town during the summers asking for contributions and gradually accumulated a fund. Mother Veronica found an abandoned 70-acre estate in the countryside in 1898 called Ridgewood and purchased it for $2,000 with a one-third down payment. It had five large solid buildings but they were in poor condition. This was a lovely site for a motherhouse and orphanage although some miles outside town and inconvenient. That same year, four sisters came from Poland to help with the 24 orphans.

Life at Ridgewood was demanding. Sisters gathered firewood for their kitchen stove and open fireplaces, hauled water from a spring and well, and walked each day with their orphaned students to and from St. Mary's School and Church. Their nagging money problems became acute when they had to close St. Mary's School for a time and nearly could not meet their mortgage payments. They once again sought alms from the local citizens and factory workers. Neighboring farmers helped with the heavy work and donated produce for the sisters and orphans.

One year, a severe winter storm left the sisters snowbound and they ran low on food. Concerned for the sisters and orphans, Mother Veronica gathered the sisters in chapel to pray to St. Joseph. Several hours later, Sister Colette answered a knock at the convent door to find what appeared to be a bearded farmer standing there. At the foot of the stairs was a hand-drawn sled filled with rice and flour. Sister Colette unloaded the food, then called to Mother Veronica and the other sisters to come thank the farmer. When the sisters got to the door, he had disappeared, leaving no tracks in the virgin snow. The sisters all called out, "Thank you, St. Joseph." This story has remained a fond tradition among the Bernardines.

The Vatican granted permission to the congregation in 1901 to establish a novitiate and the sisters vested six postulants with the Franciscan habit, repeating the ancient rite for the their first time in the United States. With each passing year, the small congregation began to realize the need for a convent much closer to town if it was to grow and expand its ministries. Walking the two miles to school each morning and back again to the convent each evening was a tiresome burden and unnecessary loss of time. Monsignor George Bornemann, who became their friend and benefactor, purchased a 10-acre tract of land in Reading for a new convent/orphanage. Mother Veronica raised money for the building by opening a turkey farm at Ridgewood. She then sold Ridgewood.

The sisters moved into the newly constructed convent/orphanage in 1906 and named it Mt. Alvernia after the place where St. Francis of Assisi had received the stigmata. This new motherhouse marked the beginning of real growth for the order: 31 sisters in 1907, 90 in 1912, 260 in 1920, and 1,300 at its peak. They staffed numerous parochial schools and orphanages.

In 1920, Mother Hedwig, who succeeded Mother Veronica in 1912, accepted 50 Polish girls in the Reading orphanage. Soviet Russia had exiled Polish families to Siberia for political reasons and the children were stranded when their parents died. The Catholic Union in Chicago arranged for 100 orphans to come to the United States until they could be repatriated to Poland by the Red Cross.

The Bernardines later became a haven for 50 refugee Polish girls by a strange turn of events. In 1939, occupying Soviets exiled more than a million Poles to the wastelands of Kazakhstan where many died of overwork, exposure, and starvation. General Sikorski, Prime Minister of the Polish Government-in-Exile in London, arranged for about 1,000 of the children to be released by Russia in 1941; many of them ended up in refugee camps in India, but Indian hospitality ceased after the war. The young people could return to Poland, now under Communist control, or seek refuge elsewhere. Father Casimir Bobrowski approached Mother Zygmunta, provincial-superior of the Bernardine Sisters in Scranton. He explained about the girls in India and stated that 50 of them had expressed a desire to join the Bernardine order but lacked funds for travel to the United States. Mother Zygmunta notified Superior-General Edmund. An intensive campaign raised $35,000 and the girls left India in January 1947. Their trip to the Bernardine convent at Villa Maria in Stamford, Connecticut, was a veritable victory parade. Polish-American societies met them at train stops and feted them with banquets and gifts. After their arrival in Villa Maria, 19 of the girls changed their minds about the religious life. Catholic colleges across the country came to the rescue with scholarships. The other 31 girls became Bernardines. These unusual incidents exemplify the Bernardine commitment to the care of orphans.

The American Bernardines broke away from the Polish motherhouse in 1919 because of the many difficulties resulting from the war and breakdown in communications. A Polish missionary priest serving in Brazil, Salesian Father Konstanty, returned to Poland in 1923 for a visit. While home, he informed the Bernardines of the plight of poor Polish immigrants in Brazil and asked for workers to minister to them. In response to this call, four Bernardine sisters, excused from cloister, went to Dom Feliciano to teach, care for the sick in their homes, and provide religious instruction. In 1936, poverty forced the Polish Bernardines to turn to the American Bernardines for help. Despite the Great Depression in the United States, the American Bernardines responded by immediately sending five sisters to Brazil, the first of 50. Their missionary accomplishments and adventures are a fascinating story. In time,

Brazilian vocations swelled their ranks and the Americans returned home. Brazilian Bernardines became a province of the American branch, a role reversal that would have astounded Mother Jadwiga. Following an appeal from Pope Pius XII in 1957 for assistance for Africa, Bernardines went to Liberia and established schools and clinics in Cape Palmas and Monrovia. Today the 740 American Bernardine sisters serve in 11 states plus Brazil and Liberia.

Sisters of St. Joseph of the Third Order of St. Francis (SSJ-TOSF-3930)

Since Poles often gravitated to areas previously settled by Germans, the two ethnic groups often mingled. Polish-German marriages were not uncommon and German-American businessmen frequently hired Polish workers. Poles recognized that they were latecomers to the American scene and needed time in order to match the already established German-Americans. Poles were patient and adopted a positive outlook on this challenge. Polish girls with a religious vocation often joined ethnic German orders and were well-received. German orders such as the School Sisters of Notre Dame staffed some schools in Polish parishes due to the shortage of Polish sisters. Polish women who joined these orders normally taught in those schools.

Despite the mutual respect and common Catholicity of Germans and Poles, tensions based on Old World antagonisms arose from time to time. Polish immigrants could not forget generations of Prussian and Austrian domination. Wealthier and better educated German-Americans tended to assume a superior attitude toward Polish immigrants from the rural peasant class. Sisters were not immune to these sources of ethnic friction.[30] Such problems occasioned the development of the Sisters of St. Joseph of the Third Order of St. Francis.[31]

The School Sisters of St. Francis experienced phenomenal growth in the 1880's and 1890's. They numbered 452 sisters and taught in 93 parochial schools in 1897. Often located where Poles settled in ever increasing numbers, this German order attracted and accepted Polish girls. Starting around 1890, they began supplying teachers to parochial schools in Polish parishes. By 1900, when the order had grown to almost 700 sisters, between 80 and 90 were of Polish extraction. Many, but not all, Polish-American sisters joined with the expectation of teaching in Polish parishes. Naturally, not all Polish recruits were assigned to classrooms. Since Polish schools were in desperate need of teachers, Poles resented the fact that some candidates who were capable and motivated to teach were instead assigned to domestic duties such as work in the sanitarium.

Some other suggestions of ethnic prejudice came into play as the number of Polish sisters increased and their presence became more visible and audible. On several occasions, Polish-language prayer books were taken from them. At times, German superiors in convents seemed to treat Polish sisters coldly and in a few instances even forbade them to speak Polish. It must be remembered how important to self-identification and self-esteem one's native language was to the immigrant and to their first- and second-generation descendants. To disparage that language was an affront to the person and to her people. In short, the Polish sisters in this German order did experience some incidents of ethnic discrimination.

Due to the large number of small rural Polish parishes in the diocese of Green Bay, Wisconsin, the bishop, priests, and laity became increasingly frustrated over the lack of Polish-language teachers. It appeared to them that existing congregations were neglecting them. This provided an incentive to seek separate status. The inevitable break was triggered by an incident in 1900 when six Polish girls from the parish in Stevens Point reported as postulants to the motherhouse in Milwaukee. They had been encouraged by the School Sisters of St. Francis teaching at the Stevens Point parochial school. Since this parish was sending a number of girls to the order, the pastor felt secure that even more teachers would be sent for his school. But the unexpected happened. None of the six postulants was given teacher training; all were instead assigned household duties. Within six months, they were dismissed and sent home. The father of one girl sent Mother Alfons an insulting letter. Mother Alfons then informed the pastor that all her sisters would be withdrawn.

The story of the separation of Polish sisters from the School Sisters of St. Francis is both confusing and complex, entailing heart-rending grief all around. The pastor of St. Peter's Church in Stevens Point took the initiative and secured the agreement of the Polish sisters in his school for a movement of separation. He organized a group of Polish priests to further this plan. Bishop Sebastian Messmer of the Green Bay Diocese, a German-Swiss, understood the situation and sympathized with the frustration of the Polish sisters. He backed the movement from the beginning. Mother Alexia was in Europe during the episode and Mother Alfons adopted a rigid position. She notified all concerned that the School Sisters of St. Francis was no longer diocesan, having just (in January 1900) attained pontifical status and thus Archbishop Frederick X. Katzer of Milwaukee could not grant permission for the separation.

Nevertheless, on July 1, 1901, in an informal service, Bishop Sebastian Messmer accepted the founding sisters as a new congregation in the Green Bay Diocese. The legal contest continued for almost a year using precedents set by Mother Seton's Daughters and their dispute over affiliation with the French Daughters of Charity back in 1850 and the split of the Franciscan Sisters in Milwaukee in 1873. Bishop Messmer wrote the apostolic delegate, Cardinal Sebastiano Martinelli, citing the shortage of sister-teachers for his poor parishes. He indicated that he had more small Polish parishes than any diocese in the country, and for that reason a new Polish congregation was an absolute necessity. Those concerned in the decision sought above all to achieve a just solution, fair to both the Polish-American community and to the School Sisters of St. Francis.

In the end, the Sacred Congregation for the Propagation of the Faith in Rome affirmed the new congregation formed by the 46 sisters who left the School Sisters of St. Francis in Milwaukee. Cardinal Martinelli issued the canonical decree on April 9, 1902. Mother Felicia Jaskulski was elected first superior and Mother Clara Bialkowski vicar-general. The sisters had already been teaching in six Polish schools through the 1901-02 school year, three in Wisconsin, one in Chicago, and one in Detroit.

As requested by the bishop, the congregation concentrated on teaching in Polish parishes for many years. They entered the health care field in 1938, opening the first of their eight hospitals. Over the years they have ministered to other ethnic groups and have sent missionaries to Puerto Rico, Peru, Brazil, and South Africa.

Until 1949, applicants had to prove Polish ancestry to ensure the continued Polish character of the congregation. Polish remained the in-house language for decades, only shifting gradually to English as second- and third-generation Polish postulants entered. Today, the president of the congregation is of Irish lineage.

There were probably some who criticized either the School Sisters of St. Francis, the Sisters of St. Joseph of St. Francis, or both, because of the split. Yet the incident, while creating tension for a time, had beneficial results. It focused attention on the needs of the rising Polish-American community, its intense Catholicity and the mounting numbers of Polish vocations to the priesthood and women religious orders. Greater sensitivity to ethnic feelings and more open acceptance of aspirants doubtlessly resulted. The Sisters of St. Joseph of the Third Order of St. Francis grew to a membership of 1,331 sisters in the ensuing 65 years. The School Sisters of St. Francis also expanded, reaching a total of 3,341 in the same span. In the long run, it would appear that everyone profited from the division.[32]

Franciscan Sisters of St. Joseph (FSSJ-1470)

This predominantly teaching congregation which engages in diverse educational, health care, and social ministries had a rather rocky beginning and owes its existence to a remarkable Polish woman, Agnes Hilbert (1865-1938), known in religion as Mother Mary Colette of the Divine Redeemer. Although founded in the United States, its foundress was a Pole who was a member of a German order that had relocated in Poland because of *Kulturkampf*. Agnes Hilbert's father was Baron Hugo von Hilbert, and her mother, Anna, was the daughter of Prince Tadeusz Siemniszko. As a result of her parents' privileged position, Agnes received a fine education from the Charity Sisters of St. Charles Borromeo in Cieszyn. She later joined that order.

On hearing that the provincial of the Holy Ghost Fathers was going to Europe, Father Anthony Jaworski, pastor of St. Stanislaus Kostka parish in Pittsburgh, asked him to seek some Polish sisters for the parish school. The request was fulfilled by the provincial. It so happened that Sister Colette had volunteered for service in Egypt in 1887 but was told to wait another year. She was selected for America because of her Polish background and command of the English language. At 23, she was the youngest of four sisters who arrived with Mother Marina Fuchs in Pittsburgh on Palm Sunday 1889.

The community and school prospered. Local vocations and reinforcements from Poland increased the number of sisters from the original five to 20. More than 700 children were attending the school after four years' operation. Young Sister Colette taught the sixth and seventh graders. The future seemed bright for this branch of the Charity Sisters of St. Charles Borromeo, but fate took a strange twist.

Borromean sisters take a fourth vow, to nurse the sick in their homes without recompense. Third-year novices were required to go to Cieszyn for a nursing course, taught in German. In order to properly prepare the four American novices for this training, the sisters provided instructions in German and conducted some devotions in that language. This requirement raised a veritable storm among the parishioners. Having been forced to speak German back in Poland, the new Americans were adamantly opposed to their daughters' going to Cieszyn and speaking that language. The upshot was that Superior-General Sophie Watteyne could not waive the requirement since it was integral to the work of her order and neither would the parents allow the novices to go to Poland. Father Jaworski was caught in the middle of this standoff and felt it prudent to replace the Borromean Sisters with Sisters of the Holy Family of Nazareth from Chicago. Mother Sophie recalled her sisters to Poland and the parents of the novices ordered their daughters to return home. However, the four novices clung to Sister Colette and begged her to remain.

Sister Colette received permission from Mother Sophie to take the novices to St. Stanislaus Church in Trenton, New Jersey, in response to a prior invitation. Permission was for one year only, leaving their status thereafter still in question. The pastor, Father Felix Baran, appealed to his Franciscan provincial for help. Father Hyacinth Fudzinski took charge. He was leaving for Europe anyway and promised Sister Colette he would visit Mother Sophie and the Archbishop of Wroclaw to secure the needed waivers. He also asked, should he be unsuccessful, whether Colette would become a Franciscan. This unexpected request posed a profound difficulty because she deeply loved her community, its sisters, and Mother Sophie. Intense prayer and fasting followed. Kneeling before a statue of the Sacred Heart, she pleaded for guidance. Was it God's will that she sacrifice her ties to the Borromeans for the sake of the American novices? Looking into the face of Jesus, she saw Him smile and nod His head. In awe, she broke into tears. Throughout her life she would burst into tears whenever she recalled that vision.

Father Fudzinski met with failure in Cieszyn but with success in Rome. Pope Leo XIII dispensed Colette from her vows and approved the foundation of a new Franciscan congregation to serve Polish-Americans. Sister Colette's letter to the Borromeo convent and one from the convent back to her bespeak the intense grief felt on both sides of the Atlantic over this separation. The letter and reply follow:

> *Most Reverend and Dearest Mother General,*
> *Dear Council Sisters, and Beloved Sisters,*
>
> *In the Most Sacred Heart of Jesus, I am writing this letter. Grief tears at my heart because I must bid farewell to you.*
> *It was under Obedience that I remained in America with the novices on the basis of that one word, "Yes" I received from our Reverend Mother. Only Our Lord knows how difficult I found doing so.*
> *The Most Reverend Father Hyacinth Fudzinski, the Provincial, went to both Cieszyn and Wroclaw with the best of intentions, the desire to stabilize in America the Community of the Charity Sisters of St. Charles Borromeo. Tragically, he did not win the confidence of the Administration. For this reason he went to the Holy See in Rome and obtained for me a dispensation from my vows and permission to establish a new branch of the Franciscan Sisters. With the aid of Our Lord and with gratitude to the Reverend Father*

*Provincial, I shall adopt the Franciscan habit. In conscience I
cannot forsake the poor novices.*

*To my beloved congregation and to you, dearest Reverend
Mother Sophie, I must say Good-bye. I humbly ask for your blessing, Most Reverend Mother. My sincere thanks and appreciation
for my excellent spiritual training, my education, and particularly
for the love I have always received from you. May the Lord repay
you with countless graces for all you have done for me. I beseech
your prayers on my behalf for God's blessing on this new undertaking to which He has led me.*

*I kiss your hand, Most Reverend Mother, and extend cordial
regards as I bid farewell to the entire Community.*

With much love and gratitude to all. . . . [33]

The reply echoed similar sentiments:

Dear Beloved Sister of Ours,

*Intense grief reigned in our midst when your letter arrived —
our Reverend Mother Sophie Watteyne had just expired. Fortunately she did not have to experience the terrible anguish which
befell the rest of us on receiving the news from America. Still
greater sorrow overwhelmed us on learning that you, our beloved
Sister, are severing ties with our Community. Two heavy crosses
were given us to bear in one day: in the morning, the death of our
beloved and revered Mother Sophie; in the afternoon, the loss of
one of our cherished Sisters.*

*But if in God's presence you have reflected well and prayed
much over your decision, and if you love the novices even more
than our Congregation, then may Our Lord, the Blessed Mother,
St. Joseph, and your newly selected patron — St. Francis of Assisi
— assist you in all the difficulties which befall you.*

*We send you our blessing, dear Sister. Most likely our deceased
Reverend Mother is doing so from heaven. (How frequently she la-
mented having sent that Yes.) May Our Lord sustain you with His
grace to fulfill faithfully your new obligations. May your little
band increase for the glory of God.*

*Farewell, dear sister. God bless you and grant you success.
Loving regards from all of us — the orphaned Council and the entire Congregation.*

*P.S. If ever, dear sister, you should be in need, our doors and
our hearts are always open to receive you because we love you.* [34]

The five former Borromean sisters were vested in the Franciscan habit
and became the Franciscan Sisters of St. Joseph in Trenton on September 8,

1897. Sister Collette was now a "mother." When Franciscan Father Baran was transferred and a diocesan priest was assigned to St. Stanislaus parish, the people withheld contributions in protest and forced the parish school to close. Mother Colette faced yet another crisis and Father Fudzinski stepped in once again to assist. He arranged for their transfer to the new Corpus Christi parish in Buffalo, New York, to serve the many Poles settling in that industrial center. This second uprooting was no less painful than the first in Pittsburgh. Happily, Buffalo proved to be fertile ground for the community, which grew quietly under the inspired leadership of Mother Colette. The sisters assumed parochial schools in Polish parishes in Connecticut, Pennsylvania, Massachusetts, and Wisconsin. By 1920 the order numbered almost 300 members.

Financial management was not a strong point with Mother Colette. The pressure of debts caused the Franciscan provincial to relieve her as superior-general in 1921, a painful experience yet a step he deemed necessary for the governance of the growing congregation. She suffered other slights in the following years, yet remained cheerful and an inspiration for postulants and younger sisters. She spent her final years in prayerful retirement at the motherhouse, relocated in 1928 to Hamburg just outside Buffalo.

Father Fudzinski died in 1925. Mother Mary Colette Hilbert, heroic foundress and dedicated Borromean and Franciscan, expired on July 13, 1938, at the age of 72. Hilbert College in Hamburg bears her name. Her gravestone in St. Stanislaus Cemetery in Cheektowaga (formerly part of Buffalo) carries the simple title of "Fundatorka," Polish for "Foundress." One is tempted to think she may have preferred the title "Mateczka" — "Mother."

A much smaller community, the **Daughters of Mary of the Immaculate Conception (DM-0860)**, was founded in New Britain, Connecticut, by Monsignor Lucian Bojnowski in 1904. The founding sisters were M. Agnes Waltosz, M. Lucy Bobrowsks, M. Colette Bermard, M. Rosalie Wolk, and M. Germaine Mysliwiec. Polish-speaking sisters were needed in Connecticut to serve the growing number of Poles. Their original work was with orphans and the elderly and later became educators with a grade school and a girls' academy. Still later they entered health care work in this and other dioceses.

The six Polish-American foundations just described and three others had a profound impact.[35] Six of the eight based their constitutions on the Rule of St. Francis. They located in the midst of Polish concentrations and as quickly as vocations permitted they sent sisters to minister in other Polish parishes, strengthening their ties to the Polish laity. So many Polish-American women and girls have joined practically every order in the United States over the years that their representation in religious communities exceeds the Polish proportion of the Catholic population.

The Polish people, their intense fidelity to the faith, and their holy women have been a blessing for the United States and the Catholic Church.

Orders from Central and Eastern Europe

Peoples from Central and Eastern Europe joined the last of the great immigrant waves pouring into the country. As the immigration statistics in Table III (p. 271) indicate, some four million came between 1890 and 1917. This immigrant wave was a complex mixture of peoples and religions. They were Lithuanians, Ukrainians, Czechs, Slovaks, Croats, Slovenians, Serbs, Estonians, Latvians, Ruthenians, Russians, and Hungarians.[36] Not all were Roman Catholics. Large numbers belonged to the various Orthodox churches not in union with Rome, many were Jews, and some were even followers of the prophet Mohammed. Some Ukrainians were members of Russian Orthodox churches while others were Uniates[37] in communion with Rome. Many of the Baltic immigrants were Lutherans. Each ethnic group had its own particular experiences in settling into a new country, and those accounts are so extensive that generalization must suffice.

Slavic peoples generally paralleled the Poles in establishing themselves in the United States. The industrial complexes of the Midwest and Pennsylvania attracted large numbers while colonies sprang up in the large cities of the East. During these years, few newly arrived or first- and second- generation Slavs ventured to the West or South. Steel mills, mines, factories and the like provided employment. While some stayed in New York, New Jersey, and Connecticut, the majority gravitated to Cleveland, Chicago, Detroit, Gary, Omaha, Milwaukee, Pittsburgh and other industrial towns and cities. Each cluster had its own city ghetto. A small proportion, mainly Czechs and Ukrainians, sought farming opportunities in Minnesota, the Dakotas, Montana, Iowa, Kansas, and Nebraska while others purchased farms from relocating Yankees in Massachusetts and Connecticut. Russian-Germans and Hungarian-Germans moved into the Dakotas in large numbers.

No single Slavic group comprised as many immigrants as did the Poles nor did any one have access to native priests and sisters to the same degree. Yet each ethnic group passionately desired its own ethnic church, pastor, and teaching sisters, going to great lengths to secure them. Czechs, Lithuanians, and Slovaks were generally more successful in securing ethnic priests, but all had difficulty in obtaining ethnic sisters. As a result, many immigrant children attended established parochial schools. Polish and German parishes were generally friendly and helpful, but Irish pastors tended to be insensitive to the needs of Slavic immigrants. The Irish-dominated hierarchy was often just as insensitive to the aspirations of these new and different Catholics and to their cultural religious practices. This was particularly true of Byzantine-rite Slavs who were not familiar with the Latin rite. Ukrainian Uniates, one of the most numerous Catholic Slavic groups, received disgraceful treatment from certain dioceses because their priests could marry. Archbishop John Ireland, not noted for modesty or moderation, flatly refused permission for Ukrainian priests to function in his archdiocese.[38] His liberal views on other matters hardly deterred him from exercising this prejudice. Such treatment drove almost a third of the newcomers into the Russian Orthodox Church.

The reasons why some orders did not come to the United States was because their educational and social services were outlawed. Struggling in the home country, they seldom had the resources or personnel to support their ethnic brethren in the United States. For these reasons, Slavic immigrants had fewer women religious to minister to their needs than almost any other ethnic group.

The Croatian **Sisters of St. Francis of Christ the King (OSF-1520)** came to Kansas City, Kansas in 1909 to teach Croatian and Slovenian children. The **Notre Dame Sisters (ND-2900)** came to teach Czech children and settled in Omaha in 1910. The Czech **School Sisters of the Third Order of St. Francis (OSF-1690)** settled in Pittsburgh where Benedictine sisters provided kindness and assistance. An offshoot from this order **(1700)** was formed in Bethlehem, Pennsylvania.

The world's oldest existing woman religious order, the **Sisters of the Order of St. Basil the Great (OSMB-3730)**, sent a founding group of sisters from the Ukraine in 1911 who settled in Philadelphia to teach Ukrainians of the Ukrainian Byzantine rite. In 1921, a branch was established in Pittsburgh to serve the Ruthenian Byzantine rite Catholics. Both groups are commonly called "Basilian Sisters."

The only congregation with Russian roots is the **Sisters of the Holy Spirit (SHS-2040),** founded by Mother Josephine Finatowitz (1861-1936) in Rome in 1890. Born in Smolensk, she converted to Roman Catholicism at age 13, later going to Rome to enter a Carmelite monastery. She ardently desired to convert Russia. After leaving the monastery for health reasons, she founded the new order for that purpose, naming it the Congregation of Perpetual Adoration of the Most Blessed Sacrament. In 1905, Mother Josephine and several sisters went to Russia, where they suffered persecution and hardships. Before leaving for Russia, she sent Sister Anthony Kolasa and another sister to the United States to seek financial help and to eventually establish a foundation. She also changed the community title about this time. Sister Anthony visited Mother Josephine in Russia in 1912, and finding her in danger of arrest, helped her leave Russia for the United States. Over the years, the community grew with American sisters although Mother Josephine experienced trials and disappointments. Dispossessed by Bishop Francis R. Canevin of the first community established by Sister Anthony, she eventually founded another group in Cleveland. These were not united until after her death. The community lists April 25, 1913 as its American foundation date. Over the years the sisters have focused on education, health care, and homes for the aged poor. They also promote devotion the Holy Spirit. This small community maintains its motherhouse in Pittsburgh.

The **Sisters of the Divine Redeemer (SDR-1020)** came from Hungary. At first they settled in McKeesport, Pennsylvania, but later moved to Elizabeth, New Jersey.

The Slavic surnames common in numerous orders reflect the vocations these devout peoples have supplied the Church. A number of existing communities made strenuous efforts to assist these newcomers. For example, sisters from the Congregation of the Third Order of St. Francis of Mary Immaculate, in Joliet, Illinois, took over St. Wenceslas parochial school, the first school for Czech children in Chicago, without a single sister-teacher able to speak Czech. They hired a lay teacher to instruct in Czech. Sister Delphine studied the language but died before teaching a single day. Sisters from this community took over the St. Procopius parish school with 60 pupils in 1876. By 1900 this was the largest Czech-language school in the United States with over 1,000 pupils. In 1879, they took over a Slovak parish school in Streator, Illinois, the first Slovak parochial school in the western hemisphere. In another instance, the School Sisters of Notre Dame provided leaders for the infant community of Sisters of the Holy Spirit between 1913 and 1918.

The first Slovakian community, the **Sisters of Saints Cyril and Methodius (SS.C.M.-3780)** were begun in 1903 by three Slovak priests who gained the cooperation of Mother M. Cyril, then superior of the IHM's in Scranton, Pennsylvania, to prepare several candidates for work among Slovak immigrants. Receiving their novitiate training in Scranton, three young women, Sisters Mary Mihalek, M. Joseph Bazrtek, and M. Emmanual Pauly, took vows on September 11, 1909. Mother Mary Mihalek and Father Matthew Jankola are considered co-founders. The community had 12 novices at that time. Within just a few years the sisters had taken over schools in Wilkes-Barre, Pittston, and Olyphant in Pennsylvania as well as one in Bridgeport, Connecticut where they taught 1,200 students. In 1915, with the help of The Slovak Catholic Union who defrayed building expenses, the sisters were invited to the Diocese of Harrisburg by Bishop J. W. Shanahan where the motherhouse remains.

American-founded in 1907 in Scranton, Pennsylvania, the **Sisters of St.**

Casimir (SSC-3740) was founded by Lithuanians for Lithuanians. Catholic religious orders were not permitted in the homeland. A devout woman, Casimira Kaupas (1880-1940) left Lithuania for the United States in 1897 to act as housekeeper for her brother, Father Anthony Kaupas, in Scranton. She witnessed the dire need of Lithuanian immigrants and determined to found a community to serve them.[39] With the help of Lithuanian-American priests, Bishop John W. Shanahan of Harrisburg and Mother M. Cyril, IHM, this congregation began its ministerial life. Sister M. Boniface, IHM, acted as both superior and novice-mistress while she formed the new sisters for religious life. In 1911, they moved to Chicago, where there was a large concentration of Lithuanians, and opened a school and later two hospitals. In 1920, Mother Maria Kaupas, SSC, established a community of her congregation in Lithuania that became autonomous in 1934, another role reversal. In 1937, the sisters broadened their ministries to non-Lithuanian parishes.[40] The **Sisters of the Immaculate Conception of the Blessed Virgin Mary (Lithuanian) (2140)** was founded after the establishment of Lithuania's independence in 1918. This congregation sent a founding group to the United States in 1938, which now ministers in Connecticut and Vermont.

Other Immigrant Orders

As they had since the early 19th century, dynamic orders in Canada continued to send founding sisters south of the border in response to pleas by American bishops and priests. Strong vocations and a long tradition of support for the French-Canadian Catholics of New England engendered a positive attitude toward these requests. Twelve more orders[41] made foundations during this era.

During the 1891-1917 era, the anticlerical French government and its laws of suppression[42] against religious orders triggered an exodus of 19 more communities to the United States, bringing the total of French immigrant orders to 63, more than from any other country.[43]

England sent two orders. In addition to the Omaha Servites mentioned earlier, it sent **Sisters of the Little Company of Mary (LCM-2270)** to Chicago in 1893. They specialize in health services and praying for the dying.

Spain sent three orders. The **Society of St. Teresa of Jesus (STJ-4020)**, commonly called "Teresian Sisters," is large worldwide but small in the United States. Another large international order, the **Sister Servants of Mary (SM-3600)**, came via Mexico and have several hundred sisters engaged in general ministry. The **Mothers of the Helpless (MD-2920)** maintain a day nursery in New York City.

Revolution in 1910 and persecution of the Catholic Church in Portugal caused two orders to migrate here: the **Institute of the Sisters of St. Dorothy (SSD-3790)** and the **Congregation of the Dominican Sisters of St. Catherine of Siena of Kenosha (OP-1070)**.

Switzerland contributed two more orders: the **Sisters of St. Francis of the Holy Eucharist (OSF-1560)** and the **Sisters of Mercy of the Holy Cross (SCSC-2630)**.

Although the vast majority of Mexicans are nominal Roman Catholics, the Church has been plagued by persecutions going back to Mexican independence from Spain. The Free Masons were strong in intellectual and political circles, and radical revolutionaries found the Catholic Church a convenient whipping boy for Mexico's troubles. Thus, when the Mexican revolutionary government in 1910 began serious persecution of the Catholic Church, many priests and sisters fled to the United States. Some of these refugee sisters joined existing American orders, including Carmelite nuns who fled in terror when authorities crudely violated their convents.

American-Founded Orders

America's third order of black sisters, **Franciscan Handmaids of the Most Pure Heart of Mary (FHM-1260)**, was founded in Savannah, Georgia, in 1916. The community soon moved to New York City, the present site of their motherhouse. This community affiliated with the Franciscan order in 1929 and added the word "Franciscan" to their original title. Today, this diocesan community is open to all races. Sisters serve in teaching preschool and elementary school children, pastoral care to the sick and unwed mothers, religious education, and outreach to the homeless. Like this community, most of the new American-founded congregations of this era were and are small.[44]

An interesting beginning concerns the **Mission Helpers of the Sacred Heart (MHSH-2720)**. Father Herbert Vaughan, an English priest, founded an order of priests and brothers in 1866 to propagate the faith among unevangelized peoples.[45] Founded at Mill Hill in London, they soon became known as the Mill Hill Fathers. Their first mission in the United States was in Baltimore in 1871. This order became the independent Josephite Fathers in 1893 and now labors among blacks. Stirring appeals for help by these priests drew an unusual woman, Anna Hartwell (1855-1910), to Baltimore from New York. Anna, a Chicago native, was a widow and convert to Catholicism. Father Slattery, the Josephite superior, was delighted to have her help and Anna immediately joined a small group of ladies in St. Peter Claver parish calling itself "St. Joseph's Guild." A woman of charm, Anna soon assumed leadership. The ladies taught Sunday school, visited homes, and conducted classes for black girls in sewing, cooking, and reading. Anna, who assumed the title of "Sister Joseph," wanted to found a religious order to minister to blacks and approached Bishop (later Cardinal) James Gibbons. He approved and commended their work to Providence and to the Josephite Fathers to determine success or failure. Father Slattery assumed oversight of this proposed foundation. In contrast to the foundation experiences of so many communities, both the foundress and the assigned priest mentor proved to be ineffective in leadership roles, making the community's survival and subsequent successes the more remarkable.

Anna Hartwell met Mary Frances Cunningham (1859-1940) one day at St. Peter Claver parish. Mary Frances had moved to Baltimore from Washington with her family when she was 10 years old. One of 13 children, she attended school taught by the Sisters of Mercy until age 14, when she went to work in a garment factory. Mary Frances was highly intelligent and in short order became the bookkeeper. Her parish, St. Martin's, had numerous black children who were receiving no religious training, and Mary Frances got permission to open catechism classes in the basement of the parish school. Her development of methods for teaching the catechism and later for teaching the deaf attest to her brilliance.

That day in 1890 at St. Peter Claver parish when the two women fell into conversation, Mary Frances decided on the spot to join forces with Anna. Father Thomas Broydrick, her pastor, was cautious and advised waiting to see if this new community could survive. When she pressed him for permission, he said he would confer with Bishop Gibbons for a decision. The bishop said, "Let her go. Something may come of it." She joined the Mission Helpers and took the religious name of Sister Demetrias. Anna Hartwell was now known as Mother Joseph. Since the early members shared a deep devotion to the Sacred Heart of Jesus, they incorporated Sacred Heart into their title of Mission Helpers.

Ministries in the early years included teaching catechism, visiting private homes, alms-houses, prisons, and reform schools, ministering to the deaf and blind, and caring for orphans taken into the motherhouse. They established an industrial school for black girls. When local pastors noticed that black children were better instructed in the faith than their white parishioners, these priests insisted that the sisters expand that ministry to include white children.

While poverty in the early stages of new orders is often characteristic, this community struggled more than most. Mother Joseph seemed incapable of financial management, quickly assuming new ministries for the sisters without adequate financial resources. In addition, Father Slattery neglected his oversight responsibilities, failing to insure a rule for the new community and allowing Mother Joseph to incur heavy debts. He failed to provide sufficient clarity of vision with regard to the community mission. Confusion erupted with regard to spiritual matters as well as financial issues. The sisters were forced to beg alms and operate a commercial laundry that increasingly required more sister-workers and longer hours in the steamy ironing rooms. When Cardinal Gibbons learned of the situation in 1895, he relieved Father Slattery and appointed Father Peter Tarro to oversee the floundering community.

Mother Joseph's general health gradually deteriorated and · Sister Demetrias had to assume greater and greater responsibility. Mother Joseph left with increasing frequency, spending two years in Puerto Rico establishing a mission and going to spas in Europe for treatment. As a recent convert to Catholicism, she was ill-prepared for the leadership of a religious community. She increased the financial burdens by purchasing religious statues, articles, and art (including her own portrait) and scheduling trips abroad. Mother Joseph would often turn administration over to Sister Demetrias only to abruptly resume control. She expanded ministries without adequate financial support: a school for the deaf in Baltimore, the mission in Puerto Rico, a nursery in Trenton, and a new convent in New York. By 1906, the Mission Helpers were in a state of crisis. Even so, Mother Joseph continued expansion plans, sending sisters to Guam and departing once more for Europe herself. Sister Demetrias struggled with debts and overworked sisters who needed both spiritual and physical nourishment.

Matters came to a head in 1906 when Cardinal Gibbons directed Father Tarro to call for the first Chapter of Elections. Mother Joseph received a letter in Europe announcing the chapter and the urgent need for a constitution. It requested her immediate return and she set out for New York. Upon arrival she resigned her position as superior and then sent another letter resigning from the community. Her declining mental and physical health had taken its toll.

Sister Demetrias was elected unanimously and became Mother in title as well as fact. She is considered the order's foundress. Anna Hartwell went to Rome with her mother in 1907 and died in 1910 while under the care of the Sisters of the Little Company of Mary. Her contributions attest to the mystery of God's call and designs. Mother Demetrias and all the sisters prayed for their departed and separated co-foundress.

Mother Demetrias served two six-year terms as superior and rectified the unsatisfactory situation. This relatively small order has done outstanding work with their unusual ministries. A feature that distinguishes them is their close identification with the laity wherever they serve. They go out to minister rather than having recipients come to them. Today they operate in 51 missions, plus one in Puerto Rico and one in Venezuela. It seems that after all "something did come of it."

In an unusual move, this order recently joined forces with the Sisters of

Mercy in Baltimore for the care of elderly sisters of both communities in a single facility — a harbinger of things to come.[46]

Sisters of the Holy Cross, Sisters of St. Joseph of St. Louis, Sisters of Charity of Emmitsburg, Maryland with lay nurses and Father Bader, Camp Hamilton, Lexington, Kentucky, 1898.
Courtesy Archives, Bertrand Hall, Saint Mary's, Notre Dame, Indiana

War-Nurses Again

The United States went to war with Spain in 1898 and within a matter of months won a stunning victory. Americans suffered very few battle casualties, but, as during the Civil War, disease created havoc. Rapid mobilization and massing of recruits in training camps set the scene for dysentery and typhoid epidemics. Large numbers of occupation troops in Cuba and Puerto Rico contracted malaria. When the call for volunteer nurses sounded, Catholic sister-nurses stepped forward once again.

The Daughters of Charity supplied around 200 of the roughly 300 sister-nurses who served with the military. They opened their many hospitals to military patients, as did the Sisters of St. Francis of Philadelphia, the Sisters of the Holy Cross, and several other communities. Most of the other 100 sister-nurses came from the Sisters of Mercy in Baltimore and the Sisters of St. Joseph of Carondelet in St. Louis.[47] Sister-nurses adapted quickly to the military routine with its bugle calls such as reveille, mess call, recall and taps, governing the pulse of life. A teaching order, the Sisters of the Holy Names of Jesus and Mary in Key West, Florida, converted their convent and school into a hospital. Trained civilian nurses supervised the sister-teachers, who quickly learned the basics of nursing and performed satisfactorily. This was the first hospital to receive casualties following the Battle of Santiago.

Some sisters served on hospital ships evacuating the sick from Cuba and Puerto Rico, but most of them served in the camps on the mainland where thousands of sick soldiers required their help. One example of these experiences comes from the memoirs of a Sister of the Holy Cross who served at Camp Hamilton in Lexington, Kentucky:

> *About one o'clock we reached the camp. . . . Some of the soldiers told us afterwards that our entrance into the hospital grounds was the most beautiful sight they ever saw; but the reality of what we were facing dawned on us at the sight of the long rows of tents, and so we did not feel fine at all. . . . Not much preparation had been made for our coming. . . . We were introduced to Major Stewart, who placed us in charge of the Typhoid Ward, containing over fifty patients, most of them very ill. . . . We learned that there were over six hundred sick, who were in tents all around us. . . . The sisters went to the wards immediately after breakfast (six o'clock in the morning) and stayed until ten at night, barely taking time for their meals. . . . Between ministrations, they wrote letters for the men. . . .*[48]

After the war, Surgeon-General George M. Sternberg sent each community a letter of appreciation and testimony to their efficient, intelligent, and faithful service. In a letter to the Daughters of Charity that reflected the attitudes towards all sister-nurses, Dr. L. Brechemin, the surgeon of a large military hospital set up in Chickamauga, Georgia, wrote the following:

> *I can hardly tell you in words strong enough how much of an assistance and comfort you have been to me — I worked hard for them and they did the same for me — never failed me. They took superb care of the patients. They helped me in every department of my hospital and if it was a success a great part of the credit is due to them. . . .*[49]

Theodore Roosevelt's "splendid little war" ended quickly. Once the patient loads diminished, the nursing sisters returned to their convents and places of regular ministry. Before the next war, both the U.S. Army and U.S. Navy would have their own nursing corps and only one community of Catholic sisters would participate as nurses in an overseas battle zone.

End of an Era

As wars have a way of doing, World War I punctuated the end of the Age of Immigration that began with Germans fleeing *Kulturkampf* in the 1870's. Close to 25 million immigrants arrived during those 40-plus years. The ethnic composition of the American population underwent a profound change as did the Catholic Church. The title "Immigrant Church" has a solid foundation, and the sisters who came to the United States during those years were critical to that foundation. As Father Dabrowski wrote from his country Wisconsin parish to Felician sisters in Poland in 1874: "Without a Catholic school here for the Polish child of immigrants, all will be lost for God and country," this sentiment rang true for many Italians, Slavs, and other nationalities during this period. It was the impetus for many sisters who came to America to minister in schools, orphanages, and hospitals. They became culture-carriers to the New World.

The end of World War I initiated what most consider to be the "modern age," treated in later chapters. While we have been concentrating on new and different peoples and new religious orders in the post-Civil War years, other important events and developments were transpiring. Probably the most important Church conclave in United States history took place during the Third Plenary Council of Baltimore in 1884. As we shall see, sisters enabled the explosive expansion of Catholic education that the council mandated. Concurrently, sisters founded hospitals at an unprecedented rate as they expanded their health services. Therefore, we are not ready to leave the 1866-1917 years quite yet. The next chapter fills in many of the gaps of sister-history missed along the way.

Endnotes

1. When urged to make peace with the Cathodic Church because of the ill effects for Germany created by persecution and the diplomatic break with the Vatican, Bismarck is reputed to have remarked, "I will not go to Canossa." This was a reference to Holy Roman Emperor Henry IV's excommunication by Pope Gregory VII in 1076. Seeking relief, the emperor walked over the Alps in winter, approached the castle at Canossa where the pope was staying, and, barefoot in the snow, prostrated himself before the pope at the castle gate.
2. George Brown Tindell, *America: A Narrative History* (New York, NY: W.W. Norton & Co., 1984), p. 744.
3. Sr. Mary Ewens, OP, *The Role of the Nun in Nineteenth-Century America* (Salem, NH: Ayer Company Publishers, Inc., 1971), p. 294.
4. The Knights of Columbus was founded in 1882 by Father Michael J. McGivney (1852-1890) in New Haven, Connecticut. This fraternal organization of Catholic laymen has raised huge sums of money with its life insurance policies and has

made thousands of mortgage loans for the construction of Catholic churches and institutions.

5. Sr. Dolores Liptak, RSM, *Immigrants and their Church* (New York, NY: Macmillan Publishing Company, Inc. 1989), p. 78.

6. Typical were Sisters of Mercy from Ireland who began work in New Hampshire in 1857. Fifty-five percent of those joining their community between 1857 and 1880 were Irish-born. Between 1881 and 1908, the percentage dropped to 29 percent.

7. Archbishop John Ireland's treatment of Mother Alexia is one example of "forcibly."

8. Giovanni Schiavo, *Italian-American History, Vol. II: The Italian Contribution to the Catholic Church in America* (New York, NY: The Vigo Press, 1949), pp. 503-504.

9. Michael La Sorte, *La Merica: Images of Italian Greenhorn Experience* (Philadelphia, PA: Temple University Press, 1985), p. 84.

10. Episcopalian groups were especially active in attempting to proselytize Italians. Today, Italian surnames occur with surprising frequency among the Episcopalian clergy.

11. A relic is part of the human remains or some object intimately associated with a saint or martyr. Veneration of relics goes back to the earliest days of Christianity when the faithful sought them for edification. The traditional expression "raised to the honors of the altar," used when a saint is canonized, refers to the ancient practice of digging up the remains and "raising" a bone to the altar stone of a church. The cult of relics has been a matter of dispute within the Church. In some eras relics were the source of abuse and scandal. Non-Catholics generally view veneration of relics as pure superstition. Catholic theology on relics is complex, ranging from stout defense to near condemnation. Because of its antiquity, the Church allows the cult within bounds, because of the purpose of veneration, to pray to and pay homage to its source. Canon law is strict concerning identification and handling of relics — excommunication is imposed for selling one. Eastern Orthodox churches place great store on relics and their veneration while modern American Catholics are generally ambivalent on the subject.

12. Mother Saverio De Maria, MSC, *Mother Frances Xavier Cabrini* (Chicago, IL: Missionary Sisters of the Sacred Heart, 1984), p. 42.

13. Ibid., p. 130.

14. Also see Sr. Mary Louise Sullivan, MSC, *Mother Cabrini: "Italian Immigrant of the Century."* (New York, NY: Center for Migration Studies, 1992). Considerable information was derived from this book.

15. St. Lucy Filippini was canonized in 1930. Her statue occupied the last remaining niche reserved for founders and foundresses of religious orders at the Basilica of St. Peter in Rome.

16. Like many sister-teachers of this age, the Filippini teachers received the paltry pay of $12 per month, and sewed at night to supplement this meager wage.

17. Sr. Margherita Marchione, MPF, Religious Teachers Filippini in the United States, *U.S. Catholic Historian,* Vol. 6, No. 4, p. 357. Also see *A Pictorial History of the Saint Lucy Filippini Chapel* (Prato, Italy: Edizioni del Palazzo, 1992), p. 130.

18. One of the first to send congratulations upon his appointment as bishop and one of the first to call on him was Sister Ninetta. During the interview, Sister Ninetta mentioned that they had so few chairs that they had to carry them along when moving from room to room. The bishop handed her a folded bill that she was too modest to examine until leaving the bishop's residence. It was a $100 bill, something she had never before seen. The ecstatic Sister Ninetta and her sister companion rode the streetcar home instead of walking.

19. The others are —
    Sisters of the Divine Savior (SDS-1030).
    Sisters of St. John the Baptist (CSJB-3820).
    Daughters of Charity of the Most Precious Blood (DCPB-0740).
    Sisters of the Resurrection (CR-3480).
    Apostles of the Sacred Heart of Jesus (ASCJ-0130).
    Religious Venerini Sisters (MPV-4180).
    Mantellate Sisters, Servants of Mary of Blue Island (OSM-3570).

20. This was not the first Servite foundation in the United States. In 1887, Mother Mary Celestia and seven Servite sisters came to Chicago from Italy and operated an orphanage, academy, and novitiate. In 1897, the sisters had a dispute with Archbishop Patrick A. Feehan over title to the property they occupied. He excommunicated the sisters and the community dissolved.

21. In 1854, Father Leopold Moczgemba came with 100 families from Upper Silesia to Texas seeking religious freedom, economic opportunity, and escape from Austrian domination. They settled in Panna Maria, the first Polish settlement in the United States. From here they founded the towns of St. Hedwig, Kosciuszko, and Bandera. Father Moczgemba is considered the "Patriarch of American Polonia" by Polish-Americans. He died in Dearborn, Michigan, in 1891 and was buried in Detroit. His remains were transferred to Panna Maria in 1974.

22. In 1913, Connecticut had the highest percentage of Poles of any state — 18 percent of the state's population.

23. Rudolph Vecoli, "Prelates and Peasants: Italian Immigrants and the Catholic Church" (*Journal of Social Studies,* Spring, 1969), p. 238.

24. The Old Catholic Church is a loose confederation of small national churches brought together in 1889 by the Union of Utrecht. These churches refused to accept the papal infallibility that was promulgated by the Council of Vatican I in 1870.

25. A failed order, termed the Sisters of the Immaculate Conception and commonly called Blue Sisters because of their habits, was established in Panna Maria, Texas, in 1875. Father Felix Zwiardowski organized the group with local Polish girls and designated them Sisters of the Immaculate Conception over the objections of Mother Marcellena, the superior of this order in Poland. It grew to 30 sisters but disbanded four years after foundation on orders of the bishop because of mismanagement by Father Felix. Some of the women joined other orders while the rest returned home. Although the first Polish religious community in one sense, this small group cannot be considered a canonically defined religious congregation.

26. Sr. Mary Jane Kadyscewdki, CCSF, *One of the Family: History of the Felician*

Sisters, Our Lady of the Sacred Heart Province, Corapolis, Pennsylvania, 1920-1977 (Pittsburgh, PA: Wolfson Publishing Co., Inc., 1982), p. 28.

27. Father Dabrowski's accomplishments were not limited to overseeing the Felicians. He opened Sts. Cyril and Methodius Seminary in 1886 which became a critical institution for Polish communities all over the United States. He administered the seminary for 26 years and was a no-nonsense superior. In 1903, a group of seminarians used unethical tactics in organizing a protest against his strict rules. Despite protests from the Polish clergy and press, he dismissed 29 seminarians. He was also suspicious of the "Americanization" movement, fearful that it would hasten the loss of Polish culture and weaken loyalty to the Church.

28. During World War II, seven of the Polish convents of the Sisters of the Holy Family of Nazareth came under first German and then Russian military control. Of the 353 sisters, 100 ended up in concentration camps, 35 in prison, and the balance dispersed. On August 1, 1943, German authorities marched 11 sisters of the Nowogrodek convent into the countryside where the sisters were forced to dig a ditch. They were then shot and tossed into this grave. One sister who had eluded the Germans discovered the rude grave a few days later. Today, these heroic women who were executed because they dispensed charity to the wounded, sick, and escapees are honored with a monument near a chapel in that city. On October 11, 1990, the first official step was taken introducing the cause for canonization of Sister M. Stella and her ten companions.

29. See Katherine Burton, *Where There Is Love: The Life of Mother Mary Frances Siedliska of Jesus the Good Shepherd* (New York, NY: P. J. Kenedy & Sons, 1951). Also see Antonio Ricciardi. Translated by Regis N. Burwig, *His Will Alone: The Life of Mother Mary of Jesus of the Good Shepherd* (Oshkosh, WI: Castel-Pierce Press, 1971).

30. Ethnic friction in general society carried over into religious communities in rare instances. Non-Irish sisters, especially Italians, sometimes felt discrimination in Irish-American communities and Hispanic sisters were sometimes treated as second-class religious in Texas and the Southwest.

31. The original title of this congregation was Polish Sisters of St. Joseph. In 1925, it was changed to Sisters of St. Joseph and finally, in 1931, to its present title.

32. Sr. Josephine Marie Peplinski, SSJ-TOSF, *A Fitting Response: The History of the Sisters of St. Joseph of the Third Order of St. Francis, Part 1, The Founding* (South Bend, IN: The Sisters of St. Joseph, 1982). Most of the account is derived from this book.

33. Sr. M. Edwina Bogle, FSSJ, and Sr. Jane Marie Brach, FSSJ, *In All Things Charity: A Biography of Mother M. Colette Hilbert* (Hamburg, NY: Franciscan Sisters of St. Joseph, 1983), pp. 58-59. Most of the account is derived from this book.

34. Ibid., p. 59.

35. The others were —

    Sisters of Resurrection (CR-3480).
    Franciscan Sisters of Chicago (OSF-1210).
    Franciscan Sisters of Our Lady of Perpetual Help (OSF-1430).

36. Hungarians and Lithuanians are not Slavs, but are often mistakenly included

with them since they arrived about the same time from similar regions and had similar experiences. Cleveland became a national center for Hungarian-language newspapers and societies.

37. Ukrainian Catholics are not particularly fond of the term "Uniate," but accept it as descriptive.

38. Approximately 500,000 Ukrainian immigrants arrived between 1870 and 1914.

39. Sr. Dolores Liptak, RSM, *Immigrants and Their Church* (New York, NY: Macmillan Publishing Co., 1989), p. 137.

40. See Rev. John M. Lozano, CMF, *Founding of the Sisters of St. Casimir: Mother Maria Kaupas* (Chicago, IL: Claretian Publications, 1981). The account is derived from this book.

41. They were —

Sisters of Charity of Quebec (SCQ-0560).
Sisters of the Assumption (SASV-0150).
Religious Hospitallers of St. Joseph (RHSH-3440).
Society of the Sisters, Faithful Companions of Jesus (FCJ-4048).
Congregation of Our Lady of the Holy Rosary (RSR-3100).
The Little Sisters of the Holy Family (PSSF-2320). (They support
   priests with prayer and domestic services.)
Daughters of Wisdom (DW-0960).
Sisters of Ste. Jeanne D'Arc (SJA-3815).
Ursuline Nuns (OSU-4110).
Congregation of the Daughters of Jesus (FJ-0830).
Sisters Auxiliary of the Apostolate (SAA-0140).
Sister Adorers of the Precious Blood (APB-0110).*
   * Contemplatives with six autonomous monasteries: Brooklyn, NY;
      Watertown, NY; Manchester, NH; Portland, OR; Portland, ME;
      and Lafayette, LA.

42. An indication of the severity of French governmental suppression during these years was the closure of 514 convents of the Daughters of Charity.

43. The 19 new arrivals were —

Dominican Sisters of the Perpetual Rosary (OP-1050).
Little Sisters of the Assumption (LSA-2310).
Benedictine Sisters of Our Lady of Belloc (no longer existing).
Society of Helpers (HHS-1890).
Congregation of Notre Dame de Sion (NDS-2950).
Religious of Our Lady of the Retreat in the Cenacle (RC-3110).
Sisters of St. Ursula (SU-4040).
Daughters of the Holy Spirit (DHS-0820).
Sisters of St. Mary of the Presentation (SMP-2450).
Sisters of St. Chretienne (SSCH-3750).
Sisters of the Sacred Heart of Jesus (SSCJ-3670).
Religious of Christian Education (RCE-3410).
Congregation of the Infant Jesus (CIJ-2230).
Daughters of Charity of the Sacred Heart of Jesus (FCSCJ-0750).

> Dominican Sisters of Charity of the Presentation of the Blessed
> Virgin Mary (OP-1100).
> French Benedictine Sisters (no longer existing).
> Sisters of St. Joseph (Lyons, France)(CSJ-3870).
> Sisters of Charity of St. Louis (SCSL-0620).
> Franciscan Missionaries of Our Lady (OSF-1380).

44. They were —

> Sisters of St. Francis of the Immaculate Conception (OSF-1580).
> Sisters of Reparation of the Congregation of Mary (SRCM-3470).
> Daughters of Mary of the Immaculate Conception (DM-0860).
> Sisters of Our Lady of Christian Doctrine (RCD-3080).
> Missionary Servants of the Most Blessed Trinity (MSBT-2790).
> Maryknoll Sisters of St. Dominic (MM-2470). (See Chapter 9.)
> Franciscan Handmaids of the Most Pure Heart of Mary (FHM-1260).

45. Father Vaughan later became Cardinal Archbishop of Westminster.
46. Carol Clark Croteau, *Heart Touching Heart* (Baltimore, MD: Mission Helpers of the Sacred Heart, 1990). Also see John C. Murrett, MM, *The Mary of St. Martin's* (Westminster, MD: The Newman Press, 1960).
47. Father Craft and the four Indian nurses (see next chapter) are not included since they did not belong to a recognized order and the sisters were not properly trained nurses.
48. Sr. Ursula Stepsis, CSA, and Sr. Dolores Liptak, RSM, eds., *Pioneer Healers: History of Women Religious in American Health Care* (New York, NY: Crossroad, 1989), p. 62. Much of the information in this chapter and Appendix C on hospitals and nursing schools has been derived from this book.
49. Ibid., p. 65.

CHAPTER 8

Gathering Bouquets (1866-1917)

✝ — ✝

THE HALF-CENTURY reported in the preceding two chapters constitutes a fascinating period of sister-history. Yet the story of how women religious performed their varied ministries was left incomplete amid the vortex of massive immigration, ethnic strains, immigrant orders and new American foundations, dramatic increases in sister-population, and movement into the West with its accompanying adventures and struggles. Their apostolates were critical to preservation of the faith and economic advancement of millions of Catholics, immigrant and native-born, as well as to the fortunes of the Catholic Church. These ministries and the women religious who performed them require more than the brief glimpses provided in the foregoing two chapters since they set the patterns of religious life and service that would govern for the next half-century. We follow the laborers into their many gardens.

Parochial Schools

Nothing in American Catholic history compares in scope to the increase in parochial schools during this era, an accomplishment made possible by the herculean efforts of thousands of selfless women religious devoting their lives to this ministry. World history records no comparable complex of private schools operated without government support.

The parochial school, as that institution is understood today, became the central feature of American Catholicity in the final decades of the 19th century. The Third Plenary Council of Baltimore in 1884 focused on the subject and issued declarations designed to create a massive increase. While parochial schools existed in America going back to Mother Seton's free school in Emmitsburg and increased quietly all during the antebellum years, the 19th-century slogan "school first, church second" illustrates the emphasis on Catholic education.[1]

In presenting statistics about this institution, a definition problem arises. The correct and common understanding today of a "parochial" school is one attached to the parish that builds it, underwrites its operations, and employs sister-teachers from some religious community. However, this neat arrangement was not always the case. During the first two thirds of the 19th century, women religious often built schools with their own funds and operated them without any allegiance to a particular parish. The combination academy, free school, and orphanage was a common arrangement. The same applies to boys' schools operated by orders of priests and brothers.[2] The statistical count of parochial schools in the 19th century contains many schools that do not fit today's definition.

With those caveats, we can accept the numbers of those who have examined the subject. For instance, John O'Kane Murray wrote in 1876 that there were 1,645 "parish" schools and 557 academies and "select schools."[3] His count must be considered highly accurate since he concentrated on establishing statistics concerning American Catholics. His count of "select schools" refers to female academies, boys' boarding schools and college preparatory schools. Father Harold Buetow, a noted Catholic education historian, lists 2,246 parochial schools in 1880, just four years later.[4] This figure seems to include the select schools. It is clear that well over 2,000 Catholic schools were in operation before the Third Plenary Council of 1884, and the greater portion were "parochial" by any definition.

Free broad-based public education emerged toward the end of the antebellum period and expanded rapidly following the Civil War. Anti-Catholic and anti-immigrant attitudes and practices permeated the expanding complex of public schools. The Protestant establishment made use of the Protestant Bible and textbooks with anti-Catholic slants.[5] Protestant teachers and school administrators assumed a decidedly anti-Catholic posture that often shook the faith of Catholic children.

Each gathering of the nation's bishops in provincial and plenary councils had urged creation of more Catholic schools. At the Second Plenary Council in 1865, the American bishops once again encouraged parochial schools. During the Third Plenary Council in 1884, they more forcibly addressed this pressing problem and decreed that every parish must have a parochial school.[6] Among their many proclamations, the following are remembered as some of the most important to the American Catholic experience:

> *Article I: Near each church, where it does not exist, a parochial school is to be erected within two years of the proclamation of this Council, and it is to be maintained in perpetuum, unless the*

> *Bishop, on account of grave difficulties, judges that a postpone-*
> *ment may be allowed.*
>
> *Article IV: All Catholic parents are bound to send their children*
> *to the parochial schools, unless either at home or in some other*
> *Catholic schools they may be sufficiently and evidently certain of*
> *the Christian education of their children, or unless it be lawful to*
> *send them to other schools on account of a sufficient cause, ap-*
> *proved by the Bishop, and with opportune cautions and remedies.*
> *As what is a Catholic school is left to the judgment of the Ordinary*
> *to define.*[7]

At first, the council declarations were not universally accepted. Prelates such as Archbishop John Ireland of St. Paul agitated for accommodation with the public sector, seeking financial aid, shared time, and less burdensome remedies; but most bishops and the laity supported the position of the council and attempted full compliance.

While education was one of the important ministries of Catholic women religious before 1884 and usually their chosen one, it now became overriding. During the 52-year span from 1866 to 1917, more than 50,000 sisters devoted their entire religious lives to teaching in parochial schools. The Baltimore decision was historic and profound in dimension. The statistics disclose an average *annual increase* of 107 parochial schools and 33,860 students covering 40 years. Such phenomenal expansion would have been impossible without sacrificial giving by the laity and commitment by the rapidly increasing numbers of sisters who taught without remuneration beyond bare subsistence. The results are graphically portrayed in Table IV.

Parochial School Statistics
1880-1920

Year	Pupils	Catholic Population	Parochial Schools
1880	405,234	6,143,222	2,246
1890	633,238	8,277,039	3,194
1900	854,523	10,129,677	3,811
1910	1,237,251	14,347,027	4,845
1920	1,701,219	17,753,553	6,551

Table IV

Local bishops had extraordinary authority over women religious and pressured orders and congregations to enter or expand their teaching ministry. Orders with rules restricting them to teaching girls were asked to amend their constitutions and accept boys.[9] Newly established immigrant and domestic orders often had limited choice in the matter. Women religious generally accepted the challenge and strained to accommodate the needs. Intense focusing of energies and personnel produced a private school complex unmatched in American history.

Catholic children ordinarily entered the labor force upon completion of primary school. Both sexes went to work at an early age and child labor was a continuing problem. First-, second- and even third-generation immigrant families were usually more interested in employment, savings, and security than in education beyond the basics.[10] As each immigrant group moved upward on the economic and social ladders, even larger immigrant groups replaced it on the lowest rung. Continuing escalation of the size of the Catholic lower class kept pressure on the sisterhood to address the fundamental and overwhelming need for primary education. Critics of the Church for its weak support of secondary and higher education often ignore this fact.

The Third Plenary Council also urged better preparation of teachers, including educational courses during the novitiate period. For the most part, the larger and stronger communities adopted these recommendations, but many small congregations including the host of new immigrant communities were frequently unable to effect them. As late as the 1930's, some sisters began their teaching careers poorly prepared, regardless of their own level of education. Untrained sister-teachers concerned prelates such as Bishop John Lancaster Spalding of Peoria, who called for a central Catholic normal school. Unfortunately, his recommendation was never implemented. Many congregations included education courses in their novitiates, but this practice was only partially successful. The pressure for teachers often resulted in novices being sent to the classroom before they completed even this minimal preparation.

The mounting requirements for teacher certification by local and state governments was a mixed blessing for women religious. Bishops could not override this requirement no matter how desperate the need for teachers and sometimes had to allow sisters to earn college-level credits for certification. The fortunate ones attended sister-operated normal schools. Arrangements were also made for courses conducted during the summers, normally a time for retreats and vacations.[11] Correspondence courses and evening classes were helpful. Sisters had to study for their own exams during the evenings and weekends in addition to attending religious services, performing personal devotions, discharging domestic duties, grading papers, and preparing classes. It sometimes took many years to obtain all the credits needed for full certification. Such a life would be near impossible without spiritual motivation.

Critics of Catholic education tend to compare the training level and teaching competence of sisters to those of public school teachers, with sisters falling short in both categories. During this era, the teaching skills of some young sisters beginning their careers were deficient. Also, lack of proficiency in English sometimes hampered immigrant sister-teachers, causing them to fall temporarily below the norm. However, the truth is that sisters were better educated overall than their public school peers. Normal schools to prepare public school teachers began appearing in this era, but the majority of public school teachers taught in one-room schools all over the nation with just a minimal education and no formal training. Turnover was high due to the proclivity of young women to teach only briefly before marrying. Conversely, numerous well-educated Catholic women entered orders and taught the balance of their active lives. European-born sisters frequently had excellent educations and once they mastered English, their superior qualifications asserted themselves. Mothers-superior not only recognized but were acutely conscious of the need for upgrading their sister-teachers and made strenuous and ongoing efforts to rectify deficiencies and upgrade skills. Priest-professors from Catholic colleges and universities commonly gave lectures and classes at convents in the summer. On the whole, Catholic sister-teachers were superior to public school teachers in both education and teaching skills.

Another fallacy is that curricula and teaching methods were haphazard and highly diverse. On the contrary, orders had the advantage of teaching methods handed down for generations. For example, the Ursulines had their *Reglements*; in 1884 the *Teaching Manual of the Sisters of St. Joseph of Carondelet* was published and widely used by other teaching orders. Newer orders were quick to adopt such guidelines and adapt them to local needs. Sister-principals paid close attention to local public school curricula and took steps to adopt what they deemed appropriate.

A shortage of satisfactory textbooks was a nettlesome problem until late in the 19th century. Catholic textbooks were published in limited quantities as early as 1809, but public school textbooks were better. Because these books often offended Catholic sensibilities, publishers sometimes expurgated them for Catholic use. The William Sadlier Company of New York began publishing textbooks for Catholic school use in 1875, followed by other publishers such as the Benzinger Brothers.

Another nagging disadvantage was the quality of physical facilities that in many parishes were inferior to those of the public schools. With the passage of time pastors managed to upgrade them to something close to par. The laity were conscious of the quality needs and sacrificed generously to improve them. By 1917, with the exception of newly opened schools in missions and poor parishes, physical structures generally equaled and at times surpassed the quality of public school buildings.

The critics are right about class size. Classes of up to 60 children did occur and classes of 40 to 50 were not uncommon. While not desirable for the best results, these oversize classes are a testament to the teaching quality of the sisters who nonetheless insured a superior basic education. Another testament to the quality of parochial schools is the widespread enrollment of Jewish and Protestant children — a seeming anomaly in an age of widespread anti-Catholicism.

While willing to lead sacrificial lives in the educational ministry, the sisters were not always willing to accept abuse from pastors or even bishops. Mothers-superior recalled their sisters from parishes when conflicts arose over teacher assignments, administration, curriculum, lay teachers, finances, or other matters. Support from the clergy varied widely, often diminishing once the sisters arrived and established themselves or when new priests and bishops replaced the original supplicants. Priests and bishops accrued reputations that were communicated among the sisterhood; therefore, when a pastor purposely drove one community away in order to replace it with a more cooperative group, he learned about the "old-girl" network to his dismay. The demand for sister-teachers was so great that many mothers-superior could exercise considerable selectivity in their assignments. In seeking sister-teachers, many bishops were not the least bashful about courting communities with large memberships outside their dioceses.[12]

Local bishops and archbishops sometimes exercised tight control over the communities in their jurisdictions, using their authority to impose rigid directives on allocation of sisters to ministries, on teacher salaries, on financial expenditures, and on their obtaining permission to attend Catholic and secular colleges. The many diocesan communities were subject to complete episcopal control over their affairs. Often, pontifical orders had such large investments in real estate and local traditions (original foundation, benefactors, and vocations) that they could not move away to escape authoritarian bishops. While such unhappy situations were the exception, most bishops were highly supportive and reasonable.

The phrase "parochial school system" is something of a misnomer since a true integrated system has never evolved on a national scale. Terms such as "diocesan system" or "Dominican system" would be more accurate. Jurisdiction over teaching methods, textbooks, curriculum, and school administration was often the province of the order furnishing the teachers. Mothers-superior frequently stipulated these prerogatives before signing contracts with parishes. Beginning with New York archdiocese in 1886, bishops gradually appointed school superintendents, established school boards, and exercised other forms of oversight. This process did not solidify until well into the 1930's. Individual pastors and sister-principals exercised considerable autonomy; situations frequently varied from parish to parish. Differing ethnic circumstances dictated the curriculum, and sisters from differing communities exercised their own particular educational philosophies.

Despite minor differences, a certain uniformity in daily routine marked practically all parochial schools. The day began in class with roll call and the children praying the *Morning Offering*. Then with military-like precision students marched in single file to Mass, students seated in ascending order class by class, with the first grade in the front pew and a sister-teacher at the end of the pew differentiating the grades. Each class opened and closed with prayer, included the *Angelus* at noon and closed with a final prayer. Religious principles were integrated into all subjects. Many students were instructed to write the initials J.M.J. (Jesus, Mary, and Joseph) or similar aspirations on the heading of all papers. Children often wore prescribed uniforms. Schools closed on holy days, a custom much envied by public school students. Classroom discipline was enforced. Frequent tests and assigned homework were routine.

Economic and ethnic diversity did prevail among parishes and schools, however. For example, an old German or Irish parish in one section of a city might be heavily middle class while in another neighborhood a new Italian or Polish parish might be working class.[13] Part-time instruction in foreign languages complicated matters but also challenged students and teachers. For the most part, the schools met that challenge successfully, something often overlooked in evaluating the quality of bilingual parochial schools. Starting with the New York Archdiocese in 1886, dioceses gradually established school boards, school superintendents, and other forms of oversight. This was an uneven and drawn-out process that did not solidify until well into the 1930's.

The standard religious teaching tool for Catholic children from 1885 to 1965 was the famous catechism emanating from the Third Plenary Council of Baltimore, commonly called the *Baltimore Catechism*. It was intimately familiar to American Catholics for the next 80 years. It contained 421 questions and answers, usually printed on 72 pages. Its sequence was Creed, Sacraments, Prayers, Commandments, and Last Things. Learning was by rote. Children had to give the correct answers before making First Communion and receiving Confirmation. Parochial school curricula allotted a certain number of hours to its study while Catholic children attending public schools had to attend Sunday School and recite the answers. Like any learning method, rote can be carried to extremes.[14] Modern pedantry scorns this teaching method; however, rote learning proved to be highly effective in inculcating the precepts of the Catholic faith in generations of Catholics.[15]

There is no parallel in history to parochial school education in the United States. Millions upon millions of Catholic children of primary school age have attended these thousands of schools made possible by the sacrificial services of sisters.[16] Their dedication to this ministry was the lifeblood of the Church, sustaining its growth. Tuition, Sunday collections, and donations underwrote this vast complex. Sisters also taught music and other subjects after school hours, ran bazaars and socials, and drew funds from their academy or hospital, if they operated one, to help defray expenses.

The parochial school complex was the agency most responsible for keeping millions of Catholics Catholic, for the economic and social elevation of millions of immigrants and for the growth of the Catholic Church to its present status. Without the sisters and their parochial schools, that status would be much diminished. Therein lies a tremendous tribute to women religious and their teaching ministry.

High Schools and Academies

Following the Civil War, public high schools began to emerge and by 1880 there were around 800 in operation. Thereafter they increased rapidly: 10,000 by 1900 and 14,000 in 1920. However, secondary education for Catholic youth was slow in evolving and never was able to accommodate more than a fraction of children graduating from parochial schools. The first Catholic high school was in Philadelphia, opened in 1890 as a central diocesan school, a practice others adopted in subsequent years. In 1900, there were only 53 Catholic high schools, 263 in 1910, and still only 1,552 in 1920. Reasons for this deficiency were grounded in finances and shortages of personnel. Since the entire Catholic educational establishment was already straining resources in opening and operating parochial schools, the higher costs of a high school seemed prohibitive. Laity, mostly lower middle-class working families, could ill afford the much higher tuition of a high school.

Girls' academies operated by sisters and nuns retained the high repute earned in the antebellum years. Academic standards were generally so high that those academies would almost qualify as junior colleges today. For example, academies operated by Mother Duchesne's Society of the Sacred Heart had required courses in philosophy, Bible history, rhetoric, chemistry, and Christian ethics. Academies generated vocations and had secured desperately needed support for the Church among the upper classes during the nativist and Know-Nothing heyday. Academies also contributed to the growth of parochial schools by underwriting the cost of connected free schools for local children that evolved into parochial schools. For example, the Sisters of Mercy established this model with their first academy in 1843 and continued to follow it with subsequent academies.

Despite the demand for teachers in expanding parochial schools, female academies increased during this era, albeit not at such a frantic rate. There were slightly over 200 academies at the end of the Civil War, and they increased rapidly thereafter: to 511 in 1880, to 557 in 1885, to 624 in 1890, to 662 in 1900 and to 709 in 1910.[17] Academy experience promoted female independence, scholarship, intellectual curiosity, and created networks often lasting a lifetime. These institutions remained the crown jewels of Catholic education well into the 20th century.

Academies for boys were operated by various male religious orders. Jesuits and orders of brothers[18] generally catered to the Catholic middle and upper classes.[19] While some of their academies were the academic equals of the elitist Episcopal and private prep schools, they never achieved the wide reputation of academies operated by sisters and nuns.

Colleges

Catholic colleges for men emerged early, beginning with Georgetown University in 1791. There were 14 Catholic colleges and universities in operation by 1860. The Jesuits and other male religious orders opened colleges across the nation. At the turn of the century, the total had risen to 63, still a small number considering the size of the Catholic population. Colleges for Catholic women were even slower in appearing, despite the fact that women were attending institutions of higher learning in considerable numbers. Women's colleges such as Mount Holyoke, Wellesley, Vassar, and Bryn Mawr began much earlier and achieved distinction. Shortly after the Civil War, the Midwestern states of Ohio and Michigan opened admission for women to state colleges — a movement which gradually spread over the nation.[20]

Saint Mary's Academy in Notre Dame, Indiana, maintained a postgraduate department offering college level courses but did not grant a bachelor's degree until 1898. Ursuline College in Cleveland, Ohio, was established in 1871 and granted a bachelor's degree in 1872. It did not proceed from an academy as did so many Catholic women's colleges, but was established to be a women's college and is given credit for being the first Catholic women's college organized and chartered explicitly for the purpose of college education. In 1895, the School Sisters of Notre Dame received a charter from the state of Maryland to award degrees and began extending their academy to include college-level courses.[21] In 1899, their College of Notre Dame of Maryland granted bachelor degrees to six women. In 1904, under the leadership of Mother Irene Gill, Ursulines opened the College of New

Rochelle (originally the College of St. Angela) in New York, the first Catholic women's college in that state.

In 1900, the Sisters of Notre Dame de Namur founded Trinity College in Washington, D.C. to take advantage of the faculty, library, and cultural activities of The Catholic University of America.[22] This was the second sister-founded college that did not spring from an existing academy. Since then, thousands of sisters have taken courses at Trinity College.

Participation of young Catholic women in higher education ran counter to the psychology of the times, especially among the clergy, hierarchy, and lower and lower-middle classes. Increasing numbers of upper- and upper-middle class Catholic families could afford college for daughters as well as sons, and each year more young Catholic women enrolled in secular colleges and universities. Agitation among sister-teachers for college credits for teacher certification mounted annually. These pressures forced the hierarchy to grant grudging approval for Catholic women's colleges, and by 1917 the total of sister-operated colleges reached 47. Of these, 44 are still in operation (see Appendix D).

Hospitals

As Table V demonstrates, the growth of hospitals operated by sisters during these years was no less dynamic than the educational drive, although far fewer sisters were involved. They founded 479 hospitals across the country, expanding a ministry begun during the antebellum years. Following the Civil War, the nation needed more and better hospitals to meet the demands of a fast growing population and an aroused awareness of the need for better medical care. Improved medical education, advances in medical knowledge, nursing schools, and such simple inventions as flush toilets, bathtubs, and central heating enabled hospitals to dispense vastly improved health care and to adapt better to the needs of the sick and injured.

Mother Seton's daughters were prominent in hospital work in the antebellum era and continued this ministry, opening 58 hospitals. The Sisters of Mercy entered the field in Pittsburgh in 1847 and founded their second hospital in Chicago in 1854. Following their involvement in Civil War nursing, they rapidly expanded this ministry and became foundation leaders with 79 hospital foundations— reflecting their expansion into the largest group of congregations in the country. The many Franciscan congregations opened 57 hospitals. The Sisters of St. Joseph and St. Joseph of Carondelet combined to establish 35 new hospitals. With each passing decade, more orders entered hospital work (see Appendix C). This expansion is a reflection of increases in sister-population and the numbers of congregations, although hospitals grew in far greater proportion. Some orders established hospitals in all regions of the country; others concentrated on specific areas, such as the Sisters of Providence in the West and Northwest. Others answering the "call of the West" included the Sisters of Charity of Leavenworth, Sisters of Charity of Cincinnati, Benedictine Sisters of Pontifical Jurisdiction, Sisters of the Presentation of the Blessed Virgin Mary, and Sisters of St. Joseph of Carondelet. The impoverished South received attention primarily from the Sisters of Mercy and the Daughters of Charity, while the Congregation of the Sisters of the Incarnate Word founded hospitals in their home territory of Texas. The Far West had fewer congregations than the East and Midwest, reflected in fewer hospital foundations.

Sister-Founded Hospitals 1866-1917

Decade	East	Mid-West	Far West	West	South	Total
1870-79	12	20	7	3	4	46
1880-89	10	31	27	7	5	80
1890-99	30	36	23	11	4	104
1900-09	31	53	30	8	14	136
1910-19	26	33	35	10	9	113
Totals	109	173	122	39	36	479

Note: Texas is counted as "South." Maryland and Washington are under "East." Kansas and Nebraska are under "West."

Table V

Many factors combined in motivating communities to expand or enter hospital operations. For some it was a natural follow-up to antebellum or Civil War experiences while for others it was response to obvious needs in their localities. Newly arriving immigrant orders with nursing experience quickly entered the field. The opening West with its great distances and rugged conditions prompted a number of orders to provide desperately needed medical facilities for settlers, miners, railroad workers, and local natives. The wisdom of having facilities for their own sick and aged sisters, as well as the income generated by hospitals, were also contributing factors.

Some orders founded hospitals in response to ethnic needs. During this Age of Immigration poor immigrants were often unable to communicate their symptoms in English in public hospitals. Frequently encountering outrageous anti-Catholic and anti-immigrant prejudice from doctors and hospital administrators, they were often neglected or even denied proper treatment.

A number of hospitals sprang up to serve German patients. The Franciscan Sisters of the Poor sent sisters to New York from Cincinnati in 1865 to establish St. Francis Hospital on the lower East Side where many poor Germans lived. Orders fleeing Germany because of *Kulturkampf* were especially attuned to the needs of their countrymen. Members of the **Franciscan Sisters, Daughters of the Sacred Hearts of Jesus and Mary (OSF-1240)**, who arrived from Germany in 1872 assumed responsibility for St. Boniface Hospital in Carondelet, Missouri. This institution burned down in 1877, but the sisters remained active in hospital work in Missouri, Illinois, Iowa, and Colorado. The **Sisters of St. Francis of Perpetual Adoration (OSF-1640)** fled Westphalia in 1875 and found a home in Fort Wayne, Indiana. Within eight months, they began construction of St. Elizabeth Hospital on two lots donated by a kind benefactor. In 1884, they dispatched Sisters Leonarda and Alexa to Cleveland, where they opened St. Alexa Hospital. Twenty sisters from the **Hospital Sisters of the Third Order of St. Francis (OSF-1820)** left Germany in 1875 for Springfield, Illinois, where they nursed the sick in their homes and later opened St. John's Hospital. The **Franciscan Sisters of Mary (FSM-1415),** who departed Germany in 1872, opened a hospital in St. Louis in 1877 to serve the large German population in that city. Later, they established two more hospitals in Missouri and others in Wisconsin and Illinois. These hospitals were all open to everyone but essentially catered to German-Americans.

The Felician Sisters arrived in Wisconsin in 1874 to minister to immigrant Poles. They opened a 10-bed hospital in Manitowoc in addition to an orphanage and home for the aged. The Congregation of the Sisters of the Holy Family of Nazareth came to Chicago in 1885 and began their ministry with a school in a Polish parish. They also opened St. Mary of Nazareth Hospital in 1894, the first one in Chicago for the burgeoning Polish population. Inhabitants of the French quarter in New York derived great satisfaction when the French-speaking Sister Marianites of the Holy Cross came to nurse in the French Hospital. The Sisters of Mercy were closely identified with the Irish, although they founded some hospitals in areas not predominantly Irish. We have seen Mother Cabrini's work in establishing hospitals to serve Italians. Without exception, these Catholic hospitals served people of all faiths and nationalities.

Sister-operated hospitals in many locations were semipublic institutions partially underwritten with public funds. For example, Providence Hospital in Washington, D.C., operated by the Daughters of Charity was the only hospital in the city serving civilians during the Civil War. A special relationship developed from this experience, and Congress routinely appropriated monies to support the institution's care of indigent patients. When Congress appropriated $30,000 in 1897 to build an isolation ward at Providence Hospital, the bill was challenged on the grounds of separation of church and state.

The case reached the Supreme Court in *Bradfield v. Roberts*. The court held that the religious affiliation of the hospital was immaterial and the government's contract was valid. Another unusual relationship between the Daughters of Charity and the federal government began with the 1903 contract for the community to furnish nurses for the United States Soldier's Home and Hospital in Washington, D.C.

During the 1870's and 1880's, accidents, violence, and sickness plagued pioneers, miners, ranchers, and railroad construction crews in the opening West, prompting sisters to give special attention to this region. The places where they founded hospitals read like locales in a Western novel: Deer Lodge, Lead City, Deadwood, Georgetown, Cripple Creek, Ogden, Laramie City, Leadville, Butte, Denver, Fort Scott, Prescott, Nogales, Hearne, Temple, Missoula, Salt Lake City, Wichita, Tucson, and so on (see Appendix C). Their ministrations in these and other locations throughout the West encompass a host of adventures, hardships, and accomplishments. With little financial support available, the sisters begged in the mining camps and among the construction crews, usually with success. They also sent sisters "back East" to beg alms. It was Catholic sisters who initiated what has now become a national institution — hospitalization insurance. They sold policies for five dollars per year that guaranteed treatment. Lumber camps and mills of the upper Midwest also attracted the sisters, who opened hospitals in such locations as Big Rapids, Manistee, Cadillac, Muskegon, and Saginaw. This little known story of how the sisters served so valiantly in providing health services in the West and upper Midwest during these years deserves more attention. Perhaps someone will perform the necessary research and reporting while the records still exist.

Nursing care for the poor in their homes attracted several orders. The Franciscan Sisters of Mary, who settled in St. Louis, began their American ministry by visiting the worst slums of this city along the banks of the Mississippi River. Sisters of the **Congregation of Bon Secours (CBS-0270)** came to Baltimore from France in 1881. This order was founded specifically to treat the sick poor in their homes and they activated this ministry in Baltimore. This order later engaged in hospital work and founded several institutions. Visitation to the homes of the sick poor was not restricted to these orders and attracted sisters from many orders to this charitable ministry.

War with Spain in 1898 once again pulled sister-nurses into military nursing. While it was not on the scale of Civil War participation, this experience showed the willingness of Catholic women religious to serve their country in time of need, and acted as an example of selfless service for the nation's youth.

Nursing Schools

Florence Nightingale made nursing a respectable profession in England following the Crimean War.[23] It became a true profession in the United States after the Civil War, with medical education for professional nurses becoming requisite by the end of the 19th century. Numerous schools came into existence during the 1880's and 1890's. Bellevue Hospital in New York City and Massachusetts General Hospital in Boston set the standards and provided leadership. In 1886, the Hospital Sisters of St. Francis established the first Catholic nursing school at St. John's Hospital in Springfield, Illinois. In 1889, the Sisters of Charity of Cincinnati established Good Samaritan School of Nursing, the Sisters of Mercy founded one in Chicago, and the Daughters of Charity founded schools in Brooklyn and Buffalo. Admission was for sisters only in these early Catholic schools. St. Joseph's Hospital School of Nursing in Denver operated by the Sisters of Charity of Leavenworth admitted laywomen in 1900. The practice spread rapidly thereafter. At the turn of the century, 59 of the nation's 393 schools of nursing were operated by Catholic sisters. Sisters would continue to open and operate nursing schools in conjunction with their hospitals — the total peaked at 403 schools in 1931.

Increasing medical knowledge about germs and transmission of diseases sometimes caused doctors to criticize the clothing worn by sister-nurses. They believed that heavy wool habits made natural habitats for germs that could be picked up from one patient and transported to another. In some cases, the sisters were quick to adapt and developed white linen habit-uniforms, perfectly suited for nursing while retaining a religious identification. Unfortunately, tradition was so strong in some communities that nursing sisters had great difficulty in obtaining permission to wear proper garb. All sister-nurses eventually adjusted to modern sanitation demands.

Most nursing schools, public and religious, were patterned after the Nightingale School of Nursing in London. Florence Nightingale insisted that any nursing school be associated with a medical school in a teaching hospital. Residence for students should be suitable for formation of character and discipline. One person, the matron, should have final authority for the entire program. She was convinced that regardless of the auspices under which it was practiced, nursing must always be carried on in a deeply religious manner. A spiritual atmosphere for hospitals was encouraged, and, to a lesser degree, this outlook was emulated in the United States. Nursing had come full circle after over three centuries of neglect with American sister-nurses in the vanguard of change.

Orphanages

Historical accounts repeatedly mention sisters caring for orphans. At times they operated institutional orphanages and at others simply took children into their academies and convents. During the antebellum years, many immigrants endured horrible conditions in crossing the Atlantic and more health hazards in poverty-ridden slums. These deplorable conditions and epidemics resulted in numerous orphans. Conditions moderated in the second half of the 19th century, reducing the number of newly orphaned children. The nation's improving economic conditions and the upgrading of living standards resulted in relatively fewer orphans in proportion to the population. However, the actual number of orphans increased because of the flood of immigrants, especially poor ones.

Sister Rose White of the Sisters of Charity in Emmitsburg opened the first Catholic orphanage in Philadelphia in 1816.[24] She also took charge of the second one in New York. Thereafter, orphan care by Catholic sisters increased rapidly, with most communities becoming involved in this ministry.

Following the Civil War, the federal government supported institutions caring for the children of Union soldiers killed during the war. This improved attitude towards civic responsibility for orphans removed much pressure from the sisters. The foundation and operation of the Children's Aid Society by Protestant clergyman Reverend Charles Loring Brace (1826-1890) also decreased demands on the sisters. The society's commendable concept was to remove children from institutional orphanages and locate them in private homes. By 1875 it had placed 35,000 children; when disbanded in 1929 it had placed 150,000. It sent children to settler families in the Midwest and West. However, the society ignored both the religion of the child and that of the adopting family. Once aware of this practice, Catholic orphanages withdrew their support.

The 272 Catholic orphanages of 1885 increased to 322 in 1900 and were caring for 83,000 children in 1908. By the end of the 19th century, Catholics had greatly improved their orphanages with sturdy, well-heated buildings, good food, adequate clothing, and structured education for the children. It was no longer a case of impoverished sisters accepting even poorer orphans in their convents and combination schools.

As the 20th century progressed, health care and economic conditions improved, and the number of orphans gradually decreased. Governmental social service agencies and foster home programs accelerated the decline. While Catholic sisters continued and expanded their orphan-care ministry from 1866 to 1917, it peaked just as the era closed and would decrease thereafter until it practically disappeared in the late 20th century.[25] In the context

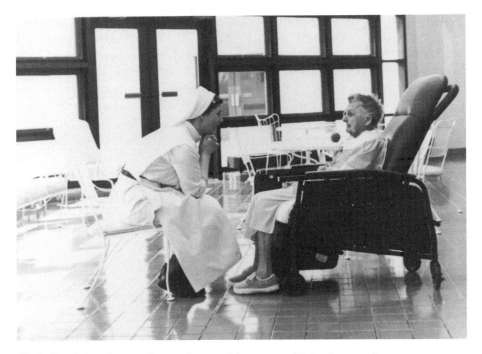

Catholic sisters honor those advanced in years with loving service.
Dominican Sisters of the Relief of Incurable Cancer, St. Rose's Home, New York

of needs in its time, the sisters' ministry to orphans ranks as a superb testimonial to their religious calling.

Aged Poor

The elderly destitute have always been part of the American scene. We recall how in 1843 Mother Henriette Delille and her Congregation of the Sisters of the Holy Family in New Orleans opened the first Catholic home for the aged poor in the United States. With rapid urbanization and lessening family cohesion, the numbers of elderly poor mounted. Increased longevity contributed as did the scarcity of pension and retirement provisions by business and industry. The federal government felt that responsibility for the elderly poor rested with local communities and state governments, and many of them did take credible actions to provide relief for those victims of old-age poverty. However, these actions and the efforts of local religious and charitable societies were inadequate, especially in an urban society that tended to ignore the problem. Catholic sisters had been keenly aware of this problem for most of their history, and many communities established homes for the elderly poor in addition to their primary ministries. But no American order had this ministry as its sole apostolate until 1868.

The congregation of the **Little Sisters of the Poor (LSP-2340)**, founded in France in 1839 by Jeanne Jugan (1792-1879), had already spread to the British Isles, Belgium, and Spain before the Little Sisters arrived in New York in 1868. Their entry was prepared by a zealous French priest, Father Ernest Lelievre, who gave up the prospect of a brilliant law career to devote his life to furthering the work of the Little Sisters. He secured the necessary permissions from bishops for American foundations. Thereupon, the sisters opened homes for the aged poor in Brooklyn, Cincinnati, New Orleans, and Baltimore. During the next four years they established nine homes in nine more cities. By 1901, the Little Sisters had opened homes as far west as San Francisco, all based on Jeanne Jugan's concepts of respect for the dignity of each elderly person ("The Poor are Our Lord") and the involvement of the laity in supporting and caring for their less fortunate brothers and sisters. American girls, attracted by the radical form of Gospel charity they saw practiced in these homes, crossed the Atlantic to offer themselves as candidates at the motherhouse in France.

These American postulants were dear to the heart of the foundress, known to them only as Sister Mary of the Cross. Although she had taken in the first aged persons, had instituted the collection of alms to supply their needs, and had founded homes based on complete dependence on Divine Providence, her true role as foundress was obscured in her later years by regrettable circumstances. A priest took the title of founder for himself and sent Sister Mary of the Cross to live as an ordinary sister at the motherhouse for the last 27 years of her life. Her example of heroic self-effacement and charity under these circumstances was not lost on the generations of young postulants and novices who were in daily contact with her. Providentially, she was able to transmit her charism to the younger generations by example and word. Pope John Paul II praised this same example when he beatified her in 1982 in the presence of pilgrims from all over the world.

In 1902, the congregation opened a novitiate in Queens, New York, that has received a steady stream of vocations ever since. As homes built in the 19th century became obsolete, new modern ones replaced them, made possible by a vast network of friends and benefactors. These new homes included apartments for self-sustaining elderly people and day centers for the elderly poor of the neighborhood. In 1958, the Fraternity Jeanne Jugan was formed, composed of laywomen who wish to associate themselves with the spirituality and apostolate of the Little Sisters.

Following Vatican II, the Little Sisters revised their constitutions, seeking to apply Jeanne Jugan's charism to modern situations. They live in communities large enough for them to care for their residents personally, with the help of a trained staff. Little Sisters strive to be truly "little sisters" to the elderly poor of all religious and ethnic backgrounds, caring for them as they would for their own family members until death. The hallmark of these homes is "family spirit" and includes residents, their families, staff members, volunteers, and friends. The Little Sisters recently renewed their commitment to the poorest aged and to the continued missionary expansion of the congregation. An American mission for the Navajo Indians in Gallup, New Mexico, opened in 1983. Four thousand Little Sisters, serving in 30 countries, are meeting a new challenge by speaking out against euthanasia and for respect for the lives of the elderly.

Another example of how this ministry attracts women religious concerns the **Franciscan Sisters of Chicago (OSF-1210)**, which sprang from the efforts of a devout Polish immigrant girl to care for poor old people in St. Stanislaus Kostka parish in Chicago. Josephine Dudzik (1860-1917) began taking helpless people into her home for care while she was a Franciscan tertiary. An entry from her *Chronicle* indicates her deep spirituality and charitable impulses:

> *. . . I felt the misery of suffering of others, and it seemed to me that I could not love Jesus, or even expect heaven if I were concerned only about myself . . . not suffering any inconvenience, but simply living in comfort. Very often, I felt drawn to greater sacrifice for others. Consequently, I was preoccupied with the thought of how I could be of service to the needy and the poor. In my mind, I was already arranging the beds and preparing all things necessary for this purpose. The thought haunted me day and night even though I was unaware of the means by which this could be accomplished. . . .*[26]

Josephine (Mother Mary Theresa) did in fact find the means to effect this ministry. She and her friend Rosalie Wysinski (Mother Mary Anna, 1850-1917) founded a Franciscan community for this purpose in 1894. The story of their struggles, near failures, and final establishment of St. Joseph Home for the Aged and Crippled is inspiring. This Franciscan community grew and expanded their ministries of orphan care, teaching, and other charities. In 1940, they accepted an invitation from Father Edward J. Flanagan to supply sisters to help at his famous Boys Town outside Omaha, Nebraska. Action has been taken to enter Mother Mary Theresa's cause for canonization.

Ministry to the American Indian and Black Population

While touring Europe in 1887 with her two sisters, Katharine Mary Drexel had an interview with Pope Leo XIII. She described the plight of

American Indians and how she had offered to erect a boarding school in Wyoming for the Arapaho and Shoshone. She stated that Bishop James O'-Connor had located sisters for these missions but could not secure priests. Expecting the pope to offer priests of some order, she was astonished at his reply: "Why not, my child, yourself become a missionary?" Katharine repeated that sisters were available but the Indian missions needed priests. After the interview, Katharine broke down in uncontrollable weeping to the dismay of her two sisters. She did not explain her interior struggle about a religious vocation or how the pope's unexpected and perceptive remark had seared her soul. Later that year, 14-year-old Thérèse Martin (the Little Flower) also left in tears after an interview with the pope, who refused to grant permission for her to enter a Carmelite monastery until she was of age. The following year Francesca Cabrini left her interview smiling. Pope Leo XIII seems to have met more than his quota of saintly women during those two years.

Katharine was born into a socially prominent and wealthy Philadelphia family. Sadly, Mrs. Drexel died shortly after Katharine's birth but Mr. Drexel's second wife, Emma Bouvier, was a dear mother to her in every way. Mr. Drexel, a prominent banker, was a dedicated Catholic of Austrian extraction. Katharine had an older sister, Elizabeth, and a younger half-sister, Louise. Mr. Drexel insured a superior education for his daughters, employing the best tutors. He took the girls on European tours several times to broaden their knowledge and on trips in his private railroad car to the West where they visited Yellowstone and other interesting sights. After making their debuts, the sisters participated in the social life of Philadelphia, mingling with visiting royalty. All three Drexel girls were highly intelligent and charming.

The Drexel household was noted for kindness and piety and the servants there were treated like family members. No sister, priest, or person in need left the Drexel home without help. When Emma developed cancer, suffering terribly during her final two years, she and Katharine became close. Jokingly, Katharine threatened to enter a convent if Emma did not get better. Mrs. Drexel died in 1883 when Katharine was 25 years old. Compounding the family's sadness, Mr. Drexel died two years later.

Mr. Drexel's will received wide publicity. He left an estate of $15.5 million — a monumental sum in those days, the equivalent of over $300 million today. His will directed that 10 percent go to a long list of specified Catholic charities; the balance was placed in trust for his three daughters. To protect them from fortune hunters, he specified that his daughters receive only the income for life. If any died without issue, the other two or one would receive the entire income. If all three died without children, the estate would go to the original beneficiaries of his charity.

The three sisters wasted no time in applying their income to charity, with Elizabeth, the oldest, leading the way. She loved the orphanages her father supported but felt they did not provide trade skills to prepare the orphans for entering the working world. Consequently, she funded St. Francis de Sales Industrial School in Eddington, Pennsylvania, as a memorial to her father; here thousands of young men have learned a trade. Louise, the youngest, focused her generosity on the Josephite Fathers, a society dedicated to helping blacks. She and her husband, Colonel Edward Morrell, established St. Emma's Industrial and Agricultural Institute, a military school on 1,600 acres overlooking the James River near Richmond, Virginia. The three sisters joined in donating $50,000 to The Catholic University of America, funding the Francis A. Drexel Chair of Moral Theology.

Katharine's story deserves more detail. Several weeks after Mr. Drexel's death, the sisters were in the upstairs sitting room when the butler announced that two priests were downstairs. Katharine was delegated to receive them. One was Bishop Martin Marty, then Vicar-Apostolic of Northern Minnesota and the other was Monsignor Joseph Stephen, Director of the Bureau of Catholic Indian Missions. They came seeking financial aid for missionary work among the Indians.

The Bureau of Catholic Indian Missions requires some explanation. In 1870, President Ulysses Grant proclaimed his Peace Policy to Congress intending that the program pacify the Indians, make them wards of the state, and redress past injustices. The federal government assumed responsibility for their welfare and education. Unfortunately, it turned out to be a rerun of the Andrew Jackson "removal policy," forcing tribes off their hunting grounds and onto reservations in Oklahoma and miserable wastelands in the West. Railroads, gold seekers, and settlers coveted large portions of the reservations and routinely violated treaties.[27]

A key feature of the Peace Policy was to award Indian agencies to "such religious denominations that had hitherto established missioners among the Indians and perhaps to some other denominations who would undertake the work on the same terms." Although highly sensible in conception, the policy was thwarted in execution as the phrase "hitherto established" was violated outrageously. Catholics had clear claim to 34 agencies but only received eight.[28] The other 66 went to Episcopal, Baptist, Quaker, and Presbyterian denominations. Finding protest to no avail, the bishops established the Bureau of Catholic Indian Missions in Washington in order to be better heard and to centralize and coordinate missionary endeavors. The Third Plenary Council of 1884 made this a permanent Church office.[29]

Katharine and her sisters responded positively to Bishop Marty's and Monsignor Stephen's appeals and funneled sizable contributions through the bureau, insisting that their aid be kept anonymous in order to prevent slackening by others. In 1887 and again in 1888, the three sisters toured the West with Monsignor Stephen and Bishop O'Connor, Katharine's spiritual director. At the Pine Ridge Agency in South Dakota, Katharine presented gifts to Chief Red Cloud and his wife. These visits to remote poverty-stricken Indian reservations were more than romantic girlish adventures as they enabled Katharine to visualize the Indians' practical needs.

On returning to Philadelphia, she retained an architect to design schools and chapels that would use prefabricated materials and be easily erected. Over the next five years the Drexel sisters funded boarding schools and missions for an extensive list of tribes: Puyallups in Washington, Cheyenne and Arapahos in Wyoming, Sioux in the Dakotas, Coeur d'Arlene and Nez Perce in Idaho, Mission Indians in California, Chippewas in Wisconsin, Crows and Blackfeet in Montana, Comanches and Osage in Oklahoma, and the Pueblos in New Mexico. Katharine developed a set procedure. She paid for the land and buildings and then deeded the property to the Bureau of Catholic Indian Missions. Monsignor Stephen was usually able to secure a government grant of $100 per year per Indian pupil.

While continuing her philanthropic work with the Indians, Katharine considered becoming a religious against the advice of her spiritual guide, Bishop James O'Connor. Katharine was 14 when she first met him, then pastor of St. Dominic's parish in Holmesburg, Pennsylvania, near the Drexel summer home. St. Michael's was no ordinary summer home — it had an altar and the requirements for saying Mass. As local pastor and frequent visitor, Father O'Connor came to know Katharine well, and she turned to him for religious guidance. After becoming Bishop of Omaha in 1885, the relationship intensified and their voluminous correspondence has been preserved. It graphically tells the story of her spiritual struggles and journey towards God's vineyard. Katharine kept insisting she wished to become a religious, preferably a contemplative, while Bishop O'Connor kept advising her to "think, pray and wait." He felt her true vocation was as a lay leader and example to others by service and financial support to charities. Katharine placed herself under obedience to him in spiritual matters, but persisted in seeking his permission to enter religious life.

By 1889, Katharine had made a firm decision to join a religious community and investigated her options. She was drawn to the Franciscan Sisters of Philadelphia. Bishop O'Connor, recognizing her determination, decided that she should not join an existing community but rather should establish a congregation to minister to Indians and blacks. However, the thought of be-

Sisters of the Blessed Sacrament, Franciscan Friary, Chinle, Arizona.
Courtesy of Sisters of the Blessed Sacrament, Bensalem, Pennsylvania

coming a foundress frightened and disturbed Katharine — Pope Leo's admonition suddenly took on new meaning. She finally relented and placed herself entirely under Bishop O'Connor's direction.

Bishop O'Connor had a high regard for the Sisters of Mercy in Pittsburgh and decided that Katharine should undergo her novitiate with them. The announcement that Katharine was founding a new congregation to provide ministry to Indians and blacks immediately drew applicants. With childlike simplicity, she accepted the demands of spiritual formation in poverty and obedience yet did not lose her sense of humor, entertaining the other novices with Indian dances and chants during their recreation period. During novitiate, word arrived of the massacre of helpless Indian women and children at Wounded Knee. Katharine had visited the Pine Ridge Reservation several years earlier and funded the Holy Rosary School. The **Sisters of St. Francis of Penance and Christian Charity (OSF-1630)** from Stella Niagra, New York, taught the children. Father Jutz and the sisters refused to leave the mission despite impending violence. Chief Red Cloud threatened to join the soldiers if the enraged braves harmed the "blackrobes." Happily, the priest and sisters were spared. Katharine remembered her small gifts to the chief and gave thanks.

Bishop O'Connor's final illness and death shattered Katharine's life of withdrawal from the world but Archbishop Ryan, realizing what this loss meant to her, offered to share her burden by volunteering to become her mentor. He assisted in establishing the **Sisters of the Blessed Sacrament for Indians and Colored People (SBS-0260),** helped draw up a rule, and was her primary advisor for many years. Katharine went to Rome in 1907 to seek approval for her rule, which it received in six years, a relatively short time for this procedure.

After professing her vows in Pittsburgh, Katharine bought land in Cornwells Heights, Pennsylvania, for the future motherhouse, staying at St. Michael's while it was under construction. The words "colored people" in the title of her congregation aroused local bigotry. Workers discovered dynamite on the grounds during the dedication ceremony, but disposed of it before any destruction occurred.

After both Elizabeth and Louise died without children, all income from the estate came to Mother Katharine. Her contributions to all sorts of worthy causes reads like a government appropriations bill: schools, chapels, missions, a college, and on and on. The motherhouse became a regular "port of call" for bishops, priests, and sisters from other communities coming to ask for help. She always received them graciously and did what she could. Mother Drexel traveled constantly, studying the desperate needs of poor blacks in the South and visiting Indian reservations all over the West. Whenever she gave money for some specific purpose such as a school she required that legal forms be signed stipulating that the money had to be refunded if the structure were abandoned or if the school, church, or land be used for other than Negro or Indian needs. She was shrewd and careful with her money. Requests came from every quarter.

One of the first visitors to Mother Drexel was Archbishop Francis Janssens of New Orleans. He came asking help for the blacks of his diocese. She promised aid and over the years invested heavily in Louisiana. Father Augustus Tolton,[30] the first black priest ordained to minister to blacks in the United States, wrote Mother Katharine a letter that bespeaks his appreciation for her work and his personal travail:

> *Dear Mother Catharine (sic):*
>
> *I deem it necessary to write you this letter to ask you to please forgive me for vexing you. A priest wrote me stating that all of us fathers in the Colored Missions were almost setting you crazy, that you had too many to attend to. Of course, I, for one, cannot tell you how to conduct myself when I see one person at least, showing her love for the Colored race. One thing I do know; it took the Catholic Church 100 years here in America to show forth such a*

person as yourself. This is the reason why you have so much bother now and so many extending their hands to get a lift.

In the whole history of the Church in America we cannot find one person who has sworn to give her treasury for the sole benefit of the Colored and Indians. As I stand alone as the first Negro priest of America, so you, Mother Catherine, stand alone as the first one to make such a sacrifice for the cause of a downtrodden race. Hence the South looks on with an angry eye. The North in many places is criticizing every act, just as it is watching every move I make. I suppose that is the reason why we had no Negro priests before this day. They watch us the same as Pharisees did Our Lord. They watched Him. I really feel there will be a stir all over the United States when I begin my church. I shall work and pull at it as long as God gives me life, for I see that I have principalities to resist everywhere and everywhere I go.

The world is indeed a great book and I have read all of its pages. So this letter is to ask if you will excuse me if I have bothered you. I know that you have a lot to do, for I am sure you have letters from all parts of America and even outside of it. . . .[31]

In 1904, the Sisters of the Blessed Sacrament for Indians and Colored People numbered 104 members. They served in Santa Fe, Rock Castle in Virginia, St. Michael's in Arizona, and at the motherhouse in Cornwells Heights. Mother Drexel used the Bureau of Catholic Indian Missions as a conduit for the millions of dollars she expended on those missions. This procedure enabled her to create and sustain schools and chapels operated by others without having to furnish sisters from her small congregation.

Support for blacks in the South presented a monumental challenge. Very few blacks were Catholic outside of the scattered parishes of the Gulf Coast. Only a few Catholics lived outside Richmond, Norfolk, Charleston, Nashville, Vicksburg, Memphis, New Orleans, Mobile, and the larger Southern towns. The region was slowly emerging from the economic consequences of the Civil War and Reconstruction with blacks the poorest of all. Fundamentalist and even mainline Protestant ministers thrived on the rich lode of anti-Catholicism. Prejudice was deep and pervasive. Catholic priests and sisters who ministered to blacks aroused strong resentment.

Louise Morrell also made an appropriation to aid blacks, funding St. Emma's Industrial and Agricultural Institute for black boys, named in honor of Mrs. Drexel. It was located near Rock Castle along the James River in Virginia, and Christian Brothers operated it in the early years, while later Benedictine fathers from Latrobe, Pennsylvania, managed it. Louise's glowing accounts of the beauty of the countryside and the obvious needs for educational opportunity for black girls captured Katharine's imagination. So she bought a nearby 600-acre plantation for a school for black girls.

Mother Katharine and another sister left the motherhouse to oversee the progress of the building at Rock Castle. Because of mixed-up arrangements, the two sisters found themselves outside the railroad station in Richmond in the dead of night. The waiting room was locked and their train for the school did not leave until late the next morning. Neither knew any sisters in Richmond or where to go. As they stood on the dark street, a black coachman drove up and asked if they were the ones the sisters on Duval Street were expecting. Thinking perhaps someone had sent word ahead, they climbed into his carriage. He let them out at the convent steps and drove off. Mother Drexel knocked on the door and it seemed forever before a sister came to see who it was so late at night. After protracted consultation inside the convent, they were admitted. Mother Drexel explained how they happened to be there, but the sisters disclaimed any knowledge about their coming or any coachman. Enquiries the following day into all possible sources for arranging the coachman produced negative results. Mother Katharine concluded that St. Joseph did not want the two sisters out on the dark street alone at night.

With the completion in 1899 of St. Francis de Sales High School, named in memory of her father, Katharine and another sister set out to oversee opening preparations and to check on accommodations for the sisters assigned to live and teach there. News on arrival at St. Francis de Sales was that someone had torched the barn in the night and that insurance covered only part of the loss. Such incidents never intimidated Mother Drexel in her missionary endeavors for blacks. A bit later, she determined to build a school for the black girls of Nashville, Tennessee, when that community closed the only public school open to them in 1905. In the process, she bought a large house in a white neighborhood. Bitter opposition resulted, including a threat to construct a street right through the middle of the property. Newspapers published her private correspondence and aroused public indignation. Even black preachers opposed the school for fear that it would draw away support. However, Mother Drexel persisted and the school opened and prospered for many years.

The brightest jewel in Mother Katharine's crown is probably Xavier University, which she established in New Orleans in 1915. At that time, there were three Protestant colleges for blacks in southern Louisiana and one public college, Southern University. Catholic black students in the Protestant colleges were required to attend chapel services and some tended to lose their faith. As a result, black Catholic parents favored Southern University. This college was situated on the outskirts of New Orleans near the Mississippi River, but over the years a white community grew up around it. The inhabitants resented the black students and petitioned the legislature to move the college elsewhere. When the state relocated it to Baton Rouge in 1912, Archbishop Janssens contacted Mother Drexel about the situation. The old college property was to be sold at public auction and he sensed it would go cheaply. Armed with her agreement, he bid it off for only $18,000. The neighbors became frantic when it became public that a new black college was taking the place of the old one, but they had already used up their political credits in getting Southern University moved.

Mother Drexel funded the new foundation and sent sisters to operate it. Initially, it functioned as a normal school educating black teachers. It became a fully accredited college in 1925. Over the years, it secured university status with the addition of graduate schools in pharmacy, education, history, and English. It moved to a new and larger campus in 1932. Tens of thousands of black students have attended Xavier University from all over the nation as well as from the Caribbean and Africa.

On a much smaller scale but indicative of Mother Drexel's influence, the parish in the small hamlet of Newton Grove, North Carolina, received gifts from her for construction of the rectory and for expansion of both the white and black schools. Dominican sisters taught and raised the educational level of black children so high that graduates left the area because the only available jobs were performing fieldwork. As a consequence, a tiny but thriving black Catholic community scattered. Today the mostly white congregation at Our Lady of Guadalupe Church in Newton Grove offers prayers weekly for Blessed Katharine Drexel's canonization. They treasure her memory.

Mother Drexel suffered a severe heart attack in 1935 and lived for the next 20 years in prayerful retirement, almost as an invalid. She refused to contest her father's will and break the trust despite urgings from various quarters. Upon her death, the estate was distributed to the still functional institutions that Mr. Drexel had treated so generously back in 1885. At the time of Mother Drexel's death in 1955, more than 15,000 students were attending the 69 schools for Indians and blacks she had founded or supported.

A number of people predicted that the congregation would wither after Mother Drexel died and the income ceased. Those persons failed to grasp that her legacy was not money but rather a spirit of love and service to the most unfortunate of her countrymen. Her order, never very large, has around 300 members today.

Is Katharine Drexel a saint? Those closest to her and the sisters of her order think that she is. The first stage, certified by a miracle, has raised her to the status of "beatified." She is now Blessed Katharine Drexel. Canonization requires another clear-cut miracle. Perhaps God will see fit to provide one on some Indian reservation or in the Deep South.

Another American foundation of this period specializing in ministry to the poorest is the **Sisters of the Holy Spirit and Mary Immaculate (SHSp-2050)**, founded by Margaret Mary Healy-Murphy. In 1849, she married John B. Murphy — lawyer, slave owner, and later mayor of Corpus Christi, Texas. During her Corpus Christi years, before being widowed, Margaret ministered to sharecroppers, slaves, ranch workers and neighbors. She passed on her knowledge and love of God to the poor, sick, and dying.

While listening to the sermon at St. Mary's Church on Pentecost Sunday 1887, she was inspired to minister to freed slaves in San Antonio. She financed the building of St. Peter Claver Church and a school for black children in 1888. Since she had difficulty securing teachers, she determined to found a religious community to meet the needs of the destitute and oppressed. She recruited women in Ireland and founded her community in San Antonio in 1893. Her work included primary and secondary education for blacks and Hispanics. With the added help of lay teachers, she established 40 schools that reached a total enrollment of 13,000 children in 1964. These sisters continue to minister to the poor of Texas, Louisiana, Mississippi, Mexico, and Zambia. Margaret Mary Healy-Murphy, loving wife, charitable mistress, rich widow, foundress, educator, and benefactor to the poor is a credit to Texas and to her Irish-American heritage.

One day in New York City in 1876, Mary Walsh (1850-1922), a London-born Irish immigrant, was on her way home from the laundry where she worked when she noticed a little girl crying in a doorway. She stopped to investigate, and the child led her upstairs where Mary found three more children, a dead baby and a sick mother. The lack of food and medicine and the needs of this impoverished family led Mary to quit her job as a laundress and take care of this desperate family. She later became a parish caretaker of the poor while doing laundry work to earn a living. For the next 34 years, Mary struggled to hold together a small band of women she gathered to further this ministry. Their order started in 1879 as a community of Dominican tertiaries. Volunteers appeared from time to time, but the group was never more than a dozen. Some were unable to bear the work and several died. Poverty and desolation stalked their steps in ministering to the most helpless of New York's slums. One day when there was no food, Mother Mary crowed like a rooster to amuse her companions in their misery. A neighbor appeared at the door and thrust money into her hands with a plea to get rid of the rooster so he could get some sleep.

Through those trying years, she retained her ideal of a permanent community devoted to care of the sick poor in their homes. Mother Mary Walsh and seven companions received permission in 1907 to erect a branch of the Dominican Third Order Regular. The eight women made their Dominican novitiate, after which they became the **Dominican Sisters of the Sick Poor — Congregation of the Immaculate Conception (OP-1070-16).** These sisters ultimately became registered nurses and opened convents in numerous dioceses.[32] On reflection, one is tempted to wonder about that little girl in the doorway. Who was she, really?

American Indian Sisters

The idea of founding a congregation composed of native American women to minister to their destitute brethren on the reservations occurred to bishops and priests over the years. However, Indian women entering existing communities generally did not persevere due to deep-seated cultural differences between European and American women, discouraging a religious foundation for them. Mixed-blood women had better success, and many such vocations have been successful. Still, a Benedictine priest with some Indian blood made a serious attempt to organize a religious community of Indian women in 1890.

Father Francis M. Craft learned four Indian languages and was injured at Wounded Knee attempting to halt the slaughter. His courage was never in question. Later, he gathered a small group of Indian women to teach on the

Father Craft and the nuns in field uniforms.
Courtesy Milford Historical Society, Milford, Pennsylvania

Spanish-American War. Camp Cuba Libra, Jacksonville, Florida.
Daughters of Charity, Emmitsburg, Maryland

Fort Berthold Reservation in South Dakota. When government schools displaced them, they nursed in the homes of the sick. Turnover was high. Father Craft never had more than 12 sisters at one time in this unofficial and canonically unrecognized community.

In 1897, Father Craft became ill if not mentally unbalanced. He ignored his bishop's directives and an Indian agent accused the sisters of immoral conduct, a charge never proven but harmful nonetheless. When Father Craft actively discouraged families from sending children to the government school in Carlisle, Pennsylvania, the Secretary of the Interior banned him from all Indian reservations. Down to only four sisters and dejected, Father Craft renounced his affiliation with the Catholic Church with an advertisement in the Pierre newspaper.

When the Spanish-American War erupted in April 1898, Father Craft wired the War Department offering his sisters as war-nurses. Apparently ignorant of Father Craft's status, the War Department sent the sisters to Camp Cuba Libre in Jacksonville, Florida, with Father Craft along as an orderly. They soon transferred to Havana. However, the sisters were discharged from nursing when their lack of proper training became apparent. Sister Anthony, granddaughter of Chief Spotted Tail and niece of Chief Red Cloud, died in

Cuba and was buried with military honors. The other three sisters went home, married, and lived long lives as practicing Catholics.

Father Craft left Cuba and returned to his home in Pennsylvania suffering from yellow fever. He eventually recovered, made his peace with the Church, and became pastor in Milford where he performed satisfactorily until his death in 1920. This strange, driven priest wrote an obscure chapter in American sister-history while attempting to create a viable religious community composed of Indian women.[33]

Mother Katharine Drexel's sisters furnished the novice-mistress for the only existing community of native American sisters, the **Oblate Sisters of the Blessed Sacrament (OSBS-3010)** founded by Father Sylvester Eisenman in 1935 in St. Paul, South Dakota. It remains very small to this day.

Care of Poor Patients With Terminal Cancer

There are seven institutions dedicated to the care of indigent patients with terminal cancer operated by the **Servants of Relief for Incurable Cancer (OP-1070-23)** in the U.S. There are long waiting lists for admittance and the sisters are besieged by requests to build and operate additional facilities. Their desire to increase capacity is limited only by vocations. Patients pay nothing and receive the finest medical attention possible plus the loving care of sisters who seek to make their final days pleasant, dignified, and holy. Income to support these institutions comes from contributions by admirers and the faithful. The order accepts no payments from patients or their families, nor do they accept money from governmental sources such as Medicaid.

This singular ministry is the creation of a most unusual woman, Rose Hawthorne Lathrop (1851-1926), known in religion as Mother Mary Alphonsa Lathrop. Her story has two distinct parts. The first reads like a Greek tragedy.[34]

Rose was the daughter of Nathaniel Hawthorne, the noted American author who grew up in Salem, Massachusetts, where his ancestors had participated in the persecution of Quakers and the hanging of witches.[35] This heritage haunted him and influenced his writing. Following graduation from Bowdoin College, he launched into a writing career that would bring him permanent fame as one of the great early American authors. Best remembered today are *Twice-Told Tales, The House of the Seven Gables,* and *The Scarlet Letter*.

Nathaniel's wife, Sophia, was one of the three famous Peabody sisters. Elizabeth Peabody was at the center of the intellectual life of Boston for many years and is the American foundress of kindergartens. Mary Peabody married and worked closely with Horace Mann, known as the "father" of American public education. Nathaniel and Sophia had a happy marriage in every respect. Three children brightened their lives: Julian, Una, and baby Rose, whom Nathaniel called "Rosebud." Their Concord home, the Wayside, is a literary shrine today. Such luminaries as Ralph Waldo Emerson, Henry Thoreau, Orestes Brownson, and Louisa Alcott gathered there to discuss and argue literary matters while the children scurried in and out of the salon.

Nathaniel's income from writing did not support the family in the style of their peers and, although never truly poor, he contended with slim finances most of his life. In 1853 when Rose was two years old, Nathaniel's classmate and friend Franklin Pierce was elected President of the United States. He appointed Nathaniel the American Consul in Liverpool, which enabled gracious living for a few years. An incident during this period had a lasting effect on Rose. Nathaniel visited an asylum for sick destitute children where a small girl, hungry for affection, asked him to hug her. Nathaniel was fastidious and abhorred anything ugly. It took moral strength for him to lift this tiny child covered with putrefying sores, hold her in his arms and kiss her. Using fictitious characters, Nathaniel later described this moving scene in his journal.

After three years in Liverpool, he gave up the post and traveled widely in Europe. The family spent two years in Italy where Nathaniel and Sophia soaked up the Catholic atmosphere. He wrote: "The popish religion certainly does apply itself most closely and comfortably to human occasions."[36] He was impressed by the church's solemnity, pageantry, and the comfort and solace it afforded its members. Sophia felt uncomfortable with the attraction she and Nathaniel felt towards a religion they previously held in contempt. Their New England Unitarian attitudes underwent a deep change. Although they never became Catholics, they were forced to defend Catholic proclivities that emerged in Nathaniel's writings in such works as *The Marble Faun.*

Nathaniel died four years after their return to the United States when Rose was 13 years old. "Rosebud" was stricken at the loss of her beloved father with whom she had a special relationship. Sophia sold Wayside in 1868 and moved the family to Dresden, Germany, where Rose studied painting and music. Her striking beauty and vibrant personality blossomed despite unkindness by some schoolmates. Ever since Washington Irving spent some months enjoying the arts and music of Dresden in 1822, knowledgeable American tourists had made Dresden a must stop when touring Europe. The Hawthorne home became a mecca for visiting Americans. One such visitor was the handsome young George Lathrop, son of a New York physician. Rose and George fell madly in love although both were only 17. The Lathrop family moved to London in 1871 and Sophia followed with Rose and Una while Julian returned to the United States. Shortly afterward Sophia died. Rose lost both parents within five years. Only 19 years old and without realistic prospects, Rose and George married in London and returned to the United States. George secured a position as staff critic on the *Atlantic Monthly* in Cambridge, Massachusetts, that gave them a good start on married life.

While George wrote, Rose bore a son, Francis. Instead of the joy and happiness that a firstborn normally brings into a family, the event sent Rose into deep depression. She displayed all the symptoms of puerperal insanity, a rare but not unknown malady for women between 25 and 30 bearing a first child. George admitted her to the McLean Asylum, the best in the country at that time. Her recovery required a number of months in this institution. Sadly, little Francis died of diphtheria four years later and Rose was once again ravaged by the death of a loved one. This loss marked a turning point in the marriage. She left George shortly thereafter, but they reconciled after a year's separation, only to separate again in 1895.

During these years Rose had some light works published, but her poetry and essays were more often rejected. However, she was successful on the lecture circuit and gave an impassioned speech on women's rights in 1893 at the Catholic Congress held in conjunction with the World's Columbian Exposition in Chicago. Her speech included —

> . . . *Oh, women, the hour has struck when you are to arise and defend your rights, your abilities for competition with men in intellectual and professional endurance, the hour when you are to prove that purity and generosity are for the nation as well as the home. . . .*[37]

On March 19, 1891, newspapers nationwide reported that the Lathrops had converted to Catholicism. A number of editorial writers condemned and criticized the move, accusing them of seeking publicity and being hypocrites. A few editors bemoaned attacks on a private religious choice in this free country. The affair became a *cause célèbre* in both public and literary circles. Some attacks were so virulent that George wrote an *apologia* published by the *New York Independent* to explain how he had studied religions and that logic led him to conclude that Catholicism was the true Christian faith. Both the Lathrop and Hawthorne families expressed dismay but neither withdrew friendship or support.

Rose never attempted to explain her conversion. Surmise and deduction from other aspects of her life must suffice for tentative explanations. Her father and to some degree her mother were attracted to Catholicism. Nathaniel unconsciously incorporated much of Catholic understanding of the nature of man in his writings, including the need to expiate guilt. Rose was drawn to anything her adored father favored. The cold Calvinistic mindset of the New England milieu had repulsed him — Catholicism is the antithesis of Unitarianism. If George tested his logic and conclusions on Rose, that may have reinforced private convictions she had held for some time. She usually answered her heart rather than her mind in critical matters, but it is difficult to know for sure what finally motivated her. Both George and Rose became practicing Catholics. Rose was particularly fervent in Mass attendance, daily communion, and devotions such as novenas.

The pair went to Washington, D.C. in 1893 to research and write the history of the Visitation Order in America. In the process of researching and writing this account of nuns, Rose became enamored with the foundress, St. Jane de Chantal, who had left home and children in 17th-century France to minister to the poor and sick. Rose also became fascinated with nuns in general and concluded their life to be the nearest thing on earth to perfection.

In 1895, Rose went to Jamaica to visit her brother Julian and his family. She had determined to make a final break with George and this was the first move. After the visit, she went to Montreal for a retreat with the Grey Nuns and from there took up residence for a time with the Sisters of Charity in Cambridge, Massachusetts. George opposed the separation and sought a reconciliation, but Rose was determined and parried all his overtures. There is no doubt that George always loved Rose right up to his death. Researchers have never been able to explain satisfactorily why Rose wanted to end the marriage although his drinking was a problem. She always claimed that she loved George and had tried to keep the marriage going. She prayed for him during these trying years and continued to do so all her life. About this time she published her final literary effort, *Some Memories of Hawthorne*. Ironically, it was a smashing success.

Back in New York in 1896, Rose heard from a friend about her old seamstress who had cancer and had been sent to Blackwell's Island, a miserable warehouse for the poor with terminal cancer. Rose went to investigate. The scenes and smells of Blackwell's Island hit her like a bombshell. Sadness, despair, agony, and desperation were reflected in the faces of the dying. At that moment, Rosebud's spiritual impulses and impetuous nature dictated action. The vision of Nathaniel Hawthorne lifting a small sick English child and kissing her flashed through Rose's mind. Suddenly, she knew what God wanted of her. Later, she described this event in this way:

> *A fire was then lighted in my heart, where it still burns. I set my whole being to endeavor to bring consolation to the cancerous poor....*[38]

The next day she visited the New York Cancer Hospital to spend three

Mother Rose Hawthorne Lathrop.
Dominican Sisters of the Relief of Incurable Cancer, St. Rose's Home

months studying the treatment and care of patients. She rented a small flat on Scammel Street in a poor neighborhood on the lower East Side. From this modest address, she ventured forth into poor homes with cancer victims to cheer them and dress their sores. She let it be known that her home was open for any poor person with cancer unable to secure proper care. Mrs. Watson, whose face was disfigured with cancerous sores needing constant dressing, was Rose's first "guest." Rose steeled her nerves and suppressed her natural revulsion in tending to the old lady. This woman served both as a teaching and testing agent for Rose and her budding ministry. Mrs. Watson was extremely grateful for Rose's attentions and attempted to help in keeping the flat clean. Her grandson, institutionalized as a juvenile delinquent, became a frequent visitor, causing havoc and forcing Rose to forbid his return. This act brought about a complete reversal in Mrs. Watson's attitude as she became belligerent and complaining. Thus, with her first guest, Rose discovered that gratitude was not to be sought or expected on earth, but reserved for God alone.

As more guests appeared, Rose appealed to the public for aid with paid advertisements and articles about her work. These efforts produced gifts of linens and small contributions as well as gratis medical help from a doctor. A Jewish lawyer whose wife had died of cancer performed free legal services for Rose for the next 19 years. The ads and articles also invited helpers to join her in this work.

In December 1897, a lovely young woman of 26 appeared at Rose's door. She was Alice Huber, a native of Louisville, Kentucky, living in New York to advance her artistic career. She wanted to balance her life with some form of charity, and her spiritual director suggested she investigate Rose's work. On entering the flat crowded with cancer victims, Alice was appalled by the smell and sight of disfiguring sores. Later she wrote a description of this first encounter:

> *Everything about the place and neighborhood, the untidy woman in the kitchen, the patients upstairs, seemed perfectly repulsive to me. I certainly did not want to stay. . . . I knew nothing whatsoever about taking care of sick people and I felt great disgust to be near ordinary persons with sores, much less cancers. . . .*[39]

Alice's reaction to cancer reflected the common view of the day. New developments in the field of bacteriology discovered the tubercle bacillus and established tuberculosis as a transmittable disease. Most medical practitioners and the general public also believed that cancer was contagious. They viewed this disease much as leprosy had been all through recorded history. Victims with sufficient money could command hospital rooms or private medical attention at home. The poor and working lower-middle class were not so fortunate. Once incapacitated or in the terminal stages, these unfortunates usually ended up at alms-houses such as Blackwell's Island. Families and friends normally rejected or avoided them out of fear of contagion. On the other hand, Rose believed that cancer was not contagious and that charity demanded decent treatment for the victims, especially those in the terminal stages. To her credit, Alice agreed to help out one day a week before departing the dreary scene, leaving Rose to wonder if she would return.

Thus ended the first part of Rose Hawthorne's life, so like a Greek tragedy with its early beginnings in the witch hunts in Salem, death claiming her child, and with her experiences in Cambridge, London, Rome, Dresden, New London, Chicago, Jamaica, Montreal, and New York. In the final scene her husband died without her at his bedside.

The second part of Rose's life was more a triumphal drama. It began when Rose had a dream in which George forgave her for ending the marriage. Two weeks later she had a vision of the crucified Jesus in which He said, "I love you, and you love Me. Then what is the trouble?" This vision gave her great consolation. The following day Alice Huber moved in to become Rose's permanent helper and beloved companion in religion.

As the original flat became inadequate for the increasing numbers of poor women with terminal cancer, Rose rented larger rooms on Water Street. George's death opened the door to full religious life and Rose eagerly peered through, wanting to enter. She now made the first move towards the formation of a religious order. She cut her long reddish hair and put on a severe outfit that resembled the early habit of the Sisters of Charity. Acting on the advice of her friend and counselor, Father Clement Thuente, Rose wrote Archbishop Michael Corrigan. She described the garb and asked for an interview. He initially refused to see her, but finally agreed when Rose wrote again. The archbishop was as harsh with Rose as he had been with Mother Cabrini almost 10 years earlier. He finally consented for Rose, Alice, and Cecilia Cochrane, the third member, to wear the garb, but only in private, and he withheld both ecclesiastical approval and personal support for several years. The archbishop felt that Rose's little band could function best as an arm of some established order. He may have been dubious about the perseverance of this converted Catholic with a different background than he normally encountered. He wrote about the women: "If it is not God's work it will go to pieces, and if it is God's work it will succeed."

Still lacking church approbation, the three women began a routine of combined prayer and nursing. The arrival of ever more women in the final stages of life forced them to examine the possibilities of a much larger facility. Rose once again took up her facile pen and appealed for support from the public. She was always more successful in raising money than in securing vocations. During the three years of the group's semireligious status, around 150 women made enquiries but only three became permanent members. Some joined but left when the stress of this life proved too demanding. Others she sent away as unsuitable.

With a gift of $1,000 from a friend, Rose made a down payment on a large building on Cherry Street that she named St. Rose's Free Home for Incurable Cancer. She gave this title in honor of St. Rose of Lima, a Dominican tertiary and nurse to the poor. This larger house could accommodate as many as 20 patients and was an improvement over the miserable flat on Scammel Street and the crowded quarters on Water Street. But it too had drawbacks that would eventually force yet another move. Rose paid for the Cherry Street home within two years with donations from friends, the public, and $1,000 she saved.

Realization dawned on Rose that those outside her small circle might have nightmarish concepts about a life devoted to nursing the terminally ill.

She sought to dispel some of these fears with her writing. In an article printed in *The Catholic World* in February 1899, she wrote —

> *The subject about which I write, and which I would gladly make interesting to the general public, is one that can hardly be made agreeable; but nevertheless I can testify that such a life as I lead with a few companions in a poor district, among the sick, has many agreeable points. As it is my earnest desire to get women to join me who have a natural talent for nursing, and a natural inclination to nurse those who need it most, I think it might be well for me to present the bright side of the care of the cancerous poor. . . .*[40]

In September 1899 Archbishop Corrigan consented to the request of the three women that they "begin in a humble way and establish a Chapter in connection with the church of the Dominican Fathers."[41] Father Thuente, a Dominican, began religious instruction on their daily lives as tertiaries and approved their taking religious names and being called "sister." On September 14, 1899, Cecilia became Sister Mary Magdalen and Alice became Sister Mary Rose in honor of St. Rose of Lima. Rose Hawthorne Lathrop became Sister Mary Alphonsa.

Movement from tertiary status to sister proceeded. Archbishop Corrigan permitted Mass in their home, but withheld permission to wear the full Dominican habit for some time. Mother Alphonsa made a retreat with Dominican sisters in Caldwell, New Jersey, during the summer of 1900. She wrote her sisters-to-be that she had learned much about religious life, but that the mortifications and fasting of these sisters would not do for a nursing order. Two more women joined in 1900. On December 8 of that year this tiny community was invested with the full

Dominicans, St. Rose of Lima (c. 1942).
Courtesy Gonzaga University

Dominican habit and in January 1901 the community obtained a charter from the state of New York that would facilitate receiving gifts and legacies. Mother Alphonsa had established an official order of women religious. She now set new goals.

Up to this point Mother Alphonsa had only accepted female patients, but the time to make arrangements for men had arrived. Father Cothonay, a Dominican, was looking for a buyer for a large house in Sherman Park, a small town outside New York City. Mother Alphonsa wanted to buy it. The price was $28,000 — a most attractive figure since the Dominican fathers had over $50,000 invested in the property. It provided healthful and soothing surroundings and could accommodate both men and women. Mother Alphonsa observed that food could also be grown in this semirural environment. Archbishop Corrigan approved and Mother Alphonsa purchased it in 1901. Rosary Hill became the motherhouse and novitiate of the Servants of Relief for Incurable Cancer in the U.S.

Mother Alphonsa received many honors and achieved national fame for the work that she and her sisters performed. Vindication for her stand came when it was proven that cancer was not contagious. During these years at Rosary Hill, Mother Alphonsa nursed the dying, wrote appeals for funds and recruits, prayed, instructed, nurtured her sisters, monitored the institution, and corresponded widely. Sister Mary Rose, her dear friend Alice Huber, remained in New York to manage the St. Rose's Free Home for Incurable Cancer. Mother Alphonsa's final goal was the construction of a new fireproof sanitorium at Rosary Hill. This task required a tremendous sum, so once again she took up her pen to appeal as only a Hawthorne could. Unhappily, she did not live long enough to see its completion.

Over 100,000 indigent sufferers have spent their final days in these institutions that are open to all races, sexes, and religions. Conditions for acceptance are poverty, terminal cancer properly certified by a physician, and unavailability of home care. The "Servants" see Jesus Christ in each patient and extend their seemingly endless supply of love to each one. They take only one day a month off from this demanding work. Contrary to ordinary human expectations, individual sisters derive a tremendous amount of happiness and consolation from this ministry. Even those sisters whose primary duties are technical or backup services take turns in direct, hands-on nursing.

On the morning of July 9, 1926, the sisters found that Mother Mary Alphonsa had died peacefully in her sleep. Rosebud joined Nathaniel, Sophia, Una, George, little Francis, a small English girl, and the thousands who had died with dignity because of her love. Is she a saint? Only God knows and we await His testimony. The Hawthorne name will live on for more than literary accomplishments.

Foreign Missions

Foreign missions would become an important ministry later in the 20th century. But even as domestic demands overwhelmed the sisters, some chose to enter missionary work during this era. Early in the 19th century, American Protestants began sending missionaries overseas. They did credible work in the medical field and in conversions to Christianity. Catholic sisters followed in the final years of the 19th century.

In 1879, the Franciscan Sisters of Allegany (1180) were first, when they sent three sisters to Jamaica where the community is still active in education. They opened the first Catholic teachers' college on the island in 1897. The Sisters of Mercy from Cincinnati also sent missionaries to Jamaica in 1880, and in 1893 the Sisters of Mercy from New Orleans sent sisters to British Honduras (now Belize), as did the Congregation of the Sisters of the Holy Family in 1898. Two communities based in San Antonio, Texas, have ministered in Mexico for many years: the congregation of the Sisters of Charity of the Incarnate Word since 1885 and the Sisters of the Holy Spirit and Mary Immaculate since 1901. In 1887, Benedictine sisters from Elizabeth, New Jersey, made a foundation in Ecuador. The Sisters of Charity of St. Vincent de Paul of New York opened a mission in the Bahamas in 1889 and still labor there. Several of the Sisters of the Holy Cross joined European sisters of their order in India in 1889 but were recalled in 1896. The Sisters of Notre Dame de Namur sent missionaries to South Africa in 1889. In 1891, Mother Cabrini made her Nicaraguan foundation. Puerto Rico drew missionaries from the Mission Helpers of the Sacred Heart in 1902, from the Daughters of Charity[42] in 1905, from Dominican Sisters of Amityville, New York, in 1910 and from the School Sisters of Notre Dame in 1915. The Religious of the Sacred Heart of Mary in Tarrytown, New York, sent missionaries to Brazil in 1910 and opened a convent in Tuy, Spain in 1911 as a refuge for sisters fleeing revolution in Portugal.

Perhaps the most interesting early American missionary effort involved lepers. Hawaii was an independent kingdom in 1883 when Mother Marianne Cope (1838-1918), the provincial of the Sisters of the Third Franciscan Order (1490) of Syracuse, New York, was asked to send aid to the island's sick poor, including the victims of leprosy. She accepted the invitation and personally led a group of six sisters to Hawaii. Every member of her congregation had volunteered to accompany her.

A glimpse of her devotion to a life of charitable work is provided in one of her letters:

> *I am hungry for the work and I wish with all my heart to be one*
> *of the chosen Ones, whose privilege it will be, to sacrifice them-*

selves for the salvation of the souls of the poor Islanders. . . . I am not afraid of any disease, hence it would be my greatest delight even to minister to the abandoned "lepers." . . . Waking and sleeping, I am on the Islands. Do not laugh at me, for being so wholly absorbed in that one wish, one thought, to be a worker in that large field. . . .[43]

Mother Marianne was born in Germany and emigrated as a child with her parents and grew up in Utica, New York. At age 24, she joined the Syracuse Franciscans that two years earlier had become autonomous from the Franciscan Sisters of Philadelphia. She was elected mother-provincial in 1877, serving in that position when the call came from Hawaii.

After service in Honolulu caring for the daughters of lepers, Mother Marianne went to Molokai in 1888 where the sainted Father Damien worked and lived with his lepers. She took over management of the Baldwin House for boys with leprosy. She labored there until 1895, when she took control of Bishop House for girls suffering from the disease. She ministered in this institution until her death in 1918. Her grave at Kalaupapa is marked by a beautiful monument — a high pedestal surmounted by a statue of St. Francis embracing the crucified Savior.

Her 35 years of service to lepers were filled with the labor, love, and problems such a ministry entails. The motherhouse in Syracuse supplied recruits although a few sisters could not bear this work and had to be replaced. She encountered many of the same problems that Father Damien had with the Health Board in Honolulu. He died only six months after her arrival in Molokai. During this brief span they had a warm relationship and she was with him the day before his death. She prepared his body for burial with tears streaming down her cheeks. Today Father Damien represents Hawaii in Washington in the Statuary Hall along with Mother Joseph of Oregon. Mother Marianne Cope could well complement those saintly servants of God.

Horribly disfigured girls at the Bishop House were sometimes difficult to control and occasionally sneaked out at night. Mother Cope understood and said little. One day in May 1889 she received a visitor, Robert Louis Stevenson. Unlike most curiosity seekers, he remained a full week, although in poor health, and spent hours each day playing croquet and joshing with the disfigured girls, showing no disgust at their ugliness. A week after his departure a brand new $500 piano arrived, and shortly thereafter this handwritten and signed poem came in the mail:

Reverend Sister Maryanne, Matron of the Bishop Home:

To see the infinite pity of this place,
The mangled limb, the devastated face,

The innocent sufferers smiling at the rod,
A fool were tempted to deny his God.

He sees, and shrinks; but if he look again,
Lo, beauty springing from the breast of pain!
He marks the sisters on the painful shores,
And even a fool is silent and adores.[44]

Leprosy began to decline in 1890 when the total census dropped below 1,000 for the first time. Thereafter the number declined slowly each year as death claimed victims faster than new cases appeared. Cruel in many ways, the policy of segregation of lepers from the general population was effective.

Unlike Father Damien, Mother Marianne was never able to address her girls as "fellow lepers." Yet, research reveals her life and work to be heroic, and steps are underway to enter her cause for sainthood — a seemingly appropriate recognition for one of the earliest American Catholic sister-missionaries.

Franciscan Sisters of Syracuse still minister to the lepers on Molokai. The settlement is administered by the Hawaiian Health Department for Hansen's Disease and is staffed by six sisters. Hawaii has provided well over 100 vocations for this congregation, something that surely pleases Mother Marianne, the former novice-mistress in Syracuse. *Casa Marianna* in Pativilca, Peru, where sisters minister to poor peasants in the foothills of the Andes, is a memorial to her. Robert Louis Stevenson gave Mother Marianne her finest tribute: *"He marks the sisters on the painful shores / And even a fool is silent and adores."*

The Prayer Ministry

Throughout these years, contemplative nuns quietly expanded. The Carmelite monastery in Baltimore was a mother lode for new foundations, beginning with St. Louis in 1863. They sent founding nuns to Boston in 1890, to Brooklyn in 1907, to Seattle in 1908, and to Wheeling in 1913. Boston in turn sent founding nuns to Philadelphia in 1902 and to Santa Clara in 1908. In 1915, Mexican Carmelites fleeing persecution settled in Grand Rapids. The Poor Clares expanded in similar fashion. The contemplative part of the Sisters of the Good Shepherd, called Magdalens, increased quietly, numbering around 400 in 1900. Since they live a life of anonymity in Good Shepherd convents, little information is reported about them.

An American, Mother Mary of Jesus (Julia Crooks, 1839-1924), arrived in Newark, New Jersey in 1880 from France accompanied by three other Dominican nuns from the monastery in Oullins. These **Dominican Contemplative Nuns (OP-1050)** established the first Dominican cloistered monastery in the United States. The Monastery of St. Dominic in Newark proved a fountainhead for other monasteries. An entirely different group of Dominicans from Belgium established a monastery in 1891 in Union City, New Jersey. They in turn provided founding groups for more monasteries. In 1990, a total of 22 Dominican monasteries emanating from these two foundations existed in the U.S. and overseas.[45]

By 1917, contemplative monasteries were no longer a rarity in the United States with vigorous growth characterizing most such orders. The four Carmelites of Port Tobacco in 1790 would surely be pleased to see their mode of religious life finally taking hold in this land.

Other Ministries

An entire community of Episcopal sisters joined the Roman Catholic Church in 1909 and are known today as the **Franciscan Sisters of the Atonement (SA-1190)**. This community was originally founded in 1898 as a branch of the Anglican Society of the Atonement by Mother Lurana Mary White at Graymoor, New York. Their co-founder, Episcopal priest Paul Wattson, joined Mother Lurana in a strong belief in the primacy of the pope and the desire for unity between the Anglican communion and the Roman Catholic Church. They promoted this union at every opportunity and by whatever means they could, although their stance made them unpopular in Episcopal circles. Reverend Wattson and Mother Lurana advanced the idea of celebrating Christian union during the octave from the feast of St. Peter to that of St. Paul. This idea found a ready reception in Rome and subsequently became known as the Chair of Unity Octave. Some Anglican and Episcopal churches adopted the prayers. Other Christian churches in favor of unity felt uncomfortable with this prayer form and used prayers more to their liking and traditions. This community and its founders anticipated the spirit of ecumenism well before Vatican II.

The sisters have performed a variety of ministries over the years; today 270 sisters minister in a long list of dioceses as well as in Japan, Canada, Ireland, Brazil, and Italy. Among their many apostolates are AIDS, pastoral, hospital and prison ministries, religious education, social welfare, community development programs, home visitation, adult day care, child day care, kindergartens, camps for underprivileged youth, justice and peace work, guest and retreat house ministries. Christ's dictum that "All may be one" remains the driving force for this unique Franciscan community.

Summary

In 1917 there were 224 orders and congregations in the United States plus their many offshoots. The 84,000 sisters and nuns had convents in every state of the Union as well as schools, academies, colleges, hospitals, orphanages, and charitable institutions. A small number of sisters were serving in foreign missions. More than half served in the ever expanding complex of parochial schools.

This brief recapitulation of sister-ministry between the end of the Civil War and American entry into World War I hopefully brings into clearer focus how tens of thousands of sisters and nuns devoted their lives to working in the vineyard. More than the clergy, more than the bishops, and more than any other force, sisters and nuns molded the character of the American Catholic population. Catholic historians concentrate, with some justification, on clerics and bishops of this era, but miss the critical role played by women religious who were the veritable Catholic heroines of the Age of Immigration.

Along the way, the reader has been introduced to several of the better known sisters, including a canonized saint and a host of saintly women. As the era closed, dangerous adventures and grinding needs were past and would not recur until women religious once again ventured into places of peril — foreign missions in the Orient. We now leave this intriguing period with many stories of adventure, sacrifice, achievement, and love yet untold. The modern age beckons.

Endnotes

1. For example, St. John Nepomucene Neumann (1811-1860), Bishop of Philadelphia from 1852 until his death, founded numerous parochial schools, increased the number of students twenty-fold, and organized a diocesan "system." He secured orders of both men and women religious to teach and founded the Sisters of St. Francis of Philadelphia (1650) for that purpose.
2. Brothers of the various orders sometimes operated parochial schools. For example, the Brothers of Holy Cross conducted 79 parochial schools during the 19th century (Connelly, Rev. James T., CSC, "Educators in the Faith: The Holy Cross Congregation and their Schools in the United States, 1865-1900," paper presented at the Conference on the History of Holy Cross in the United States, New Orleans, 1990).
3. John O'Kane Murray, *Catholicity in the United States: Popular History of the Catholic Church in the U.S.* (Brooklyn, NY: 1876), p. 612.
4. Rev. Harold A. Buetow, *Of Singular Benefit: The Story of Catholic Education in the United States* (New York, NY: The Macmillan Company, 1970).
5. The *McGuffey Readers* of the 19th century are famous. Some education historians believe that those textbooks were a primary influence in shaping the American character of that age. Their strong Protestant flavor made them unacceptable to Catholics, although later editions were modified for Catholic acceptance. From the first edition in 1836 to the last one in 1920, some 120 million textbooks were sold.

6. Even the composition of the council attracted anti-Catholic criticism. Of the 72 prelates in attendance, only 24 were American-born although many of the foreign-born immigrated as children. The countries of their origins were Ireland (22), Germany (9), France (7), Belgium (4), Spain (2) and one each from Holland, Switzerland, Scotland, and Slovenia.

7. Robert T. O'Gorman, *The Church that Was a School: Catholic Identity and Catholic Education in the United States Since 1790* (Nashville, TN: The Catholic Education Futures Project, 1987), p. 15.

8. Proclamations by a national conference of bishops are not absolutely binding on its members although they exert tremendous influence. In the hierarchial structure of the Roman Catholic Church, a bishop is ultimately responsible to proclamations of universal Church councils such as Vatican II, and to the pope.

9. Rules and constitutions prohibiting members from teaching boys, or boys beyond a certain age, were an ongoing problem well into the 20th century. Some communities with European motherhouses had considerable difficulty in this regard. The "boy problem" was a frequently used term among those communities. While many communities succumbed to pressure from the hierarchy to teach boys, the Sisters of Notre de Namur were adamant about adhering to their rule and consequently had to withdraw from a number of parochial schools.

10. An economic drag on immigrant families was the need to send money to relatives in the homeland for Atlantic passage or simply to alleviate poverty. This charitable impulse continues to the present day among immigrant and first-generation immigrant families.

11. The Catholic University of America instituted a full summer course for women religious in 1911 with an initial class of 284 students.

12. Bishops calling for help from large communities was common and partially explains the wide geographical dispersion of some orders. Another factor was the ethnic pull that motivated mothers-superior to send sister-teachers to parochial schools of the community's ethnic makeup, no matter how far distant from the motherhouse.

13. Parochial schools were frequently sociological "mixers." Parents of all economic and social classes sent their children to the nearest parochial school without regard to its "class" status. Mixing became more the norm as neighborhoods and parishes diluted ethnic membership. Author's personal note: As one of the children of Catholic Army personnel at Fort Sill, Oklahoma, who daily rode into Lawton on an Army bus (now outlawed) to attend parochial school, I recall the Mexican children tying their ponies to the hitching post each day.

14. Sisters prepared boys to become altar boys. Mass was in Latin and the altar boy had to memorize a sizeable number of responses to the priest's prayers. Any gathering of Catholic men over 50 years of age will usually find one or more ex-altar boys who can still recite the Latin prayers — and who do so gleefully.

15. Following Vatican II, the American Catholic Church abandoned the *Baltimore Catechism* but failed to provide a workable substitute. Subjective religious education without a firm foundation in factual knowledge has proven largely in-

effectual. The *Universal Catechism*, officially approved June 25, 1992, should more than make up for this gap in religious education.

16. During these years, salaries paid to sister-teachers varied slightly from diocese to diocese and even within dioceses at times. For instance, the Sisters of St. Joseph in Boston in 1910 earned only $200 per year and this did not include board. The wage increased to $250 in 1921 and to $300 in 1937. See Sr. Mary J. Oates, CSJ, "The Good Sisters: The Works and Position of Catholic Churchwomen in Boston, 1870-1940," Robert E. Sullivan and James M. O'Toole, eds., *Catholic Boston: Studies in Religious Community, 1870-1970* (Boston, MA, 1985), p. 191. Such low salaries impeded the educational and intellectual development of individual sisters and left little for community overhead, care of aged sisters, or training of novices.

17. Eileen Mary Brewer, *Nuns and the Education of American Catholic Women, 1860-1920* (Chicago, IL: Loyola University Press, 1987), p. 15.

18. Orders of brothers engaged in education during these years were —
    Marist Brothers - arrived in U.S. in 1817.
    Brothers of the Congregation of the Holy Cross - 1841.
    Brothers of the Christian Schools - 1845.
    Brothers of the Sacred Heart - 1847.
    Xaverian Brothers - 1854.
    Brothers of the Poor of St. Francis - 1868.
    Orders engaged in education with both priests and brothers were —
    Jesuits - active since colonial days.
    Dominicans - arrived in U.S. in 1805.
    Vincentians - 1818.
    Society of the Precious Blood - 1843.
    Benedictines - 1846.
    Marianist Fathers and Brothers - 1849.
    Oblates of Mary Immaculate - 1849.
    Resurrectionists - 1865.
    Viatorians - 1882.
    Missionaries of Our Lady of LaSalette - 1892.
    Salvatorians - 1896.

19. Tuition and board typically ran $150-$300 per school year for the academies. Additional fees were levied for such items as music lessons, drawing, and painting. (Advertisements in *Sadlier's Catholic Directory* for 1885.) Although these prices seem small today, the average worker earned around $15 per week. An income of $3,000-$4,000 per year put one in the economic middle class.

20. State supported colleges proliferated following the Hatch Act of 1887 and the Morrill Act of 1890 that provided federal financing for land grant colleges. The late 19th-century college student population grew from 52,000 in 1870 to 237,000 in 1900.

21. Most Catholic histories credit the College of Notre Dame of Maryland with being the first Catholic women's college to grant degrees instead of Ursuline

College in Cleveland. The reason for this becomes clear in Debra Campbell's history of the college soon to be published.

22. Certain elements in the Church attempted to block the foundation of Trinity College for fear that it would be part of The Catholic University of America or become coeducational. The heroic efforts of Sister Julia McGroarty and Sister Mary Euphrasia and the backing of Cardinal James Gibbons and Archbishop John Lancaster Spalding were enough to effect the foundation. The college opened in 1900 and graduated a class of 16 in 1904.

23. In England, the head nurse of a ward is still addressed as "sister," a carryover from Florence Nightingale's insistence on a semi-religious character for nurses.

24. The first recorded orphanage in the original United States was opened in South Carolina before the American Revolution by a Jewish group.

25. For example, orphanages operated by the Daughters of Charity peaked in 1909 at 32.

26. Sr. Anne Marie Knawa, OSF, *As God Shall Ordain: A History of the Franciscan Sisters of Chicago, 1894-1987* (Chicago, IL: Worzalla Publishing Company, 1989), p. 65.

27. Over the years, the U.S. Government signed 389 treaties with Indian tribes. A high percentage were ignored or violated.

28. The eight agencies that Catholics retained were:
    1 - Cheyenne Agency, Montana.
    2 - Crow Creek Agency, Montana.
    3 - Devil's Lake Agency, North Dakota.
    4 - Pine Ridge Agency, South Dakota.
    5 - Rosebud Agency, South Dakota.
    6 - Sisseton Agency, South Dakota.
    7 - Standing Rock Agency, South Dakota.
    8 - Yankton Agency, South Dakota.

29. Thomas J. Morgan was the head of the Indian Bureau between 1889 and 1893. While a Baptist educator, he had castigated parochial schools as a challenge to true Americanism. He agitated for denominational Indian schools to be converted to nonsectarian government schools in order to thwart Catholic receipt of federal funds.

30. Augustus Tolton (1854-1897) was born to slave parents in Missouri. The owners and slaves were all Catholic. When the Civil War broke out, his father escaped and joined the Union Army, dying in St. Louis in 1865. Mrs. Tolton made a daring escape with her children and settled in Quincy, Illinois. Forced to work in a tobacco factory, Augustus managed to secure an education with the help of several priests and eventually decided that he had a vocation. When no American seminary would accept a black, he went to Rome to attend the Urban College of the Propagation of the Faith. He served the black Catholics of Quincy then Chicago before dying suddenly from heat exhaustion at age 43.

31. Sr. Consuelo Marie Duffy, SBS, *Katharine Drexel: A Biography* (Cornwells Heights, PA: Mother Katharine Drexel Guild, 1966), p. 248. Much of this account is based on this book.

32. Sr. Mary Jean Dorsey, OP, *Saint Dominic's Family: The Lives of Over 300 Famous Dominicans* (Washington, DC: Dominicana Publications, DC, 1964).

33. Lest these descriptions infer that only Indian women had vocation problems, an incident, amusing only in retrospect, took place in South Dakota in 1882. The *Yankton Press* and the *Dakotian* both printed —

> *Yankton has been considerably interested today over the marriage of Dr. V. Sebiakin-Ross to Miss Nelly Kerns. Dr. Sebiakin-Ross is a popular young Russian physician here and Miss Kerns has been known to the community and generally beloved as Sister Mary Paul, of the convent of the Sacred Heart.*

This scandal hit like a bombshell and the story went out over the wire. Newspapers all over the country printed it. To say that Bishop Martin Marty and the other sisters were upset would be an understatement. To compound the disgrace, a tobacco manufacturer named a best-selling cigar the "Mary Paul" after the former sister, perpetuating the memory of this unfortunate incident and grating on Catholic nerves for many years (Robert F. Karolevitz, *Bishop Martin E. Marty: The Blackrobe Lean Chief,* Yankton, SD: privately printed for the Benedictine Sisters of Sacred Heart Convent, 1980, p. 88).

34. Patricia Dunlavy Valenti, Ph.D., *To Myself a Stranger: A Biography of Rose Hawthorne Lathrop* (Baton Rouge, LA: Louisiana State University Press, 1991). This account is based on this book and the preliminary manuscript that Dr. Valenti was kind enough to allow me to use.

35. A witch hunt gripped Salem, Massachusetts, in 1692. Before the hysteria was brought under control, 19 people had been executed and more than 100 others had been charged with or convicted of practicing witchcraft. Contrary to popular belief, no women accused of witchcraft were "burned at the stake."

36. Ibid, p. 103.

37. James Hennesey, SJ, *American Catholics: A History of the Roman Catholic Community in the United States* (New York, NY: Oxford University Press, 1981), p. 191.

38. Sr. Mary Joseph, OP, *Out of Many Hearts* (Hawthorne, NY: The Servants of Relief for Incurable Cancer, 1965), p. 22.

39. Valenti, p. 143.

40. Ibid, p. 155.

41. Ibid, p. 156.

42. In 1875, persecution in Mexico sent 75 Daughters of Charity fleeing across the border into the United States, most into California. American Daughters of Charity sheltered them. While some joined American communities, most relocated to Spanish-speaking territories where the international order had communities — an indirect American contribution to foreign missions.

43. Sr. Mary Laurence Hanley, OSF, *A Song of Pilgrimage and Exile: The Life and Spirit of Mother Marianne of Molokai* (Chicago, IL: Franciscan Herald Press, 1980), p. 72. Most of the account was derived from this book.

44. Ibid., p. 328.

45. Daughters and granddaughters of the Newark monastery are —

Year Founded	Place
1889	Bronx, NY
1906	Farmington, MI
1915-1989*	Cincinnati, OH
1915-1970*	Albany, NY
1921	Menlo, Park, CA
1924	Los Angeles, CA
1945	Lufkin, TX
1959	Karachi, Pakistan
1977	Cocaue, Philippines

Daughters and granddaughters of the Union City monastery are —

1897	Milwaukee, MI
1899-1980*	Catonsville, MD
1900	Camden, NJ
1905	Buffalo, NY
1909	La Crosse, WI (moved to Washington, DC in 1984)
1919	Summit, NJ
1922	West Springfield, MA
1925	Lancaster, PA
1925	Syracuse, NY
1944	Elmira, NY
1945	Marbury, AL
1947	North Guilford, CT
1965	Nairobi, Kenya
1977	Cainta, Philippines

* Year closed.

CHAPTER 9

Sturdy Growth
(1918-1945)

‡ — ‡

THE 1918-1945 YEARS might well be called the Age of Violence. Beginning with World War I and ending at the close of World War II, deaths from battle, execution, bombing, lawlessness, as well as from starvation and sickness, totaled in the hundreds of millions. The Turkish persecution of Armenians, the Turko-Greek War, Italy's invasion of Ethiopia, civil wars in China and Spain, Nazi persecution of Jews, calculated Soviet starvation of Ukrainians and Kulaks, and warfare in the Balkans were part of the destruction between the great world wars that violated human rights and seriously divided peoples.

National Events

Following the end of World War I and the return of American servicemen from Europe, the nation looked inward, assumed an isolationist posture and grappled with social and economic problems. The public perceived socialism as an economic threat imported from Europe which stimulated renewed anti-immigrant passions, contributing to the passage of restrictive immigration laws. The famous Sacco-Vanzetti trial typified the unreasonable fear of socialism and dislike for the most recent waves of immigrants — Italians and Slavs. In 1920, authorities arrested Italian immigrants Bartolomeo Vanzetti and Nicola Sacco for the murder of a paymaster during a robbery in Boston. Both men were admitted anarchists and very "foreign" looking. Despite weak evidence, the court convicted and executed them, pleas for clemency from all over the world notwithstanding. The case still arouses strong feelings in some quarters.

American entry into World War I had not been universally popular. Irish-Americans and German-Americans opposed entry for ethnic reasons. However, once committed, the entire nation responded with patriotic fervor. Of the 3,989 conscientious objectors, only four were Catholics.[1] Almost two million servicemen went to France. Following the war, most Americans became disillusioned with the League of Nations, and an isolationist attitude swept the nation. The Spanish Civil War of 1936-39 divided Americans between supporters of the Communist-controlled government and the Fascist revolutionaries. Ardent anti-Communists tilted for General Franco and the revolutionaries as did most Catholics because of persecution of the Church.[2]

While World War I temporarily slowed immigration, the U.S. Congress effectively terminated it in 1921. The Emergency Immigration Act passed that year restricted entry to three percent of foreign-born Americans as listed in the census of 1910. This was the first immigration law to establish quotas for the country of origin. A second quota law in 1924 reduced this to two percent of the 1890 census — favoring Irish and Germans while overtly discriminating against Italians, Jews, Slavs, and other Central and Eastern Europeans. In 1929 Congress tightened the screws with a limitation of 150,000 immigrants per year based on national origins in the 1920 census. North Americans, Canadians, and Mexicans were exempt, although they did not immigrate to the United States in large numbers during these years.

Cultural assimilation of the 13.92 million foreign-born listed in the 1920 census was an ongoing process. The perpetuating factor keeping native languages and cultures alive gradually faded. Ethnic intermarriages increased among Catholics. Irish-Italian, Czech-Polish, German-Irish, and other combinations tended to loosen strong ethnic and cultural loyalties. As sociologists have often noted, second- and third-generations were more quickly absorbed into American culture. The Americanization of the Church promoted by some of the Irish-American hierarchy was almost complete by 1945.

The Americanization of congregations of women religious continued in parallel with their families except for the ever arriving new orders; however, that flow ceased abruptly in 1941.[3] Only one new order arrived after the entrance of the United States into World War II; it came from Mexico — the **Missionary Catechists of the Sacred Hearts of Jesus and Mary (MC-2700)**. These sisters settled in Victoria, Texas, where they have maintained their motherhouse ever since. The war impacted several thousand German-, Austro-Hungarian-, and Italian-born sisters, who suddenly found themselves "enemy aliens." They had to register and report regularly on their occupations, associations, and addresses. Special permission was needed in order to travel or change address. The law permitted no exceptions. Too many foreign-born sisters had procrastinated about securing American citizenship and learned a bitter lesson.

Political movements and passions gripped the country, resulting in two amendments to the United States Constitution that would cause great social tension. Ratified in 1919, the Eighteenth Amendment imposed the prohibition of alcoholic beverages, causing massive defiance of the law by ordinary citizens and the creation of large criminal organizations to supply the demand for illegal spirits. Protestant churches and organizations strongly supported the "noble experiment," eventually resulting in a reduction of their influence on national morality. This decline of moral authority would continue until the Protestant establishment no longer was the primary determinant of national moral values, paving the way for the rise of rampant secularism. Catholic bishops maintained low profiles in the political frays surrounding passage of the amendment. Although drunkenness by Catholics (the Irish disease) had bothered the hierarchy for years, they were disinclined to support Prohibition, feeling that it was too extreme a measure and highly unpopular with most Catholics. The Catholic Total Abstinence Union (CTAU) founded in 1872 had not been very successful, although some bishops such as Archbishop John Ireland, never one for half measures, advocated legal prohibition.

After more than a century of struggles, the Nineteenth Amendment was ratified in 1920 granting suffrage to women. Although Susan B. Anthony is the best known suffrage worker, Alice Paul and Carrie Chapman Catt secured the final victory. Bishops gave very limited support to suffrage for women, clinging tenaciously to the view that women's place was in the home. Already suspicious of higher education for women and disturbed by Catholic women entering the labor force, some bishops remained fearful that family life would deteriorate.

But, finally, more women began to achieve prominence in public life and letters. Edith Wharton won the Pulitzer Prize for *The Age of Innocence* in 1921, Edna St. Vincent Millay won it for *The Harp-Weaver and Other Poems* in 1923, and Edna Ferber won it for *So Big* in 1925. Rebecca L. Felton became the first female United States senator in 1922. Amelia Earhart was the first woman to fly solo across the Atlantic.[4] In 1931 Jane Addams shared the Nobel Peace Prize with Nicholas Butler. Frances Perkins became the first female cabinet member as Secretary of Labor under Franklin Roosevelt. Mrs. Eleanor Roosevelt became the most "activist" First Lady in American history, working for the rights of labor, women, minorities, and the disadvantaged.

Prohibition and the return of two million servicemen from France ushered in the Roaring '20s, so-called because of illegal speak-easies, short-skirted "flappers," and a daring new emphasis on sex. Margaret Sanger promoted birth control and confession magazines described the sexual exploits of movie stars. The instant popularity of Sigmund Freud's psychoanalysis theories seemed to provide an excuse for immoral behavior.[5] Millions of automobiles created newfound personal mobility, loosening family ties and reducing parental control over teenage children. The rise of the motion picture industry contributed to changing attitudes and influenced moral values. In recognition of this, Catholic bishops established the National Legion of Decency in 1934 to monitor and classify films. This move was highly popular and received the support of Protestant and Jewish leaders. Despite this and other efforts by religious leaders, the impact of these new attitudes was stronger than any previous shift of national mores. Cracks that would later develop into gaping holes appeared in the American wall of moral restraint.

Black Tuesday on Wall Street on October 29, 1929, ushered in the Great Depression. No economic crisis before or since had affected so many Americans. With 25 percent of the work force unemployed and the rest at reduced wages, true poverty stalked the land. Almost every community of women religious experienced even greater hardship, scrimping on food and other necessities and the loss of opportunities to expand existing ministries or assume new ones. One example of the thousands of burdens that the depression imposed concerns the Misericordian Hospital in New York City, operated by the Canadian-founded **Misericordia Sisters (SM-2680).** They were forced to dismiss 10 nurses in 1935 despite the desperate need for their services. Some communities had to curtail assistance for sisters in foreign missions. Sacrifices by sisters during the depression conjures up reminiscences of the 19th century.

In spite of such setbacks, the Roman Catholic Church in the United States experienced stability and realized new strength. By 1945, Catholics had increased to 20 percent of the population, and the addition of such disparate sees as Honolulu, Hawaii; Pueblo, Colorado; Raleigh, North Carolina; and Gallup, New Mexico, increased the number of dioceses to 118. The clergy trained in an expanded network of diocesan and religious order seminaries and grew to nearly 39,000 priests. Bishops had considerable clout in some sections of the country: political leaders in Washington gave their views a respectful if not always sympathetic audience.[6] American cardinals and archbishops cut wide swaths in Rome as a consequence of strong financial support for the Vatican, the staunch orthodoxy of the American Church and loyalty to the pope. However, anti-Catholicism was not dead in the United States.

Ku Klux Klan Attack

Nativist anti-Catholic impulses that took concrete form in the 19th century abated during the early years of the 20th century. The Know-Nothings, the Ku Klux Klan, and the American Protective Society that had fomented such strong anti-Catholic sentiments and harassed women religious in the 1800's were no longer a serious threat. However, that latent mean spirit revived following World War I and was embodied in a resurrected Ku Klux Klan.[7] It began its new life in Atlanta in 1915 and included Catholics, Jews, immigrants, labor unions, and blacks on its hate list. It rapidly expanded in the 1920's, reaching a membership between four and five million by the middle of the decade. Its power was demonstrated in Indiana where the Klan almost took control of the state government.[8] On August 8, 1925, 40,000 hooded Klansmen marched down Pennsylvania Avenue in Washington, D.C., flaunting their power. Although popular in its old breeding ground, the Deep South, it became more national during this time. Different from the post-Civil War secret society, the Klan now attracted middle-class Protestants, including numbers of clergymen.

The most serious anti-Catholic attack by the Ku Klux Klan occurred in Oregon where it tried to legally ban parochial schools. Existing animosity towards Jews, Asians, blacks, Catholics, and non-Nordic immigrants in the Northwest states of Oregon and Washington made this region fertile ground for the Ku Klux Klan with its slogan "100 percent American." Fundamentalist Protestant members of lodges such as the Odd Fellows and Knights of Pythias agitated for expulsion of "undesirables" with strong support from Scottish rite Masonic lodges. Anti-Catholic speakers found ready audiences in Oregon and Washington, both among the most unchurched section of the United States.[9] Within short order, Klan recruiting in Oregon resulted in 14,000 members.

Both in Oregon and other localities over the nation, school boards sometimes hired sisters to teach in public schools in heavily Catholic districts where all or most of the students were Catholic. These arrangements came under increasing pressure during the 1920's and 1930's although statutes and ordinances banning religious garb for teachers were not new. The Pennsylvania legislature passed such a law in 1895 and the New York State Superintendent of Education issued regulations to that effect in 1898. However, the Ku Klux Klan attack in Oregon was the most serious attempt in American history to outlaw Catholic parochial schools.

Because of Oregon's peculiar statute allowing a fractional percentage of the voters to initiate a law, the national Klan leadership chose this state as the best locale to launch an initiative requiring all children to attend public schools.[10] When submitted to the voters, it carried by 115,506 to 103,685 votes.[11] In January 1923, the legislature passed a "religious garb" bill prohibiting the wearing of any religious clothing (habits) by teachers in state supported schools.[12] This initiated a rough legal battle between the state of Oregon and the Roman Catholic Church. With funds supplied by the Knights of Columbus to cover legal expenses, the Church reacted, somewhat belatedly, and appealed the Oregon Compulsory School Bill in the federal courts. The Sisters of the Holy Names of Jesus and Mary, who had been in the state since 1864, joined the Episcopalians' Hill Military Academy in Portland as appellants. After hearing the legal arguments by both sides, that court declared the law unconstitutional in March 1924. Even so, a compulsory attendance law nearly passed in the state of Washington seven months later. The Klan and its Masonic supporters had done their work well and now proceeded to appeal the decision to the United States Supreme Court, confident of victory.

However, justice prevailed in *Pierce v. Society of Sisters.* On June 1, 1925, the United States Supreme Court handed down its historic decision.[13] The court was unanimous in declaring —

> *The fundamental theory of liberty upon which all governments in this Union repose excluded any general power of the state to standardize its children by forcing them to accept instruction from public teachers only. The child is not the mere creature of the state; those who nurture him and direct his destiny have the right, coupled with the high duty to recognize and prepare him for additional obligations. . . .*

Had the Supreme Court held that states' rights superseded those of parents and students, parochial schools would have been destroyed in short order in numerous states and American Catholicity would have been faced with a challenge of unprecedented proportions. Despite the travail that the case created, the precedent for private education was now established.

Although the victory resolved the legal status of parochial schools, anti-Catholicism did not end, reasserting itself vigorously in the 1928 presidential election. Republican Herbert Hoover defeated the Democratic candidate, Alfred E. Smith,[14] who was a Catholic. Numerous "safe" Democratic states voted Republican, especially in the "Solid South" and in the Southwest. Isolated instances of harassment of sisters during this era were not especially serious, but they demonstrated how slowly prejudice dies.[15] Anti-Catholicism dissipated perceptively during World War II when it was deemed unpatriotic to express prejudice against any American. The abatement of prejudice continued during the immediate postwar years. Only since John F. Kennedy's election in 1960 has overt anti-Catholicism faded and taken on more subtle forms. In retrospect, the Oregon School Case now appears to have been a critical turning point in the long history of American anti-Catholicism.

Growth of the Orders by 1945

Sister-population doubled during this era, reaching 174,000 in 1945. The vast Catholic educational complex with millions of students continued to generate vocations in large numbers. Also, the arrival of 52 immigrant communities and the domestic foundation of another 15 communities accounted for part of the overall increase. Seeking a safe haven from Nazi and Fascist persecution, 11 communities came from Germany and eight from Italy. Persecution in Mexico sent five communities fleeing across the border in 1926. Four new communities arrived from Canada and three each from Belgium, England, and Austria. France sent only two groups. Two each came from Poland and Hungary. One each came from eight other countries (see Appendix B). The larger orders, congregations, and groups are found in Table VI, p. 375.

As Table VI illustrates, Franciscans increased the most, growing from 6,461 sisters in 1900 to 30,241 in 1945 — fantastic growth of 470 percent in just 46 years. They added 13 new communities and fostered fresh offshoots to bring the total to 65 independent congregations. Factors that may explain Franciscan ascendancy are: concentration on teaching in parochial schools, the arrival of reinforcements from motherhouses in Europe and Canada, the relative ease of formation of new communities under the rule of St. Francis, and the tertiary, or third-order movement. While most tertiaries eventually married or had careers, many young women were attracted by the Franciscan spirit of love and poverty, joining communities and propelling increases in membership. Franciscans concentrated on teaching. In 1945 they were operating 1,470 grammar schools, 266 high schools, 32 academies, 11 industrial schools, two junior colleges, 12 colleges, and 62 nursing schools. Such broad exposure maximized the effects of the example of love that attracts vocations. The Polish-American Felician Sisters remained the largest of the Franciscan congregations with 3,318 members. Second were the German-American School Sisters of St. Francis with 2,222 members, third the Irish-American Sisters of St. Francis of Philadelphia with 1,713 members, and fourth the Polish-American Bernardine Sisters of the Third Order of St. Francis with 1,417 members.

Other orders with wide exposure to youths through education also enjoyed strong growth. In 1945 Mother McAuley's Sisters of Mercy of the Union in the United States and the 17 autonomous communities of the Sisters of Mercy were operating 608 grammar schools, 164 high schools, 17 academies, four industrial schools, one junior college, 10 colleges, and 66 nursing schools. Mother Caroline's School Sisters of Notre Dame were operating 418 grammar schools, 123 high schools, seven academies, one industrial school, and three colleges. Mother Seton's six daughters were

1945 Membership Totals for Larger Orders and Congregations

Order	Membership
65 Franciscan-based communities	30,241
Sisters of St. Joseph (3830)	11,876
Sisters of Mercy (2570)	10,911
Dominican Sisters (1070)	10,754
Benedictine Sisters of Pontifical Jurisdiction (0230)	7,141
Sisters of Mercy of the Union in the United States (2580)	5,990
School Sisters of Notre Dame (2970)	5,769
Sisters of St. Joseph of Carondelet (3840)	3,504
Ursuline Nuns (4110)	3,405
Congregation of the Sisters of the Holy Cross (1920)	3,698
Sisters of Notre Dame de Namur (3000)	2,339
Daughters of Charity (0760)	2,239
Sisters of Charity of Montreal (Grey Nuns)(0490)	2,126
Sisters of Charity of the Blessed Virgin Mary (0430)	2,075
Little Sisters of the Assumption (2310)	2,040
The Congregation of the Sisters of Charity of the Incarnate Word (0460)	1,699
Sisters of Charity of St. Elizabeth, Convent Station (0590)	1,641
Sisters of the Holy Family of Narareth (1970)	1,593
Sisters, Servants of the Immaculate Heart of Mary (Immaculata, PA) (2170)	1,586
Sisters of Providence of Saint Mary-of-the-Woods (3360)	1,384
Sisters of the Good Shepherd (1830)	1,382
Sisters of Charity of St. Vincent de Paul, Halifax (0640)	1,356
Sisters of Charity of Nazareth (0500)	1,351
Sisters of Charity of St. Vincent de Paul, New York (0650)	1,321
Sisters of the Presentation of the Blessed Virgin Mary (3320)	1,262
Sisters, Servants of the Immaculate Heart of Mary (Monroe, MI) (2150)	1,165
Sisters of Charity of Cincinnati (0440)	1,247

Table VI

operating 369 grammar schools, 114 high schools, 43 academies, 13 industrial schools, four colleges, and 61 nursing schools. The Benedictine Sisters of Pontifical Jurisdiction were operating 366 grammar schools, 60 high schools, 23 academies, two commercial schools, and eight nursing schools. The three branches of the Sisters, Servants of the Immaculate Heart of Mary were operating 233 grammar schools, 98 high schools, 11 academies, one industrial school, and three colleges. Numerous other congregations enjoyed a high rate of vocations because of their involvement in teaching and exposure to youths.

Growth also permitted orders to take on a wider range of ministries. For example, in 1938 the 13 communities of Dominican Sisters with a combined membership of 5,652 sisters were operating five general hospitals, two nursing schools, five orphanages, two day nurseries, one school for blind children and one for blind adults, seven retreat houses, five homes for working girls, one home for the aged poor, four social service centers, a ladies' home, a ladies' hospice, a vacation home for girls, a mission for blacks, and the orders had sister-missionaries in Cuba, Puerto Rico, and China.

Some communities of semi-cloistered women, such as the Society of the Sacred Heart and Visitation nuns, that had concentrated on operating academies and boarding schools experienced a slowdown in vocations. As the 20th century progressed, academies that had been the crown jewels of Catholic education for over 100 years began losing some of their appeal. The local high school, public and Catholic, exerted a strong attraction for teenage Catholic girls. These were the years when co-education, athletics, social activities, low cost, and basically sound academics made the neighborhood high school a favored American institution, enjoying strong popular support. By 1945, anti-Catholicism had moderated in public schools and nearly disappeared in areas with large concentrations of Catholics. Moreover, Catholic public school teachers were commonplace. Thus, teenage girls resisted parental pressure for an academy education and instead attended local high schools. Conversion of academies into small liberal arts colleges also reduced their number. The result was a slackening of vocations to communities heavily invested in academies.

Most orders required that postulants have at least a high school degree. Each passing year witnessed more postulants' arriving with some college credits, although less than five percent arrived with college degrees. The average age of postulants was higher, with more mature women joining communities in greater numbers. Very few communities would now accept a postulant below the age of 18. The struggle for advanced education and graduate degrees for sisters continued unabated, but progress on this front was painfully slow. Barriers imposed by constitutions and rules that impeded attendance at secular and even Catholic male colleges and universities gradually eroded as did the resistance of the hierarchy. However, significant improvements in sister-education remained for the post-1945 years.

The new Code of Canon Law went into effect throughout the Catholic world in 1918. It impacted women religious communities in the United States to varying degrees. For some communities the adjustment was traumatic in that considerable authority shifted from mothers-superior to local bishops. Canon 500 stated that sisters were subject to the local ordinary *in all things* unless they had an indult exempting them. Mothers-superior

Visitation Nuns, Washington, D.C. (c. 1942).
Courtesy Gonzaga University

suddenly discovered that they had to secure permission to act in matters in which they formerly felt free to do as they deemed best. The code overrode some longstanding internal procedures governing how the sisters functioned. Many women religious felt that communities were in danger of losing individual charisms and becoming homogenized. American women religious had always supported themselves financially and had never been a burden on the hierarchy, making this new legislation seem overly oppressive.[16] Recognition that the code was intended for worldwide application where conditions often differed from those in the United States did not lessen resentment. However, many communities, including monastic orders and the newer and smaller congregations, adapted easily and did not view the code as an imposition. The primary redeeming aspect of the code, universally applauded within the sisterhood, was the clear definition of their rights of appeal in disputes with Church authorities.

Dispersion of convents and monasteries over the nation prompted many communities to reorganize administrative structures by creating provinces. Some autonomous communities of the same rule began movements for formal affiliation. For example, 39 of the 60 autonomous communities of the Sisters of Mercy joined in 1929 to become the Sisters of Mercy of the Union in the United States; and in 1944 the 14 independent communities of the Sisters of Our Lady of Charity federated, becoming the North American Union of the Sisters of Our Lady of Charity. Numerous diocesan communities secured pontifical status, reducing somewhat their dependence on local bishops. Financial acumen and management ability became increasingly important, often influencing the elections of mothers-superior. In many ways, these were years of solid growth, consolidation, upgrading of institutions, expansion of ministries, and relative tranquility for American sisters and nuns — in contrast to the rivers of blood created by international violence.

Growth of Catholic Education

Nearly 2,000 new parochial schools appeared between 1918 and 1945, with the number of students doubling to almost three million. Some 63,000 sisters were teaching in this vast complex in 1945. Assured quality education by sister-teachers and the religious factor combined to keep parochial schools growing in number and size. More sisters enrolled in Catholic colleges to secure degrees and a limited few attended secular colleges. There was a consensus among all elements of the Church that the superiority of parochial schools would be maintained and the standards set by secular authorities would be met or exceeded. The laity were generous with financial support and sister-educators strained to continue upgrading the quality of Catholic education. Parochial schools continued drawing Protestant and Jewish students in surprising numbers. These statistics attest to the farsighted wisdom of the Church fathers in Baltimore in 1884 and to the marvelous dedication of women religious.

Teaching in foreign languages, even part time, had almost ceased by 1945, a reflection of the Americanization process. French was a notable exception, still spoken and taught in many of the French-Canadian communities in New England. Frequently, second- and third-generation descendants no longer had facility in their ancestral languages. Loss of bilingual ability, furthered by the abandonment of bilingual education, tended to erode ethnic pride and cultural traditions. Ethnic youths disliked seeming "different," easily succumbing to peer pressure and resisting learning their ancestral languages.

Parochial schools were where sisters had the most interaction with the laity. To this generation, a parish without sisters seemed to lack something since sisters constituted an integral and essential element of Catholic life in the eyes of the laity who held them in high esteem. Large parishes with a large school usually had a convent adjunct where all the sister-teachers lived. Another model was a central convent for sisters who issued forth daily to teach in two or more schools. Sisters of the same order always lived together, the only exception being the occasional guest from another order. Memoirs and biographies of Catholic writers repeatedly mention habited sisters as a common sight in and about parishes.

The presence of women religious had a way of increasing reverence in church and stimulating greater participation in church activities. Sisters lent an air of dignity and decorum that enhanced parish life. A knot of children usually followed a sister wherever she went about school and church grounds and neighborhood streets. The local convent was often the first place people in trouble or want visited for advice or help.

Support for High Schools

Although Catholic schools focused on primary education, in 1903 a committee of the National Catholic Educational Association (NCEA) recommended that Catholics give equal importance to secondary education. High schools, however, did not receive serious support until the 1920's. By 1945, 15,000 sister-teachers were involved in the education of more than 400,000 students in some 2,000 Catholic high schools. Bishops took the lead in establishing area high schools to serve multiple parishes and established diocesan boards and superintendents to oversee their operation.

Yet Catholic high schools were unable to educate all the youth graduating from parochial primary schools. Construction and operation of a high school was considered too burdensome to justify sufficient schools to accommodate all Catholic students. Competition from public high schools was strong and these institutions were generally academically excellent. Most Catholic parents believed that the religious grounding their children had already received in the parochial school met that need and did not hesitate to enroll them in the local public high school. Nor could many families afford the Catholic high school, if indeed there was one in the area. While parochial primary schools flourished during these years, the high school never became a strong facet of Catholic education. Girls' academies and boys' prep schools were generally outstanding institutions, but too limited in number and students to have a major impact.

Growth of Colleges

The growth of Catholic women's colleges founded by women religious orders was a response to several factors. Because only a small minority of postulants joining orders had college degrees, pressure for better education of sister-teachers was building inexorably all during this era. State and district school boards intensified requirements for degrees and certification became more difficult. Exhaustion, psychological as well as physical, became a common complaint of sister-teachers who were trying to study for certification and college degrees. Mothers-superior saw that having a community-owned college would be one answer to the ongoing problem and pursued founding a college where possible. For example, the Sisters of St. Benedict of Ferdinand, Indiana, opened St. Benedict's College as a normal school for sisters only. It became a four-year college in 1943 and admitted lay women in 1956. In some cases, the slackening demand for academy education by the laity indicated a dim future for those community-run institutions. Thus the transfer of academy facilities and personnel to collegiate usage seemed a natural procedure. Another factor was the need for collegiate access by young women in the emerging Catholic middle class. The net result of these factors was the opening of 74 sister-operated women's colleges between 1918 and 1945, bringing the total to 119 (see Appendix D). Only two colleges appeared during World War II: the Felician Sisters established Felician College in Lodi, New Jersey and the Dominican Sisters opened Tacoma Catholic College in Washington state, both in 1942.

Further stimulus for founding women's colleges came from the success of such institutions as Trinity College in Washington, the College of Notre Dame of Maryland in Baltimore, St. Mary's in Notre Dame, the College of St. Catherine in St. Paul, the College of New Rochelle in New York, and Manhattanville College in New York. These colleges achieved high degrees of academic distinction and accrued national reputations on a par with the renowned Seven Sisters.[17] Mother Pauline O'Neill, CSC, the president of St. Mary's from 1895 to 1931, demonstrated how separating the faculties of college and academy improved the quality of both. She hired lay teachers, including men, to ensure the best possible faculty for the college. Her successor as president, Sister Madeleva Wolff, a noted author, poet, and nationally recognized educator, brought St. Mary's College to its status as one of the nation's top women's colleges. In 1941, she established St. Mary's graduate school of sacred theology, the first such school for women in the United States. Sister Antonia McHugh was largely responsible for making the College of St. Catherine a leading institution and the first Catholic college to have a chapter of Phi Beta Kappa. These educators set the pace for higher education of future sister-teachers, examples not lost on other religious communities.

Manhattanville College admitted a black student in 1938 over the protests of the alumnae. Mother Grace Dammann spoke out forcefully on the evil of discrimination and put the matters to rest. Sister Madeleva admitted black students to St. Mary's in 1941 over the protests of Southern parents. However, most Catholic women's colleges conformed to the general practice of denying admittance to black youth, not so much as a belief in racial segregation but to avoid tension, loss of students and financial support, and faculty unrest.

The majority of the newly founded women's colleges were small, with student bodies generally in the 100 to 300 range. Some were academically superior. Examples include Albertus Magnus College in New Haven, Connecticut, and Ohio Dominican College in Columbus, Ohio. The Great Depression inhibited growth of colleges somewhat but in one instance triggered the foundation of a superior liberal arts college operated by the Sisters of Mercy in West Hartford, Connecticut. After several years of preparation, the sisters were ready to open a college in 1931, but Bishop John J. Nilan withheld approval of the opening because of the serious economic climate. Meanwhile, the sisters arranged for two college-level extension courses with Emerson College in Boston. These courses were so well attended that the bishop reassessed the situation. Many local women could not afford to leave home to attend college and earn the degrees needed for employment and better salaries. Even those who could afford it still could not attend local colleges because they did not admit women. Noting these facts, the bishop gave the green light in 1932 and the Sisters of Mercy inaugurated St. Joseph College with Sister Mary Rosa McDonough, Ph.D., as dean. Sister Rosa gathered an excellent faculty, lay men and women as well as religious, with credentials from such institutions as The Catholic University of America, Columbia, Radcliffe, Fordham, Yale, and noted European universities. Some 39 percent of the graduates of the first five classes enrolled in graduate programs at a wide spectrum of outstanding universities.

Conversely, some of the 72 institutions founded by women religious during these years were not strong academically and struggled financially. Some were even mediocre with weak faculties.[18] Reasons for the less than edifying results were grounded in the attitudes of the hierarchy, mothers-superior of the orders operating colleges, and a large segment of the laity. These were transition years for women in public arenas, including higher education. Many bishops still clung tenaciously to 19th-century views and only acquiesced in women's colleges in order to offset the perceived evils of Catholic girls' attending secular colleges.[19] In the bishops' eyes, coeducation, anti-Catholic professors, lack of supervision, and Protestant students all posed threats to Catholic morals. As a result, the hierarchy did not oppose women religious orders opening colleges to educate their own members, Catholic young women or a combination. The same bishops provided the colleges little financial support and reserved highly qualified priest-professors for seminaries and men's colleges. A number of sister-founded women's colleges foundered for lack of adequate funds. Leading Catholic educators such as Sister Madeleva Wolff and Mary Molloy of St. Teresa's College in

Missionary Catechists of Divine Providence, Shrine of Our Lady of San Juan, San Juan, Texas, 1980. Note earlier-worn habit near center.

Courtesy Missionary Catechists of Divine Providence

Winona, Minnesota, pleaded in vain for fewer but better colleges. Most mothers-superior wished to maintain their autonomy and were simply not attuned to the concept of coordinated joint operation of colleges.[20]

Attitudinal shifts on higher education for women were also slow to emerge among the laity. Catholics in the upper and upper-middle classes sent their daughters to college and gave strong support to the limited number of outstanding Catholic women's colleges. However, a large segment of lower-middle-class Catholics was not far removed from immigrant roots with no tradition for higher education, especially for women. Thus, the financially weaker colleges that catered to these classes of Catholics limped along with inadequate backing from both the hierarchy and laity. However, "weak" Catholic women's colleges were not failures. They filled the void for lower-middle-class Catholics that is now occupied by junior and community colleges. Sister-operated colleges provided Catholic young women an opportunity to enter the work force at a higher level than their grandmothers, aunts, and even mothers who had worked in mills and factories, sewn garments in sweatshops, or worked as domestics and retail clerks. Thousands of graduates became teachers in public schools and others went on to universities and entered the professions. As the era progressed, most of the weaker sister-operated women's colleges upgraded faculties and admission standards, becoming excellent institutions with good reputations and results.

Confraternity of Christian Doctrine

In his 1905 encyclical *Acerbo Nimis,* Pope Pius X directed catechetical instruction for Catholic youth in every parish, college, university, and secondary school in areas where religious teaching was banned in public schools. The 1917 Code of Canon Law (canon 711:2) mandated the formation of the Confraternity of Christian Doctrine (CCD) in every parish for this purpose, but the American hierarchy was slow in implementing this directive. Not until the 1930's did CCD programs become general over the United States, following this plea in 1929 from Pope Pius XI in his encyclical *Divini Illius Magistri*:

> *For the love of Jesus Christ, Our Savior, We implore pastors of souls, by every means in their power, by catechetical instructions, by word of mouth and written articles, widely distributed, to warn Christian parents of their grave obligations. . . .*[21]

Despite the increase in the number of sisters, there were simply not enough to assume this new ministry in significant numbers. Consequently, the laity undertook this responsibility, its first serious participation in Catholic religious education on a major scale. Priests and sisters trained and supervised lay instructors, forging closer bonds between sisters and lay people. The CCD program has been highly successful over the years at the primary and high school levels. However, at the collegiate level it has had mixed results. The Newman Club movement for Catholic students attending secular institutions, begun in 1893 at the University of Pennsylvania, has never enjoyed the full support of the hierarchy.

The CCD movement was indirectly responsible for the ultimate foundation of a new congregation of women religious, the **Missionary Catechists of Divine Providence, San Antonio, Texas (MCDP-2690).**[22] During the 1920's and 1930's, Mother St. Andrew's Sisters of Divine Providence provided teachers for the poor Mexican parishes in Houston. The revolution in 1910 and persecution of the Church beginning in 1926 sent thousands of Mexican Catholics fleeing across the border, many settling in Houston. Language difficulties and the need for instructors inspired Sister Benita Vermeersch, the principal of Our Lady of Guadalupe parish school, to conceive the idea of gathering some young Mexican women to handle CCD instructions. Out of this beginning, a group calling itself the Society of St. Teresa, generally referred to as the Catechists, grew and became progressively more active and closer to the Church. They took no vows, but starting in 1932 they made promises (chastity, obedience, and poverty) for a 6-month term. Like the disciples, they went out two by two to establish catechetical centers in the homes of Mexican families. Most Catechists lived together in community, others at home. They wore modified habits and with each passing year seemed more like vowed women religious. This initiative was so successful that in 1946 the Vatican approved the Society of the Missionary Catechists of Divine Providence as an adjunct to the Sisters of Divine Providence. In 1989, the society became an independent congregation — an unanticipated bonus of the CCD movement. Mother St. Andrew would surely be pleased that her order and her spiritual descendant, Sister Benitia, fostered the first Mexican-American congregation founded in the United States.

Health Care Growth

World War I's Base Hospital #102 in Vincenza, Italy, may be most famous for one of its patients — a wounded Red Cross worker named Ernest Hemingway who wrote of this wartime experience in *A Farewell to Arms*. It is also famous in sister-history as the last instance of official military nursing. This hospital was home to Sister Chrysostom Moynahan and 10 other Daughters of Charity, the only American sister-nurses overseas during the war. The hospital, in support of the 332nd Regiment from Ohio attached to the Italian Army, was the most forward military hospital serving on the front in 1918. While Mr. Hemingway lay on his cot below at night, the sister-nurses gathered on the roof to watch the flashes of shellfire from the raging Battle of Caporetto, only 15 miles away. After the war, they returned to the United States to resume their former ministries.

Recorded history's worst influenza epidemic erupted during the summer of 1918, eventually killing more than 20 million people, including 548,000 Americans. Death came quickly, usually within several days of the patient's incurring the virus. Recruits training for war service in crude encampments were especially vulnerable; 57,000 of them died — as compared to the 49,000 killed in combat in France. Hastily constructed field hospitals sprang up to house the stricken, and sisters from a long list of communities volunteered and nursed in these camp hospitals. For example, Camp Zachary Taylor near Louisville contained as many as 50,000 soldiers when the epidemic struck. In all, 14,000 men contracted influenza there. Three Catholic chaplains and 88 Catholic sisters from six different communities labored to the point of exhaustion in providing nursing care and spiritual support. Sister Jean Connor, only 28 years old, of the Sisters of Loretto contracted influenza nursing at Camp Zachary Taylor and died.[23]

Service in Italy and field hospitals in the United States marked the end of military nursing by Catholic sisters, a ministry that began at the Battle of

New Orleans in 1814. That service, continued during the Civil War and Spanish-American War, contributed enormously to improving the image and status of Catholics in the United States. Wartime sister-nurses hold a special place of honor in the American Catholic experience.

Opening 169 new hospitals during this era attests to their continued devotion to the health ministry (see Appendix C for the listings). Every section of the country benefitted from the expansion. Sisters streamlined health care, closing older hospitals that were unable to upgrade and meet modern medical standards, and consolidating smaller remote hospitals in urban centers. Sisters planning to establish hospitals entered the field prepared to meet current standards and costs. Both Catholic and Protestant philanthropists made generous grants. Cities and towns without hospitals made special provisions to enable sisters to found and operate them. Local governments normally provided the original facility and then operating income by paying a fixed daily amount for the care of indigent patients, a procedure that did not violate separation of church and state. Such towns and cities strongly supported these hospitals, and women religious experienced little anti-Catholic animosity even in heavily Protestant areas. Sisters serving in this ministry were highly respected in the medical profession and honored in the communities where they served. Many sister-operated hospitals became teaching institutions for interns. Nursing schools were a natural appendage. The highwater mark for Catholic nursing schools was in 1931 with 403 in operation. Most accepted laywomen as well as sisters. Catholic presence in health care was clearly visible throughout the nation.

A number of individual sisters achieved distinction in the fields of hospital administration, nursing, and nursing education. Sister Chrysostom Moynahan was the first registered nurse licensed by Alabama and established one of the first schools of nursing in the state in 1900. She was active in hospital and nursing education work until 1918, when she led the contingent of sister-nurses to Italy. After stints of hospital administrator in St. Louis and St. Joseph, Missouri, she returned to Alabama to assume the post of administrator of Providence Hospital in Mobile. She is remembered in Alabama's Women's Hall of Fame. In 1941, Sister Eugenia Marie Carpe of the Sisters of Charity of Cincinnati was the first Catholic sister to be elected President of the Ohio Hospital Association. Sister Mary Ignatia Gavin of the Sisters of Charity of St. Augustine was closely associated with the birth and early development of Alcoholics Anonymous. St. Thomas Hospital in Akron, Ohio, where she nursed was the first private hospital in the United States to treat alcoholism as a disease.

Of all the outstanding women religious in health care education during this era, Sister Mary Olivia Gowan, OSB, who established the School of

Nursing at The Catholic University of America, is perhaps the most famous. Since more and more lay nurses in the 1930's were obtaining graduate degrees, Sister Olivia felt that someone had to take the lead in establishing a Catholic graduate school for nurses. She accepted the challenge and, despite opposition from elements of the faculty and restricted facilities, she persevered and established a graduate school at Catholic University, which opened in 1933 and set an example for other Catholic universities. Sister Olivia, who died in 1977, received numerous awards, participated in many national organizations, and served as a consultant to the U.S. Navy, Veterans Administration, and many individual hospitals.

Sister Stanislaus, DC (Katie Malone, 1863-1949) at Charity Hospital in New Orleans for 63 years — from 1884 to 1947 — was identified in the public mind as the epitome of the caring and charitable sister-nurse.[24] During her 64-year stint at Charity Hospital she rose to superior and energized its expansion and modernization. President

Novice, Carmelite Sisters for the Aged and Infirm (c. 1942).
Courtesy Gonzaga University

Franklin D. Roosevelt made a point of meeting her when he visited New Orleans in 1934. She received an honorary Doctor of Science degree from Loyola University in 1936, was Louisiana's candidate for the prestigious Saunder's Award in 1937 and received the *Times-Picayune* Loving Cup in 1945. When she died in 1949, Postmaster-General James Farley was a pallbearer, joining archbishops, governors, congressmen, doctors, senators, and distinguished citizens of New Orleans at her funeral.

Most of the 33 orders and congregations operating hospitals in 1917 continued making foundations, having accrued decades of experience and a cadre of trained hospital administrators. Other communities entering the field during this era included the Daughters of St. Mary of Providence (0940), the Missionary Servants of the Most Blessed Trinity (2790), the Sisters of St. Casimir (3740), and the Sisters of the Little Company of Mary (2270). The numerous general hospitals, specialty institutions such as the homes for incurable cancer and (maternity) hospitals, the expansion of visitations to the sick poor in their homes, and the opening of nursing schools attest to how strongly the health care ministry attracted sisters seeking to serve God's people through this apostolate.

Service to the Aged Poor

Factors that generated orphans in such large numbers in the 19th century moderated as the 20th century progressed. Influenza in 1918 was the last large-scale epidemic that left so many orphans in its wake. Improvement in general health, better medical facilities, and economic betterment of the overall American population reduced premature adult deaths and the number of orphans.[25] Another critical ministry — care for the aged poor — assumed a higher priority.

Elderly destitute have always been part of the American scene, but their numbers mounted perceptibly with rapid urbanization and lessening family cohesion. Increased longevity contributed as did the scarcity of pension and retirement provisions by business and industry. Old age caught up with immigrants before they could accumulate adequate savings, often because of sending money to the homelands. The cold, impersonal nature of urban society generally resulted in the public ignoring the problem. The "county poor house" that many jurisdictions established and operated normally housed alcoholics, mentally retarded, poor old people. Paid staffs were not noted for kindness and loving care.

Professed, Carmelite Sisters for the Aged and Infirm (c. 1942).
Courtesy Gonzaga University

Numerous orders of Catholic women religious had been operating homes for the aged poor throughout American history and were keenly aware of this social problem. We saw how Mother Jeanne Jugan's Little Sisters of the Poor came from France in 1868 to provide this ministry and how they have grown. Another order, the **Carmelite Sisters for the Aged**

Postulants, Daughters of St. Paul.
Courtesy Daughters of St. Paul, Boston, Massachusetts

and Infirm (O.Carm-0330), was founded for this ministry in 1929 by Mother Angeline Teresa McCrory in New York City. As the problem intensified and became more visible, increasing numbers of religious communities decided that they should include this work of mercy among their apostolates. By 1945, more than 100 different communities were operating some 240 homes for the aged.

New Ministries

Among the new ministries that sisters undertook during these years were propagation of the faith through publications and home visitations. Catholic presses have poured forth books, tracts, magazines, weekly and monthly newspapers, diocesan and parish newsletters and pamphlets since the early 19th century, including foreign-language publications reflecting the immigration tides. German-Americans and Polish-Americans were especially active in publishing. In 1858 Isaac Thomas Hecker, a leading Catholic intellectual of the age, founded the Paulist Fathers (Society of the Missionary Priests of St. Paul the Apostle) with conversion of non-Catholics as its primary mission. In pursuit of this apostolate, Father Hecker started the monthly magazine *Catholic World* in 1866, ultimately resulting in a publish-

Daughters of St. Paul.

Courtesy Daughters of St. Paul, Boston, Massachusetts

ing organ known as the Paulist Press. He founded the Catholic Publishing Society as well. Jesuits, Franciscans, Benedictines, Dominicans, and other male orders have also been active in using the media for Catholic communications since the mid-19th century. Individual women religious have made notable contributions to Catholic literature and publications over the years. For example, Mother Angela Gillespie of the Congregation of the Holy Cross was co-founder and active contributor to *Ave Maria*. But no women religious order devoted exclusively to communications existed in the United States until the arrival of the **Pious Society Daughters of St. Paul (FPS-0950)** in 1932.

Father James Alberione and Mother Thecla (Teresa Merlo) founded the order in Italy in 1915. Popularly called the Daughters of St. Paul, these sisters promulgate the Catholic faith using all forms of the media. Under the leadership of Mother Paula Cordero, the sisters first settled in Staten Island, New York, but had a difficult beginning because their mission was misunderstood by the hierarchy. However, their persistence and the results of their efforts gradually won support. Today some 2,900 sisters operate in 38 countries with over 200 in the United States. They distribute their books, pamphlets, films, audiotapes, and videotapes through mail-order catalogs and from 22 media centers scattered over the country. While their ministry is extremely active, sisters live in community, wear a habit, and have a deeply Eucharistic prayer life including a daily hour of adoration. With each passing year, their apostolate becomes more important to the Catholic Church as a result of the increasing public reliance on the media for shaping religious attitudes and beliefs.

Most American active communities of women religious have performed home visitation at one time or another. Nursing orders such as the Bon Secours concentrated on this ministry. However, no community had a primary mission of evangelization by means of home visitation until 1920 when Julia Teresa Tallon (1867-1954), a former member of the Congregation of the Sisters of the Holy Cross, founded the **Parish Visitors of Mary Immaculate (PVMI-3160)** in New York City. Over the years, these devoted women have contacted many thousands of inactive Catholics and others in need of spiritual help by calling on homes and visiting with families. They often use a parish census as a means of making contact. Their evangelizing apostolate also includes catechesis for individuals, small groups, and public school children. They minister to human and social needs, giving advice and guidance and act in a liaison capacity with professionals and organized social service agencies. Mother Mary Teresa (Julia) died in 1954 after adding yet another ministry to the roster of good works of women religious.

Another example of how new communities arise to address pressing needs, in 1917 Father John Joseph Sigstein initiated the formation of a society of women to provide catechetical instruction to neglected Hispanics of the Southwest. From the start, their charism called for personal religious instruction outside any institutional setting. With strong support from Archbishop Albert T. Daeger of Santa Fe and Archbishop John F. Noll of Fort Wayne, Father Sigstein gathered volunteers, titled "Catechists." They were even addressed as "Catechist" instead of "Sister." The first two members, Julia Doyle and Marie Benes, arrived in New Mexico on August 5, 1922, their official founding date. Thereafter, the society grew rapidly, establishing a training center in Huntington, Indiana, named in part for their patron Archbishop Noll. In 1938 the Society of Missionary Helpers of Our Blessed Lady of Victory became a canonically established congregation, **Our Lady of Victory Missionary Sisters (OLVM-3130)**, and continued spreading their catechetical ministry to many parts of the United States and to Bolivia. Today, this remains a vibrant community still active in their chosen apostolate.

The Sisters of St. Joseph of Carondelet initiated ministry to the deaf in St. Louis in 1830, and since then individual sisters in numerous communities have learned sign language and taught the hearing impaired.[26] In 1915, the

Sisters of Charity of Cincinnati engaged in this ministry. There were not enough sisters available to assist at St. Rita School for the Deaf in Evandale, Ohio, so the director, Monsignor Henry J. Waldhaus, gathered a group of laywomen in 1924 to meet the need. They called themselves the Sisters of Pious Union of Our Lady of Good Counsel, although this group was not canonically recognized and was more of a confraternity. These pious women taught the deaf and went a step further, allowing the deaf and hearing impaired to become members of their group. Unable to secure canonical recognition, 20 members formally joined the Sisters of Charity of Cincinnati while continuing the ministry — another example of religious life drawing pious women engaged in works of mercy.

Feeding the hungry is one of the most fundamental of Christian charities. It is so basic that it has received little commentary in this history of American women religious. During the Great Depression that ministry assumed newer and greater proportions. Sisters operated soup kitchens, gave handouts to those calling at their doors, and expended scarce funds purchasing supplies to meet the needs. Many community chronicles speak of sisters going hungry in order to feed the less fortunate.

Growth of Contemplative Orders

Active apostolates were not the only ones flourishing during this era. Growing communities of contemplatives expanded the prayer ministry. A different branch of Poor Clares arrived in 1921 from Paris and established their first monastery in Cleveland. They were the **Poor Clares of Perpetual Adoration (PCPAS-3210)**. In 1854, while reading the Gospel account of the ten lepers ("Where are the other nine? Has none but this foreigner returned to give thanks to God?"),[27] Mother Marie Claire Bouillevaux was inspired to dedicate her order to thanksgiving for God's wondrous gift of the Eucharist. In each of their chapels, there are always two nuns at prayer before the Blessed Sacrament. They now have five monasteries in the United States. Later, we shall encounter the yet another Poor Clare community in Birmingham, Alabama, whose members practice a highly unusual ministry.

Contemplative life drew a steady stream of vocations, enabling growth and foundation of new monasteries. While it varies from order to order, the normal membership in a contemplative monastery is around 20. When it exceeds this number plans for a new foundation begin, explaining how so many new foundations can occur within a relatively short period. Financial support traditionally derives from dowries, donations by the families of nuns, and from the nuns' production of altar breads, candies, art works, candles, vestments, altar linens, and holy cards. Contemplative nuns enjoy the love and support of a strong element of the Catholic laity, who are also generous with alms and endowments. These nuns are constantly asked to pray for special causes. Many people with serious problems, including non-Catholics, often turn to them for prayer support. Near miraculous solutions are sometimes reported although nuns are extremely scrupulous in replying to questions about Divine favors being granted as a result of their prayers. They will admit to no miracles no matter how insistent the beneficiary may be about receiving one.

"Extern" and "portress" are terms describing contemplative sisters who perform duties outside the monastery, deal with workmen, escort nuns to the doctor or dentist and greet visitors. Duty may require a portress to answer the bell in the dead of the night and find a young woman who has decided to join the community standing at the door declaring, "I'm here!"[28] Since more and more contemplative communities are exposing their special charism to the laity with retreat houses, religious services, and chapels that are open to the public, live-in weeks for teenage girls and spiritual counseling to the troubled, all community members have to be involved. Nuns who have externs or have had them in the past relish stories about these sisters.

The tale is told of Sister Bernardine, an old near-deaf extern. The produce store that had donated two kegs of sauerkraut to the monastery sent a driver to pick up the empty kegs and he dealt with Sister Bernardine. At the same time, another extern was escorting two sick nuns to the hospital. Mother Abbess asked Sister Bernardine, "Did the gentleman come for the two sisters?"

"Oh, yes, Mother," replied Sister Bernardine, "and he felt so bad."

Mother Abbess was moved to think the chauffeur had such a kind heart. "What did he say?" she asked.

Sister Bernardine replied, "Well, he thought they looked terrible. And he said, next time to please fill them both up with water and stand them upside down overnight."

Mother Abbess went pale. Sister Bernardine continued, "That way, they won't shrink so much."

"Who won't shrink?" whispered Mother hoarsely. She had to shout a repeat.

Sister Bernardine responded somewhat indignantly, "Why, the sauerkraut barrels."[29]

Another supposedly true tale concerns the popular belief that Poor Clares will not ring their convent bell unless they are starving. A deaf couple lived next door to the Poor Clare convent in a Western city in the 1930's. One day their children failed to come home for supper and the worried parents rang a large bell frantically to summon them. Passing citizens mistook this for the convent bell and word spread over the city that "the nuns are starving." In the morning, automobiles and trucks appeared at the convent and kept coming all day bearing tons of groceries. The extern-sisters spent the day redirecting the gifts to hospitals, orphanages, and poor homes. They then persuaded the deaf couple to exchange their bell for a horn to call the children home.

Identical twin sisters, members of the Dominican Nuns in Farmington Hills, Michigan, took special delight in pranks. One day an electrical problem required the services of a repairman who followed one of the twins to the basement to inspect the panel. After working on it, he went upstairs to check the appliances. There he encountered the other twin, although he thought he had left her in the basement. On returning, he found her waiting for him, though he was positive that she was upstairs. After verifying that there was only one staircase, he ran upstairs leaving the sister behind. But there she was waiting for him again. The poor man was about to proclaim a miracle when the twin sister appeared. All three broke into gales of laughter and the workman left the monastery still chuckling.

Sisters in Foreign Missions

During the closing decades of the 19th and the opening decades of the 20th centuries American communities sent missionaries to Jamaica, Hawaii, Puerto Rico, British Honduras, Mexico, and the Bahamas. In 1919, Pope Benedict XV called for an overhaul and rejuvenation of missionary work in non-Christian lands in his apostolic epistle *Maximum Illiud*. He pointedly commended missionary sisters for their ongoing efforts. Thereafter, American communities expanded mission schools, medical clinics, and charitable apostolates in these mission territories.

In 1893, Sisters of Mercy from New Orleans made a foundation in Belize (British Honduras).[30] In role reversals, the Sisters of Mercy of the Union absorbed two non-American communities that were already in the missions. In 1894, Sisters of Mercy from England and Ireland established a mission in Charlestown, British Guiana. On hearing of the formation of the Sisters of Mercy of the Union, they applied for admittance and were accepted in 1934. The Union admitted a second Mercy group in British Guiana in 1939.

In 1874, the Dominican Sisters of Etrepagny, France, had arrived in Trinidad, British West Indies, to operate a leprosarium. Cut off from France during World War II, the Dominicans could no longer handle the workload because of depletion of their numbers. In 1944, the Sisters of Mercy of the Union responded to the plea of the Archbishop of Port-of-Spain to assist the Dominicans. Mother Mary Veronica Daily of the Baltimore Province sent sisters who labored there until 1955 when political upheavals forced their withdrawal. The plight of their abandoned lepers created great sadness among the sisters.

Although South America had tremendous needs, significant missionary

Foreign Mission Sisters of St. Dominic (Maryknoll).
Courtesy Gonzaga University

efforts there by women religious did not begin until after World War II. Yet they did go earlier. Sisters, Servants of the Immaculate Heart of Mary (2170) from the Philadelphia archdiocese went to Peru in 1922. The archbishop, Dennis Cardinal Dougherty, in response to a plea from the archbishop of Lima, pressured the sisters to send missionaries to open an academy to counter a prospering American supported Protestant academy. The sisters felt their call was to the poor but acquiesced, sending three foundresses. Broken promises, no convent, no school property awaited them. The Lima archdiocese was bankrupt. To their credit, the IHM's remained despite health problems, poverty, and lack of an English-speaking priest.[31] Ultimately spending over $400,000 of their community's funds they opened and operated two fine educational institutions. This community of IHM's continues its Peruvian apostolate today.[32] The other South American effort during these years was made by Bernardine sisters who went to Brazil in 1936 to assist Polish Bernardine sisters.

The Sisters of Charity of St. Elizabeth, Convent Station, had missionaries in Puerto Rico and the Virgin Islands from 1933 to 1948. While American missionary sisters increased their presence in the Caribbean and Central America during these years, in the early 1920's another region fraught with peril beckoned committed women religious — the Far East.

The Rise of Maryknoll

Maryknoll! For Catholics, this word conjures up visions of darkest Africa, steamy Latin America, the exotic Orient, and the lonely atolls of Oceania. Three generations of Catholics have been weaned on Sunday collections for the foreign missions and stories of loving charity, adventure, sacrifice, and conversions by the Catholic Foreign Mission Society of America, popularly called Maryknoll. School children saved their pennies, collected used clothing, tore used postage stamps off envelopes, and made spiritual bouquets for missionaries.

Fathers James A. Walsh (1867-1936) of Boston and Thomas F. Price (1860-1919) of Raleigh shared a dream of an American foreign missionary society that would transform the United States from a beneficiary mission land into a benefactor nation. In the spirit of *Maximum Illiud,* the American archbishops approved the concept as a result of strong support from Cardinal James Gibbons, Cardinal William O'Connell, and the apostolic delegate, Cardinal Diomede Falconio. With Pope Pius X's approval, the Catholic Foreign Mission Society formed and opened its seminary in 1911 in Maryknoll, near Ossining, New York. American Catholics reacted positively to the new society and provided strong, broad-based support.

A small group of women who had been working with Father Walsh in Boston moved to Maryknoll shortly after the society was founded to assist him in publishing the society's news magazine, *The Field Afar.* Prominent among them was Mary Josephine Rogers (1882-1955), a graduate of Smith College. These women soon realized that they wanted to be part of Maryknoll and began calling themselves Teresians in honor of the famous Carmelite saint. Sisters from the Scranton branch of the Sisters, Servants of the Immaculate Heart of Mary provided religious training from 1914 to 1916. Dominican Sisters of Sinsinawa came in 1917 to provide canonical novitiate training. In 1920, the group became the Foreign Mission Sisters of St. Dominic, which changed to **Maryknoll Sisters of St. Dominic (MM-2470)** in 1954 when they secured pontifical status. The obvious leader and first mother-superior was Mary Josephine Rogers, recognized as foundress. When word of this new society spread, aspirants appeared asking for admittance and by 1921 it had 115 members. That year, Maryknoll sisters were ready for their first foreign mission — China.

China Missions

China has been a magnet for missionaries for centuries. The potential for conversion of the teeming millions exerts an irresistible pull. Nestorians from Syria were the first Christians to penetrate the Middle Kingdom, arriving in the seventh century to introduce Christianity with limited success. From the Nestorians on, China has alternately tolerated and persecuted Christians within its borders. When Marco Polo arrived in China in 1275, he found a few Nestorians still active who had somehow survived persecutions. In 1307, Franciscan friars became the first Catholic missionaries to penetrate China, but their foothold was soon aborted by persecution. A Jesuit missionary, Matteo Ricci, secured approbation from the Ming emperor in 1552, and during his 18 years in China this intrepid Jesuit laid Christian foundations that would partially survive future persecutions.[33] St. Francis Xavier, the famous Jesuit missionary who converted thousands in India and gained entry into Japan, died on an offshore island never achieving his dream of entering China. Chinese leaders killed over a dozen European missionaries along with an unknown number of Chinese Catholics during the persecutions of 1648 and 1700. Ten French Daughters of Charity suffered martyrdom during the persecution of 1856. During the Boxer Rebellion of 1900, the revolutionaries summarily executed seven Irish sisters of the Franciscan Missionaries of Mary. One Chinese sister was spared, but the Boxers forced her to witness the executions. Pope Pius XII beatified the seven Irish sisters in 1946. Disruptions that the revolt generated throughout China resulted in the deaths of thousands of Chinese Christians, Catholic and Protestant.

In 1842, the great European powers imposed the first of a series of trade treaties on the weakened Manchu emperor that included clauses protecting missionaries. However, enforcement from Peking was not totally effective and missionaries, especially in the interior, were in constant danger from local officials, bandits, and warlords. China was not a very safe place for foreigners during most of the 19th century. Despite the perils, a long list of European religious orders sent sisters to found orphanages, hospitals, schools, and charitable houses. For example, French Daughters of Charity arrived in 1847, the Sisters of St. Paul of Chartres in 1848, the Helpers of the Holy Souls in 1867, the Franciscan Missionaries of Mary in 1886 and the Dominican Sisters in 1889. Italy sent Daughters of Charity of Canossa in 1860. By 1900 there were 10 orders of sisters in China. The two million Chinese Catholics of 1921 attest to the contributions of those early European missionaries. Protestant missionaries from England and the United States became active in the 19th century and performed many commendable charities over the years.[34]

Chinese history after the fall of the Manchu dynasty in 1911 is extremely complex. No central government ever had complete control over this huge country until the Communists finally gained the upper hand in 1947. Civil war characterized the country. Japan and Russia interfered in Chinese internal affairs as well. As a result of the Open Door Policy proclaimed by the United States in 1899 and faced with mounting anti-foreigner Chinese sentiments, the great European powers relinquished most of the extraterritorial concessions they had wrested from the weak Manchu government.

In seeking popular support, first one warring faction then another exploited resentment against foreigners, which translated into anti-missionary and anti-Christian feelings. American and European missionaries were usually poor by western standards, but seemed wealthy to the masses of impoverished Chinese. Communists were particularly adept at preying on the peasantry in this regard. Japan became increasingly aggressive, seizing Manchuria and forming a puppet country named Manchukuo. Full scale war broke out between China and Japan in 1937. So much turmoil intensified banditry, the plague of China for untold centuries. World War II only compounded the stresses and intensified the chaos.

For these reasons, the history of American women religious missionaries in China is equally complex.[35] In general terms, religious communities flourished in Peking and coastal cities such as Shanghai and Hong Kong, operating uninterruptedly until 1941. Experiences differed in the interior, where missionary groups found themselves constantly uprooted. They would make an establishment in one location, enjoy considerable success in providing medical services, opening orphanages, operating schools, converting natives to Catholicism, and training native catechists, only to find they had to flee on short notice.[36] Warring factions, bandits, hostile local officials, and interruptions in railroad and other transportation means contributed to the forced evacuations. Sisters sometimes moved to safer places in China, Manchuria, Korea, or the Philippines to minister until they could return to their original missions. Some even went home to the United States for a time and then back to China when they thought it safe.

The first Maryknoll overseas effort began in 1918, when Father Price and three Maryknoll priests went to South China. Father Price died within a year but other Maryknollers soon followed.[37] During the next 23 years, they established missions in China, Korea, Japan, and the Philippines. The outbreak of war in 1941 brought most of the American missionary endeavors in these countries to an abrupt halt and created untold hardships for the vineyard laborers.

Although Maryknoll fathers and brothers were the first American Catholic missionary group in China, Maryknoll sisters were not the first American women religious there. Sister Catherine Buschmann of the Daughters of Charity was first.[38] Arriving in 1896, she worked with French Daughters of Charity for the next 30 years, serving in Peking and Shanghai. When other American missionaries began arriving, she provided invaluable advice and orientation. The first group of American sister-missionaries to arrive in China came in 1920. They were Sisters of Providence of Saint Mary-of-the-Woods from Indiana.[39] By 1940, the number of American women religious orders with sisters in China had risen to 27 communities.[40]

The first Maryknoll sisters arrived in China on November 3, 1921, led by Sister Mary Paul McKenna. They split into two groups, one remaining in Hong Kong and the other going to Yeungkong in the interior to set up a refuge for abandoned babies.[41] Anti-Catholicism reared its ugly head in Hong Kong when the governor withdrew his offer for the management of a hospi-

Sister Eugena, Daughters of Charity, St. Joseph's Hospital, St. Joseph, Missouri (c. 1942).

Courtesy Gonzaga University

tal after local Anglicans objected. Even European Catholic sisters in Hong Kong were apprehensive about the arrival, fearing the Maryknollers would draw students from their schools. Although the Maryknoll sisters did begin their school, they also opened an embroidery room where poor women and girls produced church vestments for export to the United States, elevating the economic status of these exploited women. Additional groups of Maryknoll sisters arrived; by 1926 there were 26 Maryknoll sisters in China. Hong Kong became the headquarters for sisters serving in China, Korea, and Manchuria. Sister Gertrude Moore, a nurse in Yeungkong, became the first known American sister to die in China when she contracted typhoid in 1923.

From 1920 to 1941 communications with motherhouses in the United States were tenuous. Mail was sometimes lost or censored and often delayed for extensive periods. Mothers-superior in the United States had difficulty at times in appreciating the conditions under which their sisters labored. For example, it took 16 years for the Sisters of Charity of St. Elizabeth serving in Hunan Province to secure permission to modify their ponderous headdress.[42] In another instance, a photograph in an American newspaper in 1938 showed Sisters of Providence nursing wounded Chinese soldiers at the Chaffing railroad station where intermittent shelling threatened everyone, and hundreds of soldiers were suffering horribly from untreated wounds. The sisters were wearing white gowns with aprons that did not quite reach their ankles. Mother Mary Bernard at Saint Mary-of-the-Woods wrote asking why the sisters were out of prescribed habit. Her lack of understanding of the terrible conditions was a trial at times for sisters on mission.

Shortage of funds was also a constant problem requiring supplementary support from home, although the missionaries attempted to be self-supporting with tuition, private music lessons, gardens, medical fees, and English language lessons.[43] Near poverty caused sisters to cut and paste Christmas cards they had received the previous year to make new ones to send. Even so, American motherhouses provided as much financial support as they could and all the sisters took tremendous pride in the work their compatriots were doing under difficult and hazardous conditions.

Refugees were often a problem; their sheer numbers during famines and warfare exceeded the sisters' ability to shelter and feed them. In desperation, peasants abandoned babies and were prone to force daughters into prostitution. Sisters sought ways to salvage babies and protect the young women. For example, the Sisters of Charity of Saint Elizabeth in Yuanling opened a workshop during the 1925 famine that employed dozens of threatened women in making kimonos, fire screens, and vestments.[44]

Other problems compounding the challenges were the lack of adequate medical facilities, frequent shortages of supplies, intense heat and cold, lack of plumbing, exposure to diseases such as dysentery, and adjustment to Chinese food. Yet the only commonly heard complaint by the sisters was being denied Mass and ready access to the sacraments as so often happened when priests were unavailable for extended periods.

One advantage that American, English, and Irish missionaries possessed that other European missionaries sometimes envied was English, the language of international commerce and second language for educated Chinese — a highly desirable subject for students. Conversely, each new American missionary had to learn Chinese, normally requiring three or four years before becoming facile in this difficult language. Some sisters with many years in China never learned to speak it.

American sisters usually engaged in operating schools, orphanages, catechetical centers, and medical dispensaries, and a few groups operated hospitals. Sisters generally invested most of their resources in schools and orphanages for girls and in training catechists. Chinese women catechists who persevered proved to be exemplars of piety and fidelity, some of them joining American religious communities. Available trained personnel, facilities, equipment, and medical supplies determined the amount of health services the sisters could provide. For example, during one year Sister Finan Griffin of the Sisters of Charity of St. Elizabeth treated more than 25,000 patients in her dispensary and made 1,700 house calls — a prodigious effort. Embroidery shops were another arrangement providing employment for poor women who learned sewing and fancy needlework. They produced religious vestments and silken garments favored by well-off Chinese.

Training indigenous sisters was an important work pursued by most communities since building up the local church was vital. Another apostolate aggressively pursued by all Catholic missionaries, European and American, was the establishment and nourishment of the Legion of Mary for young Chinese. When the Communists later gained control of the government, the Legion of Mary became a primary target in efforts to eliminate Catholicity. This confraternity not only survived persecution but expanded and grew after the Church was outlawed. Some critics have maintained that missionary efforts were a failure because "rice Christians" quickly faded once free care and food disappeared. In view of the turmoil, displacements, chaos, and social disruptions created by wars and civil strife, it would seem that the opposite is true — that so many Chinese remained faithful to Christianity. The sisters were central to this phenomenon.

A frightening aspect of service in China, especially in the interior, was the murder of priests and the exposure of sisters to the same fate. In one instance in 1929, Reds brutally executed three American Passionist priests in Hunan Province. There were numerous instances of kidnapping for ransom; practically every mission group of sisters had this happen to one or more of their co-workers. A number of sisters were robbed at gunpoint and had their lives threatened by bandits. Bandits and Reds ransacked mission houses on numerous occasions and destroyed them with some frequency. Bishops and priests with oversight of sister-missionaries were usually quick to order them to move to safer locations when danger threatened although it was not always possible to evacuate them. Besides, the sisters would often argue for permission to remain at their stations.

When in 1937, with war declared between China and Japan, the Japanese began bombing cities and towns, more than one mission was hit. It is remarkable that so many sisters escaped violent death during these years and the courage they displayed was a credit to the American sisterhood. However, disease created serious illnesses and even claimed lives. A number of sisters died from cholera, typhoid, and weakened constitutions resulting from malaria and intestinal diseases.

Maryknoll sisters in China enjoyed several advantages that some other communities lacked. They served with Maryknoll priests, whereas many American sisters served under Italian, French, and German bishops with only an occasional visit from an American priest.[45] (The Sisters of Charity of St. Elizabeth were another exception as they worked closely with Passionist priests from Union City.) Mother Mary Joseph personally visited her Maryknoll sisters in China several times and sent an assistant when she was unable to go. She fully understood the conditions and appreciated the sisters' needs. The Maryknoll motherhouse maintained a training program for prospective missionaries that utilized both priests and sisters with mission experience as instructors. Maryknoll sisters working in the Mei Xian district went into the countryside in pairs to live with Chinese families seeking conversion, with good results. When sisters fled from violence, Maryknoll had other missions in China and Hong Kong where they could stay until they could return, an option not always available to other American sister-missionaries.

With war declared between China and Japan in 1937, many orders in the United States began withdrawing missionaries. Despite urging by the State Department for all Americans to leave China in 1941, there were still 160 sisters there on December 7 when the Japanese attacked Pearl Harbor. Sisters became instant enemy aliens to the Japanese, who interned American missionaries in areas under their control. Some sisters evaded capture and moved further inland along with millions of Chinese refugees, joining sisters already working deep in the interior or making their way to India and home. For example, Daughters of Charity fled their mission ahead of the advancing Japanese and traveled for six months by foot, sampan, bus, train, and airplane to India and then by ship to Ceylon, Australia, Panama, Miami, and finally to their St. Louis motherhouse. Sisters in areas under Nationalist control continued functioning. Those in internment camps either got repatriated on the exchange ship *Gripsholm* or spent the war in captivity. Sister-missionaries had always maintained amicable relations with Protestant missionaries, and the friendships between these two groups strengthened in the internment camps where they endured hardships together, sharing whatever they had.

Catholicism entered Korea from China in 1784, brought by Korean officials serving in Peking where they encountered Christianity for the first time. This new religion caught fire and spread rapidly. French and Chinese priests eventually arrived to convert and minister. Despite vicious persecutions beginning in 1801, missionaries and an underground church kept the faith vibrant. French Sisters of St. Paul from Chartres came in 1888 and Benedictine Sisters in 1909. After seizing control of Korea in 1910, Japanese officials tolerated Christian worship and allowed the Church to operate without governmental hinderance. Protestant mission societies in England and the United States targeted Korea for special efforts and enjoyed thousands of conversions, outpacing Catholic results despite the earlier beginning.[46] Maryknoll sent priests to Korea in 1923; the first group of sisters arrived in 1924. Maryknoll's first sister-doctor, Sister Mary Mercy, opened a clinic. When war broke out in 1941, the Japanese interned the sisters, who were later repatriated. Sister Mary Agneta Chang, a Korean, remained behind in Pyongyang with the fledgling community that Maryknoll sisters were training. They survived the war unharmed. However, in 1950 during the Korean War the Communists arrested and presumably executed Sister Agneta.

As in the rest of Asia, Christianity has had a turbulent history in Japan. For a time during the 16th century, the efforts of Jesuit and Franciscan missionaries bore fruit; and by 1623, just before persecution obliterated the Church, there were around 300,000 Catholics in Japan. Most lived on the island of Kyushu. Nagasaki and Hiroshima were Catholic centers (and the most Christian cities in Japan in 1945 when devastated by atomic bombs). Beginning with the final expulsion of missionaries in 1614, thousands of Japanese Catholics suffered martyrdom. The rulers were determined to seal off Japan from the outside world and to eliminate Christianity, which they did with unrelenting cruelty. In their efforts to unify Japan, the shoguns insisted on worship of the emperor, making Shintoism the state religion. Missionaries arriving in the mid-19th century were amazed to find a few Japanese who considered themselves Catholic. The survivors of persecution had passed the faith down generation to generation in secret, although it became distorted in all but the essentials. In the modern era, conversion to Christianity is difficult for Japanese because of hundreds of years of government-instilled anti-Christian prejudice. The austere nature of the Japanese people, centuries of paganism and their innate sense of superiority and racial cohesiveness hinder conversions.

Catholic and Protestant missionaries had one highly esteemed gift for Japan making their presence tolerable — education. The Japanese were hungry for knowledge that western institutions offered and the government gave financial support to colleges established by missionaries. Yet, Christianity made little progress among the people. For example, the Sisters of Notre Dame de Namur ran schools in Japan from 1924 to 1941 but realized few conversions. Other missionaries — male and female, European and American, Catholic and Protestant — all experienced the same results in varying degrees. Japan was not fertile ground for Christianity. The small victories of the 1920's and 1930's only broke the crust.

By contrast, the Philippines were Catholic in name — fertile ground for conversions — but desperately in need of missionaries. After the Spanish-American War most priests returned to Spain without leaving a strong native clergy behind. The populace was poorly instructed, prone to superstition, and gradually falling away from the Church. Following the war, aggressive American Protestant missionary efforts introduced anti-Catholic attitudes, while the new public school system installed by American authorities subtly introduced secularism. The Vatican appealed to Maryknoll to send priests and sisters to bolster the Catholic faith since the Philippines was now an American colony. Maryknoll responded.

Nine Maryknoll sisters went to the Philippines in 1926, and there were 53 sisters serving in the islands when the Japanese Army landed in 1941.[47] Most of them spent the war in house arrest or the prison camps, enduring privations along with other interned American civilians. Sister Trinita Logue of New York City spent nine months in the infamous Santiago Prison in Manila undergoing unspeakable tortures from Japanese interrogators demanding information she did not possess. Sister Mary Hyacinth Kunkel and two other sisters were living in house arrest in Baguio in the north of Luzon when the Japanese seized the house in 1944. The three sisters lived in caves in the mountains for the next four months. Hearing of the American landings, they joined a group of civilians moving south to cross American lines. Sister Hyacinth became separated from the column while trudging through the mountains, disappearing without a trace in the thick undergrowth. Searches failed to find her.

In a classic case of bad timing, six Holy Cross sisters sailed from San Francisco aboard the *President Grant* on November 9, 1941, bound for their mission in India.[48] While the ship was unloading supplies in Manila, the Japanese bombed Pearl Harbor. The sisters spent the next two and a half years in house arrest in convents in Manila. In July 1944, Japanese military authorities transferred two of them to the internment camp at Los Baños, 40 miles south of Manila. In this infamous camp, the sisters suffered great privation together with the other 2,000 internees, 150 of whom died of starvation. On February 23, 1945, paratroopers of the 11th Airborne Division landed, attacking the guards and freeing the prisoners (it was later learned that the Japanese intended to kill them all). The six sisters returned home in a troop ship.[49]

The several thousand American sisters who served so faithfully in the Orient over the course of these years planted seeds in hostile soil in hopes that some would survive and germinate. The evidence available today suggests that they were far more successful than they probably thought at the time. Christianity is vibrant in Korea and making slow progress in Japan. The Philippine people are staunchly Catholic, with vocations to the priesthood and sisterhood thriving. As we shall see, Catholicity in China has survived persecution and is expanding in the face of continued Communist opposition. It appears that the contributions of American missionary sisters in the Far East were far out of proportion to their numbers.

With the country at war and the Far East closed off, Maryknoll looked to Latin America for missionary efforts. Sisters opened missions in Bolivia, Panama, and Nicaragua in 1942, 1943, and 1944. These efforts initiated missionary efforts that would ultimately involve many hundred American sisters — and martyrdom.

World War II

The 44 months of American participation in World War II called over 10 million men to service in the armed forces, including 3,000 Catholic chaplains. One out of five American males between the ages of 18 and 45 joined the armed forces or was drafted. These men came from every section of the country, from rural and urban areas, from all races, from all social and economic classes, from all ethnic origins, from all religious denominations, and from all educational levels. The demographic melting pot boiled as never before or since. Living and fighting together instilled a degree of mutual understanding never before experienced by Americans. Old prejudices underwent reevaluation. Catholics lived with the unchurched and Protestants. Catholic servicemen mingled with the local populations near the many military training centers located in the South and interfaith marriages abounded. Thus the strangeness of Catholics in their midst faded and Catholicity in the South experienced vigorous growth that continues.

The war years accelerated social displacements already underway. Southern blacks migrated to industrial centers in the North and Midwest seeking decent wages. Women went to work in factories and shipyards performing manual labor normally reserved for men. "Rosie the Riveter" conveys the image of this new participation in industry. Colleges scrambled to fill empty classrooms with women, cementing once and for all the normalcy of women in higher education. Women assumed new responsibilities in family and financial management that thereafter would be considered routine. Since each armed service now had an official Nurse Corps, the only sister-nurses to participate in military hospitals were the refugees in the interior of China whom the Air Force employed briefly. Formation of the Women's Army Auxiliary Corps in 1942 formally incorporated non-nurse women in the armed forces for the first time.[50] Hired female pilots ferried airplanes across the Atlantic to England. World War II was as much a watershed in the emancipation of American women as the Nineteenth Amendment.

Religious fervor along with the patriotic fervor enveloped the nation. Practically all religious orders enjoyed increases in vocations. Cynics would point out the shortage of men of marriageable age but ignore historical precedents that demonstrate how people always turn to God in troubled times. Catholic chaplains did outstanding work and gained tremendous respect from non-Catholics for their ministrations to all servicemen regardless of religious affiliation. They lived with and died with the fighting men and a number became decorated heroes. Over and over chaplains reported non-Catholic servicemen lining up with Catholics for confession and attending Mass while in combat.[51]

Sisters and nuns continued quietly performing their numerous ministries throughout the war. They contended with ration coupons and various shortages along with everyone else. They guided the children in their schools in writing letters and becoming "pen pals" with servicemen overseas. While sisters only founded two new colleges during the war, they opened a total of 17 new hospitals — a reflection of wartime needs. The break in communications between American communities and their motherhouses in Europe was a special burden, and they prayed fervently for the safety of their sisters in Poland, France, Italy, Germany, Czechoslovakia, Hungary, and other locations embroiled in the war. Lack of information about their sisters in the Orient was another source of worry and stimulus of unceasing devotions. Like so many American families, sisters had relatives serving in the armed forces and their safety was another object of prayer.

War has a way of creating unusual friendships. During the fierce fighting for the island of Saipan in 1944, Father Arthur Tighe, an Air Force chaplain, stumbled across seven Spanish missionary sisters hiding in a cave with terrified civilians. He discovered that Sister Genevieve had already been killed by shellfire and another sister was wounded. He was able to secure medical help for the wounded sister, but Sister Genevieve was buried in a mass grave by a bulldozer. Father Tighe arranged for medical care, food, and fresh clothing and took a special interest in the remaining sisters. They became fast friends. These members of the **Mercedarian Missionaries of Berriz (MMB-2510)** had been ministering in Saipan since 1926. Their order has a fourth vow: "I will remain in the mission when there would be danger of losing my life if the good of my sisters and brothers so demands. . . ."[52] On Christmas Eve, Father Tighe and another priest celebrated Mass for 10,000 men on the beach, 4,000 of them non-Catholic. The priests ran short of hosts at communion time because of the large number of non-Catholics who came forward to receive. The priests said nothing and broke the hosts in ever smaller pieces to stretch the supply. Midway through Mass, a violent storm approached. As it neared, it suddenly parted into two separate storms passing on either side of the assembled group. The Spanish missionary sisters were present at this Mass. It seemed that God was acknowledging the cost of the fourth vow. As an outgrowth of this experience, the Spanish mother-superior dispatched a group of nuns to Kansas City in 1946 to make an American foundation.

In another unusual instance, the **Sisters of St. Rita (OSA-4010)** from Germany, were serving in Bolivia and cut off from home. They managed to get to the United States and the Augustinian fathers in New Hamburg, New York. In 1942, they moved to Racine, Wisconsin, where they continue to serve their primary apostolate of family visitation and care for the elderly in their St. Monica's Home.

Summary

Atom bombing of Hiroshima and Nagasaki punctuated the end of the Age of Violence, a 27-year span unmatched for unspeakable human slaughter. It is something of a paradox that these same years witnessed tranquility and orderly growth for most American women religious orders in the United States. The sisterhood survived the last serious assault on their teaching apostolate in the Oregon School Case and easily faced down the lingering vestiges of anti-Catholic prejudice directed against them. The 1918-1945 years were a time for bringing the construction of their magnificent edifice to near full growth.

That edifice took 218 years to build, order by order, congregation by congregation, ministry by ministry, institution by institution, and was substantially complete by 1945. All the ancient orders were established, most of the large international congregations had American components and the distinctly American-founded congregations were flourishing. Fleshing out the array, hundreds of small communities, immigrant and domestically founded, were performing a wide range of ministries. Parochial schools, high schools, and sister-operated colleges constituted the largest private educational complex in the world. No country could boast more sister-operated hospitals, more charitable houses, or more active apostolates. Italy was the only country in the world with more sisters and nuns than the 140,000 American women religious. Every section of the United States was conscious of the presence of Catholic women religious performing good works. Broadened entry into foreign missionary endeavors signaled their growing presence on the international stage.

In every sense of the word, American women religious had "matured" by 1945. Full blossoming lay just ahead.

Endnotes

1. See James Hennesey, SJ, *American Catholics: A History of the Roman Catholic Community in the United States* (New York, NY: Oxford University Press, 1981), p. 225.
2. Anarchists on the Republican side during the Spanish Civil War slaughtered thousands of priests and bishops and hundreds of sisters and nuns. They set convents on fire and then machine-gunned the fleeing nuns, while others they lined up against walls and shot mercilessly. Despite these atrocities, the American and English governments and presses supported the Republican side because of the help provided to the revolutionaries by Nazi Germany and Fascist Italy.

3. In 1945, a total of 148 American orders and congregations had motherhouses in Europe. Italy had the most with 75 because international orders have always favored Rome for the location of their primary motherhouse. France with 22 and Canada with 20 were next. Germany had 10 and the balance of the other 21 foreign motherhouses were in 10 different countries. The degree of control exercised by these motherhouses over their American communities varied considerably. Some exercised close supervision and detailed oversight while the affiliation between others was almost symbolic.

4. Amelia Earhart (1897-1937) was an editor, airline executive, pursuer of flying records, and an activist in feminist causes. She was immensely popular and the nation mourned when she disappeared over the Pacific Ocean in 1937.

5. An unlikely threesome introduced the concept of "relativism" into the American consciousness: Charles Darwin's "survival of the fittest," Albert Einstein's establishment of the "law of relativity" in physics, combined with Sigmund Freud's theory of "moral guiltlessness" to undermine acceptance of absolutes and verities accepted in the past. The inexorable rise of secularism, relativism, and situation ethics in the second half of the 20th century can be attributed in some measure to popular misunderstanding and intentional misconstruing of those theories.

6. Some of the more memorable Church leaders during these years included Archbishop Edward Mooney of Detroit, Archbishop George Mundelein of Chicago, Archbishop Samuel Stritch of Milwaukee, Archbishop Francis J. Spellman of New York, and Archbishop John T. McNicholas of Cincinnati.

7. Author's personal note: My grandfather, a cotton mill operator in Speigner, Alabama, in the 1920's refused to join the Klan and openly expressed his disdain. Rumors circulated that he would receive night visitors. Sure enough, one night a caravan of cars carrying hooded Klansmen came down the street where he lived. He got his shotgun, placed it across his lap, sat on the front porch steps and just looked at them. The cars halted but nobody got out. It was a staring contest to see if they believed that he would shoot anyone coming onto his yard to plant a burning cross. They believed he would and drove off. He was never troubled again.

8. A murder scandal and disclosures of bribery by state officers undercut the Klan's power in Indiana. In 1923, Oklahoma declared martial law to curb civil disturbances instigated by the Klan.

9. The reasons for the continuing low percentage of church affiliation in the Pacific Northwest have been examined over and over with no conclusive resolution. Theories include the fact that the original settlers were mostly unchurched, that something approaching nature-worship supplants religion, and the strong Masonic influence in the region.

10. An organization called the Public School Defense League managed to place an amendment on the ballot in Michigan outlawing parochial schools in 1920. The Ku Klux Klan was not involved. The voters of Michigan defeated the amendment overwhelmingly.

11. The Sisters of St. Mary of Oregon (Chapter 6) were duped into posing for a

photograph with their students outside a public school where the sisters taught Catholic children. To their embarrassment, this photo was used on derogatory leaflets that the Ku Klux Klan and it supporters distributed to sway voters.

12. The anti-religious garb law in Oregon, originally directed against Catholic sisters, was recently applied against a Sikh high school teacher who was fired.

13. An interesting aspect of the case concerns organizations not normally friendly to the Roman Catholic Church that filed *amicus curiae* briefs in support of the sisters. They were the Domestic and Foreign Missionary Society of the Protestant Episcopal Church, The North Pacific Conference of the Seven Day Adventists, and the American Jewish Committee.

14. Alfred E. Smith, the "happy warrior," was the first Catholic to run for president. However, an earlier warrior and Catholic, William S. Rosecrans, a Civil War Union general, almost became president. He was offered the vice-presidential slot on the Republican ticket by the convention in 1864. Secretary of War and party official Edwin M. Stanton intercepted General Rosecrans' telegram of acceptance and stuffed it in his pocket. He failed to deliver the message to the convention because of his intense dislike of the general, whose brother was incidentally a Catholic bishop. Andrew Johnson filled the ticket and became president upon the assassination of Abraham Lincoln. See Albert J. Nevins, MM, *Our American Catholic Heritage* (Huntington, IN: Our Sunday Visitor, Inc., 1972), pp. 179-180.

15. Minor harassments of sisters continued well into the 1930's. For example, when Dominican Sisters arrived in Lufkin, Texas in 1936 to open a parochial school, locals vacated the street whenever the sisters walked by. An airplane dropped flyers over the town declaring that Catholicity was a menace to Lufkin and the world. As in other non-Catholic areas beset with anti-Catholic prejudice, the examples of love and charity by the sisters soon dissipated the hostility. See Sr. Shelia Hackett, OP, *Dominican Women in Texas* (Houston, TX: D. Armstrong Company, Inc., Houston, TX, 1986), p. 356. Today, Lufkin is the home of the Monastery of the Infant Jesus, a thriving community of Contemplative Dominican Nuns (1060).

16. Women religious communities often provided financial assistance to bishops and pastors. Sisters' frugality was extreme and they managed to accrue savings to an amazing degree considering the meager wages paid. Recent studies into this phenomenon suggest that the first generation of around 25 years was the most difficult financial period for most communities, involving extreme poverty in many instances. Thereafter, many communities were able to accumulate savings, invest in real estate, and make loans. Hospitals and academies were generally profit centers.

17. The so-called Seven Sisters are Radcliffe, Bryn Mawr, Mount Holyoke, Smith, Vassar, Barnard, and Wellesley.

18. Sr. Mary J. Oates, CSJ, "The Development of Catholic Colleges for Women, 1895-1960," *Vol. 7, U.S Catholic Historian,* Fall 1988, Baltimore, MD, p. 420. She states that the American Association of University Women only recognized

one out of six Catholic women's colleges in 1930, and in 1938 only one in five was accredited by the Association of American Colleges.

19. The introduction in Congress in 1923 of the Equal Rights Amendment (ERA) by the National Woman's Party did not help soften the attitude of the bishops. Feminist activity stirred the hierarchy to form the National Council of Catholic Women (NCCW) under the supervision of the National Catholic Welfare Conference (NCWC).

20. Narrow vision concerning coordinated collegiate direction was not limited to mothers-superior. In 1933 a study recommended that each of the various Jesuit colleges select an area of excellence to emphasize so that each one could gain national prominence in the chosen discipline. Jesuit college presidents ignored the recommendation. Again, a suggested plan for a Great Lakes Jesuit University combining the resources of Marquette, Loyola, John Carroll, Canisius, University of Detroit, and the College of Buffalo got no response from the presidents. See Rev. William B. Faherty, SJ, *American Catholic Heritage: Stories of Growth* (Kansas City, MO: Sheed & Ward, 1989), p. 94.

21. *Manual of the Parish Confraternity of Christian Doctrine,* Paterson, NJ, 1961, p. 155.

22. Sr. Mary Paul Valdez, MCDP, *The History of the Missionary Catechists of Divine Providence (*San Antonio, TX: private printing, 1978).

23. Clyde F. Crews. *An American Holy Land: A History of the Archdiocese of Louisville* (Wilmington, DE: Michael Glazier, Inc. 1987), pp. 235-236.

24. Charity Hospital in New Orleans traces its lineage back to 1736, when a dying sailor left money to establish a hospital. When a hurricane destroyed it in 1779, Don Almonaster of Spain donated $114,000 to rebuild it. A fire destroyed this institution in 1806 and the state rebuilt the hospital on donated land. The legislature appropriated funds for a new hospital in 1832. The Board of Administrators invited the Daughters of Charity to assume management in 1834 and this congregation has been associated with the hospital ever since.

25. Although orphans and orphanages decreased rapidly beginning in the 1930's, the problem of children needing stable parental care increased. The numbers of divorces and separations began accelerating during the late 1930's and have continued to escalate to this day. The product is children in broken homes with one parent who is often unable to provide even minimal care because of poverty or the need to work and leave the children untended. Foster homes have replaced orphanages. A sad aspect is that millions of childless couples wanting to adopt babies are denied this opportunity because of the legal complications surrounding children of broken homes and their advanced age when parents separate. There are more children from one-parent families in school than from two-parent homes in numerous school districts.

26. In 1930, the National Association of the Deaf honored the Sisters of St. Joseph of Carondelet in Buffalo, New York, for their work with a life-sized statue of Abbé Charles M. de l'Epée. He was the originator of the "French method" of teaching the deaf. It utilizes a combination of finger spelling and signs.

27. *Luke* 17: 11-19, *The New American Bible With Revised New Testament* (Confraternity of Christian Doctrine, 1986).
28. Sister Mary of the Heart of Jesus, while a teenager from West Virginia, left her Baptist parents to join the Dominican Nuns in Detroit in the 1930's. Arriving in the dead of the night, she threw her suitcase over the wall, slipped through the grill, rang the bell and announced to the sleepy portress, "I'm here!" Her irate father tracked her down and took her back home as she was underage. But, at age 21 she returned and has remained a nun ever since (*Echoes*, June 1992, Dominican Nuns, Farmington Hills, MI).
29. Sr. Mary Francis, PCC, *A Right to be Merry* (Chicago, IL: Franciscan Herald Press, 1973), pp. 94-95.
30. Mother Austin Carroll (1835-1909) personally led her sisters to Belize and then supported them for many years from the motherhouse in New Orleans. She is famous for collecting and then editing the annals of the Sisters of Mercy. In addition to being a dynamic leader, she was a noted author. Her publications include *Life of Catherine McAuley: Foundress of the Institute of the Religious Sisters of Mercy, A Catholic History of Alabama and the Floridas, Annals* and 30 other books, plus numerous articles.
31. Hardships experienced by the IHM's in Peru over the years are a testimonial of their devotion to their apostolate. Physical stress, dietary deficiencies, and disease took their toll. Over 10 sisters returned home broken in health. In 1942, Sister Mary Flora was killed and three others suffered permanent damage when a drunken truck driver hit their bus. One problem that plagued the sisters was the long periods with no English-speaking priest to conduct a retreat or hear confessions. During the depression years the sisters were so strapped for funds that they sometimes had to walk the 14 miles between their two schools, Lima and Callao, both ways.
32. Margaret Mary Reher, "Get Thee to a (Peruvian) Nunnery: Cardinal Dougherty and the Philadelphia IHM's." Paper prepared for future presentation in the *Records of the American Catholic Historical Society of Philadelphia*. Also, "Toward Breaking the Cycle of Poverty: The IHM's in Peru." Unpublished paper, 1992.
33. Matteo Ricci adapted certain ingrained beliefs, including ancestor veneration, to Catholic liturgy, incurring Vatican disapproval. Adding cultural elements to Catholic belief is a controversial topic, as seen in Africa today.
34. Protestants formed the American Board of Commissioners for the Foreign Missions in 1810, long before the concept even occurred to American Catholics. American Protestant missionaries arrived in Hawaii in 1820 and in China in 1829. English Protestant missionaries first arrived in China in 1807. Robert Morrison translated the Bible into Chinese in 1819. See Kenneth Scott Latourette, *A History of Christian Missions in China* (New York, NY: Macmillan, 1929), pp. 211-212. A common belief among Chinese during most of the 19th century and early 20th century was that all Europeans were Catholic and all Americans were Protestant, reflecting missionary endeavors during those years.
35. Thomas A. Breslin, *China, American Catholicism, and the Missionary* (Univer-

sity Park, PA: The Pennsylvania University Press, 1980). This is an overall account of American Catholic missionary endeavors in China and served as a valuable resource in unravelling that complex story, despite its negative appraisals of missionary effectiveness.

36. The uprisings of 1925-27 so alarmed foreign powers that they recalled their nationals from the interior. Sisters of Charity left their mission in Yuanling on consular orders. When the Sisters of Loretto were slow in leaving their mission, the American consul threatened to send U.S. Marines to evacuate them. In 1930, a group of five Daughters of Charity ministering in a village near Kanchow had to flee in the middle of the night for fear of a bandit Army attacking the city. The sisters wore native dress and hid in three different Christian homes in the countryside, traveling at night seeking safer locations. These are just a few instances of the many flights.

37. Father Price had requested that his body be buried in Hong Kong and that his heart be removed and buried in France near Bernadette Soubrious of Lourdes fame. He had a deep devotion to her, praying to her constantly although she had not yet been canonized. His body was buried in Hong Kong but the transfer of his heart resulted in bureaucratic nightmares with customs officials in both China and France. His heart now resides in a small reliquary near St. Bernadette's incorrupt body and his body has been removed to Maryknoll, where it is buried beside Father Walsh.

38. In 1890, Dora Thumel married Charles Buschmann who died a year later. She joined the Daughters of Charity in Emmitsburg and took the religious name of Sister Blanche. Later, she volunteered for service with the French sisters in China. Soon after arriving in Shanghai, the French sisters asked her to change her name because they already had two Sister Blanches. She took the name of Sister Catherine in honor of St. Catherine Labouré, whose nephew was their chaplain. She died in Shanghai in 1926 after 30 years service in China. See Sr. Clara Groell, DC, *White Wings in Bamboo Land*, (Emmitsburg, MD: St. Joseph's Provincial House Press, 1973).

39. Sr. Anne Collette Wolf, SP, *Against All Odds: Sisters of Providence Mission to the Chinese, 1920-1990* (Saint Mary-of-the-Woods, IN: 1990). Entries about the Sisters of Providence in China are based on this book.

40. Sisters in China in 1937 represented the following orders: Benedictine Sisters of Pontifical Jurisdiction, Dominican Sisters, Sisters of Notre Dame de Namur, Sisters of Charity of St. Elizabeth, Sisters of Charity of Cincinnati, Daughters of Charity, Sisters of Loretto at the Foot of the Cross, Adorers of the Blood of Christ, Sisters of St. Joseph, the Society of the Sacred Heart, Missionary Sister Servants of the Holy Spirit, Sisters of Providence of Saint Mary-of-the-Woods, Ursuline Nuns of the Congregation of Paris, the Society of Helpers, and several Franciscan congregations.

41. The practice of drowning or abandoning babies by poor Chinese has always horrified Christian missionaries. During famines, parents were known to feed infants to the hogs. Unwanted infants, mostly girls, could be purchased for as little

as 30 cents and practically all missionaries operated orphanages for these unwanted children.

42. Sr. Mary Carita Pendergast, SC, *Havoc in Hunan: The Sisters of Charity in
Western Hunan, 1924-1951* (Morristown, NJ: College of St. Elizabeth Press,
1991), p. 25.

43. There was considerable competition for donations among the Society for the
Propagation of the Faith and the many religious communities with missionary
priests and sisters (Maryknollers, Passionists, Vincentians, Benedictines, Franciscans, etc.). The Great Depression of 1930-1941 compounded the financial
stresses.

44. Casper Caulfield, CP, *Only the Beginning: The Passionists in China, 1921-1931*
(Union City, NJ: Passionist Press, 1990), p. 125.

45. The presence of German and Italian bishops, priests, and sisters in China during
World War II was a blessing for many American missionaries. Since Germany
and Italy were allies of Japan, their nationals continued operating freely in areas
of China under Japanese control. They did everything possible under the circumstances to assist American missionaries. American Air Force personnel in
the interior arranged for the release of German Lutheran deaconesses from
prison, assuring Chinese Nationalist authorities that they would be responsible
for the deaconesses, who then acted as nurses and cooks for the Americans
(Pendergast, p. 132). Since Ireland was neutral, Irish sisters and priests avoided
imprisonment, but were severely restricted by the Japanese.

46. Protestants (mainly Presbyterians) claimed 19 percent of the South Korean
population in 1990 while Catholics claimed 6.4 percent. The balance were Con-
fucians, Taoists, Shamanists, uncommitted, or indifferent. No figures are available for North Korea.

47. Father William T. Cummings, a Maryknoll priest serving as an Army chaplain
during the fighting on Bataan coined the phrase "There are no atheists in fox-
holes." He endured the infamous Death March only to die aboard a Japanese
transport ship taking the prisoners to Japan.

48. Holy Cross sisters from the Notre Dame convent served briefly in Dacca from
1889 to 1896. They resumed the mission in 1927, sending seven well-trained
missionaries. Over the years they supported the mission with replacements.

49. Rev. Robert McKee, CSC, "Holy Cross P.O.W.s in the Philippines: 1941-1945"
(Wilkes Barre, PA: Paper delivered at the 1983 Conference on the History of the
Congregation of the Holy Cross, May 25-26, 1985).

50. The Women's Army Auxiliary Corps (WAAC), founded in 1942, was made an
integral branch of the Army by Congress in 1943, becoming the Women's Army
Corps (WAC). Some 140,000 women served as WAC's during the war. In 1970,
Elizabeth P. Hoisington became the first female general. In 1972 women were
admitted to the Reserve Officers Training Corps (ROTC) and in 1976 women
were admitted to West Point. The WAC was disestablished in 1978 and the
members were absorbed into the regular armed forces. The Navy and Air Force
paralleled the Army experience.

51. Author's personal note: While a paratroop company commander in Korea in

1950-51, I witnessed non-Catholic soldiers lining up with us for confession before we made a combat jump. Our chaplain had a pat formula for this situation. He imparted spiritual counseling, gave a blessing, and sent the penitent off just as relieved as we Catholics.

52. Sr. Patricia Cody, MMB, *The Major and the Miracle* (Kansas City, MO: privately printed, 1982).

CHAPTER 10

Full Bloom
(1946-1965)

‡ — ‡

BY OBJECTIVE MEASURABLE standards, women religious organizations reached their zenith during the 1946-1965 years, experiencing a great burst into full bloom. As we shall see, sister-population, parochial schools, colleges, hospitals, monasteries, foreign missions, and charitable institutions increased to historic levels. Hardly a city or town was without a convent, even in the South, and only the rare American was unfamiliar with the sight of sisters in habits. New orders, immigrant and domestically-founded, continued appearing. Sisters fought a tough battle for improved formation and education for future sister-teachers and community leaders met to form a national association for the first time in history. Sister-missionaries ventured into South America and Africa in response to calls from the pope. From a historical perspective, it appears that these were the "glory years" for American sisters and nuns.

As the era opened, Germany, Japan, and Italy lay in ruins, their leaders dead or awaiting trial for war crimes. Good had conquered evil. *Pax Americana* and the newly formed United Nations promised world peace. Never before had such feelings of power, righteousness, and optimism pervaded American society. Unhappily, the euphoria was short lived when it soon became clear that the United States had helped rid the world of one set of evil political forces only to be confronted with a more virulent one — Communism. The Cold War, the hot war in Korea, the threat of nuclear war, and Communist-inspired international terrorism preoccupied American political leadership, governing national foreign and military policy throughout the era.

On June 22, 1944 President Franklin Roosevelt signed the Servicemen's Readjustment Act, commonly called the "GI Bill of Rights." This statute provided for free tuition, basic sustenance, and book allowances for veterans seeking higher education. Over the years, some 7.6 million veterans have taken advantage of this opportunity to attend college. Such an unprecedented educational experience vaulted millions of Catholic men from working-class families into the professional and managerial ranks. Veterans Administration (VA) and Federal Housing Authority (FHA) loan guarantees for low down-payment mortgages propelled millions of Catholic families into the mush-rooming suburbs leaving the inner city neighborhoods of their parents and grandparents. Blacks from the South and Hispanics, mainly from Puerto Rico, moved into the old neighborhoods transforming them racially and eth-nically. The speed of the demographic shift was unparalleled, especially so among urban Catholics.

The end of the era was punctuated by the final session of Vatican II on December 8, 1965, when Pope Paul VI officially closed the 21st ecumenical council of the universal Catholic Church. Vatican II was a renewal council that announced the dawning of a new day for the Church. American sisters and nuns stood in the threshold in 1965 ready to participate in renewal — popularly termed *aggiornamento.*

The American Catholic Scene

During and immediately after the trauma of World War II, a religious revival swept the United States. Church attendance soared as public and private religious fervor reached fever pitch. While religious intensity tapered off with peace and return to normalcy, the revival was so strong that its ef-fects persisted throughout the 1950's and into the early 1960's. Mainline Protestant churches realized increased membership and wealth, while fun-damentalist sects gathered growing support. For a brief moment, it seemed that the Third Great Awakening of American Protestantism was at hand. However, mainline Protestant accommodation to secular values and dilution of dogmas gradually undermined their revival. Evangelical fundamentalist sects with their rigid disciplines continued to grow and prosper.

The Catholic experience was more profound and solidly based. Millions of servicemen returned from overseas with a heightened appreciation of their religion gained in the maelstrom of war. The Church reached new heights of membership, institutional strength, and active participation in its devotional life. Around 70 percent of all Catholics attended Mass on Sundays and holy days. Millions attended Mass on weekdays, especially on the first Friday of each month, a day devoted to the Sacred Heart of Jesus. On Saturday after-noons, lines formed outside confessional booths as both sinners and the devout awaited their turns to receive forgiveness of sins and the special graces of this sacrament. Catholics were noted for large families although ar-tificial birth control was increasingly used, though condemned by the

Church. The most common devotion was recitation of the prayers of the rosary. Devout Catholics prayed novenas to the Sacred Heart of Jesus, the Blessed Virgin Mary, St. Joseph, the Little Flower, St. Anthony, St. Jude, and other saints.[1] Petitioners for divine favors lighted candles before statues of Jesus, Mary, and saints to signify a desire for continual prayer to them. Millions wore scapulars[2] and holy medals, mounted small statues of St. Christopher in their automobiles, blessed themselves in public before meals, fasted before receiving Holy Communion, proudly displayed ashes on their foreheads on Ash Wednesday, and attended parish missions, religious seminars, devotions, and retreats. Women wore hats or veils in church and everyone observed silence as a mark of reverence for the Blessed Sacrament in the tabernacle. Catholics gloried in the papal declaration of the ancient belief in the Assumption of Mary as an infallible dogma of the Church during the Holy Year of 1950.[3]

Although the parish priest was no longer necessarily better educated than any member of his parish and no longer filled the role of arbitrator in secular matters, as was customary during much of the 19th century, the laity still accorded him great respect — poor preaching or lack of administrative ability notwithstanding. The laity supported parishes and contributed in second collections for foreign missions, Indians and Negroes, Peter's Pence, and special causes.[4] Catholics normally sent their children to parochial schools, and if not, to CCD classes for religious instruction. A child's First Communion was a particularly happy moment in Catholic families and a vocation to religious life by a member was cause for special joy.

Catholic lay organizations attracted hundreds of thousands of members who belonged to a wide spectrum of youth, professional, business, worker, academic, arts, and other Catholic lay organizations. Catholic Action in its many guises was vigorous. The 1960 edition of the *Catholic Almanac* listed 223 different groups, including such organizations as the Catholic Youth Organization (CYO), Legion of Mary, Grail, Serra Club, and Holy Name and St. Vincent de Paul Societies. Prayer breakfasts and scripture study clubs proliferated. The Knights of Columbus advertised in secular magazines for inquiries about Catholic beliefs and practices, sending information in plain envelopes to those who responded. Conversions to Catholicism ran in the tens of thousands annually — 126,209 recorded in 1965 — who came from a variety of sources, especially the non-Catholic partners in mixed marriages. Men were as devout as women, something of an anomaly since in most Catholic countries women outnumbered men at religious services.

Such manifestations of faith resulted from a variety of factors, including the molding of the child during the formative years and family religious practices. The parish church reinforced family teaching by the example and instruction of priests and a sacramental system that provided for the critical moments of life. Emotion also played a part in religious fervor: ethnic cultural loyalties, fear of hell, and a special love for the Blessed Virgin Mary with whom Catholics could identify and to whom it was natural to turn in time of personal trouble. But it was sisters who were central in the development of the spiritual life of the millions of Catholics who constituted the devotional Church. Reinforcing other influences, sister-teachers drilled students in the catechism, prepared them for reception of the sacraments, shepherded them to Mass each school morning, trained altar boys, encouraged vocations, provided living role models of a life dedicated to God, and molded the religious attitudes of Catholic youth. The only negative aspect was that too many parents tended to rely on sisters to perform their duties in religious formation.

Anti-Catholic prejudice in commercial and public life was subtle but generally insignificant compared to the past. Greater numbers of Catholic men found acceptance on previously restricted bank boards, in brokerage houses and law firms, in medical practices, in private clubs, and as top corporate executives. Even so, anti-Catholic prejudice persisted among a hard core of mainline Protestants and continued as a central tenant among members of fundamentalist sects. In 1947, Methodist Bishop G. Bromley Oxnam organized the Protestants and Other Americans United for the Separation of Church and State (POAU) with Paul Blanchard as principal spokesman. For a short time it seemed that this organization would become powerful, but its blatant anti-Catholicism soon rendered it impotent and its influence faded. On May 18, 1951, the 20 nurses at St. Francis Hospital in Charleston, West Virginia, walked off the job to protest the hiring of three black nurses, leaving 140 patients without care. Sister Helen Clare of the Sisters of St. Joseph of Wheeling refused to discharge the black nurses, citing Christian principles and the constitution. Sister-nurses from the order's other hospitals flew to Charleston; while some local nurses and others from out-of-town volunteered, relieving the pressure. This precedent set the pattern for Catholic hospitals over the nation. Archbishop (later Cardinal) Joseph E. Ritter of St. Louis mandated the desegregation of Catholic schools in his archdiocese in 1947. Archbishop Patrick A. O'Boyle desegregated churches and schools in the Washington archdiocese between 1948 and 1952. Bishop Vincent Waters decreed church and school integration in the Raleigh diocese in 1953. Archbishop Joseph Francis Rummel of New Orleans did so in 1962. Other bishops gradually emulated their examples. Although civil rights received support from the hierarchy, clergy, women religious, and many Catholic intellectuals, a large portion of the laity tended to be ambivalent, indifferent, or even opposed to desegregation. For example, busing of school children to achieve racial balance generally infuriated the middle class, including Catholic parents. The reappraisal and reformation of long held racial attitudes was a slow process.

Although these were "glory years" for the American Catholic Church and women religious, the triumphant mood of the Church and the full blossoming of the orders and congregations obscured certain unhealthy forces at work that would ultimately have an adverse impact on Catholicism. Family breakdown accelerated, facilitated by personal mobility and the ongoing migration from rural to urban settings. Drugs entered the scene as youth experimented with marijuana and LSD, entry drugs leading to heroin and cocaine use. Crime increased at both ends of the spectrum — street violence and the Mafia at one end and corruption in labor unions and board rooms at the other. Divorce assumed increasing magnitude each passing year. Historically, families had considered divorce as something shameful and an embarrassment but by the mid-1960's it had become socially acceptable. Protestant denominations were permissive concerning divorce and diluted their tenets to accommodate their members. Secular humanism consolidated old gains and secured new adherents in higher education settings. Trustees of the great Protestant-founded universities lost control of tenured faculties who, under the flag of academic freedom, aggressively pursued a secularist agenda, aping their peers in state-supported institutions. Accreditation agencies tended to intimidate those who might desire to retard the secularist trends. Although the Protestant establishment, popularly called WASPs (white, Anglo-Saxon, Protestant), was fast losing its traditional moral authority and accustomed control of American mores, the general public was not receptive to its replacement by the Catholic establishment.

Women Religious

By 1946, most women religious communities were financially secure, even wealthy when real estate is considered. Solid buildings with central heat, modern plumbing, and attractive furnishings typified convents over the nation. Many of the motherhouses were large imposing structures with spacious grounds and magnificent chapels. A total valuation of real estate owned by the communities would mount into the hundreds of millions of dollars when colleges, hospitals, academies, and other properties are considered. The early poverty years had instilled a deep regard for wise money management and mothers-superior were often elected for their financial acumen as well as spiritual and leadership qualities.[5] It was a cumulative process, each generation adding properties and investments. Conversely, many small communities remained basically poor, living on current income derived from teaching and other ministries. The Great Depression of the

1930's had also impoverished some orders that were heavily in debt. In short, the 1950's and 1960's found a mixture of financial conditions and their impacts on members.

Despite negative developments in American society, the institution of women religious continued to grow. Sister-population increased by 35,000 members, from 174,000 to 209,000. The tremendous growth rate of vocations started decreasing in the early 1960's, but this was considered a temporary aberration. A total of 104 new orders and congregations joined the roster over the 25-year span (see Appendix B). A brief review of the larger communities is helpful in visualizing the growth.

Franciscans

The spiritual followers of St. Francis of Assisi were the largest group of one rule in the country, with 35,699 sisters in 63 different congregations. The Polish-founded Felician Sisters (1170) with 4,155 sisters continued as the largest single Franciscan community. The School Sisters of St. Francis (1680), founded by German immigrant Mothers Alfons and Alexia, had 3,163 sisters. The Polish-derived Bernardine Sisters of the Third Order of St. Francis (1810) had 2,210 members. Founded by the sainted American bishop, John Neumann, the Sisters of St. Francis of Philadelphia (1650) was the next largest with 1,851 sisters. Five other Franciscan congregations had over 1,000 members: the Sisters of St. Joseph of the Third Order of St. Francis (3930) with 1,449 sisters; the Congregation of the Sisters of the Third Order of St. Francis of Perpetual Adoration (1780) with 1,257 sisters; the Franciscan Sisters of Christian Charity (1230) with 1,157 sisters; the Sisters of St. Francis of the Holy Family (1570) with 1,081 sisters; and Mother Moes' Sisters of the Third Order Regular of St. Francis of the Congregation of Our Lady of Lourdes (1720) with 1,034 sisters. The other 54 communities ranged in size from just under 1,000 members to less than 100. Between 1946 and 1965, Franciscans gained 5,268 new members, bolstered by 2 new domestic foundations and 9 immigrant communities (see Appendix B). In 1965 the various Franciscan congregations were operating 40 kindergartens, 2,077 parochial grammar schools, 317 high schools, 25 academies, 35 colleges, 248 hospitals, 74 nursing schools, 51 orphanages, 88 homes for the aged, 26 day nurseries, 5 sanatoria, 1 Indian school, 2 mission schools, and 33 mission houses in 15 different foreign countries.

Sisters of St. Joseph

The Sisters of St. Joseph of Carondelet (3840), originally founded in Missouri in 1836 by French sisters had 5,148 members in 1965; they were

Dominican Motherhouse, Adrian, Michigan. Novices and Postulants at prayer.
Courtesy Gonzaga University

divided into four provinces with its generalate in St. Louis, a vice-province in Hawaii, and branch communities in Savannah, Georgia, and Lewiston, Idaho. The 19 autonomous congregations of the Sisters of St. Joseph (3830) had 11,928 members. There were four other groups of St. Joseph sisters that traced their roots back to Father John Peter Médaille in Le Puy, France, the newest being the Sisters of St. Joseph of Lyons (3870) who came to Jackman, Maine, in 1906. These St. Joseph communities increased by 3,044 members, making them the second largest group of congregations in the United States. In 1965 they were operating 1,089 parochial grammar schools, 195 high schools, 56 academies, 19 colleges, 70 hospitals, 22 nursing schools, 1 sanitarium, 2 infant homes, 14 orphanages, 10 homes for the aged, 1 Indian mission, and 108 mission houses.

Dominicans

The 17,199 Dominican Sisters (1070) were organized in 30 autonomous congregations. The Congregation of St. Catherine of Siena (1070-01), founded at St. Catherine, Kentucky, in 1822, had 856 sisters. The Sinsinawa Dominican Congregation of the Most Holy Rosary (1070-03), founded by Father Samuel Mazzuchelli in 1847 in Sinsinawa, Wisconsin, had 2,097 members. Largest of the communities, the Congregation of the Most Holy Rosary (1070-13), established at Adrian, Michigan, in 1892, had 2,666 members. The Congregation of the Holy Cross (1070-05) in Amityville, New York had 1,717 members.[6] During these 20 years, the Dominican Sisters experienced a fantastic growth of 6,445 members. In 1965 the various Dominican congregations had sisters in 5 foreign missions and were operating 1,043 parochial grammar schools, six junior high schools, 227 high schools, 37 academies, two junior colleges, 22 colleges, 38 hospitals, three nursing schools, 5 convalescent homes, 3 orphanages, 7 homes for the aged, and 67 rural missions.

Sisters of Mercy

The Sisters of Mercy constituted one of the largest groups in the country with 14,537 members. One group bound together by a structure known as the Sisters of Mercy of the Union in the United States of America (2580) had 7,374 members. An association of 17 autonomous congregations, the Sisters of Mercy (2570), had 7,263 sisters. All followed the rule confirmed by Pope Gregory XVI in 1841 as amended in 1926. Founded in the United States by Irish immigrant sisters first under the leadership of Mother Francis Xavier Warde and then under several Irish sisters including Mother Baptist Russell, and fed by the vocations of Irish-American women, these communities gained 4,048 new members during this era. In 1965 Sisters of Mercy of both groups had sisters in 14 foreign missions and were operating 817 parochial grammar schools, five junior high schools, 187 high schools, 18 academies, five junior colleges, 22 colleges, 115 hospitals, 64 nursing schools, 4 convalescent homes, 18 orphanages, and 19 homes for the aged.

Mother Seton's Daughters

The six congregations comprising Mother Seton's spiritual descendants were: the Daughters of Charity of St. Vincent de Paul (0760), the Sisters of Charity of St. Vincent de Paul of New York (0650), the Sisters of Charity of Cincinnati, Ohio (0440), the Sisters of Charity of St. Vincent de Paul, Halifax (0640), the Sisters of Charity of St. Elizabeth, Convent Station (0590) and the Sisters of Charity of Seton Hill, Greensburg, (0570). The Daughters of Charity were the largest group with 2,768 members while the Sisters of Charity of Seton Hill were the smallest with 881 members. Altogether the six congregations counted 10,413 members. Education, that began with Mother Seton's parochial school in Emmitsburg, continued to be a prime apostolate. In 1965, the 6 communities were operating and staffing eight colleges, 129 high schools, 12 academies, and 474 parochial grade schools. In addition they operated an Indian School (Halifax), and 2 schools for the deaf (Cincinnati and Seton Hill). Additionally, the New York group were operating five kindergartens, a secretarial school and a home economics school while the St. Elizabeth group ran a commercial high school. Health care, begun in St. Louis in 1829 with opening of the first permanent Catholic hospital in the United States, likewise continued as a primary apostolate. In 1965, the six communities were operating 66 general hospitals, 3 mental hospitals, 2 foundling hospitals, a leprosarium (Daughters of Charity), seven infant asylums, an infirmary, a clinic, a cancer research clinic (Cincinnati), and 57 nursing schools. These sisters also operated 12 orphanages plus one in Rome, Italy (Cincinnati), various child-care homes and day-care centers, as well as 8 homes for the aged, retreat houses, catechetical centers, and social service centers.

Benedictines

Benedictine Sisters of Pontifical Jurisdiction (0230), spiritual descendants of Mother Benedicta Riepp and Abbot Boniface Wimmer, numbered 7,141 sisters. Their confederation, the Congregation of St. Scholastica, consisted of 16 motherhouses in the United States and one in Mexico, each one an autonomous community. St. Benedict's Convent in St. Joseph, Minnesota, was the largest group with 1,026 members. The Congregation of St. Scholastica gained 1,179 new members during the era. In addition, there were several unaffiliated Benedictine groups, such as the Benedictine Sisters of Perpetual Adoration of Pontifical Jurisdiction (0220), with total memberships of 984. Various Benedictine communities had sisters in 16 foreign missions and were operating 569 parochial grammar schools, 83 high schools, 20 academies, 13 colleges, 38 hospitals, 4 nursing schools, 2 orphanages, 3 Indian missions, and 21 homes for the aged.

School Sisters of Notre Dame

The School Sisters of Notre Dame (2970) was founded by Mother Teresa Gerhardinger in Bavaria in 1833. An American motherhouse was established in Milwaukee in 1850 by Mother Caroline Friess. In 1957, this international congregation's motherhouse was moved from Munich to Rome. The American branch was organized into 6 provinces, with motherhouses in Wisconsin, Maryland, Missouri, Minnesota, Connecticut, and Texas. The 1,380 member increase brought their total to 7,057 members. In 1965 these sisters were operating 23 kindergartens, 8 catechetical schools, 4 reading clinics, 539 grammar schools, 92 high and junior high schools, 1 Indian school, 12 business schools, 4 colleges, a deaf school, a home for children, and 3 orphanages.

Ursulines

Ursulines, America's oldest resident order, numbered 4,189 members. The largest group, the Congregation of Paris, had 2,463 members while the smaller Roman Union had 1,433 members.[7] The several unaffiliated communities had 293 members. In 1965 the various Ursuline communities were operating 21 kindergartens, 280 parochial grammar schools, 2 junior high schools, 41 high schools, 30 academies, 6 colleges, and 1 orphanage.

The balance of the vast array of apostolates were performed by sisters in hundreds of smaller communities. Other orders and congregations with more than 1,000 members in 1965 were —

Membership Statistics — 1965

Order	Membership	Increase (1946-1965)
Sisters of Notre Dame de Namur (3000)	3,429	1,200
Sisters of Charity of the Blessed Virgin Mary (0430)	2,576	657
Sisters, Servants of the Immaculate Heart of Mary Immaculata, Pennsylvania (2170)	2,393	859
Sisters of Charity of Montreal (0490)	1,974	344
Sisters of the Presentation of the Blessed Virgin Mary (3320)	1,910	822
Sisters of the Congregation of the Holy Cross (1920)	1,717	383
Maryknoll Sisters of St. Dominic (2470)	1,707	662
Sisters of the Holy Family of Nazareth (1970)	1,680	642
Sisters, Servants of the Immaculate Heart of Mary, Monroe, Michigan (2150)	1,647	604
Sisters of Providence of Saint Mary-of-the-Woods (3360)	1,637	286
Sisters of Charity of Narareth (0500)	1,594	312
Sisters, Servants of the Immaculate Heart of Mary, Scranton, Pennsylvania (2160)	1,303	390
Sisters of the Good Shepherd (1830)	1,244	-182
Sisters of Loretto at the Foot of the Cross (2360)	1,210	166
Sisters of the Holy Names of Jesus and Mary (1990)	1,205	24
Sisters of Christian Charity (0660)	1,177	83
Society of the Sacred Heart (4070)	1,111	112
Adorers of the Blood of Christ (0100)	1,075	162
Carmelite Nuns (0420)	1,023	566

Table VII

The vigor demonstrated by the foregoing statistics illustrates the underlying strength that motivations for religious life continued to exert on young women and the more mature in their late 20's and early 30's. This increase might seem surprising since the Catholic population was now mostly middle-class and women religious were no longer faced with the dire poverty of ethnic brethren, virulent anti-Catholicism, or numerous orphans needing housing and care. The desperate need for Catholic schools to educate children that had driven earlier vocations no longer seemed to be a such critical factor. Nonetheless the vocational momentum continued. The many Catholic families with some member already in religious life prompted consideration of a vocation.

America lost its innocence in World War II and at Hiroshima and Nagasaki. As never before, the seriousness of life was impressed on American youth with every report of national and international events. The Cold War, opposition to Communism, persecution behind the Iron Curtain, the Korean War, Chinese persecution of Christians, the civil rights movement and the Peace Corps — reinforced by the national religious revival — combined to turn idealistic young minds to God and His admonitions for charity and love. The combination of traditional-old and the horrible-new fostered vocations.

Contemplatives

The 4,037 cloistered nuns of 1965 lived in 167 monasteries scattered over the country. The contemplative life, dating back to the earliest days of Christianity, continued to exert its irresistible attraction for deeply devout women.[8] During the final decades of the 19th century and throughout the 20th century, this form of religious life expanded quietly. Although these nuns constituted a tiny fraction — 1.8 percent — of women religious in 1965, their impact far outranged their numbers. Numerous bishops petitioned orders for monasteries for their dioceses, accounting for much of the dispersion over the country. There were only 11 states without a monastery of nuns in 1965: Alaska, Arizona, Delaware, Florida, Hawaii, Idaho, Maine, Montana, South Carolina, Tennessee, and Wyoming.

Catholic parents whose daughters elected to join contemplative orders fell into two categories: (1) those who adamantly opposed this withdrawal from family contacts and secular life, and (2) those who felt privileged and happy with their daughter's vocation. Most Catholics viewed the contemplative life as the highest possible religious calling and considered nuns to be spiritual aristocrats. Lay people did not hesitate to seek prayer support from them in times of personal trouble. Cloistered nuns held a certain fascination for non-Catholics who often assumed the nuns led morose lives, were not allowed to talk, and were subject to stern mothers-superior. Even some Catholics were unaware of the joyous life inside the cloister. Monasteries acted as magnets for local Catholics who attended Mass and prayed in their chapels. Some monasteries featured retreat centers where Catholics could spend a few days in quiet prayer and spiritual reflection. If asked, many Catholics during these years would have guessed that cloistered nuns constituted a fourth or more of all women religious.[9] Such was their influence on Catholic life.

Carmelites, first nuns in the original United States, were the largest contemplative group. During these years, they gloried in yet another heroine named Teresa, slated for future canonization (beatified in 1987): Edith Stein, the daughter of devout German-Jewish parents, converted to Catholicism in 1922. She later helped convert her sister Rosa. Her study of philosophy at Göttingen University and inspiration from reading the autobiography of St. Teresa of Ávila led to her conversion. A noted intellectual, she taught and lectured at the Educational Institute in Munster. Nazi anti-Semitic laws forced her from the post in 1931 and she carried out a long-cherished wish and became a Carmelite nun in Cologne, taking the religious name of St. Teresa Benedicta of the Cross. In 1938, she moved to a Carmelite monastery in Echt, Holland, because her Jewish blood put her in peril in Germany. Rosa joined her and became a Third Order Carmelite. After the German Army overran Holland the Nazis arrested them. In August 1942 Sister Teresa (prisoner #44074) and Sister Rosa died in the gas chamber at Auschwitz. Important literary works testify to Edith Stein's intellectual capacity and spirituality: *Ways of Knowing God, Finite and Eternal Bridge, The Science of the Cross, Essays on Women,* and translations of Cardinal Newman's letters and St. Thomas Aquinas' *On Truth.* The hatred that Carmelites attract like lightning rods from enemies of Jesus Christ claimed one more saintly martyr.

American Carmelites, primarily descendants from Port Tobacco and the Baltimore monastery, plus the nuns fleeing Mexico during the persecutions of the early 20th century, numbered 1,071 members. They had 65 monasteries scattered over 35 states.[10] Visitation Nuns, the second oldest American order of cloistered nuns dating from 1799, continued operating academies even as they began to diminish in number. In 1965, the 694 Visitation Nuns were in 21 monasteries located in nine states and the District of Columbia. Poor Clares, who experienced high adventure and failures in the early years of the Republic, were permanently established by Mothers Maddalena Bentivoglio and Veronika von Elmendorff in the 1870's. Despite the history of short-term foundations, this order began its solid expansion and in 1965 numbered 658 nuns in 23 monasteries, located in 16 different states. John Creighton of Omaha, the great benefactor of the Poor Clares, could take pride in his support of their early beginnings.

Other orders had increased in like proportions. The Dominican Second Order, established in 1880, had 655 members in 21 monasteries located in 11 different states. The desire of the original Kentucky Dominican sisters to be Second Order was fulfilled — 58 years later. The Congregation of the Benedictine Sisters of Perpetual Adoration, whose foundress Mother Benedicta Riepp expected to establish such communities when she came from Bavaria in 1852, numbered 323 in 17 monasteries. The 165 Sister Adorers of Precious Blood lived in seven monasteries and the 109 Religious of the Passion of Jesus Christ lived in five monasteries. Five other small orders lived in seven monasteries.[11]

New Orders

An indication of international ferment and turmoil can be gleaned from non-traditional sources of some of the 93 immigrant groups of women religious that arrived after 1946: 14 from Spain, five from England, four from Mexico, two from Holland, and one each from Argentina, Brazil, El Salvador, Colombia, Cuba, Malta, Portugal, South Africa, Sweden, Uganda, and Yugoslavia (see Appendix B for the listings). Each new foundation was a different story — flight from Communist persecution or poverty, desire by large international orders for an American foundation, response to appeals by American priests and bishops, response to appeals by ethnic groups for sisters of their culture, and the desire for a safe haven in the United States in times of peril. However, the impact of immigrant orders was insignificant in the overall increase of 55,495 sisters and nuns. Even reinforcements from traditional European motherhouses, a factor in the past, no longer added to the total in a meaningful way. The ravages of World War II and Communist suppression of Eastern Europe cut off this source almost completely. There were also 12 new domestic foundations. Among the newcomers, the first order from Sweden arrived, the **Brigittine Sisters (OSSS-0280)**. Founded in the 14th century by St. Bridget (1303-1373), the order was suppressed in Sweden during the Reformation, but survived in Rome and a few other places in Europe. In 1911, Elizabeth Hesselblad, a Swedish convert, founded a new branch of the old order. She led the Brigettines back to Sweden in 1923 and established convents in Italy, Switzerland, India, and England. In 1957, foundresses established the order in Darien, Connecticut. Non-cloistered contemplatives, the nuns lead a prayer life and are open to those seeking spiritual renewal.

Throughout this history, the term "offshoot" has been used to designate autonomous communities of the same charism emanating from original foundations. In 1965, there were 222 offshoot communities, bringing the number of autonomous communities to a grand total of 627. Dominican Sisters are one example with their 30 autonomous communitics, as are the Sisters of St. Joseph with their 19 congregations. Each Carmelite and Poor Clare community was autonomous. Some founding groups came to the United States years after the first foundation by members of their order but did not amalgamate, remaining independent. There are numerous examples of this during the 19th century. As the 20th century progressed, the trend reversed and closer association, confederation, and outright amalgamation became more common. Examples of this are the Sisters of Mercy of the Union and the Roman Union of the Ursulines.

Growth of Apostolates

During these years of full bloom sisters and nuns were spending their lives in a multitude of activities. Around 24,000 were postulants and novices undergoing formation. Over 30,000 were in full or scmi-retirement. The 1965 *Official Catholic Directory* lists 104,314 sisters engaged in education, well over half of active professed women religious. A total of 3,700 were serving in the foreign missions. The balance were in a wide variety of activities including studying at colleges and universities, nursing, operating hospitals and nursing schools, operating orphanages, leading contemplative lives in monasteries, operating homes for the poor and aged and other charitable institutions, performing domestic and administrative duties in their communities, caring for their aged and sick members, and a host of miscellaneous apostolates.

Simultaneously with the growth of the sisterhood, there was an increase in priest-population — from 38,451 to 58,632 — mirroring the vocational experience of women religious who also had a role in stimulating priestly vocations. With few exceptions, the 58,632 Catholic priests and 48,992 seminarians studying for ordination in 596 seminaries had attended parochial schools and received religious instructions from sister-teachers. A common practice of seminarians was to secure a nun as "prayer partner" for spiritual support. Another practice in parochial schools was for sisters to poll the students to see if any had thoughts of a vocation. Those expressing such an inclination received special attention from the sisters, although most of those vocational impulses were temporary, emotional or feigned. Sisters trained altar boys; most priests in 1965 could give some credit for their vocations to those early days before the altar. It was routine, almost expected, that a new priest who owed his vocations to sisters and nuns would invite them to attend his ordination. There were thousands such sisters — a subtlc but powerful apostolate.

Immaculate Conception School, Clarksdale, Mississippi.

Courtesy Sisters of Charity, BVM

Sister-Educators

The great edifice of the parochial school complex was at its zenith. There was hardly a town of more than 30,000 inhabitants in the United States lacking a parochial school. The 10,503 schools with 4.56 million students represented an increase of 2,483 schools and 2.5 million students during the 1946-1965 years. Despite the general problem of sister education, numbers of sisters secured masters degrees and doctorates in a wide range of disciplines. Sisters held prestigious positions on faculties, as college presidents, hospital administrators, and leaders of national and international associations, agencies and organizations. Women religious counted noted poets, historians, writers, editors, artists, and even scientists in their ranks.

Rapid expansion of parochial schools required more lay teachers; by 1965 there were 73,314 in classrooms. Tensions arose between religious and lay teachers, for the latter were paid better, though their salaries remained 60-70 percent that of their public school counterparts. The necessity of increasing tuition also created tension among Catholic parents who now were faced with increased costs to send their children to school.

Public schools in most parts of the country had been undergoing a process of religious neutralization for decades along with a general upgrading of scholastic standards. To a certain extent, anti-Catholicism had diminished. Lay Catholic teachers taught in public schools almost in proportion to Protestant teachers. There were however scattered schools that still denigrated Catholicism, especially in the South and in heavily Protestant rural school districts. Even so, the preservationist motive against support of parochial school weakened. While attendance at Catholic schools reached historic levels, Catholic youth attending public schools increased as the school-age population burgeoned.

Opening 41 women's colleges (see Appendix D) attested to aspirations of sister-educators who continued to focus on small liberal arts colleges. Reflecting the drive for sister education, 39 different communities opened colleges to serve their members and to educate Catholic laywomen. The Sisters of Mercy opened four, the Felician sisters two, the Society of the Sacred Heart two, and the Benedictine Sisters of Pontifical Jurisdiction two. Seven different communities of the Dominican Sisters founded colleges as did three separate communities of the Sisters of St. Joseph. Over half (29) of the new colleges were situated in the Northeast. New York State led the parade with 13 new women's colleges; the next largest number, seven, were founded in Pennsylvania. The Midwest added six while five were begun in the South. The West added three and the Far West two. Reasons for the concentration in the Northeast are unclear, but this section has always led the nation in educational foundations and outstanding institutions. Titles of new colleges often reflected the name of heroines such as Cabrini, Seton, and Hilbert.

An unusual change-of-campus concerned Fort Wright College of the Holy Names in Spokane, Washington. When the U.S. Army announced the closing of Fort George Wright in 1960, Mother Marian Raphael Carlson purchased it. The agreement called for occupancy within 18 months; the sisters moved into the old officers' quarters and began adapting the 55 buildings on the 85-acre post to collegiate use. The original Holy Names Normal School had opened in 1907 and as certification standards increased the school upgraded, issuing its first baccalaureate degree in 1939. The new campus allowed for further upgrading and expanded curriculum.

During these years, women's colleges upgraded faculties, curricula, and admission standards. Many more joined the ranks of highly respected colleges for women. Meanwhile, the movement for state-supported junior and community colleges was growing stronger and would ultimately force the closure of numerous private small liberal arts colleges all over the country, including a number of Catholic women's colleges.

The Catholic educational establishment operated by women religious — parochial primary schools, high schools, academies, and women's colleges — constituted a magnificent structure. The flaws and occasional lack of excellence could not obscure a ministry that was a primary factor in bringing the American institutional Church to its 1965 status.

Health Ministry

The Hospital Survey and Construction Act of August 13, 1946 (Hill-Burton Act) provided federal financing for construction and upgrading of hospitals. Sisters took full advantage of this statute. No other 25-year period could equal these years for the founding of hospitals by women religious — 123 new ones opened by 53 different communities already experienced in hospital operations led the way, among them the Benedictine Sisters of Pontifical Jurisdiction with 13 new hospitals, the Dominican Sisters with 10, the Sisters of St. Joseph with 8, the Felician Sisters with 7, the Sisters of Mercy of the Union in the USA with 7, the Sisters of Mercy with 4, the Sisters of St. Joseph of Carondelet with 5, and the Congregation of Sisters of Charity of the Incarnate Word with 4. Most of the other 45 communities opened just one hospital (see Appendix C). Most of the 808 Catholic hospitals of 1965 were sister operated, as were the 341 nursing schools.

A delightful story concerns Cardinal Spellman who was walking with a Jewish friend on West 51st Street in New York City one day. The cardinal suggested that they stop and visit St. Clare's Hospital, established by the Franciscan Sisters of Allegany in 1949. The cardinal asked the elderly sister who greeted them to tell the superior that they had dropped in to pay their respects. "I'll certainly do that, Father," said the sister failing to recognize him.

The cardinal's friend, trying to correct matters, told the sister that her visitor was Cardinal Spellman. She smiled and answered. "Every priest who drops by here tells us that he's Cardinal Spellman."

The friend then pointed to His Eminence's picture in the entrance hall. The sister responded, "There is an annoying resemblance."

The cardinal then showed his driver's license to the sister. After examining it carefully, she said with a frown, "Now Father, where did you get that?"

Each chapter of American history features sister-nurses ministering to those in need. The antebellum period witnessed sister-nurses in action. These included the Ursulines in New Orleans, Mother Seton's daughters, Sisters of Mercy, Franciscan Sisters of the Poor, Sisters of St. Joseph, Sisters of St. Joseph of Carondelet, Sisters of Providence, Sisters of Charity of Montreal, and Sisters of Charity of St. Augustine. Sisters participated heroically in the trauma of the Civil War, accruing tremendous respect for themselves and the Catholic Church. Few chapters can equal their performance in the opening West. Subsequent operation of hundreds more hospitals and establishment of nursing schools in every section of the United States bore witness to Catholic charity in action. Tens of millions of Americans owe their lives and health to these women.

Foreign Missions

Beginning with Jamaica, locale of the first foreign mission by the Franciscan Sisters of Allegany in 1879, sister-missionaries began to focus attention on gaining converts in the Caribbean and Central America. We have seen how various groups of sisters opened missions in the Bahamas, Nicaragua, Ecuador, Belize, Puerto Rico, and Mexico. They also served in Hawaii and even South Africa in the late 19th century and ministered in the Far East during the early decades of the 20th century. From 1946 to 1965, the number of sister-missionaries increased dramatically — from slightly over 1,000 in 1946 to 3,706 in 1965.

A new impetus for missionary endeavors came from Rome. Pope Pius XII issued his encyclical *Evangelii praecones* in 1951, calling for increased missionary efforts. He also established the Pontifical Commission for Latin America in 1958. Pope John XXIII repeated the call in 1959 in his encyclical *Princeps pastorum*. Then in 1961, Monsignor Agostino Casaroli, repre-

Sister Elsie Monge, MM, Rural Community Development, Quito, Ecuador, 1977.

Courtesy Maryknoll Archives, Maryknoll, New York

senting the Pontifical Commission for Latin America, addressed the Second Religious Congress of the United States at Notre Dame University. He asked the religious communities to send 10 percent of their members to minister in Latin America. This radical call for missionary efforts was received with varying degrees of enthusiasm and trepidations. Some communities reacted quickly and began making plans and arrangements for missionary endeavors. Calls went out for volunteers and language studies were inaugurated. Other communities felt that they were already overextended and could not spare sisters for the new apostolate. Still other communities agreed in principle but could not respond immediately. In 1965, just four years after Monsignor Casaroli's appeal, hundreds of sister-missionaries had spread out over Latin America to minister.

While a number of communities already had experience in the Caribbean and Central America, only a few had any exposure to South America. Mother Cabrini had stationed American sisters in Argentina and Brazil in 1896, Sisters, Servants of the Immaculate Heart of Mary had gone to Peru in 1923 and Bernardine Sisters sent missionaries to help Polish Bernardines in Brazil in 1936. However, limited South American experience did not deter other communities. Peru with its poverty, isolated Andean villages, hordes of Indian peasants and shortages of priests and sisters attracted 46 different American communities. IHM's, the first in Peru, had 49 sister-missionaries there in 1965. Maryknoll sent 40. Franciscan communities focused on Brazil with 136 sister-missionaries from 17 of the 43 communities sending missionaries. Felician Sisters sent 40 sisters and Bernardine Sisters sent 30 of their members. Maryknoll was a strong presence in Chile with 55 missionary-sisters. Sisters, Servants of the Immaculate Heart of Mary from West Chester, Pennsylvania, were next with 17 sister-missionaries. Conditions in Chile were similar to those in Peru, although the European stock was a stronger element of the population. The pattern changed somewhat in Bolivia, where Sisters of Charity of Saint Elizabeth sent missionaries in 1963, joined by Maryknoll furnishing 42 missionaries and the Daughters of Charity 24 sisters. Here, poverty was especially pervasive among the Indians who constituted the largest segment of the population of any South American country. **Medical Mission Sisters (SCMM-2490)** had 26 missionaries in Venezuela. Twelve other communities sent small cadres. Six other countries were favored with American sister-missionaries. As is evident from Table VIII, Argentina and Uruguay received the fewest, but they were the most prosperous and advanced countries of South America.

Nominal Catholicity prevailed throughout Latin America although beneath the thin upper crust of society it tended to be primitive, infused with superstitions, and lacked a strong catechetical basis. Powerful strains of

Latin America Locations of Sister-Missionaries in 1965

Country	Number of Sisters
Puerto Rico	386
Peru	285
Brazil	235
Chile	164
Bolivia	129
Colombia	86
Guatemala	85
Jamaica	71
Mexico	54
Bahamas	49
Venezuela	42
Honduras	36
Guyana	24
Panama	24
Costa Rica	22
Ecuador	21
Argentina	18
Dominican Republic	12
Haiti	8
El Salvador	7
Uruguay	3
Total	1,781

Table VIII

Freemasonry and anticlericalism pervaded the upper and middle classes. Fundamentalist Protestant missionaries found fertile ground among the neglected and ignorant masses of poor peasants and were making serious conversion inroads. Centuries of oppression of the Indian and mixed blood peasantry, beginning with the Spanish *conquistadors* and continued by the powerful landowning upper classes, had produced a Latin American disaster — economic, social, and religious. Poverty was widespread, military dictatorships common and the Church generally impotent although a clerical minority struggled for equitable land distribution, just wages, humane treatment, and human rights. The ruling classes, abetted by the military, had intimidated the hierarchy for decades and only tolerated the Church as long as it restricted itself to the spiritual sphere and stood aloof from politics, social reform, and economic activity.

Latin America did not generate vocations to the religious life in significant numbers because of illiteracy, ignorance, poverty, and lack of Catholic education. Contemplative and semi-monastic women's communities had flourished in the Spain of the *conquistadors* and seemed to them the normal and proper institutions for women religious, an attitude they transported to the New World. Even Third Order congregations lived a semi-cloistered existence in keeping with Spanish tradition. These conditions explain why nominally Catholic Latin America was in desperate need of Catholic missionaries and why the pope asked for special help. American sisters clearly understood the missionary roles they would have to fill. It was not just a response to poverty.

Europeans and Americans had influenced events and conditions in Central America and the Caribbean for several centuries, resulting in wide disparity of cultures, economics, racial mixtures, religious affiliations, and educational levels. One would need to review each individual location for a specific characterization. However, poverty and ignorance were common factors that drew sister-missionaries.

Following the end of World War II, movements to free colonies gained momentum among the exhausted European powers. Agitation for independence, at times revolutionary and violent, created dilemmas for the colonial powers. They felt an obligation to prepare native populations for self-rule but were unwilling to transfer governance under threat of revolution. Great Britain and France in particular wrestled with this problem. However, because of political and economic pressures at home, those governments caved in and freed colonies apace. The sheer number of new nations confounded atlas publishers and school children studying geography (see Appendix E). The majority of the new nations were in Africa.

European missionaries had been active in sub-Saharan Africa for centuries but made weak efforts to build a native clergy, an error the Church sought to correct late in the 19th century. This failure had resulted in having to re-convert each succeeding generation at tremendous cost in energy and time. Protestant missionaries were also active from the early 19th century and provided native populations with medical services and educational opportunities although the number of converts to the various Protestant denominations was relatively small. British colonial administrations allowed Catholic

Daughters of Wisdom (c. 1942).
Courtesy Gonzaga University

Africa Locations of Sister-Missionaries in 1965	
Country	Number of Sisters
Tanzania	71
Ghana	49
Nigeria	41
Malawi	28
Uganda	25
Zambia	24
Kenya	24
South Africa	16
Basutoland	16
Rhodesia	11
Cameroon	10
Liberia	10
Republic of the Congo	8
Ethiopia	6
Egypt	6
Seven other locations	10
Total	355

Table IX

missionaries to operate freely and they enjoyed considerable conversion success. In sub-Saharan British colonies, serious competition for conversions came not from Protestant missionaries but from Islamic religious leaders, financed and supported by traditional Moslem countries. Islam had been a presence for centuries in sub-Saharan Africa, but spread rapidly in the late 19th and early 20th centuries, using anti-European propaganda and force as conversion tools.

Portuguese colonies were the oldest in Africa and a gradual conversion to Catholicity had been in progress for several centuries. The French, who arrived in sub-Saharan Africa much later, fostered Catholic conversions with some success although their efforts in Islamic North Africa were without any significant results. When European colonial administrations departed and colonies became independent nations, governmental support for Christian missionaries vanished, increasing the need for missionary support. American communities responding to African needs had sisters stationed in the countries listed in Table IX in 1965.

As might be expected, equatorial Africa presented monumental medical challenges and the Medical Mission Sisters sent 22 members to Ghana and ten to Uganda, including nine of their limited supply of doctors. The **Medical Missionaries of Mary (MMM-2480)**, founded in 1950, sent 15 missionaries. Maryknoll Sisters concentrated their efforts in Tanzania where they collaborated with the 106 Maryknoll fathers in that country. Other communities sending significant numbers to Africa included the Society of the Holy Child Jesus (4060), the Daughters of Wisdom (0960), and the Holy Spirit Missionary Sisters (3530). Other communities sent sisters in pairs or small groups to work in established missions. Political unrest and dictatorial regimes increased the normal problems. Newly created countries had no

Sister Rosemarie Milazzo, MM, Kenya Bura, 1985.
Maryknoll Mission Archives, Maryknoll, New York

tradition of democracy and sometimes succumbed to the lure of Marxism, sparking anti-Western and anti-Christian suppression of missionaries.

While South America and Africa were new territories for most American sister-missionaries, the Orient was not. With the Japanese surrender on August 14, 1945, missionaries in China found themselves suddenly released from detention camps and house arrest or free to return from exile in the interior. Sisters who fled to India and then home or repatriated directly to the United States scrambled to return. For them it was important to restore the old missions. Experiences varied. Some found their convents and schools in good repair with loyal Christians awaiting their return. Others found desolation and destruction with their former followers dead or scattered. Missionaries returning to areas under Communist control accepted tremendous risks. China exchanged one form of chaos for another as the Nationalist government with United States assistance sought to re-establish political control while the Communists with Russian backing sought to seize power.

In an obvious effort to bolster the Church's recovery, Pope Pius XII designated the Archbishop of Peking, Thomas Tien, to the College of Cardinals — the first native Chinese to be elevated to the red hat. Chinese Christians, Catholic and Protestant, rejoiced in the recognition and even non-Christians took pride in the honor bestowed on their countryman. In 1946, it seemed that once the Communists were defeated and suppressed that

China would be a peaceful country and that missionary endeavors would flourish as before. However, the Nationalist government was weak and corrupt while the Communists under Mao Tse Tung were highly disciplined, ruthless, and backed by Russia. The Communists sought to seduce as well as overpower. They claimed to be simple agrarian peasant reformers, a line swallowed by the United States State Department, who were dedicated to religious freedom and determined to redress social injustice. Communists cleverly manipulated bandits into harassing missionaries. Once in full control, the Reds then viciously eliminated banditry and the war lords, thereby gaining the support of the peasantry. Communist fellow-travelers had infiltrated Chinese universities, the media, and Nationalist government, quietly preparing the way for a Communist takeover. The Reds established stable administrations in areas under their control although most missionaries instinctively distrusted them based on years of experience with their terrorist tactics. Yet hoping for the best, they proceeded to reopen missions and import fresh missionaries from the United States. On October 1, 1949, Mao Tse-tung established the People's Republic of China and in December Chiang Kai-shek and the Nationalist government fled to Formosa (Taiwan) sealing China's fate — and that of the missions.

A total of 5,000 Catholic bishops, priests, and sisters from Europe and the United States were in China in 1949.[12] Just three years later the number had dropped to 163.[13] Stories of suffering and sacrifice that numerous missionaries endured from Communists are legion. Maryknoll Sister Paulita Hoffmann described the last Mass in Hingning, Mei Xian, as follows:

> *Late in November we had our final Sunday Mass. Father Aloysius Au, our Chinese pastor, had already received notice that for an indefinite time there were to be no further gatherings of the people in church; but he did not accept this notice as official. To avoid trouble, he told the Christians that Sunday Mass would be earlier than the usual hour. Just as the assistant priest was nearing the end of the ceremony, a Communist soldier threateningly walked in the side door of the church, hand on gun. He eyed the congregation cautiously and advanced directly to the altar rail. He commanded the priest to discontinue the Mass. Father Au, with characteristic courage, approached the soldier and quietly invited him outside for a few words. The priest was thus able quickly to complete the ceremony as the frightened Christians chanted the Mass prayers with him. He signaled the people to make no more sound and their voices dropped off gradually to whispers. As the priest left the sanctuary the Christians silently and sadly slipped away. It was the last Mass they were to hear, for their pastor was*

> *taken prisoner and placed in a labor squad. The church was*
> *closed. The sisters were placed under house arrest.*[14]

Father Au died in a labor camp several years later. Communist authorities arrested all the sisters and priests in Meixian City on December 23, 1950. Maryknoll Bishop Francis Xavier Ford and Sister Joan Marie were taken to Canton and imprisoned there in April 1951. Bishop Ford died in captivity in February 1952 at age 60 and Sister Joan Marie was expelled from China later that year. Between those dates, the two Maryknollers suffered incredibly. Bound, beaten, tried in kangaroo court, paraded before howling mobs that stoned them, confined in filthy cramped cells, interrogated for hours, and threatened with death if they did not sign confessions, the bishop and sister offered up their sufferings to God. Under the unremitting tortures, Bishop Ford's health broke and he died, ten months after his arrest. Sister Joan Marie survived despite the mistreatment.

Practically all missionaries leaving China felt deep depression and a sense of failure. Chinese bishops, priests, and sisters are known to have endured terrible tortures under the Communists. Many suffered execution and others received long prison sentences. A special sadness concerns the Chinese sisters who remained. For example, the fate of the 112 Chinese Daughters of Charity remains unknown. The fates of untold tens of thousands of the faithful may never be known.

Some modern scholars have been critical of the Church's shortfalls in converting the Chinese, claiming that its limited successes were among the lowest elements of society. The term "rice Christians" was used to describe false converts seeking free food and medical care; there were unquestionably many impoverished Chinese who took advantage of Christian charity, something clearly recognized by missionaries who nonetheless discharged Jesus' dictates. However, it is now becoming clear that after the missionaries departed the underground Catholic Church not only survived but grew. Almost all American and European missionaries had fostered youth chapters of the Legion of Mary and it seems they continued to spread the faith, not only among the humble but among the educated and professional classes. That so many Chinese were willing to suffer for their faith reaffirms that the blood of martyrs is indeed the seed of the Church.

Japanese cruelties to captured American servicemen during the war created a wide belief that missionaries received the same treatment; the Philippine experience reinforced this view. However, in Japan itself, missionaries fared decently considering the circumstances, possibly a result of the Vatican's establishment of diplomatic relations with Japan in 1942. Missionaries who did not choose repatriation endured either house arrest or restricted freedom and were usually able to maintain contacts with local

Christians. When the war ended, missionaries had little difficulty in reestablishing their ministries and recruits from the United States came in considerable numbers. South Korea likewise proved hospitable and missions flourished. All contact with missionaries in North Korea was lost. Most are presumed dead. American missionaries re-entered the Philippines to reopen missions.

In 1965, sisters were ministering in the following locations in the Far East:

Far East Location of Sister-Missionaries in 1965

Country	Number of Sisters
Philippines	181
Japan	165
Pakistan	121
India	88
Hong Kong	85
Taiwan	74
Korea	60
Thailand	12

Table X

As before the war, the number of Maryknoll Sisters predominated with 270 sister-missionaries: 87 in the Philippines, 70 in Hong Kong, 44 in South Korea, 35 in Japan, and 34 in Taiwan.[15] Franciscan Missionary Sisters of Mary (1370), Sisters of Notre Dame de Namur (3000), and the Daughters of Charity of St. Vincent de Paul (0760) also made a strong presence in the Far East.[16]

Although few in number, the Medical Mission Sisters formed a critical element of American Catholic missionary endeavors in the Far East. Anna Marie Dengal, an experienced lay missionary doctor, founded this congregation in the United States in 1925. Its members are primarily doctors, registered nurses, and medical technicians. Since in many parts of the Third World and the Orient women are inhibited about male doctors examining them, female doctors and medical personnel provided a needed service. The Medical Mission Sisters opened their first mission hospital in Rawalpindi, India, in 1927. The year 1965 found 57 members serving in Pakistan, 59 in India, nine in Vietnam, and three in the Philippines. Africa, South America, Oceania, Hawaii, Canada, Australia, and miscellaneous locations in the Middle East and Europe accounted for the balance of sister-missionaries serving outside the continental United States in 1965. Almost one-third of their members were in the United States, doing medical work, or in their Rome generalate.

Statistics fail to convey the devotion, sacrifices, and accomplishments of thousands of sisters serving in distant lands. Although physical hardships and privations were common denominators among practically all missionaries during these years, there were no martyrs or long imprisonments other than in China. In many ways this era was a peaceful interlude in the non-Chinese missions. Danger and terror would revive in the next phase of history.

It remains to be seen how history will treat the missionary efforts of American sisters and priests during the approximately 100 years between 1880 and 1980. However, several generalizations would seem to qualify for future acceptance. American missionaries played an important role in the revitalization of Catholicity in Latin America. In many of those countries the Church has reached general populations as never before. Lay apostolates, many initially stimulated by sister-missionaries, now bring charity and catechesis to the masses. In the Orient, the faith is alive and growing. Even in China under suppression, it continues to flourish in the underground church. Sub-Saharan Africa has become the fastest growing element of the worldwide Catholic Church. Missionary activities of American women religious might not seem to be critical factors in the resurgent Latin American Church and the expanding African and Asian Churches, but future's perspective may well determine that American women religious did indeed play a significant role.

The Sisters Organize

There is a general misconception that American women religious communities began to organize national organizations as a result of the pronouncements of Vatican II. This is not surprising considering that the American bishops themselves had no central organization until 1917. Following the Third Plenary Council of 1884, archbishops met annually but had no fixed mechanism for functioning between meetings until they formed the National Catholic War Council during World War I to coordinate Catholic war and relief efforts. This organization proved so effective that the archbishops transformed it into the National Catholic Welfare Conference (NCWC) as a permanent agency composed of all members of the hierarchy. In 1966 this body was replaced by the present two-tier organization; the National Conference of Catholic Bishops (NCCB) for policy and the United States Catholic Conference (USCC) for administration and participation by a broader range of Catholic agencies. It was just a matter of time before women religious would also organize nationally.

Prior to the 1950's, American women religious had no distinct national organizations outside their individual orders' administrative structures. Individual sisters belonged to national educational, health, social services, and other kinds of associations but had no national organization composed exclusively of women religious leaders. But, beginning in the 1950's, spurred by leadership from the Vatican and leadership by American sister-educators, they began to organize nationally.

Conference of Major Superiors of Congregations of Women Religious

The American women religious scene of 1950 was a mosaic composed of diocesan congregations, pontifical orders and congregations, communities with motherhouses in Europe and Canada, contemplative orders, semi-monastic orders, small active communities, large orders, and congregations with hierarchial structures. Such a seeming patchwork of women religious groups had evolved historically; it was a natural composition to those most intimately concerned — sisters and nuns, the hierarchy, and the clergy. Yet, the body of women religious contained a basic flaw that grew more serious with each passing year — namely the isolation of communities from one another. Each mother-superior was essentially alone in her efforts to educate her sisters while simultaneously insuring their religious formation and developing them as whole persons.

In 1941, Sister Bertrande Meyers, DC, conducted an in-depth survey of how the education of sisters was viewed by the nation's mothers-superior, novice-mistresses and deans of sisters' studies. She compiled her findings in a doctoral dissertation titled *"The Education of Sisters,"* soon published in book form.[17] It demonstrated that higher education *per se* was not a solution. Although essential for professional preparation of sisters for apostolates requiring special training and degrees, higher education had to be balanced with the spiritual formation of sisters and the sense of community identity had to be maintained and fostered; this balance was not so much a matter of attaining higher education as a matter of how it was to be effected. Her report indicted the haphazard methods for educating sisters and proposed far-reaching solutions, including a greater degree of collaboration among women religious leaders and resistance to sending sisters into the classroom or hospital before they were properly prepared both educationally and spiritually. Unfortunately, the timing of this report during the war year 1941 diminished its impact and its findings did not receive the attention they deserved.

During the Holy Year of 1950,[18] the major superiors of religious orders and congregations from all over the world convened in Rome in response to a call from the Sacred Congregation of Religious.[19] It gathered the male and female superiors-general for the stated purpose of effecting a renewal of religious life and adapting it to modern times. This General Assembly of Religious was the first such convocation in the 1,900-year history of the Catholic Church. Its findings were exhaustive in examining religious life in all its ramifications. Basically, it defined the theological aspects of religious life. In his message to the assembly, Pope Pius XII distinguished essentials from the extrinsic, counseled elimination of non-essentials, cautioned prudent adjustment to modern conditions, and recommended federations under papal approval.[20] While he was generally referring to cloistered nuns, the call for *aggiornamento* and adaptation of religious life to the modern world impacted orders and congregations of women religious throughout the world. This was the beginning of changes that are still unfolding.[21]

The following year, Pope Pius XII convened the First International Congress of Teaching Sisters. Among other remarks in his apostolic exhortation *Ci torna*, he said —

> *Many of your schools are being described and praised to us as being very good. But not all. It is our fervent wish that all endeavor to become excellent. This presupposes that your teaching Sisters are masters of the subjects they expound. See to it, therefore, that they are well trained and that their education corresponds in quality and academic degrees to that demanded by the State. . . . Educate yourselves, educate yourselves completely, educate yourselves with renewed effort, you who have the duty, and are the educators of so many young girls today, and of so many of the teaching women of the proximate future . . . influence depends on adequate knowledge and skill on the part of sisters . . . superiors must provide training suitable to conditions. . . .*

He also addressed the subject of habits, saying —

> *Select one of such a kind that it will be an expression of interior unaffectedness, of simplicity and religious modesty; that it will serve to edify all, even modern youth. . . .*

At the International Congress of Superiors-General of Orders and Congregations of Women in 1952, Pope Pius XII iterated his exhortation of *Ci torna* and focused on vocations. He urged superiors to preserve family spirit within their communities and to provide adequate training and opportunity for maintaining professional efficiency. He again addressed the subject of habits, stating —

> *The religious habit should express consecration. For the rest, let the habit be suitable and meet the requirements of hygiene. In sum, in non-essentials adapt yourselves as far as reason and well ordered charity make it advisable. . . .*

At first, these papal statements did not receive wide dissemination among American women religious and it was several years before they became common knowledge. Meanwhile, Pope Pius XII demonstrated his commitment to renewal in 1954 by approving the establishment of Regina Mundi Institute in Rome for the training of sisters who would teach religion at the collegiate level. The faculty was drawn from among the best of the Roman theological schools. Courses included philosophy, theology, and various scientific disciplines. Many American sisters enrolled since Saint Mary's College in South Bend was the only women's college in the United States teaching theology to women.

Following the 1950 international session of superiors of orders and congregations in Rome, the Sacred Congregation of Religious requested national meetings. The first American congress took place at Notre Dame University in 1952, the largest gathering of superiors of women religious organizations in the history of the United States. Wide-ranging topics for discussion included the necessity for special training for superiors and mistresses of novices, ways and means of prolonging the formation initiated in the novitiate, training in the positive aspects of the religious vows, special problems in the practice of the vows in modern times, theology for sisters, and the necessity for sound education in the various apostolates.[22]

Other topics for informal discussion included lay teachers in parochial schools, overcrowded classrooms, and how the numbers of Catholic children were increasing proportionally faster than sister-population. In a speech, the Prefect of the Sacred Congregation of Religious, Very Reverend Arcadio Larraona, stressed mutual support and exchange of information among the orders and congregations. The superiors formed a "Sisters Committee" to insure continuation of the initiatives and elected Mother Gerald Barry of the Adrian Dominicans as the chairperson. In retrospect, this was a profoundly significant gathering. As a follow-up, summer workshops termed Institutes on Spirituality were conducted each summer at Notre Dame University for superiors, formation sisters, and others who pursued the subjects raised in 1952.

As early as 1950, the Vatican began encouraging women religious throughout the world to organize into national conferences of major superiors. The Sisters Committee studied this proposal during the Notre Dame gathering of 1952 and the Vatican requested that the committee remain intact following the congress. Lack of progress prompted the Sacred Congregation of Religious to send Father Elio Gambari to the United States to urge action.[23] As a result, on November 24, 1956, major superiors of 235 orders and congregations established the Conference of Major Superiors of Congregations of Women Religious (CMSW) with Mother Gerald as the first president. The Vatican extended formal approval in 1962. Several years later the title was changed to Leadership Conference of Women Religious (LCWR). For the first time American mothers-superior and provincials of orders with motherhouses in Europe and Canada had a national organization with staff to facilitate formulation of policy, coordination, and mutual support to carry out the mandate issued by Pope Pius XII. This organization now had a powerful voice representing a majority of American sisters and nuns.

The Sister Formation Movement

The "baby-boom" of the late 1940's and the 1950's was the result of millions of servicemen returning home to become husbands and fathers, creating an explosion of births that intensified pressures to expand parochial schools and open new ones. Pastors and bishops sent urgent appeals to mothers-superior for more and more sister-teachers resulting in thousands of young sisters being sent into classrooms; many were just out of novitiate or in some cases had not completed teacher preparation or gained college degrees. Meanwhile, states and school districts continued upgrading qualifications for certification. Eighty-six percent of public school teachers beginning their careers in 1959 had college degrees while a much smaller percentage of sisters began teaching with one.

Pressures mounted for improved education for sister-teachers, a goal requiring time, money, and approbation from bishops. Many mothers-superior were in an impossible situation. If they sent sisters to college they lost up to four years of teaching time further intensifying stress on their sister-teachers struggling in overcrowded classrooms. Teacher salary scales were so low that it was often difficult to accrue sufficient funds to cover college expenses. Despite the certification problem, the majority of bishops and diocesan school superintendents continued to believe that the proven past accomplishments of sister-teachers demonstrated that the loss of teaching time was unnecessary. Higher costs for the increasing numbers of lay teachers also stiffened their resistance to increased training time.

These factors ignored the impact of poor educational preparation on the individual sister who thought that she had a right to be professionally prepared for her work for the Church. Her parents felt that justice and common decency demanded it. As early as 1929, Pope Pius XI had called for the full education of sister-teachers in his encyclical *Rappresentanti in terra* (The Christian Education of Youth). In 1949, Sister Madeleva Wolff, CSC, the famed educator from Saint Mary's College in South Bend, Indiana, gave two presentations at the convention of the National Catholic Educational Association (NCEA). Her first was titled "The Preparation of Teachers of Religion" and included such subjects as the preparation of lay religion teachers, the habit not automatically making a good teacher, and the quality of sister education. Her second presentation was titled "The Education of Sister Lucy." Sister Madeleva spoke forcefully about the hypothetical young Sister Lucy. Her remarks included:

If all our religious communities begin this year to complete the education of our young sisters before sending them out to teach, practically all the immediate generation will have their degrees and licenses in two or three years. After that, our teaching communities will have established this pattern of time and study training. They will have the same number of sisters to send out each year, with this incalculable difference, that they will be adequately prepared. Summer schools thereafter can be devoted to graduate work, particularly in theology, and Sister Lucy will still be "young Sister Lucy" when her teacher training has been complete. She will have the vitality, the enthusiasm, and quick mind and generosity of youth to give to her best years of teaching. How shortsighted, how stupidly extravagant we have been in squandering these. . . .[24]

Her observations were all too familiar to the women religious present but coming from a speaker of such stature the presentations brought these concerns before a national forum where they could no longer be down-played or ignored. In some ways, Sister Madeleva's presentations at the 1949 meeting of the National Catholic Educational Association was the *Magna Carta* for professional training of sister-teachers.

A new day dawned when Pope Pius XII addressed the First International Congress of Teaching Sisters in 1951. His speech became the topic of a panel discussion at the Teacher Education Section of the 1952 National Catholic Educational Association convention in Kansas City, Missouri. These discussions resulted in the formation of a special committee to survey the current status of sister-teacher education. The survey results were presented at the following year's convention in Atlantic City, New Jersey. Among other findings, the survey disclosed that 171 communities were sending sisters to teach with less than two years of college pre-service preparation and that 118 communities had no access to facilities for a four-year program. As a section of the Department of Colleges and Universities of the National Catholic Educational Association, the Sister Formation Conference (SFC) advocated radical improvements, but with limited success. As late as 1960, sisters were still calling for understanding and support for their position on spiritual and professional preparation for future sister-teachers. An extract from an article by Sister Mary Emil Penet, IHM, of the National Catholic Educational Association eloquently bespeaks the appeal:

The human spirit has its own laws, and the need for time to work lasting changes is one of them. If the Sister of tomorrow is to have more contact with the world in her apostolate, then we must remove her farther and longer from the world while we are getting

*her ready. If she is to live in surroundings of turmoil, noise, and
confusion, then we must help her a little longer to cultivate interior silence and calm. If she is going to have to work under intense
pressure during a lifetime in order to meet the demand that she be
a saint, scholar, and gentlewoman — for this is what tomorrow's
world will ask of her — then we need to give her a start on saintli-
ness, scholarship, and gentility before she goes into service. Above
all, we need to give her a chance to grow in the love of God which
will impel and sustain her through the white martyrdom of this
kind of intense life. . . .*[25]

Some of the larger and stronger communities had excellent programs,
often using their own colleges — their members among the fortunate
minority. For example, in 1949 three communities in Connecticut began a
diocesan teachers college; they were the Sisters of Mercy, the Sisters of St.
Joseph, and the Daughters of the Holy Ghost. In another instance, the Sisters
of Charity of St. Elizabeth, Convent Station (0590) instituted a program in
1954 with their sisters attending the College of St. Elizabeth. After complet-
ing novitiate, sisters entered a "juniorate" program lasting from two to four
years devoted to securing college degrees. Even so, the overall situation was
approaching the desperation stage with the onrushing tide of Catholic
children seeking admittance to parochial schools.

Sister formation was as much a grass roots movement as it was a formal
conference. Practically every order and congregation in the United States
entered into a period of intense introspection as a result of surveys initiated
by the SFC and constant updates printed in the *Sister Formation Bulletin*
edited by Sister Ritamary Bradley, CHM. Begun in 1954, that bulletin was
widely circulated among all women religious, not just among leaders. It
reported on developments in different communities for comparison by
others, on meetings of every description, and on decisions by the Vatican and
American Church leaders. Sister Emil was the heart of the formation movement and Sister Ritamary its voice. Contrary to common assumptions, the
movement encompassed more than higher education, giving impetus for better formation of the *whole sister* to include her spiritual, intellectual, and social person. Sister Emil pursued these objectives untiringly.

The juniorate took more concrete form as a result of the SFC's efforts.
While at first it was considered a time period following the novitiate for pursuing higher education, it now came to stand for an institution — a college
exclusively devoted to educating sisters of one order or many orders and
congregations. In 1956, with funding from the Ford Foundation, sisters with
PhD's convened for the summer at the so-called Everett Conference to
prepare a suggested undergraduate curriculum for future-sister-teachers.

Sister Bertrande Meyers fostered the opening of Marillac College in St. Louis in 1955 by the Daughters of Charity as a juniorate college. Sisters of St. Joseph also opened Brentwood College in Brentwood, New York, where sisters of this and other orders could earn a degree in education. The School Sisters of Notre Dame and the Sisters of Charity of Providence followed suit.

Slowly at first and then rapidly, the concept of every future sister-teacher having a complete novitiate and juniorate received acceptance among the hierarchy, clergy, and diocesan school superintendents. Data proving that poorly prepared sisters had a much greater departure rate from communities than those properly educated hastened acceptance of the proposition. It now became a matter of how soon the concept could be implemented by the various communities. By 1967, the count of sisters with at least an BA degree had risen to 62 percent. A new day was dawning for sister-teachers.

It was inevitable that the Conference of Major Superiors of Congregations of Women Religious and the Sister Formation Conference would come into conflict since both had many of the same overall objectives and the lines of decision-making became confused. The Vatican supported the CMSW as the logical body to exercise ultimate authority despite Sister Emil's feelings that formation should be far more broad-based than just major superiors. Ultimately she lost out and the SFC became a subordinate part of the CMSW. Even so, this loss of independence could not obscure that fact that Sisters Emil and Ritamary were the leading individuals in the decade-long overhaul and revamping of the formation of future sister-teachers who emerged from the 1960's as the best educated women religious in the world and the best educated large group of women in the United States.

Thus, the Vatican and American sister-educators, working along parallel lines, brought a whole new dimension to the sisterhood. After 1,600 years, women religious communities secured national and international cooperative agencies for mutual support, development of policy, and coordination. Today, the LCWR represents the majority of American orders. Its stated purpose is to promote the spiritual and apostolic calling and works of American sisters and nuns. Its membership is composed of the superiors of orders and congregations and the provincials of communities with motherhouses outside the United States. The question of adequate time for formation and education of future sister-teachers was settled. Those processes, the sister formation movement and the establishment of an association, prepared women religious organizationally and psychologically for the challenges of renewal.

The Second Vatican Council

Elected in 1958, Pope John XXIII captured the world's imagination as a kindly, generous, Italian peasant-pope. He also astounded the Church only three months after his installation by announcing that a universal Church council would be held as soon as proper preparations could be made. He enjoyed universal approval for an expression attributed to him, "Open the windows of the Church and let fresh air in." After extensive preparations involving theologians, cardinals, bishops, and priests of various scholarly disciplines, Pope John XXIII convened the council on October 11, 1962. Before the first session was completed, the pope died on June 3, 1963, mourned by the entire world. Pope Paul VI was elected his successor.

The nation and much of the world focused on Rome between 1962 and 1965 while the council was in progress. Not since the Council of Trent some 420 years earlier had such a momentous conclave of Catholic leaders convened to reshape the Church. Preconciliar announcements got world attention when they indicated the drastic changes to be considered. The secular media paid particular attention to ongoing events and kept the American public informed on developments as well as rumors and misinformation. Protestant churchmen and leaders of other world religions followed the proceedings with mounting interest. Ordinary Americans of all religious persuasions took positions concerning issues before the council and someone coined a new phrase, "the spirit of Vatican II."

An unusual aspect of this council was the invitation extended to non-Catholic delegate-observers, to Catholic lay auditors, and to women religious auditors. Nineteen American Protestant churchmen received invitations. Sister Mary Luke Tobin of the Sisters of Loretto at the Foot of the Cross represented the CMSW, and Catherine McCarthy represented the National Council of Catholic Women. While delegate-observers and auditors had no vote and could not address the council, they often had "box seats" at closed sessions of numerous commissions of the council and were often better informed than Catholic officials. Commission members frequently held informal conversations with auditors and delegates, listening to and discussing their views on a wide range of topics.

As the sessions progressed with detailed media coverage, Protestants (and many Catholics) came to the realization that the Church was not the monolithic, tightly controlled, dictatorial organization that they had been led to believe it was. American Catholics were thrilled by the attention given their Church, even though confused about much of what was happening. Introduction of English in the Mass in 1964 was the first concrete impact of the council on the average Catholic who was apprehensive about other changes that many were forecasting. It remained for the official documents to be promulgated and digested before the actual council decisions became widely known.

In 1965 when the council ended, almost one of every four Americans was

Catholic, 45.6 million strong, 24 percent of the population. By objective measurements, the Catholic Church in the United States was in "full bloom." Table XI demonstrates that status.

These statistics demonstrate the awesome magnitude of the Church. In less than 200 years it had grown from a tiny, fragile institution to the largest and most powerful religious denomination in the nation, and one of the strongest national Catholic churches in the world. We have followed that growth from infancy to full bloom. At each stage of American history, women religious played an increasingly vital role in the life of the Church, nurturing it with education, religious instruction, health care, and charitable apostolates. Without their ministrations, the Church could not possibly have achieved such a status.

In 1965, the Catholic population was so large and growing, men and women religious so dedicated, the educational complex so encompassing, the laity so loyal and supportive, devotional life so vibrant, and the institutional church so strong and comprehensive that it seemed to some observers that the United States might well become Catholic — given another century or so. American sister-history amply demon-

Catholic Statistics — 1965

Catholic Population	45,640,619
Cardinals	6
Archbishops	29
Bishops	212
Priests	58,632
Women Religious*	209,000
Brothers	12,271
Dioceses	149
Parishes	17,088
Chapels, Missions, and Stations	18,197
Colleges and Universities	304
Students	384,526
Parochial Schools	10,503
Students	4,566,809
High Schools	2,455
Students	1,095,519
General Hospitals	808
Patients in 1964	16,571,548
Special Hospitals and Sanatoria	141
Patients in 1964	324,055
Nursing Schools	341
Students	35,430
Seminaries	596
Seminarians	48,992
Orphanages	257
Children	23,379
Other Protective Institutions	141
Guests	16,300
Homes for Aged Poor	257
Guests	35,560

*See Appendix F.

Table XI

strates that if this is to transpire they will be in the vanguard. History also has a way of confounding the wisest seers, continually offering new and unexpected challenges. Few, if any, sisters or nuns in 1965 could have foreseen the challenges they would be facing in the post-1965 years.

Endnotes

1. The cult of St. Jude was popularized in the United States, not in Europe. During the 1920's, pious women in Chicago began to pray to this little known apostle and the divine favors his intercession procured earned him the title "the saint of the impossible." Since then, popular devotion to him has spread over the United States and the entire world.

2. There are around 18 different kinds of scapulars, each being a badge of some confraternity in which the wearer is enrolled (Carmelite, Sacred Heart, Franciscan, etc.). A scapular consists of two small pieces of cloth attached to a circular band of string. The badges are usually a half-inch to three inches in size, square or rectangular, with the confraternity imprint on one side. The scapular is worn around the neck under clothing with one badge hanging down the front and the other down the back.

3. Church Council Vatican I in 1870 defined the dogma of papal infallibility. This dogma holds that the pope, speaking to the entire world as pope (*ex cathedra* — from the chair) is infallible when defining dogmas of faith and morals. The basis for this dogma lies in the belief that the Holy Spirit would not allow a false teaching of this magnitude by the successor to Peter and head of the universal Church founded by Jesus Christ. The dogma does not imply infallibility under any other circumstances. Since that council, popes have only issued one infallible pronouncement: the Assumption of the Blessed Virgin Mary, a simple affirmation of an ancient belief. The dogma of papal infallibility is often misunderstood and just as often misrepresented by enemies of the Church.

4. Peter's Pence is an annual collection to support the Vatican. The term derives from England where the collection first began in 787. King Henry VIII abolished it in England in 1534.

5. Among the many devices that some mothers-superior employed seeking financial security was life insurance. These communities scrimped to pay premiums, considered a top priority over most other demands. In addition, any surplus funds were invested immediately and interest became a sustaining source of income for those making wise decisions.

6. Originally Second Order, this congregation and its offshoots were all Third Order by this time.

7. In 1900, the Roman Union was formed as an international Ursuline community with a mother-general and motherhouse in Rome at the invitation of Pope Leo XIII. Most of the American communities with origins in France (Congregation of Paris) declined the invitation to join while most communities with non-French origins joined.

8. Most sisters in apostolic communities led contemplative lives during different

periods, especially in novitiate and during their retirement years. They also found other opportunities to withdraw from active ministry and assume a daily regimen not unlike that of contemplatives in the monastery — for brief or extended periods of time. Many convents had "cloistered" areas for sisters' meditation and the "quiet hour" was a general practice. Some convents had the privilege of keeping the Blessed Sacrament in their chapels and practiced "perpetual" adoration, usually two sisters at a time. Throughout this book, maintaining the distinctions between sisters and nuns has resulted in too little being said about the deep devotional lives of active sisters. Practically all have been "contemplatives" or "near-contemplatives" at one time or another during their religious lives. The distinction between apostolic and contemplative communities was often thin or blurred — nuns in a community practicing active ministry while sisters in an apostolic one living an intense prayer life.

9. This statement is based on the author's personal impression gained during those years.

10. Discalced Carmelites (OCD) are the largest group with 62 monasteries. The majority trace their roots back to Port Tobacco. There are 15 monasteries that trace their roots to Mexico and the years that their members had to flee persecution. Four Carmels have French origins and the Carmel of Hawaii was founded from Hong Kong. One Byzantine Rite community is located in Sugarloaf, Pennsylvania. Calced Carmelites (O.Carm) have three cloistered monasteries: in North Dakota, Texas, and Wisconsin.

11. They were —

> Nuns of Perpetual Adoration of the Blessed Sacrament (3190) — 86 members.
>
> Congregation of the Handmaids of the Precious Blood (1860) — 40 members.
>
> Cistercian Nuns of the Strict Observance (Trappistines) (0670) — 87 members.
>
> Sister Servants of the Holy Spirit of Perpetual Adoration (3540) — 29 members.
>
> Pious Disciples of the Divine Master (0980) — 49 members.

12. Edward Fischer, *Maybe a Second Spring: The Story of the Missionary Sisters of St. Columban in China* (New York, NY: Crossroads, 1983), p. 188.

13. An Irish group of sisters, members of the Franciscan Missionaries of Mary, operated the only Catholic school in China after the Communist takeover until it closed in 1966. The school was in Peking and served the diplomatic community. The Communist government permitted it to operate as a rare concession to foreign sensibilities. With the advent of the Great Cultural Revolution in 1966, Red Guards shut down the school, uprooting and expelling the sisters with great physical cruelty. On reaching the border to Hong Kong, Sister Eamon O'Sullivan was unable to walk across because of the horrible treatment she had received. Chinese border guards tossed her limp body on a hand cart on which she rode half-conscious to her waiting comrades on the British side. She died the next day. The few other remaining missionaries were either imprisoned or expelled.

14. John F. Donovan, MM, *The Pagoda and the Cross: The Life of Bishop Ford of Maryknoll* (New York, NY: Charles Scribner's Sons, 1967), p. 185.

15. Between 1921 and 1953, a total of 173 Maryknoll Sisters served in China. Of these, 22 were trained nurses and two were medical doctors. See Jean-Paul Wiest, *Maryknoll in China: A History, 1918-1955* (London, England: M.E. Sharpe, Inc.,1988), p. 461.

16. A small community, the **Franciscan Missionary Sisters of Our Lady of Sorrows (OSF-1390),** had sisters in Hong Kong. Originally founded by Italian bishop Rafael Palazzi, OFM, in Hunan in 1939, it attracted four sisters from the Sisters of St. Francis of the Holy Family who joined them in 1949. Two returned to the United States in 1949 when the Communists took control of China and established the order in Beaverton, Oregon. Thus, in one more reversal, China provided foundresses for this land.

17. Bertrande Meyers, DC, *The Education of Sisters: A Plan for Integrating the Religious, Cultural, Social, and Professional Training of Sisters* (New York, NY: Sheed and Ward, 1941).

18. Senator Patrick McCarran of Nevada while visiting Rome in 1950 for the Holy Year had a private audience with Pope Pius XII. During the meeting Senator McCarran mentioned that he had two daughters who were members of the Sisters of the Holy Names of Jesus and Mary. The pope beamed and stated that this was "his" order. While a cardinal he became their "protector." After the interview, the pope wrote a personal note to the mother-general in Canada requesting that the McCarran daughters who belonged to the Oakland, California, community be allowed to come to Rome for the Holy Year. Feeling that "all go or none go," she refused the request. The daughters, Mary and Margaret, remained ignorant of the high level activities on their behalf until years later. See Ruth Montgomery, *Once There Was a Nun* (New York, NY: G. P. Putnam & Sons, 1962), pp. 252-253.

19. The Sacred Congregation of Religious is an administrative office of the Vatican. Its jurisdiction is personal without territorial limits. Pope Pius X established it as a special office of the Roman Curia in 1906. As a general rule, it handles all matters pertaining to religious orders, congregations, societies, and institutes. Thus, this department has oversight of governance and practices of women religious.

20. His address was technically an apostolic constitution titled *Sponsa Christi.*

21. Sr. Elizabeth Kolmer, ASC, *Religious Women in the United States: A Survey of the Influential Literature from 1950 to 1983* (Wilmington, DE: Michael Glazier, 1984), pp.19-25. This work was invaluable in sorting out the series of complex events taking place during these years.

22. Sr. Bertrande Meyers, DC, *Sisters for the 21st Century* (New York, NY: Sheed and Ward, 1965), p. 47.

23. Father Elio Gambari was closely associated with the formation and workings of the Conference of Major Superiors of Women (CMSW) and with the Sister Formation Conference (movement). He spoke at meetings, gave workshops, advised and provided guidance during the confusing early developments. He also

fostered and aided the follow-up organization of the Leadership Conference of Women Religious (LCWR).

24. National Catholic Educational Association, *National Catholic Educational Association Bulletin.* Proceedings of the Forty-Sixth Annual Meeting (Washington, DC: National Catholic Educational Association, 1949), p. 225.

25. Sr. Emil Mary Penet, IHM, "Why a Sister Shortage?" *The American Ecclesiastical Review, Vol. CXLII* (Washington, DC: The Catholic University of America Press, 1960), p. 27.

CHAPTER 11

Epilogue

‡ — ‡

THE YEARS SINCE 1965 are more properly *current events* — not crystallized history — and it will remain for historians of the 21st century to unravel the complexities of an extremely turbulent period, providing the clarity that only comes with hindsight. The experiences of American sisters and nuns during recent years are complex, not fully recorded, largely unreported, and still unfolding. Consequently, this last chapter of sister-history must of necessity be limited to the presentation of known facts with brief commentary on the background of an era marked by unprecedented change. The central events of the era impacting sisters and nuns were the Second Vatican Council and the precipitous rise of secularism and materialism.

Impact of Vatican II

Winds of change emanating from Vatican II were of hurricane force. The council undertook to reshape the Roman Catholic Church molded by the Council of Trent 400 years earlier — an undertaking of monumental proportions. While altering none of the fundamental dogmas or tenets of the Catholic faith, the council introduced new concepts of how the Catholic community should function in the modern world.[1] It was a pastoral rather than a doctrinal council, one conciliatory to modern views. Ecumenism, religious freedom, greater participation by the laity in liturgy and the life of the Church, emphasis on scripture study, a much greater status for the Gospel proclamation in the Mass, public worship as a community rather than as an individual function, and reestablishment of the ancient office of permanent deacon were just some of the new thrusts. This council was on a par with the Councils of Nicaea and Trent in historic dimension, one destined to influence the shape of Catholicity for centuries to come. The future shape intended by the Holy Spirit was difficult for most Catholics to discern. Like the Councils of Nicaea and Trent, Vatican II's proclamations initially found mixed reactions. For some the restoration of biblical and historical perspective was a liberating and exhilarating experience. For others, the experience was confusion, misunderstanding, and controversy — even turmoil.

Open dissent by bishops expressing divergent views, and leaks of drafts being rejected by the pope and returned for reworking, were highly publicized, creating a new sense in the Catholic world — a feeling that Church teachings were not necessarily the immutable verities accepted in the past. They could be questioned. Adding to the ferment, American bishops and priests lacked unanimity on interpretations of conciliar documents. The Catholic press debated sensitive subjects such as the parameters of papal infallibility, the limits of Vatican authority, academic freedom for professors in Catholic universities, and priestly celibacy.

Pope Paul VI's encyclical *Humanae Vitae* in 1968, dealing with the morality of artificial birth control, created a storm. Theologians and the clergy contested the pope and some priests defied their bishops on this issue.[2] Liturgical excesses by *avant garde* priests, such as allowing rock bands and dancers at Mass, priests dressed as clowns for children's Masses and other unauthorized liberties, shocked the majority of Catholics. Clashes between liberal and conservative elements within the Church were often abrasive and acrimonious. Contention over these and other issues carried over into women's religious communities, creating liberal and conservative factions.

Much like the Bible itself, conciliar documents and the later postconciliar implementing documents were so voluminous and comprehensive that they seemed to contain something for every school of thought, and were therefore subject to selective interpretation. Every faction with an agenda for change could isolate some portion of the documents to justify its position. If lacking an authoritative extract, it could always invoke the "spirit of Vatican II." Voices sounded on every side proclaiming exclusive understanding of the true meaning of the council. Secular presses issued streams of commentary and interpretations, adding to the cacophony. Some Catholic theologians hampered orderly and careful implementation of *aggiornamento* by their sometimes revolutionary interpretations of conciliar documents. As a result of these and other factors, the Catholic Church in the United States experienced convulsive turmoil and internal conflicts, inevitably impacting women religious communities.

A number of conciliar and postconciliar documents were directed to sisters and nuns. The unprecedented outpouring of official decrees on women religious included: *Perfectae Caritatis* (Decree on the Up-To-Date Renewal of Religious Life, 1965), *Ecclesiae Sanctae* (Norms for Implementing the Decree: On the Up-To-Date Renewal of Religious Life, 1966), *Renovationis Causam* (Instruction on the Renewal of Religious Life, 1969), *Venite Seorsum* (Instruction on the Contemplative Life and on the Enclosure of Nuns, 1969), *Evangelica Testificatio* (Apostolic Exhortation on the Renewal of Religious Life, 1971), *Mos Virgines Consecrandi* (Introduction to the Rite of Consecration to a Life of Virginity, 1970), *Quitte Ton Pays* (Religious Obliged to Assist Aged or Sick Parents, 1976) and *Mutuae Relationes* (Directives for Mutual Relations Between Bishops and Religious in the Church, 1978). While unintended, this plethora of official documents created considerable confusion, casting a cloud over long established practices, understandings, and norms within religious communities.

One requirement of *Ecclesiae Sanctae* (1966) was that each community convene a general chapter within two and no more than three years for the purpose of revising its constitution, reforming the structures of religious life. Over the following several years, sisters and nuns in hundreds of communities seeking to comprehend and implement the documents conducted thousands of chapter, leadership, committee, subcommittee, task force, study group, focus group, workshop, and other meetings. Reshaping the structures of religious life demanded arduous work. Collegiality in community governance required trial to determine its most workable forms; ministry needed review to see if it met the mandated "preferential option for the poor;" and the call to "peace and justice" ministry needed examination to determine its implications. Community custom books needed revision to eliminate rigid, detailed, and outdated prescriptions for personal conduct and spiritual exercises, or elimination altogether. Modernizing habits remained unfinished business. More importantly, a call was sounded to recapture the original charisms of founders or foundresses.

Questionnaires to the memberships abounded.[3] The LCWR issued bulletins with updates. Individual sisters wrote papers and books on the meaning of *aggiornamento*. Catholic presses poured out articles and books by priests, scholars, and theologians. Psychiatrists and sociologists added their analyses. Factions formed within communities, each claiming particular understanding of how the community should be reformed. In the midst of reappraisal with its tension and confusion, tens of thousands of individual women religious began to question the meaning and value of religious life — concepts that had always been taken for granted.

Disparity of speed and degree of change was widespread, some communities moving aggressively to implement what they perceived to be the required changes, while others moved cautiously with measured introduction of minimal changes. This often created tensions among community members; some unhappy with the radical changes and others displeased with the slow pace of renewal. Priests in supervisory and advisory capacities relative to women religious communities varied in their interpretations of conciliar documents, some directing or advising radical changes and others promoting caution. *Aggiornamento* was a stressful process. So much change in so short a period presented challenges never before encountered.

Many priests ordained in the 1960's and 1970's were given the impression that the Church was close to relaxing celibacy and allowing marriage, raising unrealistic false expectations. The emphasis that conciliar documents placed on "the people of God" and lay participation in the life of the Church created a perception among some of the clergy that their status as ordained ministers of God was being downgraded, creating a morale problem. Some priests were unsettled by parish councils, finance committees, lectors reading scripture from the pulpit, and eucharistic ministers distributing communion, and the loss of the exclusive nature of traditional priestly functions. Still others were exuberant about *aggiornamento* and sought to push change to extreme limits. Turmoil among the clergy only added to the confusion and intensified the questioning of religious life by sisters and nuns.

Thousands of priests either sought proper dispensation from their vows as provided by canon law in order to marry or simply walked away from their parishes and religious communities. In one four-year period alone, 1966 to 1969, some 3,400 priests departed. Only the huge number of seminarians in 1966, many of whom also left, kept priest-population from plummeting. Over the 25-year span, the total number of priests only dropped from 58,632 to 53,088. But by 1990 their average age had mounted to unprecedented levels. By 1984, 241 seminaries had closed. In 1990, there were only 6,482 seminarians studying for the priesthood as compared to 48,992 in 1965 — *an 86.8 percent reduction*. In 1990, a drastic numerical decline of the clergy lay just ahead — a looming crisis.

Thus, Vatican II's winds of change initially created a mixture of joyful acceptance, confusion, controversy, and turmoil; a not altogether surprising development considering that the council mandated a different Roman Catholic Church for the upcoming centuries. In the short term, Catholicity suffered. However, total adjustment to change in the short span of 25 years was an unrealistic expectation.

Impact of Secular Society

While it is a historical accident that the United States experienced cultural wars simultaneously with Vatican II and its aftermath, social turmoil nonetheless exacerbated the situation for the Roman Catholic Church — and women religious. Between 1966 and 1990, the speed of change in American society's perceptions of moral values was unprecedented.

The assassinations of President John F. Kennedy and Dr. Martin Luther King, civil rights marches and demonstrations, college students' disruption of campuses, the National Guard shooting of students at Kent State University, anti-war demonstrations and draft evasion, anti-nuclear protests, political strife and activist rallies combined to intensify political and cultural conflicts. "Rights" became the rallying cry for minorities, women, the handicapped, the criminally accused, consumers, refugees, students, homosexuals, the elderly, mental patients, environmentalists, and other special interest groups. Without passing judgment on the relative merits of each rights movement, it is clear that they polarized the public. Each movement engendered its own highly vocal, radical advocacy group.

A side effect of rights activism was an enhanced emphasis on personal independence and the individual's right to freedom from authority. An anti-establishment mentality took hold, with the popular media promoting personal fulfillment and rejection of authority. Catholics influenced by this attitude felt free to question Church teaching; individuals could choose the pastor and teachings that pleased, rejecting those that did not — "cafeteria" Catholics. Women religious were as exposed as the general public to the "do your own thing" culture.

Movements for women's rights are as old as the Republic. Women's suffrage was a continuing movement until passage of the Nineteenth Amendment. Thereafter, women's aspirations looked to the economic and social spheres. The term "feminist movement" conveyed different shades of meaning, including sensitivity to discrimination and activist demands for equality with men in every aspect of life. Among some Catholic women, it included ordination to the priesthood, which many Protestant churches adopted.[4] As the era progressed, the ordination of women found increasing support among women religious, adding to ferment within communities.[5]

With the assimilation process completed for the millions of Catholic descendants of the immigrant waves of the late 19th and early 20th centuries, ethnic traditions faded, including those that fostered large families, piety, and vocations. The melting pot was a reality that weakened a prime source of vocations. Unlike the earlier Irish, German, Polish, Italian, and other ethnic immigrant groups, the millions of Catholic Hispanics that immigrated during these years came without a strong tradition of vocations to religious life. However, their fidelity to the Catholic Church remains a strong vocation potential for the future.[6]

Governmental assumption of responsibility for social services accelerated during the 1930's under President Franklin Roosevelt and expanded rapidly thereafter. Welfare, Social Security, Medicare and Medicaid, Aid to Families with Dependent Children, unemployment benefits, food stamps, Workman's Compensation for job-related injuries, and other federal and state programs sought to meet needs formerly addressed by the private sector and charitable organizations such as communities of women religious. Nonetheless, needs calling for their apostolic action remained, especially among children of separated parents, deserted wives, battered women, sick old people, homeless street people, illegal immigrants, and the poor. Unfortunately, massive governmental programs tended to dim the importance of apostolates to meet those needs, impairing potential vocations.

Despite the doleful effects of these events and movements, the most damaging cultural changes for religious life were the rise of *secularism* and *materialism.*[7]

Since the moral bulwark of mainline Protestant churches had almost collapsed and the Catholic hierarchy had lost much of its influence over the Catholic population, there was no effective opposition to secularist trends. Banning prayer in public schools and tax-supported institutions was just one aspect of how secularists used separation of church and state to further their anti-religious agenda.[8] Inaugurated by the birth control pill and culminating in the Supreme Court's legalization of abortion on demand (*Roe vs. Wade*, 1972), the country acquiesced in the new morality: a development termed the "sexual revolution." New interpretations of the First Amendment triggered an explosion of pornography and explicit sex in the media. A rising tide of crime, venereal disease, addiction to drugs, child sexual abuse, and the deadly AIDS virus failed to deter morally questionable lifestyles.[9] First early calls sounded for legalized euthanasia. Almost without realizing it, the general public acquiesced in the shift to secular relativism with its attendant social decomposition.

Americans have always sought to improve their economic status, but this era witnessed a phenomenal increase of two-income families working for the "better life" rather than from necessity. Millions of couples avidly pursued more income in order to afford a better house, private schools for their one or more children, an investment portfolio, a vacation home, travel, two or more automobiles, fashionable clothing, and other luxuries. Other less economically favored couples worked to keep up with inflation. An explosion in the use of credit cards and second mortgages on homes fostered a "buy now - pay later" culture that plunged millions into debt, often beyond their ability to service. Simultaneously, financial support for churches, Catholic and Protestant, fell to new lows. Advertising and television kept the "upward mobility" and "perpetual youth" dreams ever before the public. The less privileged, who could not obtain the "good life" and enticing "things" promised in an age of relative prosperity, were confused and frustrated. Youths from poor and single-parent homes became psychological victims of consumerism, one of the many causes of crime and drug abuse. Materialism perverted and pervaded the American scene.

The so-called "devotional Church" that had emerged in the mid-19th century in the United States had provided spiritual comfort to millions, including the hordes of Catholic immigrants. Devotional life was intertwined with social life; an integral aspect of the Catholic neighborhood, centered around the parish and parochial school. Following the end of World War II, the flight of the large Catholic middle class to the suburbs effectively sapped the vitality of that way of life. Traditional devotional practices faded; even regular attendance at Sunday Mass declined, especially after the upheavals generated by Vatican II and the onslaughts of social turmoil. Council emphasis on the "people of God" as partners in promoting salvation created a sudden shift of perceived responsibility for instilling religious values in children, and seemed to relieve the clergy and religious of much of that burden. However, the majority of Catholic parents were not trained or psychologically prepared for that responsibility so soon. Consequently, with the breakdown of the devotional Church and family piety, the upcoming generation was less disposed to encouraging a religious vocation.

In probing for a descriptive term for the emerging new secularist and materialistic concepts and public policies, serious writers began using the phrase "post-Christian Age" with increasing frequency. Secularism is anti-religious by definition — rampant materialism deadens the senses to spirituality. With those forces in ascendancy, the American milieu was not supportive of religious life or conducive to fresh vocations.

Drought

The confluence of the initial reactions to Vatican II and the impact of a fast changing secularist society took its toll. The dual forces were almost impossible to accommodate simultaneously, resulting in a precipitous decline in sister-population. Table XII provides some statistics of the downward spiral.

Each decade of American history saw an increase in the number of women religious until the mid 1960's. During the 1950's and early 1960's, a running flood of vocations combined with increased longevity propelled sister-population to new heights. In 1965, they numbered 209,000. Thereafter membership totals plunged as thousands of sisters and nuns sought dispensation from their vows while fresh vocations almost disappeared. Over the 25-year span, total sister-population decreased by 102,000 members — *a shocking 48.8 percent loss*. Whereas in 1965 there were some 11,000 women in formation (postulants, novices, and those in juniorate programs), by 1990 the total had dropped to around 2,200,[10] hardly sufficient to sustain a membership being depleted by departures and deaths.

The high rate of vocations that had characterized women religious orders and congregations up to the early 1960's fell off at an alarming rate; simul-

Sister-Population — 1990

Order	1990 Membership	Change (1965-1990)
Franciscans (69 congregations)	19,346	-17,459
Dominicans	9,339	-8,877
Sisters of St. Joseph (all branches)	8,869	-8,192
Sisters of Mercy (all branches)	7,633	-7,153
Mother Seton's Daughters (six congregations)	5,385	-5,028
School Sisters of Notre Dame	4,056	-3,001
Benedictines (all branches)	4,377	-3,488
Sisters, Servants of the Immaculate Heart of Mary (three branches)	3,376	-1,967
Ursulines (all branches)	2,042	-1,854
Sisters of Notre Dame de Namur	1,691	-1,738
Carmelites (all branches)	1,539	-634
Sisters of Charity of the Blessed Virgin Mary	1,247	-1,329
Sisters of Charity of Montreal	1,025	-949
Sisters of the Presentation of the Blessed Virgin Mary	1,071	-839
Sisters of the Holy Family of Narareth	928	-752
Maryknoll Sisters of St. Dominic	847	-860
Sisters of the Congregation of the Holy Cross	839	-878
Sisters of Providence of Saint Mary-of-the-Woods	834	-803
Sisters of the Good Shepherd	762	-482
Sisters of the Holy Names of Jesus and Mary	722	-483
Society of the Sacred Heart	665	-446
Sisters of Christian Charity	589	-588
Adorers of the Blood of Christ	576	-508
Sisters of Loretto at the Foot of the Cross	555	-655
Poor Clares and Order of St. Clare	524	-134

Table XII

taneously sisters sought dispensation from their vows by the thousands.[11] Community survival became a dreaded subject seldom discussed openly.

Published statistics on sister aging and insurance industry underwriting tables allow a reasonably accurate forecast of sister-population for the near term. Overall, the 1990 median age of all sisters and nuns was 65.[12] Underwriting tables indicate that half of the 111,000 women religious will be dead by 2009, leaving around 55,000 of the 1990 women religious still alive, but with over half of them at advanced ages. Given currently established trends, new vocations will be able to offset only a small portion of the losses. Hence, the nadir of sister-population in less than two decades could well find fewer than 50,000 *active* women religious in the United States — a projected fallback of sister-population to the early 1900's level.

By 1986 the situation had become so desperate[13] that the hierarchy instituted an annual collection to provide for the care of aged women religious whose communities lacked adequate resources. Funds are disbursed on a priority of needs basis. The wide publicity given needy aging women religious created something of a "dying institution" image that tended to repel vocations. The unfolding situation triggered a vast number of articles, books, dissertations, and seminars seeking to analyze, provide solutions, and otherwise address the central issues of religious life.[14]

Establishment of new orders did not materially alter the picture. This era witnessed the fewest of any 25-year period in American history — only 17 fresh foundations; three of these did not last and the balance remained small. Yesterday's dependable sources, Canada, Italy, and Ireland, only sent one new order each. India sent three, an indication of the shift of religious vitality from the industrialized West to the emerging Third World. Clearly, religious orders in the United States could no longer rely on foreign sources for personnel.

Catholic education, so long an overwhelming need, the seed bed of vocations and the glue of American Catholicism, suffered tremendous harm in the 1970's and 1980's. Whether it was due to a drastic decrease in availability of sister-teachers or pressing economic reasons, the result was the same — parochial schools closed by the thousands.

In 1964, Mary Perkins Ryan, an activist in the liturgical movement, published *Are Parochial Schools the Answer? Catholic Education in Light of the Council.*[15] This book presented a number of well elucidated arguments for dismantling Catholic schools. Essentially she maintained that only a portion of Catholic children could attend, that Christian formation of the whole Catholic community was being neglected in favor of the schools, that public schools needed the influence of Catholic students, that ecumenism was being retarded by a narrow view of religious formation, and that the probability of receiving public funds for an ever more expensive complex of schools was not likely. This book received wide readership in Catholic clerical, hierarchical, and educational circles, creating something of a furor. A number of bishops and pastors concurred in the findings, using them as rationale for closing parochial schools as the availability of sisters declined. It was probably not so much the book as its timing in the ferment following Vatican II that created havoc. During the next 26 years a total of 3,929 Catholic elementary schools closed. Tuition soared and lay principals and teachers predominated in those remaining in operation. The number of students *decreased by 2.58 million.* High schools suffered similar losses in keeping with the trend, dropping from 2,465 to 1,379 schools, and 464,852 fewer students. An unfortunate consequence was that a high proportion of the shrinkage of students in Catholic schools came from the poor and working class; inner city schools closing while those in the suburbs serving the middle and upper classes fared somewhat better.

Even Catholic colleges closed. Half, 36 of 72, of the sister-operated women's colleges shut down during this era. As available personnel decreased, costs increased and secular institutions that proliferated following World War II began to emphasize more economic and technically oriented subjects, Catholic liberal arts colleges seemed somewhat less attractive and viable. Study of the humanities gave way to emphasis on the sciences and job-preparation.

Reasons for sisters leaving parochial schools in such large numbers are varied and interwoven with their reasons for leaving religious life. After more than 75 years of struggles for higher education of sister-teachers, communities that had recently become highly successful in enabling their members to earn bachelor and graduate degrees, now witnessed thousands abandon teaching. One factor for leaving the classroom was the higher priority placed on the "preferential option for the poor" and "peace and justice" ministries. Moreover, under revised constitutions and community rules, individual sisters now felt freer to practice ministries more in keeping with their own career desires. Also, there was a perception that the laity was fully capable of handling this function and that the time for change had arrived. Now the laity could step up to the challenge of Catholic primary education. While this attitude was well grounded, the sudden departures of sister-teachers denied a proper transition period covering several decades.

What happened in education followed a similar scenario in the health care profession. Even though few sister-operated hospitals closed, sister-nurses became a rare sight. A common practice was for the operating community to retain ownership with a lay board of trustees. This arrangement qualified the hospitals for federal funds, while retaining a resource for aging sick sisters and a source of revenue for the community. Sometimes, there was little to distinguish a Catholic hospital from a public one — another loss of a "witness" that had stimulated vocations in the past. Numerical losses also occurred among the missionary communities. The peak number of 4,105 sister-missionaries of 1968 fell to 2,345. Latin America and Africa remained the prime locations for their activities. The number of sisters on Indian reservations dwindled, as it did in a host of charitable apostolates.

Losses by contemplative communities were less severe — 24 percent shrinkage versus 49 percent for apostolic communities — and while contemplatives represented less than 3 percent of sister-population, they claimed some 15 percent of all women religious in formation in 1990. Here too, patterns changed with less austere lifestyles and greater contact by nuns with the laity. Traditional ministries, although impaired by the reduced number of sisters, did not disappear. Many groups continued living in convents, performing established ministries, wearing habits, and practicing long-standing devotional exercises. Despite their numerical losses, sisters are still teaching in parochial schools and academies, operating hospitals and colleges, caring for the aged poor and poor with incurable cancer, operating retreat centers, visiting homes, helping troubled women, and going to foreign missions. A widening of the spectrum of lifestyles and ministries characterized the era.

Religious garb, the habit, underwent a transformation after 1965. Initially, most communities adopted modified habits, discarding the ancient headdress and substituting more practical dresses cut along modern lines. Then, numerous communities went entirely to secular dress. An unusual sight at large convents was older sisters still in traditional habits, younger ones in modified habits, and still others in secular clothing with perhaps a veil or religious symbol about the neck. By 1990, the majority of women religious were in secular clothing with a sizeable minority in modified habits. A small minority clung to the traditional habit, perhaps slightly modified. It was clear

Sister Dorothy Kazel, Ursuline Nuns of Cleveland, gave her life in the service of the Church and the people of El Salvador on December 2, 1980.

Ursuline Nuns, Cleveland, Ohio

Sister Joan Sawyer, killed with seven prisoners at Lurigancho Prison, Lima, Peru on December 14, 1983.
Courtesy Missionary Sisters of St. Columban

that the time had arrived for modernizing habits, something encouraged by the Vatican. Rationale for total adoption of secular dress was based on the ideas of being "with and of the People of God," enhancing ministry effectiveness, and removing an obstacle to employment in academia and other professions. There was also a feeling that wearing a "uniform" detracted from the individualism of sisters and their personality development. The apparent negative result has been a reduction of "witness," a symbol of dedication so critical during most of American history in attracting vocations and bolstering Catholic pride.

Another change was the downgrading of communal living, manifested by the breakup of large convents as sisters moved into apartments and ordinary houses, usually in pairs and small groups. As their numbers dwindled, fewer sisters per school and new ministries involving individual sisters forced their dispersion. Consequently, thousands of convents that had traditionally housed a half dozen or so women religious devoted to one school or ministry closed. Communal devotions, life, and attendant companionship suffered.

Sister Carla Piette, MM; Sister Maura Clarke, MM; Sister Ita Ford, MM.

Courtesy Maryknoll Archives, Maryknoll, New York

However, some women religious deemed this an improvement that allowed for individual personality development and intellectual growth.

Amidst all these changes, one thing that remained was the dedication and love of women religious, even in the face of great danger. In August, 1980, while traveling to an isolated mission station in El Salvador, Maryknoll Sister Carla Piette drowned in a flash flood after saving her companion, Sister Ita Ford. Later that year, in December, Ursuline Sister Dorothy Kazel, Maryknoll Sisters Ita Ford and Maura Clarke, and lay missionary Jean Donovan suffered martyrdom, victims of a death squad that first brutalized then killed and buried them in a shallow roadside grave.[16] Although evidence points to governmental agents, those responsible for the killings have never been apprehended or punished. On December 14, 1983, Irish-born Sister Joan Sawyer of the Missionary Sisters of St. Columban (2880) in Chicago and Boston, was shot dead by police in Lima, Peru, when taken hostage by a group of prisoners. Despite the fact that safe passage had been guaranteed the prisoners and the hostages included Sister Joan, three

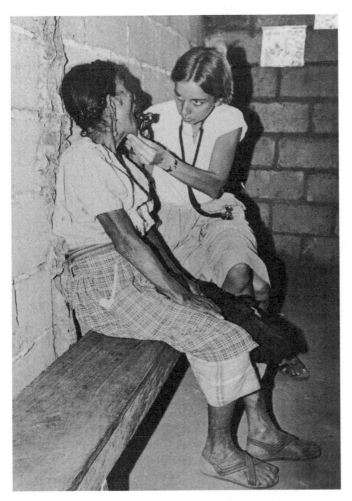

Sister Mary Lou Daoust, MM, M.D., Catarina, Guatemala, 1984.

Courtesy Maryknoll Archives, Maryknoll, New York

Marist sisters, and several social workers, police fired indiscriminately at the group as they left Lurigancho Prison in an ambulance. No official was ever convicted or punished.

United States foreign policy during these years supported Latin American governments against insurgents, despite the fact that this term was often applied to ordinary peasants and those who ministered to them. The State Department only exerted token pressure for justice in El Salvador and Peru, despite American public outrage. This United States official posture served to endanger other missionaries. Nonetheless, in El Salvador, Nicaragua, Honduras, Guatemala, and Peru, American sisters have elected to remain with the people like many of their brother missionaries, despite constant danger from terrorists who seemingly assassinate church workers, especially missionaries, as a matter of policy.[17] In several areas of Africa, danger has threatened missionaries. Total dedication by women religious to the work of Jesus Christ regardless of perils is a continuing legacy.

Simultaneously, sisters were entering new fields of ministry, reflecting in part the opening up of new areas of endeavor for women. Sisters became diocesan chancellors, judges on canonical marriage tribunals, canon lawyers, hospital chaplains, theologians, pastoral assistants, parish administrators, and professors in seminaries. They became leaders in the sanctuary movement for refugees and supporters of migrant workers and the disadvantaged in inner cities. Sisters became diocesan and parish staff members, marriage counselors, media activists, and clinical psychologists. Numerous new charitable works included homes for battered women, half-way houses for women released from prison, inner-city missions, help for AIDS patients, and work among the poor of Appalachia. Sisters sat on the boards of directors of banks and corporations, were elected to state legislatures and were active artists, authors, historians, and poets. Mother Angelica, a Poor Clare nun and foundress of Our Lady of the Angels Monastery in Birmingham, Alabama, parlayed her faith and entrepreneurial ability to inaugurate a television station, EWTN, that in just a few years developed the largest audience of any Catholic television station in the world. In 1971, Mother Teresa of Calcutta sent her **Missionaries of Charity (MC-2710)** to make their American foundation.[18] Her sisters work especially with AIDS patients in their ministries. Women religious

Mother Teresa.

OSV

continue to probe every aspect of social needs that might call for their ministry.

In the early 1980's, a religious revival began to take hold among the laity, stimulated by renewal movements such as Cursillo, and programs such as Renew and Marriage Encounter. Small charismatic groups formed to invoke the Holy Spirit. Papal visits by Pope John Paul II to the United States enhanced Catholic interest and involvement. Group pilgrimages to Fatima in Portugal, Medjugorje in Yugoslavia, Lourdes in France, and Guadalupe in Mexico City, plus shrines in the United States, such as the Basilica of the Immaculate Conception in Washington, served to gradually revitalize devotional life. Membership exploded in secular Franciscan, Carmelite, and other order-related groups. As intended by Vatican II, the laity became ever more involved in the life of the Church, exemplified by the offices of eucharistic minister, lector, and cantor. The laity assumed much greater responsibility for parish functions and leadership in promoting devotional activities. It appeared that the *aggiornamento* pendulum had reached its apex and was returning to middle ground, seeking to blend the best of the new and old. In 1990, despite the hindrances of secular society, the "spirit of Vatican II" was beginning to take hold among the "people of God."

Final Words

We have traveled the road of American history with hundreds of thousands of sisters and nuns. Along the way, the mystery and magnificence of religious life with its demands for lifelong commitment and ministry have become clearer in our questioning minds. This saga has presented brief looks at hundreds of saintly women and glimpses of hundreds more while passing over many thousands; all worthy of more detailed and deliberate examination. Foundresses, leaders, and their companions have faced and overcome challenge after challenge with courage, determination, perseverance, love, and piety. Their contributions to the Catholic Church, for the salvation of souls and to the welfare of all Americans have been enormous, enhancing the lives of many millions. Most Catholics and practically all non-Catholics are unaware of these facts.

Pessimism engendered in the current era about the future of American sisters and nuns belies that past history. Undeniably, religious orders have life cycles[19] which may cover a few years or many decades. Institutions begun by women religious in the United States only encountered serious setbacks in the late 1960's, after an exceptionally long-running success story. This is a new and puzzling time whose challenges are patently evident — as in the past, the proper responses will be forthcoming, if not in the short term, most certainly in the long one. Fresh blossoms will sprout to replace those that wither.

The lessons of history teach that foundresses and leaders, unknown to themselves or others, arise and answer God's summons in time of need. We will see other Frances Dickensons, Elizabeth Ann Setons, Alice Lalors, Maria Sansburys, Catherine Spaldings, Rose Philippine Duchesnes, Elizabeth Langes, Eliza Gillespies, Anne Therese Guérins, Henriette Delilles, Mary Francis Clarks, Ann Ross's, Catherine Moes, Colette Hilberts, Frances Cabrinis, Ninetta Ionatas, Rose Hawthorne Lathrops, Katharine Drexels, and even teenage Mary O'Neils, Teresa Barrys, and Agnes Hazottes. They are in the wings and will appear in due time.

Already, signs of consensus are starting to appear concerning formulas for revival. These include such items as the necessity for clear community identity and self-image, badly blurred in recent times. The efficacy of homogeneous lifestyles and ministry within communities is being reexamined. There is a clear niche for each type community in the apostolic spectrum; room for every kind of ministry and lifestyle. Calls are sounding for clearer focus on the spiritual nature of religious life, as opposed to the social service aspect. Studies of vocational stimulants emphasize the importance of one-on-one invitations, something that sisters have always been masterful in doing, and will do again. Fresh recognition of how important communal life is to many women religious and to aspirants is causing some communities to reappraise their practices in this regard. Melding the best of the past with the best of the new is an ongoing process, far from complete.

Historians of the 21st century will probably marvel at how quickly American women religious communities can rejuvenate. Catholics have always taken pride in how their sisters and nuns contributed to every aspect of need, offering their prayers and works to help and uplift the poor, to convert and save souls, to aid peoples in foreign lands, to instill moral values in youth, and to strengthen the Roman Catholic Church. They will still do so as American history continues unfolding.

The long range plans of the Holy Spirit include American sisters and nuns.

Endnotes

1. In its entire 2,000-year history, under the guidance of the Holy Spirit, the Catholic Church has never reversed or changed a fundamental dogma of faith or moral tenet. However, excesses, faults, crimes, lax spirituality, and un-Christian conduct have sometimes characterized its leaders. The distinction between the two aspects of the Roman Catholic Church, divine and human, is often ignored or lost on critics.

2. Archbishop Patrick O'Boyle of Washington, D.C. had to discipline priests who openly dissented with *Humanae Vitae,* revoking the authority of 51 of them to function. Of these, 25 abandoned the priesthood.
3. In 1967, the Conference of Major Superiors of Women (CMSW) issued a questionnaire answered by 139,000 individual sisters and community superiors. This was repeated in 1980 by the LCWR. Among other topics, the surveys sought to ascertain the reasons women religious listed for giving up their vocations. Answers included: no vocation, no personal fulfillment, prefers marriage, dissatisfaction with community life, new appreciation for lay role, and psychological disturbance. See Sr. Marie Augusta Neal, SNDN, *Catholic Sisters in Transition: From the 1960s to the 1980s* (Wilmington, DE: Michael Glazier, Inc., 1984), pp. 10, 22.
4. The call for women's ordination first burst upon the American Catholic consciousness on October 7, 1979, when Sister M. Theresa Kane, RSM, delivered the welcoming address to Pope John Paul II at the Shrine of the Immaculate Conception in Washington, D.C., an event covered by national television and watched by millions of Catholics. As President of the LCWR, she presumed to represent all American women religious. In this address, she forcefully called for women's opportunity to explore the full extent of ministry.
5. A phenomenon among some strongly feminist women religious was their leaving their communities to form "non-canonical" groups to practice ministry without having to be concerned necessarily with the attitudes of particular bishops. The most famous case concerns the Sisters of the Immaculate Heart of Mary (IHM-2180). This congregation came from Spain in 1871 and is not connected to the American-founded "IHMs." In 1978, Cardinal Archbishop James F. McIntyre of Los Angles strenuously objected to this group's decision to discard religious garb, change their own ministry, eliminate fixed devotions, resume baptismal names, and other innovations. After Mother-Superior Humiliata (Anita Caspary) lost an appeal to Rome, she led some 400 members out of the community to form their own non-canonical organization. Members could marry, live independently, and choose ministry. Some 50 sisters complied with the cardinal's directives, perpetuating the community. This case attracted national attention, especially among women religious. See Marcelle Bernstein, *Nuns* (London, England: Collins, 1976) for a general discussion of the "non-canonical" phenomenon.
6. Immigrants from the Philippines (1,199,851) and Vietnam (470,031) arriving during these years were mostly Catholic. Numbers of today's vocations to the priesthood and sisterhood come from these new groups.
7. For definitions of secularism and materialism, see John A. Hardon, SJ, *Modern Catholic Dictionary* (New York, NY: Doubleday, 1980), pp. 496 and 341. Essentially, secularism is a philosophy that holds that human existence and destiny are fully explainable in terms of this world without reference to eternity and denigrates Christianity's code of human conduct. There are many shades of secularism, ranging from outright atheism to diluted Christianity, the latter being the most prevalent in the United States. Carried to its extreme, materialism holds

that all is matter, with no distinction between matter and spirit; the pleasures of the body and emotions are the main reasons for human existence. As used in this chapter, the term implies that all human problems can be solved by economics and possession of material things.

8. Throughout the 19th and well into the 20th centuries, Catholics opposed prayer in public schools because of Catholic children being forced to say Protestant prayers. However, the onset of rampant secularism in the 1950's and 1960's altered this outlook considerably.

9. Violent crime increased from 20.0 incidents per 100,000 people in 1965 to 73.2 incidents in 1990 (F.B.I.).

10. Sr. Eleace King, IHM, *CARA Formation Directory for Men and Women Religious 1993* (Washington, DC: CARA/Center for Applied Research in the Apostolate, Georgetown University, 1993), p. 2.

11. The year 1970 marked the peak of departures from religious life according to the Sacred Congregation of Religious in Rome.

12. Sr. Patricia Wittberg, SC, *Creating a Future for Religious Life: A Sociological Perspective* (New York: NY: Paulist Press, 1991), p. 82. Also see Elizabeth Kolmer, *Religious Women in the U.S.* (Wilmington, DE: Michael Glazier, 1984), pp. 41, 61. Also see Sr. Marie Augusta Neal, SNDN, pp. 18-19.

13. Sisters were not able to join the Social Security system until 1972, when most did. However, their low earnings and late enrollment entitled them to meager benefits. A side effect of the financial crisis was to drive some active sisters to the best paying jobs in order to provide community support regardless of their occupational desires or qualifications.

14. A sampling of those publications includes:

> Alice Lifton, "Structural Changes in U.S. Catholic Women's Orders After 1967: Placing Religious Innovation in Sociological Context," Ph.D. Diss. Columbia Univ., New York, NY, 1985.
>
> Diarmuid O'Murchu, MSC, *Religious Life: A Prophetic Vision* (Notre Dame, IN: Ave Maria Press, 1985).
>
> Gerald A. Arbuckle, *Out of Choice: Refounding Religious Congregations* (Mahwah, NJ: Paulist Press, 1988).
>
> Joan Chittister, *Women, Ministry and the Church* (Mahwah, NJ: The Paulist Press, 1983).
>
> Lawrence Cada, *Shaping the Coming Age of Religious Life* (New York, NY: Seabury Press, 1979).
>
> Mary Ellen Muckenhirn, "The Changing Sister," *Fides*, 1965.
>
> Mary Jo Leddy, *Renewing Religious Life: Beyond the Liberal Model* (Mystic, CT: Twenty-Third Publications, 1990).
>
> Patricia Ann Haire, "An Investigation of Psychological Differences Among Roman Catholic Sisters with Respect to Lifestyles, Years in Religious Service, and Degree of Commitment to Religious Life," United States International University, San Diego, CA. 1981.
>
> Patricia Loraine Watson, "Persistent Factors in Vocational Choice," Ph.D. Diss. Univ. of Detroit, , 1985.
>
> Pontifical Commission on Religious Life, "U.S. Religious Life and the Decline of Vocations," *Origins*, Dec., 1986.

David Nygren, CM, and Sr. Miriam Ukeritis, CSJ, "Future of Religious Orders in the United States," *Origins*, Sept. 24, 1992.

Robert J. McAllister, MD, Ph.D., *Living the Vows: The Emotional Conflicts of Celibate Religious* (San Francisco, CA: HarperCollins, 1986).

Sr. Carol Wagner, RDC, "Why Religious? Why Divine Compassion?" *Sisters Today*, Mar. 1991.

Sr. Kathleen M. Cooney, OSU, "Reasons for Staying in a Religious Congregation from the Viewpoint of Women Who Entered Between 1945 and 1975," Ph.D. Diss. Case Western Reserve Univ., Cleveland, OH. 1985.

Sr. Sandra Schneiders, IHM, *New Wine, New Wineskins* (Mahwah, NJ: Paulist Press, 1988).

Rev. David Nygren and Sr. Miriam Ukeritis, CSJ, "Future of Religious Orders in the United States," *Origins, Vol. 22. No. 15,* 1992.

15. Mary Perkins Ryan, *Are Parochial Schools the Answer? Catholic Education in the Light of the Council* (New York, NY: Holt, Rinehart and Winston, 1963).

16. Sister Dorothy Kazel, OSU, took the religious name of Sister Laurentine, in memory of an Ursuline nun who was guillotined during the Reign of Terror in France.

17. Michael J. Cypher, OSF, and James F. Carney, SJ, were slain in Honduras. Lay missionaries William Woods, Stanley Rother, John D. Troyer, Francis X. Holdenried and Christian Brother James Miller were all killed in Guatemala.

18. This order has accrued numerous American vocations. An amusing incident occurred in San Francisco when the sisters were making an establishment in that city. A bystander observing the sari-clad sisters moving into their new quarters asked one where she was from. In a distinct Southern accent, the sister replied, "I'm from West Virginia. Where y'all from?"

19. Raymond Hostie, a French Jesuit made a study of the life cycles of European male religious orders, clearly establishing cycles of foundation, vitality and growth, decline, death or revival. While he did not investigate women's religious orders, he maintained they have similar cycles. See Raymond Hostie, SJ, *The Life and Death of Religious Orders: A Psycho-sociological Approach* (Washington, DC: Center for Applied Research in the Apostolates, CARA, 1983).

APPENDIX A

Order Title Abbreviations

✠ — ✠

PRACTICALLY EVERY COMMUNITY has a set of initials that designates its title. Women religious normally affix these initials after their signatures. They are also used in most publications when naming a women religious. The average reader is frequently frustrated in not knowing which order those initials identify.

As displayed in the 1990 Official Catholic Directory, those initials, the order(s) they identify, and OCD number are:

ACJ	The Handmaids of the Sacred Heart of Jesus (1870)
AD	Sisters of the Lamb of God (2260)
AP	Nuns of the Perpetual Adoration of the Blessed Sacrament (3190)
APB	The Sisters Adorers of the Precious Blood (0110)
APG	Sisters of Perpetual Adoration (3195)
AR	Handmaids of Reparation of the Sacred Heart of Jesus (1880)
ASC	Adorers of the Blood of Christ (0100)
ASCJ	Apostles of the Sacred Heart of Jesus (0130)
ASSP	Angelic Sisters of St. Paul (0120)
BVM	Sisters of Charity of the Blessed Virgin Mary (0430)
CaCh	Carmelite Sisters of Charity (0340)
CarmelDCJ	Carmelite Sisters of the Divine Heart of Jesus (0360)
CBS	Congregation of Bon Secours (0270)
CC	Carmel Community (0310)
CCVI	Congregation of the Sisters of Charity of the Incarnate Word (0460)
	Congregation of the Sisters of Charity of the Incarnate Word, Houston, Texas (0470)
CCW	Carmelite Community of the Word (0315)
CDP	Sisters of Divine Providence (0990)
	The Sisters of Divine Providence of Kentucky (1000)
	Congregation of Divine Providence, San Antonio, Texas (1010)
CDS	Congregation of the Divine Spirit (1040)

CFMM	Minim Daughters of Mary Immaculate (2675)
CHF	Congregation of the Sisters of the Holy Faith (1940)
CHM	Congregation of the Humility of Mary (2100)
CHS	Community of the Holy Spirit (2020)
CIC	Sisters of the Immaculate Conception (2120)
CIJ	Congregation of the Infant Jesus (2230)
CJC	Poor Sisters of Jesus Crucified and the Sorrowful Mother (3240)
CLHC	Congregation of Our Lady, Help of the Clergy (3090)
CMS	Comboni Missionary Sisters (0690)
	Cashel Mercy Sisters (2515)
CMST	Missionary Carmelites of St. Teresa (0390)
CND	Sisters of the Congregation De Notre Dame (2980)
CP	Religious of the Passion of Jesus Christ (Passionist Nuns)(3170)
	Sisters of the Cross and Passion (3180)
CPPS	Sisters of the Precious Blood (Dayton, Ohio)(3260)
	Sisters of the Most Precious Blood (O'Fallon, MO)(3270)
CPS	Missionary Sisters of the Precious Blood (2850)
CR	Sisters of the Resurrection (3480)
CS	The Company of the Savior (0710)
CSA	Sisters of Charity of St. Augustine (0580)
	Congregation of the Sisters of St. Agnes (3710)
CSAC	Sisters of the Catholic Apostolate (Pallottine)(3140)
CSB	Congregation of St. Brigid (3735)
CSC	Congregation of the Sisters of the Holy Cross (1920)
	Sisters of Holy Cross (1930)
CSFN	Sisters of the Holy Family of Nazareth (1970)
CSJ or SSJ	Sisters of St. Joseph (3830)
	Sisters of St. Joseph of Carondelet (3840)
CSJ or SSJ	Sisters of St. Joseph of Chambery (3850)
	Sisters of St. Joseph of Lyons, France (3870)
	Sisters of St. Joseph of Medaille (3880)
CSJB	Sisters of St. John the Baptist (3820)
CSJP	Sisters of St. Joseph of Peace (3890)
CSR	Sisters of the Holy Redeemer (2000)
CSSF	Felician Sisters (1170)
CSSp	Sisters of the Holy Spirit (2030)
CST	Carmelite Sisters of St. Therese of the Infant Jesus (0380)
CVD	Sisters of Bethany (1170)
CVI	Congregation of the Incarnate Word and Blessed Sacrament (2190)
	Religious of the Incarnate Word (3449)
DC	Daughters of Charity of St. Vincent de Paul (0760)
	Daughters of the Cross (0770)
DCPB	Daughters of Charity of the Most Precious Blood (0740)
DHM	Daughters of the Heart of Mary (0810)
DHS	Daughters of the Holy Spirit (0820)
DM	Daughters of Mary of the Immaculate Conception (0860)
	Daughters of Our Lady of Mercy (0890)

DMJ	Daughters of Mary and Joseph (0880)
DSF	Daughters of St. Francis of Assisi (0920)
DSMP	Daughters of St. Mary of Providence (0940)
DW	Daughters of Wisdom (0960)
EFMS	Eucharistic Franciscan Missionary Sisters (1150)
FC	Daughters of the Cross of Liege (0780)
FCJ	Society of the Sisters, Faithful Companions of Jesus (4048)
FCSCJ	Daughters of Charity of the Sacred Heart of Jesus (0750)

Daughters of Our Lady of Mercy (c. 1942).
Courtesy Gonzaga University

FDC	Daughters of Divine Charity (0790)
FdCC	Canossian Daughters of Charity (0730)
FDNSC	Daughters of Our Lady of the Sacred Heart (0900)
FDP	Daughters of Divine Providence (0800)
FHIC	Franciscan Hospitaller Sisters of the Immaculate Conception (1270)
FHM	Franciscan Handmaids of the Most Pure Heart of Mary (1260)
FI	Daughters of Jesus (0840)
FJ	Congregation of the Daughters of Jesus (0830)

FMA	Daughters of Mary Help of Christians (0850)
FMDC	Franciscan Missionary Sisters of the Divine Child (1340)
FMI	Congregation of the Daughters of Mary Immaculate (0870)
	Franciscan Sisters of Mary Immaculate of the Third Order of St. Francis of Assisi (1500)
FMIJ	Franciscan Missionary Sisters of the Infant Jesus (1365)
FMM	The Franciscan Missionaries of Mary (1370)
FMSC	Franciscan Missionary Sisters of the Sacred Heart (1400)
FMSJ	Mill Hill Sisters (1410)
FSE	The Institute of the Franciscan Sisters of the Eucharist (1250)
FSJ	Religious Daughters of St. Joseph (0930)
FSM	Franciscan Sisters of Mary (1415)
FSP	Pious Society Daughters of St. Paul (0950)
	Franciscan Sisters of Peace (1425)
FSPA	Congregation of the Sisters of the Third Order of St. Francis of Perpetual Adoration (1780)
FSR	Franciscan Sisters of Ringwood (1420)
FSSE	Franciscan Sisters of St. Elizabeth (1460)
FSSJ	Franciscan Sisters of St. Joseph (1470)
	Franciscan Sisters of St. Joseph (1480)
GHMS	Home Mission Sisters of America (2080)
GNSH	Grey Nuns of the Sacred Heart (1840)
HCG	Hermanas Catequistas Guadalupanas (1900)
HHS	Society of Helpers (1890)
HJ	Hermanas Josefinas (1910)
HM	Sisters of the Humility of Mary (2110)
HMSS	Religious Sisters of the Apostolate of the Blessed Sacrament (3370)
HPB	Congregation of the Handmaids of the Precious Blood (1860)
HVM	Sisters Home Visitors of Mary (2090)
IBVM	Institute of the Blessed Virgin Mary (Loretto Sisters) (2370)
	Institute of the Blessed Virgin Mary (Loreto Sisters) (2380)
ICM	Missionary Sisters of the Immaculate Heart of Mary (2750)
IHM	Sisters, Servants of the Immaculate Heart of Mary (2150)
	Sisters, Servants of the Immaculate Heart of Mary (2160)
	Sisters, Servants of the Immaculate Heart of Mary (2170)
	Sisters of the Immaculate Heart of Mary (2180)
	The California Institute of the Sisters of the Most Holy and Immaculate Heart of the Blessed Virgin Mary (2930)
IJ	Sisters of the Infant Jesus (2240)
IWBS	Congregation of the Incarnate Word and Blessed Sacrament (2200)
IWBS	Sisters of the Incarnate Word and Blessed Sacrament (2205)
LCM	Sisters of the Little Company of Mary (2270)
LHC	Lovers of the Holy Cross Sisters(2390)
LMSC	Little Missionary Sisters of Charity (2290)
LSA	Little Sisters of the Assumption (2310)
LSIC	Little Servant Sisters of the Immaculate Conception (2300)
LSJ	Little Sisters of Jesus (2330)

LSJM	Little Sisters of Jesus and Mary (2331)
LSP	Little Sisters of the Poor (2340)
MC	Consolata Missionary Sisters (0720)
	Missionary Catechists of the Sacred Hearts of Jesus and Mary (2700)

Sister of St. Elizabeth (c. 1942).
Courtesy Gonzaga University

	Missionaries of Charity (2710)
	Poor Clare Missionary Sisters (2840)
MCDP	Missionary Catechists of Divine Providence, San Antonio, Texas (2690)
MD	Mothers of the Helpless (2920)
MHS	Sisters of the Most Holy Sacrament (2940)
MHSH	Mission Helpers of the Sacred Heart (2720)
MJMJ	Missionaries of Jesus, Mary and Joseph (2770)
MM	Maryknoll Sisters of St. Dominic (2470)
MMB	Mercedarian Missionaries of Berriz (2510)
MMM	Medical Missionaries of Mary (2480)
MOM	Missionary Sisters of Our Lady of Mercy (2830)
MPF	Religious Teachers Filippini (3430)

MPV	Religious Venerini Sisters (4180)
MS	Marian Sisters of the Diocese of Lincoln (2400)
MSBT	Missionary Servants of the Most Blessed Trinity (2790)
MSC	Congregation of the Marianites of Holy Cross (2410)
	Missionary Sisters of the Most Sacred Heart of Jesus of Hiltrup (2800)
	Missionary Sisters of the Sacred Heart of Jesus (Cabrini Sisters) (2860)
MSHR	Missionary Sisters of the Holy Rosary (2730)
MSJ	Medical Sisters of St. Joseph (2500)
MSMG	Missionary Sisters of Mother of God (2810)
MSOLA	Missionary Sisters of Our Lady of Africa (2820)
MSSA	Missionary Servants of St. Anthony (2890)
MSSCB	Missionary Sisters of St. Charles Borromeo (Scalabrini Sisters) (2900)
MSSp	Mission Sisters of the Holy Spirit (2740)
MSSS	Missionary Sisters of the Most Blessed Sacrament (2780)
NAU-OLC	North American Union Sisters of Our Lady of Charity (3070)
ND	Notre Dame Sisters (2960)
NDS	Congregation of Notre Dame De Sion (2950)
OBT	Sister Oblates to the Blessed Trinity (3020)
OCarm	Calsed Carmelites (0300)
	Carmelite Nuns of the Ancient Observance (0320)
	Carmelite Sisters for the Aged and Infirm (0330)
	Carmelite Sisters (Corpus Christi) (0350)
	Congregation of Our Lady of Mount Carmel (0400)
	Institute of the Sisters of Our Lady of Mount Carmel (0410)
OCD	Discalced Carmelite Nuns (0420)
	Carmelite Sisters of the Most Sacred Heart of Los Angeles (0370)
OCIST	Cistercian Nuns (0680)
OCSO	Cistercian Nuns of the Strict Observance (0670)
ODN	Company of Mary (0700)
OLM	Sisters of Charity of Our Lady of Mercy (0510)
OLS	Sisters of Our Lady of Sorrows (3120)
OLVM	Our Lady of Victory Missionary Sisters (3130)
OMO	Oblates of the Mother of Orphans (3035)
OP	Dominican Contemplative Nuns (1050)
	Dominican Contemplative Sisters (1060)
	Dominican Sisters (1070)
	Dominican Sisters of Bethany Congregation (1080)
OP	Marian Society of Dominican Catechists (1090)
	Dominican Sisters of Charity of the Presentation of the Blessed Virgin (1100)
	Dominican Sisters of the Roman Congregation (1120)
	Dominican Rural Missionaries (1130)
	Eucharistic Missionaries of St. Dominic (1140)
OSA	Augustinian Nuns of Contemplative Life (0160)
	Congregation of Augustinian Sisters Servants of Jesus and Mary (2145)
	Sisters of St. Rita (4010)
OSB	Benedictine Nuns of the Congregation of Solesmes (0170)

Benedictine Nuns of the Primitive Observance (0180)
Benedictine Sisters (0190)
Benedictine Sisters (Regina Pacis) (0200)
Missionary Benedictine Sisters (0210)
Congregation of the Benedictine Sisters of Perpetual Adoration
of Pontifical Jurisdiction (0220)

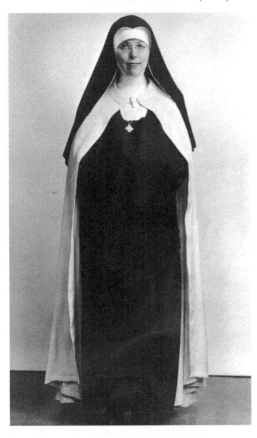

Professed, Corpus Christi Carmelite.
Courtesy Gonzaga University

Benedictine Sisters of Pontifical Jurisdiction (0230)
Benedictine Nuns (0233)
Olivetan Benedictine Sisters (0240)
Congregation of Jesus Crucified (2250)

OSBM	Sisters of the Order of St. Basil the Great (3730)
OSBS	Oblate Sisters of the Blessed Sacrament (3010)
OSC	Sisters of St. Clare (3770)
OSF	Franciscan Sisters of Allegany, New York (1180)
	The Franciscan Sisters of Baltimore (1200)
	Franciscan Sisters of Chicago (1210)

Franciscan Sisters of Christian Charity (1230)
Franciscan Sisters, Daughters of the Sacred Hearts
of Jesus and Mary (1240)
Franciscan Sisters of the Immaculate Conception (1280)
Franciscan Sisters of the Immaculate Conception and
St. Joseph for the Dying (1300)
Franciscan Sisters of Little Falls, Minnesota (1310)
Franciscan Missionary Sisters for Africa (1320)
Franciscan Missionary Sisters of the Immaculate Conception (1350)
Missionary Franciscan Sisters of the Immaculate Conception (1360)
Franciscan Missionaries of Our Lady (1380)
Franciscan Missionary Sisters of Our Lady of Sorrows (1390)
Franciscan Sisters of Our Lady of Perpetual Help (1430)
Franciscan Sisters of the Sacred Heart (1450)
Franciscan Sisters of St. Paul, MN (1485)
Sisters of the Third Franciscan Order (1490)
Sisters of St. Francis (1510)
Sisters of St. Francis of Christ the King (1520)
Sisters of St. Francis of the Congregation of Our Lady
of Lourdes, Sylvania, Ohio (1530)
Sisters of St. Francis, Clinton, Iowa (1540)
Sisters of St. Francis of the Holy Cross (1550)
Sisters of St. Francis of the Holy Eucharist (1560)
Sisters of St. Francis of the Holy Family (1570)
Sisters of St. Francis of the Immaculate Conception (1580)
Sisters of St. Francis of the Immaculate Heart of
Mary (Hankison, North Dakota) (1590)
Sisters of St. Francis of the Martyr St. George (1600)
Sisters of St. Francis of Millvale, Pennsylvania (1620)
Sisters of St. Francis of Penance and Christian Charity (1630)
Sisters of St. Francis of Perpetual Adoration (1640)
Sisters of St. Francis of Philadelphia (1650)
Sisters of Saint Francis of the Providence of God (1660)
Sisters of St. Francis of Savannah, MO (1670)
School Sisters of St. Francis (1680)
School Sisters of the Third Order of St. Francis (Pittsburgh, PA) (1690)
School Sisters of the Third Order of St. Francis (Panhandle, Texas) (1695
School Sisters of the Third Order of St. Francis (Bethlehem, PA) (1700)
The Sisters of St. Francis of Assisi (1705)
Congregation of the Third Order of St. Francis
of Mary Immaculate, Joliet, IL (1710)
Sisters of the Third Order Regular of St. Francis
of the Congregation of Our Lady of Lourdes (1720)
Congregation of the Sisters of the Third Order
of St. Francis Oldenburg, IN (1730)
Sisters of the Third Order of St. Francis of Penance
and of Charity (1760)

	The Sisters of the Third Order of St. Francis (East Peoria, Illinois) (1770)
	Sisters of St. Francis of the Third Order Regular (Williamsville, New York) (1800)
	Bernardine Sisters of the Third Order of St. Francis (1810)
	Hospital Sisters of the Third Order of St. Francis (1820)
	Congregation of the Servants of the Holy Child Jesus of the Third Order Regular of Saint Francis (1980)
OSFS	Oblate Sisters of St. Francis De Sales (3060)
OSHJ	Oblate Sisters of the Sacred Heart of Jesus (3050)
OSM	Mantellate Sisters, Servants of Mary of Blue Island (3570)
	Servants of Mary (3580)
	Servants of Mary (Servite Sisters) (3590)
OSP	Oblate Sisters of Providence (3040)
OSS	Religious of the Order of the Blessed Sacrament and of Our Lady (3490)
OSSR	Order of the Most Holy Redeemer (2010)
	Oblates of the Most Holy Redeemer (3030)
OSSS	The Brigittine Sisters (0280)
OSST	Sisters of the Most Holy Trinity (2060)
OSU	Ursuline Nuns (4110)
	Ursuline Nuns of the Congregation of Paris (4120)
	Ursuline Sisters of the Congregation of Tildonk, Belgium (4130)
	Ursuline Sisters of Belleville (4140)
	Irish Ursuline Union (4150)
PBVM	Presentation of the Blessed Virgin Mary Sisters (3280)
	Sisters of the Presentation of the BVM (3320)
	Union of the Sisters of the Presentation of the Blessed Virgin Mary (3330)
PCC or OSC	Order of St. Clare (3760)
PCJ	Sisters of the Poor Child Jesus (3220)
PCPA	Poor Clares of Perpetual Adoration (3210)
PDDM	Pious Disciples of the Divine Master (0980)
PFM	Little Franciscans of Mary (U.S.) (2280)
PHJC	Poor Handmaids of Jesus Christ (3230)
PM	Sisters of the Presentation of Mary (3310)
PSN	Poor Sisters of Nazareth (3242)
PSSF	The Little Sisters of the Holy Family (2320)
PSSJ	Poor Sisters of St. Joseph (3250)
PVMI	Parish Visitors of Mary Immaculate (3160)
RA	Religious of the Apostolate of the Sacred Heart of Jesus (3380)
	Religious of the Assumption (3390)
RC	Congregation of Our Lady of the Retreat in the Cenacle (3120)
RCD	Sisters of Our Lady of Christian Doctrine (3080)
RCE	Religious of Christian Education (3410)
RCM	Sisters of the Immaculate Conception (2130)
RDC	Sisters of the Divine Compassion (0970)
RE	Religious of the Eucharist (3420)

RGS-CGS	The Sisters of the Good Shepherd (1830)
RHSJ	Religious Hospitallers of Saint Joseph (3440)
RJM	Religious of Jesus and Mary (3450)
RMI	Claretian Missionary Sisters (0685)
	Religious of Mary Immaculate (3460)
RSC	Religious Sisters of Charity (3400)
RSCJ	Society of the Sacred Heart (4070)
RSHM	Religious of the Sacred Heart of Mary (3465)
RSM	Religious Sisters of Mercy of Alma, Michigan (2519)

Sisters of the Presentation of Mary (c. 1942).

Courtesy Gonzaga University

	Sisters of Mercy (2520)
	Sisters of Mercy of Ardagh and Clonmacnois (2523)
	Sisters of Mercy (2540)
	Sisters of Mercy (SLIGO) (2549)
	Sisters of Mercy (2550)
	Sisters of Mercy of the Americas (2575)
RSM-SM	Sisters of Mercy (2560)

RSR	Congregation of Our Lady of the Holy Rosary (3100)
SA	Franciscan Sisters of the Atonement (1190)
SAA	Sisters Auxiliaries of the Apostolate (0140)
SAC	Sisters of the Guardian Angel (1850)
	Pallottine Missionary Sisters - Queen of Apostles Province (3150)
SASV	Sisters of the Assumption (0150)
SBS	The Sisters of the Blessed Sacrament for Indians and Colored People (0260)
SC	Sisters of Charity of Cincinnati, Ohio (0440)
	Sisters of Charity of Seton Hill, Greensburg, Pennsylvania (0570)
	Sisters of Charity of St. Elizabeth, Convent Station (0590)
	Sisters of Charity of St. Vincent de Paul, Halifax (0640)
	Sisters of Charity of St. Vincent de Paul, of New York (0650)
SCC	Sisters of Christian Charity (0660)
SchP	Sisters of the Pious Schools (3200)
SCIC	Sisters of Charity of the Immaculate Conception of Ivrea (0450)
SCIF	Daughters of the Sacred Heart of Jesus (0910)
SCIM	Servants of the Immaculate Heart of Mary (3550)
SCL	Sisters of Charity of Leavenworth, Kansas (0480)
SCMC	Sisters of Charity of Our Lady, Mother of the Church (0530)
SCMM	Sisters of Charity of Our Lady, Mother of Mercy (0520)
	Medical Mission Sisters (2490)
SCN	Sisters of Charity of Nazareth (0500)
SCO	Sisters of Charity of Ottawa (0540)
SCQ	Sisters of Charity of Quebec (0560)
SCSC	Sisters of Mercy of the Holy Cross (2630)
SCSH	Sisters of Charity of St. Hyacinthe (0610)
SCSJA	Sisters of Charity of St. Joan Antida (0600)
SCSL	Sisters of Charity of St. Louis (0620)
SDR	Sisters of the Divine Redeemer (1020)
SDS	Sisters of the Divine Savior (1030)
SDSH	Sisters of the Society Devoted to the Sacred Heart (4050)
SDV	Vocationist Sisters (4210)
SFMA	Franciscan Missionary Sisters of Assisi (1330)
SFP	Franciscan Sisters of the Poor (1440)
SGM	Sisters of Charity of Montreal (0490)
SHCJ	Society of the Holy Child Jesus (4060)
SHF	Sisters of the Holy Family (1960)
SHJM	Sisters of the Sacred Hearts of Jesus and Mary (3680)
SHS	Sisters of the Holy Spirit (2040)
SHSp	Sisters of the Holy Spirit and Mary Immaculate (2050)
SIW	Sisters of the Incarnate Word and Blessed Sacrament (2210)
	Sisters of the Living Word (2350)
SJ	Servants of Jesus (3560)
SJA	Congregation of the Sisters of St. Joan of Arc (3815)
SJC	Sisters of St. Joseph of Cluny (3860)
SJS	Sister Servants of the Blessed Sacrament (3499)

SJSM	Sisters of St. Joseph of St. Mark (3910)
SJW	Sisters of St. Joseph the Worker (3920)
SL	Sisters of Loretto at the Foot of the Cross (2360)
SM	Marist Sisters Congregation of Mary (2430)
	Sisters of Mercy (2516)
	Sisters of Mercy (2518)
	Sisters of Mercy (Cork and Ross) (2600)
	Sisters of Mercy of Meath Community (2640)
	Misericordia Sisters (2680)
	Sisters Servants of Mary (3600)
SMDC	Sisters of Mercy Daughters of Christian Charity of St. Vincent de Paul (Hungary) (2610)
SMG	Poor Servants of the Mother of God (3640)
SMI	Sisters of Mary Immaculate (2440)
SMIC	Missionary Sisters of the Immaculate Conception of the Mother of God (2760)
SMP	Sisters of Mary of the Presentation (2450)
SMR	Society of Mary Reparatrix (2460)
SMSH	Sisters of St. Marthe (of St. Hyacinthe) (3940)
SMSM	Marist Missionary Sisters (Missionary Sisters of the Society of Mary) Inc. (2420)
SND	Sisters of Notre Dame (2990)
SNDdeN	Sisters of Notre Dame de Namur (3000)
SNJM	Sisters of the Holy Names of Jesus and Mary (1990)
SOLM	Sisters of Our Lady of Mercy (Mercedarians) (2670)
SP	Sisters of Providence (3340)
	Sisters of Providence (3350)
	Sisters of Providence of St. Mary-of-the-Woods, Indiana (3360)
SPC	Sisters of Saint Paul de Chartres (3980)
SRC	Servants of Our Lady, Queen of the Clergy (3650)
SRCM	Sisters of Reparation of the Congregation of Mary (3470)
SSA	Sisters of St. Ann (3718)
	Sisters of St. Anne (3720)
SSC	Missionary Sisters of St. Columban (2880)
	Sisters of St. Casimir (3740)
SSCC	Congregation of the Sacred Hearts and of Perpetual Adoration (3690)
SSCH	Sisters of St. Chretienne (3750)
SSCJ	Servants of the Most Sacred Heart of Jesus (3630)
	Sisters of the Sacred Heart of Jesus of Saint Jacut (3670)
SSCK	Sister Servants of Christ the King (3510)
SSCM	Servants of the Holy Heart of Mary (3520)
	Sisters of Saints Cyril and Methodius (3780)
SSD	Institute of the Sisters of St. Dorothy (3790)
SSE	Sisters of St. Elizabeth (3800)
SSF	Congregation of the Sisters of the Holy Family (1950)
SSHJP	Servants of the Sacred Heart of Jesus and of the Poor (3660)
SSJ	Servants of St. Joseph (3595)
	Sisters of Saint Joseph of Chestnut Hill, Philadelphia (3893)

	Sisters of St. Joseph of St. Augustine, Florida (3900)
SSJ-TOSF	Sisters of St. Joseph of the Third Order of St. Francis (3930)
SSL	The Congregation of the Sisters of St. Louis, Juilly-Monaghan (3935)
SSM	Sisters of the Sorrowful Mother (Third Order of St. Francis) (4100)
SSMI	Sisters Servants of Mary Immaculate (3610)
	Sisters Servants of Mary Immaculate (3620)
SSMN	Sisters of Saint Mary of Namur (3950)
SSMO	Sisters of St. Mary of Oregon (3960)
SSND	School Sisters of Notre Dame (2970)
SSPC	Missionary Sisters of St. Peter Claver (3990)
SSpS	Missionary Sisters Servants of the Holy Spirit (3530)
SSpSdeAP	Sister Servants of the Holy Spirit of Perpetual Adoration (3540)
SSS	Servants of the Blessed Sacrament (3500)Sisters of Social Service of Los Angeles, Inc. (4080)
	Sisters of Social Service (4090)
SSTV	Congregation of Sisters of St. Thomas of Villanova (4030)
STJ	Society of St. Teresa of Jesus (4020)
SU	Society of St. Ursula (4040)
SUSC	Religious of the Holy Union (2070)
SVM	Sisters of the Visitation of the Congregation of the Immaculate Heart of Mary (4200)
SVZ	Sisters of Charity of St. Vincent de Paul of Zagreb(0630)
VHM	Visitation Nuns (4190)
VS	Vocation Sisters (4220)
VSC	Vincentian Sisters of Charity (4160)
	Vincentian Sisters of Charity (4170)
XMM	Xaverian Missionary Society of Mary, Inc. (4230)
XS	Society of Catholic Missions Sisters of St. Francis Xavier (3810)
No Initials	Dominican Sisters of Our Lady of the Rosary and of Saint Catherine of Siena, Cabra (1110)
	Sisters of the Immaculate Conception of the Blessed Virgin Mary (Lithuanian) (2140)
	Sisters of Mercy (2517)
	Sisters of Mercy (2530)
	Sisters of Mercy (2560)
	Sisters of Mercy of the Blessed Sacrament (2590)
	Sisters of Our Lady of Mercy (2660)

APPENDIX B

Original American Foundations

(Partial Index)

THE FOLLOWING LISTING of original foundings of the orders and congregations of women religious in the United States is in chronological sequence. Some orders (Dominicans, e.g.) receive several entries inasmuch as different groups came from different places and countries with no connection to the others. Countries of origin are those from which they came, although several had different ethnic origins. Offshoots (daughters, granddaughters, etc.) that sprang from original foundations are not listed although they were often autonomous or quickly became so. Given names are sometimes used for the foundresses or first mothers-superior. Order titles are those shown in the 1990 *Official Catholic Directory* and are sometimes different from the titles at time of foundation.

The listings show the date of foundation, title, initials, OCD number of the order, the country of origin, the name of the American foundress(es) and/or founder. This is also a partial index indicating where orders first appear in the text. Order titles are not repeated in the regular Index.

An asterick (*) at the end of the listing indicates the community is no longer listed in the OCD. Some with European and Canadian motherhouses have withdrawn from the United States. Some have become defunct or amalgamated with other orders.

1727 - Ursuline Nuns of the Congregation of Paris (OSU-4110). New Orleans, LA. France. Mother M. AugustineTranchepain. Page 143.

1790 - Discalced Carmelite Nuns (OCD-0420). Port Tobacco, MD. Belgium. Mother Bernadina Matthews. Page 50.

1799 - Visitation Nuns (VHM-4190). Washington, DC. U.S. Mother Teresa Lalor. Page 54.

1809 - Sisters of Charity of St. Vincent de Paul (SC-0760).[1] Emmitsburg, MD. U.S. St. Elizabeth Ann Seton. Page 110.

1812 - Sisters of Loretto at the Foot of the Cross (SL-2360). St. Charles, KY. U.S. Mary Rhodes and Fr. CharlesNerinckx. Page 62.

1812 - Sisters of Charity of Nazareth (SCN-0500). Nazareth, KY. U.S. Mother Catherine Spalding. Page 63.

1818 - Society of the Sacred Heart (RSCJ-4070). St. Charles, MO. France. St. Philippine Duchesne. Page 66.

1822 - Dominican Sisters (OP-1070-01). St. Catharine, KY. U.S. Maria Sansbury and Rev. Thomas Wilson. Page 195.

1829 - Oblate Sisters of Providence (OSP-3040). Baltimore, MD. U.S. Mary Elizabeth Lange. Page 69.

1829 - Sisters of Charity of Our Lady of Mercy (OLM-0510). Charleston, SC. U.S. Bishop John England. Page 73.

1833 - Sisters of Charity of the Blessed Virgin Mary (BVM-0430). Philadelphia, PA. U.S. Mary Francis Clarke. Page 75.

1833 - Congregation of Our Lady of Mount Carmel (O.CARM-0400). Plattenville, LA. France. Mother Therese Chevrel. Page 75.

1836 - Sisters of Saint Joseph of Carondelet (CSJ-3840). St. Louis, MO. France. Mother Febronie Fontbonne. Page 134.

1840 - Sisters of Notre Dame de Namur (SNDdeN-3000). Cincinnati, OH. Belgium. Mother Louise de Gonzague. Page 135.

1840 - Sisters of Providence of Saint Mary-of-the-Woods, Indiana (SP-3360). Saint Mary-of-the-Woods, IN. France. Mother Theodore (Anne Therese Guérin) Page 137.

1842 - Congregation of the Sisters of the Holy Family (SSF-1950). New Orleans, LA. U.S. Mother Henriette Delille. Page 96.

1842 - The Sisters of the Good Shepherd (RGS-CGS-1830). Louisville, KY. France. Mother Marie des Ange Porcher. Page 142.

1843 - Congregation of the Sisters of the Holy Cross (CSC-1920). Notre Dame, IN. France. Rev. Edward Sorin. Page 139.

1843 - Sisters of Mercy (RSM-2570). Pittsburgh, PA. Ireland. Mother Mary Francis Xavier Warde. Page 85.

1843 - Congregation of the Marianites of Holy Cross (MSC-2410). New Orleans, LA. France. Mother Mary of the Seven Dolors (Leocadie Gascoin). Page 141.

1844 - Sisters of the Precious Blood (CPPS-3260). New Riegel, OH. Switzerland. Rev. Francis de Sales Brunner. Page 161.

1845 - Sisters, Servants of the Immaculate Heart of Mary (IHM-2150). Monroe, MI. U.S. Theresa Renauld, Charlotte Schaaf, Teresa Maxis, and Rev. Louis Florent Gillet. Page 97.

1845 - Ursuline Nuns of the Congregation of Paris (OSU-4120). St. Martin, OH. France. Mother Julia Chatfield. Page 143.

1846 - Sisters of Mercy of the Union (RSM-2580). New York, NY. Ireland. Mother M. Agnes O'Connor. Page 157.

1847 - Dominican Sisters (OP-1070-03). Sinsinawa, WI. U.S. Rev. Samuel Mazzuchelli, OP Page 100.

1847 - School Sisters of Notre Dame (SSND-2970). St. Marys, PA. Germany. Mother Mary Teresa of Jesus (Caroline Gerhardinger). Page 163.

1848 - Ursuline Nuns (OSU-4110). St. Louis, MO. Austria. Mother Magdeline Stehlen. Page 52.

1849 - Congregation of the Sisters of the Third Order of St. Francis of Perpetual Adoration (FSPA-1780). Milwaukee, WI. Germany. Mother Aemiliana Duerr (Ottilie Duerr). Page 167.

1849 - The Sisters of St. Francis of Assisi (OSF-1705). Milwaukee, WI. Germany. Mother Aemiliana Duerr. Page 167.

1850 - Ursuline Nuns of the Congregation of Paris (OSU-4120-04). Cleveland, OH. France. Mother Mary of the Annunciation (Mary Beaumont). Page 143.

1850 - Dominican Sisters of San Rafael (OP-1070-04). Monterey, CA. France. Mother Mary Goemaere. Page 145.

1851 - Congregation of the Sisters of the Third Order of St. Francis, Oldenburg, Indiana (OSF-1730). Oldenburg, IN. Austria. Mother Theresa Hackelmeier and Rev. Francis Joseph Rudulph. Page 168.

1851 - Sisters of Mercy (RSM-2580). Little Rock, AR. Ireland. Mother M. Teresa O'Farrell. Page 157.

1851 - Sisters of Charity of St. Augustine (CSA-0580). Cleveland, OH. France. Mother Bernardine Cabaret. Page 146.

1851 - Daughters of the Heart of Mary (DHM-0810). Cleveland, OH. France. Anna Romaine Pance. Page 147.

1852 - Benedictine Sisters of Pontifical Jurisdiction (OSB-0230). St. Marys, PA. Germany. Mother Benedicta Riepp, Sister Walburga Dietrich, Mother Maura Flieger. Page 169.

1853 - Congregation of the Incarnate Word and Blessed Sacrament (IWBS-2200). Brownsville, TX. France. Mother Ignatius McKeon. Page 153.

1853 - Dominican Sisters (OP-1070-05). Amityville, NY. Germany. Mother Mary Josepha Witzlhofer. Page 172.

1854 - Sisters of the Presentation of the Blessed Virgin Mary (PBVM-3320). San Francisco, CA. Ireland. Mother M. Joseph Cronin, Mother M. Teresa Comerford, Mother M. Xavier Daly. Page 156.

1854 - Sisters of Mercy (RSM-2570). San Francisco, CA. Ireland. Mother Mary Baptist Russell. Page 157.

1855 - The Sisters of St. Francis of Philadelphia (OSF-1650). Philadelphia, PA. U.S. Bishop John Neumann and Mother Francis Bachmann. Page 102.

1855 - Daughters of the Cross (DC-0770). Cocoville, LA. France. Marie Hyacinth Le Conniat. Page 154.

1855 - Sisters of Charity of Montreal (Grey Nuns) (SGM-0490). Toledo, OH. Canada. Mother Henriette Blondin. Page 150.

1855 - North American Union Sisters of Our Lady of Charity (NAU-OLC-3070). Hamburg, NY. France. Mother Mary of St. Jerome of Tourneux. Page 151.

1855 - Sisters of St. Joseph of Bourg (CSJ-3880).[2] Bay St. Louis, MS. France. Mother Eulalie Thamet. Page 151.

1856 - Sisters of Providence (SP-3350). Fort Vancouver, WA. Canada. Mother Joseph (Esther Pariseau). Page 148.

1858 - Ursuline Sisters of the Immaculate Conception (OSU-4120-03). Louisville, KY. Germany. Mary Salesia Reitmeier. Page 143.

1858 - Franciscan Sisters of the Poor (SFP-1440). Cincinnati, OH. Germany. Frances Schervier. Page 173.

1858 - Congregation of the Sisters of Saint Agnes (CSA-3710). Barton, WI. U.S. Rev. Caspar Rehrl. Page 103.

1858 - Sisters of Charity of Leavenworth, Kansas (SCL-0480). Leavenworth, KS. U.S. Mother Xavier Ross. Page 104.

1858 - Sisters of Mercy (RSM-2580). Cincinnati, OH. Ireland. Mother Teresa Maher. Page 157.

1859 - Franciscan Sisters of Allegany, New York (OSF-1180). Allegany, NY. U.S. Rev. Pamfilo da Magliano. Page 103.

1859 - Sisters of the Holy Names of Jesus and Mary (SNJM-1990). Portland, OR. Canada. Mother Mary Alphonse. Page 152.

1860 - Dominican Sisters (OP-1070-08). New Orleans, LA. Ireland. Mother Mary John Flanagan. Page 160.

1860 - Sisters of the Congregation De Notre Dame (CND-2980). Bourbonnais, IL. Canada. Mother St. Alexis of St. Joseph. Page 154.

1862 - Dominican Sisters (Congregation of St. Catherine of Siena) (OP-1070-09). Racine, WI. Germany. Mother Benedicta Bauer. Page 127.

1862 - Society of the Holy Child Jesus (SHCJ-4060). Towanda, PA. England. Cornelia Connelly. Page 123.

1863 - Sisters of St. Mary of Namur (SSMN-3950). Lockport, NY. Belgium. Emilie Keman. Page 219.

1864 - Sisters of the Humility of Mary (HM-2110). New Bedford, PA. France. Marie Anna Tabourat. Page 219.

1865 - Congregation of the Third Order of St. Francis of Mary Immaculate, Joliet, IL (OSF-1710). Joliet, IL. U.S. Rev. Pamfilo da Magliano and Mother Alfred Moes. Page 103.

1865 - Franciscan Missionary Sisters of the Sacred Heart (FMSC-1400). New York, NY. Italy. Mother Gertrude. Page 219.

1866 - Congregation of the Sisters of Charity of the Incarnate Word, Houston, Texas (CCVI-0470). Galveston, TX. France. Mother Mary Blandine Matelin, Joseph Roussin, and Ange Escudé. Page 229.

1866 - Congregation of Divine Providence, San Antonio, Texas (CDP-1010). Austin, TX. Germany. Mother St. Andrew Feltin. Page 233.

1866 - Sisters of St. Joseph of St. Augustine, Florida (SSJ-3900). St. Augustine, FL. France. Mother Marie Sidonia Rascle.

Ursulines of the Immaculate Conception (c. 1942).

Courtesy Gonzaga University

1866 - Sisters of Saint Anne (SSA-3720). Oswego, NY. Canada. Mother M. Stanislaus, Mother M. Mecthilde, Sister Marie-de-la-Purification, Mother M. Agnes-de-Jesus.

1868 - Little Sisters of the Poor (LSP-2340). Brooklyn, NY. France. Marie de la Conception. Page 336.

1868 - Sisters of Saint Francis, Clinton, Iowa (OSF-1540). Mt. Olivet, KY. U.S. Mother M. Paula Beaven.

1868 - Poor Handmaids of Jesus Christ (PHJC-3230). Hessen Cassel, IN. Germany. Mother M. Rose Blum. Page 260.

1869 - Sisters of the Third Order of St. Francis of Penance and of Charity (OSF-1760). Tiffin, OH. U.S. Rev. Joseph Bihn and Elizabeth Schaefer.

1869 - Franciscan Sisters of Christian Charity (OSF-1230). Manitowoc, WI. U.S.
Rev. Joseph Fessler, Theresa Gramlich, and Rosa Wahl. Page 419.

1870 - Adorers of the Blood of Christ (ASC-0100). Belle Prairie City, IL. Germany.
Mother Clementine Zerr. Page 260.

1871 - Sisters of the Immaculate Heart of Mary (IHM-2180). Gilroy, CA. Spain.
Raymunda Cremadell. Page 471.

1872 - Franciscan Sisters of Mary (FSM-1415).[3] St. Louis, MO. Germany. Mother
Mary Odilia Berger. Page 331.

1872 - Sisters of the Most Holy Sacrament (MHS-2940). New Orleans, LA. France.
Mother M. Augustine.

1872 - Sisters of the Holy Family (SHF-1960). San Francisco, CA. U.S. Rev. John
Prendergast and Mother Dolores (Lizzie Armer).

1872 - Franciscan Sisters, Daughters of the Sacred Hearts of Jesus and Mary
(OSF-1240). St. Louis, MO. Germany. Mother Mary Alphonsa Gormann,
Mother Mary Dorothea Lutticke, and Mother Mary Philomena Oldegeering.
Page 331.

1873 - Sisters of Providence (SP-3340). Holyoke, MA. Canada. Catherine Horan.

1873 - Missionary Franciscan Sisters of the Immaculate Conception (OSF-1360).
Belle Prairie, MN. Italy. Mother Mary Ignatius Hayes.

1873 - Sisters of Christian Charity (Daughters of the Blessed Virgin Mary of the
Immaculate Conception) (SCC-0660). New Orleans, LA. Germany. Blessed
Pauline von Mallinckrodt and Mother Mathilde Kothe. Pages 260.

1873 - Sisters of the Presentation of Mary (PM-3310). Glens Falls, NY. Canada.
Mother St. Francois-de-Borgia.

1874 - Sisters of Charity of Our Lady, Mother of Mercy (SCMM-0520). Baltic, CT.
Holland. Mother M. Carola.

1874 - Sisters of the Immaculate Conception (CIC-2120). Labadieville, LA. U.S.
Rev. Cyprian Venissat and Mother Mary (Elvina Vienne).

1874 - School Sisters of St. Francis (OSF-1680). New Cassel, WI. Germany.
Mother Alexia Hoell, Mother Alfons Schmid, and Mother Clara Seiter. Page
234.

1874 - Sisters of St. Francis of Penance and Christian Charity (OSF-1630). Buffalo,
NY. Germany. Mother Aloysia Lenders and Mother Cecilia Steffen. Page
341.

1874 - Sisters of the Presentation of the Blessed Virgin Mary (PBVM-3320). New York, NY. Ireland. Mother Mary Joseph Hickey. Page 156.

1874 - Felician Sisters (CSSF-1170). Stevens Point, WI. Poland. Mother Mary Angela (Sophia Camille Truszkowska). Page 290.

1874 - Sisters of Notre Dame (SND-2990). Cleveland, OH. Germany. Aldegonda Wolbring, Lisette Kühling. Page 245.

1874 - Congregation of the Benedictine Sisters of Perpetual Adoration of Pontifical Jurisdiction (OSB-0220). Clyde, MO. Switzerland. Mother M. Anselma Felber. Page 172.

1875 - Sisters of St. Francis of Perpetual Adoration (OSF-1640). Lafayette, IN. Germany. Mother M. Clara Thomas. Page 331.

1875 - Order of St. Clare (OSC-3760). Cleveland, OH. Italy. Maddalena and Constance Bentivoglio.

1875 - Sisters of St. Francis of the Holy Family (OSF-1570). Iowa City, IA. Germany. Mother Mary Xavier Termehr. Page 419.

1875 - Hospital Sisters of the Third Order of St. Francis (OSF-1820). Springfield, IL. Germany. Mother Angelica Ratte. Page 331.

1876 - Franciscan Sisters of the Sacred Heart (OSF-1450). Avilla, IN. Germany. Mother Anastasia Bischler. Page 260.

1876 - Sisters of Divine Providence (CDP-0990). Pittsburgh, PA. Germany. Mother Xavier Schneider. Page 260.

1876 - Dominican Sisters (OP-1070-11). New York City, NY. U.S. Mother Mary Catherine Antoninus Thorpe.

1877 - Religious of the Sacred Heart of Mary (RSHM-3465). Sag Harbor, NY. France. Rev. Mother Basil Davis.

1877 - Sisters of the Third Order Regular of St. Francis of the Congregation of Our Lady of Lourdes (OSF-1720). Rochester, MN. U.S. Mother Alfred and Barbara Moes. Page 243.

1877 - Religious of Jesus and Mary (RJM-3450). Fall River, MA. Canada. Mother Francis Xavier.

1878 - Sisters of Charity of St. Hyacinthe (SCSH-0610). Lewiston, ME. Canada. Mother Alphonsine Cote.

1879 - Sisters of St. Joseph of Cluny (SJC-3860).[4] Morrilton, AR. France and Ireland.

1879 - Dominican Sisters of the Sick Poor (OP-1070-16). New York, NY. U.S. Mary Walsh. Page 347.

1880 - Dominican Contemplative Nuns (OP-1050). Newark, NJ. France. Mother Mary of Jesus (Julia Crooks). Page 360.

1880 - Dominican Sisters (OP-1070-17). Glens Falls, NY. U.S. Bishop Francis McNierney and Mother Maria Catherine de Ricci of the Heart of Jesus (Lucy Eaton Smith).

1880 - Institute of the Blessed Virgin Mary (IBVM-2370). Joliet, IL. Canada. Mother Gonzaga Gallivan.

1881 - Sisters of St. Francis of the Holy Cross (OSF-1550). Green Bay, WI. U.S. Rev. Edward F. Daems and Christine Rousseau.

1881 - The Franciscan Sisters of Baltimore (OSF-1200). Baltimore, MD. England. Mother Mary Frances Basil.

1881 - Congregation of Bon Secours (CBS-0270). Baltimore, MD. France. Mother Ferdinand. Page 332.

1881 - Sisters of Holy Cross (CSC-1930). North Grosvenor Dale, CT. Canada. Mother Mary of St. Eugenie (Mary Fanny Decelles). Page 141.

1882 - Servants of the Immaculate Heart of Mary (SCIM-3550). Biddleford, ME. Canada. Mother Mary Josephet Fitzbach Roy (Mother Mary of the Sacred Heart).

1883 - Order of Our Lady of Lourdes. New Orleans, LA. U.S.*

1884 - Sisters of St. Joseph of Peace (CSJP-3890). Jersey City, NJ. England. Mother Mary Francis Clare Cusack.

1885 - Sisters of the Holy Family of Nazareth (CSFN-1970). Chicago, IL. Italy. Frances Siedliska. Page 293.

1885 - Sisters of St. Joseph of Chambery (CSJ-3850). Hartford, CT. France. Mother Martha of Jesus.

1886 - Religious of the Holy Union of the Sacred Hearts (SUSC-2070). Fall River, MA. France. Mother Marie Helena Daumerie.

1886 - Sisters of St. Mary of Oregon (SSMO-3960). Sublimity, OR. U.S. Archbishop William H. Gross, CSsR, and Mother M. Wilhelmina Bleily. Page 243.

1886 - Sisters of the Divine Compassion (RDC-0970). New York, NY. U.S. Mother Mary Veronica Starr and Rev. Thomas S. Preston.

1887 - Misericordia Sisters (SM-2680). New York, NY. Canada. Mother St. Stanislaus de Koska. Page 371.

1887 - Sisters of Mercy (RSM-2580). Council Bluffs, IA. Ireland. Mother M. Vincent McDermott and Mother M. Magdalene Bennett. Page 157.

1887 - Olivetan Benedictine Sisters (OSB-0240). Pocahontas, AR. Switzerland. Mother Beatrice Renggli.

1889 - Little Franciscans of Mary (PFM-2280). Worcester, MA. U.S. Rev. Ambrose Martial Fafard and Mother Mary Joseph.

1889 - Servants of the Holy Heart of Mary (SSCM-3520). Bourbonnais, IL. France. Mother Mathilde Gauvin, Sister St. Luc Lennec, Mother Lucilla Poret, and Mother Emerentia Roettgen.

1889 - Sisters of Divine Providence of Kentucky (CDP-1000). Covington, KY. Germany. Blessed Jean Martin Moye. Page 260.

1889 - Sisters of the Catholic Apostolate (CSAC-3140). New York, NY. Italy. Mother M. Pia Borzi.

1889 - Sisters of the Sorrowful Mother (SSM-4100). Wichita, KS. Italy. Mother M. Scholastica Demer.

1889 - Missionary Sisters of the Sacred Heart of Jesus (MSC-2860). New York, NY. Italy. St. Frances Xavier Cabrini. Page 275.

1890 - Mission Helpers of the Sacred Heart (MHSH-2720). Baltimore, MD. U.S. Mother Mary Demetrias Hartwell. Page 309.

1890 - Sisters of Charity of Quebec (SCQ-0560). Fall River, MA. Canada. S. S. Paschal (Henriette Pouliot). Page 318.

1890 - Ursuline Nuns (OSU-4110). York, NE. Germany. Mother Clare Cornely. Page 52.

1890 - Sisters of St. Francis of the Immaculate Conception (OSF-1580). Metamora, IL. U.S. Mary Pacifica (Margaret) Forrestal. Page 319.

1890 - The Sisters Adorers of the Precious Blood (APB-0110). Brooklyn, NY. Canada. Mary St. Gertrude de Vallerot. Page 318.

1891 - Franciscan Sisters of the Immaculate Conception of Little Falls, Minnesota (OSF-1310). Little Falls, MN. U.S. Mother Mary Frances Beauchamp.

1891 - Dominican Sisters of the Perpetual Rosary (OP-1050). West Hoboken, NJ. France. Rev. Damian Marie Saintourens, OP, and Mother Mary of Jesus (Mary Garnier). Page 360.

1891 - Little Sisters of the Assumption (LSA-2310). New York, NY. France. Mother Marie du Crist. Page 318.

1891 - Sisters of the Assumption (SASV-0150). Southbridge, MA. Canada. Mother St. Anselme. Page 318.

1891 - The Sisters of the Blessed Sacrament for Indians and Colored People (SBS-0260). Philadelphia, PA. U.S. Mother Katharine Drexel. Page 342.

1892 - Benedictine Sisters of Our Lady of Belloc (OSB). Sacred Heart, OK. France. Mother M. Philomena. Page 318.

1892 - Society of Helpers (HHS-1890). New York, NY. France. Mother Mary of St. Bernard. Page 318.

1892 - Congregation of Notre Dame De Sion (NDS-2950). Lewiston, ME. France. Mother Mary Edouard. Page 318.

1892 - Congregation of Our Lady of the Retreat in the Cenacle (RC-3110). New York, NY. France. Mother de Grimaldi.

1892 - Sisters of St. Francis of the Holy Eucharist (OSF-1560). Nevada, MO. Switzerland. Mother M. John Hau. Page 318.

1893 - Sister Servants of the Holy Spirit and Mary Immaculate (SHSp-2050). San Antonio, TX. U.S. Margaret Mary Healy-Murphy. Page 346.

1893 - Sisters of St. Francis of the Mission of the Immaculate Virgin (OSF-1510). New York, NY. U.S. Rev. John C. Drumgoale.

1893 - Sisters of the Little Company of Mary (LCM-2270). Chicago, IL. England. Mother Mary Veronica. Page 308.

1893 - Servants of Mary (OSM-3580). Mount Vernon, NE. England. Mother Mary Gertrude Guinaw. Page 287.

1893 - Franciscan Sisters of the Immaculate Conception of the Order of St. Francis (OSF).[5] Belle Prairie, MN. U.S. Mother Mary Michael.

1893 - Little Sisters of the Holy Family (PSSF-2320). Van Buren, ME. Canada. Mother Marie of the Visitation. Page 318.

1894 - Franciscan Sisters of Chicago (OSF-1210). Chicago, IL. U.S. Mother Mary Theresa Dudzik and Mother Mary Anna Wysinski. Page 337.

1894 - Religious Hospitallers of Saint Joseph (RHSJ-3440). Winooski, VT. Canada. Mother Bonneau. Page 318.

**Cloistered Contemplative. Choir sisters.
Dominican Sisters of the Perpetual Rosary of
Pontifical Jurisdiction (c. 1942).**
Courtesy Gonzaga University

1894 - Bernardine Sisters of the Third Order of St. Francis (OSF-1810). Reading,
PA. Poland. Mother Mary Veronica Grzedowska. Page 295.

1895 - Sisters of the Divine Savior (SDS-1030). Milwaukee, WI. Italy. Mother M.
Raphaela Bohnheim. Page 316.

1896 - Society of the Sisters, Faithful Companions of Jesus (FCJ-4048). Fond du
Lac, WI. U.S. Rev. Mother Philomena Higgins. Page 318.

1896 - The Servants of Relief for Incurable Cancer (OP-1070-23). New York, NY. U.S. Mother Rose Hawthorne Lathrop. Page 349.

1897 - Franciscan Sisters of St. Joseph (FSSJ-1470). Trenton, NJ. U.S. Rev. Hyacinth Fudzinski and Mother M. Colette Hilbert. Page 301.

1897 - Ursuline Nuns (OSU-4120). St. Ignace, MI. Canada. Mother Angela.

1898 - Franciscan Sisters of the Atonement (SA-1190).[6] Garrison, NY. U.S. Rev. Paul James Francis Wattson and Lurana Mary White. Page 361.

1899 - Congregation of Our Lady of the Holy Rosary (RSR-3100). Upper Frenchville, ME. Canada. Mother Marie de St. Adolphe (Marie-Anne Otis) and Mother Marie de L'Enfant Jesus (Sephora St. Croix). Page 318.

1900 - Religious of the Eucharist (RE-3420). Washington, DC. Belgium.

1900 - Sisters of the Resurrection (CR-3480). Chicago, IL. Italy. Mother Anne Strzelecka. Page 316.

1900 - The Little Sisters of the Holy Family (PSSF-2320). Canada. Page 318.

1901 - Sisters of St. Joseph of the Third Order of St. Francis (SSJ-TOSF-3930). Stevens Point, WI. U.S. Rev. Luke Pescinski, Mother Mary Clara Bialkowski, Mother Mary Felicia Jaskulski. Page 298.

1901 - Missionary Sisters Servants of the Holy Spirit (SSpS-3530). Techny, IL. Holland. Mother Leonarda Lentrup.

1901 - Franciscan Sisters of Our Lady of Perpetual Help (OSF-1430). St. Louis, MO. U.S. Mother Mary Ernestine. Page 317.

1902 - Society of St. Ursula (SU-4040). New York, NY. France. Mother Hélène Marie. Page 318.

1902 - Vincentian Sisters of Charity (VSC-4160). Braddock, PA. Austria. Mother M. Emerentiana Handovits.

1902 - Sisters of St. Joseph of Le Puy (CSJ-3830-16). Fall River, MA. France.

1902 - Daughters of the Holy Spirit (DHS-0820). Hartford, CT. France. Mother Marie Alvarez. Page 318.

1902 - Apostles of the Sacred Heart of Jesus (ASCJ-0130). Boston, MA. Italy. Mother Dominic Geminiani. Page 278.

1903 - Sisters of Mary of the Presentation (SMP-2450). Wild Rice, ND. France. Mother St. Cesaire.

1903 - Sisters of Reparation of the Congregation of Mary (SRCM-3470). New York, NY. U.S. Mother Mary Zita O'Keefe.

1903 - Sisters of St. Chretienne (SSCH-3750). Salem, MA. France. Mother Marie du Sacre Coeur.

1903 - Sisters of the Sacred Heart of Jesus (SSCJ-3670). San Antonio, TX. France. Mother Marie Bernard.

1903 - Congregation of the Daughters of Jesus (FJ-0830). Lewistown, MT. Canada.

1904 - The Franciscan Missionaries of Mary (FMM-1370). Worcester, MA. India. Mother Agnelle.

1904 - Daughters of Wisdom (DW-0960). St. Agatha, ME. Canada. Mother Marie Therese.

1904 - Dominican Sisters of the Roman Congregation (OP-1120). Lewiston, ME. France. Mother Marie Emmanuel Legigand.

1904 - Daughters of Mary of the Immaculate Conception (DM-0860). New Britain, CT. U.S. Msgr. Lucian Bojnowski, Mothers Mary Agnes Waltosz, Mary Lucy Bobrowska, Mary Colette Bernard, Mary Rosalie Wolk, Sister Mary Germaine Mysliwiec.

1905 - Religious of Christian Education (RCE-3410). Huntington, WV. France. Mother Garnier.

1905 - Congregation of the Infant Jesus (CIJ-2230). Brooklyn, NY. France. Mother Marie Antoinette.

1905 - Daughters of Charity of the Sacred Heart of Jesus (FCSCJ-0750). Newport, VT. France. Mother St. Edgar Bouju, Mother Aline de St. Laurent Courant, Mother St. Gerard Majella Guignard, Mother St. Fernand Pageot.

1906 - Sisters of St. John the Baptist (CSJB-3820). Newark, NJ. Italy. Mother Bernedine D'Auria.

1906 - Dominican Sisters of Charity of the Presentation of the Blessed Virgin (OP-1100). Fall River, MA. France. Mother Marguerite du Sacré Coeur.

1906 - Sisters of St. Joseph of Lyons, France (CSJ-3870). Jackman, ME. France. Mother Mary Philippine Coupas.

1906 - French Benedictine Sisters.[7] Ramsey, LA. France. Mother Gertrude Berho.

1907 - Sisters of St. Casimir (SSC-3740). Scranton, PA. U.S. Rev. Anthony Staniukynas and Mother Maria Kaupas. Page 308.

1907 - Servants of the Sacred Heart of Jesus and of the Poor (SSHJP-3660). Laredo, TX. Mexico. Mother Concepcion G. de Quevedo.

1908 - Society of Mary Reparatrix (SMR-2460). New York, NY. France. Mother Mary of St. Matthew.

1908 - Congregation of the Sacred Hearts and of Perpetual Adoration (SSCC-3690). Fairhaven, MA. France. Mother Beatrix.

1908 - Daughters of Mary Help of Christians (Salesian Sisters of St. John Bosco) (FMA-0850). Paterson, NJ. Italy. Mother Brigida Prandi. Page 286.

1908 - Missionary Sisters of the Most Sacred Heart of Jesus of Hiltrup (MSC-2800). Lansford, PA. Germany. Mother Mary Electa Schulte-Mesum.

1908 - Daughters of Charity of the Most Precious Blood (DCPB-0740). Bridgeport, CT. Italy. Mother Gerardina Bove and Mother Pacifica Cuozzo.

1909 - Sisters of Saints Cyril and Methodius (SSCM-3780). Scranton, PA. U.S. Mother Mary Mihalak. Page 307.

1909 - Religious Venerini Sisters (MPV-4180). Lawrence, MA. Italy. Mother Keller.

1909 - Daughters of the Eucharist. Baltimore, MD. U.S. Mother Katherine A. Dietz.*

1909 - Sisters of St. Francis of Christ the King (OSF-1520). Kansas City, KS. Yugoslavia. Mother Bonaventure Kunst, Mother M. Pulcheria Zovko, Mother M. Clotilda Strand, Mother M. Aurelia Plankar. Page 306.

1910 - Ursuline Sisters of Belleville (OSU-4140). Kenmare, ND. Germany. Mother Leonie Rodgers.*[8]

1910 - Religious of the Passion of Jesus Christ (Passionist Nuns) (CP-3170). Pittsburgh, PA. Italy. Mother Mary Hyacinth of the Sacred Heart. Page 286.

1910 - Notre Dame Sisters (ND-2960). Fenton, MO. Czechoslovakia. Mother M. Gualberta.

1910 - Society of St. Teresa of Jesus (Teresian Sisters) (STJ-4020). San Antonio, TX. Spain. Mother Dolores Aparicio.

1910 - Sisters of Our Lady of Christian Doctrine (RCD-3080). New York, NY. U.S. Marion Frances Gurney.

1910 - Religious Teachers Filippini (MPF-3430). Trenton, NJ. Italy. Mother Ninetta Ionata.

1910 - Sisters of Charity of St. Louis (SCSL-0620). Turton, SD. France. Mother St. Raymond.

1911 - Dominican Sisters (OP-1070-25). Ontario, OR. Portugal. Mother Mary Catherine Roth.

1911 - Sisters of the Order of St. Basil the Great (OSBM-3730). Philadelphia, PA. Austria. Mother Mary Helen Langevich. Page 306.

1911 - Institute of the Sisters of St. Dorothy (SSD-3790). New York, NY. Portugal. Mother Morelli.

1911 - Sisters Auxiliaries of the Apostolate (SAA-0140). Monongah, WV. Canada. Mother Mary Ursula Langowski.

1912 - Maryknoll Sisters of St. Dominic (MM-2470). Ossining, NY. U.S. Mary Josephine Rogers.

1912 - Missionary Servants of the Most Blessed Trinity (MSBT-2790). Baltimore, MD. U.S. Rev. Thomas Judge.

1912 - Pallottine Missionary Sisters - Queen of Apostles Province (SAC-3150). Richwood, WV. Germany. Mother Mary Franziska Zabel.

1912 - Carmelite Sisters of the Divine Heart of Jesus (Carmel DCJ-0360). Milwaukee, WI. Germany. Mother Maria Teresa of St. Joseph.

1912 - Sisters of Mercy of the Holy Cross (SCSC-2630). Dickinson, ND. Switzerland. Mother M. Lauda Werner.

1912 - Servants of Mary (Servite Sisters) (OSM-3590). Ladysmith, WI. U.S. Mother Mary Alphonse Bradley. Page 287.

1912 - Religious of the Order of the Blessed Sacrament and of Our Lady (Sacramentine Nuns) (OSS-3490). Yonkers, NY. France. Mother Mary of the Rosary Prevost.

1912 - Sisters of the Divine Redeemer (SDR-1020). McKeesport, PA. Hungary. Mother Mary Berchmana Berghofer, Sister Mary Frederika Mikuska, Mother Mary Cassianna Nagy, Mother Mary Sabina Horvath. Page 307.

1913 - Franciscan Missionaries of Our Lady (OSF-1380). Monroe, LA. France. Mother Mary de Bethanie Crowley.

1913 - Sisters of St. Francis of the Immaculate Heart of Mary (Hankinson, ND) (OSF-1590). Collegeville, MN. Germany. Mother Paschalina Schaflitzel.

1913 - School Sisters of the Third Order of St. Francis (OSF-1690). Pittsburgh, PA. Czechoslovakia. Mother M. Louise Kilb. Page 306.

1913 - Daughters of Divine Charity (FDC-0790). New York, NY. Hungary. Mother Valeria.

1913 - Sisters of the Holy Spirit (SHS-2040). Pittsburgh, PA. Russia. Mother Josephine Finatowitz. Page 306.

1913 - Daughters of St. Mary of Providence (DSMP-0940). Chicago, IL. Italy. Mother Rose Bertolini.

1914 - Sisters Servants of Mary (SM-3600). New Orleans, LA. Spain. Mother Anastasia Borostiaga.

1914 - Congregation of the Sisters of St. Joan of Arc (SJA-3815). Worcester, MA. Canada. Father Marie Clement Staub, AA.

1914 - Missionary Sisters of St. Peter Claver (SSPC-3990). St. Louis, MO. Germany. Hildegard Schattinger.

1915 - Sister Servants of the Holy Spirit of Perpetual Adoration (SSpSdeAP-3540). Philadelphia, PA. Holland. Mother Mary Michael and Mother Mary Baptista.

1915 - Ursuline Nuns (OSU-4120). Fulda, OH. Germany. Mother M. Salesia.

1916 - Franciscan Handmaids of the Most Pure Heart of Mary (FHM-1260). Savannah, GA. U.S. Rev. Ignatius Lissner and Mother M. Theodore Williams.

1916 - Mantellate Sisters, Servants of Mary of Blue Island (OSM-3570). Blue Island, IL. Italy. Mother Louise. Page 287.

1916 - Mothers of the Helpless (MD-2920). New York, NY. Spain. Mother Aurora De San Jose.

1916 - Missionary Daughters of the Most Pure Virgin Mary (MDPVM). Kingsville, TX. Mexico. Mother Virginia Fischer.

1917 - Carmelite Sisters of St. Therese of the Infant Jesus (CST-0380). Bentley, OK. U.S. Father Edward Soler, OCD.

1919 - Missionary Sisters of the Immaculate Heart of Mary (ICM-2750).[9] New York, NY. Belgium. Mother MarieAdrienn Moyaert.

1919 - Franciscan Sisters of the Immaculate Conception and St. Joseph for the Dying (OSF-1300). Monterey, CA. Italy. Mother M. Ottilia.

1919 - Daughters of Our Lady of Mercy (DM-0890). Springfield, MA. Italy. Mother Mary Josephine Fortune.

1919 - Religious of the Assumption (RA-3390). Philadelphia, PA. England and France. Mother Agnes Marguerite, RA.

1919 - Franciscan Sisters of St. Elizabeth (FSSE-1460). Newark, NJ. Italy. Mother Maria Tortolani.

1920 - Sisters of the Most Holy Trinity (OSST-2060). Bristol, PA. Italy. Mother Teresa of Jesus.

1920 - Carmelite Sisters (Corpus Christi) (OCARM-0350). Duluth, MN. England. Mother Mary Ellerker.

1920 - Parish Visitors of Mary Immaculate (PVMI-3160). New York, NY. U.S. Mother Mary Teresa Tallon.

1921 - Poor Clares of Perpetual Adoration (PCPA-3210). Cleveland, OH. Austria. Mother Mary Agnes Eiechler and Mother Mary Cyrilla Zotter.

1921 - Grey Nuns of the Sacred Heart (GNSH-1840). Buffalo, NY. Canada. Mother Mary Augustine.

1922 - Marist Missionary Sisters (Missionary Sisters of the Society of Mary, Inc.) (SMSM-2420). Boston, MA. France. Mother Mary Pia and Mother Mary Rose.

1922 - Missionary Sisters of the Immaculate Conception of the Mother of God (SMIC-2760). St. Bonaventure, NY. Brazil. Mother Kathleen Keefe.

1922 - Our Lady of Victory Missionary Sisters (OLVM-3130). Chicago, IL. U.S. Rev. John Joseph Sigstein.

1922 - Sisters of Saint Francis of the Providence of God (OSF-1660). Pittsburgh, PA. U.S. Rev. Michael Krusas and Rev. Magnus Kazenas.

1922 - Sisters of St. Francis of Savannah, MO (OSF-1670). Conception, MO. Austria. Mother M. Pia Feichtenschlager.

1922 - Mission Sisters of the Holy Spirit (MSSp-2740). Cleveland, OH. Hungary. Mother Hildegard Alberti-Enno.

1923 - Franciscan Sisters of St. Paul, MN (OSF-1485). St. Paul, MN. Germany. Mother Adela Schilz.

1923 - Dominican Sisters (OP-1070-26). Windber, PA. Czechoslovakia. Mother Mary de Sales Zavodnik.

1923 - Missionary Benedictine Sisters (OSB-0210). Raeville, NE. Germany. Mother M. Diemud Gerber.

1923 - Sisters of St. Francis of the Martyr St. George (OSF-1600). Alton, IL. Germany. Mother M. Columbe.

1923 - Grey Sisters of St. Elizabeth. North East, PA. Germany. Mother Michael.*

1924 - Sisters of the Holy Redeemer (CSR-2000). Baltimore, MD. Germany. Mother M. Hernelda Reinhard.

1924 - Poor Sisters of Jesus Crucified and the Sorrowful Mother (CJC-3240). Elmhurst, PA. U.S. Rev. Alphonsus Maria Urbanavicius, CP

1924 - Sisters of the Cross and Passion (CP-3180). Providence, RI. England. Mother M. Gonzaga. Page 286.

1924 - Sisters of the Poor Child Jesus (PCJ-3220). Parkersburg, WV. Holland. Mother M. Theotima Bullock.

1924 - Poor Sisters of Nazareth (PSN-3242). San Diego, CA. England. Mother St. Basil.

1924 - Ursuline Sisters of the Congregation of Tildonk, Belgium (OSU-4130). Ozone Park, NY. Belgium. Mother M. Stanislaus.

1925 - Dominican Sisters (OP-1070-29). Helena, MT. Germany. Mother Bonaventura Groh.

1925 - Medical Mission Sisters (SCMM-2490). Washington, DC. U.S. Mother Anna Marie Dengal.

1925 - Missionary Sisters of the Precious Blood (CPS-2850). Princeton, NJ. Germany. Mother M. Hilberta Soder.

1925 - Nuns of the Perpetual Adoration of the Blessed Sacrament (AP-3190). El Paso, TX. Italy. Mother Maria Concepciòn del Espiritu Santo.

1926 - Company of Mary (ODN-0700). Douglas, AZ. Mexico. Mother Ana Maria Serrano.

1926 - Sisters of Social Services of Los Angeles, Inc. (SSS-4080). Los Angeles, CA. Hungary. Mother Frederica Horvath.

1926 - Daughters of Mary and Joseph (DMJ-0880). Culver City, CA. Belgium. Mother Modwina O'Driscoll.

1926 - Little Servant Sisters of the Immaculate Conception (LSIC-2300). Reading, PA. Poland.

1926 - Sisters of Mercy of the Blessed Sacrament (HMSS-2590). Hartshorne, OK. Mexico. Mother Amparo Perez.

1926 - The Handmaids of the Sacred Heart of Jesus (ACJ-1870). Philadelphia, PA. Spain.

1926 - Congregation Del Divino Pastor. Eagle Pass, TX. Mexico.*

1926 - Cordi-Marian Missionary Sisters (MCM). Martindale, TX. Mexico. Mother Maria del Consuelo Gayon Solorzano.

1926 - Minim Daughters of Mary Immaculate (CFMM-2675). Nogales, AZ. Mexico. Pablo de Anda Padilla.

1926 - Daughters of Divine Charity (FDC-0790). Rankin, PA. Yugoslavia. Mother M. Leonora Vurnik.

1927 - Eucharistic Missionaries of St. Dominic (OP-1140). Amite, LA. U.S. Margaret Grouchey and Catherine Bostic.

1928 - Franciscan Sisters of the Immaculate Conception (OSF-1280). Belleville, NY. Germany. Mother Edetrudis.

1929 - Missionary Sisters of Our Lady of Africa (MSOLA-2820). Metuchen, NJ. France. Mother M. Sabine.

1929 - Congregation of the Servants of the Holy Infancy of Jesus (OSF-1980). Staten Island, NY. Germany. Mother Praxedis Zirkelbach.

1929 - Carmelite Sisters for the Aged and Infirm (O.CARM-0330). New York, NY. U.S. Mother M. Angeline Teresa McCrory.

1929 - Franciscan Sisters of Ringwood (FSR-1420). Passaic, NJ. U.S. Mother Angela Clare Pesce.

1929 - Missionary Servants of St. Anthony (MSSA-2890). San Antonio, TX. U.S. Rev. Peter Baque.

1930 - Missionary Catechists of Divine Providence, San Antonio, Texas (MCDP-2690). San Antonio, TX. U.S. Mother M. Benita Vermeersch.

1930 - Missionary Sisters of St. Columban (SSC-2880). Silver Creek, NY. Ireland. Mother Mary Francis de Sales Hogan.

1931 - Carmelite Nuns of the Ancient Observance (O.CARM-0300). Coopersburg, PA. Italy. Mother Therese of Jesus and Mother Clement Mary of the Guardian Angel.

1931 - Sisters of St. Elizabeth (SSE-3800). Milwaukee, WI. U.S. Mother Mary Elizabeth Ruf and Mother Mary Agnes Stippich.

1931 - School Sisters of the Third Order of St. Francis, Panhandle, Texas (OSF-1695). Panhandle, TX. Austria. Mother M. Salesia Seipelt.

1931 - The Little Daughters of St. Joseph (LDSJ). Kenmore, WA. Canada.*

1932 - Sisters of Charity of St. Joan Antida (SCSJA-0600). Milwaukee, WI. Italy. Mother Monica Tarantola.

1932 - Congregation of Antonian Sisters of Mary, Queen of the Clergy.Worcester, MA. Canada.*

1932 - Franciscan Sisters of Mary Immaculate of the Third Order of St. Francis of Assisi (FMI-1500). Amarillo, TX. Switzerland. Mother Caritas Brader.

1932 - Pious Society Daughters of St. Paul (FSP-0950) Staten Island, NY. Italy. Mother Paula Cordero. Page 389.

1935 - Oblate Sisters of the Blessed Sacrament (OSBS-3010). Marty, SD. U.S. Rev. Sylvester Eisenmann, OSB

1935 - Sisters Servants of Mary Immaculate (SSMI-3620). Baltimore, MD. Poland.

1935 - Daughters of Mary, Health of the Sick (DMHS). New York, NY. U.S. Rev. Edward F. Garesche.*

1935 - Sisters of St. Rita (OSA-4010). New Hamburg, NY. Germany. Mother Helene Wenzel.

1936 - Sisters of the Immaculate Conception of the Blessed Virgin Mary (Lithuania) (2140). Marianapolis College, CT. Lithuania. Mother Mary Aloysa.

1937 - Sisters of St. Joseph of St. Mark (SJSM-3910). Cleveland, OH. Germany. Mother M. Romana Trunk.

1939 - Sisters of Social Service (SSS). Fargo, ND. Canada.*

1941 - Missionary Sisters of St. Charles Borromeo (Scalabrini Sisters) (MSSCB-2900). Melrose Park, IL. Italy. Mother Caetana Borsatto.

1943 - Missionary Catechists of the Sacred Hearts of Jesus and Mary (MC-2700). Victoria, TX. U.S. Rev. Daniel Giorgi.

1946 - Society of Catholic Mission Sisters of St. Francis Xavier (XS-3810). Mount Clemens, MI. U.S. Cardinal Edward Mooney.

1946 - Mercedarian Missionaries of Berriz (MMB-2510). Kansas City, MO. Spain. Mother Josephine Martinez.

1946 - Daughters of St. Francis of Assisi (DSF-0920). Peru, IL. Czechoslovakia.
Mother Mary Boleslav Gazo.

1947 - Missionary Carmelites of St. Teresa (CMST-0390). Cuero, TX. Mexico.
Carmen Griselda Morales.

1947 - Congregation of the Handmaids of the Precious Blood (HPB-1860). Jemez
Springs, NM. U.S. Rev. Gerald Fitzgerald.

1947 - Sisters Oblates to the Blessed Trinity (OBT-3020).[10] New York, NY. Italy.
Mother Gloria Castra.

1947 - Poor Servants of the Mother of God (SMG-3640). High Point, NC. England.
Mother Mary Patrice.

1947 - Sisters of Our Lady of Sorrows (OLS-3120). Moreauville, LA. Italy. Mother
Rose Mini.

1947 - Servants of the Blessed Sacrament (SSS-3500). Waterville, ME. Canada.
Mother Mary Sweetland.

1947 - Institute of the Sisters of Our Lady of Mount Carmel (O.CARM-0410).
Hamilton, MA. Italy. Mother Paola Innocenti.

1948 - Pious Disciples of the Divine Master (PDDM-0980). Port Richmond, NY.
Italy. Father James Albenone.

1948 - Benedictine Nuns of the Primitive Observance (OSB-0180). Bethlehem, CT.
France. Mother Benedict Duss.

1948 - Congregation of Sisters of St. Thomas of Villanova (SSTV-4030). Norwalk,
CT. France. Mother Kevin.

1948 - Daughters of St. Mary of Leuca.Buffalo, NY. Italy.*

1949 - The Congregation of Sisters of St. Louis, Juilly-Monaghan (SSL-3935). El
Monte, CA. Ireland. Mother Mary Ronan McDonnell.

1949 - Sisters of Bethany (CVD-0250). Los Angeles, CA. El Salvador. Mother
Dolores de Maria Zea and Mother Maria de la Cruz Pinto.

1949 - Congregation of the Daughters of Mary Immaculate (FMI-0870). Somerset,
TX. Spain. Mother Mary del Pilar Diás de Guereñu.

1949 - Little Missionary Sisters of Charity (LMSC-2290). Boston, MA. Italy.
Mother Mary Concetta.

1949 - Sisters, Home Visitors of Mary (HVM-2090). Detroit, MI. U.S. Msgr. John
Ryan and Mother Mary Schutz.

1949 - Cistercian Nuns of the Strict Observance (OCSO-0670). Wrentham, MA. Ireland. Mother Bernard O'Donnell.

1949 - Oblate Sisters of the Sacred Heart of Jesus (OSHJ-3050). McDonald, OH. Italy. Mother Clara D'Amico and Mother Chiarina Antonucci.

1950 - Sisters of the Infant Jesus (IJ-2240). Colma, CA. France.*

1950 - Daughters of Jesus (FI-0840). Pinehurst, NC. Spain. Mother Isabel Tejero.

1950 - Medical Missionaries of Mary (MMM-2480). Boston, MA. Ireland. Mother Therese Stanley.

1950 - Hermanas Catequistas Guadalupanas (HCG-1900). San Antonio, TX. Mexico.

1950 - Comboni Missionary Sisters (CMS-0690). Richmond, VA. Italy. Mother Emma Gazzaniga.

1950 - Oblate Sisters of St. Francis de Sales (OSFS-3060). Childs, MD. France. Mother Bertha Gonzaga Schär.

1951 - Dominican Rural Missionaries (OP-1130). Abbeville, LA. France. Mother Marie St. Paul.

1951 - Recluse Missionaries of Jesus and Mary (RMJM). Lafayette, LA. Canada.*

1952 - Home Mission Sisters of America (Glenmary Sisters) (GHMS-2080). Cincinnati, OH. U.S. Rev. William Howard Bishop.

1952 - Sisters of St. Ann (SSA-3718). Ebensburg, PA. Italy. Mother M. Celia Richini.

1952 - Congregation of the Religious of Nazareth (RdeN). Lompoc, CA. France.*

1952 - Little Sisters of Jesus (LSJ-2330). Nome, AK. France. Mother Magdeleine of Jesus.

1952 - Mill Hill Sisters (Franciscan Missionaries of St. Joseph) (FMSJ-1410). Albany, NY. England. Mother M. Patrick Mellor.

1953 - Congregation of St. Brigid (CSB-3735). San Antonio, TX. Ireland. Mother Philomena Hickey.

1953 - Congregation of the Sisters of the Holy Faith (CHF-1940). Norwalk, CA. Ireland. Mother Mary Macken.

1953 - Religious Sisters of Charity (RSC-3400). Long Beach, CA. Ireland. Mother Agnes Gertrude MacNamara.

1953 - Sisters of the Sacred Hearts of Jesus and Mary (SHJM-3680). Atwater, CA. England. Mother Leontia Collins.

1954 - Missionary Sisters of the Holy Rosary (MSHR-2730). Philadelphia, PA. Ireland. Bishop Joseph Shanahan.

1954 - Sisters of the Pious School (SchP-3200). San Fernando, CA. Spain. Mother Maria Luisa Lopez Neira.

1954 - Daughters of Our Lady of the Snows (DLS). St. Mary's, AK. U.S. Mother Antoinette Johnson.*

1954 - Religious of Mary Immaculate (RMI-3460). San Antonio, TX. Italy.

1954 - Institute of the Blessed Virgin Mary (Loreto Sisters) (IBVM-2380). Phoenix, AZ. Belgium. Mother Kieran Deignan.

1954 - Marian Sisters of the Diocese of Lincoln (MS-2400). Lincoln, NE. U.S. Mother Marta Silna and Mother Theresa Gottvaldova.

1954 - Marian Society of Dominican Catechists (OP-1090). Alexandria, LA. U.S. Bishop Charles Greco.

1954 - Poor Clare Missionary Sisters (MC-2840). Gardena, CA. Mexico. Mother Elvira Uribe, Mother Theresa Botello, Mother Carmen Rios, Mother Theresa Velescos.

1954 - Xaverian Missionary Society of Mary, Inc. (XMM-4230). Petersham, MA. Italy. Mother Celestina Healy Bottego.

1954 - Consolata Missionary Sisters (MC-0720). Grand Rapids, MI. Italy. Mother Celsa Silvestri.

1955 - Congregation of Jesus Crucified (OSB-2250). Devon, PA. France. Mother M. Marie Des Douleurs.

1955 - Religious Daughters of St. Joseph (FSJ-0930). Los Angeles, CA. Mexico. Mother Esperanza Martinez.

1955 - Carmelite Sisters of Charity (CaCh-0340). Castro Valley, CA. Spain. Mother Dolores Blasco.

1955 - Daughters of the Sacred Heart of Jesus (Bethlemita Sisters) (SCIF-0910). Dallas, TX. Colombia. Mother Maria Isabel Andersen.

1955 - Sisters of Charity of St. Vincent De Paul (SVZ-0630). West Seneca, NY. Yugoslavia. Mother Angela Sustek.

1955 - Daughters of Our Lady of the Sacred Heart (FDNSC-0900). Bellmawr, NJ. France.

1955 - Congregation of the Oblates of the Sacred Heart of Jesus (OSC). Camden, NJ. France.*

1955 - Sisters of Mercy (RSM-2540). Deerfield Beach, FL. Ireland. Mother Enda Duffy, RSM

1955 - Sisters of St. Philip Neri (SPNT). Las Vegas, NV. Cuba. Mother Maria Paz Royo.

1955 - Missionary Sisters of Our Lady of Mercy (MOM-2830). Lackawanna, NY. Brazil. Mother Mary of the Cross.

1956 - Missionaries of Jesus, Mary and Joseph (MJMJ-2770). Corpus Christi, TX. Spain. Mother Maria Dolores de la Cruz Domingo.

1956 - Sisters of the Society Devoted to the Sacred Heart (SDSH-4050). Los Angeles, CA. Hungary. Mother Ida Peterfy.

1956 - Claretian Missionary Sisters (Religious of Mary Immaculate Claretian Missionary Sisters) (RMI-0685). Momence, IL. Spain.

1956 - Congregation of the Divine Spirit (CDS-1040). Erie, PA. U.S.

1956 - Oblate Sisters of the Assumption (OA). Worcester, MA. Holland.*

1956 - Marist Sisters (Congregation of Mary) (SM-2430). Dearborn Heights, MI. Canada. Mother Dominic Rynne, SM.

1956 - Sisters of Mercy (SM-2516). El Cerrito, CA. Ireland. Mother Gertrude Hayes.

1957 - Order of the Most Holy Redeemer (OSSR-2010). Esopus, NY. Canada. Mother Mary Catherine Parks.

1957 - The Brigittine Sisters (OSSS-0280). Darien, CT. Sweden. Mother Mary Elizabeth Hesselblad. Page 426.

1957 - Servants of St. Joseph (MSSJ-3595). Falls Church, VA. Spain.

1957 - Benedictine Sisters (Regina Pacis) (OSB-0200). Bedford, NH. U.S. Mother M. Raphaela Simonis.

1957 - Cistercian Nuns (OCist-0680). Prairie du Sac, WI. Switzerland. Mother M. Roberta Peterhans

1958 - Franciscan Sisters of the Third Order of the Immaculate Conception (FSIC). Philadelphia, PA. Spain.*

1958 - Missionary Sisters of the Asumption (MSA). Marietta, OH. South Africa.*

1958 - Sisters of the Love of God (RAD). Fairhaven, MA. Spain.*

1958 - Sisters of the Lamb of God (AD-2260). Owensboro, KY. France. Mother M. Michael.

1958 - Oblates of the Most Holy Redeemer (OSSR-3030). Duxbury, MA. Spain. Mother M. Catalina.

1958 - Handmaids of Reparation of the Sacred Heart of Jesus (AR-1880). Steubenville, OH. Italy. Mother Mary Emanuela Zattolo.

1958 - Daughters of the Cross of Liege (FC-0780). Tracy, CA. England. Mother Nora Friend.

1959 - Servants of the Most Sacred Heart of Jesus (SSCJ-3630). Portage, PA. Poland. Mother Jolanta, SSCJ.

1959 - Congregation of the Oblates of Bethany (COB). St. Louis, MO. France.*

1959 - Sisters of Charity of the Infant Mary (IM). Santa Cruz, CA. Italy.

1960 - Irish Ursuline Union (OSU-4150). Columbus, GA. Ireland. Mother Margaret Mary O'Dwyer.

1960 - Sisters of Mercy (RSM-2520). Boca Raton, FL. Ireland. Mother Mary Margaret Bushe.

1960 - Missionaries of the Third Order of St. Francis of Our Lady of the Prairies (OLP). Powers Lake, ND. U.S.

1960 - Franciscan Hospitaller Sisters of the Immaculate Conception (FHIC-1270). San Jose, CA. Portugal. Mother Teresa of the Holy Face.

1961 - Congregation of Our Lady, Help of the Clergy (Maryvale Sisters) (CLHC-3090). Higganum, CT. U.S. Mother Mary Louis and Rev. Norman J. St. Martin.

1961 - Franciscan Missionary Sisters of Assisi (SFMA-1330). Holyoke, MA. Italy. Mother Angela Maria del Giglio and Rev. Giuseppe Antonio Marcheselli.

1961 - Sisters Adorers Handmaids of the Blessed Sacrament and Charity (AASC). Dos Palos, CA. Spain.*

1961 - Sisters of St. Martha of Prince Edward Island (CSM). Portland, ME. Canada.*

1961 - Dominican Sisters of Bethany (OP-1080). Chicago, IL. Holland.

1961 - Sisters of Charity of the Immaculate Conception of Ivrea (SCIC-0450). Tarrytown, NY. Italy. Mother Aurelia Bonavopontâ.

1961 - Franciscan Missionary Sisters of the Infant Jesus (FMIJ-1365). Woodbury Heights, NJ. Italy. Mother Rosalba Piazza.

1962 - Sisters of the Immaculate Conception (RCM-2130). Clovis, CA. Spain. Mother Carmen Salles and Mother Enriqueta Azana.

1962 - Franciscan Missionaries of the Divine Motherhood (FMDM). East Greenbush, NY. England. Mother Mary Francis Spring.*

1962 - The Company of the Savior (CS-0710). Bridgeport, CT. Spain. Mother Maria Felix.

1962 - African Sisters of Our Lady of Good Counsel (OLGS). Worcester, MA. Uganda.*

1963 - Angelic Sisters of St. Paul (ASSP-0120). Youngstown, NY. Italy.

1963 - Sisters of Mercy (2560). Biloxi, MS. Ireland. Mother de Lourdes Lillis.

1963 - Sisters of Saint Paul de Chartres (SPC-3980). Marquette, MI. France. Mother Mary Carol Goodman.

1964 - Daughters of Divine Providence (FDP-0800). New Orleans, LA. Italy. Mother M. Alessandrina Lauri, FDP.

1964 - Sisters of St. Elizabeth of the Third Order Regular of St. Francis of Assisi (OSE). Hoven, SD. Canada. Mother Marcella Haag.*

1964 - Cashel Mercy Sisters (CSM-2515). Jacksonville, FL. Ireland. Mother Mary Colm Gerard.*

1965 - Poor Sisters of St. Joseph (PSSJ-3250). North East, PA. Argentina. Mother Maria E. Hoeta.

1965 - Congregation of Augustinian Sisters Servants of Jesus and Mary (OSA-2145). Brandenburg, KY. Malta. Mother Rosalba Galt.

1967 - Vocationist Sisters (SDV-4210). Newark, NJ. Italy.

1968 - Augustinian Nuns of Contemplative Life (OSA-0160). Holland, MI. Italy.

1968 - Handmaids of the Most Holy Trinity (HT). South Bend, IN. U.S. Mother Ruth McAvoy.

1970 - Sisters of Charity of Our Lady, Mother of the Church (SCMC-0530). Baltic, CT. U.S. Mother M. Marie Alma Lafond.

1970 - Community of the Holy Spirit (CHS-2020). San Diego, CA. U.S. Mother Mary Prose.

1971 - Missionaries of Charity (MC-2710). Bronx, NY. India. Mother M. Teresa.

1973 - Religious Sisters of Mercy of Alma, Michigan (RSM-2519). Alma, MI. U.S.

1973 - The Institute of the Franciscan Sisters of the Eucharist (FSE-1250). Meriden, CT. U.S. Mother Rosemae Pender, FSE, Mother Shaun Vergauwen.

1974 - Servants of Jesus (SJ-3560). Clarkston, MI. U.S. Mother Gene Rakoczy.

1975 - Sisters of the Living Word (SLW-2350). Chicago, IL. U.S. Mother Annamarie Cook.

1975 - Carmel Community (CC-0310). Columbus, OH. U.S. Mother Maria Fingerlin.

1976 - Lovers of the Holy Cross Sisters (Phat Diem) (LHC-2390). Northampton, PA. VietNam. Mother Cecilia Nguyen thi Chuyen.

1977 - Vocation Sisters (VS-4220). Falls Church, VA. England.*

1978 - Dominican Sisters of Our Lady of the Rosary and of Saint Catherine of Siena, Cabra (OP-1110). Independence, LA. Ireland.

1981 - Benedictine Nuns of the Congregation of Solesmes (OSB-0170). Westfield, VT. Canada. Mother Marguerite T. Derome.

1981 - Sisters of Mary Immaculate (SMI-2440). Leechburg, PA. India. Bishop Morrow.

1985 - Medical Sisters of St. Joseph (MSJ-2500). Wichita, KS. India.

Endnotes

1. In 1847, Sisters of Charity in New York broke away from the Sisters of Charity motherhouse in Emmitsburg, forming the Sisters of Charity of St. Vincent de Paul, of New York (SC-0650). Then, in 1850, the Emmitsburg Sisters of Charity affiliated with the Daughters of Charity in France, becoming Daughters of Charity (DC-0760). In 1852, Sisters of Charity in Cincinnati broke away from Emmitsburg, becoming the Sisters of Charity of Cincinnati, Ohio (SC-0440). (See Table I, p. 111).

2. Since 1977, this order has used the title Sisters of St. Joseph of Medaille (CSJ-3880).
3. This order was known as the Sisters of St. Mary of the Third Order of St. Francis until 1987.
4. This community returned to France in 1900. They made another American foundation in Philadelphia in 1948.
5. This order is an original foundation. The reason this community does not have an OCD number is unknown. Their archivist stated over the phone that the diocese failed to report them.
6. This order belonged to the Episcopal Church when founded in 1898. The entire community joined the Catholic Church in 1909.
7. This order is now affiliated with the Benedictine Sisters of Pontifical Jurisdiction in Fort Smith, Arkansas.
8. Originally affiliated with their motherhouse in Germany, the Congregation of Calvarienberg, this community became a diocesan community in 1983.
9. Members of this order were known as the Missionary Canonesses of St. Augustine until 1963.
10. Members of this order were formerly known as the Sisters Oblate of Divine Love.

APPENDIX C

Sister-Founded Hospitals

‡ — ‡

TITLES FOR THESE institutions varied. They were not always called hospitals and included such titles as medical center, dispensary, clinic, health center, etc.

This listing uses the original titles, although many have changed over the years. The titles of founding orders are the current ones as listed in the *Official Catholic Directory*.

An asterisk indicates the institution is no longer in operation. Some hospitals still in operation are no longer owned or operated by the original founding order.

Founding year, location, and founding order along with that order's OCD number are included with each hospital.

1829-1859

1829 — Mullanphy, St. Louis, MO, Daughters of Charity of St. Vincent de Paul (0760)

1840 — Mount St. Vincent's*, Baltimore, MD, Daughters of Charity of St. Vincent de Paul (0760)

1840 — Mount Hope Retreat*, Baltimore, MD, Daughters of Charity of St. Vincent de Paul (0760)

1845 — St. Vincent*, Donaldsonville, LA, Daughters of Charity of St. Vincent de Paul (0760)

1845 — St. Mary's*, Detroit, MI, Daughters of Charity of St. Vincent de Paul (0760)

1847 — Mercy, Pittsburgh, PA, Sisters of Mercy (2570)

1848 — Charity, Buffalo, NY, Daughters of Charity of St. Vincent de Paul (0760)

1848 — St. Mary's, Milwaukee, WI, Daughters of Charity of St. Vincent de Paul (0760)

1849 — St. Joseph's*, Philadelphia, PA, Daughters of Charity of St. Vincent de Paul (0760)

1849 — St. Vincent's, New York, NY, Sisters of Charity of St. Vincent de Paul (0650)

1849 — Mercy, Chicago, IL, Sisters of Mercy of the Union (2580)

1850 — St. Mary's, Troy, NY, Daughters of Charity of St. Vincent de Paul (0760)

1850 — Wheeling, Wheeling, WV, Sisters of St. Joseph (3830-17)

1850 — St. Vincent's, Cleveland, OH, Sisters of Charity of St. Augustine (0580)

1851 — St. Mary's, Rochester, NY, Daughters of Charity of St. Vincent de Paul (0760)

1852 — Hotel Dieu, New Orleans, LA, Daughters of Charity of St. Vincent de Paul (0760)

1852 — Good Samaritan, Cincinnati, OH, Sisters of Charity of Cincinnati (0440)

1852 — St. Joseph's*, Cleveland, OH, Sisters of Charity of St. Augustine (0580)

1852 — St. Mary's*, Buffalo, NY, Daughters of Charity of St. Vincent de Paul (0760)

1853 — St. Ann's*, St. Louis, MO, Daughters of Charity of St. Vincent de Paul (0760)

1853 — St. Joseph's, St. Paul, MN, Sisters of St. Joseph of Carondelet (3840)

1855 — St. Vincent's, Toledo, OH, Sisters of Charity of Montreal (0490)

1855 — Providence, Mobile, AL, Daughters of Charity of St. Vincent de Paul (0760)

1856 — DePaul, Norfolk, VA, Daughters of Charity of St. Vincent de Paul (0760)

1856 — St. Vincent, Los Angeles, CA, Daughters of Charity of St. Vincent de Paul (0760)

1857 — St. Mary's, San Francisco, CA, Sisters of Mercy (2570)

1858 — St. Vincent's*, St. Louis, MO, Daughters of Charity of St. Vincent de Paul (0760)

1858 — St. Joseph's*, Vancouver, WA, Sisters of Providence (3350)

1858 — St. Mary's*, Cincinnati, OH, Franciscan Sisters of the Poor (1440)

1860-1869

1860 — St. Elizabeth, Covington, KY, Franciscan Sisters of the Poor (1440)

1860 — Providence Retreat*, Buffalo, NY, Daughters of Charity of St. Vincent de Paul (0760)

1860 — St. Mary's*, Philadelphia, PA, Sisters of St. Francis of Philadelphia (1650)

1860 — St. Francis de Sales*, Richmond, VA, Daughters of Charity of St. Vincent de Paul (0760)

1860 — St. Joseph's Retreat*, Dearborn, MI, Daughters of Charity of St. Vincent de Paul (0760)

1860 — St. Anne's, Washington, DC, Daughters of Charity of St. Vincent de Paul (0760)

1861 — DePaul*, New Orleans, LA, Daughters of Charity of St. Vincent de Paul (0760)

1861 — Providence, Washington, DC, Daughters of Charity of St. Vincent de Paul (0760)

1862 — St. Agnes, Baltimore, MD, Daughters of Charity of St. Vincent de Paul (0760)

1862 — St. Mary's*, Cairo, IL, Congregation of the Sisters of the Holy Cross (1920)

1863 — Carney, Boston, MA, Daughters of Charity of St. Vincent de Paul (0760)

1863 — St. Mary's, Hoboken, NJ, Franciscan Sisters of the Poor (1440)

1864 — St. John, Leavenworth, KS, Sisters of Charity of Leavenworth (0480)

1864 — St. Joseph's, Baltimore, MD, Sisters of St. Francis of Philadelphia (1650)

1864 — St. Francis, Jersey City, NJ, Franciscan Sisters of the Poor (1440)

1864 — Spencer*, Meadville, PA, Sisters of St. Joseph (3830-09)

1864 — St. Peter's*, Brooklyn, NY, Franciscan Sisters of the Poor (1440)

1864 — St. Peter's, Albany, NY, Sisters of Mercy (2570)

1865 — St. Joseph's*, Alton, IL, Daughters of Charity of St. Vincent de Paul (0760)

1865 — St. Francis, Columbus, OH, Franciscan Sisters of the Poor (1440)

1865 — St. Francis, Pittsburgh, PA, Sisters of St. Francis of Millvale, PA (1620)

1865 — St. Vincent's*, Santa Fe, NM, Sisters of Charity of Cincinnati (0440)

1866 — St. Mary, Quincy, IL, Franciscan Sisters of the Poor (1440)

1866 — St. Mary's, Galveston, TX, Congregation of the Sisters of Charity of the Incarnate Word (0470)

1866 — St. Francis*, New York, NY, Franciscan Sisters of the Poor (1440)

1866 — St. Elizabeth, Utica, NY, Sisters of the Third Franciscan Order (1490)

1867 — St. Joseph's, Paterson, NJ, Sisters of Charity of St. Elizabeth, Convent Station (0590)

1867 — St. John's, Lowell, MA, Daughters of Charity of St. Vincent de Paul (0760)

1867 — St. Michael's, Newark, NJ, Franciscan Sisters of the Poor (1440)

1868 — St. Joseph, Chicago, IL, Daughters of Charity of St. Vincent de Paul (0760)

1868 — St. Elizabeth, Boston, MA, Franciscan Sisters of Allegany, New York (1180)

1868 — Holy Family, Brooklyn, NY, Sisters of Charity of St. Vincent de Paul (0650)

1869 — St. Joseph's, Fort Wayne, IN, Poor Handmaids of Jesus Christ (3230)

1869 — Mercy, Davenport, IA, Sisters of Mercy of the Union (2580)

1869 — Providence*, Smithfield, MI, Daughters of Charity of St. Vincent de Paul (0760)

1869 — St. Joseph's*, St. Joseph, MO, Daughters of Charity of St. Vincent de Paul (0760)

1869 — St. Joseph's, Syracuse, NY, Sisters of the Third Franciscan Order (1490)

1869 — St. Mary's*, Albany, NY, Sisters of Mercy (2570)

1869 — Santa Rosa, San Antonio, TX, Congregation of the Sisters of Charity of the Incarnate Word (0460)

1869 — St. John's*, New York, NY, Sisters of Charity of St. Vincent de Paul (0650)

1870-1879

1870 — St. Catherine's*, Brooklyn, NY, Dominican Sisters (1070-05)

1870 — St. Elizabeth of Hungary*,New York, NY, Franciscan Sisters of Allegany, New York (1180)

1871 — St. John's Mercy, St. Louis, MO, Sisters of Mercy of the Union (2580)

1872 — St. Mary's, Evansville, IN, Daughters of Charity of St. Vincent de Paul (0760)

1872 — St. John*, Helena, MT, Sisters of Charity of Leavenworth (0480)

1872 — St. Mary's*, Boston, MA, Daughters of Charity of St. Vincent de Paul (0760)

1873 — St. Joseph's*, Cincinnati, OH, Sisters of Charity of Cincinnati (0440)

1873 — St. Ann's*, Cleveland, OH, Sisters of Charity of St. Augustine (0580)

1873 — St. Joseph's*, Deer Lodge, MT, Sisters of Charity of Leavenworth (0480)

1873 — St. Joseph, Denver, CO, Sisters of Charity of Leavenworth (0480)

1873 — Mercy, Iowa City, IA, Sisters of Mercy of the Union (2580)

1873 — Providence, Holyoke, MA, Sisters of Providence (3340)

1873 — St. Francis, Trenton, NJ, Sisters of St. Francis of Philadelphia (1650)

1873 — St. Patrick, Missoula, MT, Sisters of Providence (3350)

1873 — St. Joseph, Reading, PA, Sisters of St. Francis of Philadelphia (1650)

1873 — Providence, Southfield, MI, Daughters of Charity of St. Vincent de Paul (0760)

1874 — St. Mary & Elizabeth, Louisville, KY, Sisters of Charity of Nazareth (0500)

1874 — Mercy, Baltimore, MD, Sisters of Mercy of the Union (2580)

1874 — St. Margaret, Boston, MA, Daughters of Charity of St. Vincent de Paul (0760)

1874 — Child's*, Albany, NY, Society of the Holy Child Jesus (4060)

1874 — St. Mary's, Saginaw, MI, Daughters of Charity of St. Vincent de Paul (0760)

1874 — St. Joseph, Kansas City, MO, Sisters of St. Joseph (3830-15)

1875 — St. Joseph's, Savannah, GA, Sisters of Mercy of the Union (2580)

1875 — St. Anthony's, Effingham, IL, Hospital Sisters of the Third Order of St. Francis (1820)

1875 — St. Elizabeth, Belleville, IL, Hospital Sisters of the Third Order of St. Francis (1820)

1875 — St. John's, Springfield, IL, Hospital Sisters of the Third Order of St. Francis (1820)

1875 — St. Francis, Litchfield, IL, Hospital Sisters of the Third Order of St. Francis (1820)

1875 — St. Francis, Cape Girardeau, MO, Franciscan Sisters, Daughters of the Sacred Hearts of Jesus and Mary (1240)

1875 — St. Vincent, Portland, OR, Sisters of Providence (3350)

1875 — St. Vincent, Erie, PA, Sisters of St. Joseph (3830-09)

1875 — Holy Cross, Salt Lake City, UT, Congregation of the Sisters of the Holy Cross (1920)

1876 — St. Elizabeth, Lafayette, IN, Sisters of St. Francis of Perpetual Adoration (1640)

1876 — Soldier's Home*, Washington, DC, Daughters of Charity of St. Vincent de Paul (0760)

1876 — Louisiana Retreat*, New Orleans, LA, Daughters of Charity of St. Vincent de Paul (0760)

1876 — St. Joseph's*, Laramie, WY, Sisters of Charity of Leavenworth (0480)

1877 — St. Mary's, St. Louis, MO, Franciscan Sisters of Mary (1415)

1877 — Providence, Seattle, WA, Sisters of Providence (3350)

1878 — St. Mary's, Decatur, IL, Hospital Sisters of the Third Order of St. Francis (1820)

1878 — St. Joseph, Highland, IL, Hospital Sisters of the Third Order of St. Francis (1820)

1878 — St. Francis, Peoria, IL, Sisters of the Third Order of St. Francis (1770)

1878 — St. Elizabeth, Dayton, OH, Franciscan Sisters of the Poor (1440)

1879 — Mercy, Dubuque, IA, Sisters of Mercy of the Union (2580)

1879 — St. Joseph, Wichita, KS, Sisters of St. Joseph (3830-18)

1879 — St. Joseph, Lexington, KY, Sisters of Charity of Nazareth (0500)

1879 — St. Mary, Walla Walla, WA, Sisters of Providence (3350)

1879 — St. Mary's*, Columbus, NE, Sisters of St. Francis of Perpetual Adoration (1640)

1879 — St. Vincent's, Harrison, NY, Sisters of Charity of St. Vincent de Paul (0650)

1880-1889

1880 — St. Mary's, Tucson, AZ, Sisters of St. Joseph of Carondelet (3840)

1880 — St. Joseph, Atlanta, GA, Sisters of Mercy of the Union (2580)

1880 — St. Joseph, Bloomington, IL, Sisters of the Third Order of St. Francis (1770)

1880 — St. Joseph*, Omaha, NE, Sisters of St. Francis of Perpetual Adoration (1640)

1880 — St. Mary's*, Astoria, OR, Sisters of Providence (3350)

1880 — St. Vincent's*, Leadville, CO, Sisters of Charity of Leavenworth (0480)

1881 — St. Vincent, Indianapolis, IN, Daughters of Charity of St. Vincent de Paul (0760)

1881 — St. James, Butte, MT, Sisters of Charity of Leavenworth (0480)

1882 — St. Mary's, Racine, WI, Franciscan Sisters, Daughters of the Sacred Hearts of Jesus and Mary (1240)

1882 — St. Francis Xavier, Charleston, SC, Sisters of Charity of Our Lady of Mercy (0510)

1882 — Mercy, Durango, CO, Sisters of Mercy of the Union (2580)

1882 — St. Joseph, South Bend, IN, Congregation of the Sisters of the Holy Cross (1920)

1882 — St. Elizabeth, Danville, IL, Franciscan Sisters of the Sacred Heart (1450)

1882 — St. Joseph, Joliet, IL, Franciscan Sisters of the Sacred Heart (1450)

1882 — St. Mary's, Pueblo, CO, Sisters of Charity of Cincinnati (0440)

1882 — St. Vincent's*, Chicago, IL, Daughters of Charity of St. Vincent de Paul (0760)

1882 — St. Joseph's*, New York, NY, Franciscan Sisters of the Poor (1440)

1882 — St. Joseph's*, Keokuk, IA, Sisters of the Third Order of St. Francis (1770)

1882 — St. Anthony*, Terre Haute, IN, Sisters of St. Francis of Perpetual Adoration (1640)

1883 — St. Francis, LaCrosse, WI, Congregation of the Sisters of the Third Order of St. Francis of Perpetual Adoration (1780)

1883 — St. Joseph, Lancaster, PA, Sisters of St. Francis of Philadelphia (1650)

1883 — St. Mary's*, Emporia, KS, Sisters of St. Francis of Perpetual Adoration (1640)

1884 — St. Alexis, Cleveland, OH, Sisters of St. Francis of Perpetual Adoration (1640)

1884 — Providence, Kansas City, KS, Sisters of Charity of Leavenworth (0480)

1884 — St. Francis, Escanaba, MI, Sisters of the Third Order of St. Francis (1770)

1884 — St. Joseph's*, Ashland, WI, Poor Handmaids of Jesus Christ (3230)

1884 — Emergency Hospital*, Buffalo, NY, Daughters of Charity of St. Vincent de Paul (0760)

1884 — St. Anthony's, Rock Island, IL, Franciscan Sisters of the Immaculate Conception (1310)

1884 — St. Joseph's Mercy*, Chariton, IA, Sisters of Mercy (2570)

1884 — St. Joseph's, Milwaukee, WI, Franciscan Sisters, Daughters of the Sacred Hearts of Jesus and Mary (1240)

1885 — St. Joseph, Chippewa Falls, WI, Hospital Sisters of the Third Order of St. Francis (1820)

1885 — St. Alexis, Bismarck, ND, Benedictine Sisters of Pontifical Jurisdiction (0230)

1885 — St. Joseph, St. Charles, MO, Franciscan Sisters of Mary (1415)[1]

1885 — St. Johnsbury*, St. Johnsbury, VT, Sisters of Providence (3350)

1885 — St. Mary's*, Marquette, MI, Sisters of the Third Order of St. Francis (1770)

1885 — St. Joseph's*, Menominee, MI, Sisters of the Third Order of St. Francis (1770)

1885 — St. Cloud, St. Cloud, MN, Benedictine Sisters of Pontifical Jurisdiction (0230)

1885 — A. Barton Hepburn*, Ogdensburg, NY, Sisters of Charity at Ottawa (0540)

1885 — St. Vincent's*, Philadelphia, PA, Daughters of Charity of St. Vincent de Paul (0760)

1886 — Sacred Heart, Spokane, WA, Sisters of Providence (3350)

1886 — Mt. Carmel, Columbus, OH, Congregation of the Sisters of the Holy Cross (1920)

1886 — St. Elizabeth, Chicago, IL, Poor Handmaids of Jesus Christ (3230)

1886 — St. Francis*, Burlington, IA, Sisters of the Third Order of St. Francis (1770)

1886 — St. Clara's*, Lincoln, IL, Hospital Sisters of the Third Order of St. Francis (1820)

1886 — St. Clare's*, Ft. Benton, MT, Sisters of Providence (3350)

1886 — St. Ann's*, Juneau, AK, Sisters of St. Anne (3720)

1886 — Texas Pacific*, Marshall, TX, Congregation of the Sisters of Charity of the Incarnate Word (0460)

A Brooklyn Dominican Sister of the American Congregation of the Holy Cross (c. 1942).
Courtesy Gonzaga University

1887 — St. Francis, Colorado Springs, CO, Sisters of St. Francis of Perpetual
    Adoration (1640)

1887 — St. Mary's, Streator, IL, Hospital Sisters of the Third Order of St. Francis
    (1820)

1887 — Mercy, Fort Scott, KS, Sisters of Mercy of the Union (2580)

1887 — St. Mary's, Minneapolis, MN, Sisters of St. Joseph of Carondelet (3840)

1887 — St. Francis, Grand Island, NE, Sisters of St. Francis of Perpetual Adoration
    (1640)

1887 — Misericordia*, New York, NY, Misericordia Sisters (2680)

1887 — St. Peter, Olympia, WA, Sisters of Providence (3350)

1887 — St. Joseph, Houston, TX, Congregation of the Sisters of Charity of the
    IncarnateWord (0470)

1887 — St. Margaret's, Kansas City, KS, Franciscan Sisters of the Poor (1440)

1887 — St. Bernard's*, Council Bluffs, IA, Sisters of Mercy of the Union (2580)

1887 — St. Mary's*, LaSalle, IL, Franciscan Sisters of the Sacred Heart (1450)

1888 — Mt. St. Raphael*, Trinidad, CO, Sisters of Charity of Cincinnati (0440)

1888 — St. Francis, Cincinnati, OH, Franciscan Sisters of the Poor (1440)

1888 — St. Joseph's, Yonkers, NY, Sisters of Charity of St. Vincent de Paul (0650)

1888 — St. Joseph's, Hot Springs, AR, Sisters of Mercy of the Union (2580)

1888 — St. Vincent, Little Rock, AR, Sisters of Charity of Nazareth (0500)

1888 — St. Mary's, Lewiston, ME, Sisters of Charity of St. Hyacinthe (0610)

1888 — St. Mary's, Duluth, MN, Benedictine Sisters of Pontifical Jurisdiction
    (0230)

1888 — St. Agnes, Philadelphia, PA, Sisters of St. Francis of Philadelphia (1650)

1888 — St. Vincent, Green Bay, WI, Hospital Sisters of the Third Order of St.
    Francis (1820)

1888 — Trinity*, Arcata, CA, Sisters of St. Joseph (3830-03)

1889 — Glockner, Colorado Springs, CO, Sisters of Charity of Cincinnati (0440)

1889 — St. Francis*, Superior, WI, Poor Handmaids of Jesus Christ (3230)

1889 — St. Joseph's*, San Francisco, CA, Franciscan Sisters of the Sacred Heart
    (1450)

1889 — St. Anne's*, Anaconda, MT, Sisters of Charity of Leavenworth (0480)

1889 — O'Connor, San Jose, CA, Daughters of Charity of St. Vincent de Paul
    (0760)

1889 — St. Francis, Wichita, KS, Sisters of the Sorrowful Mother (Third Order of
    St. Francis) (4100)

1889 — Borges, Kalamazoo, MI, Sisters of St. Joseph (3830-11)

1889 — St. Mary's, Rochester, MN, Sisters of the Third Order Regular of St.
    Francis of the Congregation of Our Lady of Lourdes (1720)

1889 — St. Elizabeth, Lincoln, NE, Sisters of St. Francis of Perpetual Adoration
    (1640)

1889 — St. Joseph, Memphis, TN, Sisters of St. Francis of Perpetual Adoration
    (1640)

1889 — St. Joseph, Fort Worth, TX, Congregation of the Sisters of Charity of the Incarnate Word (0460)

1889 — Sacred Heart, Eau Claire, WI, Hospital Sisters of the Third Order of St. Francis (1820)

1890-1899

1890 — St. Mary's, East St. Louis, IL, Hospital Sisters of the Third Order of St. Francis (1820)

1890 — St. James, Newark, NJ, Sisters of the Third Franciscan Order (1490)

1890 — St. James Mercy, Hornell, NY, Sisters of Mercy (2570)

1890 — St. Anthony Mercy, Columbus, OH, Franciscan Sisters of the Poor (1440)

1890 — St. Joseph, Bellingham, WA, Sisters of St. Joseph of Peace (3890)

1890 — St. Nicholas, Sheboygan, WI, Hospital Sisters of the Third Order of St. Francis (1820)

1890 — Mercy, San Diego, CA, Sisters of Mercy (2570)

1890 — Mercy*, Manistee, MI, Sisters of Mercy of the Union (2580)

1890 — St. Francis*, Freeport, IL, Franciscan Sisters of the Sacred Heart (1450)

1890 — St. Joseph's*, Scranton, PA, Sisters, Servants of the Immaculate Heart of Mary (2150)

1890 — St. John's*, Port Townsend, WA, Sisters of Providence (3350)

1890 — St. Joseph's Mercy*, Sioux City, IA, Sisters of Mercy of the Union (2580)

1891 — St. Joseph's, Marshfield, WI, Sisters of the Sorrowful Mother (Third Order of St. Francis) (4100)

1891 — St. Joseph's, Tacoma, WA, Sisters of St. Francis of Philadelphia (1650)

1891 — St. Elizabeth, Yakima, WA, Sisters of Providence (3350)

1891 — St. John's, Springfield, MO, Sisters of Mercy of the Union (2580)

1891 — St. John's Queen, Elmhurst, NY, Sisters of St. Joseph (3830-05)

1891 — Roselia Foundling*, Pittsburgh, PA, Sisters of Charity of Seton Hill (0570)

1891 — All Souls*, Morristown, NJ, Sisters of Charity of Montreal (0490)

1891 — Providence*, Wallace, ID, Sisters of Providence (3350)

1891 — St. Mary's*, Oshkosh, WI, Sisters of the Sorrowful Morther (Third Order of St. Francis) (4100)

1892 — St. Joseph's Mercy, Clinton, IA, Sisters of Mercy of the Union (2580)

1892 — St. Joseph*, Aberdeen, WA, Dominican Sisters (1070-21)

1892 — St. Gabriel's, Little Falls, MN, Franciscan Sisters of the Immaculate Conception (1310)

1892 — Columbus, Great Falls, MT, Sisters of Providence (3350)

1892 — Mercy, Hamilton, OH, Sisters of Mercy of the Union (2580)

1892 — Hotel Dieu*, El Paso, TX, Daughters of Charity of St. Vincent de Paul (0760)

1892 — St. Joseph, Providence, RI, Sisters of St. Francis of Philadelphia (1650)

1892 — St. Joseph, Lorain, OH, Sisters of the Humility of Mary (2110)

1892 — Notre Dame de Lourdes, Manchester, NH, Sisters of Charity of St. Hyacinthe (0610)

1892 — St. John's, Cleveland, OH, Sisters of Charity of St. Augustine (0580)

1892 — Sacred Heart*, Manchester, NH, Sisters of Mercy (2570)

1892 — Mercy*, Prescott, AZ, Sisters of Mercy (2570)

1892 — St. Francis*, Port Jervis, NY, Sisters of St. Francis of the Mission of the Immaculate Virgin (1510)

1892 — St. Anthony's, Denver, CO, Sisters of St. Francis of Perpetual Adoration (1640)

1893 — Mercy*, Anamosa, IA, Sisters of Mercy (2570)

1893 — Mercy*, Burlington, IA, Sisters of St. Francis of Clinton, IA (1540)

1893 — St. Vincent, Worcester, MA, Sisters of Providence (3340)

1893 — Sacred Heart, Milwaukee, WI, School Sisters of St. Francis (1680)

1893 — Sacred Heart-Rhinelander, WI, Sisters of the Sorrowful Mother (Third Order of St. Francis) St. Mary's (4100)

1893 — Mercy, Des Moines, IA, Sisters of Mercy of the Union (2580)

1893 — St. Mary's, Grand Rapids, MI, Sisters of Mercy of the Union (2580)

1893 — Holy Ghost, Cambridge, MA, Sisters of Charity of Montreal (0490)

1893 — Municipal*, Chicago, IL, Poor Handmaids of Jesus Christ (3230)

1893 — St. Ignatius*, Colfax, WA, Sisters of Providence (3350)

1893 — Sacred Heart, Tomahawk, WI, Sisters of the Sorrowful Mother (Third Order of St. Francis) (4100)

1894 — St. John's Hickey, Anderson, IN, Congregation of the Sisters of the Holy Cross (1920)

1894 — Daly City, Daly City, CA, Daughters of Charity of St. Vincent de Paul (0760)

1894 — St. Mary of Nazareth, Chicago, IL, Sisters of the Holy Family of Nazareth (1970)

1894 — St. Alphonsus, Boise, ID, Congregation of the Sisters of the Holy Cross (1920)

1894 — Mercy, Laredo, TX, Sisters of Mercy of the Union (2580)

1894 — St. Francis, Maryville, MO, Franciscan Sisters of Mary (1415)

1894 — St. Agnes*, Watertown, NY, Sisters of Mercy of the Union (2580)

1894 — Seton Memorial, New York, NY, Sisters of Charity of St. Vincent de Paul (0650)

1894 — St. Mary's*, Superior, WI, Poor Handmaids of Jesus Christ (3230)

1894 — Fanny Allen, Winooski, VT, Religious Hospitallers of St. Joseph (3440)

1895 — Mercy, Sacramento, CA, Sisters of Mercy (2570)

1895 — St. Mary's, Passaic, NJ, Sisters of Charity of St. Elizabeth, Convent Station (0590)

1895 — St. Joseph, Phoenix, AZ, Sisters of Mercy (2570)

1896 — Our Savior*, Jacksonville, IL, Congregation of the Sisters of the Holy Cross (1920)

1896 — St. Agnes, Fond Du Lac, WI, Congregation of the Sisters of St. Agnes (3710)

1896 — St. Mary's, Grand Junction, CO, Sisters of Charity of Leavenworth (0480)

1896 — St. Paul, Dallas, TX, Daughters of Charity of St. Vincent de Paul (0760)

1896 — Mercy, Springfield, MA, Sisters of Providence (3340)

1896 — St. Anthony's*, Las Vegas, NM, Sisters of Charity of Leavenworth (0480)

1896 — St. John's General*, Pittsburgh, PA, Sisters of Divine Providence (0990)

1896 — St. Rose's*, New York, NY, The Servants of Relief for Incurable Cancer (1070-23)

1896 — Pittsburgh*, Pittsburgh, PA, Sisters of Charity of Seton Hill (0570)

1897 — St. Anthony, Chicago, IL, Franciscan Sisters of the Sacred Heart (1450)

1897 — St. Mary, Kankakee, IL, Servants of the Holy Heart of Mary (3520)

1897 — Sacred Heart, Yankton, SD, Benedictine Sisters of Pontifical Jurisdiction (0230)

1897 — St. Francis, Hartford, CT, Sisters of St. Joseph of Chambery (3850)

1897 — St. Elizabeth, Baker, OR, Sisters of St. Francis of Philadelphia (1650)

1897 — Hotel Dieu, Beaumont, TX, Congregation of the Sisters of Charity of the Incarnate Word (0470)

1897 — San Antonio*, Kenton, OH, Sisters of Charity of Cincinnati (0440)

1897 — St. Joseph's*, Mankato, MN, Sisters of the Sorrowful Mother (Third Order of St. Francis) (4100)

1897 — San Gabriels*, Gabriels, NY, Sisters of Mercy of the Union (2580)

1897 — St. Joseph's*, Deadwood, SD, Benedictine Sisters of Pontifical Jurisdiction (0230)

1897 — St. Andrew's*, Murphysboro, IL, Franciscan Sisters, Daughters of the Sacred Hearts of Jesus and Mary (1240)

1898 — St. Elizabeth's, Wabasha, MN, Sisters of the Sorrowful Mother (Third Order of St. Francis) (4100)

1898 — Holy Family, Manitowoc, WI, Franciscan Sisters of Christian Charity (1230)

1898 — St. Mary's, Pierre, SD, Benedictine Sisters of Pontifical Jurisdiction (0230)

1898 — St. Thomas, Nashville, TN, Daughters of Charity of St. Vincent de Paul (0760)

1898 — St. Anthony, St. Louis, MO, Franciscan Sisters, Daughters of the Sacred Hearts of Jesus and Mary (1240)

1898 — DuBois*, DuBois, PA, Sisters of Mercy (2570)

1898 — Mercy, Wilkes-Barre, PA, Sisters of Mercy of the Union (2580)

1898 — St. Margaret, Hammond, IN, Sisters of St. Francis of Perpetual Adoration (1640)

1898 — St. Anthony, Oklahoma City, OK, Franciscan Sisters of Mary (1415)

1898 — St. Vincent, Birmingham, AL, Daughters of Charity of St. Vincent de Paul (0760)

1898 — Georgetown, Washington, DC, Sisters of St. Francis of Philadelphia (1650)

1898 — St. John's*, Long Island, NY, Sisters of St. Joseph (3830-05)

1899 — St. Elizabeth, Appelton, WI, Franciscan Sisters, Daughters of the Sacred Hearts of Jesus and Mary (1240)

1899 — St. Anthony, Rockford, IL, Sisters of the Third Order of St. Francis (1770)

1899 — St. Joseph's, Mt. Clemens, MI, Sisters of Charity of Cincinnati (0440)

1899 — St. Francis, Breckenridge, MN, Franciscan Sisters of the Immaculate Conception (1310)

1899 — St. Vincent, Billings, MT, Sisters of Charity of Leavenworth (0480)

1899 — St. Joseph, Stockton, CA, Dominican Sisters (1070-04)

1899 — St. Vincent*, Montclair, NJ, Sisters of Charity of St. Elizabeth, Convent Station (0590)

1899 — Cabrini Medical New York, NY, Missionary Sisters of the Sacred Heart (2860)

1899 — Mercy*, Bay City, MI, Sisters of Mercy of the Union (2580)

1899 — House of Calvary, Bronx, NY , Dominican Sisters (1070-15)

1899 — St. Joseph's, Breese, IL, Poor Handmaids of Jesus Christ (3230)

1899 — St. Joseph's*, Hancock, MI, Sisters of St. Joseph of Carondelet (3840)

1900-1909

1900 — St. Francis, Evanston, IL, Sisters of St. Francis of Perpetual Adoration (1640)

1900 — Farren Memorial*, Turner Falls, MA, Sisters of Providence (3340)

1900 — St. Joseph's, Asheville, NC, Sisters of Mercy (2570)

1900 — St. John's, Fargo, ND, Sisters of St. Joseph of Carondelet (3840)

1900 — Mercy*, Vicksburg, MS, Sisters of Mercy (2570)

1900 — St. Joseph's, Belvidere, IL, Sisters of St. Joseph (3830-15)

1900 — St. Bernard's, Jonesboro, AR, Olivetan Benedictine Sisters (0240)

1900 — St. Clement, Red Bud, IL, Adorers of the Blood of Christ (0100)

1900 — St. Mary's*, Syracuse, NY, Daughters of Charity of St. Vincent de Paul (0760)

1900 — St. John's, Joplin, MO, Sisters of Mercy of the Union (2580)

1900 — St. Charles*, Aurora, IL, Franciscan Sisters of the Sacred Heart (1450)

1900 — St. Vincent's*, Kansas City, MO, Daughters of Charity of St. Vincent de Paul (0760)

1900 — Mt. St. Rose*, St. Louis, MO, Franciscan Sisters of Mary (1415)

1900 — Our Lady of Lourdes*, Hot Springs, SD, Benedictine Sisters of Pontifical Jurisdiction (0230)

1900 — St. Joseph's Mercy, Ann Arbor, MI, Sisters of Mercy of the Union (2580)

1900 — Holy Family*, LaPorte, IN, Poor Handmaids of Jesus Christ (3230)

1901 — St. Anthony, Louisville, KY, Sisters of St. Francis of Perpetual Adoration (1640)

1901 — St. Luke's, Aberdeen, SD, Sisters of the Presentation of the Blessed Virgin Mary (3320)

1901 — Rosary Hill, Hawthorne, NY, The Servants of Relief for Incurable Cancer (1070-23)

1901 — St. Anthony, Pendleton, OR, Sisters of St. Francis of Philadelphia (1650)

1901 — St. Anthony's, Amarillo, TX, Congregation of the Sisters of Charity of the Incarnate Word (0460)

1901 — Bendictine, Kingston, NY, Benedictine Sisters of Pontifical Jurisdiction (0230)

1901 — Mercy Denver, CO, Sisters of Mercy of the Union (2580)

1901 — St. Joseph's*, Louisville, KY, Sisters of Charity of Nazareth (0500)

1901 — Kneipp Springs*, Rome City, IN, Adorers of the Blood of Christ (0100)

1902 — Mary Immaculate, Jamaica, NY, The Servants of Relief for Incurable Cancer (1070-23)

1902 — Good Samaritan, Suffern, NY, Sisters of Charity of St. Elizabeth, Convent Station (0590)

1902 — Mercy, Council Bluffs, IA, Sisters of Mercy of the Union (2580)

1902 — Seton, Austin, TX, Daughters of Charity of St. Vincent de Paul (0760)

1902 — St. Anthony, Michigan City, IN, Sisters of St. Francis of Perpetual Adoration (1640)

1902 — St. Joseph's, Albuquerque, NM, Sisters of Charity of Cincinnati (0440)

1902 — St. Joseph's, Brainerd, MN, Benedictine Sisters of Pontifical Jurisdiction (0230)

1902 — Mercy, Devils Lake, ND, Sisters of Mercy of the Union (2580)

1902 — Providence, Sandusky, OH, Sisters of St. Francis of the Congregation of Our Lady of Lourdes (1720)

1902 — St. Joseph, Elgin, IL, Franciscan Sisters of the Sacred Heart (1450)

1902 — St. Margaret*, Montgomery, AL, Daughters of Charity of St. Vincent de Paul (0760)

1902 — St. Joseph's, Parkersburg, WV, Sisters of St. Joseph (3830-17)

1902 — Providence, Oakland, CA, Sisters of Providence (3350)

1902 — St. Joseph's, Lewiston, ID, Sisters of St. Joseph of Carondelet (3840)

1902 — St. Francis*, Kewanee, IL, Franciscan Sisters of the Immaculate Conception of the Third Order of St. Francis

1902 — Sacred Heart*, Garrett, IN, Franciscan Sisters of the Sacred Heart (1450)

1902 — St. Edward's*, New Albany, IN, Sisters of St. Francis of Perpetual Adoration (1640)

1902 — St. Vincent's*, Crookston, MN, Benedictine Sisters of Pontifical Jurisdiction (0230)

1902 — Our Lady of Perpetual Help*, Manchester, NH, Sisters of Mercy (2570)

1902 — St. James*, Perham, MN, Franciscan Sisters of the Immaculate Conception (1310)

1902 — St. Joseph's*, Pittsburgh, PA, Sisters of St. Joseph (3830-13)

1902 — St. Vincent's*, Sherman, TX, Daughters of Charity of St. Vincent de Paul (0760)

1902 — St. Thomas Mercy*, Marshalltown, IA, Sisters of Mercy of the Union (2580)

1903 — Mercy, Cedar Rapids, IA, Sisters of Mercy (2570)

1903 — St. Mary's, Green Bay, WI, Misericordia Sisters (2680)

1903 — St. Mary's, Amsterdam, NY, Sisters of St. Joseph of Carondelet (3840)

1903 — St. Vincent's, Staten Island, NY, Sisters of Charity of St. Vincent de Paul (0650)

1903 — St. Anne's*, Chicago, IL, Poor Handmaids of Jesus Christ (3230)

1903 — St. Vincent's, Bridgeport, CT, Daughters of Charity of St. Vincent de Paul (0760)

1903 — Mount Carmel, Pittsburg, KS, Sisters of St. Joseph (3830-18)

1903 — Halstead, Halstead, KS, Sisters of St. Joseph (3830-18)

1903 — Mercy, Muskegon, MI, Sisters of Mercy of the Union (2580)

1903 — St. Joseph, Concordia, KS, Sisters of St. Joseph (3830-18)

1903 — St. Margaret, Spring Valley, IL, Sisters of Mary of the Presentation (2450)

1903 — St. Mary's*, Winfield, KS, Sisters of St. Joseph (3830-18)

1903 — St. Francis*, Macomb, IL, Sisters of St. Francis of Clinton, IA (1540)

1903 — St. Bernard's, Chicago, IL, Religious Hospitallers of St. Joseph (3440)

1903 — St. Rose, Great Bend, KS, Dominican Sisters (1070-24)

1904 — Providence, Waco, TX, Daughters of Charity of St. Vincent de Paul (0760)

1904 — St. Mary's*, Clarksburg, WV, Sisters of St. Joseph (3830-17)

1904 — St. Joseph's*, Hillsgrove, RI, Franciscan Sisters of Allegany, New York (1180)

1904 — St. Anthony's*, Sabetha, KS, Sisters of St. Joseph (3830-15)

1904 — St. Joseph's Mercy*, Waverly, IA, Sisters of Mercy of the Union (2580)

1905 — Spohn, Corpus Christi, TX, Congregation of the Sisters of Charity of the Incarnate Word (0460)

1905 — St. Anthony, Carroll, IA, Congregation of the Sisters of the Third Order of St. Francis of Perpetual Adoration (1780)

1905 — Oak Park, Oak Park, IL, Misericordia Sisters (2680)

1905 — St. Mary's, Jefferson City, MO, Franciscan Sisters of Mary (1415)

1905 — Columbus-Cuneo, Chicago, IL, Missionary Sisters of the Sacred Heart (2860)

1905 — Alleghany, Cumberland, MD, Daughters of Charity of St. Vincent de Paul (0760)

1905 — St. Elizabeth, Elizabeth, NJ, Sisters of Charity of St. Elizabeth, Convent Station (0590)

1905 — Good Samaritan, Zanesville, OH, Franciscan Sisters of Christian Charity (1230)

1905 — Providence, Everett, WA, Sisters of Providence (3350)

1905 — St. Francis, Bluc Island, IL, Franciscan Sisters of Mary (1415)

1905 — St. Edward Mercy, Fort Smith, AR, Sisters of Mercy of the Union (2580)
1905 — St. Joseph*, Boonville, MO, Benedictine Sisters of Pontifical Jurisdiction (0230)
1905 — St. Joseph's*, Queens, NY, Sisters of St. Joseph (3830-05)
1905 — St. Louis*, Berlin, NH, Sisters of Charity of St. Hyacinthe (0610)
1905 — St. Joseph's*, West Point, NE, Franciscan Sisters of Christian Charity (1230)
1905 — St. Vincent, Taylorsville,IL, Adorers of the Blood of Christ (0100)
1906 — Mercy, Charlotte, NC, Sisters of Mercy (2570)
1906 — Mary Immaculate, Newport News, VA, Bernardine Sisters of the Third Order of St. Francis (1810)
1906 — St. Mary's*, Orange, NJ, Sisters of St. Francis of the Mission of the Immaculate Virgin (1510)
1906 — St. Joseph, Mitchell, SD, Sisters of the Presentation of the Blessed Virgin Mary (3320)
1906 — St. Raphael, New Haven, CT, Sisters of Charity of St. Elizabeth, Convent Station (0590)
1906 — St. Anne's, Fall River, MA, Dominican Sisters of Charity of the Presentation of the Blessed Virgin (1100)
1906 — St. Mary's*, Rosewell, NM, Sisters of the Sorrowful Mother (Third Order of St. Francis) (4100)
1906 — Holy Cross, Nogales, AZ, Sisters of St. Joseph of St. Augustine (3900)
1906 — St. Elizabeth, Red Bluff, CA, Sisters of Mercy of the Union (2580)
1906 — Northern Maine General*, Eagle Lake, ME, Little Franciscan Sisters of Mary (2280)
1906 — Mercy*, North Bend, OR, Sisters of Mercy of the Union (2580)
1906 — St. Joseph's*, Nogales, AZ, Sisters of Mercy (2570)
1906 — St. Leo*, Greensboro, NC, Daughters of Charity of St. Vincent de Paul (0760)
1907 — St. Peter's, New Brunswick, NJ, Sisters of Charity of Montreal (0490)
1907 — St. James, Pontiac, IL, Sisters of the Third Order of St. Francis (1770)
1907 — St. Ansgar, Moorhead, MN, Franciscan Sisters of the Immaculate Conception (1310)
1907 — St. Helen*, Chehalis, WA, Dominican Sisters (1070-21)
1907 — St. Mary's, Gary, IN, Poor Handmaids of Jesus Christ (3230)
1907 — St. Mary's*, Columbus, WI, Sisters of the Divine Savior (1030)
1907 — St. Michael's*, Grand Forks, ND, Sisters of St. Joseph of Carondelet (3840)
1907 — St. Mary's*, Wausau, WI, Sisters of the Divine Savior (1030)
1907 — Mercy Palmer Memorial*, Janesville, WI, Sisters of Mercy of the Union (2580)
1907 — Joseph's Mercy*, Webster City, IA, Sisters of Mercy (2570)
1907 — St. Vincent's*, Sioux City, IA, Benedictine Sisters of Pontifical Jurisdiction (0230)

1908 — St. Mary's, Galesburg, IL, Sisters of the Third Order of St. Francis (1770)
1908 — St. Ann's, Westerville, OH, Sisters of St. Francis of Penance and Christian Charity (1630)
1908 — St. Mary's, Reno, NV, Dominican Sisters (1070-04)
1908 — Timken Mercy, Canton, OH, Sisters of Charity of St. Augustine (0580)
1908 — St. Francis, Santa Barbara, CA, Franciscan Sisters of the Sacred Heart (1450)
1908 — St. Joseph's, Elmira, NY, Sisters of St. Joseph (3830-14)
1908 — St. Agnes, White Plains, NY, Sisters of St. Francis of the Mission of the Immaculate Virgin (1510)
1908 — St. Patrick's, Lake Charles, LA, Congregation of the Sisters of Charity of the Incarnate Word (0470)
1908 — St. Francis, New Castle, PA, Sisters of St. Francis of Millvale, PA (1620)
1908 — St. Joseph, Del Norte, CO, Sisters of St. Joseph (3830-15)
1908 — Mercy Cadillac, MI, Sisters of Mercy of the Union (2580)
1908 — Misericordia*, Milwaukee, WI, Misericordia Sisters (2680)
1908 — St. Joseph's*, Logansport, IN, Sisters of St. Francis of Perpetual Adoration (1640)
1908 — St. Joseph's*, Williamantic, CT, Sisters of Charity of Our Lady, Mother of Mercy (0520)
1908 — St. Joseph's*, Lewiston, MT, Congregation of the Daughters of Jesus (0830)
1908 — St. Joseph's, Nashua, NH, Sisters of Charity of Montreal (0490)
1908 — St. Anthony's*, Dodge City, KS, Sisters of St. Joseph (3830-18)
1908 — St. Joseph's*, Troy, NY, Sisters of St. Joseph of Carondelet (3840)
1908 — St. Joseph's Mercy*, Fort Dodge, IA, Sisters of Mercy of the Union (2580)
1909 — St. Mary's, Waterbury, CT, Sisters of St. Joseph of Chambery (3850)
1909 — Mount St. Mary's, Niagara Falls, NY, Sisters of St. Francis of the Third Order Regular (1800)
1909 — St. Mary's, Centralia, IL, Poor Handmaids of Jesus Christ (3230)
1909 — Mercy, Roseburg, OR, Sisters of Mercy of the Union (2580)
1909 — St. Francis, Topeka, KS, Sisters of Charity of Leavenworth (0480)
1909 — St. Anthony, Hays, KS, Congregation of the Sisters of St. Agnes (3710)
1909 — St. Mary's*, Kansas City, MO, Franciscan Sisters of Mary (1415)
1909 — Providence*, Beaver Falls, PA, Sisters of Charity of Seton Hill (0570)
1909 — St. Charles, Port Jefferson, NY, Daughters of Wisdom (0960)

1910-1919

1910 — Mercy, Johnstown, PA, Sisters of Mercy of the Union (2580)
1910 — St. John's, San Angelo, TX, Congregation of the Sisters of Charity of the Incarnate Word (0460)
1910 — Mercy, Altoona, PA, Felician Sisters (1170)

1910 — Mercy, Bakersfield, CA, Sisters of Mercy (2570)

1910 — St. Joseph's Mercy, Centerville, IA, Sisters of Mercy of the Union (2580)

1910 — St. Joseph, Mishawaka, IN, Poor Handmaids of Jesus Christ (3230)

1910 — Holy Rosary, Miles City, MT, Sisters of the Presentation of the Blessed Virgin Mary (3320)

1910 — St. Catherine's*, Omaha, NE, Sisters of Mercy of the Union (2580)

1910 — St. James*, St. James, MN, Sisters of the Third Order Regular of St. Francis of the Congregation of Our Lady of Lourdes (1720)

1910 — Champlain Valley*, Plattsburgh, NY, Sisters of Charity at Ottawa (0540)

1910 — St. Mary's of the Lake*, Saranac Lake, NY, Sisters of Mercy of the Union (2580)

1910 — St. Joseph*, Alliance, NE, Sisters of St. Francis of Penance and Christian Charity (1630)

1910 — Kalispell General*, Kalispell, MT, Sisters of Mercy (2570)

1910 — Mercy, Independence, KS, Sisters of Mercy of the Union (2580)

1910 — Loretto*, New Ulm, MN, Poor Handmaids of Jesus Christ (3230)

1911 — St. Joseph's Mercy*, Cresco, IA, Sisters of Mercy of the Union (2580)

1911 — Schumpert, Shreveport, LA, Congregation of the Sisters of Charity of the Incarnate Word (0470)

1911 — St. Elizabeth, Youngstown, OH, Sisters of the Humility of Mary (2110)

1911 — St. Joseph's, Paris, TX, Congregation of the Sisters of Charity of the Incarnate Word (0460)

1911 — Holy Rosary, Ontario, OR, Dominican Sisters (1070-25)

1911 — McKennan, Sioux Falls, SD, Sisters of the Presentation of the Blessed Virgin Mary (3320)

1911 — Providence, Medford, OR, Sisters of Providence (3350)

1911 — Mercy, Grayling, MI, Sisters of Mercy of the Union (2580)

1911 — St. Joseph, Minot, ND, Sisters of St. Francis of Penance and Christian Charity (1630)

1911 — St. James, Chicago Heights, IL, Sisters of St. Francis of Perpetual Adoration (1640)

1911 — Sacred Heart*, Havre, MT, Sisters of St. Francis of Penance and Christian Charity (1630)

1911 — St. Joseph's, Aurora, IL, Sisters of Mercy of the Union (2580)

1911 — Mother Cabrini Memorial, Chicago, IL, Missionary Sisters of the Sacred Heart (2860)

1911 — Alabama*, Mobile, AL, Daughters of Charity of St. Vincent de Paul (0760)

1911 — Mercy*, Parsons, KS, Sisters of St. Joseph (3830-18)

1912 — Holy Innocents*, Portland, ME, Sisters of Charity of Our Lady, Mother of Mercy (0520)

1912 — St. Francis, Waterloo, IA, Franciscan Sisters, Daughters of the Sacred Hearts of Jesus and Mary (1240)

1912 — St. Mary's, Madison, WI, Franciscan Sisters of Mary (1415)

1912 — St. Joseph's, Dickinson, ND, Sisters of Mercy of the Holy Cross (2630)

1912 — St. Mary's Hill, Milwaukee, WI, School Sisters of St. Francis (1680)

1912 — St. Michael's, Stevens Point, WI, Sisters of the Sorrowful Mother (Third Order of St. Francis) (4100)

1912 — John B. Murphy Memorial*, Chicago, IL, Sisters of Mercy (2570)

1912 — Mary's Help*, San Francisco, CA, Daughters of Charity of St. Vincent de Paul (0760)

1912 — Sacred Heart*, Ft. Madison, IA, Sisters of the Third Order of St. Francis (1770)

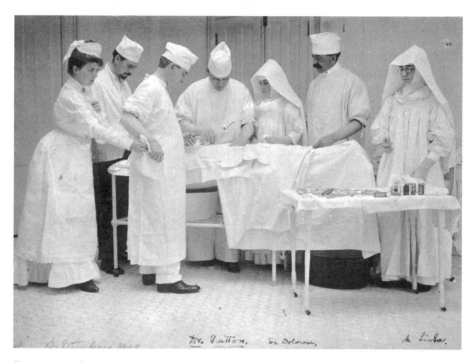

Surgery at Good Samaritan Hospital,1902. Dr. Sutton is the surgeon. The two sisters are, left to right, Sister Dolorose Goetzler and Sister Lioba Guelig, Zanesville, Ohio.

Courtesy Franciscan Sisters of Christian Charity

1912 — St. John's*, Iola, KS, Sisters of St. Joseph (3830-18)

1912 — Grey Lock*, Adams, MA, Sisters of Providence (3340)

1912 — St. Joseph's Mercy*, Detroit, MI, Sisters of Mercy of the Union (2580)

1913 — St. Francis, Monroe, LA, Franciscan Missionaries of Our Lady (1380)

1913 — Mercy, Tiffin, OH, Sisters of Mercy of the Union (2580)

1913 — St. Andrew's, Bottineau, ND, Sisters of Mary of the Presentation (2450)

1913 — St. Francis, Poughkeepsie, NY, Sisters of St. Francis of the Mission of the Immaculate Virgin (1510)

1913 — St. Francis, Charleston, WV, Sisters of St. Joseph (3830-17)

1913 — Sacred Heart*, Richwood, WV, Pallottine Missionary Sisters - Queen of Apostles Province (3150)

1913 — St. Francis, Beech Grove, IN, Sisters of St. Francis of Perpetual Adoration (1640)

1913 — St. John's, Oxnard, CA, Sisters of Mercy (2570)

1913 — St. Joseph's*, Dodgeville, WI, Franciscan Sisters of the Immaculate Conception (1310)

1913 — Huber Memorial*, Pana, IL, Misericordia Sisters (2680)

1913 — Mt. St. Agnes, Louisville, KY, Sisters of Charity of Nazareth (0500)

1913 — Sisters*, Waterville, ME, Daughters of Charity of St. Vincent de Paul (0760)

1913 — Mercy*, Hempstead, NY, Congregation of the Infant Jesus (2230)

1913 — St. Francis*, Darby, PA, Congregation of Bon Secours (0270)

1914 — St. Joseph*, Ottumwa, IA, Congregation of the Humility of Mary (2100)

1914 — Sacred Heart, Hanford, CA, Dominican Sisters (1070-25)

1914 — St. John's, Salina, KS, Sisters of St. Joseph (3830-15)

1914 — Trinity*, Jamestown, ND, Sisters of St. Joseph of Carondelet (3840)

1914 — St. Mary's*, McAlester, OK, Congregation of the Sisters of Charity of the Incarnate Word (0460)

1914 — St. Mary's*, Watertown, WI, Missionary Sisters Servants of the Holy Spirit (3530)

1914 — St. Anthony's*, Woodhaven, NY, Franciscan Sisters of the Poor (1440)

1914 — Holy Family*, St. Ignatius, MT, Sisters of Providence (3350)

1914 — Madigan Memorial*, Houlton, ME, Sisters of Mercy (2570)

1914 — St. Agnes*, Hartford, CT, Sisters of Mercy (2570)

1915 — St. Mary's, Sparta, WI, Congregation of the Sisters of the Third Order of St. Francis of Perpetual Adoration (1780)

1915 — Sacred Heart, Pensacola, FL, Daughters of Charity of St. Vincent de Paul (0760)

1915 — Mercy, Port Jervis, NY, Sisters of Mercy of the Union (2580)

1915 — St. Elizabeth*, Hannibal, MO, Franciscan Sisters of Mary (1415)

1915 — St. Charles, Bend, OR, Sisters of St. Joseph (3830-10)

1915 — A. N. Brady*, Albany, NY, Sisters of Charity of St. Vincent de Paul (0650)

1915 — Mercy*, Jackson, MI, Sisters of Mercy of the Union (2580)

1916 — St. Joseph, Polson, MT, Religious Hospitallers of St. Joseph (3440)

1916 — St. Joseph Mercy, Mason City, IA, Sisters of Mercy of the Union (2580)

1916 — Our Lady of Lourdes, Pasco, WA, Sisters of St. Joseph of Carondelet (3840)

1916 — St. Michael, Texarkana, AR, Congregation of the Sisters of Charity of the Incarnate Word (0470)

1916 — St. Vincent, Jacksonville, FL, Daughters of Charity of St. Vincent de Paul (0760)

1916 — St. Mary's*, Conrad, MT, Dominican Sisters (1070-03)

1916 — St. Anthony's*, Wenatchee, WA, Sisters of St. Joseph of Peace (3890)

1916 — St. Mary's Keller*, Scranton, PA, Bernardine Sisters of the Third Order of St. Francis (1810)

1916 — Columbus*, Seattle, WA, Missionary Sisters of the Sacred Heart (2860)

1917 — Divine Savior, Portage, WI, Sisters of the Divine Savior (1030)

1917 — St. Catherine's, Kenosha, WI, Dominican Sisters (1070-25)

1917 — Catherine McAuley, Ann Arbor, MI, Sisters of Mercy of the Union (2580)

1917 — Mercy, Toledo, OH, Sisters of Mercy of the Union (2580)

1917 — St. Joseph, New Hampton, IA, Missionary Sisters Servants of the Holy Spirit (3530)

1917 — St. Jerome, Batavia, NY, Sisters of Mercy (2570)

1917 — Sacred Heart, Allentown, PA, Missionary Sisters of the Most Sacred Heart of Jesus of Hiltrup (2800)

1917 — Mercy, Scranton, PA, Sisters of Mercy of the Union (2580)

1917 — Mercy, Nampa, ID, Sisters of Mercy of the Union (2580)

1917 — St. Francis Xavier*, Carlsbad, NM, Adorers of the Blood of Christ (0100)

1917 — St. Joseph*, Rice Lake, WI, Sisters of St. Joseph of the Third Order of St. Francis (3930)

1917 — Sacred Heart*, LeMars, IA, Sisters of St. Francis of the Holy Family (1570)

1918 — St. Mary's*, Gallup, NM, Sisters of St. Francis of Perpetual Adoration (1640)

1918 — Lee Memorial, Dowagiac, MI, Sisters of Mercy of the Union (2580)

1918 — St. Rita's, Lima, OH, Sisters of Mercy of the Union (2580)

1918 — Mercy, Oshkosh, WI, Sisters of the Sorrowful Mother (Third Order of St. Francis) (4100)

1918 — St. Luke*, Pittsfield, MA, Sisters of Providence (3340)

1918 — St. Anthony Mercy*, Pocatello, ID, Sisters of Mercy of the Union (2580)

1918 — Misericordia, Philadelphia, PA, Sisters of Mercy (2570)

1918 — St. Mary's*, Ladysmith, WI, Servants of Mary (3590)

1918 — Renger*, Hallettsville, TX, Sisters of the Incarnate Word and Blessed Sacrament (2210)

1919 — St. Joseph's, Ponca City, OK, Sisters of St. Joseph (3830-18)

1919 — Our Lady of Victory, Lackawanna, NY, Sisters of St. Joseph (3830-06)

1919 — Mercy Urbana, IL, Servants of the Holy Heart of Mary (3520)

1919 — Bon Secours, Baltimore, MD, Congregation of Bon Secours (0270)

1919 — Mercy*, Auburn, NY, Sisters of the Third , Franciscan Order (1490)

1919 — Mercy General*, Tupper Lake, NY, Sisters of Mercy of the Union (2580)

1919 — St. Joseph's, Superior, WI, Sisters of St. Joseph of Carondelet (3840)

1919 — Queens*, Portland, ME, Sisters of Mercy (2570)

1919 — St. Joseph's*, St. Cloud, MN, Benedictine Sisters of Pontifical Jurisdiction (0230)

1919 — Hinde Ball Mercy*, Mt. Vernon, OH, Sisters of Charity of Nazareth (0500)

1920-1929

1920 — St. Bernard, Milbank, SD, Daughters of St. Mary of Providence (0940)

1920 — St. Joseph, Eureka, CA, Sisters of St. Joseph (3830-03)

1920 — Mercy, Williston, ND, Sisters of Mercy of the Union (2580)

1920 — Good Samaritan, Baltimore, MD, Daughters of Charity of St. Vincent de Paul (0760)

1920 — St. Lawrence, Lansing, MI, Sisters of Mercy of the Union (2580)

1920 — Warner Brown*, Eldorado, AR, Sisters of Mercy of the Union (2580)

1920 — St. Vincent's*, Lansdowne, PA, Daughters of Charity of St. Vincent de Paul (0760)

1920 — St. Joseph's*, Hartford, WI, Religious Hospitallers of St. Joseph (3440)

1920 — St. Mary's*, Modesto, CA, Sisters of Mercy (2570)

1920 — St. Francis*, Grinnell, IA, Sisters of St. Francis of Clinton, IA (1540)

1920 — St. Elizabeth's*, Hutchison, KS, Sisters of Mercy (2570)

1920 — St. Joseph of Nazareth*, Clayton, NM, Sisters of the Holy Family of Nazareth (1970)

1921 — Good Samaritan, Pottsville, PA, Missionary Sisters of the Most Sacred Heart of Jesus of Hiltrup (2800)

1921 — St. Joseph's, Buckhannon, WV, Pallottine Missionary Sisters - Queen of the Apostles Province (3150)

1921 — St. Joseph, Flint, MI, Sisters of St. Joseph (3830-11)

1921 — Mercy, Portsmouth, OH, Sisters of the Third Order Regular of St. Francis of the Congregation of Our Lady of Lourdes (1720)

1921 — St. Catherine of Siena*, McCook, NE, Dominican Sisters (1070-01)

1921 — Loretto*, Cold Springs, NY, Franciscan Missionary Sisters of the Sacred Heart (1400)

1921 — Misericordia*, Chicago, IL, Sisters of Mercy (2570)

1921 — St. Elizabeth*, San Francisco, CA, Daughters of Charity of St. Vincent de Paul (0760)

1921 — St. Elizabeth, Granite City, IL, Sisters of Divine Providence (0990)

1922 — Yoakum Catholic, Yoakum, TX, Congregation of the Incarnatre Word and Blessed Sacrament (2200)

1922 — Santa Marta, Los Angeles, CA, Religious Daughters of St. Joseph (0930)

1922 — St. Mary's*, DeKalb, IL, Sisters of Mercy of the Union (2580)

1922 — Mercy*, Brownsville, TX, Sisters of Mercy of the Union (2580)

1922 — St. Mary's, Baraboo, WI, Franciscan Sisters of Mary (1415)

1923 — Ketchikan, Ketchikan, AK, Sisters of St. Joseph of Peace (3890)

1923 — St. Mary's, Long Beach, CA, Congregation of the Sisters of Charity of the Incarnate Word (0470)

1923 — Good Samaritan, Kearney, NE, Sisters of St. Francis of Perpetual Adoration (1640)

1923 — Our Lady of Lake, Baton Rouge, LA, Franciscan Missionaries of Our Lady (1380)

1923 — St. Francis, Wilmington, DE, Sisters of St. Francis of Philadelphia (1650)

1923 — Holy Cross*, Deming, NM, Congregation of the Sisters of the Holy Cross (1920)

1923 — St. Valentine's*, Wendell, ID, Benedictine Sisters of Pontifical Jurisdiction (0230)

1924 — Sacred Heart, Eugene, OR, Sisters of St. Joseph of Peace (3890)

1924 — St. Joseph Riverside, Warren, OH, Sisters of the Humility of Mary (2110)

1924 — St. John's, Longview, WA, Sisters of St. Joseph of Peace (3890)

1924 — St. Mary's, Huntington, WV, Pallottine Missionary Sisters - Queen of the Apostles Province (3150)

1924 — Mercy, New Orleans, LA, Sisters of Mercy of the Union (2580)

1924 — Bishop de Goesbriand*, Burlington, VT, Religious Hospitallers of St. Joseph (3440)

1924 — Mercywood, Ann Arbor, MI, Sisters of Mercy of the Union (2580)

1925 — Holy Name, Teaneck, NJ, Sisters of St. Joseph of Peace (3890)

1925 — Our Lady of Lourdes, Binghampton, NY, Daughters of Charity of St. Vincent de Paul (0760)

1925 — Holy Name of Jesus, Gadsden, AL, Missionary Servants of the Most Blessed Trinity (2790)

1925 — St. Anthony's, Morrilton, AR, Benedictine Sisters of Pontifical Jurisdiction (0230)

1925 — St. Anthony's, Alton, IL, Sisters of St. Francis of the Martyr St. George (1600)

1926 — St. John, Tulsa, OK, Sisters of the Sorrowful Mother (Third Order of St. Francis) (4100)

1926 — Mercy, Elwood, IN, Sisters of St. Joseph (3830-10)

1926 — Holy Cross, Merrill, WI, Sisters of Mercy of the Holy Cross (2630)

1926 — Mercy, Oelwein, IA, Sisters of Mercy (2570)

1926 — Queen of Angels, Los Angeles, CA, Franciscan Sisters of the Sacred Heart (1450)

1926 — St. Joseph's, Carbondale, PA, Sisters, Servants of the Immaculate Heart of Mary (2160)

1926 — St. John's*, Rapid City, SD, Benedictine Sisters of Pontifical Jurisdiction (0230)

1926 — St. Francis*, Washington, MO, Hospital Sisters of the Third Order of St. Francis (1820)

1926 — Mercy*, Slaton, TX, Sisters of Mercy of the Union (2580)

1927 — St. Mary's, Nebraska City, NE, Franciscan Sisters of Mary (1415)

1927 — St. Francis, Miami Beach, FL, Franciscan Sisters of Allegany, New York (1180)

1927 — St. Francis, Honolulu, HI, Sisters of the Third, Franciscan Order (1490)

1927 — Lecla, Battle Creek, MI, Sisters of Mercy of the Union (2580)

1927 — St. Joseph's, El Paso, TX, Sisters of St. Joseph (3830-15)

1927 — St. Joseph Mercy, Pontiac, MI, Sisters of Mercy of the Union (2580)

1927 — St. Benedict's*, Sterling, CO, Benedictine Sisters of Pontifical Jurisdiction (0230)

1927 — Sacred Heart*, Lynch, NE, Benedictine Sisters of Pontifical Jurisdiction (0230)

1927 — St. Cecelia's*, Brooklyn, NY, Dominican Sisters (1070-05)

1927 — Municipal*, Hamtrack, MI, Sisters of St. Francis of the Congregation of Our Lady of Lourdes (1530)

1928 — Mercy, Valley City, ND, Sisters of Mercy of the Union (2580)

1928 — St. Catherine, East Chicago, IN, Poor Handmaids of Jesus Christ (3230)

1928 — Holy Cross, Chicago, IL, Sisters of St. Casmir (3740)

1928 — Mt. Mercy*, Hammond, IN, Sisters of Mercy (2570)

1928 — St. Thomas*, Akron, OH, Sisters of Charity of St. Augustine (0580)

1928 — Mercy, Buffalo, NY, Sisters of Mercy (2570)

1929 — St. Francis, Shakopee, MN, Franciscan Sisters of St. Paul, MN (1485)

1929 — St. Theresa, Waukegan, IL, Missionary Sisters, Servants of the Holy Spirit (3530)

1929 — St. Joseph, Orange, CA, Sisters of St. Joseph (3830-03)

1929 — St. Agnes, Fresno, CA, Congregation of the Sisters of the Holy Cross (1920)

1930-1939

1930 — St. Mary's, Cottonwood, ID, Benedictine Sisters of Pontifical Jurisdiction (0230)

1930 — St. Mary's, Knoxville, TN, Sisters of Mercy of the Union (2580)

1930 — St. Mary, Port Arthur, TX, Congregation of the Sisters of Charity of the Incarnate Word (0470)

1930 — Little Company of Mary, Evergreen Park, IL, Sisters of the Little Company of Mary (2270)

1930 — St. Joseph's, Chewelah, WA, Dominican Sisters (1070-29)

1930 — St. Joseph's, Lowell, MA, Sisters of Charity of Ottawa (0540)

1930 — Sacred Heart, Philadelphia, PA, The Servants of Relief of Incurable Cancer (1070-23)

1930 — Mother of Good Counsel*, Normandy, MO, Franciscan Sisters of the Poor (1440)

1931 — Sante Fe*, Temple, TX, Congregation of the Sisters of Charity of the Incarnate Word (0470)

1931 — St. Bernardine, San Bernardino, CA, Congregation of the Sisters of Charity of the Incarnate Word (0470)

1931 — St. Anthony*, Milwaukee, WI, School Sisters of St. Francis (1680)

1931 — St. Anthony's, St. Petersburg, FL, Franciscan Sisters of Allegany, New York (1180)

1931 — St. Catherine, Garden City, KS, Dominican Sisters (1070-24)
1932 — Good Samaritan, Dayton, OH, Sisters of Charity of Cincinnati (0440)
1932 — St. Francis, Greenville, SC, Franciscan Sisters of the Poor (1440)
1932 — Rose Hawthorne Lathrop, Fall River, MA, The Servants of Relief for
   Incurable Cancer (1070-23)
1933 — Incarnate Word, St. Louis, MO, Congregation of the Sisters of Charity of
   the Incarnate Word (0460)
1933 — St. Luke*, Pasadena, CA, Sisters of St. Joseph of Carondelet (3840)
1933 — Langlade, Antigo, WI, Religious Hospitallers of St. Joseph (3440)
1933 — Fitzgerald-Mercy, Darby, PA, Sisters of Mercy (2570)
1934 — St. Joseph's, Tampa, FL, Franciscan Sisters of Allegany, New York (1180)
1934 — Arcadia Valley, Pilot Knob, MO, Franciscan Sisters of Mary (1415)
1934 — St. Benedict, Parkston, SD, Benedictine Sisters of Pointifical Jurisdiction
   (0230)
1935 — Bethania, Wichita Falls, TX, Sisters of the Holy Family of Nazareth (1970)
1935 — St. Joseph, Bryan, TX, Sisters of St. Francis of the Congregation of Our
   Lady of Lourdes (1530)
1935 — Our Lady of Lourdes, Norfolk, NE, Missionary Benedictine Sisters (0210)
1936 — St. Joseph, Arcadia, WI, Franciscan Sisters of St. Paul, MN (1485)
1936 — St. Mary, Manhattan, KS, Sisters of St. Joseph (3830-18)
1936 — St. Joseph, Kokomo, IN, Sisters of St. Joseph (3830-10)
1936 — Sacred Heart, Norristown, PA, Missionary Sisters of the Most Sacred Heart
   of Jesus of Hiltrup (2800)
1937 — St. Mary's, Enid, OK, Adorers of the Blood of Christ (0100)
1937 — Mother FrancesTyler, TX, Sisters of the Holy Family of Nazareth (1970)
1937 — Providence, Columbia, SC, Sisters of Charity of St. Augustine (0580)
1938 — St. Francis, Olean, NY, Franciscan Sisters of Allegany, New York (1180)
1938 — Mercy of Watertown, Watertown, NY, Sisters of Mercy of the Union
   (2580)
1938 — St. Anthony, Warwick, NY, Franciscan Sisters of the Poor (1440)
1938 — St. Aloisius, Harvey, ND, Sisters of Mary of the Presentation (2450)
1938 — St. Mary's, West Palm Beach, FL, Franciscan Sisters of Allegany, New
   York (1180)
1938 — St. Mary's, Athens, GA, Missionary Sisters of the Most Sacred Heart of
   Jesus of Hiltrup (2800)
1938 — St. Thomas More, Canon City, CO, Benedictine Sisters of Pontifical
   Jurisdiction (0230)
1939 — Providence, Anchorage, AK, Sisters of Providence (3350)
1939 — Loretto, Chicago, IL, Sisters of St. Casmir (3740)
1939 — Our Lady of Perpetual Help, Atlanta, GA, The Servants of Relief for
   Incurable Cancer (1070-23)
1939 — Mount Carmel, Detroit, MI, Sisters of Mercy of the Union (2580)

1939 — St. Mary's, Detroit Lakes, MN, Benedictine Sisters of Pontifical
      Jurisdiction (0230)

1939 — City*, New Rockford, ND, Sisters of the Presentation of the Blessed Virgin
      Mary (3320)

1939 — St. Mary of Plains, Lubbock, TX, Sisters of St. Joseph (3830-03)

1939 — St. Clare, Monroe, WI, Congregation of the Sisters of St. Agnes (3710)

1940-1949

1940 — Marian, Santa Maria, CA, Sisters of St. Francis of Penance and Christian
      Charity (1630)

1940 — Nazareth, Philadelphia, PA, Sisters of the Holy Family of Nazareth (1970)

1940 — Holy Cross*, Austin, TX, Missionary Sisters of the Immaculate
      Conception of the Mother of God (2760)

1940 — Presentation Rolla, ND, Sisters of Mary of the Presentation (2450)

1940 — St. Dominic-Jackson, Jackson, MS, Dominican Sisters (1070-10)

1941 — St. Michael, Milwaukee, WI, Franciscan Sisters, Daughters of the Sacred
      Hearts of Jesus and Mary (1240)

1941 — Providence, Portland, OR, Sisters of Providence (3350)

1941 — Our Lady of Good Counsel, St. Paul, MN, The Servants of Relief for
      Incurable Cancer (1070-23)

1941 — St. Alphonsus, Port Washington, WI, Sisters of the Sorrowful Mother
      (Third Order of St. Francis) (4100)

1942 — St. John's, Santa Monica, CA, Sisters of Charity of Leavenworth (0480)

1942 — Our Lady of Mercy, Cincinnati, OH, Sisters of Mercy of the Union (2580)

1942 — Divine Savior, York, SC, Sisters of Charity of Our Lady of Mercy (0510)

1942 — St. Joseph, Stamford, CT, Sisters of St. Joseph of Chambery (3850)

1942 — Our Lady of Mercy, Dyer, IN, Sisters of Mercy of the Union (2580)

1942 — St. Jude, Fullerton, CA, Sisters of St. Joseph (3830-03)

1943 — Mercy, Portland, ME, Sisters of Mercy (2570)

1943 — St. Eugene, Dillon, SC, Franciscan Sisters of Mary (1415)

1943 — St. Francis*, Buffalo, NY, Sisters of St. Francis of the Third Order Regular
      (1800)

1944 — Holy Family, Estherville, IA, Sisters of the Sorrowful Mother (Third Order
      of St. Francis) (4100)

1944 — Good Samaritan, Mount Vernon, IL, Sisters of St. Francis of the
      Providence of God (1660)

1944 — St. Vincent's, Monett, MO, Vincentian Sisters of Charity (4170)

1944 — St. Joseph, Burbank, CA, Sisters of Providence (3350)

1945 — Holy Cross, Detroit, MI, Sisters of St. Francis of the Congregation of Our
      Lady of Lourdes (1530)

1945 — Bon Secours, Grosse Point, MI, Congregation of Bon Secours (0270)

1945 — Holy Trinity, Graceville, MN, Missionary Benedictine Sisters (0210)

1945 — Maryview, Portsmouth, VA, Congregation of Bon Secours (0270)
1945 — Sacred Heart*, Loup City, NE, Sisters of St. Joseph of the Third Order of St. Francis (3930)
1945 — St. Francis, Lynwood, CA, Sisters of St. Francis of Penance and Christian Charity (1630)
1946 — Marymount, London, KY, Sisters of Charity of Nazareth (0500)
1946 — Okarche Memorial*, Okarche, OK, Felician Sisters (1170)
1946 — St. Edward*, Cameron, TX, Congregation of the Sisters of Charity of the Incarnate Word (0470)
1946 — St. Benedict's, Ogden, UT, Benedictine Sisters of Pontifical Jurisdiction (0230)
1946 — St. Joseph's, Park Rapids, MN, Sisters of St. Joseph of Medaille (3880)
1946 — St. Francis*, Marceline, MO, Franciscan Sisters of Mary (1415)
1947 — St. Elizabeth*, Houston, TX, Missionary Sisters of the Immaculate Conception of the Mother of God (2760)
1947 — Mercy, Oklahoma City, OK, Sisters of Mercy of the Union (2580)
1947 — St. Rose of Lima, Henderson, NV, Dominican Sisters (1070-13)
1947 — Villa St. John, Downingtown, PA, Sisters of Mercy (2570)
1947 — Our Lady of the Way, Martin, KY, Sisters of Charity of Cincinnati (0440)
1947 — St. Joseph, Bangor, ME, Felician Sisters (1170)
1948 — St. Mary's, Norton, VA, Poor Servants of the Mother of God (3640)
1948 — Sancta Marie*, Cambridge, MA, Daughters of Mary of the Immaculate Conception (0860)
1948 — St. Joseph's, Hillsboro, WI, Congregation of the Sisters of the Third Order of St. Francis of Perpetual Adoration (1780)
1948 — Mercy Owensboro, KY, Sisters of Mercy of the Union (2580)
1948 — St. Joseph of the Pines, Southern Pines, NC, Sisters of Providence (3340)
1948 — St. Joseph, Florence, CO, Sisters of Charity of Cincinnati (0440)
1948 — St. Joseph of the Plains*, Cheyenne Wells, CO, Sisters of St. Joseph of the Third Order of St. Francis (3930)
1949 — Mercy, Merced, CA, Dominican Sisters (1070-25)
1949 — St. Michael, Tyndall, SD, Benedictine Sisters of Pontifical Jurisdiction (0230)
1949 — Our Lady of Lourdes, Lafayette, LA, Franciscan Missionaries of Our Lady (1380)
1949 — St. Joseph, Hazelton, PA, Bernardine Sisters of the Third Order of St. Francis (1810)
1949 — St. Clare's, Schenectady, NY, Franciscan Sisters of the Poor (1440)
1949 — Marymount, Garfield Heights, OH, Sisters of St. Joseph of the Third Order of St. Francis (3930)
1949 — St. Clare's, New York, NY, Franciscan Sisters of Allegany, New York (1180)

1949 — Franciscan Children's, Boston, MA, Franciscan Missionaries of Mary (1370)

1949 — Carrington, Carrington, ND, Sisters of the Presentation of the Blessed Virgin Mary (3320)

1950-1959

1950 — Dominican Santa Cruz, Santa Cruz, CA, Dominican Sisters (1070-13)

1950 — St. Margaret's Mercy*, Fredonia, KS, Sisters of Mercy of the Union (2580)

1950 — St. Frances Cabrini, Alexandria, LA, Congregation of the Sisters of Charity of the Incarnate Word (0470)

1950 — Pratt*, Pratt, KS, Sisters of St. Joseph of Carondelet (3840)

1950 — Trinity, Baudette, MN, Sisters of St. Joseph of Medaille (3880)

1950 — Bon Secours, Methuen, MA, Congregation of Bon Secours (0270)

1950 — Mercy, Springfield, OH, Sisters of Mercy of the Union (2580)

1950 — Santa Rosa Memorial, Santa Rosa, CA, Sisters of St. Joseph of Carondelet (3840)

1950 — Mercy, Miami, FL, Sisters of St. Joseph of St. Augustine (3900)

1950 — Holy Family, New Ricmond, WI, Sisters of St. Joseph of Carondelet (3840)

1950 — Our Lady of Lourdes, Camden, NJ, Franciscan Sisters of Allegany, New York (1180)

1950 — St. Benedict's*, San Antonio, TX, Benedictine Sisters of Pontifical Jurisdiction (0230)

1950 — St. Ann's*, Watertown, SD, Benedictine Sisters of Pontifical Jurisdiction (0230)

1950 — St. Francis, West Point, NE, Franciscan Sisters of Christian Charity (1230)

1950 — St. Francis, Columbus, GA, Sisters of St. Francis of Millvale, PA (1620)

1951 — St. Mary-Rogers, Rogers, AR, Dominican Sisters (1070-10)

1951 — Mercy Memorial, Urbana, OH, Sisters of Mercy of the Union (2580)

1951 — St. Joseph Memorial, Larned, KS, Dominican Sisters (1070-24)

1951 — Flaget Memorial, Bardstown, KY, Sisters of Charity of Nazareth (0500)

1951 — St. John's*, Red Lake Falls, MN, Benedictine Sisters of Pontifical Jurisdiction (0230)

1951 — Yorktown Memorial*, Yorktown, TX, Felician Sisters (1170)

1951 — Kenmore Mercy, Kenmore, NY, Sisters of Mercy (2570)

1951 — Divine Providence, Williamsport, PA, Sisters of Christian Charity (0660)

1951 — Mercy, Corning, IA, Felician Sisters (1170)

1951 — Memorial, Jasper, IN, Sisters of the Little Company of Mary (2270)

1951 — St. Benedict's, Jerome, ID, Benedictine Sisters of Pontifical Jurisdiction (0230)

1951 — St. Joseph's*, Huntingburg, IN, Benedictine Sisters of Pontifical Jurisdiction (0230)

1952 — Gettysburg Memorial, Gettysburg, SD , Bernardine Sisters of the Third
      Order of St. Francis (1810)

1952 — Mount Carmel, Colville, WA, Dominican Sisters (1070-29)

1952 — Queen of Peace, New Prague, MN, Benedictine Sisters of Pontifical
      Jurisdiction (0230)

1952 — St. Anthony's, O'Neill, NE, Sisters of St. Francis of Penance and Christian
      Charity (1630)

1952 — Garrison Memorial, Garrison, ND, Benedictine Sisters of Pontifical
      Jurisdiction (0230)

1952 — DePaul, Cheyenne, WY, Sisters of Charity of Leavenworth (0480)

1952 — St. Ansgar's, Park River, ND, Sisters of the Presentation of the Blessed
      Virgin Mary (3320)

1952 — Memorial, Chattanooga, TN, Sisters of Charity of Nazareth (0500)

1952 — St. John, Detroit, MI, Sisters of St. Joseph (3830-11)

1952 — St. Joseph's, Augusta, GA, Sisters of St. Joseph of Carondelet (3840)

1953 — St. Gerard, Hankinson, ND, Sisters of St. Francis of the Immaculate Heart
      of Mary (1590)

1953 — Resurrection, Chicago, IL, Sisters of Resurrection (3480)

1953 — St. Charles, Oregon, OH, Sisters of Mercy of the Union (2580)

1953 — Towner County, Cando, ND, Sisters of St. Francis of the Immaculate Heart
      of Mary (1590)

1953 — St. Clare's-Riverside, Denville, NJ, Sisters of the Sorrowful Mother (Third
      Order of St. Francis) (4100)

1953 — Regina Memorial, Hastings, MN, Sisters of Charity of Our Lady, Mother
      of Mercy (0510)

1953 — Tawas St. Joseph, Tawas City, MI, Sisters of St. Joseph (3830-11)

1953 — Mercy, Redding, CA, Sisters of Mercy (2570)

1954 — Daniel Freeman, Marina Del Rey, CA, Sisters of St. Joseph of Carondelet
      (3840)

1954 — St. Joseph, Kirkwood, MO, Sisters of St. Joseph of Carondelet (3840)

1954 — Mercy, Port Huron, MI, Sisters of Mercy of the Union (2580)

1954 — Our Lady of Bellefonte, Ashland, KY, Franciscan Sisters of the Poor (1440)

1954 — Daniel Freeman, Inglewood, CA, Sisters of St. Joseph of Carondelet (3840)

1954 — St. Jude, Brenham, TX, Sisters of St. Francis of the Congregation of Our
      Lady of Lourdes (1530)

1954 — St. Francis, Roslyn, NY, Franciscan Missionaries of Mary (1370)

1954 — Terrebonne*, Houma, LA, Sisters of St. Joseph (3830-15)

1954 — Waupun Memorial, Waupun, WI, School Sisters of St. Francis (1680)

1955 — St. Joseph*, Blackwell, OK, Sisters of St. Joseph (3830-18)

1955 — Community Mercy, Onamia, MN, Franciscan Sisters of the Immaculate
      Conception (1310)

1955 — Divine Providence, Pittsburgh, PA, Sisters of Divine Providence (0990)

1956 — Santa Teresita, Duarte, CA, Carmelite Sisters of the Most Sacred Heart of Los Angeles (0370)
1956 — Holy Family, Cleveland, OH, The Servants of Relief for Incurable Cancer (1070-23)
1956 — St. Francis, Milwaukee, WI, Felician Sisters (1170)
1956 — Oakes Community, Oakes, ND, Sisters of St. Francis of the Immaculate Heart of Mary (1590)
1956 — St. John's*, Brownsville, MN, Benedictine Sisters of Pontifical Jurisdiction (0230)
1956 — Cardinal Glennon, St. Louis, MO, Franciscan Sisters of Mary (1415)
1956 — St. Mary's, Apple Valley, CA, Benedictine Sisters of Pontifical Jurisdiction (0230)
1956 — St. Francis, Mountain View, MO, Daughters of St. Francis of Assisi (0920)
1956 — Holy Cross, Fort Lauderdale, FL, Sisters of Mercy (2570)
1957 — Mercy*, Jourdanton, TX, Sisters of the Incarnate Word and Blessed Sacrament (2210
1957 — Holy Spirit, Camp Hill, PA, Sisters of Christian Charity (0660)
1958 — Queen of Valley, Napa City, CA, Sisters of St. Joseph of Carondelet (3840)
1958 — Trinity Memorial, Cuhady, WI, Sisters of St. Joseph of Medaille (3880)
1959 — Marcum & Wallace, Irvine, KY, Benedictine Sisters of Pontifical Jurisdiction (0230)
1959 — Lourdes, Paducah, KY, Sisters of the Third Order of St. Francis of Penance and of Charity (1760)
1959 — St. Mary's, Livonia, MI, Felician Sisters (1170)
1959 — Sacred Heart, Chester, PA, Bernardine Sisters of the Third Order of St. Francis (1810)
1959 — Jeannette, Jeannette, PA, Sisters of Charity of Seton Hill (0570)
1959 — Holy Redeemer, Meadowbrook, PA, Sisters of the Holy Redeemer (2000)

1960-1969

1960 — Little Company of Mary, Torrance, CA, Sisters of the Little Company of Mary (2270)
1960 — St. Mary's, Winsted, MN, Benedictine Sisters of Pontifical Jurisdiction (0230)
1960 — St. Joseph, Cheektowaga, NY, Franciscan Sisters of St. Joseph (1490)
1960 — Seventh Ward*, Hammond, LA, Dominican Sisters (1070-08)
1960 — St. Francis, Green Springs, OH, Franciscan Sisters of Our Lady of Perpetual Help (1430)
1960 — St. Francis, Tulsa, OK, Congregation of the Sisters of Charity of the Incarnate Word (0470)
1960 — St. Joseph, Murphysboro, IL, Adorers of the Blood of Christ (0100)

1960 — St. John's, Steubenville, OH, Sisters of St. Francis of the Congregation of Our Lady of Lourdes (1720)

1961 — St. Joseph's, Tucson, AZ, Sisters of St. Joseph of Carondelet (3840)

1961 — Holy Family, Des Plaines, IL, Sisters of the Holy Family of Nazareth (1970)

1961 — Holy Cross, Mission Hills, CA, Congregation of the Sisters of the Holy Cross (1920)

1962 — St. Joseph's, Port Charlotte, FL, Felician Sisters (1170)

1962 — Divine Redeemer, South St. Paul, MN, Sisters of the Divine Redeemer (1020)

1962 — St. Rose, Hayward, CA, Sisters of St. Joseph (3830-18)

1962 — Frank Cuneo*, Chicago, IL, Missionary Sisters of the Sacred Heart (2860)

1962 — Queen of Valley, West Covina, CA, Franciscan Sisters of the Sacred Heart (1450)

1963 — Holy Cross, Silver Spring, MD, Congregation of the Sisters of the Holy Cross (1920)

1963 — St. Claire, Morehead, KY, Sisters of Notre Dame (2990)

1964 — Holy Family, Spokane, WA, Dominican Sisters (1070-29)

1966 — St. Mary's, Richmond, VA, Congregation of Bon Secours (0270)

1966 — St. Anthony*, Houston, TX, Congregation of the Sisters of Charity of the Incarnate Word (0470)

1967 — Mercy San Juan, Carmichael, CA, Sisters of Mercy (2570)

1967 — Divine Providence, Ivanhoe, MN, Sisters of St. Mary of Oregon (3960)

1968 — Whitman Community*, Colfax, WA, Sisters of Providence (3350)

1968 — Cardinal Cushing, Brockton, MA, Sisters of Charity of Nazareth (0500)

1969 — Foster G. McGraw, Maywood, IL, Dominican Sisters (1070-10)

1969 — Mercy Catholic*, Philadelphia, PA, Sisters of Mercy (2570)

1970-1979

1971 — St. Lawrence, Lawrenceville, NJ, Sisters of St. Francis of Philadelphia (1650)

1971 — Providence, Cincinnati, OH, Franciscan Sisters of the Poor (1440)

1972 — Palos Community*, Palos Heights, IL, Misericordia Sisters (2680)

1972 — St. Stanislaus*, Nanticoke, PA, Bernardine Sisters of the Third Order of St. Francis (1810)

1973 — Clermont Mercy, Batavia, OH, Sisters of Mercy of the Union (2580)

1973 — St. Mary, Langhorne, PA, Sisters of St. Francis of Philadelphia (1650)

1973 — St. Mary, Hobart, IN, Poor Handmaids of Jesus Christ (3230)

1974 — St. Anthony, Crown Point, IN, Franciscan Sisters of Chicago (1210)

1974 — Marianjoy, Wheaton, IL, Franciscan Sisters, Daughters of the Sacred Hearts of Jesus and Mary (1240)

1974 — St. Anthony, Westminster, CO, Sisters of St. Francis of Perpetual Adoration (1640)

1974 — Redwood Memorial, Fortuna, CA, Sisters of St. Joseph (3830-03)

1974 — St. John of God, Brighton, MA, Daughters of Charity of St. Vincent de Paul (0760)

1974 — Archbishop Bergan Mercy, Omaha, NE, Sisters of Mercy of the Union (2580)

1974 — Elmbrook, Brookfield, WI, Franciscan Sisters, Daughters of the Sacred Hearts of Jesus and Mary (1240)

1977 — Marion, Sioux City, IA, Sisters of Mercy of the Union (2580)

1979 — St. Luke Institute, Suitland, MD Daughters of Charity of St. Vincent de Paul (0760)

1979 — Samaritan, Detroit, MI, Sisters of Mercy of the Union (2580)

1979 — Providence Wayne, NE, Missionary Benedictine Sisters (0210)

1980-1989

1980 — St. John's, Richmond, VA, Congregation of Bon Secours (0270)

1981 — St. Mary's, Blue Springs, MO, Franciscan Sisters of Mary (1415)

1981 — St. John's, Nassau Bay, TX, Congregation of the Sisters of Charity of the Incarnate Word (0470)

1985 — Mercy, Folsom, CA, Sisters of Mercy (2570)

1985 — Bon Secours, North Miami, FL, Congregation of Bon Secours (0270)

1985 — St. Catherine, Moss Beach, CA, Daughters of Charity of St. Vincent de Paul (0760)

1985 — St. Joseph, Dahlonega, GA, Sisters of Mercy of the Union (2580)

1985 — Monte Ville, Morgan Hill, CA, Daughters of Charity of St. Vincent de Paul (0760)

1985 — Mercy-St. Mary's, Dyersville, IA, Sisters of Mercy of the Union (2580)

1985 — Mercy, Mansfield, MO, Sisters of Mercy of the Union (2580)

1985 — Spohn Kleberg, Kingsville, TX, Congregation of the Sisters of Charity of the Incarnate Word (0460)

1985 — Holy Cross Parkview, Plymouth, IN, Congregation of the Sisters of the Holy Cross (1920)

1985 — Kenmare Community, Kenmare, ND, Sisters of St. Francis of Penance and Christian Charity (1630)

1985 — St. John Westlake, Westlake, OH, Sisters of Charity of St. Augustine (0580)

1985 — Providence Seaside, Seaside, OR, Sisters of Providence (3350)

1985 — St. Francis, Federal Way, WA, Sisters of St. Francis of Philadelphia (1650)

1985 — Snoqualmie Valley, Snoqualmie, WA, Sisters of St. Joseph of Peace (3890)

1985 — Mercy, Waldron, AR, Sisters of Mercy of the Union (2580)

1985 — Holy Cross, West Jordan, UT, Congregation of the Sisters of the Holy Cross (1920)

1985 — St. Joseph, Flushing, NY, Dominican Sisters (1070-05)

1987 — Providence, Centralia, WA, Sisters of Providence (3350)

1987 — Providence Central, Toppenish, WA, Sisters of Providence (3350)

1987 — St. Louise, Morgan Hill, CA, Daughters of Charity of St. Vincent de Paul (0760)

1987 — Providence Milwaukie, Milwaukie, OR, Sisters of Providence (3350)

1988 — Emerson A North, Cincinnati, OH, Franciscan Sisters of the Poor (1440)

1988 — St. Dominics, Manteca, CA, Dominican Sisters (1070-04)

1988 — St. Joseph Lake, St. Louis, MO, Franciscan Sisters of Mary (1415)

1989 — Albany Area, Albany, MN, Franciscan Sisters of the Immaculate Conception (1310)

1989 — Peace Harbor, Florence, OR, Sisters of St. Joseph of Peace (3890)

The orders that founded various numbers of hospitals from 1829 to 1990 were:

91 - Sisters of Mercy of the Union (2580)

70 - Daughters of Charity (0760)

44 - Sisters of Mercy (2570)

44 - Sisters of St. Joseph (3830)

35 - Benedictine Sisters of Pontifical Jurisdiction (0230)

35 - Dominican Sisters (1070) & The Servants of Relief for Incurable Cancer (1070-23)

27 - Sisters of Providence (3350)

22 - Franciscan Sisters of the Poor (1440)

22 - Sisters of St. Joseph of Carondelet (3840)

22 - Sisters of St. Francis of Perpetual Adoration (1640)

18 - Franciscan Sisters of Mary (1415)

15 - Congregation of the Sisters of Charity of the Incarnate Word, Houston (0470)

15 - Poor Handmaids of Jesus Christ (3230)

15 - Sisters of St. Francis of Philadelphia (1650)

14 - Sisters of Charity of Leavenworth (0480)

14 - Sisters of the Sorrowful Mother (Third Order of St. Francis) (4100)

14 - Hospital Sisters of the Third Order of St. Francis (1820)

13 - Congregation of the Sisters of the Holy Cross (1920)

12 - Franciscan Sisters of the Sacred Heart (1450)

12 - Sisters of Charity of Cincinnati (0440)

11 - Sisters of the Third Order of St. Francis (1770)

10 - Sisters of Charity of Nazareth (0500)

10 - Franciscan Sisters of Allegany (1180)

10 - Congregation of the Sisters of Charity of the Incarnate Word, San Antonio (0460)

10 - Franciscan Sisters, Daughters of the Sacred Hearts of Jesus and Mary (1240)

8 - Sisters of Saint Francis of Penance and Christian Charity (1630)

8 - Congregation of Bon Secours (0270)

8 - Sisters of Charity of St. Vincent de Paul of New York (0650)

8 - Felician Sisters (1170)

8 - Franciscan Sisters of the Immaculate Conception, Little Falls (1310)

8 - Sisters of St. Joseph of Peace (3890)

8 - Sisters of Charity of St. Augustine (0580)

7 - Sisters of the Presentation of the Blessed Virgin Mary (3320)

7 - Sisters of Providence (3340)

6 - Sisters Charity of St. Elizabeth, Convent Station (0590)

6 - Adorers of the Blood of Christ (0100)

6 - Sisters of the Third Franciscan Order (1490)

6 - Bernardine Sisters of the Third Order of St. Francis (1810)

6 - Religious Hospitallers of St. Joseph (3440)

6 - Sisters of the Holy Family of Nazareth (1970)

6 - Misericordia Sisters (2680)

5 - Missionary Sisters of the Sacred Heart of Jesus (2860)

5 - Sisters of the Third Order Regular of St. Francis of the Congregation of Our
       Lady of Lourdes (1720)

5 - Sisters of Charity of Montreal (0490)

4 - Sisters of St. Francis of the Mission of the Immaculate Virgin (1510)

4 - Sisters of Charity of Seton Hill, Greensburg, Pennsylvania (0570)

4 - Franciscan Sisters of Christian Charity (1230)

4 - Sisters of St. Francis of the Congregation of Our Lady of Lourdes (1530)

4 - School Sisters of St. Francis (1680)

4 - Congregation of the Sisters of the Third Order of St. Francis of Perpetual
       Adoration (1780)

4 - Sisters of Mary of the Presentation (2450)

4 - Missionary Sisters of the Most Sacred Heart of Jesus of Hiltrup (2800)

4 - Sisters of St. Joseph of the Third Order of St. Francis (3930)

The balance of the hospitals were established by 17 communities with three
       hospitals each, 11 with two, and 34 with one hospital each (see listings
       above).

Endnotes

1. In 1987, the Sisters of St. Mary of the Third Order of St. Francis and the Sisters
   of St. Francis of Maryvale amalgamated and became the Franciscan Sisters of
   Mary (1415). Hospitals were founded by both the formerly separate congregations.

APPENDIX D

Sister-Founded Colleges

‡ — ‡

THESE COLLEGES ARE listed in chronological order of original foundation — usually as academies and not colleges. In some instances they received state charters many years before actually graduating students and granting four-year degrees. Dual dates indicate the institution is closed. The numbers in parentheses following the location list the enrollment in 1990.

1809-1973 (1902) — **St. Joseph College**, Emmitsburg MD - Daughters of Charity of St. Vincent de Paul (0760).

1814[1] (1920) — **Spalding University**, Louisville KY (1,141) - Sisters of Charity of Nazareth (0500).

1840 (1923) — **Fontbonne College**, St. Louis MO (1,036) - Sisters of St. Joseph of Carondelet (3840).

1841 (1909) — **St. Mary-of-the-Woods College**, St. Mary-of-the-Woods, IN (910) - Sisters of Providence (3360).

1843 (1901) — **Clarke College**, Dubuque IA (830) - Sisters of Charity of the Blessed Virgin Mary (0430).

1844 (1903) — **Saint Mary College**, Notre Dame IN (1,821) - Congregation of the Sisters of the Holy Cross (1920).

1847 (1915) — **St. Xavier College**, Chicago IL (2,641) - Sisters of Mercy of the Union (2580).

1847 (1910) — **College of Mount St. Vincent**, Riverdale NY (1,120) - Sisters of Charity of St. Vincent de Paul of New York (0650).

1851 (1953)[2] — **College of Notre Dame**, Belmont CA (2,461) - Sisters of Notre Dame de Namur (3000).

1851 (1936) — **Marian College**, Indianapolis IN (1,215) - Congregation of the Sisters of the Third Order of Saint Francis, Oldenburg Indiana (1730).

1852-1972 (1922) — **Siena College**, Memphis TN - Dominican Sisters (1070-01).

1859-1974 (1923) — **Mt. St. Scholastica College**, Atchison KS - Benedictine Sisters of Pontifical Jurisdiction (0230).

1859 (1893) — **Marylhurst College**, Marylhurst OR (1,005) - Sisters of the Holy Names of Jesus and Mary (1990).

1890-1971 — **Mt. St. Agnes College**, Baltimore MD - Sisters of Mercy of the Union (2580).

1866 (1916) — **Avila College**, Kansas City MO (1,620) - Sisters of St. Joseph of Carondelet (3840).

1868 (1924) — **Holy Names College**, Oakland CA (720) - Sisters of the Holy Names of Jesus and Mary (1990).

1871[3] — **Ursuline College**, Pepper Pike OH (1,297) - Ursuline Nuns of the Congregation of Paris (4120).

1871 (1927) — **Edgewood College**, Madison WI (1,100) - Dominican Sisters (1070-03).

1872 (1925) — **Maryville College** - St. Louis, St. Louis, MO (2,934) - Society of the Sacred Heart (4070).

1873 — **College of Notre Dame of Maryland**, Baltimore MD (2,461) - School Sisters of Notre Dame (2970).

1878-1988 (1921) — **St. Mary College of O'Fallon**, O'Fallon MO - Sisters of the Most Precious Blood (3270).

1880 (1890) — **St. Francis College of Fort Wayne**, Fort Wayne IN (1,031) - Sisters of St. Francis of Perpetual Adoration (1640)

1881 — **Incarnate Word College**, San Antonio TX (2,240) - Congregation of the Sisters of Charity of the Incarnate Word (0460).

1881-1968 (1917) — **Duchesne College**, Omaha NE - Society of the Sacred Heart (4070).

1887 — **Alverno College**, Milwaukee WI (2,191) - School Sisters of St. Francis (1680).

1887 (1913) — **College of St. Benedict**, St. Joseph MN (2,196) - Benedictine Sisters of Pontifical Jurisdiction (0230).

1890 (1932) — **Viterbo College**, LaCrosse WI (1,067) - Congregation of the Sisters of the Third Order of Saint Francis of Perpetual Adoration (1780).

1890 (1920)[4] — **Dominican College of San Rafael**, San Rafael CA (714) - Dominican Sisters (1070-04).

1891-1988 (1918) — **Loretto Heights College**, Denver CO - Sisters of Loretto at the Foot of the Cross (2360).

1896 (1919) — **Siena Heights College**, Adrian MI (1,599) - Dominican Sisters (1070-13).

1897 — **Trinity College**, Washington DC (1,125) - Sisters of Notre Dame de Namur (3000).

1897-1967 — **Loretto Normal School**, Nerinx KY - Sisters of Loretto at the Foot of the Cross (2360).

1898 (1916) — **Webster College**, Webster Groves MO - Sisters of Loretto at the Foot of the Cross (2360).

1899 — **College of St. Elizabeth**, Convent Station NJ (1,040) - Sisters of Charity of Saint Elizabeth, Convent Station (0590).

1901 — **Rosary College**, River Forest IL (1,625) - Dominicans of Sinsinawa (1070-03).

1904 — **College of New Rochelle**, New Rochelle NY (2,240) - Ursuline Nuns (4110).

1905-1978 (1922) — **Immaculata College**, Washington DC - Sisters of Providence (3360).

1905 — **College of St. Catherine**, St. Paul MN (2,729) - Sisters of St. Joseph of Carondelet (3840).

1906 — **College of St. Scholastica**, Duluth MN (1,835) - Benedictine Sisters of Pontifical Jurisdiction (0230).

1907-1990 — **College of St. Teresa**, Winona MN - Sisters of the Third Order Regular of St. Francis of theCongregation of Our Lady of Lourdes (1720).

1907 (1919) — **Marymount College**, Tarrytown NY (1,247) - Religious of the Sacred Heart of Mary (3465).

1907-1982 (1938) — **Fort Wright College of the Holy Names**, Spokane WA - Sisters of the Holy Names of Jesus and Mary (1990).

1908 — **D'Youville College**, Buffalo NY (1,100) - Grey Nuns of the Sacred Heart (1840).

1908 — **Georgian Court College**, Lakewood NJ (2,054) - Sisters of Mercy (2570).

1908-1965 — **Mount St. Mary College,** Plainfield NJ - Sisters of Mercy of New Jersey (2570).

1910 — **Marygrove College**, Detroit MI (1,235) - Sisters, Servants of the Immaculate Heart of Mary (2150).

1911 (1928) — **Ohio Dominican College**, Columbus OH (1,331) - Dominican Sisters (1070-02).

1911 — **Loyola Marymount University**, Los Angeles CA (4,869) - Religious of the Sacred Heart of Mary (3465) and Sisters of St. Joseph of Orange (3830-03).

1911 — **Our Lady of the Lake University of San Antonio**, San Antonio TX (2,245) - Sisters of Divine Providence (1010).

1912 — **St. Joseph College**, North Windham ME (622) - Sisters of Mercy (2570).

1913 — **Mt. Mary College**, Milwaukee WI (1,366) - School Sisters of Notre Dame (2970).

1915 — **Marywood College**, Scranton PA (2,395) - Sisters, Servants of the Immaculate Heart of Mary (2160).

1915-1935 — **College of the Sacred Heart**, Cincinnati OH - Society of the Sacred Heart (4070).

1916 — **Our Lady of the Holy Cross College**, New Orleans LA (848) - Congregation of the Sisters Marianites of Holy Cross (2410).

1916 — **St. Joseph's College**, Brooklyn NY (794) - Sisters of St. Joseph (3830-05).

1916-1974 — **Immaculate Heart College**, Los Angles CA - Sisters of the Immaculate Heart of Mary (2180).

1917 — **Manhattanville College of the Sacred Heart**, New York NY - Society of the Sacred Heart (4070).

1918 — **Mallinckrodt College**, Wilmette IL (275) - Sisters of Christian Charity (0660).

1918 — **Seton Hill College**, Greensburg PA (870) - Sisters of Charity of Seton Hill, Greensburg, Pennsylvania (0570).

1919 — **Barat College**, Lake Forest IL (674) - Society of the Sacred Heart (4070).

1919 — **Emmanuel College**, Boston MA (973) - Sisters of Notre Dame de Namur (3000).

1920 — **College of St. Rose**, Albany NY (2,853) - Sisters of St. Joseph of Carondelet (3840).

1920 — **College of St. Francis**, Joliet IL (1,856) - Congregation of the Third Order of St. Francis of Mary Immaculate (1710).

1920 — **College of Mount St. Joseph**, Cincinnati OH (2,566) - Sisters of Charity of Cincinnati (0440).

1920 — **Memorial***, Immaculata College, Immaculata PA (2,100) - Sisters, Servants of the Immaculate Heart of Mary (2170).

1920 — **College of the Sacred Heart**, Menlo Park CA - Society of the Sacred Heart (4070).

1921 — **Thomas More College**, Crestview Hills KY (1,120) - Sisters of Notre Dame (2990).

1921 — **Rosemont College**, Rosemont PA (613) - Society of the Holy Child Jesus (4060).

1922 — **Notre Dame College of Ohio**, Cleveland OH (751) - Sisters of Notre Dame (2990).

1922 — **Aquinas College**, Grand Rapids MI (2,535) - Dominican Sisters (1070-14).

1922-1978 — **Mary Manse College**, Toledo, OH - Sisters of Mercy of the Union (2580).

1922 — **Marymount College**, Salina KS - Sisters of St. Joseph (3830-15).

1923 — **College of St. Mary**, Omaha NE (1,133) - Sisters of Mercy (2570).

1923 — **St. Mary College**, Leavenworth KS (1,071) - Sisters of Charity of Leavenworth (0480)

1923-1980 — **Good Counsel College**, White Plains NY - Sisters of the Divine Compassion (0970).

1924 — **Chestnut Hill College**, Philadelphia PA (1,031) - Sisters of St. Joseph of Chestnut Hill (3893).

1924 — **Nazareth College**, Rochester NY (2,935) - Sisters of St. Joseph (3830-14).

1924 — **Nazareth College**, Kalamazoo MI (730) - Sisters of St. Joseph (3830-11).

1924 — **Misericordia College**, Dallas PA (1,114) - Sisters of Mercy of the Union (2580).

1925 — **Villa Maria College**, Erie PA (686) - Sisters of St. Joseph (3830-09).

1925 — **Trinity College**, Burlington VT (999) - Sisters of Mercy of the Union (2580).

1925 — **Mount St. Mary College**, Los Angeles CA (1,203) - Sisters of St. Joseph of Carondelet (3840).

1925 — **Brescia College**, Owensboro KY (646) - Ursuline Nuns of the Congregation of Paris (4120-05).

1925 — **Albertus Magnus College**, New Haven CT (500) - Dominican Sisters (1070-02).

1925-1981 — **Ottumwa Heights College**, Ottumwa IA - Congregation of the Humility of Mary (2100).

1925 — **Xavier University of Louisiana**, New Orleans LA (2,528) - The Sisters of the Blessed Sacrament for Indians and Colored People (0260).

1926 — **Mercyhurst College**, Erie PA (2,037) - Sisters of Mercy (2570).

1927 — **Regis College**, Weston MA (1,025) - Sisters of St. Joseph (3830-01).

1927-1987 — **De Lourdes College**, Des Plaines IL (139) - Sisters of the Holy Family of Nazareth (1970).

1928 — **Elms College**, Chicopee MA (1,046) - Sisters of St. Joseph (3830-16).

1928 — **Mount Mercy College**, Cedar Rapids IA (1,568) - Sisters of Mercy (2570).

1928 — **Mount St. Clare College**, Clinton IA (335) - Sisters of St. Francis, Clinton, Iowa (1540).

1928-1958 — **St. Mary-of-the-Wasatch**, Salt Lake City UT - Congregation of the Sisters of the Holy Cross (1920).

1929 — **Mundelein College**, Chicago IL (1,010) - Sisters of Charity of the Blessed Virgin Mary (0430).

1929 — **Carlow College**, Pittsburgh PA (962) - Sisters of Mercy of the Union (2580).

1929 — **Springfield Junior College in Illinois**, Springfield IL - Ursuline Nuns of the Congregation of Paris (4120-05).

1929-1937 — **Seattle Junior College of the Sacred Heart**, Seattle WA - Society of the Sacred Heart (4070).

1930 — **Briar Cliff College**, Sioux City IA (1,103) - Sisters of St. Francis of the Holy Family (1570).

1930 — **Queen of Holy Rosary College**, Fremont CA - Dominican Sisters (1070-12).

1931 — **St. Catherine Junior College**, St. Catherine KY (280) - Dominican Sisters (1070-01).

1931-1973 — **Mary Rogers College**, Maryknoll NY - Maryknoll Sisters of St. Dominic (2470).

1932 — **St. Joseph College**, West Hartford CT (1,310) - Sisters of Mercy (2570).

1932 — **College of Great Falls**, Great Falls MT (1,200) - Sisters of Providence (3350).

1932 (1954) — **Mount St. Mary College**, Newburgh NY (1,241) - Dominican Sisters (1070-06).

1933 — **Rivier College**, Nashua NH (2,500) - Sisters of the Presentation of Mary (3310).

1933 — **Kansas Newman College**, Wichita KS (691) - Adorers of the Precious Blood (0100).

1933-1980 — **Ladycliff College**, Highland Falls NY - Franciscan Missionary Sisters of the Sacred Heart (1400).

1934 — **Salve Regina** - The Newport College, Newport RI (2,552) - Sisters of Mercy of the Union (2580).

1935 — **Silver Lake College**, Manitowoc WI (795) - Franciscan Sisters of
    Christian Charity (1230).

1935-1987 — **Sacred Heart College**, Belmont NC - Sisters of Mercy of the Union (2580).

1935-1974 — **Dominican College**, Racine WI - Dominican Sisters (1070-09).

1935-1973 — **Dunbarton College**, Washington DC - Congregation of the Sisters of
    the Holy Cross (1920).

1936 — **Mount Marty College**, Yankton SD (871) - Benedictine Sisters of
    Pontifical Jurisdiction (0230).

1936 — **Marymount Manhattan College**, New York NY (1,300) - Religious of
    the Sacred Heart of Mary (3465).

1936 — **Marian College of Fond du Lac**, Fond du Lac WI (859) - Congregation of
    the Sisters of St.Agnes (3710).

1937 — **Cardinal Stritch College**, Milwaukee WI (3,050) - The Sisters of St.
    Francis of Assisi (1705).

1937 — **Ancilla Junior College**, Donaldson IN (630) - Poor Handmaids of Jesus
    Christ (3230).

1937 — **Medaille College**, Buffalo, NY - Sisters of St. Joseph (3830-06).

1939 — **Marycrest College**, Davenport IA - Congregation of the Humility of Mary
    (2100).

1939 — **Caldwell College**, Caldwell NJ (666) - Dominican Sisters (1070-18).

1939 — **Mount Aloysius Junior College**, Cresson PA (824) - Sisters of Mercy of
    the Union (2580).

1940 — **Barry University**, Miami FL (5,238) - Dominicans Sisters (1070-13).

1941 — **Mercy College of Detroit**, Detroit MI (2,325) - Sisters of Mercy of the
    Union (2580).

1941-1980 — **Annhurst College**, Woodstock CT - Daughters of the Holy Spirit
    (0820).

1942 — **Felician College**, Lodi NJ (647) - Felician Sisters (1170).

1942-1966 — **Tacoma Catholic College**, Tacoma WA - Dominican Sisters
    (1070-20).

1946 — **Anna Maria College**, Paxton MA (1,060) - Sisters of St. Anne (3720).

1946 — **Newton College**, Newton MA - Society of the Sacred Heart (4070).

1947 — **Madonna College**, Livonia MI (4,400) - Felician Sisters (1170).

1947 — **Manor Junior College**, Jenkintown PA (450) - Sisters of the Order of St.
    Basil the Great (3730).

1947 — **Rosary Hill College**, Buffalo NY - Sisters of St. Francis of Penance and
    Christian Charity (1630).

1948 — **Gwynedd-Mercy College**, Gwynedd PA (1,812) - Sisters of Mercy (2570).

1949 — **San Diego University**, Alcala Park, San Diego CA (5,858) - Society of the
    Sacred Heart (4070).

1950 — **Marymount University**, Arlington VA (2,977) - Religious of the Sacred
    Heart of Mary (3465).

1950 — **Notre Dame College**, Manchester NH (772) - Sisters of Holy Cross (1930).

1951 — **Presentation Junior College**, Aberdeen SD (500) - Sisters of the
    Presentation of the Blessed Virgin Mary (3320).

1952 — **St. Mary of the Plains College**, Dodge City KS (908) - Sisters of St. Joseph (3830-18).

1952 — **Dominican College of Blauvelt**, Orangeburg NY (1,442) - Dominican Sisters (1070-15).

1952 — **St. Thomas Aquinas College**, Sparkill NY (2,063) - Dominican Sisters (1070-11).

1952 — **Villa Julie College**, Stevenson MD (1,279) - Sisters of Notre Dame de Namur (3000).

1952-1972 — **Cardinal Cushing College**, Brookline MA - Congregation of the Sisters of the Holy Cross (1920).

1952-1974 — **Mercy Junior College**, St. Louis MO - Sisters of Mercy of the Union (2580).

1952 — **Assumption College for Sisters**, Mendham NJ (36) Sisters of Christian Charity (0660).

1952 — **College of St. Joseph the Provider**, Rutland VT (434) - Sisters of St. Joseph (3830-07).

1953-1978 — **Mount St. Joseph**, Wakefield RI - Sisters of the Cross and Passion (3180).

1954 — **Holy Family College**, Philadelphia PA (1,685) - Sisters of the Holy Family of Nazareth (1970).

1954-1978 — **Mount Angel College**, Mount Angel OR - Benedictine Sisters of Pontifical Jurisdiction (0230).

1955-1971 — **Brentwood College**, Brentwood NY - Sisters of St. Joseph (3830-05).

1955 — **Molloy College**, Rockville Center NY (1,384) - Dominican Sisters (1070-05).

1956-1984 — **Harriman Junior College**, Harriman NY - Sisters of the Catholic Apostolate (3140).

1957 — **Cabrini College**, Radnor PA (1,264) - Missionary Sisters of the Sacred Heart of Jesus (2860).

1957 — **Hilbert Junior College**, Hamburg NY (729) - Franciscan Sisters of St. Joseph (1470).

1958 — **Lourdes College**, Sylvania OH (773) - Sisters of St. Francis of the Congregation of Our Lady of Lourdes, Sylvania, Ohio (1530).

1958 — **Alvernia College**, Reading PA (1,076) - Bernardine Sisters of the Third Order of St. Francis (1810).

1958 — **Juniorate at O'Fallon**, O'Fallon MO - Sisters of the Most Precious Blood, (O'Fallon, MO) (3270).

1958 — **Trocaire Junior College**, Buffalo NY (849) - Sisters of Mercy (2570).

1959 — **University of Mary**, Bismarck ND (1,352) - Benedictine Sisters of Pontifical Jurisdiction (0230).

1959-1968 — **DeLisle Junior College**, New Orleans LA - Congregation of the Sisters of the Holy Family (1950).

1960 — **Mater Dei College**, Ogdensburg NY (550) - Sisters of St. Joseph (3830-12).

1960 — **Villa Maria Junior College**, Buffalo NY (541) - Felician Sisters (1170).

1960 — **Elizabeth Seton College**, Yonkers NY - Sisters of Charity of St. Vincent de Paul of New York (0650).

1961 — **Aquinas Junior College**, Nashville TN (400) - Dominican Sisters (1070-07).

1963 — **LaRoche College**, Pittsburgh PA (1,852) - Sisters of Divine Providence (0990).

1963 — **Maria Junior College**, Albany NY (927) - Sisters of Mercy (2570).

1963 — **Castle Junior College**, Windham NH (212) - Sisters of Mercy (2570).

1963-1970 — **St. Dominic College**, St. Charles IL - Dominican Sisters (1070-13).

1964-1975 — **Dominican College**, Houston TX - Dominican Sisters (1070-19).

1964-1978 — **Tombrock College**, West Paterson NJ - Missionary Sisters of the Immaculate Conception of the Mother of God (2760).

1964 — **St. Mary's Junior College**, Minneapolis MN (850) - Sisters of St. Joseph of Carondelet (3840).

1965 — **Neumann College**, Aston PA - Sister of St. Francis of Philadelphia (1650).

1971 — **Chatfield College**, St. Martin OH - Ursulines of Brown County (4120).

1976-1980 — **Southern Benedictine College**, St. Bernard AL, (formed by merger of Cullman Jr. College and St. Bernard College) Benedictine Sisters and Monks.

Endnotes

1. In 1814, Nazareth Academy was established near Bardstown, Kentucky. In 1822, it moved to Nazareth. In 1920, Nazareth College was established in Louisville as a four-year liberal arts college for women. In 1921, Nazareth Academy became a junior college for women, upgrading to a senior college in 1938. In 1963, Nazareth College in Louisville was renamed Catherine Spalding College. The two colleges merged in 1969 using the title Spalding College, with dual campuses. The Nazareth campus closed in 1971. Spalding College became Spalding University in 1984.

2. This institution received a charter from the state of California to grant degrees in 1868. However, it did not actually grant a baccalaureate degree until 1953. In 1922 the campus was moved from San Jose to its present site in Belmont.

3. This is the first Catholic women's college established in the United States. It did not eminate from an academy but was founded to be a four-year college.

4. The Dominican Sisters of San Rafael secured Articles of Incorporation for the Dominican College of San Rafael in 1890 from the state of California although it was many years before a four-year college became a reality. In 1916, the secondary school was upgraded to a junior college. Despite the junior college status, BA degrees were awarded as early as 1917. Since the charter authorized granting degrees, several sisters took courses and satisfied the faculty of the University of California. After expansion to a full college in 1920, the first BA degrees awarded to lay students was in 1922.

APPENDIX E

Sisters in Foreign Missions

‡ — ‡

The U.S. Catholic Mission Association lists the following numbers of sister-missionaries for various years:

1956 - 2,212	1974 - 2,916
1958 - 2,532	1976 - 2.840
1960 - 2,827	1978 - 2,673
1962 - 2,764	1980 - 2,592
1964 - 3,137	1982 - 2,560
1966 - 3,706	1984 - 2,492
1968 - 4,105	1986 - 2,481
1970 - 3,824	1988 - 2,495
1972 - 3,121	1990 - 2,347

The statistics below for 1966 are taken from the January 1, 1966, report of the U.S. Mission Secretariat, Washington, D.C., titled U.S. Missionary Personnel Overseas. It reported 3,706 sister-missionaries. Statistics for 1990 are taken from the 1990-91 report of the U.S. Catholic Mission Association, Washington, D.C. which reported 2,347 sister-missionaries. Europe is not included, as presumably sisters there were studying or on assignment at motherhouses. A total of 10 or more sisters were stationed in each of the following countries during the indicated years:

Country	1966	1990
Peru	285	245
Brazil	235	169
Hawaii	295	121
Mexico	54	121
Chile	164	100
Guatemala	85	98

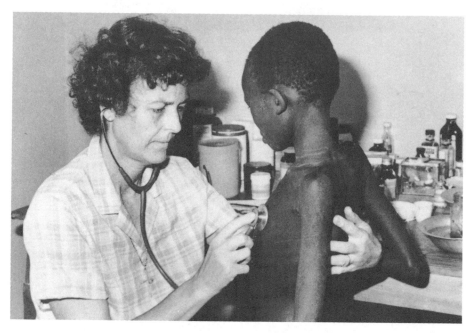

Sister Marilyn Norris, MM, Kworijik, Sudan, 1985. Photo taken by Sister Jeri Stokes, MM.

Courtesy Maryknoll Archives, Maryknoll, New York

Country	1966	1990
Bolivia	29	93
Kenya	24	90
Japan	165	81
Alaska	52	77
Taiwan	74	75
Canada	29	73
Puerto Rico	386	71
Papua, New Guinea	78	64
Philippines	181	60
Tanzania	71	53
Hong Kong	85	52
Ghana	49	51
Korea	60	44
Jamaica	71	43
Nicaragua	21	41
Australia	38	36
Haiti	8	30
India	88	30
Belize	0	30

Country	1966	1990
South Africa	16	29
Venezuela	42	29
Liberia	10	28
Honduras	36	27
El Salvador	7	27
Zimbabwe	0	26
Columbia	86	22
Zambia	24	22
Nigeria	41	22
Bangladesh	0	21
Thailand	12	21
Cameroon	10	19
Uganda	25	18
Pakistan	121	17
Ecuador	21	17
Zaire	0	16
Dominican Republic	12	15
Mariana Islands	0	15
Sierra Leone	0	15
Caroline Islands	0	14
Bahamas	49	13
Panama	24	14
Ethiopia	6	13
Israel	6	12
Marshall Islands	0	12
Costa Rica	22	11
Malawi	28	11

The following orders had 10 or more sisters in missions in 1966 or 1990:

Order	1966	1990
Maryknoll Sisters of St. Dominic (2470)	700	356
Dominican Sisters (1970)	192	112
School Sisters of Notre Dame (2870)	116	100
Sisters of St. Joseph (3830)	128	66
Sisters of St. Joseph of Carondelet (3840)	71	58
Sisters of Notre Dame de Namur (3000)	67	53
Daughters of St. Vincent de Paul (0760)	69	51
Marist Missionary Sisters (2420)	136	48
Sisters of Mercy (2570)	62	45
Congregation of the Sisters of the Holy Cross (1920)	42	42

Order	1966	1990
Medical Mission Sisters (2490)	149	41
Benedictine Sisters of Pontifical Jurisdiction (0230)	73	35
Ursuline Nuns of the Roman Union (4110)	69	34
Sisters, Servants of the Immaculate Heart of Mary, (Immaculata, PA) (2170)	77	32
Franciscan Missionaries of Mary (1370)	68	30
Sisters of the Union in the USA (2580)	73	29
Franciscan Sisters of Allengany (1180)	0	26
Sisters, Servants of the Immaculate Heart of Mary (Monroe, MI) (2150)	35	25
Sisters of Our Lady of the Good Shepherd (3070)	0	25
Little Sisters of the Poor (2340)	13	23
Sisters of the Holy Family of Nazareth (1970)	15	22
Missionary Sisters, Servants of the Holy Spirit (3530)	47	22
Sisters of Notre Dame (2990)	22	22
Sisters of the Third Franciscan Order (1490)	0	20
Congregation of the Third Order of St. Francis (1730)	11	20
Adorers of the Precious Blood of Christ (0110)	15	18
Sisters of the Presentation of the Blessed Virgin Mary (3320)	1	18
Religious of the Sacred Heart (4070)	25	18
Sisters of St. Francis of Philadelphia (1650)	0	17
Immaculate Heart of Mary Missionary Sisters (2750)	29	16
Missionary Sisters of St. Columban (2880)	9	16
Sisters of the Assumption of the Blessed Virgin Mary (0150)	6	15
Sisters of Charity of Leavenworth (0480)	6	15
Franciscan Sisters of Christian Charity (1230)	15	15
Sisters of the Holy Names of Jesus and Mary (1990)	7	15
School Sisters of St. Francis (1680)	0	15
Daughters of Saint Paul (0950)	0	15
Missionary Franciscan Sisters of the Immaculate Conception (OSF-1360)	0	14
Sisters of the Holy Family (SHF-1960)	12	14
Medical Missionaries of Mary (MMM-2480)	11	13
Society of the Holy Child Jesus (SHCJ-4060)	27	12
Daughters of the Holy Spirit (DHS-0820)	16	12
Sisters of Providence (SP-3350)	34	12
Sisters of St. Joseph of Peace (CSJP-3890)	22	12
Sisters of Charity of Halifax (SC-0640)	0	11
Sisters of Charity of St. Vincent de Paul of New York (SC-0650)	22	11

Order	1966	1990
Franciscan Sisters of the Atonement (OSF-1190)	22	11
Sisters, Servants of the Immaculate Heart of Mary (IHM-2160) (Scranton)	0	11
Missionary Sisters of Our Lady of Africa (MSOLA-2820)	0	11
Oblate Sisters of Providence (OSP-3040)	0	11
Bernardine Sisters (OSF-1810	36	11
Missionary Sisters of the Sacred Heart (MSC-2860)	0	10
Sisters of St. Anne (SSA-3720)	0	10
Hospital Sisters of the Third Order of St. Francis (OSF-1820)	16	10
Congregation of the Third Order of St. Francis of Mary Immaculate (OSF-1710)	0	10
Sisters of Saint Francis of Millvale (OSF-1620)	0	10
Sisters of St. Francis of the Holy Family (OSF-1570)	0	10

Some 119 orders had sisters serving in the missions in 1990. In addition to those above, there were 62 communities with less than ten sister-missionaries. Some operated small missions and some were working with other American missionaries such as Maryknollers. There were 25 countries with nine or fewer sister-missionaries in 1990: Algeria, Antigua, Argentina, Barbados, Benin, Bermuda, Botswana, Dominica, Egypt, Fiji Islands, Guyana, Indonesia, Ivory Coast, Jordan, Lebanon, Lesotho, Macau, Madagascar, Mali, Mauritania, Namibia, Nepal, New Caledonia, New Zealand, Paraguay, St. Lucia, St. Vincent, Samoa, Senegal, Singapore, Solomon Islands, Sri Lanka, Sudan, Swaziland, Trinidad, Uruguay, Vanuatu, and the Virgin Islands.

Sister-Population Statistics, 1830-1990

✝ — ✝

19th Century

During the early stages of research for this book, the lack of specific information on the numbers of women religious in the United States during the 19th century was frustrating. Figures for the 20th century seemed readily available using the *Official Catholic Directory*. At my behest, Sister Catherine Ann Curry, PVBM, in San Francisco, investigated 19th-century sister-population figures. As it turned out, this project was far more involved and demanding than either of us at first thought. Nonetheless, she persevered for over a year and produced a 120-page report, the best study ever made of this subject, providing the most authorative figures in existence.

Sister Catherine used a variety of sources and states in her summary:

> *Religious Women includes novices and postulants in most cases although some orders only counted professed religious. These estimates are based on the following directories: Creagh, 1822, 1840, 1850; Dunigan, 1860; Sadlier, 1870, 1880; Hoffmann-Wiltzius, 1890, 1900. Individual listings note use of supplemental directories for missing listings and basis for estimates where main directories had no statistics. Directories usually give a conservative count. Numbers of priests and Catholics are from Gerald Shaughnessy, Has the Immigrant Kept the Faith? (1925), pp. 71, 262. They, too, are on the conservative side, as some dioceses, some of them large, sent in no statistics. Figures for US population are from Historical Statistics of the United States (1976). Even today there is no totally accurate count of women religious, so my figures are probably short, though as accurate as resources permitted. A number of orders arrived around 1900 which are not noted in the directory. Some orders not included arrived and left between the census years, such as the Ursulines who briefly came*

to Bloomingdale, NY, between 1812 and 1814. Any statistical study which relies on essentially fragmentary sources cannot be completely accurate. These statistics are offered as being far more accurate than any thing available, and a basis for studies of religious life in the United States. The individual listings make it possible to note the centers of religious life and the spread of religious life throughout the country.

Sister Catherine lists a number of sources in the individual sections of the report. Those books she listed include:

Benedictine Sisters in America.

Borden, Lucille, *Francesca Cabrini* (New York, NY: Macmillian, 1945).

Brewer, *Nuns and the Education of American Catholic Women.**

Brown, Sr. Rita Marie, "History of the Immaculate Conception Academy, San Francisco" (University of San Francisco, MA Thesis, 1953).

Burns, James A., *The Catholic School System in the United States* (New York, NY: Benziger Bros., 1908).

Callahan, *The History of the Sisters of Divine Providence, San Antonio.**

Callan, *The Society of the Sacred Heart in North America.**

Carroll, Sr. Mary Teresa Austin, RSM, *Leaves from the Annals of the Sisters of Mercy*, Vol. 3 (New York, NY: Catholic Publication Society, 1889)

Catalogue de la Societe du Sacre Coeur de Jesus, 1887-1888.

Currier, *Carmel in America.**

Dehey, *Religious Orders of Women in the United States.**

Duffy, Sr. Consuela Marie, *Katharine Drexel.**

Duratschek, *Under the Shadow of His Wings.**

Flanagan, Sr. M. Rita, *The Work of the Sisters of St. Dominic of the Congregation of St. Thomas Aquinas in the Diocese of Seattle, 1888-1951* (Seattle, WA: 1951).

Herron, Sr. M. Evita, RSM, *The Sisters of Mercy in the United States* (New York, NY: Macmillian, 1929).

In Harvest Fields by Sunset Shores: Sisters of Notre Dame on the Pacific Coast, 1851-1926 (San Francisco: CA, Gilmartin, 1926).

In the Early Days: From the Pages of the Sisters of Charity of the Blessed Virgin Mary, Third Edition (Dubuque, IA: 1943).

Kavanaugh, Rev. Dennis J., SJ, *The Holy Family Sisters* (San Francisco, CA: Gilmartin, 1922).

Morgan, Sr. Mary Evangelist, Mercy, *Generation to Generation* (San Francisco, CA: Fearon, 1957).

Morkin and Seigel, *Wind in the Wheat.**

Perry, Mary Dorothea, "History of the Educational Work of the Sisters of the Holy Names" (San Rafael, CA: The Catholic University of America, MA Thesis, 1954).

Sheridan, Sr. M. Athanasius, SM, *And Some Fell on Good Ground* (New York, NY: Carlton Press, 1982).

Shea, *History of the Catholic Church in the United States.**
Silver Jubilee Memorial: Convent of Our Lady of the Sacred Heart, Oakland, Cal.,
    1868-1893 (San Francisco, CA: San Francisco Printing Co., 1893).
Sisters of the IHM (New York, NY: P. J. Kenedy, 1921).
Sisters of Notre Dame de Namur, *In Harvest Fields.*
Thomas, Evangeline, *Women Religious History Sources.**
Thomas, *Footprints on the Frontier.*
Toll, David W., *Committment to Caring* (Reno, NV: Academic Press, 1983).
Vincentia, Sr. Mary, SND, *Their Quiet Tread: Growth and Spirit of the
    Congregation of the Sisters of Notre Dame Through its First One Hundred
    Years, 1850-1950* (Milwaukee, WI: Brice, 1955).
Walsh, *Sisters of Charity of New York.**
Walsh, T. J., *Nano Nagle and the Presentation Sisters* (Dublin, Ireland: M. H. Gill,
    1959).

* See Bibliography.

Sister Catherine Ann Curry's in-depth study resulted in the statistical estimates displayed in the following table:

19th-Century Sister Population

1830 —	448	1870 —	11,424
1840 —	902	1880 —	21,835
1850 —	1,941	1890 —	32,534
1860 —	5,090	1900 —	46,583

Table XIII

20th Century

When I began to compile the order-by-order totals for the 20th century, the grand totals did not agree with those displayed in the General Summary of the *Official Catholic Directory*. My totals were consistently larger. This discrepancy initiated a project that resulted in hundreds of worker-hours. Three assistants went through the census-year issues of the OCD, adding up the memberships of each order and congregation as displayed in their individual entries. Each count produced higher grand totals for all women religious than shown on the General Summary of the OCD; discrepancies ran as high as 8,212 (1990). Totals were checked and re-checked. It occurred to us that the OCD totals might include only professed sisters and nuns. But this did not work out either. Our totals include postulants, novices, juniors, and professed.

It came to my attention that the OCD relies on dioceses for numbers of sisters and nuns rather than totaling the individual entries. It does not take much imagination to picture how annual reports from the nearly 200 dioceses have been compiled over the years. In general, it appears that those reports sometimes omitted many communities for unknown reasons, missed many women religious serving outside their motherhouse dioceses, over-looked new communities, and that old figures were sometimes used when lacking a current report. In order to further cross-check and seek to authenti-cate the counts, I sent questionnaires on sister-population to 369 community archivists. The 167 returns generally confirmed our figures. The following table displays the results of these efforts to produce more accurate sister-population statistics for the 20th century:

20th-Century Sister Population

1910 — 61,944	1960 — 194,353*
1920 — 90,558	1965 — 209,000**
1930 — 134,339	1970 — 194,941
1940 — 164,273	1980 — 141,115
1950 — 179,657	1990 — 111,481

*This figure is grossly understated. The 1960 OCD only listed 266 communities whereas its 1965 issue listed 433. It remains for someone to secure listings from the missing communities.

**This figure is a close estimate. A number of communities used their international totals, which were inadvertently listed in the 1965 OCD.

Table XIV

How Many?

These studies raise an intriguing question. How many women have belonged to religious communities in the United States between 1790 and 1990? An authoritative answer would require a tremendous research effort by numerous scholars, not likely in view of the costs in time and funds. I tried to work out a formula, with little success. So, my personal answer to the question is highly problematical. I *estimate* 350,000.

APPENDIX G

Non-Catholic Women Religious

‡ — ‡

THIS CATHOLIC HISTORY makes no mention of women of other Christian denominations who have dedicated their lives to service of God. It would be an injustice not to make reference to Protestant women who answered His call. Catholic understanding of the term "women religious" clearly includes certain Episcopal and Orthodox communities. Conversely, the term "deaconess" is clearly Protestant, but also denotes women serving their churches, fellow humans, and God. This book about Catholic women religious would be incomplete without at least a brief overview of American non-Catholic women's organizations.

Religious

The Protestant Reformation eliminated religious communities for several centuries in England. In the 1830's and 1840's, the Oxford Movement revived interest in formalized religious life. Marion Hughes became the first Protestant nun when she made her profession before Dr. Edward Pusey[1] in 1841. Thereafter seven Anglican orders quickly sprang up: the Community of St. Thomas the Martyr in 1847, the Community of St. Mary the Virgin in 1848, the Sisters of Mercy of Devonport and Plymouth in 1848, the Society of the Holy Trinity in 1849, the Community of St. John the Baptist in 1852, the Society of St. Margaret in 1855, and the Society of the All Saints Sisters of the Poor in 1856. Recovery of a long lost tradition was soon echoed in the United States.

In 1845, Anne Ayres became the first American to make a profession of vows in the Episcopal Church. This she did almost in secrecy so great was the opposition to "Roman ways." She wore no habit and did not call herself or her associates "sister." In 1852, she went public and named the community the Sisterhood of the Holy Communion. However, these sisters did not make vows, rather promises for three-year terms, and avoided the appearance of being Catholic nuns — no habits, no scheduled devotions, and freedom to leave at any time. This half-hearted approach to religious life caused three members to leave in 1866 and found the Community of St. Mary in New York City. They made lifelong vows and adopted a more devotional life. During the following seven years, four more communities appeared: the Sisterhood of the Good Shepherd (Baltimore, 1863), the Sisterhood of the Good Shepherd (New York, 1869), the Sisterhood of St. John the Evangelist (Brooklyn, 1872) and the Sisterhood of the Holy Child Jesus (Albany, 1872). These communities engaged in traditional ministries such as operating schools, orphanages, homes for the elderly, training schools, hospitals, and parish support work. They wore habits and became almost indistinguishable from Catholic nuns.

Opposition to Episcopal women religious appeared early. In 1867, members of the Community of St. Mary had to abandon a rescue center for women and children in New York City, the St. Barnabas House, when a group of Low Church visitors discovered the chapel. They made a public outcry against the "mawkish Mariolatry," "ritualism," and "Roman extravagance" they saw.[2] Stiff resistance also caused this community to abandon a children's home, The Sheltering Arms, in 1870 when pamphlets warned Episcopalians about the "Catholic" rituals being performed. Episcopalian women religious had difficult beginnings in the United States.

Opposition melted perceptibly as a result of the heroic actions of members of the Community of St. Mary during the yellow fever epidemic of 1878 in Memphis. Sisters in the branch house in Memphis refused to leave when thousands were dying (see Chapter 6). Several members from their houses in Peekskill and Boston joined them in nursing the stricken and caring for orphans. Four of these sisters died during the plague and Episcopalians all over the country lauded "their" heroic women religious, as well they should.

In 1962, a short-lived community, the Sisters of St. Paul, was founded in Gresham, Oregon, by four ladies. It disbanded six years later because of lack of vocations.

Residual opposition to "Catholic ways" continued to hamper the growth of Episcopal women religious communities, although some sisters such as members of the Community of the Holy Spirit in New York wear traditional habits and follow a traditional regimen of prayer. However, by 1900 Episcopal communities only had slightly over 100 members. Today, there are 14 Episcopal communities[3] with a combined membership of just under 300.[4] Such low numbers belie the accomplishments of these women who have founded numerous hospitals, foreign missions, orphanages, schools, homes for the aged, retreat houses, and other charitable endeavors that have often been secularized and continued functioning after the sisters ceased participation.

Women religious orders of the Orthodox Church have an unbroken monastic tradition going back to the fourth century and St. Basil the Great, predating Western monasticism. Communities of Orthodox women religious have been present in Greece, Russia, the Near East, and wherever Orthodoxy took root. The strongest and largest communities developed in Russia, where special devotion to the Blessed Virgin Mary combined with Russian monastic instincts resulted in thousands of monasteries and convents. The Bolsheviks began destroying them in 1917 and tens of thousands of nuns dispersed. The Soviet government did not permit new foundations and the orders have practically died out.

Today, there are four Orthodox women communities in the United States, all very small and all recently founded — the Community of Myrrhbearers in Ontego, New York; the Nuns of New Skete[5] in Cambridge, New York; the Community of the Holy Cross in Point Reyes, California; and the Skete of the Holy Virgin of Kazan in Santa Rosa, California. The fractured Orthodox churches in the United States (10 denominations) are gradually forming closer alliances. Given proper exposure, it would seem that the Orthodox monastic tradition, deep devotion to the Blessed Virgin Mary, and an end to persecution in Eastern Europe should produce vocations to these Orthodox women religious communities and suggest a bright future.

Deaconesses

The Deaconess Movement in Protestant denominations began in Kaisersworth, Germany, in 1836. While reading scripture, Lutheran pastor Thedor Fleidner was inspired to resurrect that early Christian role for women and initiated the movement. It spread rapidly into Switzerland, France, and Scandinavia, and by 1884 there were 56 communities of deaconesses with over 5,000 members in those countries. Depending on the individual church and country, these women took vows, or made promises, or simply indicated a commitment to service. Some wore distinctive dress and most specialized in hospital work, in addition to traditional ministries. They had no formal role or office in the Lutheran Church. Thus began a movement that caught fire and generally prospered on both sides of the Atlantic for the next 100 years.

While many Protestant denominations and sects have used the title "deaconess" for women church workers, the American Deaconess Movement was centered in the Lutheran, Episcopalian, Methodist, and Mennonite churches. Since the movement varied from denomination to denomination, even within their churches, and its form changed over the years, this recounting of the movement is in general terms.

In response to a request from Dr. William Alfred Passavant, four German Lutheran deaconesses came to Pittsburgh in 1849 and worked in Passavant Hospital, the first Protestant hospital in the Western Hemisphere. In 1884, eight German deaconesses came to Philadelphia to take charge of the German Hospital. During the final decades of the 19th century, deaconesses came from Sweden, Norway, and Denmark to serve their ethnic brethren, primarily in hospitals and health services. Individual Lutheran synods operated training schools for deaconesses, and in 1940 there were over 1,000 deaconesses in the country, most of whom performed hospital work. In 1953, the last Lutheran training center closed. The movement then withered for complex reasons: lack of official standing in the church, no clear structure, and the fractured condition of the Lutheran Church in the United States. Today, there are fewer than 100 active deaconesses who operate from four communities: the Lutheran Deaconess Motherhouse in Milwaukee, Wisconsin; Eben-Ezer Lutheran Care Center in Brush, Colorado; The Deaconess Community, Lutheran Church in America, in Gladwyne, Pennsylvania; and the Lutheran Deaconess Association in Valparaiso, Indiana.

In 1864, a group of Episcopal women opened an orphanage in Mobile and called themselves the Order of Deaconesses of the Diocese of Alabama. This is the first mention of deaconesses in American Episcopal history. In 1889, the church sanctioned the Order of Deaconesses, giving it formal status, and the New York Training School for Deaconesses opened in 1890. Graduates generally filled parish positions such as coordinator of charitable and social works, administrator of parish societies, and project assistant to the pastor. In 1897, Susan Knapp, a graduate of the training school and a highly talented woman, became its dean. She had studied the deaconess movement in England and held fixed ideas on the role, proper training, and church status of deaconesses. For the next 17 years she produced outstanding graduates in the mold she advocated who served in foreign missions, performed traditional ministries and became a force in parishes where they served. However, as happens to many strong-willed leaders, she ran afoul of her governing board of directors — in her case over finances. When the board demoted her to house mother, she resigned and, without any public complaint of her treatment, went to Tokyo and taught Bible classes until her death in 1941. Her departure signaled the gradual demise of the movement in the Episcopal Church. Today the movement has been swallowed up in the newer offices of deacon, open to both men and women, and priest, also open to women. For a time the movement prospered, but structural weaknesses, lack of broad-based support, and the advent of newer roles for women all combined to terminate the movement.

Lucy Rider, a graduate of Oberlin College in Ohio, is credited with initiating the deaconess movement in the Methodist Church. With little support, she opened a training school in Chicago in 1885 and the Methodist Episcopal Church endorsed the office of Deaconess in 1888. Other branches of the Methodist Church[6] opened training schools and deaconesses served in foreign missions, hospitals, home missions, and performed numerous charities. Between 1890 and 1900, 20 deaconess houses opened with over 300 members. Today, with women being ordained in the Methodist Church and for the typical reasons already mentioned, the movement has diminished considerably.

Mennonites initiated a deaconess movement in 1903 with the organization of the Bethel Deaconess Home and Hospital Society in Newton, Kansas. Led by Freida Kaufman, the first Mennonite woman to seek a vocation as deaconess, three women were ordained in 1908. Over the ensuing 50 years, Mennonite deaconesses concentrated their ministry on hospital work. This close association with hospitals created a problem with the Mennonite Conference leadership, who felt they had lost control of the movement, resulting in a loss of interest and support that ultimately doomed the program.

Did Protestant deaconesses during those 100 years fit the definition of women religious in the Catholic understanding of the term? If taking vows, wearing distinctive dress, living in community, having a clear organizational structure with a constitution and following a devotional regimen are qualifying characteristics, the answer would have to be negative. Yet, these women were spiritually motivated and devoted their lives to Christian service. And some groups almost fit the full definition for short periods.

Before closing the account of non-Catholic women religious, it should be noted that millions of devout American Protestant women have engaged in charitable and missionary enterprises and have given generously of their time, talents, and money. It is regrettable that prejudice and suspicion of things Catholic have prevented Protestant denominations from evolving permanent and strong organizations of women religious. Perhaps, in this ecumenical age, with broader understanding and less antipathy, the impulse will revive and a second effort succeed.

Endnotes

1. Along with John Henry Newman, Dr. Pusey founded the Oxford Movement. However, Dr. Pusey (1800-1882) did not become a Roman Catholic as did Newman, future cardinal and current candidate for canonization.
2. Mary Sudman Donovan, *A Different Call* (Wilton, CT: Morehouse Barlow, 1986), p. 40.

3. They are —
   Saints Sisters of the Poor, Catonsville, MD.
   Community of the Holy Spirit, Brewster, NY.
   The Community of St. Francis, Bethlehem, PA.
   Community of St. John the Baptist, Mendham, NJ.
   The Community of St. Mary (3 autonomous provinces), Peekskill,
      NY, Sewanee, TN, and Milwaukee, WI.
   Community of the Transfiguration, Cincinnati, OH.
   The Order of Poor Clares of Reparation, Mt. Sinai, NY.
   The Order of Saint Anne (4 autonomous houses), Cambridge, MA,
      Chicago, IL, Denver, CO, and Lincoln, MA.
   Order of St. Helena, Vails Gate, NY.
   The Order of the Teachers of the Children of God, Sag Harbor, NY.
   Sisterhood of the Holy Nativity, Fond du Lac, WI.
   Sisters of Charity, Boulder City, NV.
   Society of Saint Margaret, Roxbury, MA.
   The Order of Julian of Norwich, Waukesha, WI (includes both monks
      and nuns).
4. The Anglican Church in England claimed 815 women religious in 1990.
5. These foundresses were formerly Roman Catholic Poor Clares.
6. The United Methodist Church was formed in 1968 from the Methodist Episcopal Church, the Methodist Protestant Church, the Evangelical United Brethren, and the Methodist Episcopal Church, South.

Glossary

(Terms used in this history with reference to sisters and nuns)

ABBEY: Term used by orders of a certain type (e.g., Benedictine) to designate buildings occupied by a community of sufficient size (at least 12 professed); ruled by an abbess.

ACTIVE ORDER: Religious life organized for Christian activity, as the chief means of growing in spirituality, as opposed to a cloistered order. See "apostolic."

AD LIMINA: Abbreviation of *ad limina Apostolorum* (to the threshold of the Apostles). This phrase refers to the mandatory visit to Rome and the tombs of Sts. Peter and Paul by bishops. Every ordinary is required to make such a visit every ten years and submit a written report on his diocese every five years. In modern times, most bishops make an *ad limina* visit to Rome every five years, submit their reports, and meet with the pope.

ANCHORESS: A woman who withdraws from the world to live as a hermit, devoting her life to prayer and penance. Usually a member of a monastic community, returning from time to time to community life.

ANNALS (CHRONICLES): Chronological records kept by a community on a regular basis.

ANTICLERICALISM: A movement or personal reaction of hostility to members of the clergy, also extending to the Church as a whole. Most prevalent in those countries where Catholicism is the religion of the state or is favored by the ruling group.

APOSTOLIC: An all-encompassing word that includes the ministerial, social, cultural, evangelical, and educational outreach of the Church.

ASPIRANT: One who aspires (has ambition) to do something. One who wants to become a sister or nun.

AUTONOMOUS HOUSE: Self-governing religious community as opposed to a branch under the jurisdiction of a motherhouse, etc.

BRANCH HOUSE: Group of women religious living apart from the motherhouse of the community, but under its jurisdiction and general supervision.

CANON: Usually refers to a church law, a portion of the Mass, or a member of the clergy.

CANON LAW: The body of Church law contained in the Code of Canon Law.

CANONICAL STATUS: Under Church law, communities have either pontifical or diocesan status. Pontifical status means primary accountability to the pope. Diocesan means primary accountability to the local bishop. Other communities, not recognized, are said to be "non-canonical."

CARMEL: Autonomous community of Carmelites. It is often used in preference to other terms such as monastery.

CLOISTER: Enclosed building, set of buildings, or part of a building in which only members of a religious community may enter.

CLOISTERED ORDER: A community that is enclosed by its rule — as opposed to an active order.

CHAPTER: Meeting of a community for the purpose of elections or altering governance. To be distinguished from a "Chapter of Fault" wherein members declare their faults to the local community as acts of mortification.

COIF: Hoodlike cap usually white and worn under the veil by many American congregations. It is interchangable with a "wimple," a linen cover arranged in folds about the head.

COMMUNITY: Body of women who are voluntarily under a common rule. Also a generic term used to identify an order or any subdivision of one.

CONCORDAT: A formal treaty between the Vatican State and a secular state.

CONGREGATION: Community of women religious with simple vows.

CONSTITUTION: The official document establishing the legal existence of a community, its internal procedures, statutes, identifying the rule and charism of the community, specifying its ministries and external relationships. Constitutions must be approved by the Vatican for pontifical status or by the local bishop for diocesan status.

CONTEMPLATIVE LIFE: Religious life organized for prayer and missionary presence; sometimes existing without "enclosure."

CONVENT: Place of residence where a group of religious live community life.

COUNCIL: Governing group acting as advisors to the superior.

DAUGHTER HOUSE: Autonomous community that has been established from an older and previously established community.

EVANGELICAL COUNSELS: Refers to three general counsels of poverty, chastity, and obedience as recorded in the New Testament; called counsels because they are not mandatory for Christians as are the Commandments, although after religious profession they become obligatory.

EXTERN: A member of a contemplative or cloistered community who performs duties outside the monastery. See "portress."

FEDERATION: Group of autonomous communities or congregations associated together because of a common spiritual ideal or founder.

FRIAR: A professed religious male, normally a priest, working under a central director. The term is especially used by the Dominican, Franciscan, Carmelite, Augustinian, Minim, Trinitarian, and Mercedarian orders.

GALLICANISM: Perspective that emphasizes the autonomy of the national church for authority at the expense of the Vatican as opposed to "ultramontanism," the claim for papal primacy over national episcopal jurisdiction.

GENERALATE: Central administrative offices of a congregation that has subordinate, provincial, or regional administrations.

HABIT: Distinctive dress or uniform worn by a religious as a sign of membership in an established community and "witness" to religious life.

HOLY SEE: Catholics frequently use the term "Holy See" when referring to the pope or the Vatican.

INCARDINATE: Official recognition of a priest and acceptance of him by the bishop of a diocese, giving him authority to exercise his sacramental office in that diocese.

INDULT: Grant of a special faculty by the Holy See to bishops or others in authority to do something not otherwise permitted by the general law of the church.

INTERDICT: A formal censure whereby certain sacraments and religious services are denied to an individual, group, or parish. It does not exclude from Church membership. Innocent parties may still marry and receive the Eucharist. The dying may receive the sacrament of reconciliation and healing. This censure is only exercised in extreme cases where all else has failed to secure adherence to Church law.

MAGISTERIUM: The power inherent in the Church to teach with infallibility, based on the mission given the Church by Jesus Christ (Mt. 28:19-20).

MIRACLE: A phenomenon in nature clearly seen and outside the ordinary laws of nature, thus brought about by some power beyond nature — God.

MISSAL: A book with both fixed and variable parts, used by those who attend Mass. Prior to 1963, when use of the vernacular was approved, the missal displayed the prayers in both Latin and English, enabling one to follow the priest throughout the Mass which he recited in Latin.

MISSION: (1) Small house of temporary accommodation for religious living away from the motherhouse; (2) particular assignment of work such as with defined groups (Indians) or foreign missions; or (3) small or dependent community.

MITER: Distinctive liturgical headdress worn by popes, cardinals, abbots, and bishops of the Latin rite. A mark of office.

MODERNISM: The broad-based heresy that seeks to alter teachings of the Church by making it conform to modern science, thereby questioning the legitimacy of scripture, revelation, faith, and the authority of the Church.

MONASTERY: Autonomous religious house of a community, usually contemplative.

MOTHERHOUSE: Headquarters of a community organized with branch houses.

MOTHER SUPERIOR: Title, official or ordinary usage, of the head of an order, congregation, or community.

NOVENA: Devotion that continues nine consecutive days of recitation of specific prayers. There are numerous novenas, most devoted to the Virgin Mary, St. Joseph, or certain saints. The origin of this ancient devotion lies in the nine days that Mary and the disciples spent in prayer between Ascension Thursday and Pentecost Sunday.

NOVICE: Person who has been received into the novitiate (by being clothed with the habit or specially signed) as a candidate for full membership in the community.

NOVITIATE: Place or period of training that precedes the taking of vows and becoming a professed member.

NUN: Used popularly for any woman religious, but, strictly, a member of an order with solemn vows whose chief purpose and work is to worship in a cloistered setting; thus all sisters are not nuns. Nuns are normally addressed as Sister.

ORDER: Used popularly to denote any religious community, but, strictly, a community professing the religious life in accordance with a Rule approved by the Church and recognized as having the obligation of solemn vows.

ORDINARY: The bishop of a diocese. The 1983 Code of Canon Law uses the term "diocesan bishop."

PALLIUM: A vestment consisting of an inch-wide white wool band marked with six small crosses. Worn by the pope and archbishops as an outward sign of office and union with the Holy See.

POSTULANT: Person who has been received as a candidate for membership in a religious community; the stage previous to receiving the habit of a novice.

PORTRESS: A sister or nun who tends the "door" of the monastery. See "extern."

PRIORY: Term used by orders of a certain type (e.g. Dominican, Benedictine) to designate buildings occupied by religious and ruled by a prioress. It is smaller in size and jurisdiction than an abbey.

PROFESSED: Sister or nun who has taken either temporary or final vows and entered into full membership of a community.

PROVINCE: Administrative subdivision of a large congregation with a generalate as its central headquarters.

RELIGIOUS: Popularly used as a noun to refer to a person who has vowed to live according to the three evangelical vows (chastity, poverty, and obedience) through a Rule of life in a community that exists for the purpose of carrying out these counsels. All sisters and nuns are religious as well as priests and brothers who are members of a religious congregation or order. Secular priests and deacons are not "religious."

RELIGIOUS LIFE: Refers to living as a member of a religious community.

RESCRIPT: An official written response of the pope (normally a Vatican official) to a request, petition, question, or report. It is usually treated as authorization for some action.

RULE: Guide for life formulated by a religious community or its founder to aid its members in living the evangelical counsels. Technically, there are only four Church-recognized rules, those of St. Basil, St. Augustine, St. Benedict, and St. Francis. The words "rule" and "constitution" are frequently used interchangeably.

SACRAMENT: A visible sign of God's grace imparted by one authorized by the Church. The Catholic Church celebrates seven sacraments: Baptism, Eucharist (Holy Communion), Reconciliation (Confession and Penance), Matrimony, Anointing of the Sick, Confirmation, and Holy Orders (Ordination).

SECULAR INSTITUTE: An institute of secular life in which certain persons strive for the perfection of charity and endeavor for the sanctification of the world (New Code of Canon Law). Their work is centered in the world "as a leaven" for strengthening the Church. These societies are for men, women, and may include priests. Members do not take public vows or live in community, but seek perfection in everyday life.

SECULARISM: A movement, attitude, or view of life that limits itself to a material perspective of reality. Practically, it excludes God from human thinking and acting.

SEE: The official seat or jurisdiction of a bishop.

SEMI-MONASTIC ORDER: An order or subdivision of an order with a monastic rule that engages in some limited ministry — usually within the confines of the convent.

SISTER: Member of a congregation of women religious and used as a title of address. The majority of women religious are sisters. All sisters and nuns are "women religious."

SISTERHOOD: All encompassing term to designate women religious.

SOLEMN & SIMPLE VOWS: Solemn vows are taken publicly, are perpetual, and are found only in certain ancient orders carrying very strict obligations. Other vows, private and public, are called simple, and are for stated time periods or for life.

SPIRITUAL BOUQUET: A devotional practice whereby specific spiritual exercises are performed as a gift for someone. Popular among children in Catholic schools.

SUFFRAGAN: A bishop under the leadership of an archbishop. While a suffragan bishop yields the place of honor to his archbishop, even in his own diocese, the archbishop has only limited authority over his suffragan.

TEMPORARY VOWS: Those taken for a specified time period.

THIRD ORDER REGULAR (TERTIARY): Non-cloistered religious community or congregation, male or female, living a common life under vows and affiliated with a major order (Franciscan, etc.) to which a third order is attached. Communities called "third" order distinguish them from first and second orders having the same family name; the first being the order for men and the second being the associated order of cloistered women.

UNIATE: Refers to Eastern Rite churches that are in union with the Roman Catholic Church and recognize the pope. Their rites and liturgies originated in Antioch, Alexandria, and Byzantium. The term "uniate" is seldom used by these churches.

VATICAN: Refers to the Vatican State in Rome, residence of the pope. Also a descriptive term for the official office of the Church and its government.

VICAR-APOSTOLIC: A representative of the Vatican, normally assigned to a territory not ready for diocesan status.

VICAR-GENERAL: A priest within a diocese who is empowered with the authority of the bishop as specified. Normally, he handles matters related to certain personnel in the diocese.

VISITATION: Refers to Mary's visit to her cousin Elizabeth (Lk 1:39-45) — a term used by many religious congregations.

VOW: Promise deliberately made to God. Religious vows are of two kinds; private and public; public vows may be simple or solemn.

Select Bibliography

‡ — ‡

General

Marty, Martin E. *An Invitation to American Catholic History.* Chicago, IL: Thomas More Press, 1986.

_____

Ashley, Benedict M., OP. *The Dominicans.* Collegeville, MN: The Liturgical Press, 1990.

Baltzell, Digby E. *The Protestant Establishment: Aristocracy and Caste in America.* New York, NY: Random House, 1964.

Bellah, Robert N., and Green, Spahn, eds. *Uncivil Religion: Interreligious Hostility in America.* New York, NY: Crossroad Publishing Company, 1987.

Buetow, Rev. Harold A. *Of Singular Benefit: The Story of Catholic Education in the United States.* New York, NY: The Macmillan Company, 1970.

Breslin, Thomas A. *China, American Catholicism, and the Missionary.* University Park, PA: The Pennsylvania University Press, 1980.

Catholic Almanac. Huntington, IN: Our Sunday Visitor Publishing Division, 1990 edition.

Cogley, John, and Allen, Van Rodger. *Catholic America: Expanded and Updated Edition.* Kansas City, MO: Sheed and Ward, 1986.

Connelly, Rev. James T., CSC. "Educators in the Faith: The Holy Cross Congregation and their Schools in the United States, 1865-1900." Paper presented at the Conference on the History of the Congregation of Holy Cross, New Orleans, 1990.

_____. "Holy Cross Congregations in the Civil War." Paper presented at the Conference on the History of the Congregation of the Holy Cross, Austin, TX, 1993.

Crews, Clyde F. *An American Holy Land: A History of the Archdiocese of Louisville.* Wilmington, DE: Michael Glazier, Inc., 1987.

Davis, Cyprian. *The History of Black Catholics in the United States.* New York, NY: Crossroad Publishing Company, 1990.

Delaney, Bernard J. *The True History of Maria Monk.* London, England: Catholic Truth Society, nd (mid 1940's).

Dolan, Jay P. *The American Catholic Experience: A History from Colonial Times to the Present.* Garden City, NY: Doubleday & Company, 1985.

_____. General Editor. *The American Catholic Parish: A History from 1850 to the Present,* 2 vol. New York, NY: Paulist Press, 1987.

Eberhardt, Rev. N. C. *American Church History.* St. Louis, MO: H. Herder Book Company, 1964.

Ellis, Rev. John Tracy. *American Catholicism.* Chicago, IL: University of Chicago Press, 1956.

_____. *Documents of American Catholic History,* 3 vol. Wilmington DE: Michael Glazier, Inc., 1987.

Faherty, William B., SJ. *American Catholic Heritage: Stories of Growth.* Kansas City, MO: Sheed & Ward, 1991.

Hardon, John A., SJ. *Modern Catholic Dictionary.* New York, NY: Doubleday, 1880.

Hennesey, James, SJ. *American Catholics: A History of the Roman Catholic Community in the United States.* New York, NY: Oxford University Press, 1981.

Jacoby, George Paul. *Catholic Child Care in Nineteenth Century New York.* New York, NY: Arno Press, 1974.

Kardong, Terrence, OSB. *The Benedictines.* Wilmington, DE: Michael Glazier, 1988.

Kennelly, James K. *The History of American Catholic Women.* New York, NY: Crossroad Publishing Company, 1990.

Lane, Francis E. *American Charities and the Child of the Immigrant.* New York, NY: Arno Press, 1974.

La Sorte, Michael. *La Merica: Images of Italian Greenhorn Experience.* Philadelphia, PA: Temple University Press, 1985.

Latourette, Kenneth Scott. *A History of Christian Missions in China.* New York, NY: Macmillan, 1929.

Manual of Parish Confraternity of Christian Doctrine. Paterson, NJ: 1961. Publisher not shown.

Maynard, Theodore. *The Story of American Catholicism.* New York, NY: The Macmillan Co., 1946.

McAvoy, Thomas T. *A History of the Catholic Church in the United States.* Notre Dame, IN: University of Notre Dame Press, 1969.

Miller, Sr. Miriam, OSF. *A History of the Early Years of the Roman Catholic Diocese of Charlotte.* Charlotte, NC: Laney-Smith Inc., 1984.

Minnick, N. *Studies in Catholic History in Honor of John Tracy Ellis.* Wilmington, DE: Michael Glazier, 1985.

Moorman, John A. *A History of the Franciscan Order from its Origins to the Year 1517.* Chicago, IL: Franciscan Herald Press, 1968.

Murray, John O'Kane. *Catholicity in the United States: Popular History of the Catholic Church in the U.S.* Brooklyn, NY: Publisher not shown, 1876.

National Catholic Educational Association. *National Catholic Educational Association Bulletin.* The Proceedings of the Forty-Sixth Annual Meeting, Washington, DC, 1949.

Nevins, Albert J. *Builders of Catholic America.* Huntington, IN: Our Sunday Visitor Publishing Division, 1985.

New American Bible With Revised New Testament, The. Confraternity of Christian Doctrine, 1986.

New Catholic Encyclopedia, 17 vols. Washington, DC: The Catholic University of America, 1967.

O'Brien, David. *Public Catholicism.* New York, NY: Macmillan Publishing Company, 1989.

Official Catholic Directory. Wilmette, IL: P. J. Kenedy & Sons, 1990 edition.

Oxford Dictionary of the Christian Church. New York, NY: Oxford University Press, 1983.

Perko, Rev. F. Michael, SJ. *Catholic & American.* Huntington, IN: Our Sunday Visitor Publishing Division, 1989.

Pillar, James J. *The Catholic Church in Mississippi, 1837-1865.* New Orleans, LA: Hauser Press, 1964.

Power, Edward J. *A History of Catholic Higher Education in the United States.* Milwaukee, WI: The Bruce Publishing Company, 1958.

Pou, Virginia Doughton. *The Atlantic Hotel.* Raleigh, NC. Privately printed, 1991.

Prest, James E. *American Catholic History.* Lanham, MD: University Press of America, 1991.

Schiavo, Giovanni. *Italian-American History, Vol. II: The Italian Contribution to the Catholic Church in America.* New York, NY: The Vigo Press, 1949.

Schoenberg, Wilfred P. SJ. *A History of the Catholic Church in the Pacific Northwest, 1743-1983.* Washington, DC: Pastoral Press, 1987.

Shea, John Gilmary. *History of the Catholic Church in the United States*, 4 vol. New York, NY: Arno Press, 1978.

Short, William J., OSF. *The Franciscans.* Wilmington, DE: Michael Glazier Inc., 1990.

Doris, Rev. Edward, CSC. *The Chronicles of Notre Dame du Lac.* Notre Dame, IN: University of Notre Dame Press, 1992.

Stritch, Thomas. *The Catholic Church in Tennessee: The Sesquicentennial Story.* Nashville, TN: The Catholic Center, 1987.

Thompson, James J. *The Church, the South and the Future.* Westminster, MD: Christian Classics, Inc., 1988.

Thompson, Margaret Susan. "Women and American Catholicism, 1789-1989." *Perspectives on the American Catholic Church 1789-1989.* Virchio, Stephen J. and Geiger, Sr. Virginia, SSDN, eds. Westminster, MD: Christian Classics, 1989.

_____. "Women, Feminism and New Religious History: Catholic Sisters as a

Case Study." *Belief and Behavior: Essays in the New Religious History.* VanderMeer, Philip and Swierenga, Robert eds. New Brunswick, NJ: Rutgers University Press, 1991.

U.S. Department of Commerce, Bureau of the Census. *Historical Statistics of the United States, Colonial Times to 1970, Part 1.* Washington, DC: GPO, 1975.

Watkin, E. I. *Roman Catholicism in England from the Reformation to 1950.* London, England: Oxford University Press, 1957.

White, James M. *The Diocesan Seminary in the United States: A History from the 1780s to the Present.* Notre Dame, IN: University of Notre Dame Press, 1989.

United States History

Johnson, Paul. *Modern Times: The World from the Twenties to the Nineties.* New York, NY: HarperCollins Publishers, 1983.

Kennedy, John F. *A Nation of Immigrants.* New York, NY: HarperCollins Publishers, 1964.

McCaffrey, Lawrence J. *The Irish Diaspora in America.* Washington, DC: The Catholic University of America Press, 1976.

McCraw, Thomas K. "The Strategic Vision of Alexander Hamilton," *The American Scholar* (Washington, DC, Winter 1994).

McPherson, James, M. *Battle Cry of Freedom.* New York, NY: Oxford University Press, 1988.

Miller, Robert Ryal. *Shamrock and Sword: The Saint Patrick's Battalion in the U.S.-Mexican War.* Norman, OK: University of Oklahoma Press, 1989.

Tindall, George Brown. *America: A Narrative History.* New York, NY: W. W. Norton & Company, 1984.

Vescoli, Rudolph. "Prelates and Peasants: Italian Immigrants and the Catholic Church." *Journal of Social Studies*, Spring 1969.

Wandel, Joseph. *The German Dimension of American History.* Chicago, IL: Nelson-Hall, 1979.

Women Religious — General

Bernsrein, Marcelle. *Nuns*. Ondon, England. Collins, 1976.

Brewer, Mary Eileen. *Nuns and the Education of American Catholic Women, 1860-1920*. Chicago, IL: Loyola University Press, 1887.

Caulfield, Caspar, CP. *Only a Beginning: The Passionists in China, 1921-1931*. Union City, NJ: Passionist Press, 1990.

Clark, Elizabeth A. *Women in the Early Church*. Wilmington, DE: Michael Glazier, Inc., 1987.

Defferrari, Roy. *A Complete System of Catholic Education is Necessary: A Reply to "Are Catholic Schools the Answer?"* Boston, MA: Daughters of St. Paul, 1964.

Dehey, Elinor Tong. *Religious Orders of Women in the United States: Accounts of their Origin, Works and Most Important Institutions*. Hammond, IN: W.B. Conkey Company, 1930.

Dorsey, Sr. Mary Jean, OP. *Saint Dominic's Family: The Lives of Over 300 Famous Dominicans*. Washington, DC: Dominican Publications, 1964.

Ewens, Sr. Mary, OP. *The Role of the Nun in Nineteenth-Century America*. Salem, NH: Ayer Company Publishers, Inc., 1971.

Guide to Religious Communities for WOMEN. Chicago, IL: National Sisters Vocation Conference, 1983.

Guide to Religious Ministries: For Catholic Men and Women. New Rochelle, NY: The Catholic News Publishing Company, 1988 edition.

Hostie, Raymond, SJ. *The Life and Death of Religious Orders: A Psycho-sociological Approach*. Washington, DC: CARA/Center for Applied Research in the Apostolate, 1983.

Kennelly, Sr. Karen, CSJ. *American Catholic Women: A Historical Exploration*. New York, NY: Macmillan Publishing Company, 1989.

King, Sr. Elace, IHM. *CARA Formation Directory for Men and Women Religious 1993*. Washington, DC: CARA/Center for Applied Research in the Apostolate, Georgetown University, 1993.

Kolmer, Sr. Elizabeth, ASC. *Religious Women in the United States: A Survey of the*

Influential Literature from 1950 to 1983. Wilmington, DE: Michael Glazier Inc., 1984.

Liptak, Sr. Dolores, RSM. *Immigrants and Their Church*. New York, NY: Macmillan Publishing Company, 1989.

_____. *Perspectives on the American Catholic Church, 1789-1989*. Westminster, MD: Christian Classics, Inc., 1989.

McCarthy, Rev. Thomas P., CSV. *Guide to the Catholic Sisterhoods in the United States*. Washington, D.C: The Catholic University of America Press, 1952.

McNamara, Jo Ann. *A New Song, Celibate Women in the First Three Centuries*. New York, NY: Harrington Press, 1983.

_____. *Word and Spirit: A Monastic Review: Women in Monasticism*. Petersham, MA: St. Bede's Publications, 1989.

Meyers, Sr. Bertrande, DC. *Sisters for the 21st Century*. New York, NY: Sheed and Ward, 1965.

Misner, Barbara, "A Comparative Social Study of the Members and Apostolates of the First Eight Permanent Communities of Women Religious Within the Original Boundaries of the United States, 1790-1850." Ph.D. Diss. Washington, DC, The Catholic University of America, 1980.

Moss, Doley C. *Of Cell and Cloister: Catholic Religious Orders Through the Ages*. Milwaukee, WI: Bruce Publishing Company, 1957.

Neal, Sr. Marie Augusta, SNDN. *Catholic Sisters in Transition: From the 1960s to the 1980s*. Wilmington, DE: Michael Glazier, Inc., 1984.

_____. *From Nuns to Sisters: An Expanding Vocation*. Mystic, CT: Twenty-Third Publications, 1990.

Nygren, Rev. David and Ukeritis, Sr. Miriam, CSJ. "Future of Religious Orders in the United States." *Origins, Vol. 22, No. 15*, 1992.

O'Gorman, Robert T. *The Church that was a School: Catholic Identity and Catholic Education in the United States Since 1790*. Nashville, TN: The Catholic Education Futures Project, 1987.

Penet, Sr. Emil Mary, IHM. "Why a Sister Shortage?" *The American Eccelesiastical Review, CXLII*. 1960.

Perlmann, Joel. *Ethnic Differences: Schooling and Social Structure Among the Irish, Italians, Jews and Blacks in an American City, 1880-1935*. New York, NY: Cambridge University Press, 1988.

Religious Community Life in the United States: Proceedings of the Sisters' Section of the First National Congress of Religious of the United States. New York, NY: The Paulist Press, 1952.

Reuther, Rosemary Radford, and Keller, Rosemary Skinner. *Women and Religion in America,* 3 vol. San Francisco, CA: HarperCollins Publishers, 1986.

Rippinger, Joel, OSB. *The Benedictine Order in the United States: An Interpretive History*. Collegeville, MN: The Liturgical Press, 1990.

Ryan, Mary Perkins. *Are Parochial Schools the Answer? Catholic Education in the Light of the Council*. New York, NY: Holt, Rinehart and Winston, 1964.

Stepsis, Sr. Ursula, CSA, and Liptak, Sr. Dolores, RSM. *Pioneer Healers: History of Women Religious in American Health Care*. New York, NY: Crossroad, 1989.

Sullivan, Robert E., and O'Toole, James M., eds. *Catholic Boston: Studies in Religious Community, 1870-1970*. Boston, MA: 1985.

Taves, Ann. *The Household of Faith: Roman Catholic Devotions in Mid-Nineteenth Century America*. Notre Dame, IN: University of Notre Dame Press, 1986.

Theodore, Sr. Mary. *Heralds of Christ the King: Missionary Records of the North Pacific, 1837-1878*. New York, NY: P. J. Kenedy and Sons, 1939.

Thomas, Sr. Evangeline, CSJ. *Women Religious History Sources: A Guide to Repositories in the United States*. New York, NY: R. R. Bowker Company, 1983.

Walsh, James Joseph. *These Splendid Sisters*. Freeport, NY: Books for Libraries Press, 1927.

Wittberg, Sr. Patricia, SC. *Creating a Future for Religious Life: A Sociological Perspective*. New York, NY: Paulist Press, 1991.

Women Religious — Accounts

Alma, Sr. Maria, IHM. *Sisters, Servants of the Immaculate Heart of Mary*. Lancaster, PA: Dolphin Press, 1967.

Ames, Sr. Aloysia, CSJ. *The St. Mary's I Knew*. Tucson, AZ: St. Mary's Hospital of Tucson, 1970.

A School Sister of Notre Dame. *Mother Caroline and the School Sisters of Notre Dame in North America, 1892-1928*, 2 vols. St. Louis, MO: Woodward and Tiernan Co., 1928.

Bogle, Sr. M. Edwina, FSSJ, and Brach, Sr. Jane Marie, FSSJ. *In All Things Charity: A Biography of Mother M. Colette Hilbert*. Hamburg, NY: Franciscan Sisters of St. Joseph, 1983.

Borgia, Sr. Francis M., OSF. *He Sent Two: The Story of the Beginning of the School Sisters of St. Francis*. Milwaukee, WI: The Bruce Publishing Co., 1965.

Boyden, Anna L. *Echoes from the Hospital and White House*. Boston, MA: Lathrop, 1869.

Brett, Donna Whitson, and Edward T. *Murdered in Central America: The Story of Eleven U.S. Missionaries*. Maryknoll, NY: Orbis Books, 1988.

Brown, Sr. Mary Borromeo. *The History of the Sisters of Providence of Saint Mary-of-the-Woods: Vol. I. (1806-1856)*. New York, NY: Benziger Brothers, Inc., 1949.

Buckner, Sr. Mary, SCL. *History of the Sisters of Charity of Leavenworth*. Kansas City, MO: Hudson-Kimberly Publishing Co., 1898.

Burton, Katherine. *According to the Pattern: The Story of Dr. Agnes McLaren and the Society of Catholic Medical Missionaries*. New York, NY: Longmans, Green and Co., 1946.

_____. *The Bernardines*. Patterson, NJ: St. Anthony Guild Press, 1964.

_____. *Lily and Sword and Crown: The History of the Congregation of the Sisters of St. Casimir, Chicago, Illinois, 1907-1957*. Milwaukee, WI: Catholic Life Publications, 1958.

_____. Where There is Love: The Life of Mother Mary Frances Siedliska of Jesus the Good Shepherd. New York, NY: P. J. Kenedy & Sons, 1951.

Byrne, Patricia, CSJ. "French Roots of a Women's Movement: The Sisters of St. Joseph, 1650-1836." Ph.D. Diss. Boston College, 1985.

Callahan, Sr. Mary Generosa, CDP. *The History of the Sisters of Divine Providence, San Antonio, Texas*. Milwaukee, WI: Catholic Life Publications, 1954.

Callan, Sr. Louise, RSCJ. *The Society of the Sacred Heart in North America*. New York, NY: Longmans, Green and Co., 1937.

Campbell, Sr. M. Anne Francis, OLM. "Bishop England's Sisterhood, 1829-1929." Ph.D. Diss. St. Louis University, 1968.

Cody, Sr. Patricia, MMB. *The Major and the Miracle*. Kansas City, MO: privately printed, 1982.

Convent Annals. *Life of the Rev. Mother Amadeus of the Heart of Jesus*. New York, NY: The Paulist Press, 1923.

Croteau, Carol Clark. *Heart Touching Heart*. Baltimore, MD: Mission Helpers of the Sacred Heart, 1990.

Crumlish, Sr. John Mary, DC. *The Union of the American Sisters of Charity with the Daughters of Charity, Paris*. Emmitsburg, MD: St. Joseph's Provincial House, 1950.

Currier, Rev. Charles Warren. *Carmel in America, A Centennial History of the Discalced Carmelites in the United States*. Darien, IL: Carmelite Press, 1989.

Curry, Sr. Lois, OP. *Women After His Own Heart: The Sisters of Saint Dominic of the American Congregation of the Sacred Heart of Jesus, Caldwell, New Jersey, 1881-1981*. New York, NY: New City Press, 1966.

Darrah, Mary C. *Sister Ignatia: Angel of Alcoholics Anonymous*. Chicago, IL: Loyola University Press, 1992.

Deacon, Sr. Florence, OSF. "More than Just a Shoe String and a Prayer: How Women Religious Helped Finance the Nineteenth Century Social Fabric." Paper delivered at History of Women Religious Conference, Marymount College, Tarrytown, NY, 1992.

DeCock, Sr. Mary, BVM. "Turning Points in the Spirituality of an American Congregation." *U.S. Catholic Historian* 10 (1991): 59-69.

Degnan, Sr. M. Bertrand, RSM. *Mercy Unto Thousands: Life of Mother Mary Catherine McAuley, Foundress of the Sisters of Mercy*. Westminster, MD: Newman Press, 1957.

De Maria, Mother Saverio, MSC. *Mother Frances Xavier Cabrini*. Chicago, IL: Missionary Sisters of the Sacred Heart, 1984.

Desobry, Jean, Abbe. *Memoires de las Societe des Antiquaires de Picardie*. Amiens, France: Au Siege de la Societe, 1986.

Dominican Nuns. *Echoes*. Farmington Hills, MI: Dominican Nuns, 1992.

Donovan, John F., MM. *The Pagoda and the Cross: The Life of Bishop Ford of Maryknoll*. New York, NY: Charles Scribner's Sons, 1967.

Duffy, Sr. Consuelo Marie, SBS. *Katharine Drexel: A Biography*. Cornwell Heights, PA: Mother Katharine Drexel Guild, 1966.

Duratschek, Sr. M. Claudia, OSB. *Crusading Along Sioux Trails: A History of Catholic Indian Missions Among the South Dakota Sioux, 1839-1945*. St. Meinrad, SD: Grail Publications, 1947.

_____. *Under the Shadow of His Wings: History of Sacred Heart Convent of Benedictine Sisters, Yankton, South Dakota, 1880-1970*. Aberdeen, SD: North Plains Press, 1971.

Echoes. Farmington Hills, MI. June 1992. Dominican Nuns.

Erskine, Marjory. *Mother Philippine Duchesne*. New York, NY: Longmans, Green and Co., 1926.

Fischer, Edward. *Maybe a Second Spring: The Story of the Missionary Sisters of St. Columban in China*. New York, NY: Crossroad Publishing Company, 1983.

Fitzgerald, Sr. Constance, OCD, ed. *The Carmelite Adventure: Clare Joseph Dickenson's Journal of a Trip to America and Other Carmelite Sources, Volume II*. Baltimore MD: Carmelite Sisters, 1990.

Founding of the Sisters of St. Casimir: Mother Maria Kaupas. Introduced by John M. Lozano, CMF. Chicago, IL. Clarentian Publications, 1981.

Francis, Sr. Mary, PCC. *A Right to be Merry*. Chicago, IL: Franciscan Herald Press, 1973.

Francis, Sr. M. Michael, OSU. *The Broad Highway: A History of the Ursuline Nuns in the Diocese of Cleveland, 1850-1950*. Cleveland, OH: The Ursuline Nuns, 1951.

Gallagher, Sr. Ann Miriam, RSM. "Catherine Seton, 1800-1891: Mercy Prison Sister." Paper delivered at History of Women Religious Conference, Marymount College, Tarrytown, NY, 1992.

George, Sr. M. Louise, OSB. "Mother Paula O'Riley." Pamphlet. No publisher or place shown. 1985.

Gilmore, Sr. Julia, SCJ. *We Came North, Centennial Story of the Sisters of Charity of Leavenworth*. Meinrad, IN: Abbey Press, 1961.

Groell, Sr. Clara, DC. *White Wings in Bamboo Land*. Emmitsburg, MD: St. Joseph's Provincial House Press, 1973.

Hackett, Sr. Shelia, OP. *Dominican Women in Texas: From Ohio to Galveston and Beyond*. Houston, TX: D. Armstrong Company, Inc., 1986.

Hanley, Sr. Mary Laurence, OSF. *A Song of Pilgrimage and Exile: The Life and Spirit of Mother Marianne of Molokai*. Chicago, IL: Franciscan Herald Press, 1980.

Hannefin, Sr. Daniel, DC. *Daughters of the Church: A Popular History of the Daughters of Charity in the United States, 1809-1987*. Brooklyn, NY: New York City Press, 1989.

Healy, Kathleen. *Francis Warde: American Founder of the Sisters of Mercy*. New York, NY: Seabury Press, 1973.

Hipisch, Stepanus, OSB. *History of Benedictine Nuns*. Collegeville, MN: St. John' Abbey Press, 1958.

Historical Sketch of the Convent and Academy of the Sisters of St. Francis in Oldenburg, Indiana amd of the Work of their Community in the United States. Oldenburg, IN. Published by the Community, 1901.

Jolly, Ellen Ryan. *Nuns of the Battlefield*. Providence, RI: The Providence Visitor Press, 1927.

Joseph, Sr. Mary, OP. *Out of Many Hearts*. Hawthorn, NY: The Servants of Relief for Incurable Cancer, 1965.

Kadyscewdki, Sr. Mary Jane, CCSF. *One of the Family: History of the Felician Sisters, Our Lady of the Sacred Heart Province, Corapolis, Pennsylvania, 1920-1977*. Pittsburgh, PA: Wolfson Publishing Co,. Inc., 1982.

Karolevitz, Robert F. *Bishop Martin Marty: "The Black Robe Lean Chief."* Yankton, SD: Benedictine Sisters of Sacred Heart Convent, 1980.

Kleber, Albert, OSB, STD. *A Bentivoglio of the Bentivoglio: Servant of God, Mary Maddalena of the Sacred Heart of Jesus, Countess Annetta Bentivoglio, 1834-1905.* Evansville, IN: Monastery of St. Clare, 1984.

Knawa, Sr. Anne Marie, OSF. *As God Shall Ordain: A History of the Franciscan Sisters of Chicago, 1894-1987.* Chicago, IL: Worzalla Publishing Company, 1989.

Koester, Sr. Mary Camilla, PCC. *Into This Land: A Centennial History of the Cleveland Poor Clare Monastery of the Blessed Sacrament.* Chicago, IL: Robert J. Liererbach, 1980.

Kraman, Sr. Carlan, OSF. *Odyessy in Faith: The Story of Mother Alfred Moes.* Rochester, MN: Sisters of St. Francis, Assisi Heights, 1990.

Logan, Sr. Eugenia, SP, MA. *The History of the Sisters of Providence of Saint Mary-of-the-Woods. Vol. II (1856-1894).* Terre Haute, IN: Moore-Langen Printing Company, 1978.

Ludwig, Sr. M. Mileta, FSPA. *A Chapter of Franciscan History, 1849-1949.* New York, NY: Bookman Associates, 1950.

Madeleva, Sr. M. *My First Seventy Years.* New York, NY: Macmillan Company, 1959.

Maher, Sr. Mary Denis, CSA. *To Bind up the Wounds: Catholic Sister Nurses in the U.S. Civil War.* Women's Studies #107. Westport, CT: Greenwood Press, 1989.

Marchione, Sr. Margherita, MPF. "Religious Teachers Filippini in the United States." U.S. Catholic Historian 6 (1987): 351-372.

Marie, Sr. Jeanne, MM. *Maryknoll's First Lady.* New York, NY: Dodd, Mead and Company, 1964.

McAllister, Anna Shannon. *Flame in the Wilderness: Life and Letters of Mother Angela Gillespie, CSC, 1824-1887, American Foundress of the Sisters of the Holy Cross.* Patterson, NJ: St. Anthony Guild Press, 1944.

McCrosson, Sr. Mary of the Blessed Sacrament, SP, Leopoldine, Sr. Mary, SP, and Theresa, Sr. Mary, SP. *The Bell and the River.* New York, NY: Pacific Books, 1957.

McDonald, Sr. M. Grace, OSB. *With Lamps Burning.* St. Joseph, MN: St. Benedict's Priory Press, 1957.

McGreal, Sr. Mary Nona, OP. *Samuel Mazzuchelli, OP: Kaleidoscope of Scenes from His Life.* Sinsinawa, WI: Sinsinawa Dominicans. Privately printed. Undated.

McKee, Robert, CSC. "Holy Cross P.O.W.s in the Philippines: 1941-1945." Paper delivered at the 1985 Conference on the History of the Congregation of Holy Cross, Wilkes Barre, PA, 1985.

Melville, Annabelle M. *Elizabeth Bayley Seton: 1774-1821.* New York, NY: Charles Scribner's Sons, 1951.

Milcent, Paul. *Jeanne Jugan: Foundress of the Little Sisters of the Poor.* London, England: Darton, Longman & Todd, 1980.

Minogue, Anna C. *Loretto: Annals of the Century.* New York, NY: The American Press, 1912.

Montgomery, Ruth. *Once There Was a Nun.* New York, NY: G. P. Putnam's Sons, 1962.

Morkin, Sr. M. Louise, OSB and Seigel, Sr. M. Theopane, OSB. *Wind in the Wheat: A Century of Prayer and Work in Erie, 1856-1956.* Erie, PA: McCarty Printing Company, 1956.

Murrett, John C., MM. *The Mary of St. Martin's.* Westminster, MD: The Newman Press, 1960.

Noffke, Sr. Suzanne, OP. *The Letters of Catherine of Siena, Vol. 1.* Binghampton, NY: Medieval & Renaissance Texts & Studies, 1988.

Oates, Sr. Mary J., CSJ. "The Development of Catholic Colleges for Women, 1895-1960" *U.S. Catholic Historian* 7 (1988): 413-428.

_____. "The Good Sisters: The Works and Position of Catholic Churchwomen in Boston, 1870-1940." Robert E. Sullivan and James O'Toole, eds., *Catholic Boston: Studies in Religious Community, 1870-1970.* Boston, MA: 1985.

O'Sullivan, Sr. Mary Cecilia, CBS. *A Century of Caring: The Sisters of Bon Secours in the United States, 1881-1981.* New York, NY: Maple Press Company, 1982.

Pendergast, Sr. Mary Carita, SC. *Havoc in Hunan: The Sisters of Charity in Western Hunan, 1924-1951.* Morristown, NJ: College of St. Elizabeth Press, 1991.

Peplinski, Sr. Josephine Marie, SSJ-TOSF. *A Fitting Response: The History of the Sisters of St. Joseph of the Third Order of St. Francis, Part 1, The Founding.* South Bend, IN: Privately printed, 1982.

A Pictorial History of the Saint Lucy Filippini Chapel. Prato, Italy. Edizione del Palazzo, 1992. Author unnamed.

Ricciardi, Antonio. *His Will Alone: The Life of Mother Mary of Jesus the Good Shepherd.* Translated by Regis N. Burwig. Oshkosh, WI: Castle-Pierce Press, 1971.

Ryan, Edward A., SJ. The Sisters of Mercy: An Important Chapter in Church History, *Theological Studies, Vol. 18.* Woodstock, MD: June, 1957.

Savage, Sr. Mary Lucida, Ph.D. *The Congregation of Saint Joseph of Carondelet: A Brief Account of its Origins and its Works in the United States, 1650-1922.* St. Louis, MO: B. Herder Book Co., 1923.

Schoenberg, Wilfred P., SJ. *These Valiant Women: History of the Sisters of St. Mary of Oregon, 1886-1986.* Beaverton, OR: Sisters of St. Mary of Oregon, 1986.

Segale, Sr. Blandina, SC. *At the End of the Santa Fe Trail.* Milwaukee, WI: The Bruce Publishing Co., 1948.

Sisters of the Holy Names of Jesus and Mary. *Gleanings of Fifty Years.* Portland, OR: Press of Glass & Prudhomme Co., 1909. (Sr. Mary Flavia, SNJM, author.)

Sullivan, Sr. Mary Christiana, MA. "Some Non-Permanent Foundations of Religious Orders and Congregations of Women in the United States (1793-1850)" *Historical Records and Studies, United States Historical Society,* Vol. XXXI. New York, NY: The United States Catholic Historical Society, 1940. Pp. 7-72.

Sullivan, Sr. Mary Louise, MSC. *Mother Cabrini: "Italian Immigrant of the Century."* New York, NY: Center for Migration Studies, 1992.

Valdez, Sr. Mary Paul, MCDP. *The History of the Missionary Catechists of Divine Providence.* San Antonio, TX: Privately printed, 1978.

Valenti, Dr. Patricia Dunlavy. *To Myself a Stranger: A Biography of Rose Hawthorne Lathrop.* Baton Rouge, LA: Louisiana State University Press, 1991.

Vincentia, Sr. Mary, SND. *Their Quiet Tread: Growth and Spirit of the Congregation of the Sisters of Notre Dame, 1850-1950.* Milwaukee, WI: Bruce Press, 1955.

Von Le Fort, Gertrude. *The Song of the Scaffold.* Kirkwood, MO: Catholic Authors Press, 1933.

Wadham, Juliana. *The Case of Cornelia Connelly.* New York NY: Pantheon Books, Inc., 1957.

Walsh, Sr. Marie De Lourdes, SC. *The Sisters of Charity of New York, 1809-1959,* Vol. III. New York, NY: Fordham University Press, 1960.

Washington, Sr. M. Kathleen, ASC. *A Century of Christian Witness in America, 1870-1970: A Short History of the Adorers of the Blood of Christ.* Belleville, IL: Record Printing and Advertising Co. Undated.

Werntz, Sr. Mary Regina, RSM. *Our Beloved Union: A History of the Sisters of Mercy of the Union.* Westminster, MD: Christian Classics, Inc., 1989.

Wiest, Jean-Paul. *Maryknoll in China: A History, 1918-1955.* London, England: M.E. Sharpe, Inc., 1988.

Wolf, Sr. Anne Collette, SP. *Against All Odds: Sisters of Providence Mission to the Chinese, 1920-1990.* Saint Mary-of-the-Woods, IN: Privately printed, 1990.

Ziolkowski, Sr. Mary Janice, CSSF. *The Felician Sisters of Livonia, Michigan.* Detroit, MI: Harlo Press, 1984.

Index

(Orders and Congregations are not listed here. See Appendix B)

— D —

— I —

— J —

— K —

— O —

— P —